Access 2003 Programming by Example with VBA, XML, and ASP

Julitta Korol

Wordware Publishing, Inc.

Library of Congress Cataloging-in-Publication Data

Korol, Julitta.
  Access 2003 programming by example with VBA, XML, and ASP / by Julitta Korol.
    p. cm.
  Includes index.
  ISBN-13: 978-1-55622-223-8
  ISBN-10: 1-55622-223-8 (pbk.)
  1. Microsoft Access.   2. Database management.   I. Title.
  QA76.9.D3K6573 2005
  005.75'65--dc22   2004030068
                                                CIP

© 2005, Wordware Publishing, Inc.

All Rights Reserved

2320 Los Rios Boulevard
Plano, Texas 75074

No part of this book may be reproduced in any form or by
any means without permission in writing from
Wordware Publishing, Inc.

Printed in the United States of America

ISBN-13: 978-1-55622-223-8
ISBN-10: 1-55622-223-8
10 9 8 7 6 5 4 3 2
0501

All inquiries for volume purchases of this book should be addressed to Wordware Publishing, Inc.,
at the above address. Telephone inquiries may be made by calling:

(972) 423-0090

Contents

Part II — Creating and Manipulating Databases with ADO

Part III — Programming with the Jet Data Definition Language

Part IV — Event Programming in Forms and Reports

Part V — Taking Your VBA Programming Skills to the Web

Acknowledgments

Nobody works alone. In order for this book to become a reality, I had to enlist the help of numerous individuals. For example, while I was sleeping, far away in Hawaii Tana-Lee Rebhan was proofreading and testing all the hands-on exercises and custom projects that had just been written. She was the first person to see what went into this book, and her honest comments made me actually change a number of things to make this book easier to understand from a reader's standpoint. We worked so well as a team that we've decided to work together on future projects. Thank you, Tana-Lee, for showing up in my professional life!

When after several months of hard work by our Julittana team the book was finally finished, the manuscript was sent over to the folks at Wordware Publishing. Martha McCuller had her hands full having to do the first edit and the design of hundreds of pages of not-so-easy technical stuff. Martha's edits helped make this book even friendlier. While Martha was busy editing and designing, Denise McEvoy was desktop publishing and Alan McCuller was designing the book cover. These two people have used the best of their artistic skills to make this book visually pleasing. And when the page proofs were ready, Beth Kohler, senior editor, took over. I cannot begin to tell you how important Beth's final edits and comments were to the success of this book. And this entire book project was coordinated by publisher Wes Beckwith. I appreciate very much Wes's patience and understanding of all the obstacles that one faces in every endeavor, not to mention writing a book. Thanks, everyone!

Introduction

For many years now, Microsoft Access has allowed users all over the world to design and develop Windows-based database applications. Microsoft Office Access 2003 continues to be the world's most popular database. This book is for people who have already mastered the use of Microsoft Access databases and now are ready for the next step — programming. *Access 2003 Programming by Example with VBA, XML, and ASP* takes non-programmers through the detailed steps of creating Access databases from scratch and then shows them how to retrieve and manage their data programmatically using various programming languages and techniques. With this book at hand, users can quickly build the toolset required for developing their own database solutions. This book proves that, given the right approach, programming an Access database from scratch and controlling it via programming code can be as easy as designing and maintaining databases with Access built-in tools. Anyone interested in learning how to get started with VBA programming in Access will benefit from this book's 303 hands-on examples and 11 step-by-step projects.

This book gives a practical overview of many programming languages and techniques necessary in programming and maintaining today's Access databases.

Prerequisites

To use *Access 2003 Programming by Example with VBA, XML, and ASP*, you don't need any programming experience. The only prerequisite is that you already know how to manually design an Access database and perform database tasks by creating and running various types of queries. This book also assumes that you know how to create more complex forms with embedded subforms, combo boxes, and other built-in controls. If you don't have these skills, there are countless books on the market that can teach you step by step how to build simple databases or use the sample Northwind database that comes with Microsoft Access. If you do meet these criteria, this book will take you to the Access programming level by example. You will gain a working knowledge immediately by performing concrete tasks and without having to read long descriptions of concepts. A true learning by example begins with the first step, followed by the next step, and the next one, and so on. By the time you complete all of the steps in a hands-on or custom project, you should be able to effectively apply the same technique again and again in your own database projects.

How This Book Is Organized

This book is divided into five parts (29 chapters) that progressively introduce you to programming Microsoft Access databases. An appendix in the form of a PDF file is available to download from www.wordware.com/files/access.

Part I introduces you to Access 2003 VBA programming. Visual Basic for Applications (VBA) is the programming language for Microsoft Office Access. In this part of the book you acquire the fundamentals of VBA that you will use over and over again in building real-life Microsoft Access database applications.

Part I consists of the following nine chapters:

Chapter 1 — Procedures and Modules
In this chapter you learn about types of Access procedures that you can write, and learn how and where they are written.

Chapter 2 — The Visual Basic Editor (VBE)
In this chapter you learn almost everything you need to know about working with the Visual Basic Editor window, commonly referred to as VBE. Some of the programming tools that are not covered here are discussed and put to use in Chapter 9.

Chapter 3 — Variables, Data Types, and Constants
In this chapter you are introduced to basic VBA concepts that allow you to store various pieces of information for later use.

Chapter 4 — Passing Arguments to Procedures and Functions
In this chapter you find out how to provide additional information to your procedures and functions before they are run.

Chapter 5 — Decision Making with VBA
In this chapter you learn how to control your program flow with a number of different decision-making statements.

Chapter 6 — Repeating Actions in VBA
In this chapter you learn how you can repeat the same actions by using so-called looping structures.

Chapter 7 — Working with Arrays
In this chapter you learn the concept of static and dynamic arrays that you can use for holding various values.

Chapter 8 — Custom Collections and Class Modules
In this chapter you learn how to create and use your own objects and collections of objects.

Chapter 9 — Debugging VBA Procedures and Handling Errors
In this chapter you begin using built-in debugging tools to test your programming code and trap errors.

The skills obtained in Part I of this book are fairly portable. They can be utilized in programming other Microsoft Office applications that also use VBA as their native programming language (Excel, Word, PowerPoint, or Outlook).

Part II introduces you to a set of programming objects known as ActiveX Data Objects (ADO) that enable Microsoft Office Access and other client applications to access and manipulate data. In this part of the book you learn how to use ADO objects in your VBA code to connect to a data source; create, modify, and secure database objects; as well as read, add, update, delete, and replicate data.

Part II consists of the following nine chapters:

Chapter 10 — Accessing Data Using ADO
   In this chapter you start your encounter with ADO objects by learning several ways of accessing data from various data sources (Microsoft Access, Excel, and dBASE, as well as text files).

Chapter 11 — Creating and Accessing Tables and Fields with ADO
   In this chapter you learn how to create, copy, link, and delete database tables programmatically. You also learn how to write code to add and delete fields, as well as create listings of existing tables in a database and fields in a table.

Chapter 12 — Setting up Indexes and Table Relationships with ADO
   In this chapter you learn how to write VBA code to add primary keys and indexes to your database tables. You also learn how to use objects from the ADOX library to create relationships between your tables.

Chapter 13 — ADO Techniques for Finding and Reading Records
   In this chapter you practice various methods of using programming code to open a set of database records commonly referred to as a recordset. You learn how to move around in a recordset, and find, filter, and sort the required records, as well as read their contents.

Chapter 14 — Working with Records
   In this chapter you learn how to perform essential database operations such as adding, updating, and deleting records. You also learn how to render your database records into three popular formats (Excel, Word, and a text file).

Chapter 15 — Creating and Running Queries with ADO
   In this chapter you learn how to use VBA code instead of the Query Design view to create and run various types of database queries.

Chapter 16 — Using Advanced ADO Features
   In this chapter you learn several advanced ADO features such as how to disconnect a recordset from a database, save it in a disk file, clone it, and shape it. You also learn about database transactions.

Chapter 17 — Implementing Database Security with ADOX and JRO
   In this chapter you learn how to secure a Microsoft Access database from VBA procedures by using various methods that are available in the ADOX and JRO object libraries. This is a chapter to refer to if you need to create user and group accounts, set database and user passwords, and grant/revoke database permissions.

Chapter 18 — Database Replication
   In this chapter you learn how to make a database available in various

geographical locations by using database replication.

You will find the skills obtained in Part II of this book essential in accessing, manipulating, and securing Access databases.

Part III introduces the Data Definition Language (DDL), an important component of the Structured Query Language (SQL). Like ADO (covered in Part II) and DAO (covered in Appendix A), DDL is used for defining database objects (tables, views, stored procedures, primary keys, indexes, and constraints) and managing database security. In this part of the book, you learn how to use DDL statements with Jet databases, ADO, and the Jet OLE DB provider.

Part III consists of the following five chapters:

Chapter 19 — Creating, Modifying, and Deleting Tables and Fields

In this chapter you learn special Data Definition Language commands for creating a new Access database, as well as creating, modifying, and deleting tables. You also learn commands for adding, modifying, and deleting fields and indexes.

Chapter 20 — Enforcing Data Integrity and Relationships between Tables

In this chapter you learn how to define rules regarding the values allowed in table fields to enforce data integrity and relationships between tables.

Chapter 21 — Defining Indexes and Primary Keys

In this chapter you learn DDL commands for creating indexes and primary keys.

Chapter 22 — Database Security

In this chapter you learn how to use DDL commands to manage security in the Microsoft Access database. You learn how to quickly create, modify, and remove a database password, and manage user-level accounts.

Chapter 23 — Views and Stored Procedures

In this chapter you work with two powerful database objects: views and stored procedures. You learn how views are similar to Select queries, and how stored procedures can perform various actions similar to what Access Action queries and Select queries with parameters can do.

The skills you learn in Part III of this book will allow you to create, manipulate, and secure your Microsoft Access databases using SQL DDL statements. Numerous Access SQL/DDL statements and concepts introduced here are important in laying the groundwork for moving into the client/server environment (porting your Microsoft Access database to SQL Server).

Part IV introduces you to responding to events that occur in Access forms and reports. The behavior of the Microsoft Access objects such as forms, reports, and controls can be modified by writing programming code known as event procedures or event handlers. In this part of the book you learn how you can make your forms, reports, and controls do useful things by writing event procedures in class modules.

Part IV consists of the following four chapters:

Chapter 24 — Using Form Events

In this chapter you learn the types of events that can occur on an Access form and write event procedures to handle various form events.

Chapter 25 — Using Report Events

In this chapter you learn about events that are triggered when the Access report is run. You write your own event procedures to specify what happens when the report is opened, activated/deactivated, or closed.

Chapter 26 — Events Recognized by Controls

In this chapter you work with a custom application and write event procedures for various controls that are placed on an Access form.

Chapter 27 — More about Event Programming

In this chapter you learn about advanced concepts in event programming. You learn how to respond to events in standalone class modules to make your code more manageable and portable to other objects. You also learn how to create and raise your own events.

The skills acquired in Part IV of this book will allow you to enhance and alter the way users interact with your database application.

Part V introduces you to programming Microsoft Access databases for Internet access. Gone are the times when working with Access required the presence of the Microsoft Access application on a user's desktop. Thanks to the development of Internet technologies, you can now publish both static and dynamic Access data to the web. In this part of the book you learn how Active Server Pages (ASP) and Extensible Markup Language (XML) are used with Microsoft Access to develop database solutions for the World Wide Web.

Part V consists of the following two chapters:

Chapter 28 — Access and Active Server Pages

In this chapter you learn how to use the Microsoft-developed Active Server Pages (ASP) technology to view, insert, delete, and modify records stored in a Microsoft Access database from a web browser. Before you go on to explore numerous examples of database access presented in this chapter, you are walked through the installation of the Internet Information Services (IIS) on your computer.

Chapter 29 — XML Features in Access 2003

In this chapter you learn how to use the Extensible Markup Language (XML) with Access. You learn how to manually and programmatically export Access data to XML files as well as import an XML file to Access and display its data in a table. You also learn how to use stylesheets and transformations to present Access data to a user in a desired format.

The skills acquired in Part V of the book will make your Access applications Internet and intranet ready. You are now able to connect to, read from, and write to Access databases from within a web browser using two important Microsoft technologies.

This book would not be complete without giving you some overview and practice with the older but still quite popular method of accessing database data from VBA procedures using Data Access Objects (DAO). In order to make this book user-friendly in the sense of portability, Appendix A, which can be downloaded from www.wordware.com/files/access, provides an overview of DAO. This appendix covers a variety of topics about working with a database, including creating and linking tables, creating indexes and queries, working with records, and implementing database security.

How to Work with This Book

This book has been designed as a tutorial and should be followed chapter by chapter. As you read each chapter, perform the tasks you read about. Be an active learner by getting totally involved in the book's hands-on exercises and custom projects. When you get totally involved you learn things by doing rather than studying, and you learn faster. Do not move to new information until you've fully grasped the current topic. Allow your brain to sort things out and put them in proper perspective before you move on. Take frequent breaks between learning sessions as some chapters in this book cover a large amount of material. Do not try to do everything in one sitting. It's better to divide the material into smaller units than attempt to master all there is to learn at once. That said, however, never stop in the middle of a hands-on; finish the exercise before taking a break. Having learned a particular technique or command, try to think of ways to apply it to your own work. As you work with this book, create small sample procedures for yourself based on what you've learned up to this particular point. These procedures will come in handy when you need to review the subject in the future or simply need to steal some ready-made code.

Companion Files

The companion files can be downloaded from www.wordware.com/files/access. These include example databases and other files used in the book's hands-on activities and custom projects. Additionally, an appendix is included that provides an introduction to using Data Access Objects.

PART I

Introduction to Access 2003 VBA Programming

Visual Basic for Applications (VBA) is the programming language for Microsoft Office Access.

In this part of the book, you acquire the fundamentals of VBA that you will use over and over again in building real-life Microsoft Access database applications.

Chapter 1

Procedures and Modules

Programming boils down to writing procedures. A procedure is a group of instructions that allows you to accomplish specific tasks when your program runs. When you place instructions (programming code) in a procedure, you can call this procedure whenever you need to perform that particular task.

You create and store procedures in modules, which can contain one or more procedures. Each procedure in the same module must have a unique name. Procedures in different modules can have the same name. Each module begins with a Declaration section that lists various settings and declarations that apply to every procedure in the module. Following the Declaration section is the Procedure section, which holds the module's procedures.

Procedure Types

VBA has three types of procedures: subroutine, function, and property.

■ **Subroutine procedures** (subroutines, subprocedures)

These procedures perform useful tasks, but never return values. They begin with the keyword Sub and end with the keywords End Sub. *Keywords* are words that carry a special meaning in Visual Basic. Between these keywords you place the VBA instructions (statements) the procedure needs to execute. You can pass information to a procedure using *arguments*, which are the values that are needed for a procedure to do something. One or more arguments are entered after the procedure name. Multiple arguments are separated by commas.

Subroutines are written from scratch in modules located in the Visual Basic Editor window. You can also invoke the built-in Command Button Wizard from the toolbox in the Design view to automatically write procedures that automate database maintenance, form and report operations, record navigation, and other tasks.

■ **Function procedures** (functions)

Functions perform specific tasks and can return values. They begin with the keyword Function and end with the keywords End Function. Because functions return values, you can use them in expressions. Similar to procedures, functions can accept arguments. Function procedures can be executed from a subroutine.

■ **Property procedures**

Property procedures are used with custom objects. With property procedures you can set and get the value of an object's property or set a reference to an object.

Module Types

As mentioned earlier, procedures are created and stored in modules. In Access 2003 there are two types of modules: standard and class.

■ **Standard modules**

These modules are listed in the Microsoft Office Access Database window by selecting the Modules object in the left pane (see Figure 1-1). Standard modules are used to hold subprocedures and function procedures that are not associated with any particular form or report and, therefore, can be run from anywhere in the application. You can create a standard module by clicking Modules from the Objects list in the Database window and clicking the New button, or you can create them from the Visual Basic Editor window by choosing Insert | Module.

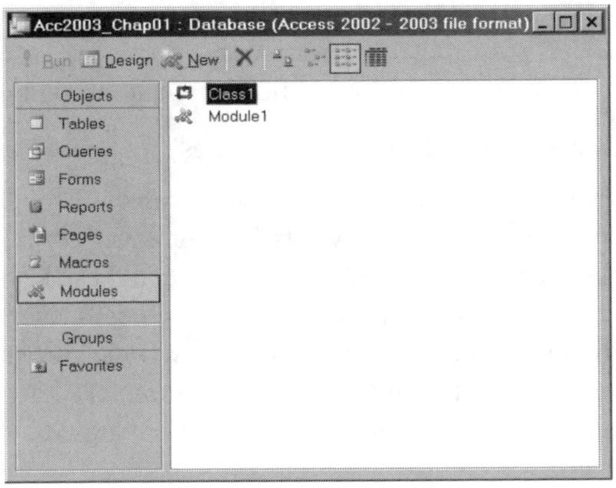

Figure 1-1: To list standard and standalone class modules that exist in a Microsoft Office Access database, click the Modules object in the left pane of the Database window.

■ **Class modules**

Class modules come in three varieties: standalone class modules, form modules, and report modules.

- **Standalone class modules** — These modules are used to create your own custom objects with their own properties and methods. You create a standalone class module by choosing Insert | Class Module in the Visual Basic Editor window. Access will create a default class module named Class1 and will list it in the Class Modules folder in the Project Explorer window (see Figure 1-3). You will work with standalone class modules in Chapter 8.
- **Form modules and report modules** — Each Access form can contain a form module, and each report can contain a report module. These

modules are special types of class modules that are saved automatically whenever you save the form or report.

To allow quick access to them, forms and reports don't have modules associated with them when they're first created. All newly created forms and reports are *lightweight* by design. They load and display faster than the forms and reports with modules. These lightweight forms and reports have their Has Module property set to No (see Figure 1-2).

When you open a form or report in Design view and choose View | Code or click the Code button in the toolbar, Access creates a form or report module. The Has Module property of a form or report is automatically set to Yes to indicate that the form or report now has a module associated with it. Note that this happens even if you have not written a single line of VBA code. Access opens a module window and assigns a name to the module that consists of three parts: the name of the object (e.g., form or report), an underscore character, and the name of the form or report. For example, a newly created form that has not been saved is named Form_Form1, a form module in the Customers form is named Form_Customers, and the report module in the Customers report is named Report_Customers.

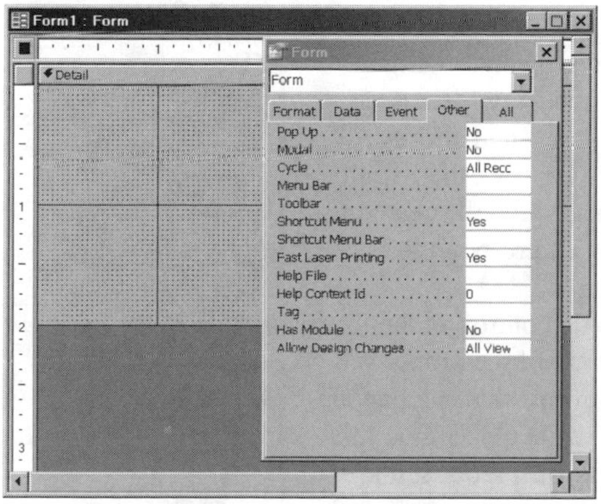

Figure 1-2: When you begin designing a new form in the Microsoft Office Access user interface, the form does not have a module associated with it. Notice that the Has Module property on the Form properties sheet is set to No.

As with report modules, form modules store event procedures for events recognized by the form and its controls, as well as general function procedures and subprocedures. You can also write Property Get, Property Let, and Property Set procedures to create custom properties for the form or report. The procedures stored in their class modules are available only while you are using that particular form or report.

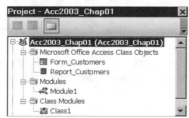

Figure 1-3: Microsoft Office Access organizes database modules in folders. Form and report modules are listed in the Microsoft Office Access Class Objects folder. Standard modules can be found under the Modules folder. The Class Modules folder organizes standalone class modules.

Events, Event Properties, and Event Procedures

In order to customize your database applications or to deliver products that fit your users' specific needs, you'll be doing quite a bit of event-driven programming. Access 2003 is an *event-driven* application. This means that whatever happens in an Access application is the result of an event that Access has detected. *Events* are things that happen to objects and can be triggered by the user or by the system, such as clicking a mouse button, pressing a key, selecting an item from a list, or changing a list of items available in a list box. As a programmer, you will often want to modify the application's built-in response to a particular event. Before the application processes the user's mouse clicks and keypresses in the usual way, you can tell the application how to react to the activity. For example, if a user clicks a Delete button on your form, you can display a custom delete confirmation message to ensure that the user selected the intended record for deletion.

For each event defined for a form, form control, or report, there is a corresponding event *property*. If you open any Microsoft Access form in Design view and choose View | Properties, and then click the Event tab of the property sheet, you will see a long list of events your form can respond to (see Figure 1-4).

By selecting a specific control on the form and clicking the Event tab of the property sheet, you can see the events that can happen to the selected control while the form is running (see Figure 1-5). Forms, reports, and the controls that appear on them have various event properties you can use to trigger desired actions. For example, you can open or close a form when a user clicks a command button, or you can enable or disable controls when the form loads.

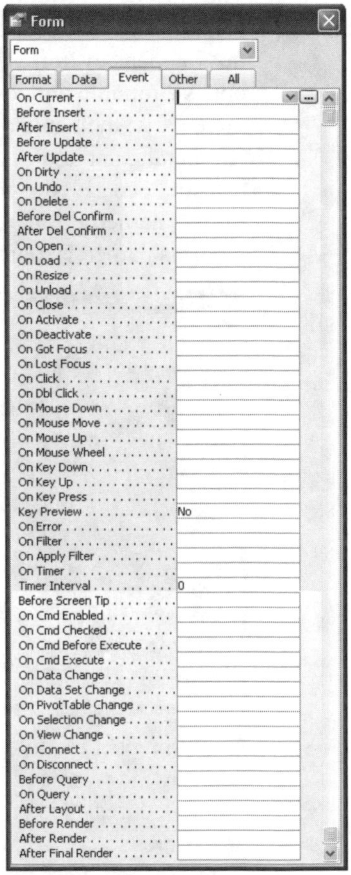

Figure 1-4: Event properties for a form.

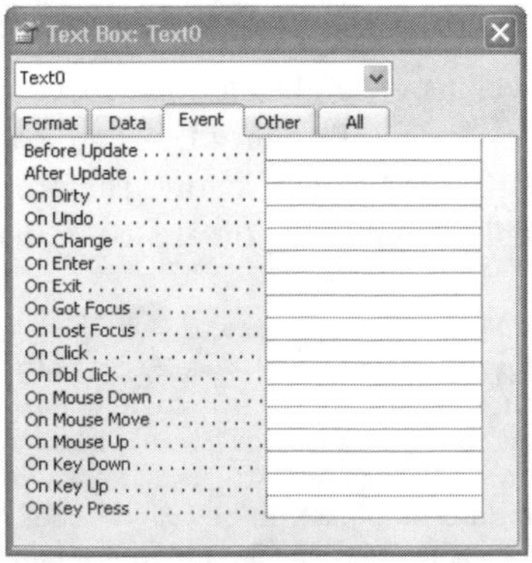

Figure 1-5: Event properties for a text box control placed on a form.

To specify how a form, report, or control should respond to events, you write *event procedures*. In your programming code, you may need to describe what should happen if a user clicks on a particular command button or makes a selection from a combo box. When you design a custom form, for example, you should anticipate and program events that can occur at run time (while the form is being used). The most popular event is the Click event. Every time a command button is clicked, it triggers the appropriate event procedure to respond to the Click event for that button. When you assign a program to an event property, you set an *event trap*. Trapping gives you considerable control in handling events. When you trap an event, you basically interrupt the default processing that Access would normally carry out in response to the user's keypress or mouse click. If a user clicks a command button to save a form, whatever programming code you've written in the Click event of that command button will happen. Keep in mind that code entered as an event procedure cannot be used as a standalone procedure. The event programming code is stored as a part of a form, report, or control and is triggered only when user interaction with a form or report generates a specific event.

Why Use Events?

By using events you can make your applications dynamic and interactive. To handle a specific event, you need to select the appropriate event property on the properties sheet and write an event handling procedure. If you don't care about a specific event, you don't need to write any code, as Access will provide its own default response to those events. Events cannot be defined for tables, queries, or data access pages.

Walking Through an Event Procedure

If you've never created an event procedure, the following hands-on exercise will show you how to get started. Your task is to change the background color of a text box control on a form when the text box is selected, and return to the default background color when you tab or click out of that text box.

⊚ Hands-On 1-1: Writing an Event Procedure

1. Open the **Acc2003_Chap01.mdb** database file from the book's downloadable file. This file contains a copy of the Customers table and the Customers form from the Northwind database that comes with Microsoft Office Access.

2. Open the **Customers** form in Design view.

3. Right-click the **ContactName** text box control on the form, and choose **Properties** from the shortcut menu.

4. Click the **Event** tab of the Text Box: ContactName property sheet. The list of event procedures available for the text box control appears (see Figure 1-6).

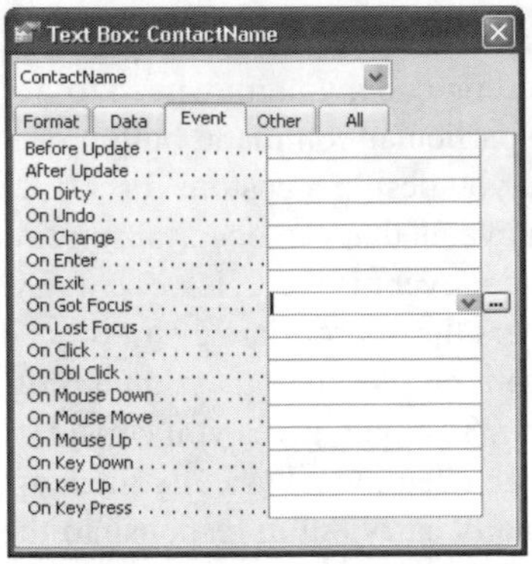

Figure 1-6: Use the Build button, which is displayed as an ellipsis (...), to create an event procedure. This button is not available unless an event is selected.

5. Click the **Build** button (...) to the right of the On Got Focus event procedure (Figure 1-6). This will bring up the Choose Builder dialog box, as shown in Figure 1-7.

Figure 1-7: To write VBA programming code for your event procedure, choose Code Builder in the Choose Builder dialog box.

6. Select **Code Builder** in the Choose Builder dialog box and click **OK**. This will display a VBA code module in the Visual Basic Editor window (see Figure 1-8). This window (often referred to as VBE) is discussed in detail in Chapter 2.

Take a look at Figure 1-8. The name of the event procedure consists of three parts: the object name (ContactName), an underscore character (_), and the name of the event (GotFocus) occurring to that object. The word Private indicates that the event procedure cannot be triggered by an event from another form. The word Sub in the first line denotes the beginning of the event procedure. The words End Sub in the last line denote the end of the event procedure. The statements to be executed when the event occurs are written between these two lines. Notice that each procedure name ends with a pair of empty parentheses ( ). Words such as Sub, End, or Private have special meaning to Visual Basic and are called *keywords* (reserved words). Visual Basic displays keywords in blue, but you can change the color of your keywords from the Editor Format tab in the Options window (choose Tools | Options in the Visual Basic Editor window). All VBA keywords are automatically capitalized.

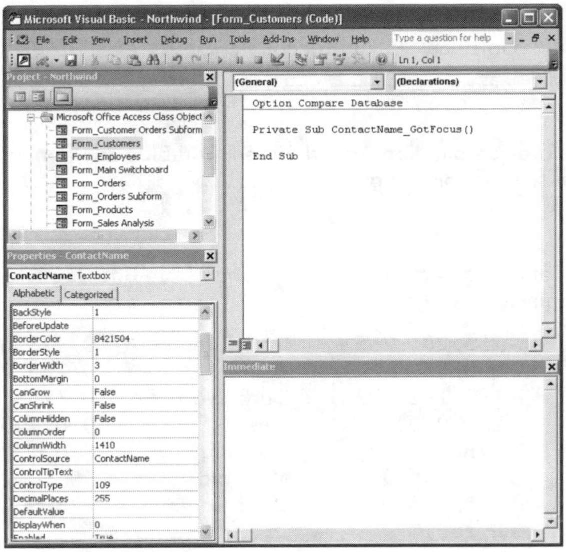

Figure 1-8: The Code Builder displays the event procedure Code window with a blank event procedure for the selected object. Here you can enter the code Access will run when the specified Got Focus procedure is triggered.

In the Code window (see Figure 1-8 above), there are two drop-down list boxes just below the title bar. The one on the left is called Object. This box displays the currently selected control. The box on the right is called Procedure. If you position the mouse over one of these boxes, the tool tip indicates the name of the box. By clicking on the down arrow to the right of the Procedure box, a list of all possible event procedures associated with the object type selected in the Object box will be displayed. You can close the drop-down list box by clicking anywhere in the unused portion of the Code window.

7. To change the background color of a text box control to green, enter the following statement between the existing lines:

```
Me.ContactName.BackColor = 65280
```

Notice that when you type each period, Visual Basic displays a list containing the possible item choices. This feature, called List Properties/Methods, is a part of Visual Basic's on-the-fly syntax and programming assistance, and is covered in Chapter 2. When finished, your first event procedure should look as follows:

```
Private Sub ContactName_GotFocus()
    Me.ContactName.BackColor = 65280
End Sub
```

The statement you just entered tells Visual Basic to change the background color of the ContactName text box to green when the cursor is moved into that control. You can also specify the color by using the RGB function like this:

```
Me.ContactName.BackColor = RGB(0, 255, 0)
```

The above statement is equivalent to the statement you used earlier in the ContactName_GotFocus event procedure.

RGB Colors

Color values are combinations of red, green, and blue components. The RGB function has the following syntax:

```
RGB(red, green, blue)
```

The intensity of red, green, and blue can range from 0 to 255. Here are some frequently used colors:

White	255, 255, 255	Dark Green	0, 128, 0
Black	0, 0, 0	Cyan	0, 255, 255
Gray	192, 192, 192	Dark Cyan	0, 128, 128
Red	255, 0, 0	Blue	0, 0, 255
Dark Red	128, 0, 0	Dark Blue	0, 0, 128
Yellow	255, 255, 0	Magenta	255, 0, 255
Dark Yellow	128, 128, 0	Dark Magenta	128, 0, 128
Green	0, 255, 0		

8. In the Visual Basic Code window, choose **File | Close and Return to Microsoft Office Access**. Notice that [Event Procedure] now appears next to the On Got Focus event property in the property sheet for the selected ContactName text box control (see Figure 1-9).

Figure 1-9: [Event Procedure] in the property sheet denotes that the text box's Got Focus event has an event procedure associated with it.

9. To test your On Got Focus event procedure, activate the **Customers** form and choose **View | Form View**.

10. Click in the **ContactName** text box and notice the change in the background color.

11. Now, click on any other text box control.

Notice that the ContactName text box does not return to the original color. So far, you've only told Visual Basic what to do when the specified control receives the focus. If you want the background color to change when the focus moves to another control, there is one more event procedure to write — On Lost Focus. The code of this procedure is shown below. To create this procedure, return your form to Design view, click the **ContactName** control, and activate the properties sheet for this control. Click the **Build** button to the right of the On Lost Focus event property on the Event tab, select **Code Builder,** and proceed to write the statement that switches the background color to whatever it was before.

The completed On Lost Focus procedure looks like this:

```
Private Sub ContactName_LostFocus()
    Me.ContactName.BackColor = 13434879
End Sub
```

12. Switch to the **Customers** form and run it by choosing **View | Form View.** Test the events by clicking in and out of the ContactName text box.

Because objects recognize a sequence of events, it's important to understand what fires the events and the order in which they occur. In Part IV of this book, you'll learn what events can be used for a particular task to make your application smarter.

Compiling Your Procedures

The VBA code you write in the Visual Basic Editor's Code window is automatically compiled by Microsoft Access before you run it. The syntax of your VBA statements is first thoroughly checked for errors and then your procedures are converted into executable format. If an error is discovered during the compilation process, Access stops compiling and displays an error message. It also highlights the line of code that contains the error. The compiling process can take from a few seconds to a few minutes or longer, depending on the number of procedures written and the number of modules used.

To ensure that your procedures have been compiled, you can explicitly compile them by choosing Debug | Compile in the Visual Basic Editor window.

Microsoft Access saves all the code in your database in its compiled form. Compiled code runs more quickly when you open it in the future. Remember to always save your modules after you compile them. In Chapter 9 you will learn how to test and troubleshoot your procedures. Refer to this chapter often as you write the procedures demonstrated in this book.

As a final note for this chapter, choose Debug | Compile to compile the event procedures you've written in this chapter.

Chapter Summary

In this chapter, you learned that procedures in Microsoft Access 2003 can be written in standard modules or class modules. You also found out that VBA has three types of procedures (subroutines, functions, and property procedures) and that it can respond to various events triggered by the user or by the system. You learned how to modify the application's built-in response to a particular event by writing two simple event procedures in a form class module.

Chapter 2

The Visual Basic Editor (VBE)

Now that you know how to write event procedures in modules placed behind a form or a report, let's spend some time in the Visual Basic Editor window and become familiar with several of its features. With the tools located in the Visual Basic Editor window, you can:

- Write your own VBA procedures
- Create custom forms
- View and modify object properties
- Test VBA procedures and locate errors

In addition to accessing the Visual Basic Editor window from the properties sheet of a form or report (while the form or report is in Design view), you can enter the VBA programming environment in any of the following ways:

- From the Database window, by choosing Tools | Macro | Visual Basic Editor
- From the keyboard, by pressing Alt+F11
- From the Database window, by clicking the Modules button, and then New on the toolbar to create a new standard module, or by double-clicking any existing standard module you want to view

Understanding the Project Explorer Window

The Project Explorer window provides access to modules behind forms and reports via the Microsoft Office Access Class Objects folder (see Figure 2-1). The Modules folder lists only standard modules that are not behind a form or report.

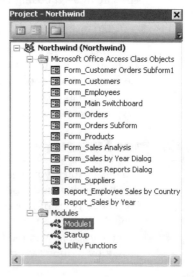

Figure 2-1: The Project Explorer window is an easy entry port to your VBA procedure code.

In addition to the Microsoft Office Access Class Objects and Modules folders, the VBA Project Explorer window can contain class modules, which are used for creating your own objects as demonstrated in Chapter 8. Using the Project Explorer window, you can easily move between modules currently loaded into memory.

You can activate the Project Explorer window in one of three ways:

■ From the View menu by selecting Project Explorer
■ From the keyboard by pressing Ctrl+R
■ From the Standard toolbar by clicking the Project Explorer button ▓ as shown in Figure 2-2

> **Note:** If the Project Explorer window is visible but not active, activate it by clicking the Project Explorer title bar.

Buttons on the Standard toolbar (Figure 2-2) provide a quick way to access many Visual Basic features.

Figure 2-2: Use the toolbar buttons to quickly access frequently used features in the VBE window.

Notice that the Project Explorer window (see Figure 2-3 on the next page) contains three buttons:

■ **View Code** — Displays the Code window for the selected module
■ **View Object** — Displays the selected form or report in the Microsoft Office Access Class Objects folder. This button is disabled when an object in the Modules or Class Modules folder is selected.
■ **Toggle Folders** — Hides and unhides the display of folders in the Project Explorer window

Understanding the Properties Window

The Properties window allows you to review and set properties for the currently selected Access class or module. The name of the selected object is displayed in the Object box located just below the Properties window title bar. Properties of the object can be viewed alphabetically or by category by clicking on the appropriate tab. The Properties window displays the current settings for the selected object. Figure 2-3 displays the properties of the ContactName text box located in the Customers form. In order to access these properties, highlight Form_Customers in the Project Explorer window. Next, click the View Object button as shown in Figure 2-3. This will open the selected form in Design view. Now, return to the Code window. The Properties window will be filled with the properties for the Customers form. To view the properties of the ContactName text box as shown in Figure 2-3, select ContactName from the drop-down list located below the Properties window title bar.

- **Alphabetic tab** — Alphabetically lists all properties for the selected object. You can change the property setting by selecting the property name, then typing or selecting the new setting.

- **Categorized tab** — Lists all properties for the selected object by category. You can collapse the list so that you see only the category names or you can expand a category to see the properties. The plus (+) icon to the left of the category name indicates that the category list can be expanded. The minus (−) indicates that the category is currently expanded.

The Properties window can be accessed in one of the following three ways:

- From the View menu by selecting Properties Window
- From the keyboard by pressing F4
- From the toolbar by clicking the Properties Window button located to the right of the Project Explorer button (see Figure 2-2)

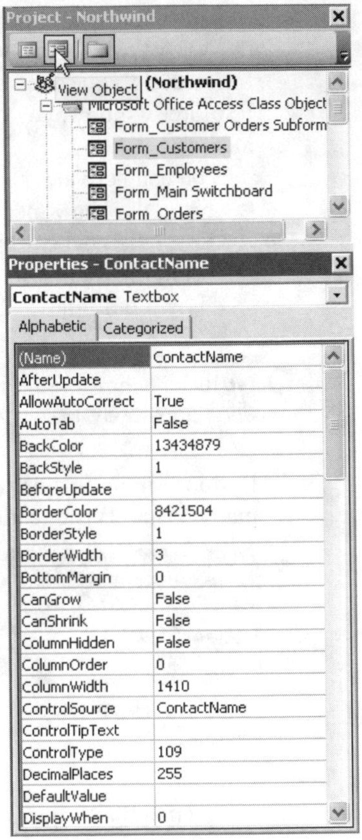

Figure 2-3: You can edit object properties in the Properties window, or you can edit them in the properties sheet when a form or report is open in Design view.

Understanding the Code Window

The Code window is used for Visual Basic programming as well as for viewing and modifying the code of existing Visual Basic procedures. Each VBA module can be opened in a separate Code window.

There are several ways of activating the Code window:

- From the Project Explorer window, choose the appropriate module and then click the View Code button
- From the VBE menu, choose View | Code
- From the keyboard, press F7

At the top of the Code window there are two drop-down list boxes that allow you to move quickly within the Visual Basic code. In the Object box on the left side of the Code window you can select the object whose code you want to view.

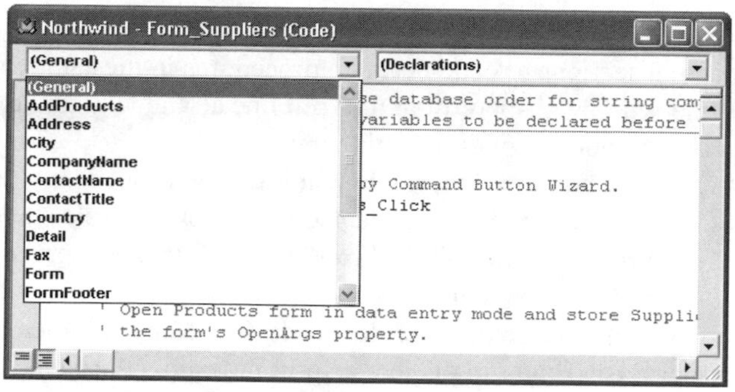

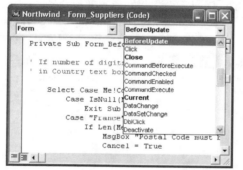

Figure 2-4: The Object drop-down box lists objects that are available in the module currently selected in the Project Explorer window.

The box on the right side of the Code window lets you select a procedure to view. When you open this box, the names of all procedures located in a module are listed alphabetically. If you select a procedure in the Procedure box, the cursor will jump to the first line of that procedure.

Figure 2-5. The Procedure drop-down box lists events the object selected in the Object drop-down box can respond to. If the selected module contains events written for the indicated object, the names of these events appear in bold type.

By dragging the split bar down to a selected position in the Code window or choosing Window | Split, you can divide the Code window into two panes, as shown in Figure 2-6.

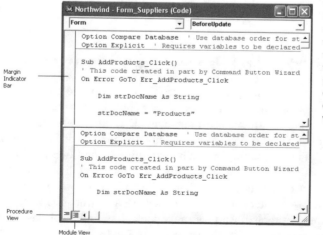

Figure 2-6: By splitting the Code window you can view different sections of a long procedure or a different procedure in each window pane.

Setting up the Code window for the two-pane display is useful for copying, cutting, and pasting sections of code between procedures in the same module. To return to a one-window display, drag the split line all the way to the top of the Code window or choose Window | Split again.

Two icons are at the bottom of the Code window. The Procedure View icon displays only one procedure at a time in the Code window. To select another procedure, use the Procedure drop-down box. The Module View icon displays all the procedures in the selected module. Use the vertical scroll bar in the Code window to scroll through the module's code. The Margin Indicator bar is used by the Visual Basic Editor to display helpful indicators during editing and debugging.

Other Windows in the VBE

In addition to the Code window, other windows are frequently used in the Visual Basic environment. The Docking tab in the Options window (select Tools | Options in the Visual Basic Editor window) displays a list of available windows and allows you to choose which windows you want to be dockable.

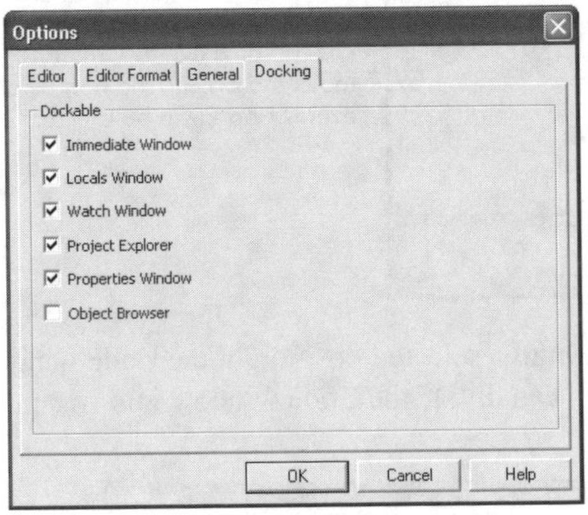

Figure 2-7: You can use the Docking tab in the Options window to control which windows are currently displayed in the Visual Basic programming environment.

On-the-Fly Syntax and Programming Assistance

Writing procedures in Visual Basic requires that you use hundreds of built-in instructions and functions. Because most people cannot memorize the correct syntax of all the instructions available in VBA, IntelliSense technology provides you with syntax and programming assistance on demand during the course of entering instructions. While working in the Code window, you can have special windows pop up and guide you through the process of creating correct VBA code. The Edit toolbar in the VBE window contains several buttons that let you enter correctly formatted VBA instructions with speed and ease. If the Edit toolbar isn't currently docked in the Visual Basic Editor window, you can turn it on by choosing View | Toolbars.

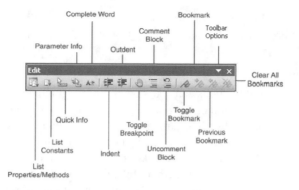

Figure 2-8: The Edit toolbar provides timesaving buttons while entering VBA code.

List Properties/Methods

Each object can contain one or more properties and methods. When you enter the name of the object in the Code window followed by a period that separates the name of the object from its property or method, a pop-up menu may appear. This menu lists the properties and methods available for the object that precedes the period. To turn on this automated feature, choose Tools | Options. In the Options window, click the Editor tab, and make sure the Auto List Members check box is selected. While entering the VBA instructions, Visual Basic suggests properties and methods that can be used with the particular object, as demonstrated in Figure 2-9.

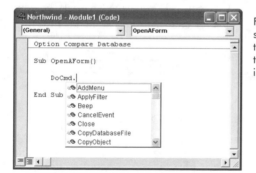

Figure 2-9: When Auto List Members is selected, Visual Basic suggests properties and methods that can be used with the particular object as you are entering the VBA instructions.

To choose an item from the pop-up menu, start typing the name of the property or method you want to use. When the correct item name is highlighted, press Enter to insert the item into your code and start a new line, or press the Tab key to insert the item and continue writing instructions on the same line. You can also double-click the item to insert it in your code. To close the pop-up menu without inserting an item, press Esc. When you press Esc to remove the pop-up menu, Visual Basic will not display the menu for the same object again. To display the properties/methods pop-up menu again, you can:

■ Press Ctrl+J

■ Use the Backspace key to delete the period, then type the period again

■ Right-click in the Code window, and select List Properties/Methods from the shortcut menu

- Choose Edit | List Properties/Methods
- Click the List Properties/Methods button 🖼 on the Edit toolbar

Parameter Info

Some VBA functions and methods can take one or more arguments (or parameters). If a Visual Basic function or method requires an argument, you can see the names of required and optional arguments in a tip box that appears just below the cursor as soon as you type the open parenthesis or enter a space. The Parameter Info feature (see Figure 2-10) makes it easy for you to supply correct arguments to a VBA function or method. In addition, it reminds you of two other things that are very important for the function or method to work correctly: the order of the arguments and the required data type of each argument. To see how this works, enter the following instruction in the Code window:

```
DoCmd.OpenForm
```

As soon as you enter a space after the OpenForm method, a tip window appears just below the cursor. The current argument is displayed in bold. Then as soon as you supply the first argument and enter the comma, Visual Basic displays the next argument in bold. Optional arguments are surrounded by square brackets [ ]. To close the Parameter Info window, press Esc. To open the tip window using the keyboard, enter the instruction or function, followed by the left parenthesis, and press Ctrl+Shift+I. You can also click the Parameter Info button 🖳 on the Edit toolbar or choose Edit | Parameter Info from the menu bar.

Figure 2-10: A tip window displays a list of arguments utilized by a VBA function or method.

To display the Parameter Info window when entering a VBA function, type the following in the Immediate window:

```
Mkdir(
```

You should see the MkDir(Path As String) tip window just below the cursor. Now, type "C:\NewFolder" followed by the ending parenthesis. When you press Enter, Visual Basic will create a folder named NewFolder in the root directory of your computer. Activate the Explorer and check it out!

List Constants

If the Options window (Editor tab) has a checkmark next to the Auto List Members setting, Visual Basic displays a pop-up menu listing the constants that are valid for the property or method. A *constant* is a value that indicates a specific state or result. Access and other members of the Microsoft Office suite have some predefined, built-in constants. Suppose you want to open a form in Design view. In Microsoft Access, a form can be viewed in: Design view (acDesign), DataSheet view (acFormDS), PivotChart view (acFormPivot-Chart), PivotTable view (acFormPivotTable), Form view (acNormal), and Print Preview (acPreview). Each of these options is represented by a built-in constant. Microsoft Access constant names begin with the letters ac. As soon as you enter a comma and a space following your instruction in the Code window (e.g., DoCmd.OpenForm "Products"), a pop-up menu will appear with the names of valid constants for the OpenForm method.

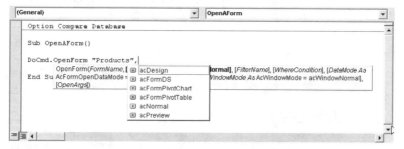

Figure 2-11: The List Constants pop-up menu displays a list of constants that are valid for the property or method typed.

The List Constants menu can be activated by pressing Ctrl+Shift+J or by clicking the List Constants button 🔳 on the Edit toolbar.

Quick Info

When you select an instruction, function, method, procedure name, or constant in the Code window and then click the Quick Info button 🔳 on the Edit toolbar (or press Ctrl+I), Visual Basic will display the syntax of the highlighted item as well as the value of its constant. The Quick Info feature can be turned on or off using the Options window. To use the feature, click the Editor tab, and make sure there is a checkmark in the box next to Auto Quick Info.

```
Northwind - Module1 (Code)
(General)                    OpenAForm
    Option Compare Database

    Sub OpenAForm()

    DoCmd.OpenForm "Products", acDesign
    DoCmd As DoCmd
    End Sub
```

Figure 2-12: The Quick Info feature provides a list of function parameters, as well as constant values and VBA statement syntax.

Complete Word

Another way to increase the speed of writing VBA procedures in the Code window is with the Complete Word feature. As you enter the first few letters of a keyword and click the Complete Word button ▣ on the Edit toolbar, Visual Basic will save you time by completing the keyword entry for you.

For example, enter the first three letters of the keyword DoCmd in the Code window, and click the Complete Word button on the Edit toolbar:

    DoC

Visual Basic will complete the rest of the command you started, and in the place of DoC you will see the entire instruction, DoCmd.

If there are several VBA keywords that begin with the same letters, when you click the Complete Word button on the Edit toolbar Visual Basic will display a pop-up menu listing all of them. To try this, enter only the first three letters of the word Application, press the Complete Word button on the toolbar, and select the appropriate word from the pop-up menu.

Indent/Outdent

The Editor tab in the Options window contains many settings you can turn on to make automated features available in the Code window.

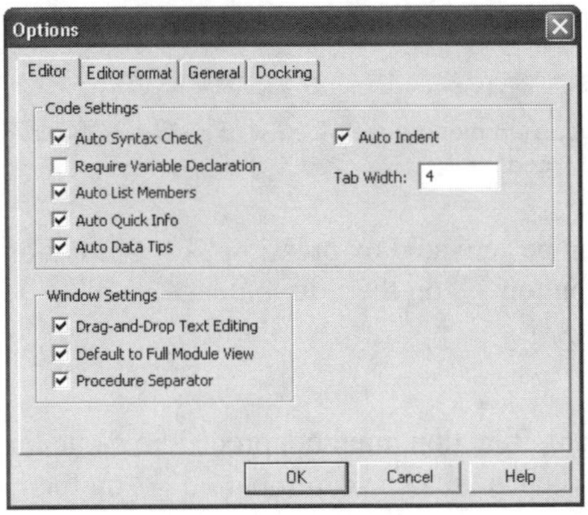

Figure 2-13: The Options window lists features you can turn on and off to fit the VBA programming environment to your needs.

If the Auto Indent option is turned on, you can automatically indent the selected lines of code the number of characters specified in the Tab Width text box. The default entry for Auto Indent is four characters. You can easily change the tab width by typing a new value in the text box. Why would you want to use indentation in your code? Indentation makes your VBA procedures more readable and easier to understand. Indenting is especially recommended for entering lines of code that make decisions or repeat actions.

Let's see how you can indent and outdent lines of code using the Orders form in the Northwind database.

◎ Hands-On 2-1: Using the Indent/Outdent Feature

1. Open the **Acc2003_Chap02.mdb** file from the book's downloadable files. This file is a copy of the Northwind sample database that comes with Microsoft Access.

2. Press **Alt+F11** to switch to the Visual Basic Editor window.

3. In the Project Explorer window, double-click on the **Form_Orders** object in the Microsoft Office Access Class Objects folder. The Code window should now show the event procedures written for this form.

4. In the Code window, select any block of code beginning with the keyword If and ending with the keywords End If.

5. Click the **Indent** button ▣ on the Edit toolbar or press **Tab** on the keyboard. The selected block of instructions will move four spaces to the right. You can adjust the number of spaces to indent to your liking by choosing **Tools | Options** and entering the appropriate value in the Tab Width box on the Editor tab.

6. Click the **Outdent** button ▣ on the Edit toolbar or press **Shift+Tab** to return the selected lines of code to the previous location in the Code window. The Indent and Outdent options are also available from the Visual Basic Editor's Edit menu.

Comment Block/Uncomment Block

The apostrophe placed at the beginning of a line of code denotes a comment. Besides the fact that comments make it easier to understand what the procedure does, comments are also very useful in testing and troubleshooting VBA procedures. For example, when you execute a procedure, it may not run as expected. Instead of deleting the lines of code that may be responsible for the problems encountered, you may want to skip these lines for now and return to them later. By placing an apostrophe at the beginning of the line you want to avoid, you can continue checking the other parts of your procedure. While commenting one line of code by typing an apostrophe works fine for most people, when it comes to turning entire blocks of code into comments, you'll find the Comment Block and Uncomment Block buttons on the Edit toolbar very handy and easy to use. To comment a few lines of code, select the lines and click the Comment Block button ▣. To turn the commented code back into VBA instructions, click the Uncomment Block button ▣.

If you don't select a block of text, when you click the Comment Block button the apostrophe is added only to the line of code where the cursor is currently located.

Using the Object Browser

If you want to move easily through the myriad of VBA elements and features, examine the capabilities of the Object Browser. This special built-in tool is available in the Visual Basic Editor window.

To access the Object Browser, use any of the following methods:

- Press F2
- Choose View | Object Browser
- Click the Object Browser button ▓ on the toolbar

The Object Browser allows you to browse through the objects available to your VBA procedures, as well as view their properties, methods, and events. With the aid of the Object Browser, you can quickly move between procedures in your database application, as well as search for objects and methods across various type libraries.

The Object Browser window is divided into several sections. The top of the window displays the Project/Library drop-down list box with the names of all currently available libraries and projects. A *library* is a special file that contains information about the objects in an application. New libraries can be added via the References dialog box (select Tools | References). The entry for <All Libraries> lists the objects of all libraries installed on your computer. While the Access library contains objects specific to using Microsoft Office Access, the VBA library provides access to three objects (Debug, Err, and Collection) as well as a number of built-in functions and constants that give you flexibility in programming by allowing you to send output to the Immediate window, get information about run-time errors, work with the Collection object, manage files, deal with text strings, convert data types, set date and time, and perform mathematical operations.

Below the Project/Library drop-down list box is a search box (Search Text) that allows you to quickly find information in a particular library. This field remembers the last four items you searched for. To find only whole words, right-click anywhere in the Object Browser window and choose Find Whole Word Only from the shortcut menu. The Search Results section of the Object Browser displays the Library, Class, and Member elements that met the criteria entered in the Search Text box. When you type the search text and click the Search button 🔍, Visual Basic expands the Object Browser window to show the search results. You can hide or show the Search Results section by clicking the button located to the right of the binoculars.

In the lower section of the Object Browser window, the Classes list box displays the available object classes in the selected library. If you select the name of the currently open database (e.g., Northwind) in the Project/Library list box, the Classes list will display the objects as listed in the Explorer window. In Figure 2-14, the Form_Employees object class is selected. When you highlight a class, the list on the right side (Members) shows the properties, methods, and events available for that class. By default, members are listed alphabetically. You can, however, organize the Members list by group type (properties,

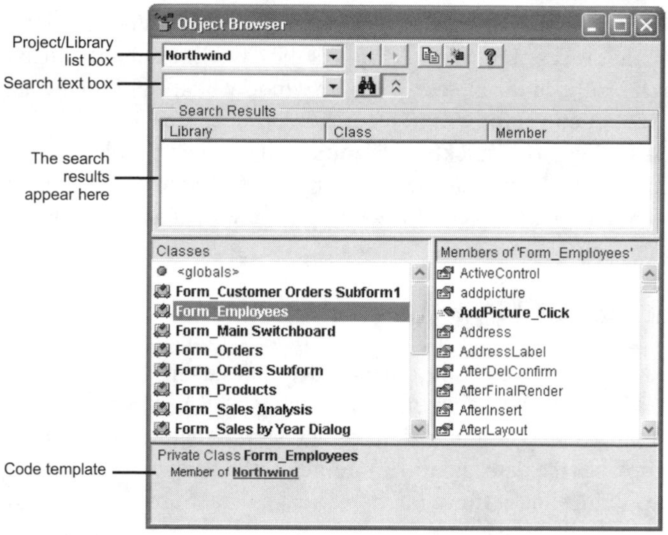

Figure 2-14: The Object Browser window allows you to browse through all the objects, properties, and methods available to the current VBA project.

methods, or events) using the Group Members command from the Object Browser shortcut menu (right-click the Object Browser to display this menu).

If you select the Northwind project in the Project/Library list box, the Members list box will list all the procedures available in this project. To examine a procedure's code, double-click its name. If you select a VBA library in the Project/Library list box, you will see the Visual Basic built-in functions and constants. If you need more information on the selected class or member, click the question mark button located at the top of the Object Browser window.

The bottom of the Object Browser window displays a code template area with the definition of the selected member. If you click the green hyperlink text in the code template, you can jump to the selected member's class or library in the Object Browser window. Text displayed in the code template area can be copied and pasted to a Code window. If the Code window is visible while the Object Browser window is open, you can save time by dragging the highlighted code template and dropping it into the Code window.

You can easily adjust the size of the various sections of the Object Browser window by dragging the dividing horizontal and vertical lines.

Now that are familiar with the Object Browser, you can put it to use in VBA programming. Let's assume that you want to write a VBA procedure to control a check box placed on a form and would like to see the list of properties and methods that are available for working with check boxes.

◎ Hands-On 2-2: Using the Object Browser

1. Switch to the Visual Basic Editor window and press **F2** to open the Object Browser.

2. In the Project/Library list box of the Object Browser, click the drop-down arrow and select the **Access** library.

3. Enter **checkbox** in the Search Text box and click the **Search** button (🔍).

Make sure you don't enter a space in the search string. Visual Basic begins to search the Access library and displays the search results. By analyzing the search results in the Object Browser window, you can find the appropriate VBA instructions for writing your VBA procedures. Looking at the Members list, you can quickly determine that you can enable or disable a check box by setting the Enabled property. To get detailed information on any item found in the Object Browser, select the item and press **F1** to activate online help.

Using the VBA Object Library

While the Access library contains objects specific to using Microsoft Access, the VBA Object Library provides access to many built-in VBA functions grouped by categories. These functions are general in nature. They allow you to manage files, set the date and time, interact with users, convert data types, deal with text strings, or perform mathematical calculations. In the following exercise, you will see how to use one of the built-in VBA functions to create a new subfolder without leaving Access.

⊚ Hands-On 2-3: Using Built-in VBA Functions

1. In the Database window of the currently open Acc2003_Chap02.mdb file, click the **Modules** button, and then click **New** to create a new standard module.

2. In the Code window, enter the name of the procedure: **Sub NewFolder()**.

3. Click the **Enter** key. Visual Basic will enter the ending keywords: End Sub.

4. Press **F2** to activate the Object Browser.

5. Click the drop-down arrow in the Project/Library list box and select **VBA**.

6. Enter **file** in the Search Text box and press **Enter**.

7. Scroll down in the Members list box and highlight the **MkDir** method.

8. Click the **Copy** button in the Object Browser window to copy the selected method name to the Windows clipboard.

9. Close the Object Browser window and return to the Code window. Paste the copied instruction inside the NewFolder procedure.

10. Now, enter a space, followed by **"C:\Study"**. Be sure to enter the name of the entire path in the quotation marks. The NewFolder procedure is shown below.

```
Sub NewFolder()
    MkDir "C:\Study"
End Sub
```

11. Choose **Run | Run Sub/UserForm** to run the NewFolder procedure.

When you run the NewFolder procedure, Visual Basic creates a new folder on drive C. To see the folder, activate Windows Explorer. After creating a new folder, you may realize that you don't need it after all. Although you could easily delete the folder while in Windows Explorer, how about getting rid of it programmatically?

The Object Browser contains many other methods that are useful for working with folders and files. The RmDir method is just as simple to use as the MkDir method. To remove the Study folder from your hard drive, replace the MkDir method with the RmDir method and rerun the NewFolder procedure. Or create a new procedure called RemoveFolder, as shown below:

```
Sub RemoveFolder()
    RmDir "C:\Study"
End Sub
```

When writing procedures from scratch, it's a good idea to consult the Object Browser for names of the built-in VBA functions.

Using the Immediate Window

The Immediate window is a sort of VBA programmer's scratch pad. Here you can test VBA instructions before putting them to work in your VBA procedures. It is a great tool for experimenting with your new language. Instructions that you enter in this window immediately display results. To activate the Immediate window, switch to the Visual Basic Editor window and choose View | Immediate Window.

The Immediate window can be moved anywhere on the Visual Basic Editor screen, or it can be docked so that it always appears in the same area of the screen. The docking setting can be turned on and off from the Docking tab in the Options window (Tools | Options). To access the Immediate window, press Ctrl+G while in the Visual Basic Editor screen. To close the Immediate window, click the Close button in the top right corner of the window.

The Immediate window allows you to type VBA statements and test their results immediately without having to write a procedure. Use it to try out your statements. If the statement produces the expected result, you can copy the statement from the Immediate window into your procedure (or you can drag it right onto the Code window, if it is visible).

The following hands-on demonstrates how to use the Immediate window to check instructions and get answers.

◎ Hands-On 2-4: Experiments in the Immediate Window

1. Switch to the VBE window by pressing **Alt+F11**.

2. Press **Ctrl+G** to activate the Immediate window or choose **View | Immediate Window**.

3. In the Immediate window, type the instruction shown below, and press **Enter**:

```
DoCmd.OpenForm "Suppliers"
```

If you entered the above VBA statement correctly, Visual Basic opens the form Suppliers, assuming the Northwind database is currently open.

4. Enter the following instruction in the Immediate window:

```
Debug.Print Forms!Suppliers.RecordSource
```

When you press **Enter**, Visual Basic indicates that Suppliers is the RecordSource for the Suppliers form.

Every time you type an instruction in the Immediate window and press Enter, Visual Basic executes the statement on the line where the insertion point is located. If you want to execute the same instruction again, click anywhere in the line containing the instruction and press Enter. For more practice, rerun the statements shown in Figure 2-15. Start from the instruction displayed in the first line of the Immediate window. Execute the instructions one by one by clicking in the appropriate line and pressing Enter.

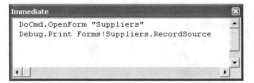

Figure 2-15: Use the Immediate window to evaluate and try out Visual Basic statements.

So far you have used the Immediate window to perform some actions. The Immediate window also allows you to ask questions. Suppose you want to find out the answers to "How many controls are in the Suppliers form?" or "What's the name of the current application?" When working in the Immediate window, you can easily get answers to these and other questions.

In the preceding exercise, you entered two instructions. Let's return to the Immediate window to ask some questions. Access remembers the instructions entered in the Immediate window even after you close this window. The contents of the Immediate window are automatically deleted when you exit Microsoft Access.

◎ Hands-On 2-5: Asking Questions in the Immediate Window

1. Click in a new line of the Immediate window and enter the following statement to find out the number of controls in the Suppliers form:

```
?Forms!Suppliers.Controls.Count
```

When you press **Enter**, Visual Basic enters the number of controls on a new line in the Immediate window.

2. Click in a new line of the Immediate window, and enter the following question:

```
?Application.Name
```

When you press **Enter**, Visual Basic enters the name of the active application on a new line in the Immediate window.

3. In a new line in the Immediate window, enter the following question:

```
?12/3
```

When you press **Enter**, Visual Basic shows the result of division on a new line. But what if you want to know the result of 3 + 2 and 12 * 8 right away? Instead of entering these instructions on separate lines, you can enter them on one line as in the following example:

```
?3+2:?12*8
```

Notice the colon separating the two blocks of instructions. When you press the Enter key, Visual Basic displays the results 5 and 96 on separate lines in the Immediate window.

Here are a couple of other statements you may want to try out on your own in the Immediate window:

```
?Application.GetOption("Default Database Directory")
?Application.CodeProject.Name
```

Instead of using the question mark, you may precede the statement typed in the Immediate window with the Print command like this:

```
Print  Application.CodeProject.Name
```

Later in this book you will learn how to run VBA procedures and functions from the Immediate window. To delete the instructions from the Immediate window, highlight all the lines and press Delete.

Chapter Summary

Programming in Access 2003 requires a working knowledge of objects and collections of objects. In this chapter you explored several methods of learning about Visual Basic. Here's the summary of when to use a specific tool:

- When in doubt about objects, properties, or methods in an existing VBA procedure, highlight the instruction in question and fire up the online help by pressing F1.
- If you need a quick listing of properties and methods for every available object, or have trouble locating a hard-to-find procedure, go with the Object Browser.
- If you want to experiment with VBA and see the results of VBA commands immediately, activate the Immediate window.

Chapter 3

Variables, Data Types, and Constants

In Chapter 2, while working in the Immediate window, you tried several Visual Basic instructions that returned some information. For example, when you entered ?Forms!Suppliers.RecordSource, you found out that the Suppliers form was based on Suppliers. However, outside the Immediate window, when you write Visual Basic procedures, you can't use the question mark. So how do you obtain your answers while doing real programming? If you enter the Forms!Suppliers.RecordSource statement in your procedure, Visual Basic won't suddenly stop to tell you the result of this instruction. To find out what a particular statement has returned, you must tell Visual Basic to memorize it. You do this by using variables.

What Is a Variable?

A *variable* is a name used to refer to an item of data. Each time you want to remember a result of a VBA instruction, think of a name that will represent it. For example, if you want to keep track of the number of controls on a particular form, you can make up a name such as NumOfControls, TotalControls, or FormsControlCount.

The names of variables can contain characters, numbers, and some punctuation marks except for the following: , # $ % & @ !

The name of a variable cannot begin with a number or contain a space. If you want the name of the variable to include more than one word, use the underscore (_). Although a variable name can contain as many as 254 characters, it's best to use short and simple names. Using short names will save you typing time when you need to reuse the variable in your Visual Basic procedure. Visual Basic doesn't care whether you use uppercase or lowercase letters in variable names; however, most programmers use lowercase letters. When the variable name is comprised of more than one word, most programmers capitalize the first letter of each word, as in the following: NumOfControls, First_Name.

> ### Reserved Words Can't Be Used for Variable Names
>
> You can use any label you want for a variable name except for the reserved words that VBA uses. Visual Basic function names and certain other words that have a special meaning in VBA cannot be used as variable names. For example, words such as Name, Len, Empty, Local, Currency, or Exit will generate an error message if used as a variable name.

Give your variables names that can help you remember their roles. Some programmers use a prefix to identify the variable's type. A variable name preceded with "str," for example strName, can be quickly recognized within the procedure code as the one holding the text string.

What Are Data Types?

When you create Visual Basic procedures you have a purpose in mind: You want to manipulate data. Because your procedures will handle different kinds of information, you should understand how Visual Basic stores data. The *data type* determines how the data is stored in the computer's memory. For example, data can be stored as a number, text, date, object, etc. If you forget to tell Visual Basic the type of your data, it is assigned the Variant data type. The *Variant* type has the ability to figure out on its own what kind of data is being manipulated and then take on that type. The Visual Basic data types are shown in Table 3-1. In addition to the built-in data types, you can define your own data types, known as user-defined data types. Because data types take up different amounts of space in the computer's memory, some of them are more expensive than others. Therefore, to conserve memory and make your procedure run faster, you should select the data type that uses the fewest bytes but at the same time is capable of handling the data that your procedure has to manipulate.

Table 3-1: VBA data types

Data Type	Storage Size	Range
Byte	1 byte	0 to 255
Boolean	2 bytes	True or False
Integer	2 bytes	–32,768 to 32,767
Long (long integer)	4 bytes	–2,147,483,648 to 2,147,483,647
Single (single-precision floating-point)	4 bytes	–3.402823E38 to –1.401298E–45 for negative values; 1.401298E–45 to 3.402823E38 for positive values
Double (double-precision floating-point)	8 bytes	–1.79769313486231E308 to –4.94065645841247E–324 for negative values; 4.94065645841247E–324 to 1.79769313486232E308 for positive values
Currency (scaled integer)	8 bytes	–922,337,203,685,477.5808 to 922,337,203,685,477.5807

Data Type	Storage Size	Range
Decimal	14 bytes	+/–79,228,162,514,264,337,593,543,950,335 with no decimal point; +/–7.9228162514264337593543950335 with 28 places to the right of the decimal; smallest non-zero number is +/–0.0000000000000000000000000001
Date	8 bytes	January 1, 100, to December 31, 9999
Object	4 bytes	Any Object reference
String (variable-length)	10 bytes + string length	0 to approximately 2 billion
String (fixed-length)	Length of string	1 to approximately 65,400
Variant (with numbers)	16 bytes	Any numeric value up to the range of a Double
Variant (with characters)	22 bytes + string length	Same range as for variable-length String
User-defined (using Type)	Number required by elements	The range of each element is the same as the range of its data type.

Creating Variables

You can create a variable by declaring it with a special command or by just using it in a statement. When you declare your variable, you make Visual Basic aware of the variable's name and data type. This is called *explicit variable declaration*.

Advantages of Explicit Variable Declaration

Explicit variable declaration:

- Speeds up the execution of your procedure. Since Visual Basic knows the data type, it reserves only as much memory as is absolutely necessary to store the data.

- Makes your code easier to read and understand because all the variables are listed at the very beginning of the procedure.

- Helps prevent errors caused by misspelling a variable name. Visual Basic automatically corrects the variable name based on the spelling used in the variable declaration.

If you don't let Visual Basic know about the variable prior to using it, you are implicitly telling VBA that you want to create this variable. *Implicit variables* are automatically assigned the Variant data type (see Table 3-1). Although implicit variable declaration is convenient (it allows you to create variables on the fly and assign values to them without knowing in advance the data type of the values being assigned), it can cause several problems.

> ### Disadvantages of Implicit Variable Declaration
>
> - If you misspell a variable name in your procedure, Visual Basic may display a run-time error or create a new variable. You are guaranteed to waste some time troubleshooting problems that could easily have been avoided had you declared your variable at the beginning of the procedure.
> - Since Visual Basic does not know what type of data your variable will store, it assigns it a Variant data type. This causes your procedure to run slower, because Visual Basic has to check the data type every time it deals with your variable. And because Variant variables can store any type of data, Visual Basic has to reserve more memory to store your data.

Declaring Variables

You declare a variable with the Dim keyword. Dim stands for "dimension." The Dim keyword is followed by the variable's name and type.

Suppose you want the procedure to display the age of an employee. Before you can calculate the age, you must feed the procedure the employee's date of birth. To do this, you declare a variable called DateOfBirth, as follows:

```
Dim DateOfBirth As Date
```

Notice that the Dim keyword is followed by the name of the variable (DateOfBirth). If you don't like this name, you are free to replace it with another word, as long as the word you are planning to use is not one of the VBA keywords. You specify the data type the variable will hold by including the As keyword followed by one of the data types from Table 3-1. The Date data type tells Visual Basic that the variable DateOfBirth will store a date.

To store the employee's age, you will declare the age variable, as follows:

```
Dim age As Integer
```

The age variable will store the number of years between today's date and the employee's date of birth. Since age is displayed as a whole number, the age variable has been assigned the Integer data type.

You may also want your procedure to keep track of the employee's name, so you declare another variable to hold the employee's first and last name:

```
Dim FullName As String
```

Since the word Name is on the VBA list of reserved words, using it in your VBA procedure would guarantee an error. To hold the employee's full name, we used the variable FullName and declared it as the String data type because the data it will hold is text. Declaring variables is regarded as good programming practice because it makes programs easier to read and helps prevent certain types of errors.

Informal (Implicit) Variables

Variables that are not explicitly declared with Dim statements are said to be implicitly declared. These variables are automatically assigned a data type called Variant. They can hold numbers, strings, and other types of information. You can create an informal variable by assigning some value to a variable name anywhere in your VBA procedure. For example, you implicitly declare a variable in the following way: DaysLeft = 100.

Now that you know how to declare your variables, let's write a procedure that uses them.

◎ Hands-On 3-1: Using Variables

This chapter's hands-on exercises are provided in the Acc2003_Chap03.mdb file included in the book's downloadable files.

1. Open **Acc2003_Chap03.mdb** from the downloadable files or, if you'd like to start from scratch, create a new Microsoft Office Access 2003 database.

2. Click the **Modules** button in the Database window and then click the **New** button to create a new module. When the Visual Basic Editor window appears you will notice Module1 under the Modules folder in the Project Explorer window.

3. In the [Module1 (Code)] window that appears in the center of the screen, enter the code of the AgeCalc procedure shown below.

4. If the Immediate window is not open, press **Ctrl+G** or choose **View |
    Immediate Window**. Since the example procedure writes the results to the Immediate window, you should ensure that this window is open prior to executing step 5 below.

5. To run the procedure, click any line between the Sub and End Sub keywords and press **F5**.

```
Sub AgeCalc()
    ' variable declaration
    Dim FullName As String
    Dim DateOfBirth As Date
    Dim age As Integer

    ' assign values to variables
    FullName = "John Smith"
    DateOfBirth = #1/3/1967#

    ' calculate age
    age = Year(Now()) - Year(DateOfBirth)

    ' print results to the Immediate window
    Debug.Print FullName & " is " & age & " years old."
End Sub
```

Notice that in the AgeCalc procedure the variables are declared on separate lines at the beginning of the procedure. If you want, you can declare several variables on the same line, separating each variable name with a comma, as shown in the example below:

```
Dim FullName As String, DateOfBirth As Date, age As Integer
```

When you list all your variables on one line, the Dim keyword appears only once at the beginning of the variable declaration line.

What Is the Variable Type?

You can find out the type of a variable used in your procedure by right-clicking the variable name and selecting Quick Info from the shortcut menu.

When Visual Basic executes the variable declaration statements, it creates the variables with the specified names and reserves memory space to store their values. Then specific values are assigned to these variables. To assign a value to a variable, you begin with a variable name followed by an equals sign. The value entered to the right of the equals sign is the data you want to store in the variable. The data you enter here must be of the type stated in the variable declaration. Text data should be surrounded by quotation marks and the date by # characters.

Using the data supplied by the DateOfBirth variable, Visual Basic calculates the age of an employee and stores the result of the calculation in the variable called age. Then, the full name of the employee as well as the age are printed to the Immediate window using the instruction Debug.Print.

Concatenation

You can combine two or more strings to form a new string. The joining operation is called concatenation. You have seen an example of concatenated strings in the AgeCalc procedure above. Concatenation is represented by an ampersand (&) character. For instance, "His name is " & FirstName will produce a string like: His name is John or His name is Michael. The name of the person is determined by the contents of the FirstName variable. Notice that there is an extra space between "is" and the ending quotation mark: "His name is ". Concatenation of strings can also be represented by a plus sign (+); however, many programmers prefer to restrict the plus sign to numerical operations to eliminate ambiguity.

Specifying the Data Type of a Variable

If you don't specify the variable's data type in the Dim statement, you end up with the *untyped* variable. Untyped variables in VBA are always assigned the Variant data type. Variant data types can hold all the other data types (except for user-defined data types). This feature makes Variant a very flexible and popular data type. Despite this flexibility, it's highly recommended that you create typed variables. When you declare a variable of a certain data type, your

VBA procedure runs faster because Visual Basic does not have to stop to analyze the variable to determine its type.

Visual Basic can work with many types of numeric variables. Integer variables can only hold whole numbers from –32,768 to 32,767. Other types of
numeric variables are Long, Single, Double, and Currency. The Long variables
can hold whole numbers in the range –2,147,483,648 to 2,147,483,647. As
opposed to Integer and Long variables, Single and Double variables can hold
decimals.

String variables are used to refer to text. When you declare a variable of the
String data type, you can tell Visual Basic how long the string should be. For
instance, Dim extension As String * 3 declares the fixed-length String variable
named extension that is three characters long. If you don't assign a specific
length, the String variable will be *dynamic*. This means that Visual Basic will
make enough space in computer memory to handle whatever amount of text is
assigned to it.

After you declare a variable, you can only store in it the type of information
that you stated in the declaration statement. Assigning string values to numeric
variables or numeric values to string variables results in the error message
"Type Mismatch" or causes Visual Basic to modify the value. For example, if
your variable was declared to hold whole numbers and your data uses decimals, Visual Basic will disregard the decimals and use only the whole part of
the number.

Let's use the MyNumber procedure in Hands-On 3-2 below as an example
of how Visual Basic modifies the data according to the assigned data types.

◎ Hands-On 3-2: Understanding the Data Type of a Variable

1. If the Visual Basic window is not open, press **Alt+F11** to open it. Next,
    choose **Insert | Module** to add a new module.

2. Enter the code of the procedure MyNumber in the new module's Code
    window.

3. To run the procedure, click any line between the Sub and End Sub
    keywords and press **F5** or choose **Run | Run Sub/UserForm**.

```
Sub MyNumber()
    Dim intNum As Integer

    intNum = 23.11
    MsgBox intNum
End Sub
```

When you run the above procedure, Visual Basic displays the contents of the
variable intNum as 23, and not 23.11, because the intNum variable was
declared as an Integer data type.

Using Type Declaration Characters

If you don't declare a variable with a Dim statement, you can still designate a type for it by using a special character at the end of the variable name. For example, to declare the FirstName variable as String, you append the dollar sign to the variable name as shown:

```
Dim FirstName$
```

The above is the same as Dim FirstName As String. Other type declaration characters are shown in Table 3-2.

Notice that the type declaration characters can only be used with six data types. To use the type declaration character, append the character to the end of the variable name.

Table 3-2: Type declaration characters

Data Type	Character
Integer	%
Long	&
Single	!
Double	#
Currency	@
String	$

◎ Hands-On 3-3: Using Type Declaration Characters in Variable Names

1. If the Visual Basic window is not open, press **Alt+F11** to open it. Next, choose **Insert | Module** to add a new module.

2. Enter the code of the AgeCalc2 procedure in the new module's Code window.

3. To run the procedure, click any line between the Sub and End Sub keywords and press **F5** or choose **Run | Run Sub/UserForm**.

```
Sub AgeCalc2()
    ' variable declaration
    Dim FullName$
    Dim DateOfBirth As Date
    Dim age%

    ' assign values to variables
    FullName$ = "John Smith"
    DateOfBirth = #1/3/1967#

    ' calculate age
    age% = Year(Now()) - Year(DateOfBirth)

    ' print results to the Immediate window
    Debug.Print FullName$ & " is " & age% & " years old."
End Sub
```

> **Declaring Typed Variables**
>
> The variable type can be indicated by the As keyword or by attaching a type symbol. If you don't add the type symbol or the As command, VBA will default the variable to the Variant data type.

Assigning Values to Variables

Now that you know how to correctly name and declare variables, it's time to start using them.

◎ Hands-On 3-4: Assigning Values to Variables

1. If the Visual Basic window is not open, press **Alt+F11** to open it. Next, choose **Insert | Module** to add a new module.

2. Enter the code of the CalcCost procedure in the new module's Code window.

3. To run the procedure, click any line between the Sub and End Sub keywords and press **F5** or choose **Run | Run Sub/UserForm**.

```
Sub CalcCost()
    slsPrice = 35
    slsTax = 0.085
    cost = slsPrice + (slsPrice * slsTax)

    strMsg = "The calculator total is " & "$" & cost & "."
    MsgBox strMsg
End Sub
```

The CalcCost procedure uses four variables: slsPrice, slsTax, cost, and strMsg. Because none of these variables have been explicitly declared, they all have the same data type — Variant. The variables slsPrice and slsTax were created by assigning some values to variable names at the beginning of the procedure. The cost variable was assigned a value that is the result of the calculation slsPrice + (slsPrice * slsTax). The cost calculation uses the values supplied by the slsPrice and slsTax variables. The strMsg variable puts together a text message to the user. This message is then displayed with the MsgBox function.

When you assign values to variables, you follow the name of the variable with an equals sign. After the equals sign you enter the value of the variable. This can be a number, expression, or text surrounded by quotation marks. While the values assigned to the variables slsPrice, slsTax, and cost are easily understood, the value stored in the strMsg variable is a little more involved.

Let's examine the content of the strMsg variable:

```
strMsg = "The calculator total is " & "$" & cost & "."
```

- The string "The calculator total is " begins and ends with quotation marks. Notice that there is an extra space before the ending quotation mark.

- The & character allows one string to be appended to another string or to the contents of a variable.
- The $ is used to denote the currency type. Because the dollar symbol is a character, it is surrounded by quotation marks.
- The & character must be used every time you want to append a new piece of information to the previous string.
- The cost variable is a placeholder. The actual cost of the calculator will be displayed here when the procedure runs.
- The & character attaches yet another string.
- The period is surrounded by quotation marks. When you require a period at the end of the sentence, you must attach it separately when it follows the name of a variable.

> **Variable Initialization**
>
> Visual Basic automatically initializes a new variable to its default value when it is created. Numerical variables are set to zero (0), Boolean variables are initialized to False, string variables are set to the empty string (" "), and Date variables are set to December 30, 1899.

Notice that the cost displayed in the message box has three decimal places. To display the cost of a calculator with two decimal places you need to use a function. VBA has special functions that allow you to change the format of data. To change the format of the cost variable you should use the Format function. This function has the following syntax:

```
Format(expression, format)
```

where *expression* is a value or variable you want to format and *format* is the type of format you want to apply.

⊚ Hands-On 3-4: (Continued)

1. Change the calculation of the cost variable in the CalcCost procedure, as shown below:

```
cost = Format(slsPrice + (slsPrice * slsTax), "0.00")
```

2. To run the modified procedure, click any line between the Sub and End Sub keywords and press **F5** or choose **Run | Run Sub/UserForm**.

After having tried out the CalcCost procedure, you may wonder why you should bother declaring variables if Visual Basic can handle undeclared variables so well. The CalcCost procedure is very short, so you don't need to worry about how many bytes of memory will be consumed each time Visual Basic uses the Variant variable. In short procedures however, it is not the memory that matters but the mistakes you are bound to make when typing variable names. What will happen if the second time you use the cost variable you omit the "o" and refer to it as cst?

```
strMsg = "The calculator total is " & "$" & cst & "."
```

And what will you end up with if, instead of slsTax, you use the word tax in the formula?

```
cost = Format(slsPrice + (slsPrice * tax), "0.00")
```

When you run the procedure with the above errors introduced, Visual Basic will not show the cost of the calculator because it does not find the assignment statement for the cst variable. And because Visual Basic does not know the sales tax, it displays the price of the calculator as the total cost. Visual Basic does not guess. It simply does what you tell it to do. This brings us to the next section, which explains how to make sure that errors of this sort don't occur.

➔ **Note:** Before you continue with this chapter, be sure to replace the names of the variables cst and tax with cost and slsTax.

Forcing Declaration of Variables

Visual Basic has an Option Explicit statement that you can use to automatically remind you to formally declare all your variables. This statement has to be entered at the top of each of your modules. The Option Explicit statement will cause Visual Basic to generate an error message when you try to run a procedure that contains undeclared variables.

◎ Hands-On 3-5: Forcing Declaration of Variables

1. Return to the Code window where you entered the CalcCost procedure (see Hands-On 3-4).

2. At the top of the module window (in the first line), enter

   ```
   Option Explicit
   ```

   and press **Enter**. Visual Basic will display the statement in blue.

3. Position the insertion point anywhere within the CalcCost procedure and press **F5** to run it. Visual Basic displays the error message: "Compile error: Variable not defined."

4. Click **OK** to exit the message box. Visual Basic selects the name of the variable, slsPrice, and highlights in yellow the name of the procedure, Sub CalcCost(). The title bar displays "Microsoft Visual Basic — Acc2003_Chap03 [break] — [Module4 (Code)]." The Visual Basic break mode allows you to correct the problem before you continue. Now you have to formally declare the slsPrice variable.

5. Enter the declaration statement

   ```
   Dim slsPrice As Currency
   ```

   on a new line just below Sub CalcCost() and press **F5** to continue. When you declare the slsPrice variable and rerun your procedure, Visual Basic will generate the same Compile error as soon as it encounters another variable name that was not declared. To fix the remaining problems in this procedure with the variable declaration, choose **Run | Reset** to exit the break mode.

6. Enter the following declarations at the beginning of the CalcCost procedure:

```
' declaration of variables
Dim slsPrice As Currency
Dim slsTax As Single
Dim cost As Currency
Dim strMsg As String
```

7. To run the procedure, click any line between the Sub and End Sub keywords and press **F5** or choose **Run | Run Sub/UserForm**. Your revised CalcCost procedure looks like this:

```
Sub CalcCost() ' revised CalcCost procedure
    ' declaration of variables
    Dim slsPrice As Currency
    Dim slsTax As Single
    Dim cost As Currency
    Dim strMsg As String

    slsPrice = 35
    slsTax = 0.085
    cost = Format(slsPrice + (slsPrice * slsTax), "0.00")
    strMsg = "The calculator total is " & "$" & cost & "."

    MsgBox strMsg
End Sub
```

The Option Explicit statement you entered at the top of the module (see step 2) forced you to declare variables. Because you must include the Option Explicit statement in each module where you want to require variable declaration, you can have Visual Basic enter this statement for you each time you insert a new module.

To automatically include Option Explicit in every new module you create, follow these steps:

1. Choose **Tools | Options**.

2. Make sure the Require Variable Declaration check box is selected in the Options window (Editor tab).

3. Choose **OK** to close the Options window.

From now on, every new module will be added with the Option Explicit statement in line 1. If you want to require variables to be explicitly declared in a module you created prior to setting the Require Variable Declaration in the Options window, you must enter the Option Explicit statement manually by editing the module yourself.

> **More about Option Explicit**
>
> Option Explicit forces formal (explicit) declaration of all variables in a particular module. One big advantage of using Option Explicit is that misspellings of variable names will be detected at compile time (when Visual Basic attempts to translate the source code to executable code). The Option Explicit statement must appear in a module before any procedures.

Understanding the Scope and Lifetime of Variables

Variables can have different ranges of influence in a VBA procedure. *Scope* defines the availability of a particular variable to the same procedure or other procedures. A variable's scope can be procedure-level or module-level. In addition to scope, variables have a *lifetime*. The lifetime of a variable determines how long a variable retains its value.

Procedure-Level (Local) Variables

From this chapter you already know how to declare a variable using the Dim statement. The position of the Dim statement in the module determines the scope of a variable. Variables declared with the Dim statement placed within a VBA procedure have a *procedure-level* scope. Procedure-level variables can also be declared by using the Static statement (see "Understanding and Using Static Variables" later in this chapter).

Procedure-level variables are frequently referred to as *local* variables. Local variables can only be used in the procedure where they were declared. Undeclared variables always have a procedure-level scope.

A variable's name must be unique within its scope. This means that you cannot declare two variables with the same name in the same procedure. However, you can use the same variable name in different procedures. In other words, the CalcCost procedure can have the slsTax variable, and the ExpenseRep procedure in the same module can have its own variable called slsTax. Both variables are independent of each other.

> **Local Variables: with Dim or Static?**
>
> When you declare a local variable with the Dim statement, the value of the variable is preserved only while the procedure in which it is declared is running. As soon as the procedure ends, the variable dies. The next time you execute the procedure, the variable is reinitialized.
>
> When you declare a local variable with the Static statement, the value of the variable is preserved after the procedure in which the variable was declared has finished running. Static variables are reset when you quit the Microsoft Access application or when a run-time error occurs while the procedure is running.

Module-Level Variables

Often you want the variable to be available to other VBA procedures after the procedure in which the variable was declared has finished running. This situation requires that you change the scope of a variable. Instead of a procedure-level variable, you will want to declare a *module-level* variable.

Module-level variables are declared at the top of the module (above the first procedure definition) by using the Dim or Private statement. These variables are available to all of the procedures in the module in which they were declared, but are not available to procedures in other modules.

For instance, to make the slsTax variable available to any other procedure in the module, you could declare this variable by using the Dim or Private statement:

```
Option Explicit
Dim slsTax As Single      ' module-level variable declared with Dim statement

Sub CalcCost()
    ...Instructions of the procedure...
End Sub
```

Notice that the slsTax variable is declared at the top of the module, just below the Option Explicit statement (and before the first procedure definition). You could also declare the slsTax variable like this:

```
Option Explicit
Private slsTax As Single  ' module-level variable declared with Private
                          ' statement

Sub CalcCost()
    ...Instructions of the procedure...
End Sub
```

Note: There is no difference between module-level variables declared with Dim or Private statements.

Before you can see how module-level variables actually work, you need another procedure that also uses the slsTax variable.

Hands-On 3-6: Understanding Module-Level Variables

This hands-on requires the prior completion of Hands-On 3-4 and 3-5.

1. In the Code window, in the same module where you entered the CalcCost procedure, cut the declaration line Dim slsTax As Single and paste it at the top of the module sheet, below the Option Explicit statement.

2. Enter the code of the ExpenseRep procedure shown below in the same module where the CalcCost procedure is located.

3. Click anywhere inside the CalcCost procedure and press **F5** to run it.

4. As soon as the CalcCost procedure finishes executing, run the ExpenseRep procedure.

```
Sub ExpenseRep()
    Dim slsPrice As Currency
    Dim cost As Currency

    slsPrice = 55.99
    cost = slsPrice + (slsPrice * slsTax)

    MsgBox slsTax
    MsgBox cost
End Sub
```

The ExpenseRep procedure declares two Currency type variables: slsPrice and cost. The slsPrice variable is then assigned a value of 55.99. The slsPrice variable is independent of the slsPrice variable declared within the CalcCost procedure.

The ExpenseRep procedure calculates the cost of a purchase. The cost includes the sales tax. Because the sales tax is the same as the one used in the CalcCost procedure, the slsTax variable has been declared at the module level. After Visual Basic executes the CalcCost procedure, the contents of the slsTax variable equals 0.085. If slsTax were a local variable, upon the termination of the CalcCost procedure, the contents of this variable would be empty. The ExpenseRep procedure ends by displaying the value of the slsTax and cost variables in two separate message boxes.

After running the CalcCost procedure, Visual Basic erases the contents of all the variables except for the slsTax variable, which was declared at a module level. As soon as you attempt to calculate the cost by running the ExpenseRep procedure, Visual Basic retrieves the value of the slsTax variable and uses it in the calculation.

Public Variables

In the previous section, you learned that by declaring a variable with the Dim or Private statement at the top of the module, you can make this variable available to other procedures in that module. But what if you want your variable to be available to all other procedures in all modules in the current Microsoft Access database as well as in other Microsoft Access databases that your procedure code may be referencing? To meet this demand, you need a module-level variable with a Public scope. Module-level variables declared with the Public statement can be used in any Visual Basic for Applications module. When you want to work with a variable in all the procedures in your application, declare it with the Public keyword, like this:

```
Option Explicit
Public slsTax As Single

Sub CalcCost()
    ...Instructions of the procedure...
End Sub
```

The slsTax variable declared at the top of the module with the Public statement will now be available to any other procedure in your application.

> **Public Variables and the Option Private Statement**
>
> If you declare a public variable in a module that contains the Option Private statement, this variable will be available only to procedures in the current database. The Option Private statement can be used at the module level to indicate that the entire module is private.

Understanding and Using Static Variables

A variable declared with the Static keyword is a special type of local variable. *Static* variables are declared at the procedure level. As opposed to the local variables declared with the Dim keyword, static variables remain in existence and retain their values after termination of the procedure in which they were declared.

The CostOfPurchase procedure (see Hands-On 3-7) demonstrates the use of the Static variable named allPurchase. The purpose of this variable is to keep track of the running total.

⊚ Hands-On 3-7: Using Static Variables

1. If the Visual Basic window is not open, press **Alt+F11** to open it.

2. Choose **Insert | Module** to add a new module.

3. Enter the code of the CostOfPurchase procedure shown below in the new module's Code window.

4. To run the procedure, click any line between the Sub and End Sub keywords and press **F5** or choose **Run | Run Sub/UserForm**.

```
Sub CostOfPurchase()
    ' declare variables
    Static allPurchase
    Dim newPurchase As String
    Dim purchCost As Single

    newPurchase = InputBox("Enter the cost of a purchase:")
    purchCost = CSng(newPurchase)
    allPurchase = allPurchase + purchCost

    ' display results
    MsgBox "The cost of a new purchase is: " & newPurchase
    MsgBox "The running cost is: " & allPurchase
End Sub
```

The above procedure begins with declaring a Static variable named allPurchase and two local variables: newPurchase and purchCost. The InputBox function used in this procedure displays a dialog box and waits for the user to enter the value. As soon as the user inputs the value and clicks OK, Visual Basic assigns this value to the newPurchase variable. The InputBox function allows you to get a user's input while the procedure is running. Because the result of the InputBox function is always a string, the newPurchase variable was declared as the String data type. You can't, however, use strings in mathematical calculations. That's why the next instruction uses a *type conversion* function (CSng) to translate the text value into a numeric variable of the Single data type. The CSng function requires one argument: the value you want to translate. The number obtained as the result of the CSng function is then stored in the purchCost variable.

Type Conversion Functions

To find out more about the CSng function (and other type conversion functions), position the insertion point anywhere within the word CSng and press F1.

The next instruction, allPurchase = allPurchase + purchCost, adds the new value supplied by the InputBox function to the current purchase value. When you run this procedure for the first time, the content of the allPurchase variable is the same as the content of the purchCost variable. When you run the procedure the second time, the value of the static variable is increased by the new value entered in the dialog box. You can run the CostOfPurch procedure as many times as you want. The allPurch variable will keep the running total for as long as the project is open.

To try out the CostOfPurchase procedure shown above, follow these steps:

◎ Hands-On 3-7 (Continued)

1. Position the insertion point anywhere within the CostOfPurch procedure and press **F5**.

2. When the dialog box appears, enter a number. For example, type **100** and press **Enter**. Visual Basic displays the message "The cost of a new purchase is: 100."

3. Click **OK** in the message box. Visual Basic displays the second message "The running cost is: 100."

4. Rerun the same procedure.

5. When the input box dialog appears, enter another number. For example, type **50** and press **Enter**. Visual Basic displays the message "The cost of a new purchase is 50."

6. Click **OK** in the message box. Visual Basic displays the second message "The running cost is: 150."

7. Run the procedure a couple of times to see how Visual Basic keeps track of the running total.

Declaring and Using Object Variables

The variables you've learned so far are used to store data. Storing data is the main reason for using "normal" variables in your procedures. In addition to the normal variables that store data, there are special variables that refer to the Visual Basic objects. These variables are called *object* variables. Object variables don't store data. They store the location of the data. You can use them to reference databases, forms, and controls as well as objects created in other applications. Object variables are declared in a similar way as the variables you already know. The only difference is that after the As keyword you enter the type of object your variable will point to. For instance:

```
Dim myControl As Control
```

The statement above declares the object variable called myControl of type Control.

```
Dim frm As Form
```

This statement declares the object variable called frm of type Form.

You can use object variables to refer to objects of a generic type such as Application, Control, Form, or Report, or you can point your object variable to specific object types such as TextBox, ToggleButton, CheckBox, CommandButton, ListBox, OptionButton, Subform or Subreport, Label, BoundObjectFrame or UnboundObjectFrame, and so on. After declaring an object variable, you also have to assign a specific value to the object variable before you can use this variable in your procedure. You assign a value to the object variable by using the *Set* keyword. The Set keyword is then followed by the equals sign and the value that the variable refers to. For example:

```
Set myControl = Me!CompanyName
```

The above statement assigns a value to the object variable called myControl. This object variable will now point to the CompanyName control on the active form. If you omit the word Set, Visual Basic will display the error message "Run-time error 91: Object variable or With block variable not set."

Again, it's time to see a practical example. The HideControl procedure in Hands-On 3-8 below demonstrates the use of the object variables frm and myControl.

Hands-On 3-8: Working with Object Variables

1. Load another instance of Microsoft Office Access 2003 and open the **Acc2003_Chap01.mdb** file that you worked with in Chapter 1. Both instances need to be open for this example.

2. Press **Alt+F11** to open Visual Basic Editor window.

3. Choose **Insert | Module** to add a new module.

4. Enter the code of the HideControl procedure shown below in the new module's Code window.

5. To run the procedure, click any line between the Sub and End Sub keywords and press **F5** or choose **Run | Run Sub/UserForm**.

```
Sub HideControl()
    ' this procedure is run against the open Customers form
    ' in the Northwind database
    Dim frm As Form
    Dim myControl As Control
    Set frm = Forms!Customers
    Set myControl = frm.CompanyName
    myControl.Visible = False
End Sub
```

The procedure begins with the declaration of two object variables called frm and myControl. The object variable frm is set to reference the Customers forms. For the procedure to work, the referenced form must be open. Next, the myControl object variable is set to point to the CompanyName control located on the Customers form.

The statement

```
Set myControl = frm.CompanyName
```

is the same as

```
Set myControl = Forms!Customers.CompanyName
```

Instead of using the object's entire address, you can use the shortcut — the name of the object variable. The purpose of this procedure is to hide the control referenced by the object variable myControl. After running the HideControl procedure, switch to the Microsoft Access window containing the open Customers form. The CompanyName control should not appear on the form. To make the control reappear, modify the last line of this procedure by setting the Visible property of myControl to True and rerun the procedure.

Advantages of Using Object Variables

The advantages of object variables are:

- They can be used instead of the actual object.
- They are shorter and easier to remember than the actual values they point to.
- You can change their meaning while your procedure is running.

When the object variable is no longer needed, you can assign Nothing to it. This frees up memory and system resources:

```
Set frm = Nothing
Set myControl = Nothing
```

Finding a Variable Definition

When you find an instruction that assigns a value to a variable in a VBA procedure, you can quickly locate the definition of the variable by selecting the variable name and pressing Shift+F2. Alternately, you can choose View | Definition. Visual Basic will jump to the variable declaration line. To return your mouse pointer to its previous position, press Ctrl+Shift+F2 or choose View | Last Position. Let's try it out.

◎ Hands-On 3-9: Finding a Variable Definition

This hands-on requires prior completion of Hands-On 3-8.

1. Locate the code of the procedure HideControl you created in Hands-On 3-8.

2. Locate the statement myControl.Visible = True.

3. Right-click the variable name and choose **Definition** from the shortcut menu.

4. Return to the previous location by pressing **Ctrl+Shift+F2**.

What Type Is This Variable?

Visual Basic has a built-in *VarType* function that returns an integer indicating the variable's type. Let's see how you can use this function in the Immediate window.

◎ Hands-On 3-10: Asking Questions about the Variable Type

1. Open the Immediate window and type the following statements that assign values to variables:

```
age = 28
birthdate = #1/1/1981
firstName = "John"
```

2. Now, ask Visual Basic what type of data each variable holds:

```
?varType(age)
```

When you press **Enter**, Visual Basic returns 2. The number 2 represents the Integer data type.

```
?varType(birthdate)
```

Now Visual Basic returns 7 for Date. If you make a mistake in the variable name (let's say you type birthday instead of birthdate), Visual Basic returns zero (0).

```
?varType(firstName)
```

From this statement Visual Basic tells you that the value stored in the firstName variable is a string (8).

Table 3-3: Values returned by the VarType function

Constant	Value	Description
vbEmpty	0	Empty (uninitialized)
vbNull	1	Null (no valid data)
vbInteger	2	Integer
vbLong	3	Long integer
vbSingle	4	Single-precision floating-point number
vbDouble	5	Double-precision floating-point number
vbCurrency	6	Currency value
vbDate	7	Date value
vbString	8	String
vbObject	9	Object
vbError	10	Error value
vbBoolean	11	Boolean value
vbVariant	12	Variant (used only with arrays of variants)
vbDataObject	13	Data access object
vbDecimal	14	Decimal value
vbByte	17	Byte value
vbUserDefinedType	36	Variants that contain user-defined types
vbArray	8192	Array

Using Constants in VBA Procedures

The contents of a variable can change while your procedure is executing. If your procedure needs to refer to unchanged values over and over again, you should use constants. A *constant* is like a named variable that always refers to the same value. Visual Basic requires that you declare constants before you use them.

You declare constants by using the Const statement, as in the following examples:

```
Const dialogName = "Enter Data" As String
Const slsTax = 8.5
Const Discount = 0.5
Const ColorIdx = 3
```

A constant, like a variable, has a scope. To make a constant available within a single procedure, you declare it at the procedure level, just below the name of the procedure. For instance:

```
Sub WedAnniv()
    Const Age As Integer = 25
    ...instructions...
End Sub
```

If you want to use a constant in all the procedures of a module, use the Private keyword in front of the Const statement. For instance:

```
Private Const dsk = "B:" As String
```

The Private constant has to be declared at the top of the module, just before the first Sub statement.

If you want to make a constant available to all modules in your application, use the Public keyword in front of the Const statement. For instance:

```
Public Const NumOfChar = 255 As Integer
```

The Public constant has to be declared at the top of the module, just before the first Sub statement.

When declaring a constant, you can use any one of the following data types: Boolean, Byte, Integer, Long, Currency, Single, Double, Date, String, or Variant.

Like variables, constants can be declared on one line if separated by commas. For instance:

```
Const Age As Integer = 25, City As String = "Denver", PayCheck As Currency = 350
```

Using constants makes your VBA procedures more readable and easier to maintain. For example, if you refer to a certain value several times in your procedure, instead of using a value, use a constant. This way, if the value changes (for example, the sales tax goes up), you can simply change the value in the declaration of the Const statement instead of tracking down every occurrence of the value.

Intrinsic Constants

Both Microsoft Access and Visual Basic for Applications have a long list of predefined constants that do not need to be declared. These built-in constants can be looked up using the Object Browser window that was discussed in detail in Chapter 2.

Let's open the Object Browser to take a look at the list of Access's constants.

◎ Hands-On 3-11: Exploring Access's Constants

1. In the Visual Basic Editor window, choose **View | Object Browser**.

2. In the Project/Library list box, click the drop-down arrow and select the **Access** library.

3. Enter **constants** as the search text in the Search Text box and either press **Enter** or click the **Search** button. Visual Basic shows the results of the search in the Search Results area. The right side of the Object Browser window displays a list of all built-in constants available in the Microsoft Access Object Library. Notice that the names of all the constants begin with the prefix "ac."

4. To look up VBA constants, choose **VBA** in the Project/Library list box. Notice that the names of the VBA built-in constants begin with the prefix "vb."

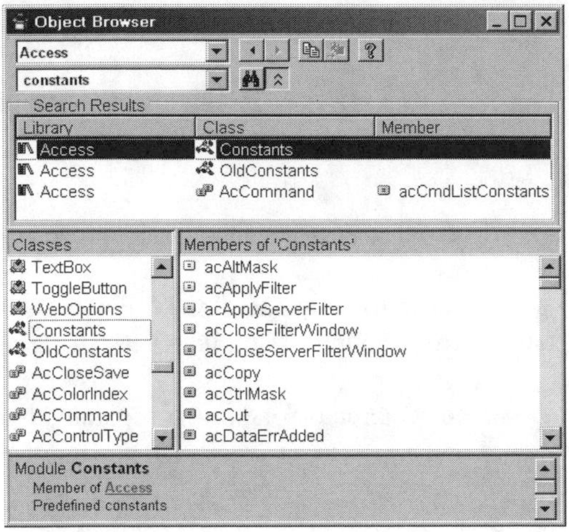

Figure 3-1: Use the Object Browser to look up any intrinsic constant.

Hands-On 3-12 illustrates how to use the intrinsic constants acFilterByForm and acFilterAdvanced to disable execution of filtering on a form.

◎ Hands-On 3-12: Using Intrinsic Constants in a VBA Procedure

1. Open any form in Design view. You can use the Customers form in the Acc2003_Chap01.mdb file that you worked with in Chapter 1.

2. In the Design view of the chosen form, choose **Edit | Select Form**.

3. Choose **View | Properties**.

4. Click the **Event** tab in the Form properties sheet.

5. Click the **Build** button (…) to the right of the On Filter property, and select **Code Builder**.

6. In the Code window, enter the Form_Filter event procedure code as shown below.

7. Switch back to Design view in the Customers form and choose **View | Form View**. If you are using your own form for this hands-on, switch to Design view of your form and open it in Form view.

8. Choose **Records | Filter | Filter By Form**. Access displays the message "You need authorization to filter records." The same message appears when you choose **Records | Filter | Advanced Filter/Sort**.

```
Private Sub Form_Filter(Cancel As Integer, FilterType As Integer)
    If FilterType = acFilterByForm Or _
        FilterType = acFilterAdvanced Then
        MsgBox "You need authorization to filter records."
        Cancel = True
    End If
End Sub
```

Chapter Summary

This chapter introduced several new VBA concepts. You found in it information about data types, variables, and constants. You learned how to declare various types of variables. You also saw the difference between a variable and a constant.

In the next chapter, you will expand your knowledge of Visual Basic for Applications by using procedures and functions with arguments. In addition, you will learn about functions that allow your VBA procedures to interact with the user.

Chapter 4

Passing Arguments to Procedures and Functions

So far you have created simple VBA procedures that carried out specific tasks. These procedures did not require that you provide additional data before they could be run. However, in real life, procedures (both subroutines and functions) often take arguments. Arguments are one or more values needed for a procedure to do something. Arguments are always entered between parentheses. Multiple arguments are separated with commas.

Writing a Function Procedure

Function procedures can perform calculations based on data received through arguments. When you declare a function procedure, you list the names of arguments inside a set of parentheses, as shown in Hands-On 4-1.

◉ Hands-On 4-1: Writing a Function Procedure with Arguments

This chapter's hands-on exercises are provided in the Acc2003_Chap04.mdb file included in the book's downloadable files.

1. Open **Acc2003_Chap04.mdb** from the downloadable files or, if you'd like to start from scratch, create a new Access 2003 database.

2. In the Database window, click the **Module** button to create a new module.

3. Enter the following function procedure JoinText in the Module1 Code window.

```
Function JoinText(k, o)
    JoinText = k + " " + o
End Function
```

Note that there is a space character in quotation marks concatenated between the two arguments of the JoinText function's result: JoinText = k + " " + o.

A better way of adding a space is by using one of the built-in functions as shown below:

```
JoinText = k + Space(1) + o
```

or

```
JoinText = k + Chr(32) + o
```

The Space function returns a string of spaces consisting of the number of spaces indicated in the parentheses. The Chr function returns a string containing the character associated with the specified character code.

Other control characters you may need to use when writing your VBA procedures are listed below:

Tab	Chr(9)
Line Feed	Chr(10)
Carriage Return	Chr(13)

You can execute a function procedure from the Immediate window, or you can write a subroutine to call the function. See Hands-On 4-2 for how to run the JoinText function procedure.

Hands-On 4-2: Executing a Function Procedure from the Immediate Window

This hands-on requires prior completion of Hands-On 4-1.

1. Choose **View | Immediate Window**, and enter the following statement:

   ```
   ?JoinText("function", " procedure")
   ```

   Notice that as soon as you enter the beginning parenthesis, Visual Basic displays the arguments that the function expects. Type the value of the first argument, enter the comma, and supply the value of the second argument. Finish off by entering the ending parenthesis.

2. Press **Enter** to execute the above statement from the Immediate window. When you press Enter, the string "function procedure" appears in the Immediate window.

You can also execute a function procedure programmatically as outlined in Hands-On 4-3.

Hands-On 4-3: Executing a Function Procedure from a Subroutine

This hands-on requires prior completion of Hands-On 4-1.

1. In the same module where you entered the JoinText function procedure, enter the following EnterText subroutine:

   ```
   Sub EnterText()
       Dim strFirst As String, strLast As String, strFull As String

       strFirst = InputBox("Enter your first name:")
       strLast = InputBox("Enter your last name:")
       strFull = JoinText(strFirst, strLast)

       MsgBox strFull
   End Sub
   ```

2. Place the cursor anywhere inside the code of the EnterText procedure and press **F5** to run it.

As Visual Basic executes the statements of the EnterText procedure, it collects the data from the user and stores the values of the first and last names in the variables strFirst and strLast. Then these values are passed to the JoinText function. Visual Basic substitutes the variables' contents for the arguments of the JoinText function and assigns the result to the name of the function (JoinText). When Visual Basic returns to the EnterText procedure it stores the function's value in the strFull variable. The MsgBox function then displays the contents of the strFull variable in a message box. The result is the full name of the user (first and last name separated by a space).

More about Arguments

Argument names are like variables. Each argument name refers to whatever value you provide at the time the function is called. You write a subroutine to call a function procedure. When a subroutine calls a function procedure, it passes it the required arguments as variables. Once the function does something, the result is assigned to the function name. Notice that the function procedure's name is used as if it were a variable.

Specifying the Data Type for a Function's Result

Like variables, functions can have types. The result of your function procedure can be a String, Integer, Long, etc. To specify the data type for your function's result, add the As keyword and the name of the desired data type to the end of the function declaration line. For example:

```
Function MultiplyIt(num1, num2) As Integer
```

If you don't specify the data type, Visual Basic assigns the default type (Variant) to your function's result. When you specify the data type for your function's result, you get the same advantages as when you specify the data type for your variables — your procedure uses memory more efficiently, and therefore it runs faster.

Let's take a look at an example of a function that returns an integer number, although the arguments passed to it are declared as Single in a calling subroutine.

⊚ Hands-On 4-4: Calling a Function From a Procedure

1. In the Visual Basic Editor window, choose **Insert | Module** to add a new module.

2. Enter the following HowMuch subroutine in the Code window:

```
Sub HowMuch()
    Dim num1 As Single
    Dim num2 As Single
    Dim result As Single

    num1 = 45.33
    num2 = 19.24
```

```
    result = MultiplyIt(num1, num2)

    MsgBox result
End Sub
```

3. Enter the following MultiplyIt function procedure in the Code window below the HowMuch subroutine:

```
Function MultiplyIt(num1, num2) As Integer

    MultiplyIt = num1 * num2

End Function
```

4. Click anywhere within the HowMuch procedure and press **F5** to run it. Because the values stored in the variables num1 and num2 are not whole numbers, to ensure that the result of multiplication is a whole number, you may want to assign the Integer type to the result of the function. If you don't assign the data type to the MultiplyIt function's result, the HowMuch procedure will display the result in the data type specified in the declaration line of the result variable. Instead of 872, the result of the multiplication will be 872.1492.

5. To make the MultiplyIt function more useful, instead of hard coding the values to be used in the multiplication, you can pass different values each time you run the procedure by using the InputBox function. Take a few minutes to modify the HowMuch procedure on your own, following the example of the EnterText subroutine that was created in the preceding hands-on. To pass a specific value from a function to a subroutine, assign the value to the function name. For example, the NumOfDays function shown below passes the value of 7 to the subroutine DaysInAWeek.

```
Function NumOfDays()
    NumOfDays = 7
End Function


Sub DaysInAWeek()
    MsgBox "There are " & NumOfDays & " days in a week."
End Sub
```

Subroutines or Functions: Which Should You Use?

Create a subroutine when you...

- Want to perform some actions.
- Want to get input from the user.
- Want to display a message on the screen.

Create a function when you...

- Want to perform a simple calculation more than once.
- Must perform complex computations.
- Must call the same block of instructions more than once.
- Want to check if a certain expression is true or false.

Passing Arguments by Reference and by Value

In some procedures, when you pass arguments as variables, Visual Basic can suddenly change the value of the variables. To ensure that the called function procedure does not alter the value of the passed arguments, you should precede the name of the argument in the function's declaration line with the ByVal keyword. Let's practice this with an example.

⊚ Hands-On 4-5: Passing Arguments to Subroutines and Functions

1. In the Visual Basic Editor window, choose **Insert | Module** to add a new module.

2. In the Code window, type the subroutine and function procedure as shown below.

```
Sub ThreeNumbers()
    Dim num1 As Integer, num2 As Integer, num3 As Integer

    num1 = 10
    num2 = 20
    num3 = 30

    MsgBox MyAverage(num1, num2, num3)
    MsgBox num1
    MsgBox num2
    MsgBox num3
End Sub

Function MyAverage(ByVal num1, ByVal num2, ByVal num3)
    num1 = num1 + 1
    MyAverage = (num1 + num2 + num3) / 3
End Function
```

The ThreeNumbers subroutine assigns values to three variables, and then calls the MyAverage function to perform and return the average of the numbers stored in these variables. The function's arguments are the names of the variables: num1, num2, and num3. Notice that all variable names are preceded with the ByVal keyword. Also, notice that prior to the calculation of the average, the MyAverage function changes the value of the num1 variable. Inside the function procedure, the num1 variable equals 11 (10 + 1). Therefore, when the function passes the calculated average to the ThreeNumbers procedure, the MsgBox function displays the result as 20.3333333333333 and not 20, as expected. The next three functions show the contents of each of the variables. The values stored in these variables are the same as the original values assigned to them: 10, 20, and 30.

What will happen if you omit the ByVal keyword in front of the num1 argument in the MyAverage function's declaration line? The function's result will still be the same, but the content of the num1 variable displayed by the MsgBox num1 is now 11. The MyAverage function has not only returned the unexpected result (20.3333333333333 instead of 20), but also has modified the original data stored in the num1 variable. To prevent Visual Basic from permanently changing the values supplied to the function, use the ByVal keyword.

Know Your Keywords: ByRef and ByVal

Because any of the variables passed to a function procedure (or a subroutine) can be changed by the receiving procedure, it is important to know how to protect the original value of a variable. Visual Basic has two keywords that give or deny the permission to change the contents of a variable: ByRef and ByVal.

By default, Visual Basic passes information to a function procedure (or a subroutine) by reference (ByRef keyword), referring to the original data specified in the function's argument at the time the function is called. So, if the function alters the value of the argument, the original value is changed. You will get this result if you omit the ByVal keyword in front of the num1 argument in the MyAverage function's declaration line. If you want the function procedure to change the original value, you don't need to explicitly insert the ByRef keyword, because passed variables default to ByRef.

When you use the ByVal keyword in front of an argument name, Visual Basic passes the argument by value. It means that Visual Basic makes a copy of the original data. This copy is then passed to a function. If the function changes the value of an argument passed by value, the original data does not change — only the copy changes. That's why when the MyAverage function changed the value of the num1 argument, the original value of the num1 variable remained the same.

Using Optional Arguments

At times, you may want to supply an additional value to a function. Let's say you have a function that calculates the price of a meal per person. Sometimes, however, you'd like the function to perform the same calculation for a group of two or more people. To indicate that a procedure argument isn't always required, you precede the name of the argument with the *Optional* keyword. Arguments that are optional come at the end of the argument list, following the names of all the required arguments. Optional arguments must always be the Variant data type. This means that you can't specify the Optional argument's type by using the As keyword.

In the preceding section, you created a function to calculate the average of three numbers. Suppose that sometimes you would like to use this function to calculate the average of two numbers. You could define the third argument of the MyAverage function as optional. To preserve the original MyAverage function, let's create the Avg function to calculate the average for two or three numbers.

Hands-On 4-6: Using Optional Arguments

1. In the Visual Basic Editor window, choose **Insert | Module** to add a new module.

2. Type the following Avg function procedure in the Code window:

```
Function Avg(num1, num2, Optional num3)
    Dim totalNums As Integer

    totalNums = 3
    If IsMissing(num3) Then
        num3 = 0
        totalNums = totalNums - 1
    End If
    Avg = (num1 + num2 + num3) / totalNums
End Function
```

3. Call this function from the Immediate window:

    ```
    ?Avg(2, 3)
    ```

    As soon as you press **Enter**, Visual Basic displays the result: 2.5.

    ```
    ?Avg(2, 3, 5)
    ```

    This time the result is: 3.3333333333333.

> **Note:** If you are working with Acc2003_Chap04.mdb file from the book's downloadable files and you entered the Avg function in a brand new module, the ambiguous name message will pop up because this function is already entered in another module. If you run into this problem, simply replace all the occurrences of Avg in your module with another name.

As you've seen, the Avg function allows you to calculate the average of two or three numbers. You decide what values and how many values (two or three) you want to average. When you start typing the values for the function's arguments in the Immediate window, Visual Basic displays the name of the optional argument enclosed in square brackets.

Let's take a few minutes to analyze the Avg function. This function can take up to three arguments. Arguments num1 and num2 are required. Argument num3 is optional. Notice that the name of the optional argument is preceded with the Optional keyword. The Optional argument is listed at the end of the argument list. Because the types of the num1, num2, and num3 arguments are not declared, Visual Basic treats all of these arguments as Variants.

Inside the function procedure, the totalNums variable is declared as an Integer and then assigned a beginning value of 3. Because the function has to be capable of calculating an average of two or three numbers, the handy built-in function IsMissing checks for the number of supplied arguments. If the third (optional) argument is not supplied, the IsMissing function puts the value of zero (0) in its place, and deducts the value of 1 from the value stored in the totalNums variable. Hence, if the optional argument is missing, the totalNums is 2. The next statement calculates the average based on the supplied data, and the result is assigned to the name of the function.

Using the IsMissing Function

The IsMissing function called from within Hands-On 4-6 allows you to determine whether or not the optional argument was supplied. This function returns the logical value of True if the third argument is not supplied, and returns False when the third argument is given. The IsMissing function is used here with the decision-making statement If…Then (discussed in Chapter 5). If the num3 argument is missing (IsMissing), then (Then) Visual Basic supplies a zero (0) for the value of the third argument (num3 = 0), and reduces the value stored in the argument totalNums by 1 (totalNums = totalNums – 1).

Testing a Function Procedure

To test whether a custom function does what it was designed to do, write a simple subroutine that will call the function and display its result. In addition, the subroutine should show the original values of arguments. This way, you'll be able to quickly determine when the argument value was altered. If the function procedure uses optional arguments, you'll also need to check those situations in which the optional arguments may be missing.

Built-in Functions

VBA comes with many built-in functions that can be looked up in the Visual Basic online help. To access an alphabetical listing of all VBA functions, choose Help | Microsoft Visual Basic Help in the Visual Basic Editor window. On the Contents tab, open the Visual Basic Language Reference folder, then click Functions.

One of the features of a good program is its interaction with the user. When you work with Microsoft Access, you interact with the application by using various dialog boxes such as message boxes and input boxes. When you write your own procedures, you can use the MsgBox function to inform the users about an unexpected error or the result of a specific calculation. So far you have seen a simple implementation of this function. In the next section, you will find out how to control the appearance of your message. Then you will learn how to get information from the user with the InputBox function.

Using the MsgBox Function

The MsgBox function you have used so far was limited to displaying a message to the user in a simple, one-button dialog box. You closed the message box by clicking the OK button or pressing the Enter key. You create a simple message box by following the MsgBox function name with the text enclosed in quotation marks. In other words, to display the message "The procedure is complete." you should prepare the following statement:

```
MsgBox "The procedure is complete."
```

You can try out the above instruction by entering it in the Immediate window. When you type this instruction and press Enter, Visual Basic displays the message box shown in Figure 4-1.

Figure 4-1: To display a message to the user, place the text as the argument of the MsgBox function.

The MsgBox function allows you to use other arguments that make it possible to determine the number of buttons that should be available in the message box or to change the title of the message box from the default. You can also assign your own help topic. The syntax of the MsgBox function is shown below.

```
MsgBox (prompt [, buttons] [, title], [, helpfile, context])
```

Notice that while the MsgBox function has five arguments, only the first one, prompt, is required. The arguments listed in square brackets are optional.

When you enter a long text string for the prompt argument, Visual Basic decides how to break the text so it fits the message box. Let's do some exercises in the Immediate window to learn various text formatting techniques.

◉ Hands-On 4-7: Formatting the Message Box

1. Enter the following instruction in the Immediate window. Make sure to enter the entire text string on one line, and then press **Enter**.

```
MsgBox "All done. Now open ""Test.doc"" and place an empty disk in the diskette
drive. The following procedure will copy this file to the disk."
```

As soon as you press **Enter**, Visual Basic shows the resulting dialog box. If you get the Compile error, click **OK**. Then, make sure that the name of the file is surrounded by double quotation marks — ""Test.doc"".

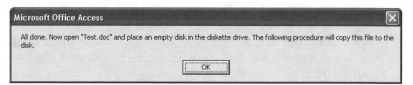

Figure 4-2: This long message will look more appealing to the user when you take the text formatting into your own hands.

When the text of your message is particularly long, you can break it into several lines using the VBA Chr function. The Chr function requires a number from 0 to 255, and returns a character represented by this number. For example, Chr(13) returns a carriage return character (this is the same as pressing the Enter key), and Chr(10) returns a linefeed character (this is useful for adding spacing between the text lines).

2. Modify the instruction entered in the previous step in the following way:

```
MsgBox "All done." & Chr(13) & "Now open ""Test.doc"" and place" & Chr(13) & "an
empty disk in the diskette drive." & Chr(13) & "The following procedure will
copy this file to the disk."
```

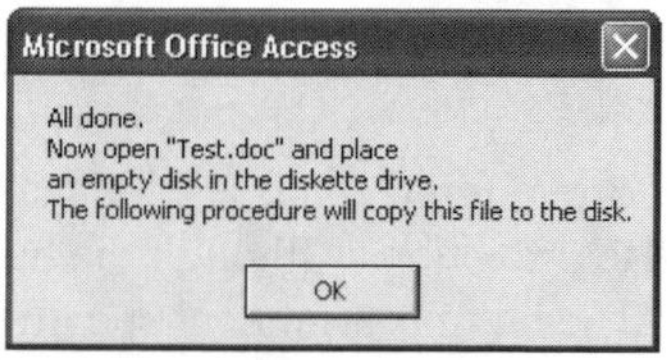

Figure 4-3: You can break a long text string into several lines by using the Chr(13) function.

You must surround each text fragment by quotation marks. Quoted text embedded in a text string requires an additional set of quotation marks, as in ""Test.doc"". The Chr(13) function indicates a place where you'd like to start a new line. The string concatenation character & is used to add a carriage return character to a concatenated string. When you enter exceptionally long text messages on one line, it's easy to make a mistake. An underscore (_) is a special line continuation character in VBA that allows you to break a long VBA statement into several lines. Unfortunately, the line continuation character cannot be used in the Immediate window.

3. Now add a new module by choosing **Insert | Module**.

4. In the Code window, enter the MyMessage subroutine as shown below. Make sure to precede each line continuation character with a space.

```
Sub MyMessage()
    MsgBox "All done." & Chr(13) _
    & "Now open ""Test.doc"" and place" & Chr(13) _
    & "an empty disk in the diskette drive." & Chr(13) _
    & "The following procedure will copy this file to the disk."
End Sub
```

When you run the MyMessage procedure, Visual Basic displays the same message as the one illustrated in Figure 4-3. As you can see, the text entered on several lines is more readable, and the code is easier to maintain. To improve the readability of your message, you may want to add more spacing between the text lines by including blank lines. To do this, use two Chr(13) or two Chr(10) functions, as shown in the following step.

5. Enter the following MyMessage2 procedure:

```
Sub MyMessage2()
    MsgBox "All done." & Chr(10) & Chr(10) _
    & "Now open ""Test.doc"" and place" & Chr(13) _
    & "an empty disk in the diskette drive." & Chr(13) & Chr(13) _
    & "The following procedure will copy this file to the disk."
End Sub
```

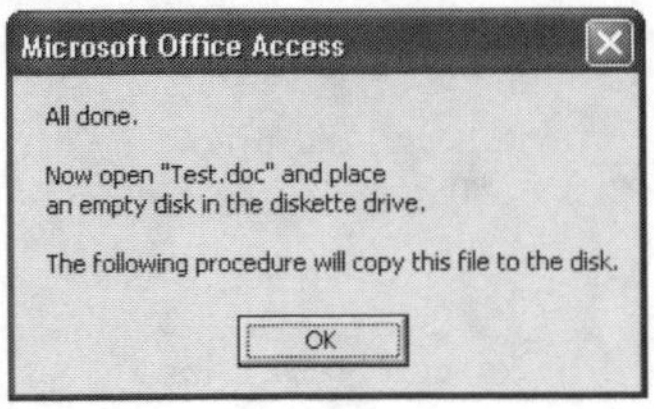

Figure 4-4: You can increase the readability of your message by increasing spacing between selected text lines.

Now that you have mastered the text formatting techniques, let's take a closer look at the next argument of the MsgBox function. Although the buttons argument is optional, it's frequently used. The buttons argument specifies how many and what types of buttons you want to appear in the message box. This argument can be a constant (see Table 4-1) or a number. If you omit this argument, the resulting message box includes only the OK button, as you've seen in the preceding examples.

Table 4-1: The MsgBox buttons argument's settings

Constant	Value	Description
Button settings		
vbOKOnly	0	Displays only an OK button. This is the default.
vbOKCancel	1	OK and Cancel buttons
vbAbortRetryIgnore	2	Abort, Retry, and Ignore buttons
vbYesNoCancel	3	Yes, No, and Cancel buttons
vbYesNo	4	Yes and No buttons
vbRetryCancel	5	Retry and Cancel buttons
Icon settings		
vbCritical	16	Displays the Critical Message icon
vbQuestion	32	Displays the Question Message icon
vbExclamation	48	Displays the Warning Message icon
vbInformation	64	Displays the Information Message icon
Default button settings		
vbDefaultButton1	0	The first button is default
vbDefaultButton2	256	The second button is default
vbDefaultButton3	512	The third button is default
vbDefaultButton4	768	The fourth button is default
Message box modality		
vbApplicationModal	0	The user must respond to the message before continuing to work in the current application.
vbSystemModal	4096	On Win16 systems, this constant is used to prevent the user from interacting with any other window until he or she dismisses the message box. On Win32 systems, this constant works like the vbApplicationModal constant (see above) with the following exception: The message box always remains on top of any other programs you may have running.
Other MsgBox display settings		
vbMsgBoxHelpButton	16384	Adds the Help button to the message box
vbMsgBoxSetForeground	65536	Specifies the message box window as the foreground window

Constant	Value	Description
vbMsgBoxRight	524288	Text is right aligned
vbMsgBoxRtlReading	1048576	Text appears as right-to-left reading on Hebrew and Arabic systems

When should you use the buttons argument? Suppose you want the user of your procedure to respond to a question with Yes or No. Your message box may then require two buttons. If a message box includes more than one button, one of them is considered a default button. When the user presses Enter, the default button is selected automatically.

Because you can display various types of messages (critical, warning, information), you can visually indicate the importance of the message by including in the buttons argument the graphical representation (icon) for the chosen message type. In addition to the type of message, the buttons argument can include a setting to determine if the message box must be closed before the user switches to another application. It's quite possible that the user may want to switch to another program or perform another task before he responds to the question posed in your message box. If the message box is application modal (vbApplication Modal), then the user must close the message box before continuing to use your application.

For example, consider the following message box:

```
MsgBox "How are you?", vbOKOnly + vbApplicationModal, "Application Modal"
```

If you type the above message box in the Immediate window and press Enter, a message box will pop up and you won't be able to work with your currently open Microsoft Office Access application until you respond to the message box.

On the other hand, if you want to keep the message box visible while the user works with other open applications, you must include the vbSystemModal setting in the buttons argument, like this:

```
MsgBox "How are you?", vbOKOnly + vbSystemModal, "System Modal"
```

Note: Use the vbSystemModal constant when you want to ensure that your message box is always visible (not hidden behind other windows).

The buttons argument settings are divided into five groups: button settings, icon settings, default button settings, message box modality, and other MsgBox display settings (see Table 4-1). Only one setting from each group can be included in the buttons argument. To create a buttons argument you can add up the values for each setting you want to include. For example, to display a message box with two buttons (Yes and No), the question mark icon, and the No button as the default button, look up the corresponding values in Table 4-1, and add them up. You should arrive at 292 (4 + 32 + 256).

To see the message box using the calculated message box argument, enter the following statement in the Immediate window:

```
MsgBox "Do you want to proceed?", 292
```

The resulting message box is shown in Figure 4-5.

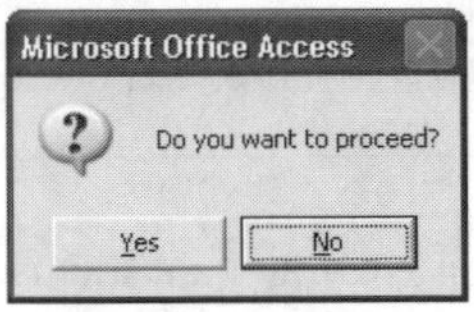

Figure 4-5: You can specify the number of buttons to include in the message box by using the optional buttons argument.

When you derive the buttons argument by adding up the constant values, your procedure becomes less readable. There's no reference table where you can check the hidden meaning of 292. To improve the readability of your MsgBox function, it's better to use the constants instead of their values. For example, enter the following revised statement in the Immediate window:

```
MsgBox "Do you want to proceed?", vbYesNo + vbQuestion + vbDefaultButton2
```

The above statement produces the same result as shown in Figure 4-5. The following example shows how to use the buttons argument inside the Visual Basic procedure.

⊙ Hands-On 4-8: Using the MsgBox Function with Arguments

1. In the Visual Basic Editor window, choose **Insert | Module** to add a new module.

2. In the Code window, enter the MsgYesNo subroutine as shown below.

```
Sub MsgYesNo()
    Dim question As String
    Dim myButtons As Integer

    question = "Do you want to open a new report?"
    myButtons = vbYesNo + vbQuestion + vbDefaultButton2
    MsgBox question, myButtons
End Sub
```

In the above subroutine, the question variable stores the text of your message. The settings for the buttons argument are placed in the myButtons variable. Instead of using the names of constants, you can use their values, as in following:

```
myButtons = 4 + 32 + 256
```

However, by specifying the names of the buttons argument constants, you make your procedure easier to understand for yourself and others who may work with this procedure in the future.

The question and myButtons variables are used as arguments for the MsgBox function. When you run the procedure, you see the result displayed as shown in Figure 4-5. Notice that the No button is now selected. It's the default button for this dialog box. If you press Enter, Visual Basic removes the message box from the screen. Nothing happens because your procedure does not have more instructions following the MsgBox function. To change the default button, use the vbDefaultButton1 setting instead.

The third argument of the MsgBox function is title. While this is also an optional argument, it's very handy because it allows you to create procedures that don't provide visual clues to the fact that you programmed them with Microsoft Access. Using this argument, you can set the title bar of your message box to any text you want.

Suppose you want the MsgYesNo procedure to display the text "New report" in its title. The following MsgYesNo2 procedure demonstrates the use of the title argument.

```
Sub MsgYesNo2()
    Dim question As String
    Dim myButtons As Integer
    Dim myTitle As String

    question = "Do you want to open a new report?"
    myButtons = vbYesNo + vbQuestion + vbDefaultButton2
    myTitle = "New report"
    MsgBox question, myButtons, myTitle
End Sub
```

The text for the title argument is stored in the myTitle variable. If you don't specify the value for the title argument, Visual Basic displays the default text "Microsoft Access." Notice that the arguments are listed in the order determined by the MsgBox function.

If you would like to list the arguments in any order, you must precede the value of each argument with its name, as shown below:

```
MsgBox title:=myTitle, prompt:=question, buttons:=myButtons
```

The last two arguments, helpfile and context, are used by more advanced programmers who are experienced with using help files in the Windows environment. The helpfile argument indicates the name of a special help file that contains additional information you may want to display to your VBA procedure user. When you specify this argument, the Help button will be added to your message box. When you use the helpfile argument, you must also use the context argument. This argument indicates which help subject in the specified help file you want to display. Suppose HelpX.hlp is the help file you created and 55 is the context topic you want to use. To include this information in your MsgBox function, you would use the following instruction:

```
MsgBox title:=myTitle, _
    prompt:=question _
    buttons:=myButtons _
    helpfile:= "HelpX.hlp", _
    context:=55
```

The above is a single VBA statement broken down into several lines with the line continuation character.

Returning Values from the MsgBox Function

When you display a simple message box dialog with one button, clicking the OK button or pressing the Enter key removes the message box from the screen. However, when the message box has more than one button, your procedure should detect which button was pressed. To do this, you must save the result of the message box in a variable. Table 4-2 shows values that the MsgBox function returns.

Table 4-2: Values returned by the MsgBox function

Button Selected	Constant	Value
OK	vbOK	1
Cancel	vbCancel	2
Abort	vbAbort	3
Retry	vbRetry	4
Ignore	vbIgnore	5
Yes	vbYes	6
No	vbNo	7

The MsgYesNo3 procedure is a revised version of MsgYesNo2. It shows how you can find out which button the user chose.

◎ Hands-On 4-9: Returning Values from the MsgBox Function

1. In the Visual Basic Editor window, choose **Insert | Module** to add a new module.

2. In the Code window, enter the code of the MsgYesNo3 procedure as shown below.

```
Sub MsgYesNo3()
    Dim question As String
    Dim myButtons As Integer
    Dim myTitle As String
    Dim myChoice As Integer

    question = "Do you want to open a new report?"
    myButtons = vbYesNo + vbQuestion + vbDefaultButton2
    myTitle = "New report"
    myChoice = MsgBox(question, myButtons, myTitle)
    MsgBox myChoice
End Sub
```

In the above procedure, you assigned the result of the MsgBox function to the variable myChoice. Notice that the arguments of the MsgBox function are now listed in parentheses:

```
myChoice = MsgBox(question, myButtons, myTitle)
```

MsgBox Function — With or without Parentheses?

Use parentheses around the MsgBox function argument list when you want to use the result returned by the function. By listing the function's arguments without parentheses, you tell Visual Basic that you want to ignore the function's result. Most likely, you will want to use the function's result when the message box contains more than one button.

When you run the MsgYesNo3 procedure, a two-button message box is displayed. By clicking on the Yes button, the statement MsgBox myChoice displays the number 6. When you click the No button, the number 7 is displayed.

Using the InputBox Function

The InputBox function displays a dialog box with a message that prompts the user to enter data. This dialog box has two buttons: OK and Cancel. When you click OK, the InputBox function returns the information entered in the text box. When you select Cancel, the function returns the empty string (" "). The syntax of the InputBox function is as follows:

```
InputBox(prompt [, title] [, default] [, xpos] [, ypos] [, helpfile, context])
```

The first argument, prompt, is the text message you want to display in the dialog box. Long text strings can be entered on several lines by using the Chr(13) or Chr(10) functions. (See examples of using the MsgBox function earlier in this chapter.) All the remaining InputBox arguments are optional.

The second argument, title, allows you to change the default title of the dialog box. The default value is "Microsoft Access."

The third argument of the InputBox function, default, allows the display of a default value in the text box. If you omit this argument, the empty edit box is displayed.

The following two arguments, xpos and ypos, let you specify the exact position where the dialog box should appear on the screen. If you omit these arguments, the input box appears in the middle of the current window. The xpos argument determines the horizontal position of the dialog box from the left edge of the screen. When omitted, the dialog box is centered horizontally. The ypos argument determines the vertical position, from the top of the screen. If you omit this argument, the dialog box is positioned vertically approximately one-third of the way down the screen. Both xpos and ypos are measured in special units called *twips*. One twip is the equivalent of approximately 0.0007 inches.

The last two arguments, helpfile and context, are used in the same way as the corresponding arguments of the MsgBox function discussed earlier in this chapter.

Now that you know the meaning of the InputBox arguments, let's see some examples of using this function.

◎ Hands-On 4-10: Using the InputBox Function

1. In the Visual Basic Editor window, choose **Insert | Module** to add a new module.

2. In the Code window, type the Informant subroutine shown below.

```
Sub Informant()
    InputBox prompt:="Enter your place of birth:" & Chr(13) _
    & " (e.g., Boston, Great Falls, etc.) "
End Sub
```

The above procedure displays a dialog box with two buttons. The input prompt is displayed on two lines (see Figure 4-6). Similar to using the MsgBox function, if you plan on using the data entered by the user in the dialog box, you should store the result of the InputBox function in a variable.

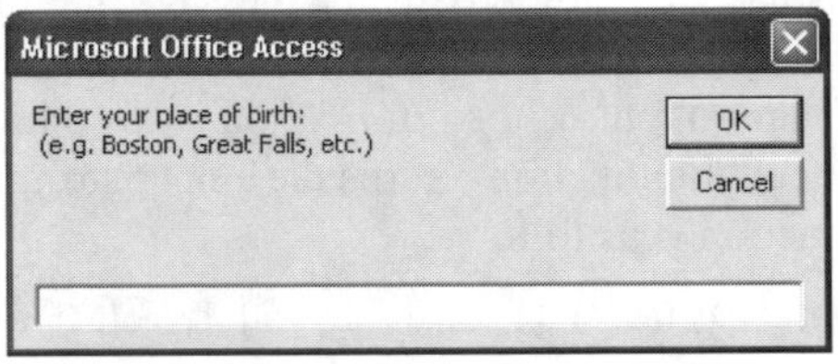

Figure 4-6: A dialog box generated by the Informant subroutine.

3. The Informant2 procedure shown below assigns the result of the InputBox function to the town variable.

```
Sub Informant2()
    Dim myPrompt As String
    Dim town As String

    Const myTitle = "Enter data"
    myPrompt = "Enter your place of birth:" & Chr(13) _
    & "(e.g., Boston, Great Falls, etc.)"
    town = InputBox(myPrompt, myTitle)

    MsgBox "You were born in " & town & ".", , "Your response"
End Sub
```

Notice that this time, the arguments of the InputBox function are listed in parentheses. Parentheses are required if you want to use the result of the InputBox function later in your procedure. The Informant2 subroutine uses a constant to specify the text to appear in the title bar of the dialog box. Because the constant value remains the same throughout the execution of your procedure, you can declare the input box title as a constant.

However, if you'd rather use a variable, you still can. When you run a procedure using the InputBox function, the dialog box generated by this function always appears in the same area of the screen. To change the location of the dialog box, you must supply the xpos and ypos arguments, explained earlier.

4. To display the dialog box in the top left-hand corner of the screen, modify the InputBox function in the Informant2 procedure, as follows.

```
town = InputBox(myPrompt, myTitle, , 1, 200)
```

Notice that the argument myTitle is followed by two commas. The second comma marks the position of the omitted default argument. The next two arguments determine the horizontal and vertical position of the dialog box. If you omit the second comma after the myTitle argument, Visual Basic will use the number 1 as the value of the default argument. If you precede the values of arguments by their names (for example, prompt:=myPrompt, title:=myTitle, xpos:=1, ypos:=200), you won't have to remember to place a comma in the place of each omitted argument.

What will happen if, instead of the name of town, you enter a number? Because users often supply incorrect data in the Input dialog box, your procedure must verify that the data the user entered can be used in further data manipulations. The InputBox function itself does not provide a facility for data validation. To validate user input, you must use other VBA instructions that are presented in the next chapter.

Converting Data Types

The result of the InputBox function is always a string. So if a user enters a number, its *string* value must be converted to a *numeric* value before your procedure can use the number in mathematical computations. Visual Basic is able to automatically convert many values from one data type to another that weren't possible in earlier versions of Microsoft Access.

Hands-On 4-11: Converting Data Types

1. In the Visual Basic Editor window, choose **Insert | Module** to add a new module.

2. In the Code window, enter the AddTwoNums procedure as shown below.

```
Sub AddTwoNums()
    Dim myPrompt As String
    Dim value1 As String
    Dim mySum As Single

    Const myTitle = "Enter data"

    myPrompt = "Enter a number:"
    value1 = InputBox(myPrompt, myTitle, 0)
    mySum = value1 + 2

    MsgBox mySum & " (" & value1 & " + 2)"
End Sub
```

3. Place the cursor anywhere inside the code of the AddTwoNums procedure and press **F5** to run it.

The above procedure displays the dialog box shown in Figure 4-7. Notice that this dialog box has two special features that are obtained by using the InputBox function's optional arguments: title and default value. Instead of the default title, "Microsoft Access," the dialog box displays a text string as defined by the contents of the myTitle constant. The zero (0) entered as the default value in the edit box suggests that the user enter a number instead of text. Once the user provides the data and clicks OK, the input is assigned to the variable value1.

```
value1 = InputBox(myPrompt, myTitle, 0)
```

Figure 4-7: To suggest that the user enter a specific type of data, you may want to provide a default value in the edit box.

Define a Constant

To ensure that all the title bars in a particular VBA procedure display the same text, assign the title text to a constant. By following this tip, you will save yourself the time of typing the title text more than once.

The data type of the variable value1 is String. You can check the data type easily if you follow the above instruction with this statement:

```
MsgBox varType(value1)
```

When Visual Basic runs the above line, it will display a message box with the number 8. Recall that this number represents the String data type. The next line,

```
mySum = value1 + 2
```

adds 2 to the user's input and assigns the result of the calculation to the variable mySum. And because the value1 variable's data type is String, prior to using this variable's data in the computation, Visual Basic goes to work behind the scenes to perform the data type conversion. Visual Basic has the brains to understand the need for conversion. Without it, the two incompatible data types (text and number) would generate a Type Mismatch error.

The procedure ends with the MsgBox function displaying the result of the calculation and showing the user how the total was derived.

Avoid a Type Mismatch Error

If you attempt to run the AddTwoNums procedure in previous versions of Microsoft Access (prior to version 2000), you will get a Type Mismatch error when Visual Basic tries to execute the following line of code:

```
mysum = value1 + 2
```

To avoid the Type Mismatch error, use the built-in CSng function to convert the string stored in the value1 variable to a Single type number. You would write the following statement:

```
mysum = CSng(value1) + 2
```

Using Master Procedures and Subprocedures

When your VBA procedure gets larger, it may be difficult to maintain its many lines of code. To make your program easier to write, understand, and change, you should use a *structured* approach. When you create a structured program, you break a large problem into small problems that can be solved one at a time. In VBA, you do this by creating a master procedure and one or more subordinate procedures. Because both master procedures and subordinate procedures are subroutines, you declare them with the Sub keyword. The master procedure can call the required subroutines and pass arguments to them. It may also call functions.

The following hands-on exercise demonstrates the AboutUser procedure. The procedure requests the user's full name, then extracts the first and last name from the fullName string. The last statement displays the user's last name followed by a comma and the first name. As you read further, this procedure will be broken down into several tasks to demonstrate the concept of using master procedures, subprocedures, and functions.

Hands-On 4-12: Breaking Up Large Procedures

1. In the Visual Basic Editor window, choose **Insert | Module** to add a new module.

2. In the Code window, enter the code of the AboutUser procedure as shown below.

```
Sub AboutUser()
    Dim fullName As String
    Dim firstName As String
    Dim lastName As String
    Dim space As Integer

    ' get input from user
    fullName = InputBox("Enter first and last name:")

    ' get first and last name strings
    space = InStr(fullName, " ")
    firstName = Left(fullName, space - 1)
    lastName = Right(fullName, Len(fullName) - space)
```

```
    ' display last name, first name
    MsgBox lastName & ", " & firstName
End Sub
```

The AboutUser procedure can be divided into smaller tasks. The first task is obtaining the user's full name. The next task requires that you divide the user-supplied data into two strings: last name and first name. These tasks can be delegated to separate functions (for example: GetLast and GetFirst). The last task is displaying a message showing the reordered full name string. Now that you know what tasks you should focus on, let's see how you can accomplish each task.

3. Insert a new module and save it as **MasterProcedures**.

4. Enter the following AboutUserMaster procedure in the MasterProcedures module window:

```
Sub AboutUserMaster()
    Dim first As String, last As String, full As String

    Call GetUserName(full)

    first = GetFirst(full)
    last = GetLast(full)

    Call DisplayLastFirst(first, last)
End Sub
```

The master procedure shown above controls the general flow of your program by calling appropriate subprocedures and functions. The master procedure begins with the declaration of variables. The first statement, Call GetUserName (full), calls the GetUserName subroutine (see step 5 below), and passes an argument to it — the contents of the full variable. Because the variable full is not assigned any value prior to the execution of the Call statement, it has the value of an empty string (" "). Notice that the name of the subprocedure is preceded by the Call statement. Although you are not required to use the Call keyword when calling a procedure, you must use it when the call to the procedure requires arguments. The argument list must be enclosed in parentheses.

5. In the MasterProcedures module, enter the following GetUserName subroutine:

```
Sub GetUserName(fullName As String)

    fullName = InputBox("Enter first and last name:")

End Sub
```

The GetUserName procedure demonstrates two very important Visual Basic programming concepts: how to pass arguments to a subprocedure and how to pass values back from a subprocedure to a calling procedure.

In the master procedure (see step 4), you called the GetUserName procedure and passed one argument to it — the variable full. This variable is received by a fullName parameter declared in the GetUserName subprocedure's Sub statement. Because the variable full contained an empty string, when Visual Basic called the GetUserName subprocedure, the fullName parameter received the same value — an empty string (" "). When Visual Basic displays the dialog box and gets the user's last name, the name is assigned to the fullName parameter. A value assigned to a parameter is passed back to the matching argument after the subprocedure is executed. Therefore, when Visual Basic returns to the master procedure, the full variable will contain user's last name.

Arguments passed to a subprocedure are received by *parameters*. Notice that the parameter name (fullName) is followed by the declaration of the data type (As String). Although the parameter's data type must agree with the data type of the matching argument, different names may be used for an argument and its corresponding parameter.

Arguments vs. Parameters

- An argument is a variable, constant, or expression that is passed to a subprocedure.
- A parameter is a variable that receives a value passed to a subprocedure.

---

6. In the MasterProcedures module, enter the following GetFirst function procedure:

```
Function GetFirst(fullName As String)
    Dim space As Integer

    space = InStr(fullName, " ")
    GetFirst = Left(fullName, space - 1)
End Function
```

The second statement in the master procedure (see step 4), first = GetFirst(full), passes the value of the full variable to the GetFirst function. This value is received by the function's parameter — fullName. To extract the first name from the user-provided fullName string, you must find the location of the space separating the first name and last name. Therefore, the function begins with a declaration of a local variable — space. The next statement uses the VBA built-in function InStr to return the position of a space character (" ") in the fullName string. The obtained number is then assigned to the variable space. Finally, the Left function is used to extract the specified number of characters (space −1) from the left side of the fullName string. The length of the first name is one character less than the value stored in the variable space. The result of the function (user's first name) is then assigned to the function's name. When Visual Basic returns to the master procedure, it places the result in the variable first.

7. In the MasterProcedures module, enter the following GetLast function procedure:

```
Function GetLast(fullName As String)
    Dim space As Integer

    space = InStr(fullName, " ")
    GetLast = Right(fullName, Len(fullName) - space)
End Function
```

The third statement in the master procedure (see step 4), last = GetLast(full), passes the value of the full variable to the GetLast function. This function's purpose is to extract the user's last name from the user-supplied fullName string. The GetLast function uses the built-in Len function to calculate the total number of characters in the fullName string. The Right function extracts the specified number of characters (Len(fullName) – space) from the right side of the fullName string. The obtained string is then assigned to the function name and is stored in the variable last upon returning to the master procedure.

8. In the MasterProcedures module, enter the following DisplayLastFirst subroutine:

```
Sub DisplayLastFirst(firstName As String, lastName As String)

    MsgBox lastName & ", " & firstName

End Sub
```

The fourth statement in the master procedure (see step 4), Call DisplayLastFirst(first, last), calls the DisplayLastFirst subroutine and passes two arguments to it: first and last. To receive these arguments, the DisplayLastFirst subprocedure is declared with two matching parameters: firstName and lastName. Recall that different names can be used for arguments and their corresponding parameters. The DisplayLastFirst subprocedure then displays the message box showing the user's last name followed by a comma and the first name.

Advantages of Using Subprocedures

- It's easier to maintain several subprocedures than one large procedure.
- A task performed by a subprocedure can be used by other procedures.
- Each subprocedure can be tested individually before being placed in the main program.
- Different people can work on individual subprocedures that constitute a larger procedure.

Chapter Summary

In this chapter, you learned the difference between the subroutine procedures that perform actions and function procedures that return values. You saw examples of function procedures called from another Visual Basic procedure. You learned how to pass arguments to functions, and determine the data type of a function's result. You increased your repertoire of VBA keywords with the ByVal, ByRef, and Optional keywords. Finally, you learned how, with the help of parameters, subprocedures can pass values back to the calling procedures.

After working through this chapter, you should be able to create some custom functions of your own that are suited to your specific needs. You should also be able to interact easily with your users by employing the MsgBox and InputBox functions.

Chapter 5

Decision Making with VBA

You can make decisions in your VBA procedures by using conditional expressions inside the special control structures. A *conditional* expression is an expression that uses a relational operator (see Table 5-1), a logical operator (see Table 5-2), or a combination of both. When Visual Basic encounters a conditional expression in your program, it evaluates the expression to determine whether it is true or false.

Table 5-1: Relational operators in VBA

Operator	Description
=	Equal to
< >	Not equal to
>	Greater than
<	Less than
> =	Greater than or equal to
< =	Less than or equal to

Table 5-2: Logical operators in VBA

Operator	Description
AND	All conditions must be true before an action can be taken.
OR	At least one of the conditions must be true before an action can be taken.
NOT	If a condition is true, NOT makes it false. If a condition is false, NOT makes it true.

Boolean Expressions

Conditional expressions and logical operators are also known as *Boolean*. George Boole was a nineteenth-century British mathematician who made significant contributions to the evolution of computer programming. Boolean expressions can be evaluated as true or false.

For example:

One meter equals 10 inches.	False
Two is less than three.	True

If...Then Statement

The simplest way to get some decision making into your VBA procedure is by using the If...Then statement. Suppose you want to choose an action depending on a condition. You can use the following structure:

```
If condition Then statement
```

For example, a quiz procedure might ask the user to guess the number of weeks in a year. If the user's response is other than 52, the procedure should display the message "Try Again."

◎ Hands-On 5-1: Using the If...Then Statement

This chapter's hands-on exercises are provided in the Acc2003_Chap05.mdb file included in the book's downloadable files.

1. Open **Acc2003_Chap05.mdb** from the book's downloadable files or, if you'd like to start from scratch, create a new Access 2003 database.

2. In the Visual Basic Editor window, choose **Insert | Module** to add a new module.

3. In the Code window, enter the SimpleIfThen procedure shown below.

```
Sub SimpleIfThen()
    Dim weeks As String

    weeks = InputBox("How many weeks are in a year:", "Quiz")
    If weeks<>52 Then MsgBox "Try Again"
End Sub
```

The SimpleIfThen procedure stores the user's answer in the weeks variable. The variable's value is then compared with the number 52. If the result of the comparison is true (that is, if the value stored in the variable weeks is not equal to 52), Visual Basic will display the message "Try Again."

4. Run the SimpleIfThen procedure and enter a number other than 52.

5. Rerun the SimpleIfThen procedure and enter the number **52**. When you enter the correct number of weeks, Visual Basic does nothing. The procedure ends. It would be nice to also display a message when the user guesses right.

6. Enter the following instruction on a separate line before the End Sub keywords:

```
If weeks = 52 Then MsgBox "Congratulations!"
```

7. Run the SimpleIfThen procedure again and enter the number 52. When you enter the correct answer, Visual Basic does not execute the Try Again statement. When the procedure is executed, the statement to the right of the Then keyword is ignored if the result from evaluating the supplied

condition is false. As you recall, a VBA procedure can call another procedure. Let's see if it can also call itself.

8. Modify the first If statement in the SimpleIfThen procedure as follows:

```
If weeks <> 52 Then MsgBox "Try Again" : SimpleIfThen
```

We added a colon and the name of the SimpleIfThen procedure to the end of the existing If…Then statement. If the user enters the incorrect answer, he will see a message, and as soon as he clicks the OK button in the message box, he will get another chance to supply the correct answer. The user will be able to keep on guessing for a long time. In fact, he won't be able to exit the procedure gracefully until he supplies the correct answer. If he clicks Cancel, he will have to deal with the unfriendly "Type Mismatch" error message. For now, you may want to revise your SimpleIfThen procedure as follows:

```
Sub SimpleIfThen2()
    Dim weeks As String

    On Error GoTo VeryEnd
    weeks = InputBox("How many weeks are in a year:", "Quiz")
    If weeks <> 52 Then MsgBox "Try Again":SimpleIfThen2
    If weeks = 52 Then MsgBox "Congratulations!"
VeryEnd:
End Sub
```

If Visual Basic encounters an error, it will jump to the VeryEnd label placed at the end of the procedure. The statements placed between On Error GoTo VeryEnd and the VeryEnd label are ignored. In the last section of this chapter you will find other examples of trapping errors in your VBA procedures.

9. Run the SimpleIfThen2 procedure a few times by supplying incorrect answers. The error trap that you added to your procedure will allow you to quit guessing without having to deal with the ugly error message.

Multi-Line If…Then Statement

Sometimes you may want to perform several actions when the condition is true. Although you could add other statements on the same line by separating them with colons, your code will look clearer if you use the multi-line version of the If…Then statement, as shown below:

```
If condition Then
    statement1
    statement2
    statementN
End If
```

For example, you could modify the SimpleIfThen procedure to include additional statements.

◎ Hands-On 5-2: Using the Multi-Line If...Then Statement

1. Insert a new module and enter the SimpleIfThen3 procedure as shown below.

```
Sub SimpleIfThen3()
    Dim weeks As String
    Dim response As String

    weeks = InputBox("How many weeks are in a year?", "Quiz")
    If weeks <> 52 Then
        MsgBox "The correct answer is 52."
        response = MsgBox("Would you like to try again?", _
        vbYesNo + vbInformation + vbDefaultButton1, _
        "Continue Quiz?")
        If response = vbYes Then
            Call SimpleIfThen3
        End If
    End If
End Sub
```

In the above example, the statements between the Then and the End If keywords don't get executed if the variable weeks is equal to 52. Notice that the multi-line If...Then statement must end with the keywords End If. How does Visual Basic make a decision? Simply put, it evaluates the condition it finds between the If...Then keywords.

Two Formats of the If...Then Statement

The If...Then statement has two formats: a single line format and a multi-line format. The short format is good for statements that fit on one line, like:

```
If secretCode <> "01W01" Then MsgBox "Access denied"
```

 or

```
If secretCode = "01W01" Then alpha = True : beta = False
```

In the above examples, secretCode, alpha, and beta are the names of variables. In the first example, Visual Basic displays the message "Access denied" if the value of the secretCode variable is not equal to 01W01. In the second example, Visual Basic will set the value of the variable alpha to True and the value of variable beta to False when the secretCode value is equal to 01W01. Notice that the second statement to be executed is separated from the first one by a colon. The multi-line If...Then statement is more clear when there are more statements to be executed when the condition is true, or when the statement to be executed is extremely long.

Decisions Based on More Than One Condition

The SimpleIfThen procedure you worked with earlier evaluated only a single condition in the If...Then statement. This statement, however, can take more than one condition. To specify multiple conditions in an If...Then statement, you use the logical operators AND and OR (see Table 5-2 at the beginning of the chapter). Here's the syntax with the AND operator:

```
If condition1 AND condition2 Then statement
```

In the above syntax, both condition1 and condition2 must be true for Visual Basic to execute the statement to the right of the Then keyword. For example:

```
If sales = 10000 AND salary < 45000 Then SlsCom = sales * 0.07
```

In this example, *condition1* is sales = 10000, and *condition2* is salary < 45000.

When AND is used in the conditional expression, both conditions must be true before Visual Basic can calculate the sales commission (SlsCom). If any of these conditions is false or both are false, Visual Basic ignores the statement after Then. When it's good enough to meet only one of the conditions, you should use the OR operator. Here's the syntax:

```
If condition1 OR condition2 Then statement
```

The OR operator is more flexible. Only one of the conditions has to be true before Visual Basic can execute the statement following the Then keyword. Let's look at this example:

```
If dept = "S" OR dept = "M" Then bonus = 500
```

In the above example, if at least one condition is true, Visual Basic assigns 500 to the bonus variable. If both conditions are false, Visual Basic ignores the rest of the line.

Now, let's look at a complete procedure example. Suppose you can get a 10% discount if you purchase 50 units of a product priced at $7.00. The IfThenAnd procedure demonstrates the use of the AND operator.

⊚ Hands-On 5-3: Using the If...Then...AND Conditional Statement

1. Insert a new module and enter the following IfThenAnd procedure in the module's Code window.

```
Sub IfThenAnd()
    Dim price As Single
    Dim units As Integer
    Dim rebate As Single

    Const strMsg1 = "To get a rebate you must buy an additional "
    Const strMsg2 = "Price must equal $7.00"

    units = 234
    price = 7

    If price = 7 And units >= 50 Then
        rebate = (price * units) * 0.1
```

```
            MsgBox "The rebate is: $" & rebate
        End If

        If price = 7 And units < 50 Then
            MsgBox strMsg1 & "50 - units."
        End If

        If price <> 7 And units >= 50 Then
            MsgBox strMsg2
        End If

        If price <> 7 And units < 50 Then
            MsgBox "You didn't meet the criteria."
        End If
    End Sub
```

The IfThenAnd procedure shown above has four If...Then statements that are used to evaluate the contents of two variables: price and units. The AND operator between the keywords If...Then allows more than one condition to be tested. With the AND operator, all conditions must be true for Visual Basic to run the statements between the Then...End If keywords.

Indenting If Block Instructions

To make the If blocks easier to read and understand, use indentation. Compare the following:

```
If condition Then           If condition Then
action1                         action
End If                       End If
```

Looking at the If...Then block statement on the right side, you can easily see where the block begins and where it ends.

If...Then...Else Statement

Now you know how to display a message or take an action when one or more conditions are true or false. What should you do, however, if your procedure needs to take one action when the condition is true and another action when the condition is false? By adding the Else clause to the simple If...Then statement, you can direct your procedure to the appropriate statement depending on the result of the test.

The If...Then...Else statement has two formats: single line and multi-line. The single-line format is as follows:

```
If condition Then statement1 Else statement2
```

The statement following the Then keyword is executed if the condition is true, and the statement following the Else clause is executed if the condition is false. For example:

```
If sales > 5000 Then Bonus = sales * 0.05 Else MsgBox "No Bonus"
```

If the value stored in the variable sales is greater than 5,000, Visual Basic will calculate the bonus using the following formula: sales * 0.05. However, if the variable sales is not greater than 5,000, Visual Basic will display the message "No Bonus."

The If...Then...Else statement should be used to decide which of two actions to perform. When you need to execute more statements when the condition is true or false, it's better to use the multi-line format of the If...Then...Else statement:

```
If condition Then
    statements to be executed if condition is True
Else
    statements to be executed if condition is False
End If
```

Notice that the multi-line (block) If...Then...Else statement ends with the End If keywords. Use the indentation as shown above to make this block structure easier to read.

```
If Me.Dirty Then
    Me!btnUndo.Enabled = True
Else
    Me!btnUndo.Enabled = False
End If
```

In the above example, if the condition (Me.Dirty) is true, Visual Basic will execute the statements between Then and Else, and will ignore the statement between Else and End If. If the condition is false, Visual Basic will omit the statements between Then and Else, and execute the statement between Else and End If. The purpose of this procedure fragment is to enable the Undo button when the data on the form has changed and keep the Undo button disabled if the data has not changed. Let's look at the procedure example.

◎ Hands-On 5-4: Using If...Then...Else Conditional Statement

1. Insert a new module and enter the following WhatTypeOf Day procedure in the module's Code window.

```
Sub WhatTypeOfDay()
    Dim response As String
    Dim question As String
    Dim strMsg1 As String, strMsg2 As String
    Dim myDate As Date

    question = "Enter any date in the format mm/dd/yyyy:" _
            & Chr(13)& " (e.g., 11/22/1999)"
    strMsg1 = "weekday"
    strMsg2 = "weekend"
    response = InputBox(question)
    myDate = Weekday(CDate(response))

    If myDate >= 2 And myDate <= 6 Then
        MsgBox strMsg1
    Else
```

```
        MsgBox strMsg2
    End If
End Sub
```

The above procedure asks the user to enter any date. The user-supplied string is then converted to the Date data type with the built-in CDate function. Finally, the Weekday function converts the date into an integer that indicates the day of the week (see Table 5-3). The integer is stored in the variable myDate. The conditional test is performed to check whether the value of the variable myDate is greater than or equal to 2 (>=2) and less than or equal to 6 (<=6). If the result of the test is true, the user is told that the supplied date is a weekday; otherwise, the program announces that it's a weekend.

Table 5-3: The Weekday function values

Constant	Value
vbSunday	1
vbMonday	2
vbTuesday	3
vbWednesday	4
vbThursday	5
vbFriday	6
vbSaturday	7

2. Run the procedure a few times, each time supplying a different date. Check the Visual Basic answers against your desktop or wall calendar.

If...Then...ElseIf Statement

Quite often you will need to check the results of several different conditions. To join a set of If conditions together, you can use the ElseIf clause. Using the If...Then... ElseIf statement, you can evaluate more conditions than is possible with the If...Then...Else statement that was the subject of the preceding section. Here's the syntax of the If...Then...ElseIf statement:

```
If condition1 Then
    statements to be executed if condition1 is True
ElseIf condition2 Then
    statements to be executed if condition2 is True
ElseIf condition3 Then
    statements to be executed if condition3 is True
ElseIf conditionN Then
    statements to be executed if conditionN is True
Else
    statements to be executed if all conditions are False
End If
```

The Else clause if optional; you can omit it if there are no actions to be executed when all conditions are false.

> ### ElseIf Clause
>
> Your procedure can include any number of ElseIf statements and conditions. The ElseIf clause always comes before the Else clause. The statements in the ElseIf clause are executed only if the condition in this clause is true.

Let's look at the following procedure fragment:

```
If myNumber = 0 Then
    MsgBox "You entered zero."
ElseIf myNumber > 0 Then
    MsgBox "You entered a positive number."
ElseIf myNumber < 0 Then
    MsgBox "You entered a negative number."
End if
```

This example checks the value of the number entered by the user and stored in the variable myNumber. Depending on the number entered, an appropriate message (zero, positive, negative) is displayed. Notice that the Else clause is not used. If the result of the first condition (myNumber = 0) is false, Visual Basic jumps to the next ElseIf statement and evaluates its condition (myNumber > 0). If the value is not greater than zero, Visual Basic skips to the next ElseIf and the condition myNumber < 0 is evaluated.

Nested If...Then Statements

You can make more complex decisions in your VBA procedures by placing an If...Then or If...Then...Else statement inside another If...Then or If...Then...Else statement. Structures in which an If statement is contained inside another If block are referred to as *nested* If statements. To understand how nested If...Then statements work, it's time for another hands-on.

◎ Hands-On 5-5: Using Nested If...Then Statements

1. Create a simple form with two text boxes and one command button.

2. Set the properties of the controls you placed on the form as follows:

Control Type	Name Property	Caption Property
Text Box	txtUser	
Text Box	txtPwd	
Command Button	cmdOK	OK
Label (in front of txtUser)		User
Label (in front of txtPwd)		Password

3. Right-click the **OK** button and choose **Build Event** from the shortcut menu. In the Choose Builder dialog box, select **Code Builder** and click **OK**.

4. Enter the code for the cmdOK_Click event procedure as shown below.

```
Private Sub cmdOK_Click()
```

```
        If txtPwd = "FOX" Then
                MsgBox "You are not authorized to run this report."
        ElseIf txtPwd = "DOG" Then
                If txtUser = "John" Then
                        MsgBox "You are logged on with restricted privileges."
                ElseIf txtUser = "Mark" Then
                        MsgBox "Contact the Admin now."
                ElseIf txtUser = "Anne" Then
                        MsgBox "Go home."
                Else
                        MsgBox "Incorrect User name."
                End If
        Else
                MsgBox "Incorrect password or user name"
        End If
        Me.txtUser.SetFocus
End Sub
```

5. Save your form as **frmTestNesting**.

To make the cmdOK_Click procedure easier to understand, the conditional statements are shown with different formatting (bold and underlined).

The procedure first checks if the txtPwd text box placed on the form holds the text string "FOX." If this is true, the message is displayed, and Visual Basic skips over the ElseIf and Else clauses until If finds the matching End If (see the bolded conditional statement).

If the text box strPwd holds the string "DOG," then we use a nested If…Then…Else statement (underlined) to check if the content of the txtUser text box is set to John, Mark, or Anne, and display the appropriate message. If the user name is not one of the specified names, then the condition is false and we jump to the underlined Else to display a message stating that the user entered an incorrect user name.

The first If block (in bold) is called the *outer* If statement. This outer statement contains one *inner* If statement (underlined).

Nesting Statements

Nesting means placing one type of control structure inside another control structure. You will see more nesting examples with the looping structures discussed in Chapter 6.

Select Case Statement

To avoid complex nested If statements that are difficult to follow, you can use the Select Case statement instead. The syntax of this statement is as follows:

```
Select Case testExpression
    Case expressionList1
        statements if expressionList1 matches testExpression
    Case expressionList2
        statements if expressionList2 matches testExpression
```

```
Case expressionListN
    statements if expressionListN matches testExpression
Case Else
    statements to be executed if no values match testExpression
End Select
```

You can place any number of cases to test between the keywords Select Case and End Case. The Case Else clause is optional. Use it when you expect that there may be conditional expressions that return False. In the Select Case statement, Visual Basic compares each expressionList with the value of testExpression.

Here's the logic behind the Select Case statement. When Visual Basic encounters the Select Case clause, it makes note of the value of testExpression. Then it proceeds to test the expression following the first Case clause. If the value of this expression (expressionList1) matches the value stored in testExpression, Visual Basic executes the statements until another Case clause is encountered, and then jumps to the End Select statement. If, however, the expression tested in the first Case clause does not match the testExpression, Visual Basic checks the value of each Case clause until it finds a match. If none of the Case clauses contain the expression that matches the value stored in testExpression, Visual Basic jumps to the Case Else clause and executes the statements until it encounters the End Select keywords. Notice that the Case Else clause is optional. If your procedure does not use Case Else, and none of the Case clauses contain a value matching the value of testExpression, Visual Basic jumps to the statements following End Select and continues executing your procedure.

Let's look at the example of a procedure that uses the Select Case statement. As you already know, the MsgBox function allows you to display a message with one or more buttons. The result of the MsgBox function can be assigned to a variable. Using the Select Case statement you can decide which action to take based on the button the user pressed in the message box.

◎ Hands-On 5-6: Using the Select Case Statement

1. Insert a new module and enter the following TestButtons procedure in the module's Code window.

```
Sub TestButtons()
    Dim question As String
    Dim bts As Integer
    Dim myTitle As String
    Dim myButton As Integer

    question = "Do you want to preview the report now?"
    bts = vbYesNoCancel + vbQuestion + vbDefaultButton1
    myTitle = "Report"
    myButton = MsgBox(prompt:=question, buttons:=bts, Title:=myTitle)

    Select Case myButton
        Case 6
            DoCmd.OpenReport "Sales by Year", acPreview
```

```
        Case 7
            MsgBox "You can review the report later."
        Case Else
            MsgBox "You pressed Cancel."
    End Select
End Sub
```

The first part of the TestButtons procedure displays a message with three buttons: Yes, No, and Cancel. The value of the button selected by the user is assigned to the variable myButton.

If the user clicks Yes, the variable myButton is assigned the vbYes constant or its corresponding value 6. If the user selects No, the variable myButton is assigned the constant vbNo or its corresponding value 7. Lastly, if Cancel is pressed, the contents of the variable myButton equals vbCancel, or 2.

The Select Case statement checks the values supplied after the Case clause against the value stored in the variable myButton. When there is a match, the appropriate Case statement is executed. The TestButtons procedure will work the same if you use constants instead of button values:

```
Select Case myButton
    Case vbYes
        DoCmd.OpenReport "Sales by Year", acPreview
    Case vbNo
        MsgBox "You can review the report later."
    Case Else
        MsgBox "You pressed Cancel."
End Select
```

You can omit the Else clause. Simply revise the Select Case statement as follows:

```
Select Case myButton
    Case vbYes
        DoCmd.OpenReport "Sales by Year", acPreview
    Case vbNo
        MsgBox "You can review the report later."
    Case vbCancel
        MsgBox "You pressed Cancel."
End Select
```

2. Run the TestButtons procedure three times, each time selecting a different button. (An error message will pop up when you select Yes. Click **End**.)

Capture Errors with Case Else

Although using Case Else in the Select Case statement isn't required, it's always a good idea to include one just in case the variable you are testing has an unexpected value. The Case Else is a good place to put an error message.

Using Is with the Case Clause

Sometimes a decision is made based on whether the test expression uses the greater than, less than, equal to, or some other relational operator (see Table 5-1). The Is keyword lets you use a conditional expression in a Case clause. The syntax for the Select Case clause using the Is keyword is shown below.

```
Select Case testExpression
    Case Is condition1
        statements if condition1 is true
    Case Is condition2
        statements if condition2 is true
    Case Is conditionN
        statements if conditionN is true
End Select
```

For example, let's compare some numbers:

```
Select Case myNumber
    Case Is <= 10
        MsgBox "The number is less than or equal to 10."
    Case 11
        MsgBox "You entered 11."
    Case Is >= 100
        MsgBox "The number is greater than or equal to 100."
    Case Else
        MsgBox "The number is between 12 and 99."
End Select
```

Assuming that the variable myNumber holds 120, the third Case clause is true, and the only statement executed is the one between the Case Is >= 100 and the Case Else clause.

Specifying a Range of Values in a Case Clause

In the preceding example you saw a simple Select Case statement that uses one expression in each Case clause. Many times, however, you may want to specify a range of values in a Case clause. You do this by using the To keyword between the values of expressions, as in the following example:

```
Select Case unitsSold
    Case 1 To 100
        Discount = 0.05
    Case Is <= 500
        Discount = 0.1
    Case 501 To 1000
        Discount = 0.15
    Case Is >1000
        Discount = 0.2
End Select
```

Let's analyze the above Select Case block with the assumption that the variable unitsSold currently has a value of 99. Visual Basic compares the value of the variable unitsSold with the conditional expression in the Case clauses. The first and third Case clauses illustrate how to use a range of values in a conditional expression by using the To keyword. Because unitsSold equals 99, the condition in the first Case clause is true; thus, Visual Basic assigns the value 0.05 to the variable Discount.

Well, how about the second Case clause, which is also true? Although it's obvious that 99 is less than or equal to 500, Visual Basic does not execute the associated statement Discount = 0.1. The reason for this is that once Visual Basic locates a Case clause with a true condition, it doesn't bother to look at the remaining Case clauses. It jumps over them and continues to execute the procedure with the instructions that may follow the End Select statement.

To get more practice with the Select Case statement, let's use it in a function procedure. As you recall from Chapter 4, function procedures allow you to return a result to a subroutine. Suppose a subroutine has to display a discount based on the number of units sold. You can get the number of units from the user and then run a function to figure out which discount applies.

◎ Hands-On 5-7: Using the Select Case Statement

1. Insert a new module and enter the following DisplayDiscount procedure in the Code window.

```
Sub DisplayDiscount()
    Dim unitsSold As Integer
    Dim myDiscount As Single

    unitsSold = InputBox("Enter the number of sold units:")
    myDiscount = GetDiscount(unitsSold)
    MsgBox myDiscount
End Sub
```

2. In the same module, enter the following GetDiscount function procedure.

```
Function GetDiscount(unitsSold As Integer)
    Select Case unitsSold
        Case 1 To 200
            GetDiscount = 0.05
        Case 201 To 500
            GetDiscount = 0.1
        Case 501 To 1000
            GetDiscount = 0.15
        Case Is > 1000
            GetDiscount = 0.2
    End Select
End Function
```

3. Place the insertion point anywhere within the code of the DisplayDiscount procedure and press **F5** to run it.

The DisplayDiscount procedure passes the value stored in the variable unitsSold to the GetDiscount function. When Visual Basic encounters the Select Case statement, it checks whether the value of the first Case clause expression matches the value stored in the unitsSold parameter. If there is a match, Visual Basic assigns a 5% discount (0.05) to the function name, and then jumps to the End Select keywords. Because there are no more statements to execute inside the function procedure, Visual Basic returns to the calling procedure DisplayDiscount. Here it assigns the function's result to the variable myDiscount. The last statement displays the value of the retrieved discount in a message box.

Specifying Multiple Expressions in a Case Clause

You may specify multiple conditions within a single Case clause by separating each condition with a comma:

```
Select Case myMonth
    Case "January", "February", "March"
        Debug.Print myMonth & ": 1st Qtr."
    Case "April", "May", "June"
        Debug.Print myMonth & ": 2nd Qtr."
    Case "July", "August", "September"
        Debug.Print myMonth & ": 3rd Qtr."
    Case "October", "November", "December"
        Debug.Print myMonth & ": 4th Qtr."
End Select
```

Multiple Conditions within a Case Clause

The commas used to separate conditions within a Case clause have the same meaning as the OR operator used in the If statement. The Case clause is true if at least one of the conditions is true.

Chapter Summary

Conditional statements, introduced in this chapter, let you control the flow of your procedure. By testing the truth of a condition, you can decide which statements should be run and which should be skipped over. In other words, instead of running your procedure from top to bottom, line by line, you can execute only certain lines. Here are a few guidelines to help you determine what kind of conditional statement you should use:

- If you want to supply only one condition, the simple If…Then statement is the best choice.
- If you need to decide which of two actions to perform, use the If…Then…Else statement.
- If your procedure requires two or more conditions, use the If…Then…ElseIf or Select Case statements.
- If your procedure has many conditions, use the Select Case statement. This statement is more flexible and easier to comprehend than the If…Then…ElseIf statement.

Sometimes decisions have to be repeated. The next chapter teaches you how to perform the same steps over and over again.

Chapter 6

Repeating Actions in VBA

Now that you've learned how conditional statements can give your VBA procedures decision-making capabilities, it's time to get more involved. Not all decisions are easy. Sometimes you will need to perform a number of statements several times to arrive at a certain condition. On other occasions, however, after you've reached the decision, you may need to run the specified statements as long as a condition is true or until a condition becomes true. In programming, performing repetitive tasks is called *looping*. VBA has various looping structures that allow you to repeat a sequence of statements a number of times. In this chapter, you learn how to loop through your code.

Visual Basic has two types of Do loop statements that repeat a sequence of statements either as long as or until a certain condition is true: Do...While and Do...Until.

Using the Do...While Loop

The Do...While loop lets you repeat an action as long as a condition is true. This loop has the following syntax:

```
Do While condition
    statement1
    statement2
    statementN
Loop
```

When Visual Basic encounters this loop, it first checks the truth value of the condition. If the condition is false, the statements inside the loop are not executed, and Visual Basic will continue to execute the program with the first statement after the Loop keyword or will exit the program if there are no more statements to execute. If the condition is true, the statements inside the loop are run one by one until the Loop statement is encountered. The Loop statement tells Visual Basic to repeat the entire process again as long as the testing of the condition in the Do...While statement is true.

Let's see how you can put the Do...While loop to good use in Microsoft Access. Curious to find out how to continuously display an input box until the user enters the correct password? Here's the hands-on that demonstrates this.

◎ Hands-On 6-1: Using the Do...While Loop

This chapter's hands-on exercises are provided in the Acc2003_Chap06.mdb file included in the book's downloadable files.

1. Open **Acc2003_Chap06.mdb** from the downloadable files or, if you'd like to start from scratch, create a new Microsoft Office Access 2003 database.

2. In the Database window, choose **Tools | Macro | Visual Basic Editor** or press **Alt+F11** to switch to the Visual Basic Editor window.

3. Choose **Insert | Module** to add a new module.

4. In the Code window, enter the AskForPassword procedure shown below.

```
Sub AskForPassword()
    Dim pWord As String

    pWord = ""
    Do While pWord <> "DADA"
        pWord = InputBox("What is the Report password?")
    Loop
        MsgBox "You entered the correct Report password."
End Sub
```

In the above procedure, the statement inside the Do...While loop will be executed as long as the variable pWord is not equal to the string DADA. If the user enters the correct password (DADA), Visual Basic leaves the loop and executes the MsgBox statement after the Loop keyword.

To allow the user to exit the procedure gracefully and cancel out the input box if he does not know the correct password, you should add the following statement on an empty line before the Loop keyword:

```
    If pWord = "" Then Exit Do
```

The Exit Do statement is discussed toward the end of this chapter. This statement tells Visual Basic to exit the Do Loop if the variable pWord does not hold any value. Therefore, when the input box appears, the user can leave the text field empty and click OK or Cancel to stop the procedure. Without the above statement, the procedure will keep on asking the user to enter the password until the correct value is supplied.

To forgo displaying the informational message when the user has not provided the correct password, you may want to use the conditional statement If...Then that you learned in the previous chapter. Below is the revised AskForPassword procedure.

```
Sub AskForPassword2()
    Dim pWord As String

    pWord = ""
    Do While pWord <> "DADA"
        pWord = InputBox("What is the Report password?")
        If pWord = "" Then Exit Do
    Loop
```

```
        If pWord <> "" Then
            MsgBox "You entered correct password."
    End If
    End Sub
```

What Is a Loop?

A *loop* is a programming structure that causes a section of program code to execute repeatedly. VBA provides several structures to implement loops in your procedures: Do...While, Do...Until, For...Next, and For Each...Next.

Another Approach to the Do...While Loop

The Do...While loop has another syntax that lets you test the condition at the bottom of the loop:

```
Do
    statement1
    statement2
    statementN
Loop While condition
```

When you test the condition at the bottom of the loop, the statements inside the loop are executed at least once. Let's try this in the following hands-on:

Hands-On 6-2: Using the Do...While Loop with a Condition at the Bottom of the Loop

1. In the Visual Basic Editor window, insert a new module and type the SignIn procedure as shown below.

```
Sub SignIn()
    Dim secretCode As String

    Do
        secretCode = InputBox("Enter your secret code:")
        If secretCode = "sp1045" Then Exit Do
    Loop While secretCode <> "sp1045"
End Sub
```

Notice that by the time the condition is evaluated, Visual Basic has already executed the statements one time. In addition to placing the condition at the end of the loop, the SignIn procedure shows again how to exit the loop when a condition is reached. When the Exit Do statement is encountered, the loop ends immediately.

To exit the loop in the SignIn procedure without entering the password, you may revise it as follows:

```
Sub SignIn2()
    Dim secretCode As String

    Do
        secretCode = InputBox("Enter your secret code:")
```

```
            If secretCode = "sp1045" Or secretCode = "" Then Exit Do
        Loop While secretCode <> "sp1045"
    End Sub
```

Avoid Infinite Loops

If you don't design your loop correctly, you can get an *infinite loop* — a loop that never ends. You will not be able to stop the procedure by using the Escape key. The following procedure causes the loop to execute endlessly because the programmer forgot to include the test condition:

```
Sub SayHello()
    Do
        MsgBox "Hello."
    Loop
End Sub
```

To stop the execution of the infinite loop, you must press Ctrl+Break. When Visual Basic displays the message box "Code execution has been interrupted," click End to end the procedure.

Using the Do...Until Loop

Another handy loop is Do...Until, which allows you to repeat one or more statements until a condition becomes true. In other words, Do...Until repeats a block of code as long as something is false. Here's the syntax:

```
Do Until condition
    statement1
    statement2
    statementN
Loop
```

Using the above syntax, you can now rewrite the previously written AskFor-Password procedure as shown in the following hands-on.

◎ Hands-On 6-3: Using the Do...Until Loop

1. In the Visual Basic Editor window, insert a new module and type the AskForPassword3 procedure.

```
Sub AskForPassword3()
    Dim pWord As String

    pWord = ""
    Do Until pWord = "DADA"
        pWord = InputBox("What is the Report password?")
    Loop
End Sub
```

The first line of this procedure says: Perform the following statements until the variable pWord holds the value DADA. As a result, until the correct password is supplied, Visual Basic executes the InputBox statement inside the loop. This process continues as long as the condition pWord = "DADA" evaluates to False.

> **Variables and Loops**
>
> All variables that appear in a loop should be assigned default values before the loop is entered.

You could modify the procedure as shown below to allow the user to cancel the input box without supplying the password.

```
Sub AskForPassword4()
    Dim pWord As String

    pWord = ""
    Do Until pWord = "DADA"
        pWord = InputBox("What is the Report password?")
        If pWord = "" Then Exit Do
    Loop
End Sub
```

Another Approach to the Do...Until Loop

Similar to the Do...While loop, the Do...Until loop has a second syntax that lets you test the condition at the bottom of the loop:

```
Do
    statement1
    statement2
    statementN
Loop Until condition
```

If you want the statements to execute at least once, no matter what the value of the condition, place the condition on the line with the Loop statement. Let's try out the following example that prints 27 numbers to the Immediate window.

Hands-On 6-4: Using the Do...Until Loop with a Condition at the Bottom of the Loop

1. In the Visual Basic Editor window, insert a new module and type the following procedure:

```
Sub PrintNumbers()
    Dim num As Integer

    num = 0
    Do
        num = num + 1
        Debug.Print num
    Loop Until num = 27
End Sub
```

The variable num is initialized at the beginning of the procedure to zero (0). When Visual Basic enters the loop, the content of the variable num is increased by one, and the value is written to the Immediate window with the Debug.Print statement. Next, the condition tells Visual Basic that it should execute the statements inside the loop until the variable num equals 27.

Counters

A *counter* is a numeric variable that keeps track of the number of items that have been processed. The PrintNumbers procedure shown above declares the variable num to keep track of numbers that were printed. A counter variable should be initialized (assigned a value) at the beginning of the program. This makes sure that you always know the exact value of the counter before you begin using it. A counter can be incremented or decremented by a specified value.

For...Next Loop

The For...Next loop is used when you know how many times you want to repeat a group of statements. The syntax of a For...Next loop looks like this:

```
For counter = start To end [Step increment]
    statement1
    statement2
    statementN
Next [counter]
```

The code in the brackets is optional. Counter is a numeric variable that stores the number of iterations. Start is the number at which you want to begin counting. End indicates how many times the loop should be executed. For example, if you want to repeat the statements inside the loop five times, use the following For statement:

```
For counter = 1 To 5
    statements
Next
```

When Visual Basic encounters the Next statement, it will go back to the beginning of the loop and execute the statements inside the loop again, as long as the counter hasn't reached the end value. As soon as the value of counter is greater than the number entered after the To keyword, Visual Basic exits the loop. Because the variable counter automatically changes after each execution of the loop, sooner or later the value stored in counter exceeds the value specified in end.

By default, every time Visual Basic executes the statements inside the loop, the value of the variable counter is increased by one. You can change this default setting by using the Step clause.

For example, to increase the variable counter by three, use the following statement:

```
For counter = 1 To 5 Step 3
    statements
Next counter
```

When Visual Basic encounters the above statement, it executes the statements inside the loop twice. The first time the loop runs the counter equals 1. The second time in the loop, the counter equals 4 (3+1). After the second time inside the loop, the counter equals 7 (4+3). This causes Visual Basic to exit the loop.

Note that the Step increment is optional. Optional statements are always shown in square brackets (see the syntax at the beginning of this section). The Step increment isn't specified unless it's a value other than 1. You can place a negative number after Step. Visual Basic will then decrement this value from the counter each time it encounters the Next statement. The name of the variable (counter) after the Next statement is also optional; however, it's good programming practice to make your Next statements explicit by including counter.

How can you use the For...Next loop in Microsoft Access? Suppose you want to get the names of the text boxes located on an active form. The procedure in the next hands-on demonstrates how to determine if a control is a text box and how to display its name if a text box is found.

◎ Hands-On 6-5: Using the For...Next Loop

1. Import the Customers table and Customers form from the Acc2003_ Chap01.mdb database file that you worked with in Chapter 1. To do this, choose **File | Get External Data | Import**. Specify the database name as **Acc2003_Chap01** and click **Import**. In the Import Objects dialog box, select the **Customers** table and **Customers** form and click **OK**.

2. Now, open the Customers form in Form view.

3. Switch to the Visual Basic Editor window and insert a new module.

4. In the module's Code window, enter the GetTextBoxNames procedure as shown below.

```
Sub GetTextBoxNames()
    Dim myForm As Form
    Dim myControl As Control
    Dim c As Integer

    Set myForm = Screen.ActiveForm
    Set myControl = Screen.ActiveControl

    For c = 0 To myForm.Count - 1
        If TypeOf myForm(c) Is TextBox Then
            MsgBox myForm(c).Name
        End If
    Next c
End Sub
```

The conditional statement (If...Then) nested inside the For...Next loop tells Visual Basic to display the name of the active control only if it is a text box.

> **Paired Statements**
>
> For and Next must be paired. If one is missing, Visual Basic generates the
> following error message: "For without Next."

For Each...Next Loop

When your procedure needs to loop through all of the objects of a collection or
all of the elements in an array (arrays are the subject of the next chapter), the
For Each...Next loop should be used. This loop does not require a counter
variable. Visual Basic can figure out on its own how many times the loop
should execute. The For Each...Next loop looks like this:

```
For Each element In Group
    statement1
    statement2
    statementN
Next [element]
```

Element is a variable to which all the elements of an array or collection will be
assigned. This variable has to be of the Variant data type for an array and of the
Object data type for a collection. Group is a name of a collection or an array.
Let's now see how to use the For Each...Next loop to print the names of controls in the currently open form to the Immediate window.

◉ Hands-On 6-6: Using the For Each...Next Loop

1. Ensure that the Customers form is open in Form view.
2. Switch to the Visual Basic Editor window and insert a new module.
3. In the Code window, type the GetControls procedure as shown below.

```
Sub GetControls()
    Dim myControl As Control
    Dim myForm As Form

    DoCmd.OpenForm "Customers"
    Set myForm = Screen.ActiveForm

    For Each myControl In myForm
        Debug.Print myControl.Name
    Next
End Sub
```

4. Run the GetControls procedure by choosing **Run | Run Sub/UserForm**.
5. To see the results of the procedure you just executed, press **Ctrl+G** to open
   the Immediate window or choose **View | Immediate Window**.

Exiting Loops Early

Sometimes you may not want to wait until the loop ends on its own. It's possible that a user will enter the wrong data, a procedure will encounter an error, or perhaps the task has been completed and there's no need to do additional looping. You can leave the loop early without reaching the condition that normally terminates it. Visual Basic has two types of Exit statements:

- The Exit For statement is used to end either a For…Next or a For Each…Next loop early.
- The Exit Do statement immediately exits any of the VBA Do loops.

The following hands-on demonstrates how to use the Exit For statement to leave the For Each…Next loop early.

◎ Hands-On 6-7: Early Exit from a Loop

1. In the Code window, enter the GetControls2 procedure as shown below.

```
Sub GetControls2()
    Dim myControl As Control
    Dim myForm As Form

    DoCmd.OpenForm "Customers"
    Set myForm = Screen.ActiveForm

    For Each myControl In myForm
        Debug.Print myControl.Name
        If myControl.Name = "Address" Then Exit For
    Next
End Sub
```

The GetControls2 procedure examines the names of the controls in the currently open Customers form. If Visual Basic encounters the control named "Address," it exits the loop.

Exiting Procedures

If you want to exit a subroutine earlier than normal, use the Exit Sub statement. If the procedure is a function, use the Exit Function statement instead.

Nested Loops

So far in this chapter you have tried out various loops. Each procedure demonstrated the use of each individual looping structure. In programming practice, however, one loop is often placed inside of another. Visual Basic allows you to "nest" various types of loops (For and Do loops) within the same procedure. When writing nested loops, you must make sure that each inner loop is completely contained inside the outer loop. Also, each loop has to have a unique counter variable. When you use nesting loops, you can often execute the specific task more effectively.

The GetFormsAndControls procedure shown in the following hands-on illustrates how one For Each…Next loop is nested within another For Each…Next loop.

◎ Hands-On 6-8: Using Nested Loops

1. Import the Employees table and Employees form from the Acc2003_ Chap02.mdb database available in the book's downloadable files. In the currently open database, choose **File | Get External Data | Import**. Specify the database filename (**Acc2003_Chap02.mdb**) and select the objects to import.

2. Switch to the Visual Basic Editor window and insert a new module.

3. In the module's Code window, enter the GetFormsAndControls procedure as shown below.

```
Sub GetFormsAndControls()
    Dim accObj As AccessObject
    Dim myControl As Control

    Set obj = CurrentProject.AllForms

    For Each accObj In obj
        Debug.Print accObj.Name & "---Form"
        If Not accObj.IsLoaded Then
            DoCmd.OpenForm accObj.Name
            For Each myControl In Forms(accObj.Name).Controls
                Debug.Print Chr(9) & myControl.Name
            Next
            DoCmd.Close
        End If
    Next
End Sub
```

The GetFormsAndControls procedure shown above uses two For Each… Next loops to print the name of each currently open form and its controls to the Immediate window. To enumerate through the form's controls, the form must be open. Notice the use of the IsLoaded function. The procedure will only open the form if it is not yet loaded. The control names are indented in the Immediate window thanks to the Chr(9) function. This is like pressing the Tab key once. To get the same result, you can replace Chr(9) with a VBA constant: vbTab.

After reading the names of the controls, the form is closed and the next form is processed in the same manner. The procedure ends when no more forms are found in the AllForms collection of CurrentProject.

Chapter Summary

In this chapter you learned how to repeat certain groups of statements in procedures by using loops. While working with several types of loops, you saw how each loop performs repetitions in a slightly different way. As you gain experience, you'll find it easier to choose the appropriate flow control structure for your task.

In the following chapters of this book, there are many additional examples of using loops. In the next chapter, for instance, you will see how, by using arrays and nested loops, you can create your own VBA procedure to pick your lottery numbers. The next chapter also shows you how to work with larger sets when your procedure requires a large number of variables.

Chapter 7

Working with Arrays

In previous chapters you worked with many VBA procedures that used variables to hold specific information about an object, property, or value. For each single value you wanted your procedure to manipulate, you declared a variable. But what if you have a series of values? If you had to write a VBA procedure to deal with larger amounts of data, you would have to create enough variables to handle all of the data.

Can you imagine the nightmare of storing currency exchange rates for all the countries in the world in your program? To create a table to hold the necessary data, you'd need at least three variables for each country: country name, currency name, and exchange rate. Fortunately, Visual Basic has a way to get around this problem. By clustering the related variables together, your VBA procedures can manage a large amount of data with ease. In this section, you'll learn how to manipulate lists and tables of data with arrays.

In Visual Basic an *array* is a special type of variable that represents a group of similar values that are of the same data type (String, Integer, Currency, Date, etc.). The two most common types of arrays are one-dimensional arrays (lists) and two-dimensional arrays (tables).

A one-dimensional array is sometimes referred to as a *list*. A shopping list, a list of the days of the week, or an employee list are examples of one-dimensional arrays. A one-dimensional array is simply a numbered list. Each value in the list has an index. Below is a diagram of a list that contains six elements (items):

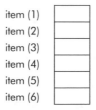

item (1)
item (2)
item (3)
item (4)
item (5)
item (6)

Notice that the column representing the one-dimensional array is currently empty. If you want to fill this array with data, instead of six individual labels, simply use one variable name followed by a number in parentheses. In the diagram above, item is a variable name and the numbers in parentheses — (1), (2), (3), (4), (5), and (6) — identify individual elements of the array.

All elements of the array must be of the same data type. In other words, one array cannot store both strings and integers. Below are two examples of one-dimensional arrays: a one-dimensional array, cities, is populated with text

(String data type, $), and a one-dimensional array, lotto, contains six lottery numbers (Integer data type, %).

One-dimensional array named cities$ (of String data type)			One-dimensional array named lotto% (of Integer data type)	
cities(1)	Baltimore		lotto(1)	25
cities(2)	Atlanta		lotto(2)	4
cities(3)	Boston		lotto(3)	31
cities(4)	Washington		lotto(4)	22
cities(5)	New York		lotto(5)	11
cities(6)	Trenton		lotto(6)	5

As you can see, the contents assigned to each array element match the variable type. If you want to store values of different data types in the same array, you must declare the array as Variant.

Two-dimensional arrays are tables of data represented in rows and columns. The position of each element in a table is determined by its row and column number. Below is a diagram of an empty two-dimensional array.

rows ↓	1	2	3	←columns
1	(1, 1)	(1, 2)	(1, 3)	
2	(2, 1)	(2, 2)	(2, 3)	
3	(3, 1)	(3, 2)	(3, 3)	
4	(4, 1)	(4, 2)	(4, 3)	
5	(5, 1)	(5, 2)	(5, 3)	

Notice how items in a two-dimensional array are identified with row and column indexes. In this diagram, the first element of the array is located in the first row and the first column (1, 1). The last element of the array is positioned in the fifth row and the third column (5, 3). Let's now populate this array with some values. The two-dimensional array below stores the name of the country or region, its currency, and the U.S. dollar equivalent.

Two-dimensional array named exchange (of Variant data type)		
Japan (1, 1)	Japanese Yen (1, 2)	102.76 (1, 3)
Australia (2, 1)	Australian Dollar (2, 2)	1.29083 (2, 3)
Canada (3, 1)	Canadian Dollar (3, 2)	1.20892 (3, 3)
Norway (4, 1)	Norwegian Krone (4, 2)	6.09506 (4, 3)
Europe (5, 1)	Euro (5, 2)	0.744734 (5, 3)

Although VBA arrays can have up to 60 dimensions, most people find it difficult to picture dimensions beyond 3D. A three-dimensional array is a collection of tables where each table has the same number of rows and columns.

Each element of a three-dimensional array is identified by three pieces of data: row, column, and table.

What Is an Array Variable?

An *array* is a group of variables that have a common name. While a typical variable can hold only one value, an array variable can store a large number of individual values. You refer to a specific value in the array by using the array name and an index number.

Declaring Arrays

Because an array is a variable, you must declare it the same way you declare other variables — by using the Dim statement. When you declare an array variable you set aside the required memory space to hold its values.

Let's take a look at some examples of array declarations:

```
Dim cities(6) As String
Dim daysOfWeek(7) As String
Dim lotto(6) As Integer
Dim exchange(5, 3) As Variant
```

Notice that the names of variables are followed by numbers in parentheses. One-dimensional arrays require one number between parentheses. This number specifies the maximum number of elements that can be stored in a list. The name of a two-dimensional array is always followed by two numbers; the first number is the row index and the second number is the column index. In the example above, the exchange array can hold a maximum of 15 values (5 * 3 = 15).

The last part in the array declaration is the definition of the data type the array will hold. An array can hold any of the following data types: Integer, Long, Single, Double, Variant, Currency, String, Boolean, Byte, Date.

When you declare an array, Visual Basic automatically reserves enough memory space for it. The amount of memory allocated depends on the array's size and data type. When you declare a one-dimensional array named lotto with six elements, Visual Basic sets aside 12 bytes — two bytes for each element of the array (recall that the size of the Integer data type is 2, hence 2 * 6 = 12). The larger the array, the more memory space is required to store the data. Because arrays can eat up a lot of memory and impact your computer's performance, it is recommended that you declare arrays with only as many elements as you think you'll use.

Subscripted Variables

The numbers inside the parentheses of the array variables are called *subscripts*, and each individual variable is called a subscripted variable or element. For example, cities(6) is the sixth subscripted variable (element) of the array cities().

Array Upper and Lower Bounds

By default, Visual Basic assigns zero (0) to the first element of the array. Therefore, the number 1 represents the second element of the array, number 2 the third, and so on. With numeric indexing starting at 0, the one-dimensional array cities(6) contains seven elements numbered from 0 to 6. If you'd rather start counting your array's elements at 1, you can explicitly specify a lower bound of the array by using an Option Base 1 statement. This instruction must be placed in the declaration section at the top of the VBA module, before any Sub statements. If you don't specify Option Base 1 in a procedure that uses arrays, Visual Basic assumes that the statement Option Base 0 is to be used, and begins indexing your array's elements at 0.

You can have the array indexing start at a number other than 0 or 1. To do this, you must specify the bounds of an array when declaring the array variable. The bounds of an array are its lowest and highest indexes. Let's take a look at the following example:

```
Dim cities(3 To 6) As Integer
```

The above statement declares a one-dimensional array with four elements. The numbers enclosed in parentheses after the array name specify the lower (3) and upper (6) bounds of the array. The first element of this array has the number 3, the second 4, the third 5, and the fourth 6. Notice the keyword To between the lower and upper index.

The Range of the Array

The spread of the subscripts specified by the Dim statement is called the *range* of the array. For example: Dim mktgCodes(5 To 15).

Using Arrays in VBA Procedures

After you declare an array, you must assign values to its elements. Assigning values to the array's elements is often referred to as "filling an array" or "populating an array." Let's try a VBA procedure that uses a one-dimensional array to programmatically display a list of six American cities.

⊚ Hands-On 7-1: Using a One-Dimensional Array

This chapter's hands-on exercises are provided in the Acc2003_Chap07.mdb file included in the book's downloadable files.

1. Open **Acc2003_Chap07.mdb** or, if you'd like to start from scratch, create a new Microsoft Office Access 2003 database.

2. Switch to the Visual Basic Editor window and insert a new module.

3. Enter the following FavoriteCities procedure in the Code window to start indexing array elements at 1:

```
Option Base 1
```

```
Sub FavoriteCities()
    ' declare the array
    Dim cities(6) As String

    ' assign the values to array elements
    cities(1) = "Baltimore"
    cities(2) = "Atlanta"
    cities(3) = "Boston"
    cities(4) = "Washington"
    cities(5) = "New York"
    cities(6) = "Trenton"

    ' display the list of cities
    MsgBox cities(1) & Chr(13) & cities(2) & Chr(13) _
        & cities(3) & Chr(13) & cities(4) & Chr(13) _
        & cities(5) & Chr(13) & cities(6)
End Sub
```

4. Choose **Run | Run Sub/UserForm** to execute the FavoriteCities procedure.

5. Modify the FavoriteCities procedure so that it displays the names of the cities in reverse order (from 6 to 1).

Before the FavoriteCities procedure begins, the default indexing for an array is changed. Notice that the position of the Option Base 1 statement is at the top of the module window before the Sub statement. This statement tells Visual Basic to assign the number 1 instead of the default 0 to the first element of the array. The array cities is declared with six elements of the String data type. Each element of the array is then assigned a value. The last statement in this procedure uses the MsgBox function to display the list of cities in a message box. When you run this procedure, each city name will appear on a separate line (see Figure 7-1). You can change the order of the displayed data by switching the index values.

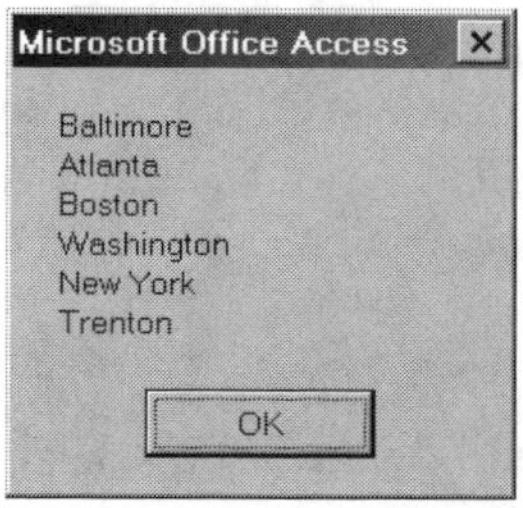

Figure 7-1: You can display the elements of a one-dimensional array with the MsgBox function.

Initial Value of an Array Element

Until a value is assigned to an element of an array, the element retains its default value. Numeric variables have a default value of zero (0), and string variables have a default value of empty string (" ").

Arrays and Looping Statements

Several looping statements you learned earlier (For…Next and For Each…Next) will come in handy now that you're ready to perform such tasks as populating an array or displaying the elements of an array. It's time to combine the skills you've learned so far.

How can you rewrite the FavoriteCities procedure so that it shows the name of each city in a separate message box? The FavoriteCities2 procedure in the following hands-on replaces the last statement of the original procedure with the For Each…Next loop.

◉ Hands-On 7-2: Using Arrays and Loops

1. In the Visual Basic Editor window, insert a new module.

2. Enter the following FavoriteCities2 procedure in the Code window.

```
Option Base 1

Sub FavoriteCities2()
    ' declare the array
    Dim cities(6) As String
    Dim city As Variant

    ' assign the values to array elements
    cities(1) = "Baltimore"
    cities(2) - "Atlanta"
    cities(3) = "Boston"
    cities(4) = "Washington"
    cities(5) = "New York"
    cities(6) = "Trenton"

    ' display the list of cities in separate messages
    For Each city In cities
        MsgBox city
    Next
End Sub
```

3. Choose **Run | Run Sub/UserForm** to execute the FavoriteCities2 procedure.

   Notice that the For Each…Next loop uses the variable city of the Variant data type. As you recall from the previous section of this chapter, the For Each… Next loop allows you to loop through all of the objects in a collection or all of the elements of an array and perform the same action on each object or element. When you run the FavoriteCities2 procedure, the loop will execute as many times as there are elements in the array.

In Chapter 4 you practiced passing arguments as variables to subroutines and functions. The procedure CityOperator in the next hands-on demonstrates how you can pass elements of an array to another procedure.

◎ Hands-On 7-3: Passing Elements of an Array to Another Procedure

1. In the Visual Basic Editor window, insert a new module.

2. Enter the following two procedures in the module's Code window.

3. Execute the CityOperator procedure (choose **Run | Run Sub/UserForm**).

```
Option Base 1

Sub CityOperator()
    ' declare the array
    Dim cities(6) As String

    ' assign the values to array elements
    cities(1) = "Baltimore"
    cities(2) = "Atlanta"
    cities(3) = "Boston"
    cities(4) = "Washington"
    cities(5) = "New York"
    cities(6) = "Trenton"

    ' call another procedure and pass
    ' the array as argument
    Hello cities()
End Sub

Sub Hello(cities() As String)
    Dim counter As Integer

    For counter = 1 To 6
    MsgBox "Hello, " & cities(counter) & "!"
    Next
End Sub
```

Notice that the declaration of the Hello procedure includes an array type argument named cities(). Passing array elements from one subroutine to another subroutine or function procedure allows you to reuse the same array in many procedures without unnecessary duplication of the program code.

Passing Arrays between Procedures

When an array is declared in a procedure, it is local to this procedure and unknown to other procedures. However, you can pass the local array to another procedure by using the array's name followed by an empty set of parentheses as an argument in the calling statement. For example, the statement Hello cities() calls the procedure named Hello and passes to it the array cities().

You can also put your newly acquired knowledge about arrays and loops to work in real life. If you're an avid lotto player who is getting tired of picking your own lucky numbers, have Visual Basic do the picking. The Lotto procedure below populates an array with six numbers from 1 to 51.

◎ Hands-On 7-4: Using Arrays and Loops in Real Life

1. In the Visual Basic Editor window, insert a new module.
2. Enter the following Lotto procedure in the module's Code window.
3. Execute the Lotto procedure (choose **Run | Run Sub/UserForm**) to get the computer-generated lottery numbers.

```
Sub Lotto()
    Const spins = 6
    Const minNum = 1
    Const maxNum = 51
    Dim t As Integer          ' looping variable in outer loop
    Dim i As Integer          ' looping variable in inner loop
    Dim myNumbers As String   ' string to hold all picks
    Dim lucky(spins) As String ' array to hold generated picks

    myNumbers = ""
    For t = 1 To spins
        Randomize
        lucky(t) = Int((maxNum - minNum + 1) * Rnd + minNum)

        ' check if this number was picked before
        For i = 1 To (t - 1)
            If lucky(t) = lucky(i) Then
                lucky(t) = Int((maxNum - minNum + 1) * Rnd + minNum)
                i = 0
        End If
        Next i
        MsgBox "Lucky number is " & lucky(t), , "Lucky number " & t
        myNumbers = myNumbers & " -" & lucky(t)
    Next t
    MsgBox "Lucky numbers are " & myNumbers, , "6 Lucky Numbers"
End Sub
```

The Randomize statement initializes the random number generator. The instruction Int((maxNum – minNum + 1) * Rnd + minNum) uses the Rnd function to generate a random value from the specified minNum to maxNum. The Int function converts the resulting random number to an integer. Instead of assigning constant values for minNum and maxNum, you can use the InputBox function to get these values from the user.

The inner For…Next loop ensures that each picked number is unique — it may not be any one of the previously picked numbers. If you omit the inner loop and run this procedure multiple times, you'll likely see some occurrences of duplicate numbers.

Using a Two-Dimensional Array

Now that you know how to programmatically produce a list (a one-dimensional array), it's time to take a closer look at how you can work with tables of data. The following hands-on creates a two-dimensional array that will hold a country or region name, name of currency, and exchange rate for three countries.

◉ Hands-On 7-5: Using a Two-Dimensional Array

1. In the Visual Basic Editor window, insert a new module.

2. Enter the following Exchange procedure in the module's Code window.

3. Execute the Exchange procedure (choose **Run | Run Sub/UserForm**).

```
Sub Exchange()
    Dim t As String
    Dim r As String
    Dim Ex(3, 3) As Variant

    t = Chr(9)  ' Tab
    r = Chr(13) ' Enter

    Ex(1, 1) = "Japan"
    Ex(1, 2) = "Japanese Yen"
    Ex(1, 3) = 102.76
    Ex(2, 1) = "Europe"
    Ex(2, 2) = "Euro"
    Ex(2, 3) = 0.744734
    Ex(3, 1) = "Canada"
    Ex(3, 2) = "Canadian Dollar"
    Ex(3, 3) = 1.20892

    MsgBox "Country " & t & t & "Currency" & t & t & "Value per US$" _
        & r & r _
        & Ex(1, 1) & t & t & Ex(1, 2) & t & Ex(1, 3) & r _
        & Ex(2, 1) & t & t & Ex(2, 2) & t & t & Ex(2, 3) & r _
        & Ex(3, 1) & t & t & Ex(3, 2) & t & Ex(3, 3), , _
        "Exchange"
End Sub
```

When you run the Exchange procedure, you will see a message box with the information presented in three columns (see Figure 7-2).

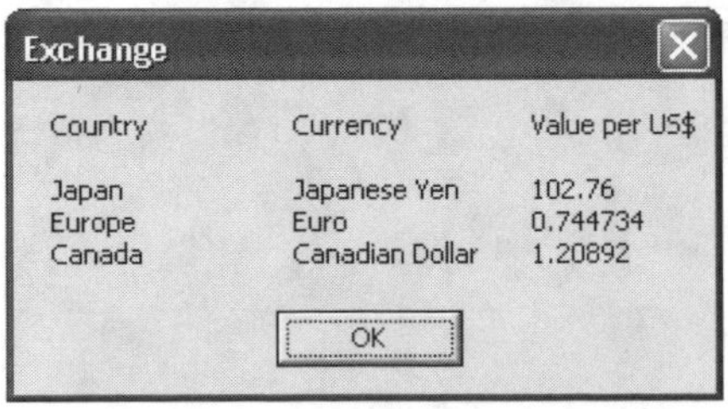

Figure 7-2: The text displayed in a message box can be custom formatted.

Static and Dynamic Arrays

The arrays introduced thus far are static. A *static array* is an array of a specific size. You use a static array when you know in advance how big the array should be. The size of the static array is specified in the array's declaration statement. For example, the statement Dim Fruits(10) As String, declares a static array called Fruits that is made up of 10 elements.

But what if you're not sure how many elements your array will contain? If your procedure depends on user input, the number of user-supplied elements might vary every time the procedure is executed. How can you ensure that the array you declare is not wasting memory?

You may recall that after you declare an array, VBA sets aside enough memory to accommodate the array. If you declare an array to hold more elements than what you need, you'll end up wasting valuable computer resources. The solution to this problem is making your arrays dynamic. A *dynamic array* is an array whose size can change. You use a dynamic array when the array size will be determined each time the procedure is run.

> **Fixed-Dimension Arrays**
>
> A static array contains a fixed number of elements. The number of elements in a static array will not change once it has been declared.

A dynamic array is declared by placing empty parentheses after the array name. For example:

```
Dim Fruits() As String
```

Before you use a dynamic array in your procedure, you must use the ReDim statement to dynamically set the lower and upper bounds of the array.

The ReDim statement redimensions arrays as the procedure code executes. The ReDim statement informs Visual Basic about the new size of the array. This statement can be used several times in the same procedure. Let's see how your procedure could use a dynamic array.

◎ Hands-On 7-6: Using a Dynamic Array

1. In a new module, enter the following DynArray procedure.

2. Execute the DynArray procedure (choose **Run | Run Sub/UserForm**).

```
Sub DynArray()
    Dim counter As Integer
    Dim myArray() As Integer      ' declare a dynamic array
    ReDim myArray(5)              ' specify the initial size of the array
    Dim myValues As String

    ' populate myArray with values
    For counter = 1 To 5
        myArray(counter) = counter + 1
        myValues = myValues & myArray(counter) & Chr(13)
```

```
    Next

    ' change the size of myArray to hold 10 elements
    ReDim Preserve myArray(10)

    ' add new values to myArray
    For counter = 6 To 10
        myArray(counter) = counter * counter
        myValues = myValues & myArray(counter) & Chr(13)
    Next counter

    MsgBox myValues
    For counter = 1 To 10
        MsgBox myArray(counter)
    Next counter
End Sub
```

In the DynArray procedure, the statement Dim myArray() As Integer declares a dynamic array called myArray. Although this statement declares the array, it does not allocate any memory to the array. The first ReDim statement specifies the initial size of myArray and reserves for it 10 bytes of memory to hold its five elements. As you know, every Integer value requires 2 bytes of memory. The For...Next loop populates myArray with data and writes the array's elements to the variable myValues. The value of the variable counter equals 1 at the beginning of the loop.

The first statement in the loop (myArray(counter) = counter +1) assigns the value 2 to the first element of myArray. The second statement (myValues = myValues & myArray(counter) & Chr(13)) enters the current value of myArray's element followed by a carriage return (Chr(13)) into the variable myValues. The statements inside the loop are executed five times. Visual Basic places each new value in the variable myValues and proceeds to the next statement: Redim Preserve myArray(10).

Normally, when you change the size of the array, you lose all the values that were in that array. The ReDim statement alone reinitializes the array. However, you can append new elements to an existing array by following the ReDim statement with the Preserve keyword. In other words, the Preserve keyword guarantees that the redimensioned array will not lose its existing data.

The second For...Next loop assigns values to the sixth through tenth elements of myArray. This time the values of the array's elements are obtained by multiplication: counter * counter.

Dimensioning Arrays

Arrays must be dimensioned in a Dim or ReDim statement before they are used. This means that you can't assign a value to an array element until you have declared the array with the Dim or ReDim statement.

Array Functions

You can manipulate arrays with five built-in VBA functions: Array, IsArray, Erase, LBound, and UBound. The following sections demonstrate the use of each of these functions in VBA procedures.

The Array Function

The Array function allows you to create an array during code execution without having to first dimension it. This function always returns an array of Variants. Using the Array function you can quickly place a series of values in a list. The CarInfo procedure in the following hands-on creates a fixed-size, one-dimensional, three-element array called auto.

⊚ Hands-On 7-7: Using the Array Function

1. In a new module, enter the following CarInfo procedure.

2. Run the CarInfo procedure and examine the results.

```
Sub CarInfo()
    Dim auto As Variant

    auto = Array("Ford", "Black", "1999")
    MsgBox auto(2) & " " & auto(1) & ", " & auto(3)

    auto(2) = "4-door"
    MsgBox auto(2) & " " & auto(1) & ", " & auto(3)
End Sub
```

The IsArray Function

Using the IsArray function you can test whether a variable is an array. The IsArray function returns True if the variable is an array or False if it's not an array. Let's do another hands-on.

⊚ Hands-On 7-8: Using the IsArray Function

1. In a new module, enter the code of the IsThisArray procedure, as shown below.

2. Run the IsThisArray procedure to examine its results.

```
Sub IsThisArray()
    ' declare a dynamic array
    Dim tblNames() As String
    Dim totalTables As Integer
    Dim counter As Integer
    Dim db As Database

    Set db = CurrentDb

    ' count the tables in the open database
    totalTables = db.TableDefs.Count
```

```
' specify the size of the array
ReDim tblNames(1 To totalTables)

' enter and show the names of tables
For counter = 1 To totalTables - 1
    tblNames(counter) = db.TableDefs(counter).Name
    Debug.Print tblNames(counter)
Next counter

' check if this is indeed an array
If IsArray(tblNames) Then
    MsgBox "The tblNames is an array."
End If
End Sub
```

The Erase Function

When you want to remove the data from an array, you should use the Erase function. This function deletes all the data held by static or dynamic arrays. In addition, the Erase function reallocates all of the memory assigned to a dynamic array. If a procedure has to use the dynamic array again, you must use the ReDim statement to specify the size of the array. The next hands-on demonstrates how to erase the data from the array cities.

◎ Hands-On 7-9: Removing Data from an Array

1. In a new module, enter the code of the FunCities procedure shown below.

2. Run the FunCities procedure.

```
' start indexing array elements at 1
Option Base 1

Sub FunCities()
    ' declare the array
    Dim cities(1 To 5) As String

    ' assign the values to array elements
    cities(1) = "Las Vegas"
    cities(2) = "Orlando"
    cities(3) = "Atlantic City"
    cities(4) = "New York"
    cities(5) = "San Francisco"

    ' display the list of cities
    MsgBox cities(1) & Chr(13) & cities(2) & Chr(13) _
        & cities(3) & Chr(13) & cities(4) & Chr(13) _
        & cities(5)

    Erase cities

    ' show all that was erased
    MsgBox cities(1) & Chr(13) & cities(2) & Chr(13) _
        & cities(3) & Chr(13) & cities(4) & Chr(13) _
```

```
        & cities(5)
    End Sub
```

After the Erase function deletes the values from the array, the MsgBox function displays an empty message box.

The LBound and UBound Functions

The LBound and UBound functions return whole numbers that indicate the lower bound and upper bound indices of an array.

◎ Hands-On 7-10: Finding the Lower and Upper Bounds of an Array

1. In a new module, enter the code of the FunCities2 procedure shown below.

2. Run the FunCities2 procedure.

```
Sub FunCities2()
    ' declare the array
    Dim cities(1 To 5) As String

    ' assign the values to array elements
    cities(1) = "Las Vegas"
    cities(2) = "Orlando"
    cities(3) = "Atlantic City"
    cities(4) = "New York"
    cities(5) = "San Francisco"

    ' display the list of cities
    MsgBox cities(1) & Chr(13) & cities(2) & Chr(13) _
        & cities(3) & Chr(13) & cities(4) & Chr(13) _
        & cities(5)

    ' display the array bounds
    MsgBox "The lower bound: " & LBound(cities) & Chr(13) _
        & "The upper bound: " & UBound(cities)
End Sub
```

When determining the lower and upper bound indices of a two-dimensional array, you must specify the dimension number: 1 for the first dimension and 2 for the second dimension.

To determine the upper and lower indices in a two-dimensional array, you may want to add the following statements at the end of the Exchange procedure that was prepared earlier in this chapter (add these lines just before the End Sub keywords):

```
MsgBox "The lower bound (first dimension) is " _
    & LBound(Ex, 1) & "."
MsgBox "The upper bound(first dimension) is " _
    & UBound(Ex, 1) & "."
MsgBox "The lower bound (second dimension) is " _
    & LBound(Ex, 2) & "."
MsgBox "The upper bound(second dimension) is " _
    & UBound(Ex, 2) & "."
```

Errors in Arrays

When working with arrays, it's easy to make a mistake. If you try to assign more values than there are elements in the declared array, Visual Basic will display the error message "Subscript out of range" (see Figure 7-3 below).

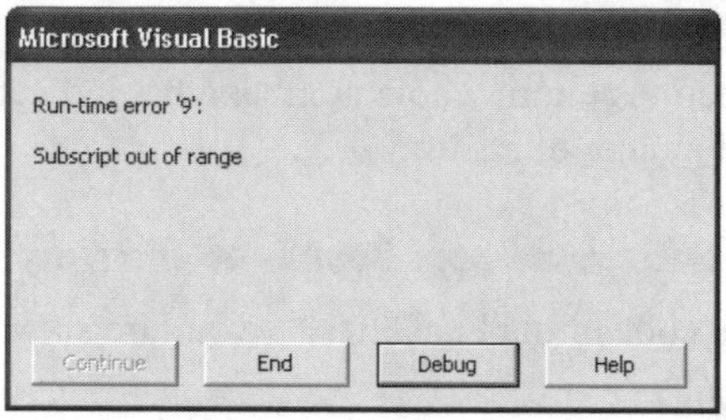
Microsoft Visual Basic
Run-time error '9':
Subscript out of range
Continue
End
Debug
Help

Figure 7-3: This error was caused by an attempt to access a nonexistent array element.

Suppose you declared a one-dimensional array that consists of six elements and you are trying to assign a value to the eighth element. When you run the procedure, Visual Basic can't find the eighth element, so it displays the above error message. If you click the Debug button, Visual Basic will highlight the line of code that caused the error (see Figure 7-4). Look at the array's declaration statement and change the index number that appears in the parentheses in the highlighted line of code.

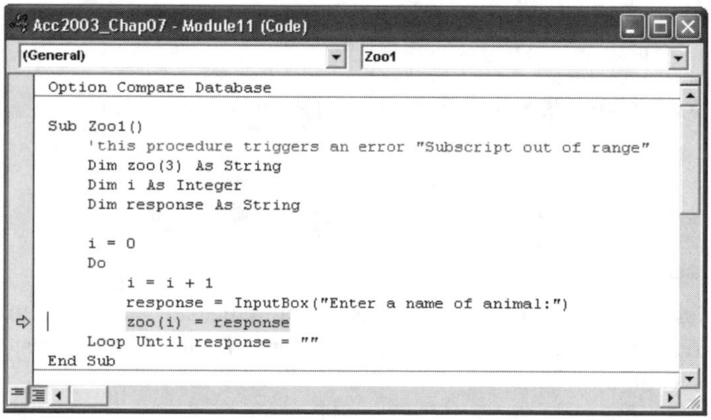
Acc2003_Chap07 - Module11 (Code)
(General)
Zoo1
Option Compare Database
Sub Zoo1()
'this procedure triggers an error "Subscript out of range"
Dim zoo(3) As String
Dim i As Integer
Dim response As String
i = 0
Do
i = i + 1
response = InputBox("Enter a name of animal:")
zoo(i) = response
Loop Until response = ""
End Sub

Figure 7-4: When you click the Debug button in the error message, Visual Basic highlights the statement that triggered the error.

The error "Subscript out of range" is often triggered in procedures using loops. The procedure Zoo1 shown in Hands-On 7-11 serves as an example of such a situation. The statements in the loop are to be executed until the user cancels out from the input box. While executing this procedure, when the variable i equals 4, Visual Basic will not be able to find the fourth element in a three-element array, so the error message will appear. The modified procedure Zoo2 demonstrates how, by using the LBound and UBound functions introduced in the preceding section, you can avoid errors caused by an attempt to access a nonexistent array element.

◎ Hands-On 7-11: Understanding Errors in Arrays

1. In a new module, enter the following procedures, Zoo1 and Zoo2, as shown below.

```
Sub Zoo1()
    ' this procedure triggers an error "Subscript out of range"
    Dim zoo(3) As String
    Dim i As Integer
    Dim response As String

    i = 0
    Do
        i = i + 1
        response = InputBox("Enter a name of animal:")
        zoo(i) = response
    Loop Until response = ""
End Sub

Sub Zoo2()
    ' this procedure avoids the error "Subscript out of range"
    Dim zoo(3) As String
    Dim i As Integer
    Dim response As String

    i = 1
    Do While i >= LBound(zoo) And i <= UBound(zoo)
        response = InputBox("Enter a name of animal:")
        If response = "" Then Exit Sub
        zoo(i) = response
        i = i + 1
    Loop

    For i = LBound(zoo) To UBound(zoo)
        MsgBox zoo(i)
    Next
End Sub
```

Another frequent error you may encounter while working with arrays is a type mismatch error. To avoid this error, keep in mind that each element of an array must be of the same data type. Therefore, if you attempt to assign to an element of an array a value that conflicts with the data type of the array, you will get a type mismatch error during the code execution. If you need to hold values of different data types in an array, declare the array as Variant.

Parameter Arrays

Earlier in this book you learned that values can be passed between subroutines or functions as required or optional arguments. If the passed argument is not absolutely required for the procedure to execute, the argument's name is preceded by the keyword Optional. Sometimes, however, you don't know in advance how many arguments you want to pass. A classic example is addition. One time you may want to add two numbers together, another time you may want to add three, ten, or fifteen numbers.

Using the keyword ParamArray you can pass to your subroutines and function procedures an array consisting of any number of elements. The following hands-on uses the AddMultipleArgs function to add as many numbers as you require. This function begins with the declaration of an array myNumbers. Notice the use of the ParamArray keyword. The array must be declared as an array of type Variant, and it must be the last argument in the procedure definition.

⊚ Hands-On 7-12: Working with Parameter Arrays

1. In a new module, enter the following AddMultipleArgs function procedure.

```
Function AddMultipleArgs(ParamArray myNumbers() As Variant)
    Dim mySum As Single
    Dim myValue As Variant

    For Each myValue In myNumbers
        mySum = mySum + myValue
    Next
    AddMultipleArgs = mySum
End Function
```

2. To try out the above function, activate the Immediate window and type the following instruction:

```
?AddMultipleArgs(1, 23.24, 3, 24, 8, 34)
```

When you press **Enter**, Visual Basic returns the total of all the numbers in the parentheses: 93.24. You can supply an unlimited number of arguments. To add more values, enter additional values in the parentheses and press Enter. Notice that each function argument must be separated by a comma.

Chapter Summary

In this chapter you learned how, by creating an array, you can write procedures that require a large number of variables. You worked with examples of procedures that demonstrated how to declare and use a one-dimensional array (list) and a two-dimensional array (table). You also learned the difference between a static and a dynamic array. This chapter ended by introducing you to five built-in VBA functions that are frequently used with arrays, as well as the ParamArray keyword. You now know all the control structures that can make your code more intelligent: conditional statements, loops, and arrays.

In the next chapter you will learn how to use collections instead of arrays to manipulate large amounts of data.

Chapter 8

Custom Collections and Class Modules

You are not limited to using objects built into Microsoft Office Access. VBA allows you to create your own objects and collections of objects, complete with their own methods and properties. In this chapter, you learn how to work with collections, including how to declare a custom Collection object. You also learn how to use class modules to create user-defined objects.

Terminology

Before diving into theory and the hands-on examples of this chapter, let's start by going over several terms that will be used throughout this chapter.

Collection — An object that contains a set of related objects.

Class — A definition of an object that includes its name, properties, methods, and events. The class acts as a sort of object template from which an instance of an object is created at run time.

Class Module — A module that contains the definition of a class, including its property and method definitions.

Event — An action recognized by an object, such as a mouse click or a keypress, for which you can define a response. Events can be caused by a user action or a VBA statement, or can be triggered by the system.

Event Procedure — A procedure that is automatically executed in response to an event initiated by the user, program code, or triggered by the system.

Form Module — A module that contains the VBA code for all event procedures triggered by events occurring in a user form or its controls. A form module is a type of class module.

Instance — A specific object that belongs to a class is referred to as an *instance of the class*. When you create an instance, you create a new object that has the properties and methods defined by the class.

Module — A structure containing subroutine and function procedures that are available to other VBA procedures and are not related to any object in particular.

Working with Collections

A set of similar objects is known as a *collection*. For example, a Microsoft Access database has a collection of tables, and each table has a collection of fields and indexes. In Microsoft Excel, all open workbooks belong to the collection of workbooks, and all the sheets in a particular workbook are the members of the worksheets collection. In Microsoft Word, all open documents belong to the collection of documents, and each paragraph in a document is a member of the paragraphs collection. Collections are objects that contain other objects.

No matter what collection you want to work with, you can do the following:

■ Refer to a specific object in a collection by using an index value.

For example, to get the name of the first control on the Customers form in the Northwind database, enter the following instruction in the Immediate window:

```
?Forms!Customers.Controls(1).name
```

■ Determine the number of items in the collection by using the Count property.

For example, when you enter this statement in the Immediate window:

```
?Forms!Customers.Controls.Count
```

VBA will return the total number of controls in the Customers form.

■ Insert new items into the collection by using the Add method.

The following example uses the Immediate window to create a new collection named myTestCollection and adds two new items to the collection:

```
set myTestCollection = New Collection
myTestCollection.Add "first member"
myTestCollection.Add "second member"
```

The following instruction returns the total number of items in myTestCollection:

```
?myTestCollection.Count
2
```

■ To find out the names of the collection members, you can type the following statements in the Immediate window:

```
?myTestCollection.Item(1)
first member
?myTestCollection(2)
second member
```

■ You can cycle through every object in the collection by using the For Each…Next loop.

For example, to remove all items from myTestCollection, enter the following looping structure in the Immediate window:

```
For Each m in myTestCollection : myTestCollection.Remove 1 : Next
```

If you did not get an error upon pressing Enter, myTestCollection should have zero members. However, to be sure, enter the following statement in the Immediate window:

```
?myTestCollection.Count
0
```

While writing your own VBA procedures, you may come across a situation where there's no built-in collection to handle the task at hand. The solution is to create a custom collection. From the previous chapter you already know how to work with multiple items of data by using dynamic or static arrays. Because collections have built-in properties and methods that allow you to add, remove, and count their elements, it's much easier to work with collections than arrays.

Declaring a Custom Collection

To create a user-defined collection, you should begin by declaring an object variable of the Collection type. This variable is declared with the New keyword in the Dim statement, as shown below:

```
Dim collection_name As New Collection
```

Adding Objects to a Custom Collection

After you've declared the Collection object, you can insert new items into the collection by using the Add method. The objects with which you populate your collection do not have to be of the same data type. The Add method looks as follows:

```
object.Add item, key, before, after
```

You are only required to specify object and item. Object is the collection name. This is the same name that was used in the declaration of the Collection object. Item is the object you want to add to the collection.

Although the other arguments are optional, they are quite useful. It's important to understand that the items in a collection are automatically assigned numbers starting with 1. However, they can also be assigned a unique key value. Instead of accessing a specific item with an index (1, 2, 3, and so on) at the time an object is added to a collection, you can assign a key for that object. For instance, to identify an individual in a collection of students or employees, you could use Social Security numbers as a key. If you want to specify the position of the object in the collection, you should use either the before or after argument (do not use both). The before argument is the object before which the new object is added. The after argument is the object after which the new object is added.

The NewEmployees procedure in the following hands-on declares the custom collection object called colEmployees.

⊚ Hands-On 8-1: Creating a Custom Collection

This chapter's hands-on exercises are provided in the Acc2003_Chap08.mdb file included in the book's downloadable files.

1. Open **Acc2003_Chap08.mdb** or, if you'd like to start from scratch, create a new Microsoft Office Access 2003 database.

2. Switch to the Visual Basic Editor window and insert a new module (**Insert | Module**).

3. In the new module, enter the NewEmployees procedure as shown below.

```
Sub NewEmployees()
    ' declare the employees collection
    Dim colEmployees As New Collection
    ' declare a variable to hold each element of a collection
    Dim emp As Variant

    ' Add 3 new employees to the collection
    With colEmployees
        .Add Item:="John Collins", Key:="128634456"
        .Add Item:="Mary Poppins", Key:="223998765"
        .Add Item:="Karen Loza", Key:="120228876", Before:=2
    End With

    ' list the members of the collection
    For Each emp In colEmployees
        Debug.Print emp
    Next

    MsgBox "There are " & colEmployees.Count & " employees."
End Sub
```

Note that the control variable used in the For Each...Next loop must be Variant or Object. When you run the above procedure, you will notice that the order of employee names stored in the colEmployees collection (as displayed in the Immediate window) may be different from the order in which these employees were entered in the program code. This is the result of using the optional argument before with the Karen Loza entry. This argument's value tells Visual Basic to place Karen before the second item in the collection.

Removing Objects from a Custom Collection

Removing an item from a custom collection is as easy as adding an item. To remove an element, use the Remove method in the following format:

```
object.Remove item
```

The object is the name of the custom collection that contains the item you want to remove. The item is the item you want to remove from the collection. To demonstrate the process of removing an item from a collection, let's work with the following hands-on that modifies the NewEmployees procedure that you prepared in Hands-On 8-1.

◎ Hands-On 8-2: Removing Objects from a Collection

This hands-on requires the prior completion of Hands-On 8-1.

1. Add the following lines to the NewEmployees procedure just before the End Sub keywords:

```
' remove the third element from the collection
colEmployees.Remove (3)
MsgBox colEmployees.Count & " employees remain."
```

Reindexing Collections

Collections are reindexed automatically when an item is removed. Therefore, to remove all items from a custom collection you can use 1 for the Index argument, as in the following example:

```
Do While myCollection.Count >0
    myCollection.Remove Index:=1
Loop
```

Creating Custom Objects

There are two module commands available in the Visual Basic Editor's Insert menu: Module and Class Module. So far you've used a standard module to create Sub and Function procedures. You'll use the class module for the first time now to create a custom object and define its properties and methods.

Creating a new, non-standard VBA object involves inserting a class module into your project and adding code to that module. However, before you do so you need a basic understanding of what a class is.

If you refer back to the terminology section earlier in this chapter, you will find out that the class is a sort of object template. A frequently used analogy is comparing an object class to a cookie cutter. Just like a cookie cutter defines what a particular cookie will look like, the definition of the class determines how a particular object should look and how it should behave. Before you can actually use an object class, you must first create a new *instance* of that class. Object instances are the cookies. Each object instance has the characteristics (properties and methods) defined by its class. Just as you can cut out many cookies using the same cookie cutter, you can create multiple instances of a class. You can change the properties of each instance of a class independently of any other instance of the same class.

A *class module* lets you define your own custom classes, complete with custom properties and methods. A *property* is an attribute of an object that defines one of its characteristics, such as shape, position, color, title, etc. A *method* is an action that the object can perform. You can create the properties for your custom objects by writing property procedures in a class module. The object methods are also created in a class module by writing the subprocedures or function procedures.

After building your object in the class module, you can use it in the same way you use other built-in objects. You can also export the object class outside the VBA project to other VBA-capable applications.

Creating a Class

The following sections of this chapter walk you through the process of creating and working with a custom object called CEmployee. This object will represent an employee. The CEmployee object will have properties such as Id, FirstName, LastName, and Salary. It will also have a method for modification of the current salary.

◎ Custom Project 8-1 (Step 1): Creating a Class Module

This chapter's custom project is provided in the Acc2003_Chap08_Custom-Project.mdb file included in the book's downloadable files.

1. In the Visual Basic Editor window, choose **Insert | Class Module**.

2. In the Project Explorer window, highlight the **Class** module and use the Properties window to rename the class module **CEmployee**.

Naming a Class Module

Every time you create a new class module, give it a meaningful name. Set the name of the class module to the name you want to use in your VBA procedures using the class. The name you choose for your class should be easily understood and should identify the "thing" the object class represents. As a rule, the object class name is prefaced with an uppercase "C."

Variable Declarations

After adding and renaming the class module, the next step is to declare the variables that will hold the data you want to store in the object. Each item of data you want to store in an object should be assigned a variable. Class variables are called *data members* and are declared with the Private statement. Using this statement in a class module hides the data members and prevents other parts of the application from referencing them. Only the procedures within the class module in which the Private variables were defined can modify the value of these variables.

Because the name of a variable also serves as a property name, use meaningful names for your object's data members. It's traditional to preface the class variable names with m_ to indicate that they are data members of a class.

◉ Custom Project 8-1 (Step 2): Declaring Class Members

1. Type the following declaration lines at the top of the CEmployee class module:

```
Option Explicit
' declarations
Private m_LastName As String
Private m_FirstName As String
Private m_Salary As Currency
Private m_Id As String
```

Notice that the name of each data member variable begins with the prefix m_.

Defining the Properties for the Class

Declaring the variables with the Private keyword guarantees that the variables cannot be accessed directly from outside the object. This means that the VBA procedures outside the class module will not be able to set or read data stored in those variables. To enable other parts of your VBA application to set or retrieve the employee data, you must add special property procedures to the CEmployee class module. There are three types of property procedures:

- **Property Let** — This type of procedure allows other parts of the application to set the value of a property.
- **Property Get** — This type of procedure allows other parts of the application to get or read the value of a property.
- **Property Set** — This type of procedure is used instead of Property Let when setting the reference to an object.

Property procedures are executed when an object property needs to be set or retrieved. The Property Get procedure can have the same name as the Property Let procedure. You should create property procedures for each property of the object that can be accessed by another part of your VBA application.

The easiest of the three types of property statements to understand is the Property Get procedure. Let's examine the syntax of the property procedures by taking a close look at the Property Get LastName procedure.

Property procedures contain the following parts: A procedure declaration line, an assignment statement, and the End Property keywords.

A procedure declaration line specifies the name of the property and the data type:

```
Property Get LastName() As String LastName
```

LastName is the name of the property and As String determines the data type of the property's return value.

An assignment statement is similar to the one used in a function procedure:

```
LastName = m_LastName LastName
```

LastName is the name of the property and *m_LastName* is the data member variable that holds the value of the property you want to retrieve or set. The m_LastName variable should be defined with the Private keyword at the top of the class module.

If the retrieved value is obtained as the result of a calculation, you can include the appropriate VBA statement:

```
Property Get Royalty()
    Royalty = (Sales * Percent) - Advance
End Property
```

The End Property keywords specify the end of the property procedure.

Immediate Exit from Property Procedures

Just as the Exit Sub and Exit Function keywords allow you to exit early from a subroutine or a procedure, the Exit Property keywords give you a way to immediately exit from a property procedure. Program execution will continue with the statements following the statement that called the Property Get, Property Let, or Property Set procedure.

Creating the Property Get Procedures

The CEmployee class object has four properties that need to be exposed to VBA procedures that reside in a standard module named EmpOperations. When working with the CEmployee object, you would certainly like to get information about the employee ID, first and last name, and current salary.

Custom Project 8-1 (Step 3): Writing Property Get Procedures

1. Type the following Property Get procedures in the CEmployee class module, just below the declaration section:

```
Property Get Id() As String
    Id = m_Id
End Property

Property Get LastName() As String
    LastName = m_LastName
End Property

Property Get FirstName() As String
    FirstName = m_FirstName
End Property

Property Get Salary() As Currency
    Salary = m_Salary
End Property
```

Each employee information type requires a separate Property Get procedure. Each of the above Property Get procedures returns the current value of the property. Notice how a Property Get procedure is similar to a function procedure. Similar to function procedures, the Property Get procedures contain an assignment statement. As you recall, in order to return a value from a function procedure, you must assign it to the function's name.

Creating the Property Let Procedures

In addition to retrieving values stored in data members (private variables) with Property Get procedures, you must prepare corresponding Property Let procedures to allow other procedures to change the values of these variables as needed. The only time you don't define a Property Let procedure is when the value stored in a private variable is meant to be *read-only*.

The example CEmployee class allows the user to assign values of the following data items by typing entries in the appropriate text boxes: last name, first name, and salary. The employee ID will be assigned automatically with a return value from a function procedure.

◎ Custom Project 8-1 (Step 4): Writing Property Let Procedures

1. Type the following Property Let procedures in the CEmployee class module below the Property Get procedures:

```
Property Let Id(ref As String)
    m_Id = ref
End Property

Property Let LastName(L As String)
    m_LastName = L
End Property

Property Let FirstName(F As String)
    m_FirstName = F
End Property

Property Let Salary(ByVal dollar As Currency)
    m_Salary = dollar
End Property
```

The Property Let procedures require at least one parameter that specifies the value you want to assign to the property. This parameter can be passed by *value* (see the ByVal keyword in Property Let Salary above) or by *reference* (ByRef is the default). If you need a refresher on the meaning of these keywords, see the section titled "Passing Arguments by Reference and by Value" in Chapter 4. The data type of the parameter passed to the Property Let procedure must have exactly the same data type as the value returned from the Property Get or Set procedure with the same name. Notice that the Property Let procedures have the same names as the Property Get procedures prepared in the preceding section.

Defining the Scope of Property Procedures

You can place the Public, Private, or Static keyword before the name of a property procedure to define its scope. To indicate that the Property Get procedure is accessible to procedures in all modules, use the following statement format:

```
Public Property Get FirstName() As String
```

To make the Property Get procedure accessible only to other procedures in the module where it is declared, use the following statement format:

```
Private Property Get FirstName() As String
```

To preserve the Property Get procedure's local variables between procedure calls, use the following statement format:

```
Static Property Get FirstName() As String
```

If not explicitly specified using either Public or Private, property procedures are Public by default. Also, if the Static keyword is not used, the values of local variables are not preserved between procedure calls.

Creating the Class Methods

Apart from properties, objects usually have one or more methods. A *method* is an action that the object can perform. Methods allow you to manipulate the data stored in a class object. Methods are created with subroutines or function procedures. To make a method available outside the class module, use the Public keyword in front of the Sub or Function definition. The CEmployee object that you create in this chapter has one method that allows you to calculate the new salary. Assume that the employee salary can be increased or decreased by a specific percentage or amount.

⊚ Custom Project 8-1 (Step 5): Writing Class Methods

1. Type the following CalcNewSalary function procedure in the CEmployee class module:

```
Public Function CalcNewSalary(choice As Integer, curSalary As Currency, _
    amount As Long) As Currency
    Select Case choice
        Case 1 ' by percent
            CalcNewSalary = curSalary + ((curSalary * amount) / 100)
        Case 2 ' by amount
            CalcNewSalary = curSalary + amount
    End Select
End Function
```

The CalcNewSalary function defined with the Public keyword in a class module serves as a method for the CEmployee class. To calculate a new salary, a VBA procedure from outside the class module must pass three arguments: choice, CurSalary, and amount. The choice argument specifies the type of the calculation. Suppose you want to increase the employee salary by 5% or by $5.00. Choice 1 will increase the salary by the specified percent, and choice 2 will add the specified amount to the current salary. The curSalary argument is the current salary figure for an employee, and the amount argument determines the value by which the salary should be changed.

About Class Methods

- Only those methods that will be accessed from outside of the class should be declared as Public. All others should be Private.

- Methods perform some operation on the data contained within the class.

- If a method needs to return a value, write a function procedure. Otherwise, create a subprocedure.

Creating an Instance of a Class

After typing all the necessary Property Get, Property Let, subprocedures, or function procedures for your VBA application in the class module, you are ready to create a new instance of a class, called an *object*. Before an object can be created, an object variable must be declared in a standard module to store the reference to the object. If the name of the class module is CEmployee, then a new instance of this class can be created with the following statement:

```
Dim emp As New CEmployee
```

The emp variable will represent a reference to an object of the CEmployee class. When you declare the object variable with the New keyword, VBA creates the object and allocates memory for it. However, the object isn't instanced until you refer to it in your procedure code by assigning a value to its property or running one of its methods.

You can also create an instance of the object by declaring an object variable with the data type defined to be the class of the object. For example:

```
Dim emp As CEmployee
Set emp = New Cemployee
```

If you don't use the New keyword with the Dim statement (as shown above), VBA does not allocate memory for your custom object until your procedure actually needs it.

⊚ Custom Project 8-1 (Step 6): Creating an Instance of a Class

1. Activate the Visual Basic Editor window and choose **Insert | Module** to add a standard module to your application. Use the Properties window to change the name of the new module to **EmpOperations**.

2. Type the following declarations at the top of the EmpOperations module:

```
Option Compare Database
Option Explicit
Dim emp As New CEmployee
Dim CEmployee As New Collection
```

The first declaration statement declares the variable emp as a new instance of the CEmployee class. The second statement declares a custom collection. The CEmployee collection will be used to store all employees' data.

Event Procedures in the Class Module

An *event* is basically an action recognized by an object. Custom classes recognize only two events: Initialize and Terminate. These events are triggered when an instance of the class is created and destroyed, respectively. The Initialize event is generated when an object is created from a class (see the preceding section on creating an instance of a class). Because the statements included inside the Initialize event are the first ones to be executed for the object, before any properties are set or any methods are executed, the Initialize event is a good place to perform initialization of the objects created from the class.

The Class_Initialize procedure uses the following syntax:

```
Private Sub Class_Initialize()
    [code to perform tasks as the object is created goes here]
End Sub
```

The Terminate event occurs when all references to an object have been released. This is a good place to perform any necessary cleanup tasks. The Class_Terminate procedure uses the following syntax:

```
Private Sub Class_Terminate()
    [cleanup code goes here]
End Sub
```

To release an object variable from an object, use the following syntax:

```
Set objectVariable = Nothing
```

When you set the object variable to Nothing, the Terminate event is generated. Any code in this event is executed then.

Creating the User Interface

Implementing our custom CEmployee object requires that you design a form to enter and manipulate employee data.

⊚ Custom Project 8-1 (Step 7): Designing a User Form

1. In the Database window, click the **Forms** object button and double-click **Create form in Design View**.

2. Save the form as **frmEmployeeSalaries**.

3. Use the toolbox to place controls on the form as shown in Figure 8-1.

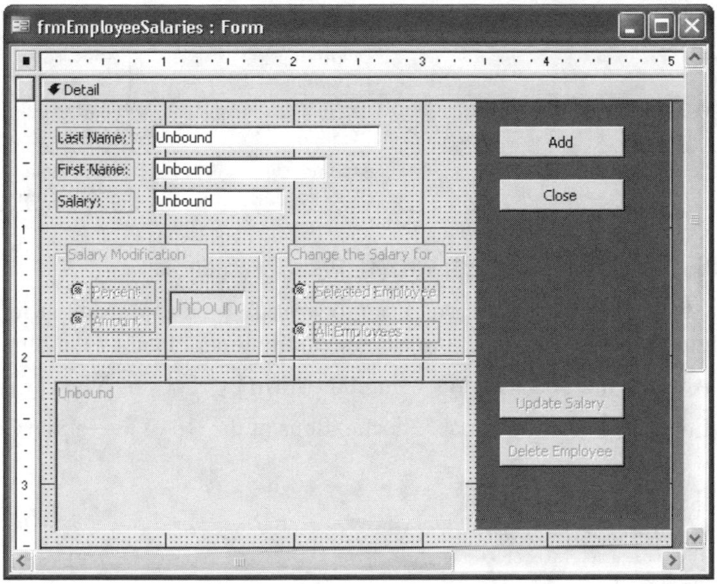

Figure 8-1: This form demonstrates the use of the CEmployee custom object.

4. Set the following properties for the form's controls:

Object	Property	Setting
Label1	Caption	Last Name
Text box next to the Last Name label	Name	txtLastName
Label2	Caption	First Name
Text box next to the First Name label	Name	txtFirstName
Label3	Caption	Salary
Text box next to the Salary label	Name	txtSalary
Frame1 (the first frame)	Name Caption	frChangeSalary Salary Modification
Text box in the frame titled "Salary Modification"	Name	txtRaise
Option button 1	Name Caption	optPercent Percent
Option button 2	Name Caption	optAmount Amount
Frame2 (the second frame)	Name Caption	frSalaryMod Change the Salary for
Option button 3	Name Caption	optSelected Selected Employee
Option button 4	Name Caption	optAll All Employees
List box	Name Row Source Type Column Count Column Widths	lboxPeople Value List 4 0.5";0.9";0.7";0.5"
Command button 1	Name Caption	cmdAdd Add

Object	Property	Setting
Command button 2	Name	cmdClose
	Caption	Close
Command button 3	Name	cmdUpdate
	Caption	Update Salary
Command button 4	Name	cmdDelete
	Caption	Delete Employee

◎ Custom Project 8-1 (Step 8): Writing Event Procedures

Now that the form is ready, you need to write few event procedures to handle various events, such as clicking a command button or loading the form.

1. Activate the Code window behind the form by choosing **View** | **Code**.

2. Enter the following variable declarations at the top of the form's Code window:

```
Option Explicit
' variable declarations
Dim choice As Integer
Dim amount As Long
```

3. Type the following UserForm_Initialize procedure to enable or disable controls on the form:

```
Private Sub UserForm_Initialize()
    txtLastName.SetFocus
    cmdUpdate.Enabled = False
    cmdDelete.Enabled = False
    lboxPeople.Enabled = False
    frChangeSalary.Enabled = False
    frChangeSalary.Value = 0
    frSalaryMod.Enabled = False
    frSalaryMod.Value = 0
    txtRaise.Enabled = False
    txtRaise.Value = ""
End Sub
```

4. Call the UserForm_Initialize procedure from the Form_Load event procedure:

```
Private Sub Form_Load()
    Call UserForm_Initialize
End Sub
```

5. Enter the following cmdAdd_Click procedure to add the employee to the collection:

```
Private Sub cmdAdd_Click()
    Dim strLast As String
    Dim strFirst As String
    Dim curSalary As Currency

    ' Validate data entry
    If txtLastName.Value = "" Or txtFirstName.Value = "" Or _
        txtSalary.Value = "" Then
```

```
        MsgBox "Enter Last Name, First Name and Salary."
        txtLastName.SetFocus
        Exit Sub
    End If

    If Not IsNumeric(txtSalary) Then
        MsgBox "You must enter a value for the Salary."
        txtSalary.SetFocus
        Exit Sub
    End If

    If txtSalary < 0 Then
        MsgBox "Salary cannot be a negative number."
        Exit Sub
    End If

    ' assign text box values to variables
    strLast = txtLastName
    strFirst = txtFirstName
    curSalary - txtSalary

    ' enable buttons and other controls
    cmdUpdate.Enabled = True
    cmdDelete.Enabled = True
    lboxPeople.Enabled = True
    lboxPeople.Visible = True
    frChangeSalary.Enabled = True
    frSalaryMod.Enabled = True
    txtRaise.Enabled = True
    txtRaise.Value = ""

    ' enter data into the CEmployee collection
    EmpOperations.AddEmployee strLast, strFirst, curSalary

    ' update list box
    lboxPeople.RowSource = GetValues

    ' delete data from text boxes
    txtLastName = ""
    txtFirstName = ""
    txtSalary = ""
    txtLastName.SetFocus
End Sub
```

The cmdAdd_Click procedure starts off with validating the user's input in the Last Name, First Name, and Salary text boxes. If the user entered correct data, the text box values are assigned to variables strLast, strFirst, and strSalary. Next, a number of statements enable buttons and other controls on the form so that the user can work with the employee data. The following statement calls the AddEmployee procedure in the EmpOperations standard module and passes the required parameters to it:

```
EmpOperations.AddEmployee strLast, strFirst, curSalary
```

Once the employee is entered into the collection, the employee data is added to the list box with the following statement:

```
lboxPeople.RowSource = GetValues
```

GetValues is the name of a function procedure in the EmpOperations module. This function cycles through the CEmployee collection to create a string of values for the list box row source.

The cmdAdd_Click procedure ends by clearing the text boxes, then setting the focus to the Last Name text box so the user can enter new employee data.

Figure 8-2: The list box control displays employee data as entered in the custom collection CEmployee.

6. Enter the following cmdClose_Click procedure to close the form:

```
Private Sub cmdClose_Click()
    DoCmd.Close
End Sub
```

7. Write the Click procedure for the cmdUpdate button as shown below:

```
Private Sub cmdUpdate_Click()
    Dim numOfPeople As Integer
    Dim colItem As Integer

    ' validate user selections
    If frChangeSalary.Value = 0 Or frSalaryMod.Value = 0 Then
        MsgBox "You must choose the appropriate option button in " & vbCr _
            & " the 'Salary Modification' and 'Change the Salary for' areas.", _
            vbOKOnly, "Insufficient selection"
        Exit Sub
    ElseIf Not IsNumeric(txtRaise) Or txtRaise = "" Then
        MsgBox "You must enter a number."
        txtRaise.SetFocus
        Exit Sub
    ElseIf frSalaryMod.Value = 1 And lboxPeople.ListIndex = -1 Then
        MsgBox "Click the employee name.", , "Missing selection in the List box"
        Exit Sub
    End If

    If frSalaryMod.Value = 1 And lboxPeople.ListIndex = -1 Then
        MsgBox "Enter data or select an option."
        Exit Sub
    End If
```

```
' get down to calculations
amount = txtRaise
colItem = lboxPeople.ListIndex + 1
If frChangeSalary.Value = 1 And frSalaryMod.Value = 1 Then
    ' by percent, one employee
    choice = 1
    numOfPeople = 1
ElseIf frChangeSalary.Value = 2 And frSalaryMod.Value = 1 Then
    ' by amount, one employee
    choice = 2
    numOfPeople = 1
ElseIf frChangeSalary.Value = 1 And frSalaryMod.Value = 2 Then
    ' by percent, all employees
    choice = 1
    numOfPeople = 2
ElseIf frChangeSalary.Value = 2 And frSalaryMod.Value = 2 Then
    ' by amount, all employees
    choice = 2
    numOfPeople = 2
End If

UpdateSalary choice, amount, numOfPeople, colItem
lboxPeople.RowSource = GetValues
End Sub
```

When the user clicks the Update Salary button, the procedure checks
whether the user selected appropriate option buttons and entered the
adjusted figure in the text box. The update can be done for the selected
employee or for all the employees listed in the list box control and collection. You can increase the salary by the specified percentage or amount.
Depending on which options are specified, values are assigned to the variables choice, amount, numOfpeople, and colItem. These variables serve as
parameters for the UpdateSalary procedure located in the EmpOperations
module. The last statement in the cmdUpdate_Click procedure sets the row
source property of the list box control to the result obtained from the
GetValues function located in the EmpOperations standard module.

8. The Delete Employee button has the following cmdDelete_Click
   procedure:

```
Private Sub cmdDelete_Click()
    ' make sure an employee is highlighted in the list box control
    If lboxPeople.ListIndex > -1 Then
        DeleteEmployee lboxPeople.ListIndex + 1
        If lboxPeople.ListCount = 1 Then
            lboxPeople.RowSource = GetValues
            UserForm_Initialize
        Else
            lboxPeople.RowSource = GetValues
        End If
    Else
        MsgBox "Click the item you want to remove."
    End If
End Sub
```

The cmdDelete_Click procedure lets you remove an employee from the custom collection CEmployee. If you click an item in the list box and then click the Delete Employee button, the DeleteEmployee procedure is called. This procedure requires one argument that specifies the index number of the item selected in the list box. After the employee is removed from the collection, the row source of the list box control is reset to display the remaining employees. After removing the last employee from the collection, the UserForm_Initialize procedure is called to tackle the task of disabling controls that cannot be used until at least one employee is entered into the CEmployee collection.

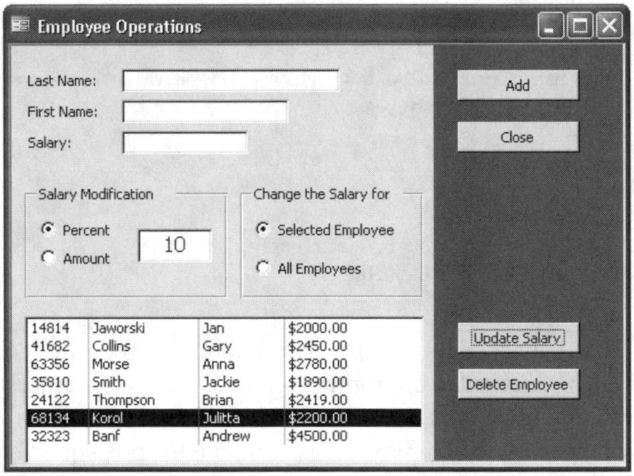

Figure 8-3: The employee salary can be increased or decreased by the specified percentage or amount.

9. Activate the EmpOperations module that you created earlier. The top of the module should contain the following lines:

```
Option Compare Database
Option Explicit
Dim emp As New CEmployee
Dim CEmployee As New Collection
```

10. In the EmpOperations standard module, enter the following AddEmployee procedure.

```
Sub AddEmployee(empLast As String, empFirst As String, _
    empSalary As Currency)
    With emp
        .Id = SetEmpId
        .LastName = empLast
        .FirstName = empFirst
        .Salary = CCur(empSalary)
        If .Salary = 0 Then Exit Sub
        CEmployee.Add emp
    End With
End Sub
```

The AddEmployee procedure is called from the cmdAdd_Click procedure attached to the form's Add button. This procedure takes three arguments.

When Visual Basic reaches the With emp construct, a new instance of the CEmployee class is created. The LastName, FirstName, and Salary properties are set with the values passed from the cmdAdd_Click procedure. The Id property is set with the number generated by the result of the SetEmpId function (see the following step). Each time VBA sees the reference to the instanced emp object, it will call upon the appropriate Property Let procedure located in the class module. (The next chapter demonstrates how to walk through this procedure step by step to see exactly when the Property procedures are executed.) The last statement inside the With emp construct adds the user-defined object emp to the custom collection called CEmployee.

11. In the EmpOperations standard module, enter the following SetEmpId function procedure:

```
Function SetEmpId() As String
    Dim ref As String

    Randomize
    ref = Int((99999 - 10000) * Rnd + 10000)
    SetEmpId = ref
End Function
```

This function's purpose is to assign a unique five-digit number to each new employee. To generate a random integer between two given integers where ending_number = 99999 and beginning_number = 10000, the following formula is used:

```
= Int((ending_number - beginning_number) * Rnd + beginning_number)
```

The SetEmpId function procedure also uses the Randomize statement to reinitialize the random number generator. For more information on using the Rnd and Integer functions, as well as the Randomize statement, search the online help.

12. Enter the GetValues function procedure as shown below. This function, which is called from the cmdAdd_Click, cmdUpdate_Click, and cmdDelete_Click procedures, provides the values for the list box control to synchronize it with the current values in the CEmployee collection.

```
Function GetValues()
    Dim myList As String

    myList = ""
    For Each emp In CEmployee
        myList = myList & emp.Id & ";" & _
            emp.LastName & ";" & _
            emp.FirstName & "; $" & _
            Format(emp.Salary, "0.00") & ";"
    Next emp
    GetValues = myList
End Function
```

13. Enter the following UpdateSalary procedure:

```
Sub UpdateSalary(choice As Integer, myValue As Long, _
    peopleCount As Integer, colItem As Integer)
    Set emp = New CEmployee

    If choice = 1 And peopleCount = 1 Then
        CEmployee.Item(colItem).Salary = _
            emp.CalcNewSalary(1, CEmployee.Item(colItem).Salary, myValue)
    ElseIf choice = 1 And peopleCount = 2 Then
        For Each emp In CEmployee
            emp.Salary = emp.Salary + ((emp.Salary * myValue) / 100)
        Next emp
    ElseIf choice = 2 And peopleCount = 1 Then
        CEmployee.Item(colItem).Salary = _
            CEmployee.Item(colItem).Salary + myValue
    ElseIf choice = 2 And peopleCount = 2 Then
        For Each emp In CEmployee
            emp.Salary = emp.Salary + myValue
        Next emp
    Else
        MsgBox "Enter data or select an option."
    End If
End Sub
```

The UpdateSalary procedure is called from the cmdUpdate_Click procedure, which is assigned to the Update Salary button on the form. The click procedure passes four parameters that the UpdateSalary procedure uses for the salary calculations. When a salary for the selected employee needs to be updated by a percentage or amount, the CalcNewSalary method residing in the class module is called. For modification of salary figures for all the employees, we iterate over the CEmployee collection to obtain the value of the Salary property of each emp object, then perform the required calculation by using a formula. By entering a negative number in the form's txtRaise text box, you can decrease the salary by the specified percentage or amount.

14. Enter the DeleteEmployee procedure as shown below:

```
Sub DeleteEmployee(colItem As Integer)
    Dim getcount As Integer

    CEmployee.Remove colItem
End Sub
```

The DeleteEmployee procedure uses the Remove method to delete the selected employee from the CEmployee custom collection. Recall that the Remove method requires one argument, which is the position of the item in the collection. The value of this argument is obtained from the cmd-Delete_Click procedure. The class module procedures were called from the standard module named EmpOperations. This was done to avoid creating a new instance of a user-defined class every time we needed to call it.

Watching the Execution of Your VBA Procedures

To help you understand what's going on when your code runs, and how your custom object works, let's walk through the cmdAdd_Click procedure. Treat this exercise as a brief introduction to the debugging techniques that are covered in detail in the next chapter.

◎ Custom Project 8-1 (Step 9): Custom Project Code Walkthrough

1. Open **frmEmployeeSalaries** in Design view and choose **View | Code**.

2. Select **cmdAdd** from the combo box at the top left of the Code window.

3. Set a breakpoint by clicking in the left margin next to the following line of code:

```
If txtLastName.Value = "" Or txtFirstName.Value = "" Or _
    txtSalary.Value = "" Then
```

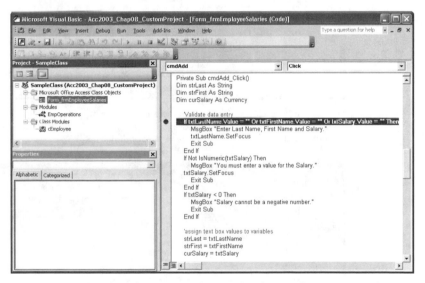

Figure 8-4: A red circle in the margin indicates a breakpoint. The statement with a breakpoint is displayed as white text on a red background.

4. Return to **frmEmployeeSalaries** in Design view and choose **View | Form View** to run the form.

5. Enter data in the Last Name, First Name, and Salary text boxes, and click the form's **Add** button. Visual Basic should now switch to the Code window because it came across the breakpoint in the first line of the cmdAdd_Click procedure.

6. Step through the code one statement at a time by pressing **F8**. Visual Basic runs the current statement and then automatically advances to the next statement and suspends execution. The current statement is indicated by a yellow arrow in the margin and a yellow background. Keep pressing **F8** to

execute the procedure step by step. After Visual Basic switches to the
EmpOperations module to run the AddEmployee procedure and encounters
the With emp statement, it will run the function to set the employee ID and
will go out to execute the Property Let procedures in the CEmployee class
module.

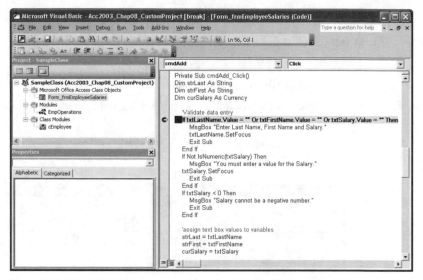

Figure 8-5: When Visual Basic encounters a breakpoint while running a procedure, it
switches to the Code window and displays a yellow arrow in the margin to the left of
the statement at which the procedure is suspended.

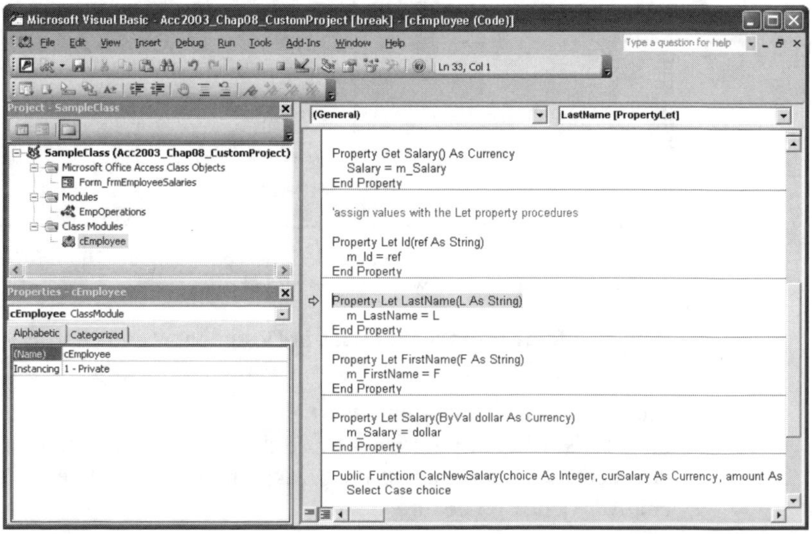

Figure 8-6: Setting the properties of your custom object is accomplished through the
Property Let procedures.

7. Using the **F8** key, trace the execution of the cmdAdd_Click procedure to the end. When VBA encounters the end of the procedure (End Sub), the yellow highlighter will be turned off. At this time, switch back to the active form. Enter data for a new employee, then click the **Add** button. When Visual Basic displays the Code window, choose **Debug | Clear All Breakpoints**. Now press **F5** to run the rest of the procedure without stepping through it.

VBA Debugging Tools

Visual Basic provides a number of debugging tools to help you analyze how your application operates, as well as locate the source of errors in your procedures. See the next chapter for details on working with these tools.

Chapter Summary

In this chapter you learned how to create and use your own objects and collections in VBA procedures. You used a class module to create a user-defined (custom) object. You saw how to define your custom object's properties using the Property Get and Property Let procedures. You also learned how to write a method for your custom object. Next, you saw how to make the class module available to the user with a custom form. Finally, you learned how to analyze your VBA application by stepping through its code.

As your procedures become more complex, you will need to start using special tools for tracing errors, which are covered in the next chapter.

Chapter 9

Debugging VBA Procedures and Handling Errors

In the course of writing or editing VBA procedures, no matter how careful you are, you're likely to make some mistakes. For example, you may misspell a word, misplace a comma or quotation mark, or forget a period or ending parenthesis. These kinds of mistakes are known as *syntax errors*. Fortunately, Visual Basic is quite helpful in spotting these kinds of errors. To have Visual Basic automatically check for correct syntax after you enter a line of code, choose Tools | Options in the Visual Basic window. Make sure the Auto Syntax Check setting is selected on the Editor tab.

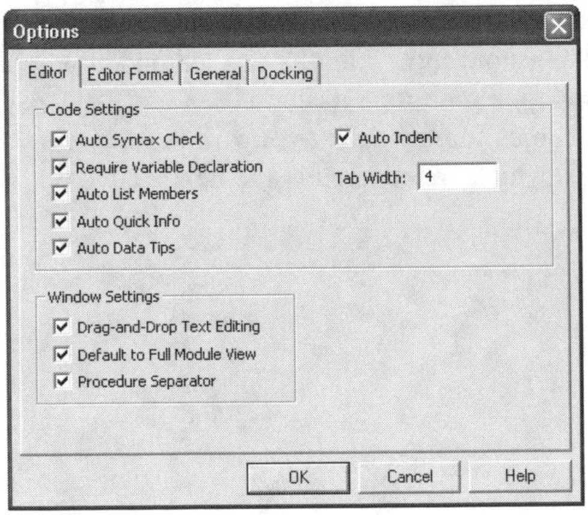

Figure 9-1: The Auto Syntax Check setting on the Editor tab of the Options dialog box lets you pick up a lot of typos in your VBA procedures.

When Visual Basic finds a syntax error, it displays an error message box and changes the color of the incorrect line of code to red, or another color as indicated on the Editor Format tab in the Options dialog box.

If the explanation of the error in the error message isn't clear, you can click the Help button for more help. If Visual Basic cannot point you in the right direction, you must return to your procedure and carefully examine the offending instruction for missed letters, quotation marks, periods, colons, equals signs, and beginning and ending parentheses. Finding syntax errors can be aggravating and time consuming. Certain syntax errors can be caught only during the execution of the procedure. While attempting to run your procedure, Visual Basic can find errors that were caused by using invalid arguments or omitting instructions that are used in pairs, such as If...End statements and looping structures.

You've probably heard that computer programs are "full of bugs." In programming, errors are called bugs, and *debugging* is a process of eliminating errors from your programs. Visual Basic provides a myriad of tools with which to track down and eliminate bugs. The first step in debugging a procedure is to correct all syntax errors. In addition to syntax errors, there are two other types of errors: run-time and logic. *Run-time errors*, which occur while the procedure is running, are often caused by unexpected situations the programmer did not think of while writing the code. For example, the program may be trying to access a drive or a file that does not exist on the user's computer. Or it may be trying to copy a file to a floppy disk without first determining whether the user had inserted a floppy disk and closed the drive door. The third type of error, a logic error, often does not generate a specific error message. Even though the procedure has no flaws in its syntax and runs without errors, it produces incorrect results. *Logic* errors happen when your procedure simply does not do what you want it to do. Logic errors are usually very difficult to locate. Those that happen intermittently are sometimes so well concealed that you can spend long hours, even days, trying to locate the source of the error.

Testing VBA Procedures

When testing your VBA procedure, use the following guidelines:

- If you want to analyze your procedure, step through your code one line at a time by pressing F8 or by choosing Debug | Step Into.
- If you suspect that an error may occur in a specific place in your procedure, use a breakpoint.
- If you want to monitor the value of a particular variable or expression used by your procedure, add a watch expression.
- If you are tired of scrolling through a long procedure to get to sections of code that interest you, set up a bookmark to quickly jump to the desired location.

Each of the above guidelines is demonstrated in a hands-on exercise in this chapter.

Stopping a Procedure

VBA offers four methods of stopping your procedure and entering into a so-called *break mode*:

- Pressing Ctrl+Break
- Setting one or more breakpoints
- Inserting the Stop statement
- Adding a watch expression

A break occurs when execution of your VBA procedure is temporarily suspended. Visual Basic remembers the values of all variables and the statement from which the execution of the procedure should resume when you decide to continue. You can resume a suspended procedure in one of the following ways:

- Click the Run Sub/UserForm button on the toolbar
- Choose Run | Run Sub/UserForm from the menu bar
- Click the Continue button in the dialog box (see Figure 9-2)

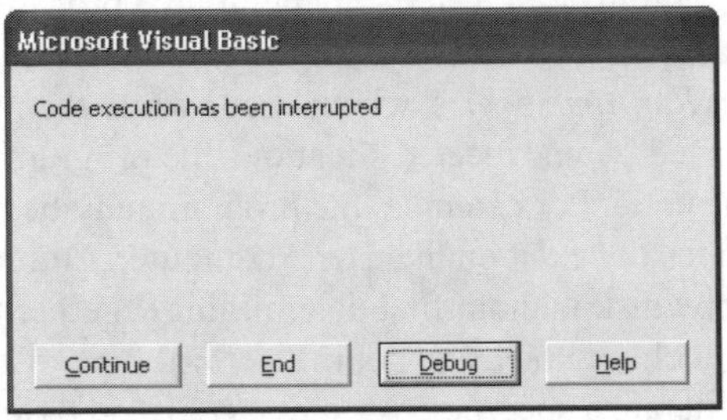

Figure 9-2: This message appears when you press Ctrl+Break while your VBA procedure is running.

The error dialog box shown in Figure 9-2 informs you that the procedure was halted. The following buttons are available:

Table 9-1: Error dialog buttons

Button Name	Description
Continue	Click this button to resume code execution. This button will be grayed out if an error was encountered.
End	Click this button if you do not want to troubleshoot the procedure at this time. VBA will stop code execution.
Debug	Click this button to enter break mode. The Code window will appear, and VBA will highlight the line at which the procedure execution was suspended. You can examine, debug, or step through the code.
Help	Click this button to view the online help that explains the cause of this error message.

Using Breakpoints

If you know more or less where there may be a problem in your procedure code, you should suspend code execution at that location (on a given line). Set a breakpoint by pressing F9 when the cursor is on the desired line of code. When VBA gets to that line while running your procedure, it will display the Code window immediately. At this point you can step through the procedure code line by line by pressing F8 or choosing Debug | Step Into.

To see how this works, let's look at the following scenario. Assume that during the execution of the ListEndDates function procedure (see Custom Project 9-1) the following line of code could get you into trouble:

```
ListEndDates = Format(((Now() + intOffset) - 35) + 7 * row, "MM/DD/YYYY")
```

◎ Custom Project 9-1: Debugging a Function Procedure

This chapter's hands-on exercises and custom project are provided in the Acc2003_Chap09.mdb file included in the book's downloadable files.

1. Open **Acc2003_Chap09.mdb** or, if you'd like to start from scratch, create a new Microsoft Office Access 2003 database.

2. Prepare the form as shown in Figure 9-3.

3. Set the following control properties:

Control Name	Property Name	Property Setting
combo box	Name Row Source Type Column Count	cboEndDate ListEndDates 1
text box controls	Name	txt1 txt2 txt3 txt4 txt5 txt6 txt7

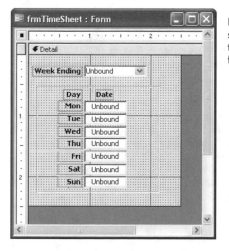

Figure 9-3: The combo box control shown on this form will be filled with the result of the ListEndDates function.

4. Save the form as **frmTimeSheet**.

5. Press **Ctrl+R** to select the form. Activate the Properties window and click the **Event** tab. Choose **[Event Procedure]** from the drop-down list next to the On Load property, then click the **Build** button (…). Type the following Form_Load procedure when the Code window appears:

```
Private Sub Form_Load()
    With Me.cboEndDate
        .SetFocus
        .ListIndex = 5     ' Select current ending date
    End With
End Sub
```

6. Choose the combo box control (cboEndDate) on the form, and activate the Properties window. Choose **[Event Procedure]** from the drop-down list next to the On Change property, then click the **Build** button (...). Enter the following code:

```
Private Sub cboEndDate_Change()
    Dim endDate As Date

    endDate = Me.cboEndDate.Value
    With Me
        .txt1 = Format(endDate - 6, "mm/dd")
        .txt2 = Format(endDate - 5, "mm/dd")
        .txt3 = Format(endDate - 4, "mm/dd")
        .txt4 = Format(endDate - 3, "mm/dd")
        .txt5 = Format(endDate - 2, "mm/dd")
        .txt6 = Format(endDate - 1, "mm/dd")
        .txt7 = Format(endDate - 0, "mm/dd")
    End With
End Sub
```

7. Choose **Insert | Module** to add a new standard module. In the properties sheet, change the Name property of Module1 to **TimeSheetProc**.

8. Enter the following function procedure in the TimeSheetProc module:

```
Function ListEndDates(fld As Control, id As Variant, _
    row As Variant, col As Variant, code As Variant) As Variant
    Dim intOffset As Integer

    Select Case code
        Case acLBInitialize
            ListEndDates = True
        Case acLBOpen
            ListEndDates = Timer
        Case acLBGetRowCount
            ListEndDates = 11
        Case acLBGetColumnCount
            ListEndDates = 1
        Case acLBGetColumnWidth
            ListEndDates = -1
        Case acLBGetValue
            ' days till ending date
            intOffset = Abs((8 - Weekday(Now)) Mod 7)

            ' start 5 weeks prior to current week ending date
            ' (7 days * 5 weeks = 35 days before next ending date)
            ' and show 11 dates

            ListEndDates = Format(((Now() + intOffset) - 35) _
                + 7 * row, "MM/DD/YYYY")
    End Select
End Function
```

9. In the ListEndDates procedure, click anywhere on the line containing the following statement:

```
ListEndDates = Format(((Now() + intOffset) - 35) + 7 * row, "MM/DD/YYYY")
```

10. Press **F9** (or choose **Debug | Toggle Breakpoint**) to set a breakpoint on the line where the cursor is located.

When you set the breakpoint, Visual Basic displays a red dot in the margin. At the same time, the line that has the breakpoint will change to white text on red (see Figure 9-4). The color of the breakpoint can be changed on the Editor Format tab in the Options dialog box (Tools menu).

Another way of setting a breakpoint is to click in the margin indicator to the left of the line on which you want to stop the procedure.

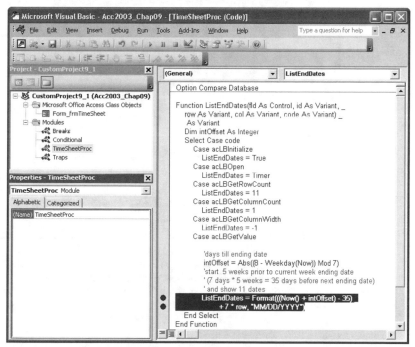

Figure 9-4: The line of code where the breakpoint is set is displayed in the color specified on the Editor Format tab in the Options dialog box.

11. Switch to the Microsoft Access Application window and open the form **frmTimeSheet** that you prepared earlier in this project.

When you open the form, Visual Basic will call the ListEndDates function to fill the combo box, executing all the statements until it encounters the breakpoint you set in step 10 above. Once the breakpoint is reached, the code is suspended and the screen displays the Code window (Figure 9-5) in break mode (notice the word "break" surrounded by the square brackets in the Code window's title bar). Visual Basic displays a yellow arrow in the margin to the left of the statement at which the procedure was suspended. At the same time, the statement appears inside a box with a yellow background. The arrow and the box indicate the current statement, or the statement that is about to be executed. If the current statement also contains a

breakpoint, the margin displays both indicators overlapping one another
(the circle and the arrow).

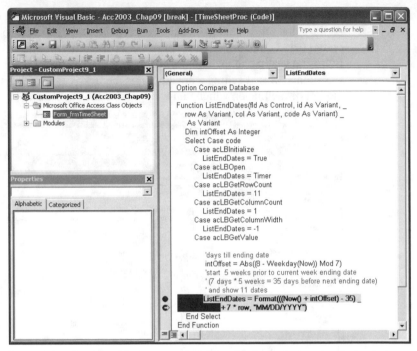

Figure 9-5: When Visual Basic encounters a breakpoint, it displays the Code window.
A yellow arrow appears in the margin to the left of the statement at which the procedure was suspended. Because the current statement also contains a breakpoint (indicated by a red circle), the margin displays both indicators overlapping one another
(the circle and the arrow).

12. Finish running your procedure by pressing **F5** to continue without stopping, or press **F8** to execute the procedure line by line.

When you step through your procedure code line by line by pressing F8,
you can use the Immediate window to further test your procedure (see the
section titled "Using the Immediate Window in Break Mode"). To learn
more about stepping through a procedure, refer to the section titled
"Stepping Through VBA Procedures" later in this chapter.

Visual Basic allows you to set any number of breakpoints in a procedure. This
way you can suspend and continue the execution of your procedure as you
please. You can press F5 to quickly move between the breakpoints. You can
analyze the code of your procedure and check the values of variables while
code execution is suspended. You can also perform various tests by typing
statements in the Immediate window.

Consider setting a breakpoint if you suspect that your procedure never executes a certain block of code.

Removing Breakpoints

When you finish running the procedure in which you had set breakpoints, Visual Basic does not automatically remove them. To remove the breakpoint, choose Debug | Clear All Breakpoints or press Ctrl+Shift+F9. All the breakpoints are removed. If you had set several breakpoints in a given procedure and would like to remove only some of them, click on the line containing the breakpoint you want to remove and press F9 (or choose Debug | Clear Breakpoint). You should clear the breakpoints when they are no longer needed. The breakpoints are automatically removed when you exit Microsoft Access.

Using the Immediate Window in Break Mode

When the procedure execution is suspended, the Code window appears in break mode. This is a good time to activate the Immediate window and type VBA instructions to find out, for instance, the name of the open form or the value of a certain control. You can also use the Immediate window to change the contents of variables in order to correct values that may be causing errors. By now, you should be an expert when it comes to working in the Immediate window. Figure 9-6 shows the suspended ListEndDates function procedure and the Immediate window with the questions that were asked of Visual Basic while in break mode.

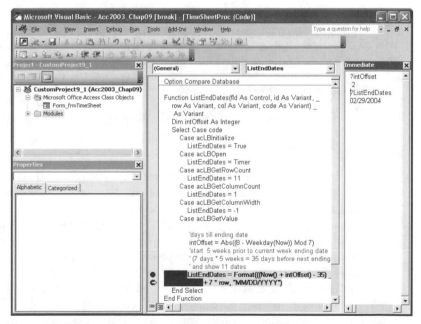

Figure 9-6: When code execution is suspended you can find answers to many questions by entering appropriate statements in the Immediate window.

In break mode, you can hold the mouse pointer over any variable in a running procedure to see the variable's value. For example, in the ListEndDates function procedure shown in Figure 9-7, the breakpoint has been set on the statement just before the End Select keywords. When Visual Basic encounters this statement, the Code window appears in break mode. Because Visual Basic has already executed the statement that stores the value of the variable intOffset, you can quickly find out the value of this variable by resting the mouse pointer over its name. The name of the variable and its current value appear in a frame. To show the values of several variables used in a procedure at once, you should use the Locals window, which is discussed later in this chapter.

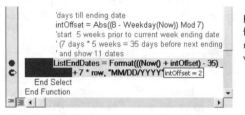

Figure 9-7: In break mode, you can find out the value of a variable by resting the mouse pointer on that variable.

Working in a Code Window in Break Mode

While in break mode, you can change code, add new statements, execute the procedure one line at a time, skip lines, set the next statement, use the Immediate window, and more. When Visual Basic is in break mode, all of the options on the Debug menu are available. You can enter break mode by pressing Ctrl+Break or F8, or setting a breakpoint. In break mode, if you change a certain line of code, VBA will prompt you to reset the project by displaying the message, "This action will reset your project, proceed anyway?" Click OK to stop the program's execution and proceed editing your code, or Cancel to delete the new changes and continue running the code from the point where it was suspended. For example, change the variable declaration. As you press F5 to resume code execution, VBA will prompt you to reset your project.

Using the Stop Statement

Sometimes you won't be able to test your procedure right away. If you set up your breakpoints and then close the database file, the breakpoints will be removed; next time, when you are ready to test your procedure, you'll have to begin by setting up your breakpoints again. If you need to postpone the task of testing your procedure until later, you can take a different approach. Insert a Stop statement into your code wherever you want to halt a procedure. Figure 9-8 shows the Stop statement before the With...End With construct. Visual Basic will suspend the execution of the cboEndDate_Change event procedure when it encounters the Stop statement and the screen will display the Code window in break mode. Although the Stop statement has exactly the same effect as setting a breakpoint, it does have one disadvantage. All Stop statements stay in the procedure until you remove them. When you no longer need to stop your procedure, you must locate and remove all the Stops.

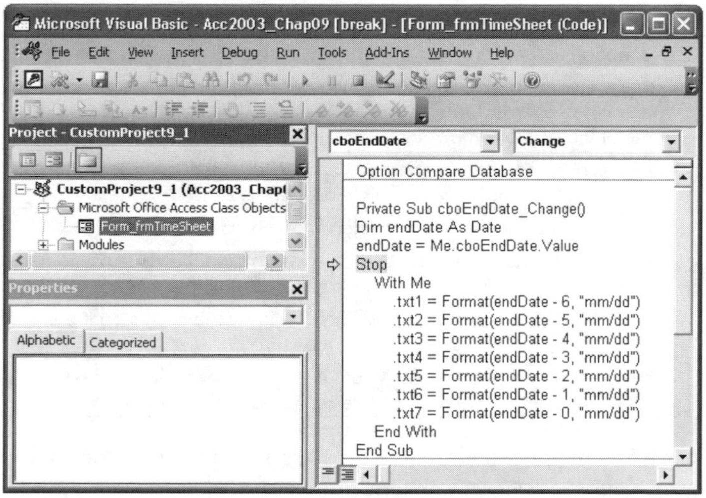

Figure 9-8: You can insert a Stop statement anywhere in your VBA procedure code. The procedure will halt when it gets to the Stop statement, and the Code window will appear with the code line highlighted.

Adding Watch Expressions

Many errors in procedures are caused by variables that assume unexpected values. If a procedure uses a variable whose value changes in various locations, you may want to stop the procedure and check the current value of that variable. Visual Basic offers a special Watch window that allows you to keep an eye on variables or expressions while your procedure is running. To add a watch expression to your procedure, select the variable whose value you want to monitor in the Code window, then choose Debug | Add Watch. The screen will display the Add Watch dialog box, as shown in Figure 9-9.

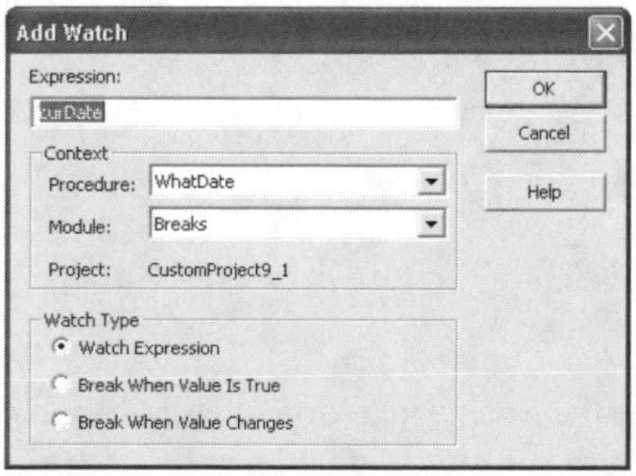

Figure 9-9: The Add Watch dialog box allows you to define conditions you want to monitor while a VBA procedure is running.

The Add Watch dialog box contains three sections, which are described in Table 9-2.

Table 9-2: Add Watch dialog sections

Section	Description
Expression	Displays the name of a variable you have highlighted in your procedure. If you opened the Add Watch dialog box without selecting a variable name, type the name of the variable you want to monitor in the Expression text box.
Context	In this section, indicate the name of the procedure that contains the variable and the name of the module where this procedure is located.
Watch Type	Specifies how to monitor the variable. If you choose: • the Watch Expression option button, you can read the value of the variable in the Watch window while in break mode. • Break When Value Is True, Visual Basic will automatically stop the procedure when the variable evaluates to true (nonzero). • Break When Value Changes, Visual Basic will automatically stop the procedure each time the value of the variable or expression changes.

You can add a watch expression before running a procedure or after suspending the execution of your procedure.

The difference between a breakpoint and a watch expression is that the breakpoint always stops a procedure in a specified location, but the watch stops the procedure only when the specified condition (Break When Value Is True or Break When Value Changes) is met. Watches are extremely useful when you are not sure where the variable is being changed. Instead of stepping through many lines of code to find the location where the variable assumes the specified value, you can put a watch breakpoint on the variable and run your procedure as normal. Let's see how this works.

◎ Hands-On 9-1: Working with the Watch Window

1. Insert a new standard module and name it **Breaks**.

2. Prepare the following WhatDate procedure as shown in Figure 9-10:

```
Sub WhatDate()
    Dim curDate As Date
    Dim newDate As Date
    Dim x As Integer

    curDate = Date
    For x = 1 To 365
        newDate = Date + x
    Next x
End Sub
```

The WhatDate procedure uses the For...Next loop to calculate the date that is x days in the future. You won't see any result when you run this procedure unless you insert the following instruction in the procedure code just before the End Sub keywords:

```
MsgBox "In " & x & " days, it will be " & NewDate
```

This time, however, you don't want to display the individual dates, day after day. Suppose that you want to stop the program when the value of the variable x reaches 211. In other words, you want to know what date will be

211 days from now. To get the answer, you could insert the following statement into your procedure before the Next x statement:

```
If x = 211 Then MsgBox "In " & x & " days it will be " & NewDate
```

But this time, you want to get the answer without introducing any new statements into your procedure. If you add watch expressions to the procedure, Visual Basic will stop the For...Next loop when the specified condition is met, and you'll be able to check the values of the desired variables.

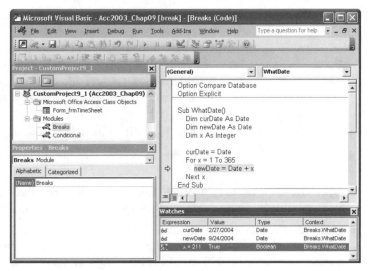

Figure 9-10: Using the Watch window.

3. Choose **Debug | Add Watch**.

4. In the Expression text box, enter the following expression: **x = 211**.

5. In the Context section, choose **WhatDate** from the Procedure combo box and **Breaks** from the Module combo box.

6. In the Watch Type section, select the **Break When Value Is True** option button.

7. Click **OK** to close the Add Watch dialog box. You have now added your first watch expression.

8. In the Code window, position the insertion point anywhere within the name of the curDate variable.

9. Choose **Debug | Add Watch** and click **OK** to set up the default watch type with the Watch Expression option.

10. In the Code window, position the insertion point anywhere within the name of the newDate variable.

11. Choose **Debug | Add Watch** and click **OK** to set up the default watch type with the Watch Expression option.

After performing the above steps, the WhatDate procedure contains the following three watches:

x = 211	Break When Value Is True
curDate	Watch Expression
newDate	Watch Expression

12. Position the cursor anywhere inside the code of the WhatDate procedure and press **F5**.

   Visual Basic stops the procedure when x = 211 (see Figure 9-10 above). Notice that the value of the variable *x* in the Watches window is the same as the value you specified in the Add Watch dialog. In addition, the Watches window shows the value of the variables curDate and newDate. The procedure is in break mode. You can press F5 to continue, or you can ask another question: What date will be in 277 days? The next step shows how to do this.

13. Choose **Debug | Edit Watch** and enter the following expression: **x = 277**.

14. Display the Edit Watch dialog box by double-clicking the expression in the Watch window.

15. Click **OK** to close the Edit Watch dialog box. Notice that the Watches window now displays a new value of the expression. The x is now false.

16. Press **F5**. The procedure stops again when the value of x = 277. The value of curDate is the same. However, the newDate variable now contains a new value — a date that is 277 days from now. You can change the value of the expression again or finish the procedure.

17. Press **F5** to finish the procedure without stopping.

   When your procedure is running and a watch expression has a value, the Watches window displays the value of the watch expression. If you open the Watches window after the procedure has finished, you will see the error "<out of context>" instead of the variable values. In other words, when the watch expression is out of context, it does not have a value.

Removing Watch Expressions

To remove a watch expression, click on the expression you want to remove from the Watches window and press Delete. Remove all the watch expressions you defined in the preceding exercise.

Using Quick Watch

If you want to check the value of an expression not defined in the Watch window, you can use Quick Watch (see Figure 9-11).

To access the Quick Watch dialog box while in break mode, position the insertion point anywhere inside a variable name or an expression you want to watch and choose Debug | Quick Watch, or press Shift+F9.

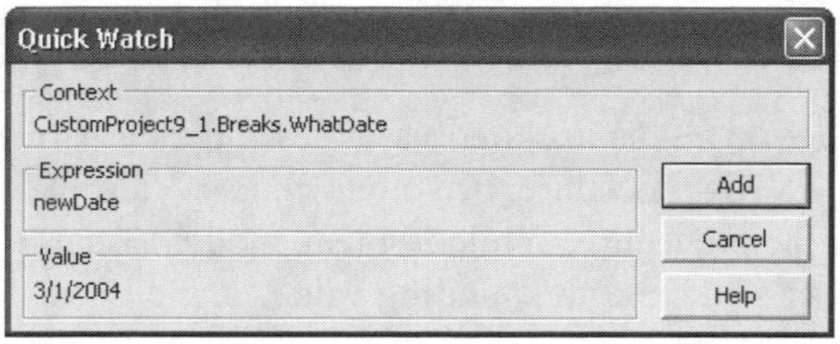

Figure 9-11: The Quick Watch dialog box shows the value of the selected expression in a VBA procedure.

The Quick Watch dialog box contains an Add button that allows you to add the expression to the Watches window. Make sure that the WhatDate procedure does not contain any watch expressions. See the preceding section on how to remove a watch expression from the Watches window. Now, let's see how to take advantage of Quick Watch.

⊚ Hands-On 9-2: Using the Quick Watch Dialog Box

1. In the WhatDate procedure, position the insertion point on the name of the variable, x.

2. Choose **Debug | Add Watch**.

3. Enter the expression **x = 50**.

4. Choose the **Break When Value Is True** option button, and click **OK**.

5. Run the WhatDate procedure. Visual Basic will suspend procedure execution when x = 50. Notice that the Watches window does not contain either the newDate or curDate variables.

   To check the values of these variables, you can position the mouse pointer over the appropriate variable name in the Code window, or you can invoke the Quick Watch dialog box.

6. In the Code window, position the mouse inside the newDate variable and press **Shift+F9**, or choose **Debug | Quick Watch**. The Quick Watch dialog boxshows the name of the expression and its current value.

7. Click **Cancel** to return to the Code window.

8. In the Code window, position the mouse inside the curDate variable and press **Shift+F9**, or choose **Debug | Quick Watch**. The Quick Watch dialog box now shows the value of the variable curDate.

9. Click **Cancel** to return to the Code window.

10. Press **F5** to continue running the procedure.

Using the Locals Window and the Call Stack Dialog Box

If you want to keep an eye on all the declared variables and their current values during the execution of a VBA procedure, be sure to choose View | Locals Window before you run the procedure. While in break mode, Visual Basic will display a list of variables and their corresponding values in the Locals window (see Figure 9-12).

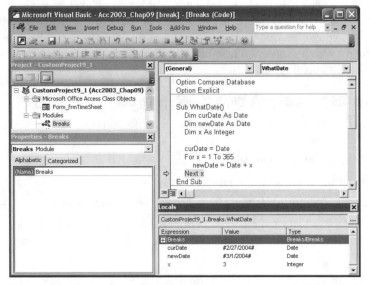

Figure 9-12: The Locals window displays the current values of all the declared variables in the current VBA procedure.

The Locals window contains three columns: Expression, Value, and Type.

The Expression column displays the names of variables that are declared in the current procedure. The first row displays the name of the module preceded by the plus sign. When you click the plus sign, you can check if any variables have been declared at the module level. Here the class module will show the system variable Me. In the Locals window, global variables and variables used by other projects aren't displayed.

The second column, Value, shows the current variable values. In this column, you can change the value of a variable by clicking on it and typing the new value. After changing the value, press Enter to register the change. You can also press Tab, Shift+Tab, up or down arrow, or click anywhere within the Locals window after you've changed the variable value.

Type, the third column, displays the type of each declared variable.

To observe the variable values in the Locals window, do the following hands-on.

Hands-On 9-3: Using the Locals Window

1. Choose **View | Locals Window**.

2. Click anywhere inside the WhatDate procedure and press **F8**. By pressing F8 you placed the procedure in break mode. The Locals window displays the name of the current module, the local variables, and their beginning values.

3. Press **F8** a few more times while keeping an eye on the Locals window.

4. Press **F5** to continue running the procedure.

   The Locals window also contains a button with an ellipsis (…). This button opens the Call Stack dialog box (see Figure 9-13), which displays a list of all active procedure calls. An *active procedure call* is the procedure that is started but not completed. You can also activate the Call Stack dialog box by choosing View | Call Stack. This option is only available in break mode.

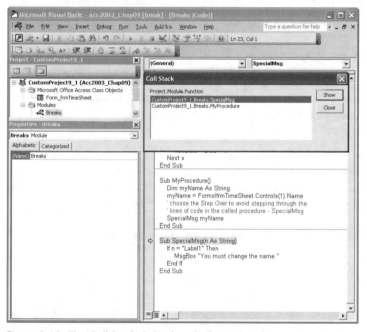

Figure 9-13: The Call Stack dialog box displays a list of procedures that are started but not completed.

The Call Stack dialog box is especially helpful for tracing nested procedures. Recall that a nested procedure is a procedure that is being called from within another procedure. If a procedure calls another, the name of the called procedure is automatically added to the Calls list in the Call Stack dialog box. When Visual Basic has finished executing the statements of the called procedure, the procedure name is automatically removed from the Call Stack dialog box. You can use the Show button in the Call Stack dialog box to display the statement that calls the next procedure listed in the Call Stack dialog box.

Stepping Through VBA Procedures

Stepping through the code means running one statement at a time. This allows you to check every line in every procedure that is encountered. To start stepping through the procedure from the beginning, place the cursor anywhere inside the code of your procedure and choose Debug | Step Into, or press F8. The Debug menu contains several options that allow you to execute a procedure in the step mode (see Figure 9-14).

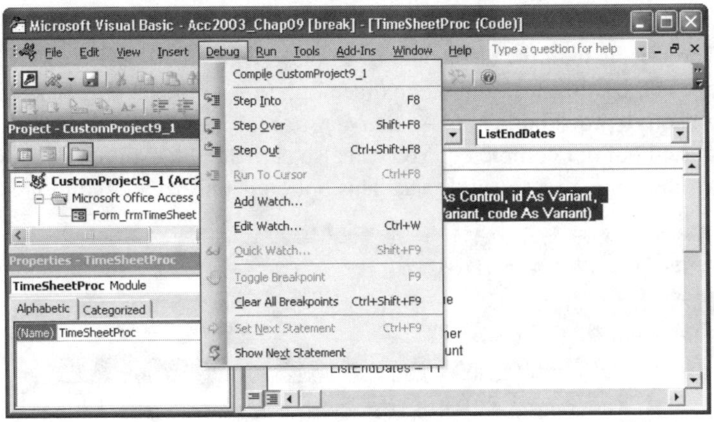

Figure 9-14: The Debug menu offers many commands for stepping through VBA procedures.

When you run a procedure one statement at a time, Visual Basic executes each statement until it encounters the End Sub keywords. If you don't want Visual Basic to step through every statement, you can press F5 at any time to run the rest of the procedure without stepping through it.

◎ Hands-On 9-4: Stepping Through a Procedure

1. Place the cursor anywhere inside the procedure you want to trace.

2. Press **F8** or choose **Debug | Step Into**. Visual Basic executes the current statement, then automatically advances to the next statement and suspends execution. While in break mode, you can activate the Immediate window, the Watches window, or the Locals window to see the effect of a particular statement on the values of variables and expressions. And, if the procedure you are stepping through calls other procedures, you can activate the Call Stack dialog to see which procedures are currently active.

3. Press **F8** again to execute the selected statement. After executing this statement, Visual Basic will select the next statement, and again the procedure execution will be halted.

4. Continue stepping the procedure by pressing **F8**, or press **F5** to continue running the code without stopping. You can also choose **Run | Reset** to

stop the procedure at the current statement without executing the remaining statements.

When you step over procedures (**Shift+F8**), Visual Basic executes each procedure as if it were a single statement. This option is particularly useful if a procedure contains calls to other procedures you don't want to step into because they have already been tested and debugged, or because you want to concentrate only on the new code that has not been debugged yet.

Stepping Over a Procedure

Suppose that the current statement in MyProcedure calls the SpecialMsg procedure. If you choose Debug | Step Over (Shift+F8) instead of Debug | Step Into (F8), Visual Basic will quickly execute all the statements inside the SpecialMsg procedure and select the next statement in the calling procedure, MyProcedure. All during the execution of the SpecialMsg procedure, Visual Basic continues to display the current procedure in the Code window.

⊚ Hands-On 9-5: Stepping Over a Procedure

This hands-on refers to the Access form named frmTimeSheet that you created in Custom Project 9-1 at the beginning of this chapter.

1. Enter the MyProcedure and SpecialMsg procedures in a new module.

```
Sub MyProcedure()
    Dim myName As String

    myName = Forms!frmTimeSheet.Controls(1).Name

    ' choose Step Over to avoid stepping through the
    ' lines of code in the called procedure - SpecialMsg
    SpecialMsg myName
End Sub

Sub SpecialMsg(n As String)
    If n = "Label1" Then
        MsgBox "You must change the name."
    End If
End Sub
```

2. Add a breakpoint at the following statement:

```
SpecialMsg myName
```

3. Place the insertion point anywhere within the code of MyProcedure and press **F5** to run it. Visual Basic halts execution when it reaches the breakpoint.

4. Press **Shift+F8** or choose **Debug | Step Over**. Visual Basic runs the SpecialMsg procedure, then execution advances to the statement immediately after the call to the SpecialMsg procedure.

5. Press **F5** to finish running the procedure without stepping through its code.

Now suppose you want to execute MyProcedure to the line that calls the SpecialMsg procedure.

6. Click inside the statement SpecialMsg myName.

7. Choose **Debug | Run to Cursor**. Visual Basic will stop the procedure when it reaches the specified line.

8. Press **Shift+F8** to step over the SpecialMsg procedure.

9. Press **F5** to execute the rest of the procedure without single stepping.

Stepping over a procedure is particularly useful when you don't want to analyze individual statements inside the called procedure (SpecialMsg).

Stepping Out of a Procedure

Another command on the Debug menu, Step Out (Ctrl+Shift+F8), is used when you step into a procedure and then decide that you don't want to step all the way through it. When you choose this option, Visual Basic will execute the remaining statements in this procedure in one step and proceed to activate the next statement in the calling procedure.

In the process of stepping through a procedure you can switch between the Step Into, Step Over, and Step Out options. The option you select depends on which code fragment you wish to analyze at a given moment.

Running a Procedure to Cursor

The Debug menu Run To Cursor (Ctrl+F8) command lets you run your procedure until the line you have selected is encountered. This command is really useful if you want to stop the execution before a large loop or you intend to step over a called procedure.

Setting the Next Statement

At times, you may want to rerun previous lines of code in the procedure or skip over a section of code that is causing trouble. In each of these situations, you can use the Set Next Statement option on the Debug menu. When you halt execution of a procedure, you can resume the procedure from any statement you want. Visual Basic will skip execution of the statements between the selected statement and the statement where execution was suspended.

Skipping Lines of Code

Although skipping lines of code can be very useful in the process of debugging your VBA procedures, it should be done with care. When you use the Next Statement option, you tell Visual Basic that this is the line you want to execute next. All lines in between are ignored. This means that certain things you may have expected to occur don't happen, which can lead to unexpected errors.

Showing the Next Statement

If you are not sure where procedure execution will resume, you can choose Debug | Show Next Statement, and Visual Basic will place the cursor on the line that will run next. This is particularly useful when you have been looking at other procedures and are not sure where execution will resume. The Show Next Statement option is available only in break mode.

Stopping and Resetting VBA Procedures

At any time while stepping through the code of a procedure in the Code window, you can press F5 to execute the remaining instructions without stepping through them, or choose Run | Reset to finish the procedure without executing the remaining statements. When you reset your procedure, all the variables lose their current values. Numeric variables assume the initial value of zero, variable-length strings are initialized to a zero-length string (" "), and fixed-length strings are filled with the character represented by the ASCII character code 0, or Chr(0). Variant variables are initialized to Empty, and the value of Object variables is set to Nothing.

Understanding and Using Conditional Compilation

When you run a procedure for the first time, Visual Basic converts your VBA statements into the machine code understood by the computer. This process is called *compiling*. You can also perform the compilation of your entire VBA project before you run the procedure by choosing Debug | Compile (name of the current VBA project). You can tell Visual Basic to include or ignore certain blocks of code when compiling and running by using conditional compilation. Your procedure may behave differently depending on the condition you set. For example, the conditional compilation is used to compile an application that will be run on different platforms (Windows or Macintosh, Win16 or Win32 bit). The conditional compilation is also useful in localizing an application for different languages. The program code excluded during the conditional compilation is omitted from the final file, thus it has no effect on the size or performance of the program.

Conditional compilation is enabled via special expressions called *directives*. First, you need to declare a Boolean (True, False) constant by using the #Const directive. Next, you check this constant inside the #If...Then... #Else directive. The portion of code that you want to compile conditionally must be surrounded by these directives. Notice that the If and Else keywords are preceded by a pound sign (#). If a portion of code is to be run, the value of the conditional constant has to be set to True (–1). Otherwise, the value of this constant should be set to False (0). You declare the conditional constant in the declaration section of the module. For example,

```
#Const User = True
```

declares the conditional constant named User.

In the hands-on that follows, data is displayed in the Spanish language when the conditional constant named verSpanish is True. The WhatDay procedure calls the DayOfWeek function, which returns the name of the day based on the supplied date. To compile the program in the English language, all you have to do is change the conditional constant to False, and Visual Basic will jump to the block of instructions located after the #Else directive.

⊚ Hands-On 9-6: Using Conditional Compilation

1. Insert a new module and name it **Conditional**.

2. Enter the WhatDay and DayOfWeek function procedures as shown below.

```
' declare a conditional compiler constant
#Const verSpanish = True

Sub WhatDay()
    Dim dayNr As Integer
    #If verSpanish = True Then
        dayNr = Weekday(InputBox("Entre la fecha, por ejemplo 01/01/2001"))
        MsgBox "Sera " & DayOfWeek(dayNr) & "."
    #Else
        WeekdayName
    #End If
End Sub

Function DayOfWeek(dayNr As Integer) As String
    DayOfWeek = Choose(dayNr, "Domingo", "Lunes", "Martes", _
        "Miercoles", "Jueves", "Viernes", "Sabado")
End Function

Function WeekdayName() As String
    Select Case Weekday(InputBox("Enter date, e.g., 01/01/2000"))
        Case 1
            WeekdayName = "Sunday"
        Case 2
            WeekdayName = "Monday"
        Case 3
            WeekdayName = "Tuesday"
        Case 4
            WeekdayName = "Wednesday"
        Case 5
            WeekdayName = "Thursday"
        Case 6
            WeekdayName = "Friday"
        Case 7
            WeekdayName = "Saturday"
    End Select
    MsgBox "It will be " & WeekdayName & "."
End Function
```

3. Run the WhatDay procedure.

Because the conditional compilation constant (verSpanish) is set to True at the top of the module, Visual Basic runs the Spanish version of the

WhatDay procedure. It asks for the user's input in Spanish and displays the result in Spanish. To run the English version of the code, change the verSpanish constant to False, and rerun the procedure.

Instead of declaring the conditional compiler constants at the top of a module, you can choose Tools | (Debugging) Properties (see Figure 9-15). When you use the Properties window, use the following syntax in the Conditional Compilation Arguments text box to enable the English version of the WhatDay procedure:

```
verSpanish = 0
```

If there are more conditional compilation constants, each of the constants must be separated by a colon.

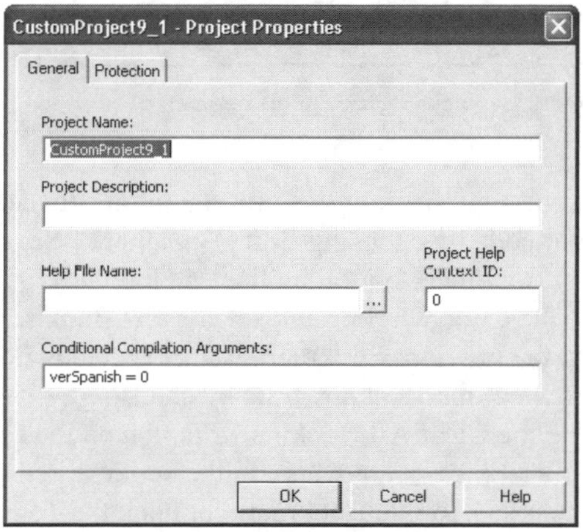

Figure 9-15: The conditional compilation constant can be declared either at the top of the module or in the Properties window, but never in both places.

4. Comment out the #Const verSpanish directive at the top of the module, and enter the conditional compilation constant in the Properties window as shown in Figure 9-15. Then run the WhatDay procedure to see how the Else branch of your program is now executed for English-speaking users.

Navigating with Bookmarks

In the process of analyzing or reviewing your VBA procedures you will often find yourself jumping to certain code areas. Using the built-in bookmark feature, you can easily mark the spots you want to navigate between.

To set up a bookmark:

1. Click anywhere in the statement you want to define as a bookmark.

2. Choose **Edit | Bookmarks | Toggle Bookmark** (or click the **Toggle Bookmark** button on the Edit toolbar). Visual Basic will place a blue, rounded rectangle in the left margin beside the statement (see Figure 9-16).

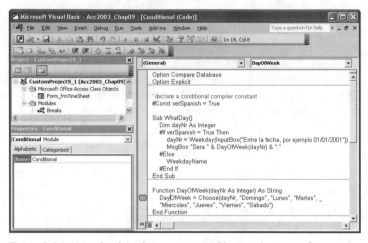

Figure 9-16: Using bookmarks, you can quickly jump between often-used sections of your procedures.

Once you've set up two or more bookmarks, you can jump between the marked locations of your code by choosing Edit | Bookmark | Next Bookmark or simply click the Next Bookmark button on the Edit toolbar. You may also right-click anywhere in the Code window and select Next Bookmark from the shortcut menu. To go to the previous bookmark, select Previous Bookmark instead. You can remove bookmarks at any time by choosing Edit | Bookmarks | Clear All or by clicking the Clear All Bookmarks button on the Edit toolbar. To remove a single bookmark, click anywhere in the bookmarked statement and choose Edit | Bookmarks | Toggle Bookmark, or click the Toggle Bookmark button on the Edit toolbar.

Trapping Errors

No one writes bug-free programs the first time. For this reason, when you create VBA procedures you have to determine how your program will respond to errors. Many unexpected errors happen at run time. For example, your procedure may try to give a new file the same name as an open file.

Run-time errors are often discovered not by a programmer, but the user who attempts to do something that the programmer has not anticipated. If an error occurs when the procedure is running, Visual Basic displays an error message and the procedure is stopped. Most often the error message that VBA displays is quite cryptic to the user. You can guard users from seeing many run-time errors by including error-handling code in your VBA procedures. This way, when Visual Basic encounters an error, instead of displaying a default error message it will show a much friendlier, more comprehensive error message, perhaps advising the user how to correct the error.

How can you implement error handling in your VBA procedure? The first step is to place the On Error statement in your procedure. This statement tells VBA what to do if an error happens while your program is running. In other words, VBA uses the On Error statement to activate an error-handling procedure that will trap run-time errors. Depending on the type of procedure, you can exit the error trap by using one of the following statements: Exit Sub, Exit Function, Exit Property, End Sub, End Function, or End Property.

You should write an error-handling routine for each procedure. See Table 9-3 for ways in which to use the On Error statement.

Table 9-3: On Error options

On Error Statement	Description
On Error GoTo Label	Specifies a label to jump to when an error occurs. This label marks the beginning of the error-handling routine. An *error handler* is a routine for trapping and responding to errors in your application. The label must appear in the same procedure as the On Error GoTo statement.
On Error Resume Next	When a run-time error occurs, Visual Basic ignores the line that caused the error and does not display an error message, but continues the procedure with the next line.
On Error GoTo 0	Turns off error trapping in a procedure. When VBA runs this statement, errors are detected but not trapped within the procedure.

Is This an Error or a Mistake?

In programming, mistakes and errors are not the same thing. A mistake — such as a misspelled or missing statement, a misplaced quotation mark or comma, or an assignment of a value of one type to a variable of a different (and incompatible) type — can be removed from your program through proper testing and debugging. But even though your code may be free of mistakes, errors can still occur. An error is a result of an event or operation that doesn't work as expected. For example, if your VBA procedure accesses a particular file on disk and someone deleted this file or moved it to another location, you'll get an error no matter what. An error prevents the procedure from carrying out a specific task.

Let's look at the example procedure in Hands-On 9-7. The OpenToRead procedure shown below demonstrates the use of the Resume Next and Error statements, as well as the Err object.

◎ Hands-On 9-7: Error Trapping Techniques

1. In the Visual Basic Editor window, insert a new module.

2. In the Code window, enter the following OpenToRead procedure.

➲ **Note:** The purpose of the OpenToRead procedure is to read the contents of the user-supplied text file character by character. When the user enters a filename, various errors can occur. For example, the filename may be wrong, the user may attempt to open a file from a diskette when there is no disk in the diskette drive, or he may try to open a file that is already open. To trap these errors, the error-handling routine at the end of the OpenToRead procedure uses the Name property of the Err object. The Err object contains information about run-time errors. If an error occurs while the procedure is running, the statement Err.Number will return the error number.

```
Sub OpenToRead()
    Dim myFile As String
    Dim myChar As String
    Dim myText As String
    Dim FileExists As Boolean

    FileExists = True

    On Error GoTo ErrorHandler
    myFile = InputBox("Enter the name of file you want to open:")
    Open myFile For Input As #1
    If FileExists Then
        Do While Not EOF(1)            ' loop until the end of file
            myChar = Input(1, #1)      ' get one character
            myText = myText + myChar    ' store in the variable myText
        Loop
        Debug.Print myText             ' print to the Immediate window
        ' Close the file - commenting out this instruction will cause
        ' error 52.
        Close #1
    End If
    Exit Sub

ErrorHandler:
    FileExists = False
    Select Case Err.Number
        Case 71
            MsgBox "The diskette drive is empty."
        Case 53
            MsgBox "This file can't be found on the specified drive."
        Case 75
            Exit Sub
        Case Else
            MsgBox "Error " & Err.Number & " :" & Error(Err.Number)
            Exit Sub
    End Select
    Resume Next
End Sub
```

Procedure Testing

You are responsible for the code you produce. This means that before you give your procedure to others to test, you should test it yourself. After all, you understand best how it is supposed to work. Some programmers think testing their own code is some sort of degrading activity, especially when they work in an organization that has a team devoted to testing. *Don't make this mistake.* The testing process at the programmer level is as important as the code development itself. After you've tested the procedure yourself, you should give it to the users to test. Users will provide you with answers to questions such as: Does the procedure produce the expected results? Is it easy and fun to use? Does it follow the standard conventions? Also, it is a good idea to give the entire application to someone who knows the least about using this particular application, and ask them to play around with it and try to break it.

If errors 71, 53, or 75 occur, Visual Basic will display the user-friendly messages given inside the Select Case block and then proceed to the Resume Next statement, which will send it to the line of code following the one that had caused the error. If another (unexpected) error occurs, Visual Basic will return its error code (Err.Number) and error description (Error(Err.Number)).

At the beginning of the procedure, the variable FileExists is set to True. If the program doesn't encounter an error, all the instructions inside the If FileExists Then block will be executed. However, if VBA encounters an error, the value of the FileExists variable will be set to False (see the first statement in the error-handling routine just below the ErrorHandler label).

If you comment the statement Close #1, Visual Basic will encounter the error on the next attempt to open the same file. Notice the Exit Sub statement before the ErrorHandler. Put the Exit Sub statement just above the error-handling routine. You don't want Visual Basic to carry out the error handling if there are no errors.

To better understand error trapping, let's perform another hands-on.

◎ Hands-On 9-8: Understanding Error Trapping

This hands-on requires prior completion of Hands-On 9-7.

1. Prepare a text file named **C:\Vacation.txt** using Windows Notepad. Enter any text you want in this file.

2. Run the **OpenToRead** procedure three times in the step mode, each time supplying one of the following:
   - The filename **C:\Vacation.txt**
   - A filename that does not exist on drive C
   - The name of any file in drive A (when the diskette slot is empty)

3. Comment the Close #1 statement and enter **C:\Vacation.txt** as the filename. Run the procedure twice. The second run will generate an error because C:\Vacation.txt will be open.

Generating Errors to Test Error Handling

You can test the ways your program responds to run-time errors by causing them on purpose:

- Generate any built-in error by entering the following syntax:

```
Error error_number
```

For example, to display the error that occurs on an attempt to divide by zero (0), type the following statement in the Immediate window:

```
Error 11
```

When you press Enter, Visual Basic will display the error message saying, "Run-time error 11. Division by zero."

■ To check the meaning of the generated error, use the following syntax:

```
Error(error_number)
```

For example, to find out what error number 7 means, type the following in the Immediate window:

```
?Error(7)
```

When you press Enter, Visual Basic returns the error description:

```
"Out of memory"
```

Chapter Summary

In this chapter, you learned how to test your VBA procedures to make sure they perform as planned. You debugged your code by stepping through it using breakpoints and watches, learned how to work with the Immediate window in break mode, found out how the Locals window can help you monitor the values of variables, and discovered how the Call Stack dialog box can be helpful in keeping track of where you are in a complex program. You also learned how to specify the parts of your procedure that you want to include or exclude upon compilation. Finally, you learned how to trap errors with error-handling routines. By using the built-in debugging tools, you can quickly pinpoint the problem spots in your procedures. Try to spend more time getting acquainted with these tools. Mastering the art of debugging can save you hours of trial and error.

PART II

Creating and Manipulating Databases with ADO

ActiveX Data Objects (ADO) is a set of programming objects that enable client applications (including Microsoft Office Access) to access and manipulate data through an OLE DB provider.

In this part of the book, you learn how to access ADO objects in your VBA code to connect to a data source; create, modify, and secure database objects; and work with data.

Chapter 10

Accessing Data Using ADO

Since its introduction in 1993, Microsoft Access has been effectively used by people all over the world for organizing and accessing data. While each new software release brought numerous changes in the design of the user interface and offered simpler ways of performing common database tasks, database access has evolved at a little slower pace.

Since Version 1.0, an integrated part of Microsoft Access has been its database engine, commonly referred to as *Microsoft Jet* or *Jet database engine*. Jet databases are stored in the familiar .mdb file format. The only way you could access a native Microsoft Access database (Microsoft Jet) programmatically in the early 1990s was by using the data access technology known as *Open Database Connectivity* (ODBC). This technology made it possible to connect to relational databases using appropriate ODBC drivers supplied by database vendors and third parties. While this technology is still in use today, it is not object-oriented and is considered by many to be quite difficult to work with. To access data via ODBC you need a specific ODBC driver installed on the computer containing the data source.

With the release of Access 2.0, Microsoft enabled programmers to efficiently access and manipulate Microsoft Jet databases with a technology called *Data Access Objects* (DAO). DAO consists of a hierarchy of objects that provide methods and properties for designing and manipulating databases. Although you will still encounter numerous Microsoft Access VBA programs that use the DAO Object Model, it is recommended that you perform your database programming tasks by using another object model known as *ActiveX Data Objects* (ADO).

Access 2000 was the first version to support ADO. Microsoft Office Access 2003 continues to use ADO as its main and preferred method of data access. ADO works with the new technology known as *OLE DB*. This technology is object-based, but it is not limited to relational databases. OLE DB can access both relational and non-relational data sources such as directory services, mail stores, multimedia, and text files, as well as mainframe data (VSAM and MVS).

To access external data with OLE DB you do not need any specific drivers installed on your computer because OLE DB does not use drivers; it uses data providers to communicate with data stores. *Data providers* are programs that enable access to data. OLE DB has many providers, such as Microsoft OLE DB Provider for SQL Server or Microsoft Jet 4.0 OLE DB Provider. There are also providers for Oracle, NT 5 Active Directory, and even a provider for ODBC.

Accessing and manipulating data programmatically with ADO requires that you establish a connection to the desired data source. The Microsoft Jet database engine enables you to access data that resides in Microsoft Jet databases, external data sources (such as Microsoft Excel, Paradox, or dBASE), and ODBC data sources. This chapter demonstrates various ways of opening both native Microsoft Jet databases as well as external data sources. You will also learn how to establish a connection to the currently open database, connect to an SQL server, create a new database, set database properties, and handle database errors.

ADO Object Model

ActiveX Data Objects (ADO) is OLE DB's main object model. ADO consists of three object models, each providing a different area of functionality (see Table 10-1). Because of this, only the objects necessary for a specific task need to be loaded at any given time.

➡ **Note:** If you're interested in programming Microsoft Office Access databases using the older Data Access Objects (DAO) (and this may be a valid requirement if you happen to be involved in a DAO to ADO conversion project), AppendixA.pdf in the book's downloadable files contains numerous DAO programming examples.

Table 10-1: Components of the ActiveX Data Object Model

Object Model	What It's Used For
ADODB — ActiveX Data Objects	Data manipulation Access and manipulate data through an OLE DB provider. With ADO objects you can connect to a data source and read, add, update, or delete data.
ADOX — ADO Extensions for DDL and Security	Data definition and security With ADOX objects you can define data such as tables, views, or indexes, as well as create and modify users and groups.
JRO — Jet and Replication Objects	Replication With JRO objects you can create, modify, and synchronize replicas. JRO can be used only with Microsoft Jet databases.

The ADODB library is the most commonly used object library, as it allows you to retrieve and manipulate data. Its objects are presented in Figure 10-1. If you installed Microsoft Office Access 2003 (or any other application in Office 2003), you should have ADO 2.5 installed on your computer.

Creating and Manipulating Databases with ADO

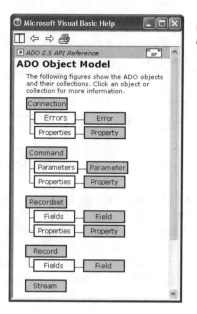

Figure 10-1: ADO Object Model.

To make sure that you have a reference to the ADODB Object Library, or to set up a reference to the ADOX and JRO Object Libraries, perform the tasks outlined in Hands-On 10-1.

◉ Hands-On 10-1: Setting Up a Reference to ADO Object Libraries

1. In the left pane of the Database window, select the **Modules** button and click **Create**.

2. From the Microsoft Visual Basic menu bar, choose **Tools | References**.

3. Make sure that **Microsoft ActiveX Data Objects 2.5 Library** is selected. Locate the entry by scrolling down the list, and click the check box to the left of the name to select it.

4. Click the check box to the left of **Microsoft ADO Ext. 2.5 for DDL and Security**.

5. From the list, select **Microsoft Jet and Replication Objects 2.5 Library**.

6. Click **OK**.

Establishing a Connection with the Data

Beore you can open a specific database in code to retrieve and manipulate data, you must establish a connection with the data source. You can do this by utilizing the ADO Connection object. You should begin by declaring an object variable of a Connection type, like this:

```
Dim conn As ADODB.Connection
```

The Connection object variable can be declared at procedure level or at module level. Recall that by declaring the variable at the top of the module you can reuse it in multiple procedures in your module.

Next, initialize the object variable by using the Set keyword:

```
Set conn = New ADODB.Connection
```

So far you've created a Connection object that doesn't point to any particular data source.

Next, you need to supply the connection information. When connecting to an unsecured Microsoft Jet database, this includes at least the Provider name and the Data Source name.

You can set the Connection object's Provider property to specify the name of the provider to be used to connect to the data source. In this example, we are connecting to a Microsoft Jet database, so we'll use the Microsoft.Jet .OLEDB.4.0 provider. The names of common data providers used with ADO are listed in Table 10-2. You need to specify additional information, such as the database path, to establish a connection by using the Connection object's ConnectionString property.

Table 10-2: Common data providers used with ADO

Provider Name	Provider Property	Description
Microsoft Jet	Microsoft.Jet.OLEDB.4.0	Used for Jet 4.0 databases. By default, this provider opens databases in Read/Write mode.
Microsoft SQL Server	SQLOLEDB	Used to access SQL Server 6.5, 7.0, and 2000 databases.
Oracle	MSDAORA	Used to access Oracle databases.
ODBC	MSDASQL	Used to access ODBC data sources without a specific OLE DB provider. This is the default provider for ADO.
Active Directory Service	ADSDSOObject	Used to access Windows NT 4.0 directory services, Novell Directory Services, and LDAP-compliant directory services.
Index Server	MSIDXS	Read-only access to Web data.

Here's the code fragment that specifies the minimum required connection information:

```
With conn
    .Provider = "Microsoft.Jet.OLEDB.4.0;"
    .ConnectionString = "Data Source=" & CurrentProject.Path & "\Northwind.mdb"
End With
```

Next, use the Connection object's Open method to open the connection to a data source:

```
conn.Open
```

ADO syntax is quite flexible. A connection to a database can also be opened like this:

```
conn.Open "Provider = Microsoft.Jet.OLEDB.4.0;" & _
    "Data Source=" & CurrentProject.Path & _
    "\Northwind.mdb"
```

As you can see in the code fragment above, the Provider name and the Data Source (path to the database) information is supplied as an argument when you call a Connection object's Open method.

Or you could open the connection like this:

```
With conn
    .Provider = "Microsoft.Jet.OLEDB.4.0;"
    .ConnectionString = "Data Source=" & CurrentProject.Path & "\Northwind.mdb"
    .Open
End With
```

After you open the connection to the database you can perform the required tasks. For now, let's display a message stating that the connection was opened:

```
MsgBox "Connection was opened."
```

When you are done with the database you connected to, you should close the connection like this:

```
conn.Close
```

The Close method of the Connection object closes the physical connection to the data source. To completely release the resources used by the Connection object, set the Connection object variable to Nothing, like this:

```
Set conn = Nothing
```

Now, to reinforce what you've just learned about establishing the connection with a data source, take a look at the three procedures below. Note that each one of these procedures performs the same task in a slightly different way. In this chapter, you will learn various methods of coding and supplying connection information.

```
Sub ConnectionExample1()
    Dim conn As ADODB.Connection

    Set conn = New ADODB.Connection

    With conn
        .Provider = "Microsoft.Jet.OLEDB.4.0;"
        .ConnectionString = "Data Source=" & _
            CurrentProject.Path & "\Northwind.mdb"
    End With

    conn.Open
    MsgBox "Connection was opened"
    conn.Close
    Set conn = Nothing
    MsgBox "Connection was closed"
End Sub
```

```
Sub ConnectionExample2()
    Dim conn As ADODB.Connection

    Set conn = New ADODB.Connection
    conn.Open "Provider = Microsoft.Jet.OLEDB.4.0;" & _
        "Data Source=" & CurrentProject.Path & _
        "\Northwind.mdb"
    MsgBox "Connection was opened"
    conn.Close
    Set conn = Nothing
    MsgBox "Connection was closed"
End Sub


Sub ConnectionExample3()
    Dim conn As ADODB.Connection
    Set conn = New ADODB.Connection
    With conn
      .Provider = "Microsoft.Jet.OLEDB.4.0;"
      .ConnectionString = "Data Source=" & _
          CurrentProject.Path & "\Northwind.mdb"
      .Open
    End With
    MsgBox "Connection was opened"
    conn.Close
    Set conn = Nothing
    MsgBox "Connection was closed"
End Sub
```

Opening a Microsoft Jet Database in Read/Write Mode

Hands-On 10-2 demonstrates how to use ADO to open a database for shared access (read/write). By default, the Connection object's Open method opens a database for shared access. The Open_ReadWrite procedure uses the Connection object's Mode property to explicitly specify the type of access to a database. The Mode property must be set prior to opening the connection because it is read-only once the connection is open. Connections can be opened read-only, write-only, or read/write. You can also specify whether other applications should be prevented from opening a connection. The value for the Mode property can be one of the constants/values specified in Table 10-3. The Mode property will work only if the provider you're using to open the connection supports it.

◉ Hands-On 10-2: Opening a Database in Read/Write Mode

1. Open the **Acc2003_Chap10.mdb** file from the book's downloadable files, or create a new Microsoft Office Access database from scratch.

2. In the Database window, press **Alt+F11** to switch to the Visual Basic Editor window.

3. In the Visual Basic Editor window, choose **Insert | Module**.

4. In the module's Code window, type the Open_ReadWrite procedure shown below.

5. Choose **Run | Run Sub/UserForm** to execute the procedure.

```
Sub Open_ReadWrite()
    Dim conn As ADODB.Connection
    Dim strDb As String

    On Error GoTo ErrorHandler
    strDb = CurrentProject.Path & "\Northwind.mdb"
    Set conn = New ADODB.Connection

    With conn
        .Provider = "Microsoft.Jet.OLEDB.4.0;"
        .Mode = adModeReadWrite
        .ConnectionString = "Data Source=" & strDb
        .Open
    End With
    MsgBox "Connection was opened."

    conn.Close
    Set conn = Nothing
    MsgBox "Connection was closed."

    Exit Sub
    ErrorHandler:
    MsgBox Err.Number & ": " & Err.Description
End Sub
```

Opening a Microsoft Jet Database in Read-Only Mode

If you'd like to open a database for read-only access you must set the Connection object's Mode property to the adModeRead constant (see Hands-On 10-3). ADO connections are opened by default for shared, updatable access. Eight mode constants are available to control the type of data access allowed.

Table 10-3: Intrinsic constants of the Connection object's Mode property

Constant Name	Value	Type of Permission
adModeUnknown	0	Permissions have not been set yet or cannot be determined. This is the default setting.
adModeRead	1	Read-only permissions
adModeWrite	2	Write-only permissions
adModeReadWrite	3	Read/write permissions
adModeShareDenyRead	4	Prevents others from opening the connection with read permissions
adModeShareDenyWrite	8	Prevents others from opening the connection with write permissions
adModeShareExclusive	12	Prevents others from opening the connection
adModeShareDenyNone	16	Prevents others from opening the connection with any permissions

⦿ Hands-On 10-3: Opening a Database in Read-Only Mode

1. In the Database window, press **Alt+F11** to switch to the Visual Basic Editor window.

2. In the Visual Basic Editor window, choose **Insert | Module**.

3. In the module's Code window, type the Open_ReadOnly procedure shown below.

4. Choose **Run | Run Sub/UserForm** to execute the procedure.

```
Sub Open_ReadOnly()
    Dim conn As ADODB.Connection
    Dim strDb As String

    On Error GoTo ErrorHandler
    strDb = CurrentProject.Path & "\Northwind.mdb"
    Set conn = New ADODB.Connection
    ' Open for read-only access
    With conn
        .Provider = "Microsoft.Jet.OLEDB.4.0;"
        .Mode = adModeRead
        .ConnectionString = "Data Source=" & strDb
        .Open
    End With
    MsgBox "Database was opened for read-only access."
    conn.Close
    Set conn = Nothing
    MsgBox "Database was closed."
    Exit Sub

ErrorHandler:
    MsgBox Err.Number & ": " & Err.Description
End Sub
```

Opening a Microsoft Jet Database Secured with a Password

If a database is secured with a password, you have to specify the Jet OLEDB:Database Password property as part of a ConnectionString property, like this:

```
"Jet OLEDB:Database Password=secret;"
```

Passwords are case sensitive. Hands-On 10-4 demonstrates how to open a Microsoft Access database after it has been secured with a password.

⦿ Hands-On 10-4: Opening a Password-Protected Database

1. Make a backup copy of the Northwind.mdb database and name it **NorthSecure.mdb**.

2. Open the **NorthSecure.mdb** database file with exclusive access. (Choose **File | Open**, switch to the folder containing the NorthSecure.mdb file, highlight the name of the file, click the arrow next to the Open button, and choose **Open Exclusive**.)

3. Set the database password to "Secret" by choosing **Tools | Security | Set Database Password** and typing **Secret**.

4. Close the NorthSecure database.

5. Switch back to the Acc2003_Chap10 database (see Hands-On 10-2) and press **Alt+F11** to activate the Visual Basic Editor window.

6. In the Visual Basic Editor window, choose **Insert | Module**.

7. In the module's Code window, type the Open_WithDbPassword procedure shown below.

8. Choose **Run | Run Sub/UserForm** to execute the procedure.

```
Sub Open_WithDbPassword()
    Dim conn As ADODB.Connection
    Dim strDb As String
    On Error GoTo ErrorHandler
    strDb = CurrentProject.Path & "\NorthSecure.mdb"
    Set conn = New ADODB.Connection
    With conn
        .Provider = "Microsoft.Jet.OLEDB.4.0;"
        .ConnectionString = "Data Source=" & strDb & ";" & _
            "Jet OLEDB:Database Password=secret;"
        .Open
    End With
    MsgBox "Password protected database was opened."
    conn.Close
    Set conn = Nothing
    MsgBox "Database was closed."
    Exit Sub
ErrorHandler:
    MsgBox Err.Number & ": " & Err.Description
End Sub
```

Opening a Microsoft Jet Database with User-Level Security

To open a database that is secured at the user level, you must supply the:

- Full path to the workgroup information file (system database)
- User ID
- Password

Specify the workgroup information file by using the Jet OLEDB:System Database property as shown in Hands-On 10-5.

⊚ Hands-On 10-5: Opening a Database Secured at the User Level

1. Create another backup copy of the original Northwind database file and name it **NorthSecureUser.mdb**.

2. Open the **NorthSecureUser.mdb** database and choose **Tools | Security | User-Level Security Wizard** to create a new workgroup information file.

3. Follow the steps of the Security Wizard. Do not change anything until you get to the screen asking for User Name and Password. Set up a user account named **Developer** with a password **WebMaster**, and click the **Add This User to The List** button. Click the **Next** button, assign Developer to the **Admin** group, and press the **Finish** button. Access will display the One-Step Security Wizard report. Print it out for your reference. Next, close the Microsoft Access application window with the NorthSecureUser database.

4. Switch back to the Acc2003_Chap10 database (see Hands-On 10-2) and press **Alt+F11** to activate the Visual Basic Editor window.

5. In the Visual Basic Editor window, choose **Insert | Module**.

6. In the module's Code window, type the Open_WithUserSecurity procedure shown below.

7. Choose **Run | Run Sub/UserForm** to execute the procedure.

```
Sub Open_WithUserSecurity()
    Dim conn As ADODB.Connection
    Dim strDb As String
    Dim strSysDb As String

    On Error GoTo ErrorHandler
    strDb = CurrentProject.Path & "\NorthSecureUser.mdb"
    strSysDb = CurrentProject.Path & "\Security.mdw"
    Set conn = New ADODB.Connection
    With conn
        .Provider = "Microsoft.Jet.OLEDB.4.0;"
        .ConnectionString = "Data Source=" & strDb & ";" & _
            "Jet OLEDB:System Database=" & strSysDb
        .Open , "Developer", "WebMaster"
    End With
    MsgBox "Secured database was opened."
    conn.Close
    Set conn = Nothing
    MsgBox "Database was closed."
    Exit Sub
ErrorHandler:
    MsgBox Err.Number & ": " & Err.Description
End Sub
```

As mentioned earlier, ADO syntax is very flexible. You can use various ways to specify property settings. The code snippet below demonstrates how to avoid formatting problems with long connection strings by using the Connection object's Properties collection.

```
With conn
    .Provider = "Microsoft.Jet.OLEDB.4.0;"
    .Properties("Jet OLEDB:System Database") = strSysDb
    .Open strDb, "Developer", "WebMaster"
End With
```

Notice that before you can reference provider-specific properties from the Connection object's Properties collection, you must indicate which provider you are using.

Opening a Microsoft Excel Spreadsheet

You can open external data sources supported by the Microsoft Jet database engine by using ADO and the Microsoft Jet 4.0 OLE DB provider. Use the Extended Properties of the Connection object to pass the connection string. Hands-On 10-6 demonstrates how to open a Microsoft Excel spreadsheet named C:\Report.xls by using ADO.

Hands-On 10-6: Opening an Excel Spreadsheet with ADO

This hands-on uses the Report.xls spreadsheet file included in the book's downloadable files. You can modify the procedure to use any other spreadsheet file.

1. In the Database window, press **Alt+F11** to switch to the Visual Basic Editor window.

2. In the Visual Basic Editor window, choose **Insert | Module**.

3. In the module's Code window, type the Open_ExcelSpread procedure shown below.

4. Choose **Run | Run Sub/UserForm** to execute the procedure.

```
Sub Open_ExcelSpread()
    Dim conn As ADODB.Connection
    Set conn = New ADODB.Connection
    conn.Open "Provider=Microsoft.Jet.OLEDB.4.0;" & _
        "Data Source=" & CurrentProject.Path & _
        "\Report.xls;" & _
        "Extended Properties=Excel 8.0;"
    MsgBox "Excel spreadsheet was opened."
    conn.Close
    Set conn = Nothing
    MsgBox "Excel spreadsheet was closed."
End Sub
```

Opening a dBASE File Using MSDASQL Provider

MSDASQL is the Microsoft OLE DB provider for ODBC. This provider works with all ODBC data sources. You can use MSDASQL to access data located in an external data source such as a dBASE file. When you connect to a database via the ODBC, you must specify the connection information. You do this by creating the DSN (Data Source Name) via the ODBC Administrator. The ODBC icon is located in the Windows Control Panel. If you are using Windows 2000 or Windows XP, open the Administrative Tools in the Control Panel, then click the Data Sources (ODBC) icon. The DSN contains information about database configuration, user security, and location. There are three types of DSNs:

- **User DSN** — A User DSN is stored locally in the Windows registry and limits database connectivity to the user who creates it.
- **File DSN** — All the information required to connect to the data source is stored in a DSN file that can be shared with other users. These files are stored by default in the Program Files\Common Files\Odbc\Data Sources folder. The File DSN provides access to multiple users and can be easily transferred from one server to another by copying DSN files.
- **System DSN** — A System DSN is stored locally in the Windows registry. The System DSN enables all users logged on to a particular server to access a database.

The procedure in Hands-On 10-7 illustrates how to open a dBASE file (Customer.dbf) via the ODBC data source named MyDbaseFile.

◎ Hands-On 10-7: Opening a dBASE file with ADO

1. Open the Control Panel, click **Administrative Tools**, and click **Data Sources (ODBC)**.

2. Click the **Add** button and add a **User DSN**.

3. Select **Microsoft dBASE driver (*.dbf)** and click **Finish**.

4. Enter the Data Source Name and Database Version as shown in Figure 10-2. Be sure to clear the Use Current Directory check box. Click the **Select Directory** button and move to the folder where the current Acc2003_Chap10.mdb file is located.

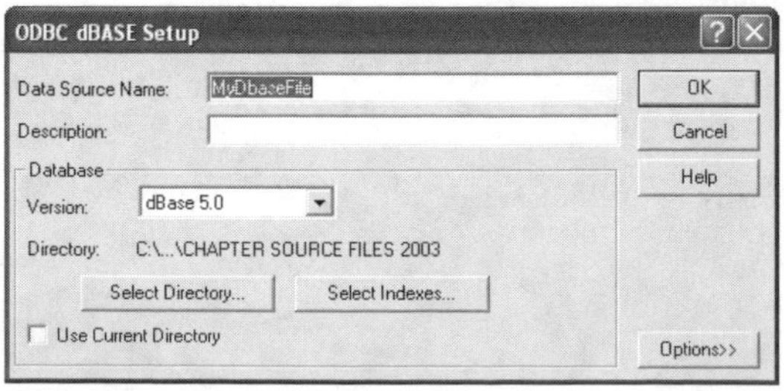

Figure 10-2: To access a data source programmatically by using the default provider (MSDASQL), you can specify the connection information by defining the Data Source Name (DSN).

5. Click **OK** to complete your entry and then close the ODBC Data Source Administrator dialog box.

6. Switch back to the Acc2003_Chap10 database and press **Alt+F11** to activate the Visual Basic Editor window.

7. In the Visual Basic Editor window, choose **Insert | Module**.

8. In the module's Code window, type the Open_dBaseFile procedure shown below.

9. Choose **Run | Run Sub/UserForm** to execute the procedure.

```
Sub Open_dBaseFile()
    Dim conn As ADODB.Connection
    Dim rst As ADODB.Recordset

    Set conn = New ADODB.Connection
    conn.Open "Provider=MSDASQL;DSN=MyDbaseFile;"
    Set rst = New ADODB.Recordset
    rst.Open "Customer.dbf", conn, , , adCmdTable
    Do Until rst.EOF
        Debug.Print rst.Fields(1).Value
        rst.MoveNext
    Loop
    rst.Close
    Set rst = Nothing
    conn.Close
    Set conn = Nothing
    MsgBox "The Immediate window contains the list of customers."
End Sub
```

After connecting to the external data source (dBASE), the Open_dBaseFile procedure opens a recordset based on the Customer.dbf table and writes the values of the first field of each record to the Immediate window. This procedure uses the Data Source Name (DSN) to connect to an external dBASE file. The DSN holds information about the location of the file as well as the required ODBC (Open Database Connectivity) driver. After connecting to the dBASE file, the procedure creates a Recordset object and uses its EOF property to loop through the recordset until the end of the file is reached. While looping, the procedure prints the values of each record's first field to the Immediate window. You will see more examples of using EOF properties in Chapter 14, "Working with Records."

Because users can modify or delete the DSN your program may fail, so it may be a better idea to use a so-called DSN-less connection. Instead of setting up a DSN, you can specify your ODBC driver and server in your connect string when using ADO. This is called a "DSN-less" ODBC connection because you do not need to set up a DSN to access your ODBC database server. All connection information is specified in code by using the DRIVER and DBQ parameters (for a dBASE connection). The following procedure demonstrates how to perform the same task as the above procedure by using a DSN-less connection to the dBASE file.

```
Sub Open_dBase_DSNLess()
    Dim conn As ADODB.Connection
    Dim rst As ADODB.Recordset

    Set conn = New ADODB.Connection
    conn.Open "DRIVER={Microsoft dBase Driver (*.dbf)};" & _
        "DBQ=" & CurrentProject.Path & "\"
    Debug.Print conn.ConnectionString
    Set rst = New ADODB.Recordset
    rst.Open "Select * From Customer.dbf", conn, _
        adOpenStatic, adLockReadOnly, adCmdText
    Do Until rst.EOF
        Debug.Print rst.Fields(1).Value
        rst.MoveNext
    Loop
    rst.Close
    Set rst = Nothing
    conn.Close
    Set conn = Nothing
    MsgBox "The Immediate window contains the list of customers."
End Sub
```

In the DSN-less connection shown above, you provide all the information required to open the connection. Notice that the dBASE filename is specified in the SQL statement.

Opening a Text File Using ADO

There are several ways to open text files programmatically. This section demonstrates how to gain access to a text file by using the Microsoft Text driver. Notice that this is a DSN-less connection (see the previous section for more information). All of the connection information is specified inside the program procedure. The following example procedure shows how to open a recordset based on a comma-separated file format and write the file contents to the Immediate window.

⊚ Hands-On 10-8: Opening a Text File with ADO

This hands-on uses the Employees.txt file provided in the book's downloadable files. This data file can be prepared from scratch by typing the following in Notepad and saving the file as Employees.txt:

"Last Name", "First Name", "Birthdate", "Years Worked"
"Krawiec","Bogdan",#1963-01-02#,3
"Górecka","Jadwiga",#1948-05-12#,1
"Olszewski","Stefan",#1957-04-07#,0

1. In the Visual Basic Editor window, choose **Insert | Module**.
2. In the module's Code window, type the Open_TextFile procedure shown below.

3. Choose **Run | Run Sub/UserForm** to execute the procedure.

```
Sub Open_TextFile()
    Dim conn As ADODB.Connection
    Dim rst As ADODB.Recordset
    Dim fld As ADODB.Field

    Set conn = New ADODB.Connection
    Debug.Print conn.ConnectionString
    conn.Open "DRIVER={Microsoft Text Driver (*.txt; *.csv)};" & _
    "DBQ=" & CurrentProject.Path & "\"
        Set rst = New ADODB.Recordset
    rst.Open "select * from [Employees.txt]", conn, adOpenStatic, _
        adLockReadOnly, adCmdText
    Do Until rst.EOF
        For Each fld In rst.Fields
            Debug.Print fld.Name & "=" & fld.Value
        Next fld
        rst.MoveNext
    Loop
    rst.Close
    Set rst = Nothing
    conn.Close
    Set conn = Nothing
    MsgBox "Open the Immediate window to view the data."
End Sub
```

Connecting to the Current Access Database

Microsoft Access provides a quick way to access the current database by referencing the ADO Connection object with the CurrentProject.Connection statement. This statement works only in VBA procedures created in Access. If you'd like to reuse your VBA procedures in other Microsoft Office or Visual Basic applications, you will be better off by using the standard way of creating a connection via an appropriate OLE DB provider.

The procedure in Hands-On 10-9 uses the CurrentProject.Connection statement to return a reference to the current database. Once the connection to the current database is established, the example procedure loops through the Properties collection of the Connection object to retrieve its property names and settings. The results are written both to the Immediate window and to a text file named C:\Propfile.txt.

◎ Hands-On 10-9: Establishing a Connection to the Current Access Database

1. In the Visual Basic Editor window, choose **Insert | Module**.

2. In the module's Code window, type the Connect_ToCurrentDb procedure shown below.

3. Choose **Run | Run Sub/UserForm** to execute the procedure.

```
Sub Connect_ToCurrentDb()
    Dim conn As ADODB.Connection
    Dim fs As Object
```

```
        Dim txtfile As Object
        Dim I As Integer

        Set conn = CurrentProject.Connection
        Set fs = CreateObject("Scripting.FileSystemObject")
        Set txtfile = fs.CreateTextFile("C:\Propfile.txt", True)

        For I = 0 To conn.Properties.Count - 1
            Debug.Print conn.Properties(I).Name & "=" & _
                conn.Properties(I).Value
            txtfile.WriteLine (conn.Properties(I).Name & "=" & _
                conn.Properties(I).Value)
        Next I
        MsgBox "Please check results in the " & _
            "Immediate window." & vbCrLf _
            & "The results have also been written to " _
            & "the 'C:\Propfile.txt' file."

        txtfile.Close
        Set fs = Nothing
        conn.Close
        Set conn = Nothing
    End Sub
```

To gain access to a computer's file system, the Connect_ToCurrentDb procedure uses the CreateObject function to access the Scripting.FileSystemObject. This function returns the FileSystemObject (fs). The CreateTextFile method of the FileSystemObject creates the TextStream object that represents a text file (txtfile). The WriteLine method writes each property and the corresponding setting to the newly created text file (C:\Propfile.txt). Finally, the Close method closes the text file.

Creating a New Access Database

You can create a new Microsoft Jet database programmatically by using the ADOX Catalog's Create method. The ADOX library is discussed in a later chapter. The Create method creates and opens a new ADO connection to the data source. An error will occur if the provider does not support creating new catalogs. The procedure in Hands-On 10-10 creates a new blank database named NewAccessDb.mdb in your computer's root directory. The error trap ensures that the procedure works correctly even if the specified file already exists. The VBA Kill statement is used to delete the file from your hard disk when the error is encountered.

◎ Hands-On 10-10: Creating a New Microsoft Access Database Using ADO

1. In the Visual Basic Editor window, choose **Insert | Module**.

2. In the module's Code window, type the CreateI_NewDatabase procedure shown below.

3. Choose **Run | Run Sub/UserForm** to execute the procedure.

```
' you must make sure that a reference to
' Microsoft ADO Ext. 2.5 for DDL and Security
' Object Library is set in the References dialog box

Sub CreateI_NewDatabase()
    Dim cat As ADOX.Catalog
    Dim strDb As String

    Set cat = New ADOX.Catalog
    strDb = "C:\NewAccessDb.mdb"

    On Error GoTo ErrorHandler
    cat.Create "Provider=Microsoft.Jet.OLEDB.4.0;" & _
        "Data Source=" & strDb
    MsgBox "The database was created (" & strDb & ")."
    Set cat = Nothing
    Exit Sub

ErrorHandler:
    If Err.Number = -2147217897 Then
        Kill strDb
        Resume 0
    Else
        MsgBox Err.Number & ": " & Err.Description
    End If
End Sub
```

While creating a database, you may specify that the database should be
encrypted by setting the Jet OLEDB:Encrypt Database property to True. You
can also include the database version information with the JetOLEDB:Engine
Type property. Simply include these properties in the connection string, as
shown in the following example:

```
cat.Create "Provider=Microsoft.Jet.OLEDB.4.0;" & _
    "Data Source=" & strDb & _
    "Jet OLEDB:Encrypt Database=True;" & _
    "Jet OLEDB:Engine Type=1;"
```

Copying a Database

ADO does not have a special method for copying files. However, you can set
up a reference to the Microsoft Scripting Runtime reference in the Microsoft
Visual Basic Editor screen to gain access to your computer file system, or use
the CreateObject function to access this library without setting up a reference.
The procedure in Hands-On 10-11 uses the CopyFile method of the
FileSystemObject from the Microsoft Scripting Runtime Library to copy
C:\NewAccessDb.mdb to the current folder on your computer. Recall that the
C:\NewAccessDb.mdb file was created by the Create_NewDatabase procedure
in Hands-On 10-10.

⊚ Hands-On 10-11: Copying a File

1. In the Visual Basic Editor window, choose **Insert | Module**.

2. In the module's Code window, type the Copy_AnyFile procedure shown below.

3. Choose **Run | Run Sub/UserForm** to execute the procedure.

```
Sub Copy_AnyFile()
    Dim fs As Object
    Dim strDb As String

    Set fs = CreateObject("Scripting.FileSystemObject")
    strDb = "C:\NewAccessDb.mdb"
    fs.CopyFile strDb, CurrentProject.Path & "\"
    Set fs = Nothing
End Sub
```

Connecting to an SQL Server

The ADO provides a number of ways of connecting to an SQL Server database. To access data residing on Microsoft SQL Server 6.5, 7.0, or 2000, you can use SQLOLEDB, which is the native Microsoft OLE DB provider for SQL.

⊚ Hands-On 10-12: Connecting to an SQL Server Database

1. In the Visual Basic Editor window, choose **Insert | Module**.

2. In the module's Code window, type the ConnectToSQL_SQLOLEDB procedure shown below.

3. Choose **Run | Run Sub/UserForm** to execute the procedure.

```
Sub ConnectToSQL_SQLOLEDB()
    Dim conn As ADODB.Connection

    Set conn = New ADODB.Connection
    ' Modify the connection information
    With conn
        .Provider = "SQLOLEDB"
        .ConnectionString = "Data Source=Mozartv4;" & _
            "database=Musicians; UserId=sa; Password=;"
        .Open
    End With
    If conn.State = adStateOpen Then
        MsgBox "Connection was established."
    End If
    conn.Close
    Set conn = Nothing
End Sub
```

Notice that in the example above, the Connection object's Provider property is set to SQLOLEDB and the ConnectionString property includes a server name, database name, user ID, and password information. You should modify the connection information in the connection string to connect to the SQL Server database you have access to.

Another way of connecting to an SQL database is by using the MSDASQL provider. This provider allows you to access any existing ODBC data sources. You can open a connection to your remote data source by using an ODBC DSN. This, of course, requires that you create a Data Source Name (DSN) entry on your workstation via the 32-bit ODBC tool in the Windows Control Panel (in Windows 2000, use Data Sources (ODBC), which is available in Administrative Tools in the Windows Control Panel).

The code example below opens then closes a connection with the remote data source based on a DSN named Pubs. You could skip setting the Provider property because MSDASQL is the default provider for ADO. All you really need to establish a connection in this case is a DSN.

```
With conn
    .Open "Provider=MSDASQL; DSN=Pubs"
    .Close
End With
```

DSN connections are inconvenient, as they require that you create a Data Source Name (DSN) on each user computer. Fortunately, there is a workaround. You can create a DSN-less connection independent of user workstations. Instead of creating a DSN on a user machine, simply provide all the connection information to the ODBC data source in your VBA code. See the two procedures in Hands-On 10-13 for the complete example of establishing DSN-less connections. (Review Hands-On 10-7 if you need more practice with DSN-less connections.)

◎ Hands-On 10-13: Connecting to an SQL Server Using a DSN-less Connection

1. In the Visual Basic Editor window, choose **Insert | Module**.

2. In the module's Code window, type the Connect_ToSQLServer and Connect_ToSQLServer2 procedures shown below.

3. Choose **Run | Run Sub/UserForm** to execute each procedure.

```
Sub Connect_ToSQLServer()
    Dim conn As ADODB.Connection

    Set conn = New ADODB.Connection
    With conn
        ' DSN-less connection using the ODBC driver
        ' (modify the data source information below)
        .Open "Driver={SQL Server};" & _
            "Server=11.22.17.153;" & _
            "UID=myId;" & _
            "PWD=myPassword;" & _
            "Database=SupportDb"
        .Close
    End With
```

```
        Set conn = Nothing
    End Sub

    Sub Connect_ToSQLServer2()
        Dim conn As ADODB.Connection

        Set conn = New ADODB.Connection
        With conn
            ' DSN-less connection using the SQLOLEDB provider
            ' (modify the data source information below)
            .Open "Provider=SQLOLEDB;" & _
                "DataSource=Mozart;" & _
                "Initial Catalog=MusicDb;" & _
                "UID=myId; Password=myPassword;"
            .Close
        End With
        Set conn = Nothing
    End Sub
```

Database Errors

In VBA, you can trap errors in your procedures by using the special On Error statements:

- On Error GoTo Label
- On Error Resume Next
- On Error GoTo 0

To determine the cause of the error, you need to check the value of the Number property of the VBA Err object. The Description property of the Err object contains the message for the encountered error number.

When using ADO to access data, in addition to the VBA Err object, you can get information about the errors from the ActiveX Data Objects (ADO) Error object. When an error occurs in an application that uses the ADO Object Model, an Error object is appended to the ADO Errors collection of the Connection object and you are advised about the error via a message box.

While the VBA Err object holds information only about the most recent error, the ADO Errors collection can contain several entries regarding the last ADO error. You can count the errors caused by an invalid operation by using the Count property of the Errors collection. By checking the contents of the Errors collection you can learn more information about the nature of the error. The Errors collection is available only from the Connection object. Errors that occur in ADO itself are reported to the VBA Err object. Errors that are provider-specific are appended to the Errors collection of the ADO Connection object. These errors are reported by the specific OLE DB provider when ADO objects are being used to access data.

The DBError procedure in Hands-On 10-14 attempts to open a nonexistent database to demonstrate the capability of the VBA Err object and the ADO Errors collection.

Creating and Manipulating Databases with ADO

◎ Hands-On 10-14: Using the VBA Err Object and ADO Errors Collection

1. In the Visual Basic Editor window, choose **Insert | Module**.

2. In the module's Code window, type the DBError procedure shown below.

3. Choose **Run | Run Sub/UserForm** to execute the procedure.

```
Sub DBError()
    Dim conn As New ADODB.Connection
    Dim errADO As ADODB.Error

    On Error GoTo CheckErrors
    conn.Open "Provider=Microsoft.Jet.OLEDB.4.0;" _
        & "Data Source=C:\my.mdb"
    CheckErrors:
    Debug.Print "VBA error number: " _
        & Err.Number & vbCrLf _
        & " (" & Err.Description & ")"
    Debug.Print "Listed below is information " _
        & "regarding this error " & vbCrLf _
        & "contained in the ADO Errors collection."
    For Each errADO In conn.Errors
        Debug.Print vbTab & "Error Number: " & errADO.Number
        Debug.Print vbTab & "Error Description: " & errADO.Description
        Debug.Print vbTab & "Jet Error Number: " & errADO.SQLState
        Debug.Print vbTab & "Native Error Number: " & errADO.NativeError
        Debug.Print vbTab & "Source: " & errADO.Source
        Debug.Print vbTab & "Help Context: " & errADO.HelpContext
        Debug.Print vbTab & "Help File: " & errADO.HelpFile
    Next
    MsgBox "Errors were written to the Immediate window."
End Sub
```

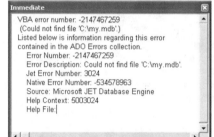

Figure 10-3: You can get information about the encountered ADO errors by looping through the Errors collection.

Compacting a Database

With frequent use over a period of time, the performance of your database may deteriorate. When objects are deleted from a database but the space isn't reclaimed, fragmentation may occur. To improve the database performance and to reduce the database file size, you can compact or repair Microsoft Office Access databases by using the ADO extension library, Microsoft Jet and Replication Objects (JRO). In order to work with this object library, choose Tools | References in the Visual Basic application window and select Microsoft Jet and Replication Objects 2.5 Library.

You can compact a Microsoft Jet database by using the CompactDatabase method of the JRO JetEngine object. To compact the database, first ensure that it is closed. Provide a new filename for the compacted database, then rename or delete the original and rename the compacted database to the original name. The procedure below demonstrates how to compact the Northwind database.

⊚ Hands-On 10-15: Compacting a Database

1. In the Visual Basic Editor window, choose **Insert** | **Module**.

2. In the module's Code window, type the CompactDb procedure shown below.

```
' use the References dialog box to set up a reference to the
' Microsoft Jet and Replication Objects Library

Sub CompactDb()
    Dim jetEng As JRO.JetEngine
    Dim strCompactFrom As String
    Dim strCompactTo As String
    Dim strPath As String

    strPath = CurrentProject.Path & "\"
    strCompactFrom = "Northwind.mdb"
    strCompactTo = "NorthwindComp.mdb"

    ' Make sure there isn't already a file with the
    ' name of the compacted database.
    On Error GoTo HandleErr

    ' Compact the database
    Set jetEng = New JRO.JetEngine
    jetEng.CompactDatabase "Data Source=" & _
        strPath & strCompactFrom & ";", _
        "Data Source=" & _
        strPath & strCompactTo & ";"

    ' Delete the original database
    Kill strPath & strCompactFrom
```

Creating and Manipulating Databases with ADO

```
        ' Rename the file back to the original name
        Name strPath & strCompactTo As strPath & strCompactFrom
        ExitHere:
        Set jetEng = Nothing
        MsgBox "Compacting completed."
        Exit Sub
    HandleErr:
        MsgBox Err.Number & ": " & Err.Description
        Resume ExitHere
    End Sub
```

Chapter Summary

In this chapter you were introduced to working with ActiveX Data Object libraries. You learned how to set up references to necessary object libraries using the References dialog box available from the Visual Basic Editor window. You also mastered the art of programmatically connecting to native Microsoft Access databases and files as well as to external databases and files. You saw how you can connect to various data sources using DSN and DSN-less connections. In addition, you created a brand new Microsoft Office Access database from scratch by using ADO. You also learned how to copy and compact a database and get information about the errors from ActiveX Data Objects.

In the next chapter, you will learn how to use ADO features to create and link tables, add and modify fields, and set up keys, indexes, and relationships between tables. In other words, you will learn which ADO objects can give you access to the structure of the database.

Chapter 11

Creating and Accessing Tables and Fields with ADO

To get going with your database design, you will need to access objects contained in the ADOX library. The full name of this library is ActiveX Data Object Extensions for DDL and Security. To use ADOX in your VBA procedures, choose Tools | References from your Visual Basic Editor screen and select Microsoft ADO Ext. 2.7 for DDL and Security. The ADOX Object Model is an extension of the ADODB library and is illustrated in Figure 11-1.

In this chapter you will use the ADOX library to programmatically create tables and add new fields.

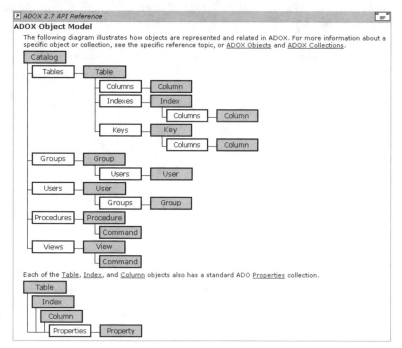

Figure 11-1: ADOX Object Model.

Creating a Microsoft Access Table

When you take a look at Figure 11-1 you will notice the Catalog object at the very top of the ADOX Object Model. The Catalog object is extremely important as it represents an entire database and contains database tables, columns, indexes, groups, users, procedures, and views. Use the ADOX Catalog object to create a table. The following steps outline the process of creating a new Microsoft Access table:

1. Declare the variables representing the Connection, Catalog, and Table objects:

```
Dim conn As ADODB.Connection
Dim cat As ADOX.Catalog
Dim tbl As ADOX.Table
```

2. Open the connection to your database:

```
set conn = New ADODB.Connection
conn.Open "Provider=Microsoft.Jet.OLEDB.4.0;" & _
    "Data Source=C:\NewAccessDb.mdb"
```

3. Supply the open connection to the ActiveConnection property of the ADOX Catalog object:

```
Set cat = New ADOX.Catalog
set cat.ActiveConnection = conn
```

4. Create a new Table object:

```
Set tbl = New ADOX.Table
```

5. Provide the name for your table:

```
tbl.Name = "tblAssets"
```

The Table object is a member of the Tables collection, which in turn is a member of the Catalog object. Each Table object has a Name property and a Type property. The Type property specifies whether a Table object is a standard Microsoft Access table, a linked table, a system table, or a view. To see an example of using the Type property, refer to the section called "Listing Database Tables" later in this chapter.

6. Append the Table object to the Catalog object's Tables collection:

```
cat.Tables.Append tbl
```

At this point your table is empty.

7. Add new fields (columns) to your new table:

```
With tbl.Columns
    .Append "SiteId", adVarWChar, 10
    .Append "Category", adSmallInt
    .Append "InstallDate", adDate
End With
```

The code fragment above creates three fields named SiteId, Category, and InstallDate. You can create new fields in a table by passing the Column object Name, Type, and DefinedSize properties as arguments of the Columns collection's Append method. Notice that ADOX uses different data types than those used in the Access user interface (see Table 11-1 for the comparison of data types).

The Table object contains the Columns collection that contains Column objects. To add a new field to a table you could create a Column object and write the following code:

```
Dim col As ADOX.Column
set col = New ADOX.Column
With col
    .Name = "SiteId"
    .DefinedSize = 10
End With
tbl.Columns.Append col
```

The last statement in the example above appends the new Column object (field) to the Columns collection of a table. The Name property specifies the name of the column. The DefinedSize property designates the maximum size of an entry in the column. To create another field, you would have to create a new Column object and set its properties. Creating fields in this manner takes longer and is less efficient than using the method demonstrated earlier.

Table 11-1: ADOX data types vs. Microsoft Access data types

ADOX Data Type	Corresponding Data Type in Access
adBoolean	Yes/No
adUnsignedTinyInt	Number (FieldSize = Byte)
adSmallInt	Number (FieldSize = Integer)
adSingle	Number (FieldSize = Single)
adDouble	Number (FieldSize = Double)
adDecimal	Number (FieldSize = Decimal)
adInteger	Number (FieldSize = LongInteger) AutoNumber
adCurrency	Currency
adVarWChar	Text
adDate	Date/Time
adLongVarBinary	OLE Object
dbMemo	Memo
adLongVarWChar	Hyperlink

◎ Hands-On 11-1: Creating a Table

1. Create a new Microsoft Office Access database or open the **Acc2003_Chap11.mdb** file from the book's downloadable files.

2. In the Database window, press **Alt+F11** to switch to the Visual Basic Editor window.

3. In the Visual Basic Editor window, choose **Insert | Module**.

4. In the module's Code window, type the Create_Table procedure shown below.

5. Choose **Run | Run Sub/UserForm** to execute the procedure.

```
' make sure to set up a reference to
' the Microsoft ADO Ext. 2.5 for DDL and Security
' Object Library

Sub Create_Table()
    Dim cat As ADOX.Catalog
    Dim myTbl As ADOX.Table

    On Error GoTo ErrorHandler

    Set cat = New Catalog
    cat.ActiveConnection = CurrentProject.Connection
    Set myTbl = New Table

    With myTbl
        .Name = "tblFilters"
        With .Columns
            .Append "Id", adVarWChar, 10
            .Append "Description", adVarWChar, 255
            .Append "Type", adInteger
        End With
    End With
    cat.Tables.Append myTbl

    Set cat = Nothing
    MsgBox "The new table 'tblFilters' was created."
    Exit Sub

ErrorHandler:
    If Err.Number = -2147217857 Then
        cat.Tables.Delete "tblFilters"
        Resume
    End If
    MsgBox Err.Number & ": " & Err.Description
End Sub
```

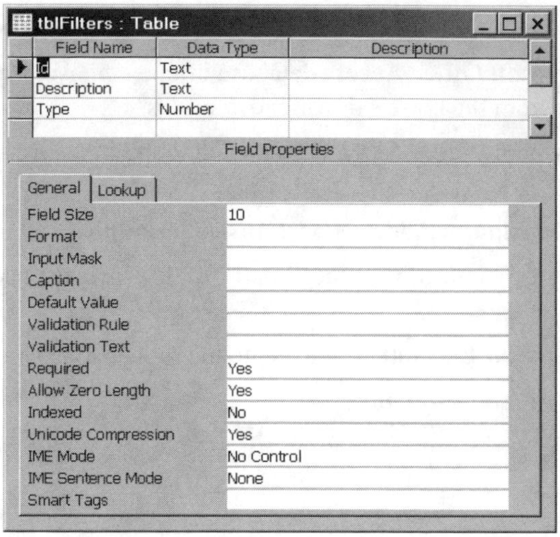

Figure 11-2: A Microsoft Access table can be created programmatically by using the Catalog object from the ADOX Object Library (see the procedure in Hands-On 11-1).

Copying a Table

The procedure in Hands-On 11-2 uses the SQL SELECT…INTO statement to select all records from the Customers table in the Northwind database into a new table called CustomersCopy. The SELECT…INTO statement is equivalent to a MakeTable query in the Microsoft Office Access user interface. This statement creates a new table and inserts data from other tables. To copy a table, the SQL statement is passed as the first argument of the Execute method of the Connection object. Note that the copied table will not have the indexes that may exist in the original table.

⊚ Hands-On 11-2: Making a Copy of a Table

➔ **Note:**   Make sure that the Northwind database is in the same folder as the currently open database, or change the path to the Northwind database in the procedure code.

1. In the Visual Basic Editor window, choose **Insert | Module**.
2. In the module's Code window, type the Copy_Table procedure shown below.
3. Choose **Run | Run Sub/UserForm** to execute the procedure.

```
Sub Copy_Table()
    Dim conn As ADODB.Connection
    Dim strTable As String
    Dim strSQL As String

    On Error GoTo ErrorHandler

    strTable = "Customers"
```

```
        strSQL = "SELECT " & strTable & ".* INTO "
        strSQL = strSQL & strTable & "Copy "
        strSQL = strSQL & "FROM " & strTable

        Debug.Print strSQL

        Set conn = New ADODB.Connection
        conn.Open "Provider=Microsoft.Jet.OLEDB.4.0;" & _
            "Data Source=" & CurrentProject.Path & _
            "\Northwind.mdb"

        conn.Execute strSQL
        conn.Close
        Set conn = Nothing
        MsgBox "The " & strTable & " table was copied."
        Exit Sub

ErrorHandler:
    If Err.Number = -2147217900 Then
        conn.Execute "DROP Table " & strTable
        Resume
    Else
        MsgBox Err.Number & ": " & Err.Description
    End If
End Sub
```

Deleting a Database Table

You can delete a table programmatically by opening the ADOX Catalog object, accessing its Tables collection, and calling the Delete method to remove the specified table from the Tables collection.

The procedure in Hands-On 11-3 requires a parameter that specifies the name of the table you want to delete.

◎ Hands-On 11-3: Deleting a Table from a Database

1. In the Visual Basic Editor window, choose **Insert | Module**.

2. In the module's Code window, type the Delete_Table procedure shown below.

```
Sub Delete_Table(strTblName As String)
    Dim cat As ADOX.Catalog

    On Error GoTo ErrorHandler
    Set cat = New ADOX.Catalog

    cat.ActiveConnection = CurrentProject.Connection
    cat.Tables.Delete strTblName
    Set cat = Nothing
    Exit Sub
```

```
ErrorHandler:
    MsgBox "Table '" & strTblName & _
        "' cannot be deleted " & vbCrLf & _
        "because it does not exist."
    Resume Next
End Sub
```

3. To run the above procedure, type the following statement in the Immediate window and press **Enter**:

```
Delete_Table("tblFilters")
```

When you press Enter, Visual Basic deletes the specified table from the current database. If the table does not exist, an appropriate message is displayed.

Adding New Fields to an Existing Table

At times you may want to programmatically add a new field to an existing table. The procedure below adds a new text field called MyNewField to a table located in the current database. The new field can hold 15 characters. For more information on adding fields to a table, refer to the section called "Creating a Microsoft Access Table" at the beginning of this chapter.

◉ Hands-On 11-4: Adding a New Field to a Table

The procedure in this hands-on references the tblFilters table in the Acc2003_Chap11 database. Since we deleted this table in the previous hands-on, you need to rerun the procedure in Hands-On 11-1 to recreate the table.

1. In the Visual Basic Editor window, choose **Insert | Module**.

2. In the module's Code window, type the Add_NewFields procedure shown below.

3. Choose **Run | Run Sub/UserForm** to execute the procedure.

```
Sub Add_NewFields()
    Dim cat As New ADOX.Catalog
    Dim myTbl As New ADOX.Table

    Set cat = New ADOX.Catalog
    cat.ActiveConnection = CurrentProject.Connection
    cat.Tables("tblFilters").Columns.Append _
        "MyNewField", adWChar, 15
    Set cat = Nothing
End Sub
```

Removing a Field from a Table

The procedure in Hands-On 11-5 illustrates how to access the ADOX Columns collection of a Table object and use the Columns collection Delete method to remove a field from a table. This procedure will fail if the field you want to delete is part of an index.

◉ Hands-On 11-5: Removing a Field from a Table

1. In the Visual Basic Editor window, choose **Insert | Module**.

2. In the module's Code window, type the Delete_Field procedure shown below.

3. Choose **Run | Run Sub/UserForm** to execute the procedure.

```
Sub Delete_Field()
    Dim cat As New ADOX.Catalog

    Set cat = New ADOX.Catalog
    cat.ActiveConnection = CurrentProject.Connection
    cat.Tables("tblFilters").Columns.Delete "Type"
    Set cat = Nothing
End Sub
```

A run-time error will occur if you attempt to delete a field that is part of an index. To see this error in action, open the tblFilters table and set a primary key on the Id column. Next, in the Delete_Field procedure, replace the statement:

```
cat.Tables("tblFilters").Columns.Delete "Type"
```

with the following line of code:

```
cat.Tables("tblFilters").Columns.Delete "Id"
```

and rerun the procedure.

Because there is an index on the Id field in the tblFilters table, Visual Basic cannot delete this field and the run-time error appears as shown in Figure 11-3.

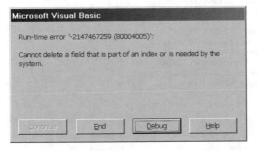

Figure 11-3: Visual Basic displays a run-time error when you attempt to delete a field that is part of an index.

To ensure that the deletion goes smoothly, include error trapping code that deletes the index if necessary. You will learn how to work with indexes by using ADO in Chapter 12.

Retrieving Table Properties

The Properties collection of an ADOX Table object allows you to set or retrieve table properties. The Properties collection exposes standard ADO properties as well as properties specific to the data provider. The following procedure accesses the table called tblFilters and lists its properties and their values in the Immediate window.

◉ Hands-On 11-6: Listing Table Properties

1. In the Visual Basic Editor window, choose **Insert | Module**.

2. In the module's Code window, type the List_TableProperties procedure shown below.

3. Choose **Run | Run Sub/UserForm** to execute the procedure.

```
Sub List_TableProperties()
    Dim cat As ADOX.Catalog
    Dim tbl As ADOX.Table
    Dim pr As ADOX.Property

    Set cat = New ADOX.Catalog
    Set cat.ActiveConnection = CurrentProject.Connection

    Set tbl = cat.Tables("tblFilters")

    ' retrieve table properties
    For Each pr In tbl.Properties
        Debug.Print tbl.Name & ": " & _
            pr.Name & "= "; pr.Value
    Next
    Set cat = Nothing
End Sub
```

```
Immediate                                                              [x]
tblFilters: Temporary Table= False
tblFilters: Jet OLEDB:Table Validation Text=
tblFilters: Jet OLEDB:Table Validation Rule=
tblFilters: Jet OLEDB:Cache Link Name/Password= False
tblFilters: Jet OLEDB:Remote Table Name=
tblFilters: Jet OLEDB:Link Provider String=
tblFilters: Jet OLEDB:Link Datasource=
tblFilters: Jet OLEDB:Exclusive Link= False
tblFilters: Jet OLEDB:Create Link= False
tblFilters: Jet OLEDB:Table Hidden In Access= False
|
```

Figure 11-4: You can list the names of table properties and their values programmatically as shown in Hands-On 11-6.

Retrieving Field Properties

The procedure in Hands-On 11-7 retrieves the field properties of the field named Id located in tblFilters in the current database.

Hands-On 11-7: Listing Field Properties

1. In the Visual Basic Editor window, choose **Insert | Module**.

2. In the module's Code window, type the List_FieldProperties procedure shown below.

3. Choose **Run | Run Sub/UserForm** to execute the procedure.

```
Sub List_FieldProperties()
    Dim cat As ADOX.Catalog
    Dim col As ADOX.Column
    Dim pr As ADOX.Property

    Set cat = New ADOX.Catalog
    Set cat.ActiveConnection = CurrentProject.Connection
    Set col = New ADOX.Column
    Set col = cat.Tables("tblFilters").Columns("Id")

    Debug.Print "Properties of the Id field " & _
        "(" & col.Properties.Count & ")"
    ' retrieve Field properties
    For Each pr In col.Properties
        Debug.Print pr.Name & "="; pr.Value
    Next

    Set cat = Nothing
End Sub
```

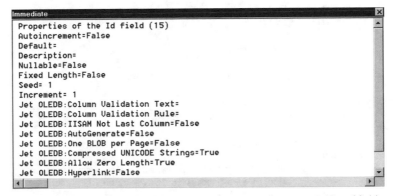

Figure 11-5: Running the procedure in Hands-On 11-7 generates a list of field properties and their values in the Immediate window.

Linking a Microsoft Access Table

In Microsoft Office Access 2003, you can create links to tables in Access databases as well as other data formats supported by Microsoft Jet's installable drivers (for example: Excel, dBASE, Paradox, Exchange/Outlook, Lotus, Text, and HTML) and ODBC drivers.

To create a linked Access table, you have to set the following table properties:

```
Jet OLEDB:LinkDatasource
Jet OLEDB:Remote Table Name
Jet OLEDB:CreateLink
```

The procedure in Hands-On 11-8 demonstrates how to establish a link to the Employees table located in the Northwind database.

◎ Hands-On 11-8: Linking a Microsoft Jet Table

1. In the Database window, press **Alt+F11** to switch to the Visual Basic Editor window.

2. In the Visual Basic Editor window, choose **Insert | Module**.

3. In the module's Code window, type the Link_JetTable procedure shown below.

4. Choose **Run | Run Sub/UserForm** to execute the procedure.

5. To access the linked Employees table after running this procedure, be sure to refresh the Database window by pressing **F5**.

```
Sub Link_JetTable()
    Dim cat As ADOX.Catalog
    Dim lnkTbl As ADOX.Table
    Dim strDb As String
    Dim strTable As String

    On Error GoTo ErrorHandler

    strDb = CurrentProject.Path & "\Northwind.mdb"
    strTable = "Employees"
    Set cat = New ADOX.Catalog
    cat.ActiveConnection = CurrentProject.Connection

    Set lnkTbl = New ADOX.Table
    With lnkTbl
        ' Name the new Table and set its ParentCatalog property to the
        ' open Catalog to allow access to the Properties collection.
        .Name = strTable
        Set .ParentCatalog = cat
```

```
        ' Set the properties to create the link
        .Properties("Jet OLEDB:Create Link") = True
        .Properties("Jet OLEDB:Link Datasource") = strDb
        .Properties("Jet OLEDB:Remote Table Name") = strTable
    End With

    ' Append the table to the Tables collection
    cat.Tables.Append lnkTbl

    Set cat = Nothing
    MsgBox "The current database contains a linked " & _
        "table named " & strTable
    Exit Sub

ErrorHandler:
    MsgBox Err.Number & ": " & Err.Description
End Sub
```

Linking a Microsoft Excel Spreadsheet

You can link an Excel spreadsheet to a Microsoft Access database by using the TransferSpreadsheet method of the DoCmd object, as shown in Hands-On 11-9. Note, however, that neither the DoCmd object nor its Transfer-Spreadsheet method are members of the ADO Object Model. The DoCmd object is built into the Microsoft Access library.

◎ Hands-On 11-9: Linking an Excel Spreadsheet

This hands-on uses the Regions.xls spreadsheet file provided in the book's downloadable files. You can revise the procedure to use any spreadsheet file that you have available.

1. In the Visual Basic Editor window, choose **Insert | Module**.

2. In the module's Code window, type the Link_ExcelSheet procedure shown below.

3. Choose **Run | Run Sub/UserForm** to execute the procedure.

```
Sub Link_ExcelSheet()
    Dim rst As ADODB.Recordset

    DoCmd.TransferSpreadsheet acLink, _
        acSpreadsheetTypeExcel8, _
        "mySheet", _
        CurrentProject.Path & "\Regions.xls", _
        -1, _
        "Regions!A1:B15"
```

```
Set rst = New ADODB.Recordset
With rst
    .ActiveConnection = CurrentProject.Connection
    .CursorType = adOpenKeyset
    .LockType = adLockOptimistic
    .Open "mySheet", , , , adCmdTable
End With

Do Until rst.EOF
    Debug.Print rst.Fields(0).Value, rst.Fields(1).Value
    rst.MoveNext
Loop
rst.Close
Set rst = Nothing
End Sub
```

The Link_ExcelSheet procedure begins by creating a linked table named mySheet from the specified range of cells (A1:B15), located in the Regions worksheet in the Regions.xls file. The –1 argument in the DoCmd statement indicates that the first row of the spreadsheet contains column headings. Next, the procedure uses the ADO Recordset object to retrieve the data from the mySheet table into the Immediate window. Notice that prior to opening the Recordset object, several properties of the Recordset object must be set.

■ The ActiveConnection property sets the reference to the current database.

■ The CursorType property specifies how the Recordset object should interact with the data source.

■ The adOpenKeyset setting tells Visual Basic that instead of retrieving all the records from the data source, only the keys are to be retrieved. The data for these keys is retrieved only as you scroll through the recordset. This guarantees better performance than retrieving big chunks of data at once.

■ The LockType property determines how to lock the data while it is being manipulated.

■ The adLockOptimistic setting locks the record only when you attempt to save it.

Opening the Recordset object also requires that you specify the data source. The data source in this procedure is the linked table named mySheet. The parameter passed depends on the source type used.

■ The adCmdTable setting indicates that all rows from the source table should be included.

You could also open the Recordset object by passing all the required parameters at once, as follows:

```
rst.Open "mySheet", _
CurrentProject.Connection, adOpenKeyset, _
adLockOptimistic, adCmdTable
```

Listing Database Tables

The procedure in Hands-On 11-10 generates a list of tables in the Northwind database. It uses the ADOX Catalog object to gain access to the database, then iterates through the Tables collection to retrieve the names of Access tables, system tables, and views. The ADOX Tables collection stores various types of Table objects, as shown in Table 11-2.

Table 11-2: Types of tables in the ADOX Tables collection

Name	Description
ACCESS TABLE	An Access system table
LINK	A linked table from a non-ODBC data source
PASS-THROUGH	A linked table from an ODBC data source
SYSTEM TABLE	A Microsoft Jet system table
TABLE	A Microsoft Access table
VIEW	A table from a row-returning, non-parameterized query

⊚ Hands-On 11-10: Creating a List of Database Tables

1. In the Visual Basic Editor window, choose **Insert | Module**.

2. In the module's Code window, type the ListTbls procedure shown below.

3. Choose **Run | Run Sub/UserForm** to execute the procedure.

```
Sub ListTbls()
    Dim cat As ADOX.Catalog
    Dim tbl As ADOX.Table

    Set cat = New ADOX.Catalog
    cat.ActiveConnection = "Provider=Microsoft.Jet.OLEDB.4.0;" & _
        "Data Source=" & CurrentProject.Path & _
        "\Northwind.mdb"

    For Each tbl In cat.Tables
        If tbl.Type <> "VIEW" And _
            tbl.Type <> "SYSTEM TABLE" And _
            tbl.Type <> "ACCESS TABLE" Then Debug.Print tbl.Name
    Next tbl
    Set cat = Nothing
    MsgBox "View the list of tables in the Immediate window."
End Sub
```

To list tables in your database you can also use the OpenSchema method of the ADO Connection object (see the section called "Listing Tables and Fields" later in this chapter).

Changing the AutoNumber

When you create a table in a Microsoft Office Access 2003 database, you can assign an AutoNumber data type to a primary key field manually using the Access user interface. The AutoNumber is a unique sequential number (incremented by 1) or a random number assigned by Microsoft Access whenever a new record is added to a table. Microsoft Office Access 2003 allows you to set the start and step value of auto-increment fields programmatically by using Jet 4.0 SQL statements (see Chapter 19 for more information).

The procedure in Hands-On 11-11 opens the ADO Recordset object based on the Shippers table located in the Northwind database, retrieves the last used AutoNumber value, and determines the current step (increment) value in effect.

◉ Hands-On 11-11: Changing the Value of an AutoNumber

1. In the Visual Basic Editor window, choose **Insert | Module**.

2. In the module's Code window, type the ChangeAutoNumber procedure shown below.

3. Choose **Run | Run Sub/UserForm** to execute the procedure.

```
Sub ChangeAutoNumber()
    Dim conn As ADODB.Connection
    Dim rst As ADODB.Recordset
    Dim strSQL As String
    Dim beginNum As Integer
    Dim stepNum As Integer

    Set conn = New ADODB.Connection
    conn.Open "Provider = Microsoft.Jet.OLEDB.4.0;" & _
        "Data Source=" & CurrentProject.Path & _
        "\Northwind.mdb"

    Set rst = New ADODB.Recordset
    With rst
        .CursorType = adOpenKeyset
        .LockType = adLockReadOnly
        .Open "Shippers", conn
        .MoveLast
    End With
    beginNum = rst(0)
    rst.MovePrevious
    stepNum = beginNum - rst(0)
    MsgBox "Last Auto Number Value = " & beginNum & vbCr & _
        "Current Step Value = " & stepNum, vbInformation, _
        "AutoNumber"

    rst.Close
    conn.Close
    Set conn = Nothing
End Sub
```

Listing Tables and Fields

Earlier in this chapter you learned how to enumerate tables in the Northwind database by accessing the Tables collection of the ADOX Catalog object. The procedures in Hands-On 11-12 and 11-13 demonstrate how to use the OpenSchema method of the ADO Connection object to obtain more information about a database table and its fields.

◉ Hands-On 11-12: Using the OpenSchema Method to List Database Tables

1. In the Visual Basic Editor window, choose **Insert | Module**.

2. In the module's Code window, type the ListTbls2 procedure shown below.

3. Choose **Run | Run Sub/UserForm** to execute the procedure.

```
Sub ListTbls2()
    ' This procedure lists database tables using the OpenSchema method
    Dim rst As ADODB.Recordset
    Set rst = CurrentProject.Connection.OpenSchema(adSchemaTables)

    Do Until rst.EOF
        Debug.Print rst.Fields("TABLE_TYPE") & " ->" _
            & rst.Fields("TABLE_NAME")
        rst.MoveNext
    Loop
End Sub
```

Obtaining the names of fields requires that you use adSchemaColumns as the parameter for the OpenSchema method. The ListTblsAndFields procedure in Hands-On 11-13 retrieves the names of fields in each table of the Northwind database.

◉ Hands-On 11-13: Listing Tables and Their Fields Using the OpenSchema Method

1. In the Visual Basic Editor window, choose **Insert | Module**.

2. In the module's Code window, type the ListTblsAndFields procedure shown below.

3. Choose **Run | Run Sub/UserForm** to execute the procedure.

```
Sub ListTblsAndFields()
    Dim conn As ADODB.Connection
    Dim rst As ADODB.Recordset
    Dim curTable As String
    Dim newTable As String
    Dim counter As Integer

    Set conn = New ADODB.Connection
    conn.Open "Provider=Microsoft.Jet.OLEDB.4.0;" _
        & "Data Source=" & CurrentProject.Path & _
        "\Northwind.mdb"
```

```
Set rst = conn.OpenSchema(adSchemaColumns)
curTable = ""
newTable = ""
counter = 1
Do Until rst.EOF
   curTable = rst!table_Name
   If (curTable <> newTable) Then
      newTable = rst!table_Name
      Debug.Print "Table: " & rst!table_Name
      counter = 1
   End If
   Debug.Print "Field" & counter & ": " & rst!Column_Name
   counter = counter + 1
   rst.MoveNext
Loop
rst.Close
conn.Close
Set rst = Nothing
Set conn = Nothing
End Sub
```

Listing Data Types

The ListDataTypes procedure in Hands-On 11-14 uses the adSchemaProvider-
Types parameter of the ADO Connection object's OpenSchema method to list
the data types supported by the Microsoft Jet OLE DB 4.0 provider.

◎ Hands-On 11-14: Listing Data Types

1. In the Visual Basic Editor window, choose **Insert | Module**.

2. In the module's Code window, type the ListDataTypes procedure shown
   below.

3. Choose **Run | Run Sub/UserForm** to execute the procedure.

```
Sub ListDataTypes()
    Dim conn As ADODB.Connection
    Dim rst As ADODB.Recordset

    Set conn=New ADODB.Connection
    conn.Open "Provider=Microsoft.Jet.OLEDB.4.0;" _
        & "Data Source=" & CurrentProject.Path & _
        "\Northwind.mdb"
    Set rst=conn.OpenSchema(adSchemaProviderTypes)
    Do Until rst.EOF
       Debug.Print rst!Type_Name & vbTab _
            & "Size: " & rst!Column_Size
       rst.MoveNext
    Loop
```

```
        rst.Close
        conn.Close
        Set rst = Nothing
        Set conn = Nothing
    End Sub
```

Chapter Summary

This chapter has shown you how to programmatically create Microsoft Access tables by using ActiveX Data Objects. You learned how to add fields to your tables and define field data types. You found out how to list both tables and fields, and investigate their properties. In addition to creating new tables from scratch, you discovered how to work with linked tables. You also learned how to copy tables and transfer data from a Microsoft Excel spreadsheet to an Access table.

The next chapter will demonstrate how to create indexes and set up table relationships from your VBA code by using ADOX objects.

Chapter 12

Setting Up Indexes and Table Relationships with ADO

Besides allowing you to create tables (see Chapter 11), the ADOX Object Model includes objects designed for adding primary keys, indexes, and relationships.

Creating a Primary Key

A *primary key* uniquely identifies a row in a table. A primary key is an index with its Unique and PrimaryKey properties set to True. There can be only one primary key per table.

- To create new keys, use the Key object from the ADOX library.
- To determine whether the key is primary, foreign, or unique, use the Key object's Type property. For example, to create a primary key, set the Key object's Type property to adKeyPrimary.

The procedure in Hands-On 12-1 demonstrates how to add a primary key to the table called tblFilters.

◎ Hands-On 12-1: Creating a Primary Key

This hands-on adds a primary key to the tblFilters table created in Hands-On 11-1 in Chapter 11. Import the module containing the Create_Table procedure code from the Acc2003_Chap11.mdb file to the current database and execute the procedure to create the tblFilters table. Or if you prefer, re-enter the Create_Table procedure code in the current database and run the procedure to create the required table.

1. Create a new Microsoft Office Access database or open the **Acc2003_Chap12.mdb** file from the book's downloadable files.

2. In the Database window, press **Alt+F11** to switch to the Visual Basic Editor window.

3. In the Visual Basic Editor window, choose **Insert | Module**.

4. In the module's Code window, type the Create_PrimaryKey procedure shown below.

5. Choose **Run | Run Sub/UserForm** to execute the procedure.

```
Sub Create_PrimaryKey()
    Dim cat As New ADOX.Catalog
    Dim myTbl As New ADOX.Table
    Dim pKey As New ADOX.Key

    On Error GoTo ErrorHandler
    cat.ActiveConnection = CurrentProject.Connection
    Set myTbl = cat.Tables("tblFilters")

    With pKey
        .Name = "PrimaryKey"
        .Type = adKeyPrimary
    End With

    pKey.Columns.Append "Id"
    myTbl.Keys.Append pKey

    Set cat = Nothing
    Exit Sub

ErrorHandler:
    If Err.Number = -2147217856 Then
        MsgBox "The 'tblFilters' is open.", _
            vbCritical, "Please close the table"
    ElseIf Err.Number = -2147217767 Then
        myTbl.Keys.Delete pKey.Name
        Resume
    Else
        MsgBox Err.Number & ": " & Err.Description
    End If
End Sub
```

Notice that after setting the Name and Type properties of the Key object, the procedure appends the Id column to the Columns collection of the Key object. Next, the Key object itself is appended to the Keys collection of the table. Because errors could occur if a table is open or it already contains the primary key, the error handler is included to ensure that the procedure runs as expected.

Creating a Single-Field Index

You can programmatically add an index to a table by using the ADOX Index object.

Before creating an index, make sure the table is not open and that it does not already contain an index with the same name.

To define an index, perform the following:

- Append one or more columns to the index by using the Append method.
- Set the Name property of the Index object and define other index properties, if necessary.
- Use the Append method to add the Index object to the table's Indexes collection.

You can use the Unique property of the Index object to specify whether the index keys must be unique. The default value of the Unique property is False.

Another property, IndexNulls, lets you specify whether Null values are allowed in the index. This property can have one of the constants shown in Table 12-1.

Table 12-1: Intrinsic constants for the IndexNulls property of the ADOX Index object

Constant Name	Description
adIndexNullsAllow	You can create an index if there is a Null value in the index field (an error will not occur).
adIndexNullsDisallow (This is the default value)	You cannot create an index if there is a Null in the index for the column (an error will occur).
adIndexNullsIgnore	You can create an index if there is a Null in the index field (an error will not occur). The Ignore Nulls property in the Indexes window in the user interface will be set to Yes.
adIndexNullsIgnoreAny (This value is not supported by the Microsoft Jet Provider)	You can create an index if there is a Null value in the index field. The Ignore Nulls property in the Indexes window in the user interface will be set to No.

The Add_SingleFieldIndex procedure in Hands-On 12-2 demonstrates how to add a single-field index called idxDescription to the table tblFilters.

◉ Hands-On 12-2: Adding a Single-Field Index to an Existing Table

This procedure uses the tblFilters table (see Hands-On 12-1).

1. In the Visual Basic Editor window, choose **Insert | Module**.

2. In the module's Code window, type the Add_SingleFieldIndex procedure shown below.

3. Choose **Run | Run Sub/UserForm** to execute the procedure.

```
Sub Add_SingleFieldIndex()
    Dim cat As New ADOX.Catalog
    Dim myTbl As New ADOX.Table
    Dim myIdx As New ADOX.Index

    On Error GoTo ErrorHandler
    cat.ActiveConnection = CurrentProject.Connection
    Set myTbl = cat.Tables("tblFilters")

    With myIdx
        .Name = "idxDescription"
        .Unique = False
        .IndexNulls = adIndexNullsIgnore
        .Columns.Append "Description"
        .Columns(0).SortOrder = adSortAscending
    End With
    myTbl.Indexes.Append myIdx
```

```
        Set cat = Nothing
        Exit Sub

    ErrorHandler:
        If Err.Number = -2147217856 Then
            MsgBox "The 'tblFilters' cannot be open.", vbCritical, _
                "Close the table"
        ElseIf Err.Number = -2147217868 Then
            myTbl.Indexes.Delete myIdx.Name
            Resume 0
        Else
            MsgBox Err.Number & ": " & Err.Description
        End If
    End Sub
```

After setting the index properties, the Description column is appended to the index, and the index sort order is set to the default (adSortAscending). To set the index field's sort order to Descending, use the adSortDescending constant. Next, the index is appended to the Indexes collection of the Table object.

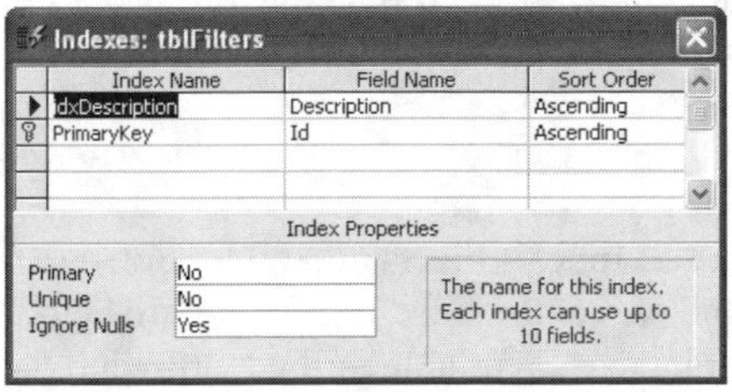

Figure 12-1: You can add indexes to an existing table programmatically by using the Key object from the ADOX Object Library. The indexes shown in this screen shot were created by running the procedures in Hands-On 12-1 and 12-2.

Adding a Multiple-Field Index to a Table

The procedure in Hands-On 12-2 demonstrated adding a single-field index to an existing table by using the ADOX Index object. You can also add a multiple-field index to a table as demonstrated in Hands-On 12-3.

Hands-On 12-3: Adding a Multiple-Field Index to an Existing Table

1. In the Visual Basic Editor window, choose **Insert | Module**.

2. In the module's Code window, type the Add_MultiFieldIndex procedure shown below.

3. Choose **Run | Run Sub/UserForm** to execute the procedure.

```
Sub Add_MultiFieldIndex()
    Dim conn As New ADODB.Connection

    With conn
        .Provider = "Microsoft.Jet.OLEDB.4.0"
        .Open "Data Source=" & CurrentProject.Path & _
            "\Northwind.mdb"
```

```
        ' Create a multifield Index named Location on City and Region fields.
        .Execute "CREATE INDEX Location ON Employees (City, Region);"
    End With

    conn.Close
    Set conn = Nothing
    MsgBox "New index (Location) was created."
End Sub
```

The Add_MultiFieldIndex procedure shown above declares the ADO Connection object and opens the connection to the Northwind database. Next, it uses the Execute method of the Connection object to run the DDL (Data Definition Language) CREATE INDEX SQL statement to add an index to the Employees table. Using SQL DDL statements is covered in detail in Part III of this book.

The CREATE INDEX statement has three parts. The name of the index to be created is followed by the keyword ON, the name of the existing table that will contain the index, and the name or names of the fields to be indexed. The field names should be listed in parentheses following the table name. The index is assumed to be ascending unless the DESC keyword is placed at the end of the CREATE INDEX statement.

Listing Indexes in a Table

The Indexes collection contains all Index objects of a table. You can retrieve all the index names from the Indexes collection. The procedure below demonstrates how to list the names of indexes available in the Northwind database's Employees table in the Immediate window.

◉ Hands-On 12-4: Listing Indexes in a Table

1. In the Visual Basic Editor window, choose **Insert | Module**.

2. In the module's Code window, type the List_Indexes procedure shown below.

3. Choose **Run | Run Sub/UserForm** to execute the procedure.

```
Sub List_Indexes()
    Dim conn As New ADODB.Connection
    Dim cat As New ADOX.Catalog
    Dim tbl As New ADOX.Table
    Dim idx As New ADOX.Index

    With conn
        .Provider = "Microsoft.Jet.OLEDB.4.0"
        .Open "Data Source=" & CurrentProject.Path & _
            "\Northwind.mdb"
    End With
    cat.ActiveConnection = conn
    Set tbl = cat.Tables("Employees")
```

```
For Each idx In tbl.Indexes
    Debug.Print idx.Name
Next idx

conn.Close
Set conn = Nothing
MsgBox "Indexes are listed in the Immediate window."
End Sub
```

Deleting Table Indexes

Although you can delete unwanted or obsolete indexes from the Indexes window in the Microsoft Office Access 2003 user interface, it is much faster to remove them programmatically.

The procedure in Hands-On 12-5 illustrates how to delete all but the primary key index from the Employees table located in the Northwind database.

⊚ Hands-On 12-5: Deleting Indexes from a Table

The procedure in this hands-on deletes all but the primary key index from the Employees table in the Northwind database. It is recommended that you prepare a backup copy of the original Northwind database prior to running this code.

1. In the Visual Basic Editor window, choose **Insert | Module**.

2. In the module's Code window, type the Delete_Indexes procedure shown below.

3. Choose **Run | Run Sub/UserForm** to execute the procedure.

```
Sub Delete_Indexes()
    ' This procedure deletes all but the primary key index
    ' from the Employees table in the Northwind database.
    ' Prior to running this procedure make a backup copy of
    ' the original Northwind database.

    Dim conn As New ADODB.Connection
    Dim cat As New ADOX.Catalog
    Dim tbl As New ADOX.Table
    Dim idx As New ADOX.Index
    Dim count As Integer

    With conn
        .Provider = "Microsoft.Jet.OLEDB.4.0"
        .Open "Data Source=" & CurrentProject.Path & _
            "\Northwind.mdb"
    End With

    cat.ActiveConnection = conn
Setup:
    Set tbl = cat.Tables("Employees")
```

```
Debug.Print tbl.Indexes.count
For Each idx In tbl.Indexes
    If idx.PrimaryKey <> True Then
        tbl.Indexes.Delete (idx.Name)
        GoTo Setup
    End If
Next idx

conn.Close
Set conn = Nothing
MsgBox "All Indexes but Primary Key were deleted."
End Sub
```

Notice that each time you delete an index from the table's Indexes collection you must set the reference to the table because current settings are lost when an index is deleted. Hence, the GoTo Setup statement sends Visual Basic to the Setup label to get the new reference to the Table object.

Creating Table Relationships

To establish a one-to-many relationship between tables, perform the following steps:

1. Use the ADOX Key object to create a foreign key and set the Type property of the Key object to adKeyForeign. A *foreign key* consists of one or more fields in a foreign table that uniquely identify all rows in a primary table.

2. Use the RelatedTable property to specify the name of the related table.

3. Use the Append method to add appropriate columns in the foreign table to the foreign key. A foreign table is usually located on the "many" side of a one-to-many relationship and provides a foreign key to another table in a database.

4. Set the RelatedColumn property to the name of the corresponding column in the primary table.

5. Use the Append method to add the foreign key to the Keys collection of the table containing the primary key.

The procedure in Hands-On 12-6 illustrates how to create a one-to-many relationship between two tables: Titles and Publishers.

◉ Hands-On 12-6: Creating a One-to-Many Relationship

1. In the current database, create the Titles and Publishers tables and add the fields as shown below:

Table Name	Field Name	Data Type	Size
Titles	TitleId	Text	8
Titles	PubId	Text	4
Titles	Title	Text	100
Titles	Price	Currency	

Table Name	Field Name	Data Type	Size
Publishers	PubId	Text	4
Publishers	PubName	Text	40
Publishers	City	Text	25
Publishers	Country	Text	25

2. Make **TitleId** the primary key for Titles and **PubId** the primary key for Publishers.

3. In the Visual Basic Editor window, choose **Insert | Module**.

4. In the module's Code window, type the CreateTblRelation procedure shown below.

5. Choose **Run | Run Sub/UserForm** to execute the procedure.

```
Sub CreateTblRelation()
    Dim cat As New ADOX.Catalog
    Dim fKey As New ADOX.Key

    On Error GoTo ErrorHandle

    cat.ActiveConnection = CurrentProject.Connection

    With fKey
        .Name = "fkPubId"
        .Type = adKeyForeign
        .RelatedTable = "Publishers"
        .Columns.Append "PubId"
        .Columns("PubId").RelatedColumn = "PubId"
    End With
    cat.Tables("Titles").Keys.Append fKey
    MsgBox "Relationship was created."

    Set cat = Nothing
    Exit Sub

ErrorHandle:
    cat.Tables("Titles").Keys.Delete "fkPubId"
    Resume
End Sub
```

You can view the relationship between the Publishers and Titles tables that was created by the above procedure in the Relationships window available in the Access user interface. To activate this window, switch to the Database window and choose Tools | Relationships or click the Relationships button on the toolbar. When the empty Relationships window appears, choose Relationships | Show Table. In the Show Table window, hold down the Ctrl key and click the Publishers and Titles table names. Click Add, then click Close. You should see the Publishers and Titles tables in the Relationships window linked together with a one-to-many relationship (see Figure 12-2).

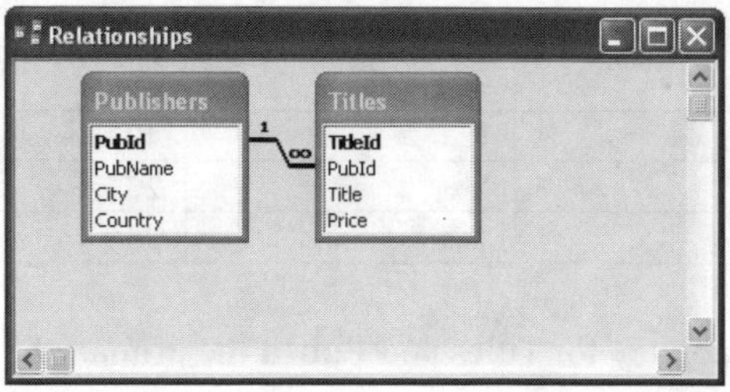

Figure 12-2: Table relationships can be created programmatically by accessing objects in the ADOX library (see the code in the CreateTblRelation procedure in Hands-On 12-6).

Chapter Summary

In this short chapter you acquired programming skills that enable you to create keys (primary keys and indexes) in Microsoft Access tables. You also learned how to use ADOX to establish a one-to-many relationship between tables.

In the next chapter, you will learn how to find and read database records.

Chapter 13

ADO Techniques for Finding and Reading Records

In order to work with data using ADO, you need to learn how to use the Recordset object to view and manipulate data. In this chapter, you will learn various methods of opening the Recordset object. You will also find out how to navigate in the recordset, and how to find, filter, read, and count the records.

Introduction to ADO Recordsets

The *Recordset object* represents a set of records in a table, or a set of records returned by executing a stored query or an SQL statement. The Recordset object is one of the three most-used ADO objects (the other two are Connection and Command). What you can do with a recordset depends entirely on the built-in capabilities of its OLE DB provider.

You can open a recordset by using the recordset's Open method. The information needed to open a recordset can be provided by first setting properties, then calling the Open method, or by using the Open method's parameters like this:

```
rst.Open [Source], [ActiveConnection], [CursorType], [LockType],
         [CursorLocation], [Options]
```

Notice that all the parameters are optional (they appear in square brackets). If you decide that you don't want to pass parameters, then you will need to use a different syntax to open a recordset. For example, examine the following code block:

```
With rst
    .Source = strSQL
    .ActiveConnection = strConnect
    .CursorType = adOpenStatic
    .LockType = adLockOptimistic
    .CursorLocation = adUseClient
    .Open Options := adCmdText
End with
```

The code segment above opens a recordset by first setting properties of the Recordset object, then calling its Open method. Notice that the names of the required recordset properties are equivalent to the parameter names listed earlier. The values assigned to each property are discussed later. You will become familiar with both methods of opening a recordset as you work with this chapter's example procedures.

Let's return to the syntax of the recordset's Open method, which specifies the parameters. Needless to say, you need to know what each parameter is and how it is used.

The Source parameter determines where you want your records to come from. The data source can be an SQL string, a table, a query, a stored procedure or view, a saved file, or a reference to a Command object. Later in this chapter you will learn how to open a recordset based on a table, a query, and an SQL statement.

The ActiveConnection parameter can be an SQL string that specifies the connection string or a reference to a Connection object. This parameter tells where to find the database as well as what security credentials to use.

Before we discuss the next three parameters, you need to know that the ADO recordsets are controlled by a cursor. The *cursor* determines whether you are permitted to scroll through the recordset backward and forward or forward only, or whether you can use it read-only or you can update the data, and whether changes made to the data are visible to other users.

The ADO cursors have three functions specified by the following parameters:

- CursorType
- LockType
- CursorLocation

Before you choose the cursor, you need to think of how your application will use the data. Some cursors yield better performance than others. It's important to determine where the cursor will reside and whether changes made while the cursor is open need to be visible immediately. The following subsection should help you in choosing the correct cursor.

Cursor Types

The CursorType parameter specifies how the recordset interacts with the data source and what is allowed or not allowed when it comes to data changes or movement within the recordset. This parameter can take one of four constants: adOpenForwardOnly (0), adOpenKeyset (1), adOpenDynamic (2), and adOpenStatic (3).

To quickly find out what types of cursors are available, switch to the Visual Basic window and open the Object Browser. Select ADODB from the Project/Library drop-down list box and type CursorType in the Search Text box, as shown in Figure 13-1.

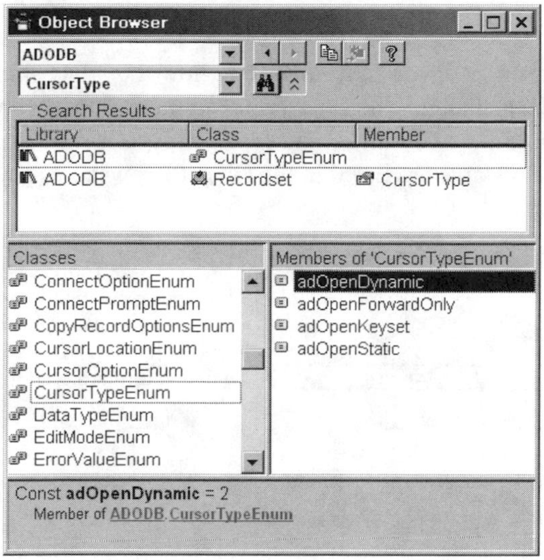

Creating and Manipulating Databases with ADO

Figure 13-1: The Object Browser lists four predefined constants you can use to specify the cursor type to be retrieved.

- When the cursor type is dynamic (adOpenDynamic = 2), users are allowed to view changes other users made to the database. The dynamic cursor is not supported by the Jet 4.0 engine in Microsoft Office Access. To use this cursor, you must use other OLE DB providers, such as MSDASQL or SQLOLEDB. Using the dynamic cursor you can move back and forth in the recordset.

- When the cursor type is forward-only (adOpenForwardOnly = 0), additions, changes, and/or deletions made by other users are not visible. This is the default and fastest cursor because it only allows you to scroll forward in the recordset.

- When the cursor type is keyset driven (adOpenKeyset = 1), you can scroll back and forth in the recordset; however, you cannot view records added or deleted by another user. Use the recordset's Requery method to overcome this limitation.

- When the cursor type is static (adOpenStatic = 3), all the data is retrieved as it was at a point in time. This cursor is desirable when you need to find data or generate a report. You can scroll back and forth within a recordset, but additions, changes, or deletions by other users are not visible. Use this cursor to retrieve an accurate record count.

You must set the CursorType property before opening the recordset with the Open method. Otherwise Access will create a forward-only recordset.

Lock Types

After you choose a cursor type, you need to specify how the ADO should lock the row when you make a change. The LockType parameter specifies whether the recordset is updatable. The default setting for LockType is read-only. The LockType predefined constants are listed in the Object Browser, as shown in Figure 13-2.

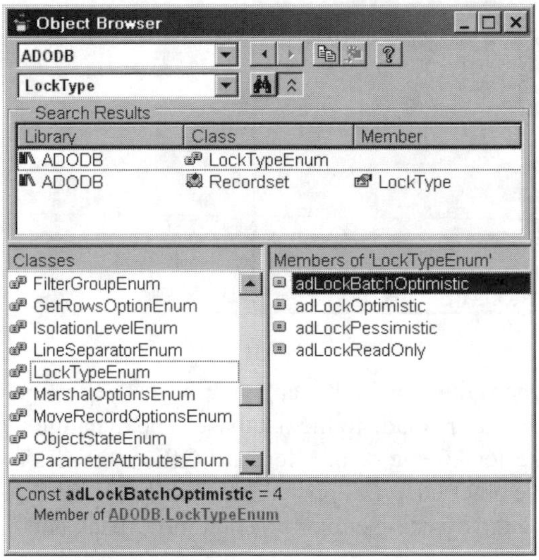

Figure 13-2: The Object Browser lists four predefined constants that you can use to specify what type of locking ADO should use when you make a change to the data.

- When the LockType property is batch optimistic (adLockBatchOptimistic = 4), batch updates made to the data are stored locally until the UpdateBatch method is called, during which all pending updates are committed all at once. Until the UpdateBatch method is called, no locks are placed on edited data. Batch optimistic locking eliminates network roundtrips that normally occur with optimistic locking (adLockOptimistic) when users make changes to one record and move to another. With batch optimistic locking a user can make all the changes to all the records, then submit them as a single operation.
- When the LockType property is optimistic (adLockOptimistic = 3), no locks are placed on the data until you attempt to save a row. Records are locked only when you call the Update method, and the lock is released as soon as the Save operation is completed. Two users are allowed to update a record at the same time. Optimistic locking allows you to work with one row at a time. If you need to make multiple updates, it's better to save them all at once by using batch optimistic locking.

■ When the LockType property is pessimistic (adLockPessimistic = 2), all the records are locked as soon as you begin editing a record. The record remains locked until the edit is committed or cancelled. This type of lock guarantees that two users will not make changes to the same record. If you use pessimistic locking, ensure that your code does not require any input from the users. You certainly don't want a scenario where a user opens a record and makes a change, then leaves for lunch without saving the record. In that case, the record is locked until the user comes back and saves or discards the edit. In this situation, it is better to use optimistic locking.

■ When the LockType property is read-only (adLockReadOnly =1), you will not be able to alter any data. This is the default setting.

Cursor Location

The CursorLocation parameter determines whether ADO or the SQL server database engine manages the cursor. Cursors use temporary resources to hold the data. These resources can be memory, a disk paging file, temporary disk files, or even temporary storage in the database.

■ When a cursor is created and managed by ADO, the recordset is said to be using a *client-side cursor* (adUseClient). With the client-side cursor, all the data is retrieved from the server in one operation and is placed on the client computer. Because all the requested data is available locally, the connection to the database can be closed and reopened only when another set of data is needed. Since the entire result set has been downloaded to the client computer, browsing through the rows is very fast.

■ When a cursor is managed by a database engine, the recordset is said to be using a *server-side cursor* (adUseServer). With the server-side cursor, all the data is stored on the server and only the requested data is sent over the network to the user's computer. This type of cursor can provide better performance than the client-side cursor when excessive network traffic is an issue. However, it's important to point out that a server-side cursor consumes server resources for every active client and, because it provides only single-row access to the data, it can be quite slow.

It is recommended that you use the server-side cursor for working with local Access databases, and the client-server cursor when working with remote Access databases or SQL Server databases.

The CursorLocation predefined constants are listed in the Object Browser, as shown in Figure 13-3.

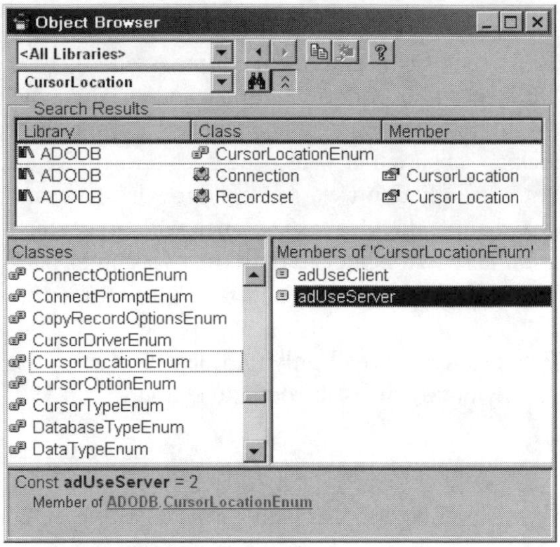

Figure 13-3: The Cursor-Location parameter of the recordset's Open method can be set by using the adUseClient or adUseServer constant.

The Options Parameter

The Options parameter specifies the data source type being used. Similar to the parameters related to cursors, the Options parameter can take one of many values, as outlined in Figure 13-4.

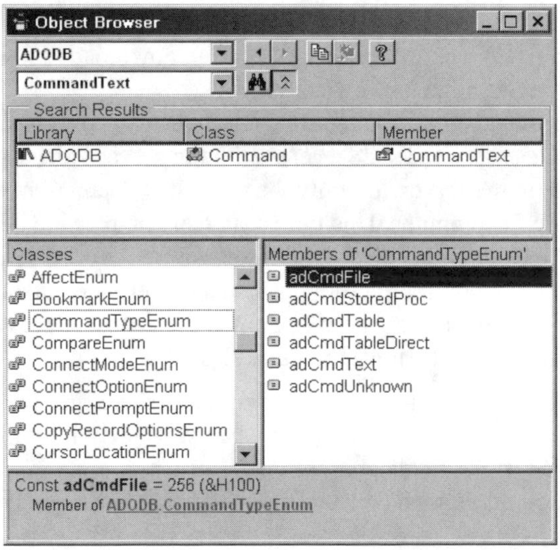

Figure 13-4: The Options parameter of the recordset's Open method is supplied by the constant values listed under the CommandText property of the Command object.

- When the Options parameter is set to adCmdFile (256), it tells the ADO that the source of the recordset is a path or filename. ADO can open recordsets based on files in different formats.
- When the Options parameter is set to adCmdStoredProc (4), it tells the ADO that the source of the recordset is a stored procedure or parameterized query.

■ When the Options parameter is set to adCmdTable (2), it tells the ADO that the source of the recordset is a table or view. The adCmdTable constant will cause the provider to generate an SQL query to return all rows from a table or view by prepending SELECT * FROM in front of the specified table or view name.

■ When the Options parameter is set to adCmdTableDirect (512), it tells the ADO that the Source argument should be evaluated as a table name. How does this constant differ from adCmdTable? The addCmdTableDirect constant is used by OLE DB providers that support opening tables directly by name, using an interface called IOpenRowset, instead of an ADO Command object. Since the IOpenRowset method does not need to build and execute a Command object, it results in increased performance and functionality.

■ When the Options parameter is set to adCmdText (1), it tells the ADO that you are using an SQL statement to open the recordset.

■ When the Options parameter is set to adCmdUnknown (8), it tells the ADO that the command type in the Source argument is unknown. This is the default, which is used if you don't specify any other option. By using the adCmdUnknown constant, or not specifying any constant at all for the Options parameter, you force ADO to make an extra roundtrip to the server to determine the source type. As you would expect, this will decrease your VBA procedure's performance; therefore you should use adCmdUknown only if you don't know what type of information the Source parameter will contain.

Note: Not all options are supported by all data providers. For example, the Microsoft Jet OLE DB Provider does not support the adCmdTableDirect cursors.

In addition to specifying the type of CommandText in the Options parameter (see Figure 13-4), you can pass additional information in the Options parameter. For example, telling ADO how to execute the CommandText property by specifying whether ADO should wait while all the records are being retrieved or should continue asynchronously.

Asynchronous Record Fetching

Asynchronous fetching is an ADO feature that allows some records to be downloaded to the client while the remaining records are still being fetched from the database. As soon as the user sees some records, he or she can begin paging through them. The user does not know that only a few records have been returned. As he or she pages through the rows backward and forward, a new connection is made to the server and more records are fetched and passed to the client. Once all records have been returned, paging is very quick because all records are on the client. Asynchronous fetching makes it seem to the user that the data retrieval is pretty fast. The downside is that records cannot be sorted until they have all been downloaded.

Additional Options parameters are listed and described below. Note that only the first three constants (adAsyncExecute, adAsyncFetch, and adAsyncFetchNonBlocking) can be used with the recordset's Open method. Other constants are used with the Command or Connection Execute method.

- adAsyncExecute (16) — This tells ADO to execute the command asynchronously, meaning that all requested rows are retrieved as soon as they are available. Using adAsyncExecute enables the application to perform other tasks while waiting for the cursor to populate.

  Note that the adAsyncExecute constant cannot be used with adCmdTableDirect.

- adAsyncFetch (32) — Using this constant requires that you specify a value greater than 1 for the recordset's CacheSize property. The CacheSize property is used to determine the number of records ADO will hold in local memory. For example, if the cache size is 100, the provider will retrieve the first 100 records after first opening the Recordset object. The adAsyncFetch constant tells ADO that the rows remaining after the initial quantity specified in the CacheSize property should be retrieved asynchronously.

- adAsyncFetchNonBlocking (64) — This option tells ADO that it should never wait for a row to be fetched. The application will continue execution while records are being continuously extracted from a very large data file. If the requested recordset row has not been retrieved yet, the current row automatically moves to the end of the file (causing the recordset's EOF property to become True). In other words, the data retrieval process will not block other processes.

  Note that adAsynchFetchNonBlocking has no effect when the adCmd-TableDirect option is used to open the recordset. Also, adAsyncFetchNon-Blocking is not supported with a Server cursor (adUseServer) when you use the ODBC provider (MSDASQL).

- adExecuteNoRecords (128) — This option tells ADO not to expect any records when the command is executed. Use this option for commands that do not return records, such as INSERT, UPDATE, or DELETE. Use the adExecuteNoRecords constant with adCmdText to improve the performance of your application. When this option is specified, ADO does not create a Recordset object and does not set any cursor properties.

  Note that adExecuteNoRecords can only be passed as an optional parameter to the Command or Connection Execute method and cannot be used when opening a recordset.

- adExecuteStream (256) — Indicates that the results of a Command execution should be returned as a stream. The adExecuteStream constant can only be passed as an optional parameter to the Command or Execute method and it cannot be used when opening a recordset.

- adExecuteRecord (512) — Indicates that the value of the CommandText property is a command or stored procedure that returns a single row as a Record object (a Record object represents one row of data).

■ adOptionUnspecified (–1) — Indicates that the command is unspecified. This is the default option.

Note that similar to adExecuteNoRecords, adExecuteStream, and adExecuteRecord, this constant can only be passed as an optional parameter to the Command or Connection Execute method and cannot be used when opening a recordset.

Opening a Recordset

ADO offers numerous ways of opening a Recordset object. To begin with, you can create ADO recordsets from scratch without going through any other object. Suppose you want to retrieve all the records from the Employees table. The code you need to write is very simple. Let's try this out in Hands-On 13-1.

◉ Hands-On 13-1: Opening a Recordset

1. Create a new Microsoft Office Access database or open the **Acc2003_ Chap13.mdb** file from the book's downloadable files. If you are creating a database from scratch, you should import the **Employees** table from the Northwind database.

2. In the Database window, press **Alt+F11** to switch to the Visual Basic Editor window.

3. In the Visual Basic Editor window, choose **Insert | Module**.

4. In the module's Code window, type the OpenRst procedure shown below.

5. Choose **Run | Run Sub/UserForm** to execute the procedure.

```
Sub OpenRst()
    Dim rst As ADODB.Recordset

    Set rst = New ADODB.Recordset
    With rst
        .Source = "Select * from Employees"
        .ActiveConnection = CurrentProject.Connection
        .Open
        Debug.Print rst.Fields.Count
        .Close
    End With
    Set rst = Nothing
End Sub
```

In the code example above, the first two lines declare a Recordset object and create a new instance of it. Next, the Source property specifies the data you want to retrieve. (The source can be a table, query, stored procedure, view, saved file, or Command object.)

The SQL SELECT statement tells VBA to select all the data from the Employees table. Next, the ActiveConnection property specifies how to connect to the data. Because the Employees table is located in the currently open database, you can use CurrentProject.Connection. Finally, the Open method retrieves the specified records into the recordset. Before we close the recordset using the recordset's Close method, we retrieve the number of fields in the open recordset by examining the recordset's Fields collection, and write the result to the Immediate window.

Opening a Recordset Based on a Table or Query

A recordset can be based on a table, view, SQL statement, or a command that returns rows. It can be opened via a Connection or Command object's Execute method or a recordset's Open method (see the example procedures below).

■ Connection.Execute method

```
Sub ConnectAndExec()
    Dim conn As ADODB.Connection
    Dim rst As ADODB.Recordset

    Set conn = New ADODB.Connection
    conn.Open "Provider=Microsoft.Jet.OLEDB.4.0;" & _
        "Data Source=" & CurrentProject.Path & _
        "\Northwind.mdb"
    Set rst = conn.Execute("Select * from Employees")
    Debug.Print rst.Source
    rst.Close
    Set rst = Nothing
    conn.Close
    Set conn = Nothing
End Sub
```

Note: Once you open the recordset, you can perform the required operation on its data. In this example, we use the recordset's Source property to write to the Immediate window the SQL command on which the recordset is based.

■ Command.Execute method

```
Sub CommandAndExec()
    Dim conn As ADODB.Connection
    Dim cmd As ADODB.Command
    Dim rst As ADODB.Recordset

    Set conn = New ADODB.Connection
    With conn
        .ConnectionString = "Provider=Microsoft.Jet.OLEDB.4.0;" & _
            "Data Source=" & CurrentProject.Path & "\Northwind.mdb"
        .Open
    End With

    Set cmd = New ADODB.Command
    With cmd
        .ActiveConnection = conn
        .CommandText = "Select * from Customers"
    End With

    Set rst = cmd.Execute
```

```
        MsgBox rst.Fields(1).Value

        rst.Close
        Set rst = Nothing
        conn.Close
        Set conn = Nothing
    End Sub
```

➡ **Note:** Once you open the recordset, you can perform the required operation on its data. In this example, we display a message with the name of the first customer.

■ Recordset.Open method

```
    Sub RecSetOpen()
        Dim rst As ADODB.Recordset
        Dim strConnection As String

        strConnection = "Provider=Microsoft.Jet.OLEDB.4.0;" & _
            "Data Source=" & CurrentProject.Path & _
            "\Northwind.mdb"

        Set rst = New ADODB.Recordset
        With rst
            .Open "Select * From Customers", _
                strConnection, adOpenForwardOnly
            .Save CurrentProject.Path & "\MyRst.dat"
            .Close
        End With
        Set rst = Nothing
    End Sub
```

➡ **Note:** Once you open the recordset, you can perform the required operation on its data. In this example, we save the entire recordset to a disk file named MyRst.data. In Chapter 16 you learn how to work with records that have been saved in a file.

The procedure in Hands-On 13-2 illustrates how to open a recordset based on a table or query.

◎ **Hands-On 13-2: Opening a Recordset Based on a Table or Query**

1. In the Database window, press **Alt+F11** to switch to the Visual Basic Editor window.

2. In the Visual Basic Editor window, choose **Insert | Module**.

3. In the module's Code window, type the OpenRst_TableOrQuery procedure shown below.

4. Choose **Run | Run Sub/UserForm** to execute the procedure.

```
Sub OpenRst_TableOrQuery()
    Dim conn As ADODB.Connection
    Dim rst As ADODB.Recordset

    Set conn = CurrentProject.Connection
    Set rst = New ADODB.Recordset

    rst.Open "Employees", conn

    Debug.Print "CursorType: " & rst.CursorType & vbCr _
        & "LockType: " & rst.LockType & vbCr _
        & "Cursor Location: " & rst.CursorLocation

    Do Until rst.EOF
        Debug.Print rst.Fields(1)
        rst.MoveNext
    Loop
    rst.Close
    Set rst = Nothing
    conn.Close
    Set conn = Nothing
End Sub
```

After opening the recordset, it's a good idea to check what type of recordset was created. Notice that the procedure above uses the CursorType, LockType, and CursorLocation properties to retrieve this information. After the procedure is run, the Immediate window displays:

```
CursorType: 0
LockType: 1
Cursor Location: 2
```

Notice that because you did not specify any parameters in the recordset's Open method, you obtained a default recordset. This recordset is forward-only (0), read-only (1), and server-side (2). (For more information, refer to the section titled "Opening a Recordset" earlier in this chapter.)

To create a different type of recordset, pass the appropriate parameters to the recordset's Open method. For example, if you open your recordset like this:

```
rst.Open "Employees", conn, adUseClient, adLockReadOnly
```

you will get the static (3), read-only (1), and client-side (2) recordset. In this recordset, you can easily find out the number of records by using the recordset's RecordCount property:

```
Debug.Print rst.RecordCount
```

Next, the procedure above uses the MoveNext method to iterate through all the records in the recordset until the end of file (EOF) is reached. The recordset's EOF property combined with a looping structure allows you to iterate through the recordset until the end of the file is reached.

Counting Records

Use the Recordset object's RecordCount property to determine the number of records in a recordset. If the number of records cannot be determined, this property will return –1. The RecordCount property setting depends on the cursor type and the capabilities of the provider. To get the actual count of records, open the recordset with the static (adOpenStatic) or dynamic (adOpenDynamic) cursor.

To quickly test the contents of the recordset, we write the employees' last names to the Immediate window. Since this recordset contains all the fields in the Employees table, you can add extra code to list the remaining field values.

Is This Recordset Empty?

A recordset may be empty. To check whether your recordset has any records in it, use the Recordset object's BOF and EOF properties. The BOF property stands for "beginning of file," and EOF indicates "end of file."

If you open a Recordset object that contains no records, the BOF and EOF properties are both set to True.

If you open a Recordset object that contains at least one record, the BOF and EOF properties are False and the first record is the current record.

You can use the following conditional statement to test whether there are any records:

```
If rst.BOF and rst.EOF Then
    MsgBox "This recordset contains no records"
End If
```

To open a recordset based on a saved query, replace the table name with your query name.

Opening a Recordset Based on an SQL Statement

The procedure in Hands-On 13-3 demonstrates how to use the Connection object's Execute method to open a recordset based on an SQL statement that selects all the employees from the Employees table in the sample Northwind database. Only the name of the first employee is written to the Immediate window. As in the preceding example, the resulting recordset is forward-only and read-only.

◎ Hands-On 13-3: Opening a Recordset Based on an SQL Statement

1. In the Database window, press **Alt+F11** to switch to the Visual Basic Editor window.

2. In the Visual Basic Editor window, choose **Insert | Module**.

3. In the module's Code window, type the CreateRst_WithSQL procedure shown below.

4. Choose **Run | Run Sub/UserForm** to execute the procedure.

```
Sub CreateRst_WithSQL()
    Dim conn As ADODB.Connection
    Dim rst As ADODB.Recordset
    Dim strConn As String

    strConn = "Provider = Microsoft.Jet.OLEDB.4.0;" & _
        "Data Source=" & CurrentProject.Path & _
        "\Northwind.mdb"

    Set conn = New ADODB.Connection
    conn.Open strConn

    Set rst = conn.Execute("Select * from Employees")
    Debug.Print rst("LastName") & ", " & rst("FirstName")

    rst.Close
    Set rst = Nothing
    conn.Close
    Set conn = Nothing
End Sub
```

Opening a Recordset Based on Criteria

Instead of retrieving all the records from a specific table or query, you can use the SQL WHERE clause to get the records that meet certain conditions. The procedure below calls the recordset's Open method to create a forward-only and read-only recordset populated with employees who do not have a manager.

◎ Hands-On 13-4: Opening a Recordset Based on Criteria

1. In the Database window, press **Alt+F11** to switch to the Visual Basic Editor window.

2. In the Visual Basic Editor window, choose **Insert | Module**.

3. In the module's Code window, type the OpenRst_WithCriteria procedure shown below.

4. Choose **Run | Run Sub/UserForm** to execute the procedure.

```
Sub OpenRst_WithCriteria()
    Dim conn As ADODB.Connection
    Dim rst As ADODB.Recordset
    Dim strConn As String

    strConn = "Provider=Microsoft.Jet.OLEDB.4.0;" & _
        "Data Source=" & CurrentProject.Path & _
        "\Northwind.mdb"

    Set conn = New ADODB.Connection
    conn.Open strConn

    Set rst = New ADODB.Recordset
    rst.Open "SELECT * FROM Employees WHERE ReportsTo is Null", _
```

```
                    conn, adOpenForwardOnly, adLockReadOnly

        Do While Not rst.EOF
            Debug.Print rst.Fields(1).Value
            rst.MoveNext
        Loop

        rst.Close
        Set rst = Nothing
        conn.Close
        Set conn = Nothing
    End Sub
```

Opening a Recordset Directly

If you are planning to open just one recordset from a specific data source, you can take a shortcut and open it directly without first opening a Connection object. This method requires you to specify the source and connection information prior to calling the Recordset object's Open method, as shown in Hands-On 13-5 below.

⊚ Hands-On 13-5: Opening a Recordset Directly

1. In the Visual Basic Editor window, choose **Insert | Module**.

2. In the module's Code window, type the OpenRst_Directly procedure shown below.

3. Choose **Run | Run Sub/UserForm** to execute the procedure.

```
Sub OpenRst_Directly()
Dim rst As ADODB.Recordset

    Set rst = New ADODB.Recordset
    With rst
        .Source = "Select * From Employees"
        .ActiveConnection = CurrentProject.Connection
        .Open
    End With
    MsgBox rst.Fields(1)

    rst.Close
    Set rst = Nothing
End Sub
```

You can also pass the required source and connection information to the Recordset object's Open method, as in the following example:

```
rst.Open "Select * From Employees", CurrentProject.Connection
```

Moving Around in a Recordset

You can navigate the ADO recordset by using the following five methods: MoveFirst, MoveLast, MoveNext, MovePrevious, and Move. The procedure in Hands-On 13-6 demonstrates how to move around in a recordset and retrieve the names of fields and their contents for each record.

⊚ Hands-On 13-6: Moving Around in a Recordset

1. In the Visual Basic Editor window, choose **Insert | Module**.

2. In the module's Code window, type the MoveAround procedure shown below.

3. Choose **Run | Run Sub/UserForm** to execute the procedure.

```
Sub MoveAround()
    Dim conn As ADODB.Connection
    Dim rst As ADODB.Recordset
    Dim fld As ADODB.Field
    Dim strConn As String

    strConn = "Provider=Microsoft.Jet.OLEDB.4.0;" & _
        "Data Source=" & CurrentProject.Path & _
        "\Northwind.mdb"

    Set conn = New ADODB.Connection
    conn.Open strConn

    Set rst = New ADODB.Recordset
    rst.Open "Select * from Customers where ContactTitle = 'Owner'", _
        conn, adOpenForwardOnly, adLockReadOnly
    Do While Not rst.EOF
        Debug.Print "New Record -------------"
        For Each fld In rst.Fields
            Debug.Print fld.Name & " = " & fld.Value
        Next
        rst.MoveNext
    Loop

    rst.Close
    Set rst = Nothing
    conn.Close
    Set conn = Nothing
End Sub
```

Finding the Record Position

Use the AbosolutePosition property of the Recordset object to determine the current record number. This property specifies the relative position of a record in an ADO recordset. The procedure in Hands-On 13-7 opens a recordset filled with employee records from the Employees table in the Northwind database and uses the AbsolutePosition property to return the record number three times during the procedure execution.

◎ Hands-On 13-7: Finding the Record Position

1. In the Visual Basic Editor window, choose **Insert | Module**.

2. In the module's Code window, type the FindRecordPosition procedure shown below.

3. Choose **Run | Run Sub/UserForm** to execute the procedure.

```
Sub FindRecordPosition()
    Dim conn As ADODB.Connection
    Dim rst As ADODB.Recordset
    Dim strConn As String

    strConn = "Provider=Microsoft.Jet.OLEDB.4.0;" & _
        "Data Source=" & CurrentProject.Path & _
        "\Northwind.mdb"

    Set conn = New ADODB.Connection
    conn.Open strConn

    Set rst = New ADODB.Recordset
    With rst
        .Open "Select * from Employees", conn, adOpenKeyset, _
            adLockOptimistic, adCmdText
    Debug.Print .AbsolutePosition
        .Move 3    ' move forward 3 records
        Debug.Print .AbsolutePosition
        .MoveLast ' move to the last record
        Debug.Print .AbsolutePosition
        Debug.Print .RecordCount
        .Close
    End With

    Set rst = Nothing
    conn.Close
    Set conn = Nothing
End Sub
```

Notice that at the beginning of the recordset, the record number is 1. Next, the FindRecordPosition procedure uses the Move method to move the cursor three rows ahead, after which the AbsolutePosition property returns 4 (1 + 3) as the current record position. Finally, the MoveLast method is used to move the cursor to the end of the recordset. The AbsolutePosition property now determines that this is the ninth record (9). The RecordCount property of the Recordset object returns the total number of records (9).

Reading Data from a Field

Use the Fields collection of a Recordset object to retrieve the value of a specific field in an open recordset. The procedure in Hands-On 13-8 uses the Do While loop to iterate through the recordset and prints the names of all the employees to the Immediate window.

⊚ Hands-On 13-8: Retrieving Field Values

1. In the Visual Basic Editor window, choose **Insert | Module**.

2. In the module's Code window, type the ReadField procedure shown below.

3. Choose **Run | Run Sub/UserForm** to execute the procedure.

```
Sub ReadField()
    Dim conn As ADODB.Connection
    Dim rst As ADODB.Recordset

    Set conn = CurrentProject.Connection

    Set rst = New ADODB.Recordset
    rst.Open "Select * from Employees", conn, adOpenStatic

    Do While Not rst.EOF
        Debug.Print rst.Fields("LastName").Value
        rst.MoveNext
    Loop

    rst.Close
    Set rst = Nothing
    conn.Close
    Set conn = Nothing
End Sub
```

Returning a Recordset as a String

Instead of using a loop to read the values of fields in all rows of the open recordset, you can use the Recordset object's GetString method to get the desired data in one step. The GetString method returns a recordset as a string-valued Variant. This method has the following syntax:

```
Variant = Recordset.GetString(StringFormat, NumRows, _
    ColumnDelimiter, RowDelimiter, NullExpr)
```

- The first argument (StringFormat) determines the format for representing the recordset as a string. Use the adAddClipString constant as the value for this argument.
- The second argument (NumRows) specifies the number of recordset rows to return. If blank, GetString will return all the rows.
- The third argument (ColumnDelimiter) specifies the delimiter for the columns within the row (the default column delimiter is tab (vbTab)).
- The fourth argument (RowDelimiter) specifies a row delimiter (the default is carriage return (vbCrLf)).
- The fifth argument (NullExpr) specifies an expression to represent Null values (the default is an empty string (" ")).

◎ Hands-On 13-9: Converting the Recordset to a String

1. In the Visual Basic Editor window, choose **Insert | Module**.

2. In the module's Code window, type the GetRecords_AsString procedure shown below.

3. Choose **Run | Run Sub/UserForm** to execute the procedure.

```
Sub GetRecords_AsString()
    Dim conn As ADODB.Connection
    Dim rst As ADODB.Recordset
    Dim varRst As Variant
    Dim fso As Object
    Dim myFile As Object

    Set conn = CurrentProject.Connection

    Set rst = New ADODB.Recordset
    rst.Open "SELECT EmployeeId, " & _
        "LastName & "", "" & FirstName as FullName " & _
        "FROM Employees", _
        conn, adOpenForwardOnly, adLockReadOnly, adCmdText

    If Not rst.EOF Then
        ' Return all rows as a formatted string with
        ' columns delimited by Tabs, and rows
        ' delimited by carriage returns

        varRst = rst.GetString(adClipString, , vbTab, vbCrLf)
        Debug.Print varRst
    End If

    ' save the recordset string to a text file
    Set fso = CreateObject("Scripting.FileSystemObject")
        Set myFile = fso.CreateTextFile(CurrentProject.Path & _
            "\RstString.txt", True)
    myFile.WriteLine varRst
    myFile.Close

    Set fso = Nothing
    rst.Close
    Set rst = Nothing
    conn.Close
    Set conn = Nothing
End Sub
```

The GetRecords_AsString procedure demonstrates how you can transform a recordset into a tab-delimited list of values using the Recordset object's GetString method. You can use any characters you want to separate columns and rows. This procedure uses the following statement to convert a recordset to a string:

```
varRst = rst.GetString(adClipString, , vbTab, vbCrLf)
```

Notice that the second argument is omitted. This indicates that we want to obtain all the records. To convert only three records to a string, you could write the following line of code:

```
varRst = rst.GetString(adClipString, 3, vbTab, vbCrLf)
```

The vbTab and vbCrLf arguments are VBA constants that denote the Tab and carriage return characters.

Because adClipString, vbTab, and vbCrLf are default values for the GetString method's arguments, you can skip them altogether. Therefore, to put all of the records in this recordset into a string, you can simply use the GetString method without arguments, like this:

```
varRst = rst.GetString
```

Sometimes you may want to save your recordset string to a file. To gain access to a computer's file system, the procedure uses the CreateObject function to access the FileSystemObject from the Microsoft Scripting Runtime Library. Using the CreateTextFile method of this object, you can easily create a File object. Notice that the second argument of the CreateTextFile method (True) indicates that the file should be overwritten if it already exists. Once you have defined your file, you can use the WriteLine method of the File object to write the text to the file. In this example, your text is the variable holding the contents of a recordset converted to a string.

Finding Records Using the Find Method

The ADO Object Model provides you with two methods for locating records: Find and Seek. This section demonstrates how to use the ADO Find method to locate all the employee records based on a condition. ADO has a single Find method. The search always begins from the current record or an offset from it. The search direction and the offset from the current record are passed as parameters to the Find method. The SearchDirection parameter can have the following values: adSearchForward and adSearchBackward.

◉ Hands-On 13-10: Finding Records Using the Find Method

1. In the Visual Basic Editor window, choose **Insert | Module**.

2. In the module's Code window, type the Find_WithFind procedure shown below.

3. Choose **Run | Run Sub/UserForm** to execute the procedure.

```
Sub Find_WithFind()
    Dim conn As ADODB.Connection
    Dim rst As ADODB.Recordset

    Set conn = New ADODB.Connection
    conn.Open "Provider=Microsoft.Jet.OLEDB.4.0;" & _
        "Data Source=" & CurrentProject.Path & _
        "\Northwind.mdb"
```

```
Set rst = New ADODB.Recordset
rst.Open "Employees", conn, adOpenKeyset, adLockOptimistic

' find the first record matching the criteria
rst.Find "TitleOfCourtesy ='Ms.'"
Do Until rst.EOF
    Debug.Print rst.Fields("LastName").Value
    ' search forward starting from the next record
    rst.Find "TitleOfCourtesy ='Ms.'", SkipRecords:=1, _
        SearchDirection:=adSearchForward
Loop

rst.Close
Set rst = Nothing
conn.Close
Set conn = Nothing
End Sub
```

To find the last record, call the MoveLast method before using Find. If none of the records meets the criteria, the current record is positioned before the beginning of the recordset (if searching forward) or after the end of the recordset (if searching backward). You can use the EOF or BOF properties of the Recordset object to determine whether a matching record was found.

The ADO Find method does not support the Is operator. To locate the record that has a Null value, use the equals (=) operator. For example:

```
' find records that do not have an entry in the ReportsTo field
rst.Find "ReportsTo = Null"

' find records that have data in the ReportsTo field
rst.Find " ReportsTo <> Null"
```

To find records based on more than one condition, use the Filter property of the Recordset object, as demonstrated in Hands-On 13-12 later in this chapter.

Finding Records Using the Seek Method

You can use the Recordset object's Seek method to locate a record based on an index. If you don't specify the index before searching, the primary key will be used. If the record is found, the current row position is changed to that row. The syntax of the Seek method looks like this:

```
recordset.Seek KeyValues, SeekOption
```

The first argument of the Seek method specifies the key values you want to find. The second argument specifies the type of comparison to be made between the columns of the index and the corresponding KeyValues.

The procedure in Hands-On 13-11 uses the Seek method to find the first company with an entry in the Region field equal to "SP":

```
rst.Seek "SP", adSeekFirstEQ
```

To find the last record that meets the same condition, use the following statement:

```
rst.Seek "SP", adSeekLastEQ
```

The type of Seek to execute is specified by the constants shown in Table 13-1.

Table 13-1: Seek constants

Constant	Value	Description
adSeekFirstEQ	1	Seeks the first key equal to KeyValues.
adSeekLastEQ	2	Seeks the last key equal to KeyValues.
adSeekAfterEQ	4	Seeks either a key equal to KeyValues or just after where that match would have occurred.
adSeekAfter	8	Seeks a key just after where a match with KeyValues would have occurred.
adSeekBeforeEQ	16	Seeks either a key equal to KeyValues or just before where that match would have occurred.
adSeekBefore	32	Seeks a key just before where a match with KeyValues would have occurred.

The Seek method is recognized only by the Microsoft Jet 4.0 databases. To determine whether the Seek method can be used to locate a row in a recordset, use the Recordset object's Supports method. This method determines whether a specified Recordset object supports a particular type of feature. The Boolean value of True indicates that the feature is supported; False indicates that it is not.

```
' find out if the recordset supports the Seek method
MsgBox rst.Supports(adSeek)
```

◎ Hands-On 13-11: Finding Records Using the Seek Method

1. In the Visual Basic Editor window, choose **Insert | Module**.

2. In the module's Code window, type the Find_WithSeek procedure shown below.

3. Choose **Run | Run Sub/UserForm** to execute the procedure.

```
Sub Find_WithSeek()
    Dim conn As ADODB.Connection
    Dim rst As ADODB.Recordset

    Set conn = New ADODB.Connection
    conn.Open "Provider=Microsoft.Jet.OLEDB.4.0;" & _
        "Data Source=" & CurrentProject.Path & _
        "\Northwind.mdb"

    Set rst = New ADODB.Recordset
    With rst
        .Index = "Region"
        .Open "Customers", conn, adOpenKeyset, adLockOptimistic, _
            adCmdTableDirect
```

```
        ' find out if this recordset supports the Seek method
        MsgBox rst.Supports(adSeek)
        .Seek "SP", adSeekFirstEQ
    End With

    If Not rst.EOF Then
        Debug.Print rst.Fields("CompanyName").Value
    End If

    rst.Close
    Set rst = Nothing
    conn.Close
    Set conn = Nothing
End Sub
```

If the Seek method is based on a multi-field index, use the VBA Array function to specify values for the KeyValues parameter. For example, the Order Details table in the Northwind database uses a multi-field index as the PrimaryKey. This index is a combination of the OrderId and ProductId fields. To find the order in which OrderId = 10295 and ProductId = 56, use the following statement:

```
rst.Seek Array(10295, 56), adSeekFirstEQ
```

Finding a Record Based on Multiple Conditions

ADO's Find method does not allow you to find records based on more than one condition. The workaround is using the Recordset object's Filter property to create a view of the recordset that only contains records matching the specified criteria. The procedure in Hands-On 13-12 uses the Filter property to find the female employees who live in the United States.

◉ Hands-On 13-12: Finding a Record Based on Multiple Criteria

1. In the Visual Basic Editor window, choose **Insert | Module**.

2. In the module's Code window, type the Find_WithFilter procedure shown below.

3. Choose **Run | Run Sub/UserForm** to execute the procedure.

```
Sub Find_WithFilter()
    Dim conn As ADODB.Connection
    Dim rst As ADODB.Recordset

    Set conn = New ADODB.Connection
    conn.Open "Provider=Microsoft.Jet.OLEDB.4.0;" & _
        "Data Source=" & CurrentProject.Path & _
        "\Northwind.mdb"

    Set rst = New ADODB.Recordset
    rst.Open "Employees", conn, adOpenKeyset, adLockOptimistic
    rst.Filter = "TitleOfCourtesy ='Ms.' and Country ='USA'"
    Do Until rst.EOF
        Debug.Print rst.Fields("LastName").Value
```

```
        rst.MoveNext
    Loop

    rst.Close
    Set rst = Nothing
    conn.Close
    Set conn = Nothing
End Sub
```

Using Bookmarks

When you work with database records you have to keep in mind that the actual number of records in a recordset can change at any time as new records are added or others are deleted. Therefore, you cannot save a record number to return to it later. Because records change all the time, the record numbers cannot be trusted. However, programmers often need to save the position of a record after they've moved to it or found it based on certain criteria. Instead of scrolling through every record in a recordset comparing the values, you can move directly to a specific record by using a bookmark. A *bookmark* is a value that uniquely identifies a row in a recordset.

Use the Bookmark property of the Recordset object to mark the record so you can return to it later. The Bookmark property is read-write, which means that you can get a bookmark for a record or set the current record in a Recordset object to the record identified by a valid bookmark. The recordset's Bookmark property always represents the current row. Therefore, if you need to mark more than one row for later retrieval, you may want to use an array to store multiple bookmarks (see Hands-On 13-13).

A single bookmark can be stored in a Variant variable. For example, when you get to a particular row in a recordset and decide that you'd like to save its location, store the recordset's bookmark in a variable, like this:

```
varMyBkmrk = rst.Bookmark
```

The varMyBkmrk is the name of a Variant variable declared with the following statement:

```
Dim varMyBkmrk As Variant
```

To retrieve the bookmark, move to another row, then use the saved bookmark to move back to the original row, like this:

```
rst.Bookmark = varMyBkmrk
```

Because not all ADO recordsets support the Bookmark property, you should use the Supports method to determine if the recordset does. Here's how:

```
If rst.Supports(adBookmark) then
    MsgBox "Bookmarks are supported."
Else
    MsgBox "Sorry, can't use bookmarks!"
End If
```

Recordsets defined with a Static or Keyset cursor always support bookmarks. If you remove the adOpenKeyset intrinsic constant from the code used in the next procedure (Hands-On 13-13), the default cursor (adOpenForwardOnly) will be used and you'll get an error because this cursor does not support bookmarks.

Another precaution to keep in mind is that there is no valid bookmark when the current row is positioned at the new row in a recordset. For example, if you add a new record with the following statement:

```
rst.AddNew
```

and then attempt to mark this record with a bookmark:

```
varMyBkmrk = rst.Book
```

you will get an error.

When you close the recordset, bookmarks you've saved become invalid. Also, bookmarks are unique to the recordset in which they were created. This means that you cannot use a bookmark created in one recordset to move to the same record in another recordset. However, if you clone a recordset (that is, you create a duplicate Recordset object), a Bookmark object from one Recordset object will refer to the same record in its clone. (See the section called "Cloning a Recordset" in Chapter 16.)

◎ Hands-On 13-13: Marking Records with a Bookmark

1. In the Visual Basic Editor window, choose **Insert | Module**.

2. In the module's Code window, type the TestBookmark procedure shown below.

3. Choose **Run | Run Sub/UserForm** to execute the procedure.

```
Sub TestBookmark()
    Dim rst As ADODB.Recordset
    Dim varMyBkmrk As Variant

    Set rst = New ADODB.Recordset
    rst.Open "Employees", _
        CurrentProject.Connection, adOpenKeyset

    If Not rst.Supports(adBookmark) Then
        MsgBox "This recordset does not support bookmarks!"
        Exit Sub
    End If

    varMyBkmrk = rst.Bookmark
    Debug.Print rst.Fields(1).Value

    ' Move to the 7th row
    rst.AbsolutePosition = 7
    Debug.Print rst.Fields(1).Value

    ' move back to the first row using bookmark
    rst.Bookmark = varMyBkmrk
```

```
        Debug.Print rst.Fields(1).Value
        rst.Close
        Set rst = Nothing
    End Sub
```

Notice that the procedure above uses the AbsolutePosition property of the Recordset object. The absolute position isn't the same as the record number. This property can change if a record with a lower number is deleted.

Using Bookmarks to Filter a Recordset

Bookmarks provide the fastest way of moving through rows. You can also use them to filter a recordset as shown in Hands-On 13-14.

⊙ Hands-On 13-14: Using Bookmarks to Filter Records

1. In the Visual Basic Editor window, choose **Insert | Module**.

2. In the module's Code window, type the Filter_WithBookmark procedure shown below.

3. Choose **Run | Run Sub/UserForm** to execute the procedure.

```
Sub Filter_WithBookmark()
    Dim rst As ADODB.Recordset
    Dim varMyBkmrk() As Variant
    Dim strConn As String
    Dim i As Integer
    Dim strCountry As String
    Dim strCity As String

    i = 0
    strCountry = "France"
    strCity = "Paris"

    strConn = "Provider=Microsoft.Jet.OLEDB.4.0;" & _
        "Data Source=" & CurrentProject.Path & _
        "\Northwind.mdb"

    Set rst = New ADODB.Recordset
    rst.Open "Customers", strConn, adOpenKeyset

    If Not rst.Supports(adBookmark) Then
        MsgBox "This recordset does not support bookmarks!"
        Exit Sub
    End If

    Do While Not rst.EOF
        If rst.Fields("Country") = strCountry And _
            rst.Fields("City") = strCity Then
            ReDim Preserve varMyBkmrk(i)
            varMyBkmrk(i) = rst.Bookmark
            i = i + 1
        End If
        rst.MoveNext
```

```
      Loop

      rst.Filter = varMyBkmrk()

      rst.MoveFirst
      Do While Not rst.EOF
         Debug.Print rst("CustomerId") & _
            " - " & rst("CompanyName")
         rst.MoveNext
      Loop
      rst.Close
      Set rst = Nothing
End Sub
```

Using the GetRows Method to Fill the Recordset

To retrieve multiple rows from a recordset, use the GetRows method, which returns a two-dimensional array. To find out how many rows were retrieved, use VBA's UBound function, as illustrated in Hands-On 13-15 below. Because arrays are zero-based by default, you must add one (1) to the result of the UBound function to get the correct record count.

Hands-On 13-15: Counting the Number of Returned Records

1. In the Visual Basic Editor window, choose **Insert | Module**.

2. In the module's Code window, type the CountRecords procedure shown below.

3. Choose **Run | Run Sub/UserForm** to execute the procedure.

```
Sub CountRecords()
    Dim conn As ADODB.Connection
    Dim rst As ADODB.Recordset
    Dim myarray As Variant
    Dim returnedRows As Integer
    Dim r As Integer 'record counter
    Dim f As Integer 'field counter

    Set conn = CurrentProject.Connection

    Set rst = New ADODB.Recordset
    rst.Open "SELECT * FROM Employees", _
        conn, adOpenForwardOnly, adLockReadOnly, adCmdText

    ' Return all rows into array
    myarray = rst.GetRows()
    returnedRows = UBound(myarray, 2) + 1

    MsgBox "Total number of records: " & returnedRows

    ' Find upper bound of second dimension
    For r = 0 To UBound(myarray, 2)
        Debug.Print "Record " & r + 1
        ' Find upper bound of first dimension
```

```
          For f = 0 To UBound(myarray, 1)
             ' Print data from each row in array
             Debug.Print Tab; _
                 rst.Fields(f).Name & " = " & myarray(f, r)
          Next f
       Next r

       rst.Close
       Set rst = Nothing
       conn.Close
       Set conn = Nothing
    End Sub
```

Notice how the CountRecords procedure prints the contents of the array to the Immediate window by using a nested loop.

Chapter Summary

In this chapter, you familiarized yourself with various methods of opening a recordset, moving around in a recordset, finding and filtering required records, and reading the contents of a recordset. You have also learned how to use the Recordset object's properties such as EOF, BOF, and RecordCount. In addition, you found out how to fill the recordset with the GetString and GetRows methods.

In the next chapter, you will gain experience performing such important data manipulation tasks as adding, modifying, copying, deleting, and sorting records.

Chapter 14

Working with Records

Now that you've familiarized yourself with various methods of opening a recordset, moving around in a recordset, finding required records, and reading the contents of a recordset, let's look at some examples of using ADO to perform such important tasks as adding, modifying, copying, deleting, and sorting records.

Adding a New Record

To add a new record, use the AddNew method of the Recordset object. Use the Update method if you are not going to add any more records. It is not necessary to call the Update method if you are moving to the next record. Calling the Move method implicitly calls the Update method before moving to the new record. For example, look at the following statements:

```
rst!LastName = "Smith"
rst.MoveNext
```

In the code fragment above, the Update method is automatically called when you move to the next record.

The procedure in Hands-On 14-1 demonstrates how to add a new record to the specified table.

Hands-On 14-1: Adding a New Record to a Table

1. Open the **Acc2003_Chap14.mdb** file from the book's downloadable files, or create this file from scratch using the Microsoft Office Access user interface.

2. Switch to the Visual Basic Editor window and insert a new module.

3. In the module's Code window, enter the Add_Record procedure as shown below.

```
' Use the References dialog box
' to set up a reference to the
' Microsoft ActiveX Data Objects Library

Sub Add_Record()
    Dim conn As ADODB.Connection
    Dim rst As ADODB.Recordset
    Dim strConn As String
```

```
    strConn = "Provider=Microsoft.Jet.OLEDB.4.0;" & _
        "Data Source=" & CurrentProject.Path & _
        "\Northwind.mdb"

    Set rst = New ADODB.Recordset
    With rst
        .Open "Select * from Employees", _
            strConn, adOpenKeyset, adLockOptimistic

        ' Add a record and specify some field values
        .AddNew
        !LastName = "Marco"
        !FirstName = "Paulo"
        !City = "Boston"

        ' Retrieve the Employee ID for the current record
        Debug.Print !EmployeeId.Value

        ' Move to the first record
        .MoveFirst
        Debug.Print !EmployeeId.Value
        .Close
    End With

    Set rst = Nothing
    Set conn = Nothing
End Sub
```

When adding or modifying records, you can set the record's field values in one of the following ways:

```
    rst.Fields("FirstName").value = "Paulo"
```

or

```
    rst!FirstName = "Paulo"
```

As mentioned earlier, when you use the AddNew method to add a new record and use the Move method, the newly added record is automatically saved without explicitly having to call the Update method. In the example procedure above we used the MoveFirst method to move to the first record; however, you can call any of the other move methods (Move, MoveNext, MovePrevious) to have ADO implicitly call the Update method. After calling the AddNew method, the new record becomes the current record.

Modifying a Record

To modify data in a specific field, find the record and set the value property of the required field to a new value. Always call the Update method if you are not planning to edit any more records. If you modify a row and then try to close the recordset without calling the Update method first, ADO will trigger a run-time error.

⊚ Hands-On 14-2: Modifying a Record

1. Switch to the Visual Basic Editor window and insert a new module.
2. In the Code window, enter the Update_Record procedure as shown below.

```
Sub Update_Record()
    Dim conn As ADODB.Connection
    Dim rst As ADODB.Recordset
    Dim strConn As String

    strConn = "Provider=Microsoft.Jet.OLEDB.4.0;" & _
        "Data Source=" & CurrentProject.Path & _
        "\Northwind.mdb"

    Set rst = New ADODB.Recordset

    With rst
        .Open "Select * from Employees Where LastName = 'Marco'", _
            strConn, adOpenKeyset, adLockOptimistic
        .Fields("FirstName").Value = "Paul"
        .Fields("City").Value = "Denver"
        .Fields("Country").Value = "USA"
        .Update
        .Close
    End With
    Set rst = Nothing
    Set conn = Nothing
End Sub
```

You can also modify several fields in a specific record by calling the Update method and passing it two arrays. The first array should specify the field names, the second one should list the new values to be entered. For example, the following statement updates the data in the FirstName, City, and Country fields with the corresponding values:

```
rst.Update Array("FirstName", "City", "Country"), Array("Paul", "Denver", "USA")
```

You can use the same technique with the AddNew method.

Canceling Changes to the Data

At times when working with records you will need to leave the record and discard the changes. To prevent ADO from automatically committing that row of data, call the recordset's CancelUpdate method. This method aborts any changes you've made to the current row.

Editing Multiple Records

ADO has the ability to perform batch updates. This means that you can edit multiple records and send them to the OLE DB provider in a single operation. To take advantage of batch updates, you must use the keyset or static cursor (see Chapter 13).

The procedure in Hands-On 14-3 finds all records in the Employees table where Title is "Sales Representative" and changes them to "Sales Rep." The changes are then committed to the database in a single update operation.

⊚ Hands-On 14-3: Performing Batch Updates

1. Switch to the Visual Basic Editor window and insert a new module.

2. In the Code window, enter the BatchUpdate_Records procedure as shown below.

```
Sub BatchUpdate_Records()
    Dim conn As ADODB.Connection
    Dim rst As ADODB.Recordset
    Dim strConn As String
    Dim strCriteria As String

    strConn = "Provider=Microsoft.Jet.OLEDB.4.0;" & _
        "Data Source=" & CurrentProject.Path & _
        "\Northwind.mdb"

    strCriteria = "[Title] = 'Sales Representative'"

    Set conn = New ADODB.Connection
    conn.Open strConn

    Set rst = New ADODB.Recordset

    With rst
        Set .ActiveConnection = conn
        .Source = "Employees"
        .CursorLocation = adUseClient
        .LockType = adLockBatchOptimistic
        .CursorType = adOpenKeyset
        .Open
        .Find strCriteria
        Do While Not .EOF
            .Fields("Title") = "Sales Rep"
            .Find strCriteria, 1
        Loop
        .UpdateBatch
    End With

    rst.Close
    Set rst = Nothing
    Set conn = Nothing
End Sub
```

The BatchUpdate_Records procedure uses the ADO Find method to locate all the records that need to be modified. Once the first record is located, it is changed in memory and the Find operation goes on to search for the next record and so on until the end of the recordset is reached. Notice that the following statement is issued to search past the current record:

```
.Find strCriteria, 1
```

Once all the records have been located and changed, the changes are all committed to the database in a single operation by issuing the UpdateBatch statement.

Updating Data: Differences between ADO and DAO

If you have ever used the older DAO Object Model to update and delete data (or plan on converting old DAO code to ADO), you must keep in mind how ADO differs from DAO in the way these operations are performed. In DAO, you were required to use the Edit method of the Recordset object prior to making any changes to your data. ADO does not require you to do this; consequently, there is no Edit method in ADO. Also, in ADO, if you modify a record, your changes are automatically saved. In DAO, leaving a row without first calling the Update method of the Recordset object will automatically discard your changes. You will find examples of working with DAO in the AppendixA.pdf file located in the book's downloadable files.

Deleting a Record

To delete a record, find the record you want to delete and call the Delete method. After you delete a record, it's still the current record. You must use the MoveNext method to move to the next row if you are planning to perform additional operations with your records. An attempt to do anything with the row that has just been deleted will generate a run-time error.

The procedure in Hands-On 14-4 deletes the record for Paul Marco which was added and then modified in earlier procedures.

⊙ Hands-On 14-4: Deleting a Record

1. Switch to the Visual Basic Editor window and insert a new module.

2. In the Code window, enter the Delete_Record procedure as shown below.

```
Sub Delete_Record()
    Dim conn As ADODB.Connection
    Dim rst As ADODB.Recordset
    Dim strConn As String
    Dim strCriteria As String

    strConn = "Provider=Microsoft.Jet.OLEDB.4.0;" & _
        "Data Source=" & CurrentProject.Path & _
        "\Northwind.mdb"

    Set conn = New ADODB.Connection
    Set rst = New ADODB.Recordset

    With rst
        .Open "Select * from Employees Where LastName ='Marco'", _
            strConn, adOpenKeyset, adLockOptimistic
        .Delete
        .Close
    End With
```

```
      Set rst = Nothing
      Set conn = Nothing
   End Sub
```

Copying Records to an Excel Spreadsheet

The procedure in Hands-On 14-5 uses automation to copy records from the Employees table to an Excel spreadsheet. Once the recordset is opened, the Excel part is handled by object variables that point to the Excel Application object (myExcel), Excel Workbook object (wkb), Excel Worksheet object (wks), and Excel Range object (StartRange). Before you can use any of these objects you must set a reference to the Microsoft Excel Object Library. The result of copying a recordset to a worksheet is shown following the procedure code.

⊚ Hands-On 14-5: Copying Records to an Excel Spreadsheet

1. Switch to the Visual Basic Editor window and insert a new module.

2. Choose **Tools | References** in the Visual Basic Editor window, scroll down to locate the Microsoft Excel Object Library, click the check box next to it, then click **OK** to exit.

3. In the Code window, enter the CopyToExcel procedure as shown below.

```
Option Compare Database
Option Explicit

' be sure to select Microsoft Excel Object Library
' in the References dialog box

Public myExcel As Excel.Application

Sub CopyToExcel()
   Dim conn As ADODB.Connection
   Dim rst As ADODB.Recordset
   Dim wbk As Excel.Workbook
   Dim wks As Excel.Worksheet
   Dim StartRange As Excel.Range
   Dim strConn As String
   Dim i As Integer
   Dim f As Variant

   On Error GoTo ErrorHandler

   strConn = "Provider=Microsoft.Jet.OLEDB.4.0;" & _
      "Data Source=" & CurrentProject.Path & _
      "\Northwind.mdb"

   Set conn = New ADODB.Connection

   ' open the recordset on the Employees table
   Set rst = New ADODB.Recordset
   With rst
```

Creating and Manipulating Databases with ADO

```
            .Open "Employees", strConn, _
                adOpenKeyset, adLockOptimistic
        End With

        ' declare a module-level object
        ' variable myExcel as Excel.Application
        ' at the top of the module
        Set myExcel = New Excel.Application

        ' create a new Excel workbook
        Set wbk = myExcel.Workbooks.Add

        ' set the reference to the ActiveSheet
        Set wks = wbk.ActiveSheet

        ' make the Excel application window visible
        myExcel.Visible = True

        i = 1

        ' Create the column headings in cells
        With rst
            For Each f In .Fields
                With wks
                    .Cells(1, i).Value = f.Name
                    i = i + 1
                End With
            Next
        End With

        ' specify the cell range that will receive the data (A2)
        Set StartRange = wks.Cells(2, 1)

        ' copy the records from the recordset
        ' and place in cell A2
        StartRange.CopyFromrecordset rst

        rst.Close
        Set rst = Nothing

        ' autofit the columns to make the data fit
        ' wks.Columns("A:Z").AutoFit
        wks.Columns.AutoFit

        ' close the workbook and save the file
        wbk.Close SaveChanges:=True, _
            FileName:="C:\ExcelDump.xls"

        ' quit the Excel application
        myExcel.Quit
        Set conn = Nothing
        Exit Sub

ErrorHandler:
    MsgBox Err.Description, vbCritical, _
        "Automation Error"
```

```
        Set myExcel = Nothing
        Exit Sub
    End Sub
```

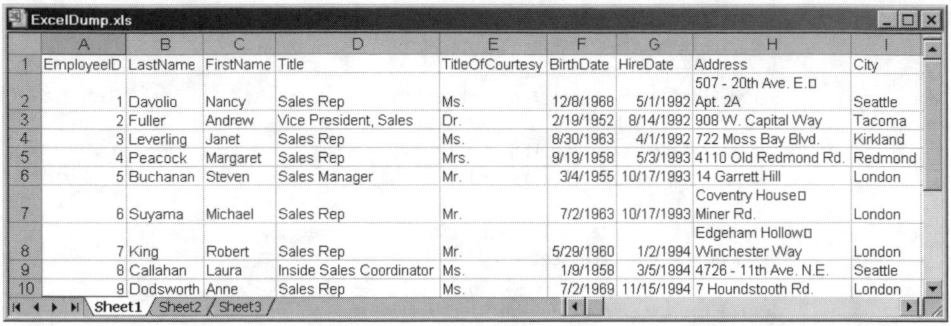

	A	B	C	D	E	F	G	H	I
1	EmployeeID	LastName	FirstName	Title	TitleOfCourtesy	BirthDate	HireDate	Address	City
2	1	Davolio	Nancy	Sales Rep	Ms.	12/8/1968	5/1/1992	507 - 20th Ave. E.□ Apt. 2A	Seattle
3	2	Fuller	Andrew	Vice President, Sales	Dr.	2/19/1952	8/14/1992	908 W. Capital Way	Tacoma
4	3	Leverling	Janet	Sales Rep	Ms.	8/30/1963	4/1/1992	722 Moss Bay Blvd.	Kirkland
5	4	Peacock	Margaret	Sales Rep	Mrs.	9/19/1958	5/3/1993	4110 Old Redmond Rd.	Redmond
6	5	Buchanan	Steven	Sales Manager	Mr.	3/4/1955	10/17/1993	14 Garrett Hill	London
7	6	Suyama	Michael	Sales Rep	Mr.	7/2/1963	10/17/1993	Coventry House□ Miner Rd.	London
8	7	King	Robert	Sales Rep	Mr.	5/29/1960	1/2/1994	Edgeham Hollow□ Winchester Way	London
9	8	Callahan	Laura	Inside Sales Coordinator	Ms.	1/9/1958	3/5/1994	4726 - 11th Ave. N.E.	Seattle
10	9	Dodsworth	Anne	Sales Rep	Ms.	7/2/1969	11/15/1994	7 Houndstooth Rd.	London

Sheet1 / Sheet2 / Sheet3 /

Figure 14-1: This Excel spreadsheet is created from Access data by running the procedure in Hands-On 14-5.

Copying Records to a Word Document

There are several techniques for placing Microsoft Access data in a Microsoft Office Word document. The procedure in Hands-On 14-6 demonstrates how to use the recordset's GetString method to insert data from the Shippers table into a newly created Word document. Another procedure (see Hands-On 14-7) shows how to format the output data using Word's Table object.

⊚ Hands-On 14-6: Copying Records to a Word Document (Example 1)

1. Switch to the Visual Basic Editor window and insert a new module.

2. Choose **Tools | References** in the Visual Basic Editor window, scroll down to locate the Microsoft Word Object Library, click the check box next to it, then click **OK** to exit.

3. In the Code window, enter the SendToWord procedure as shown below.

```
Option Compare Database
Option Explicit
' be sure to select Microsoft Word Object Library
' in the References dialog box

Public myWord As Word.Application

Sub SendToWord()
    Dim conn As ADODB.Connection
    Dim rst As ADODB.Recordset
    Dim doc As Word.Document
    Dim strSQL As String
    Dim varRst As Variant
    Dim f As Variant
    Dim strHead As String
```

Creating and Manipulating Databases with ADO

```
Set conn = New ADODB.Connection
Set rst = New ADODB.Recordset

conn.Provider="Microsoft.Jet.OLEDB.4.0;" & _
   "Data Source=" & CurrentProject.Path & _
   "\Northwind.mdb"

strSQL = "SELECT ShipperId as Id,"
strSQL = strSQL & "CompanyName as [Company Name],"
strSQL = strSQL & "Phone FROM Shippers"

conn.Open
rst.Open strSQL, conn, adOpenForwardOnly, _
   adLockReadOnly, adCmdText

' retrieve data and table headings into variables
If Not rst.EOF Then
   varRst = rst.GetString(adClipString, , vbTab, vbCrLf)
   For Each f In rst.Fields
      strHead = strHead & f.Name & vbTab
   Next
End If

' notice that Word application is declared
' at the top of the module
Set myWord = New Word.Application

' create a new Word document
Set doc = myWord.Documents.Add
myWord.Visible = True

' paste contents of variables into
' Word document
doc.Paragraphs(1).Range.Text = strHead & vbCrLf
doc.Paragraphs(2).Range.Text = varRst

   Set myWord = Nothing
End Sub
```

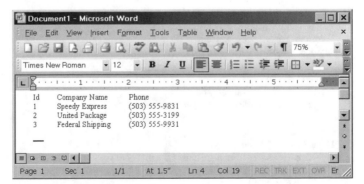

Figure 14-2: After running the procedure in Hands-On 14-6, the data
from the Shippers table is placed in a Word document.

Hands-On 14-7: Copying Records to a Word Document (Example 2)

1. In the same module where you entered the procedure in Hands-On 14-6, enter the SendToWord2 procedure as shown below.

```
Sub SendToWord2()
    Dim conn As ADODB.Connection
    Dim rst As ADODB.Recordset

    Dim doc As Word.Document
    Dim WordTbl As Word.Table
    Dim strSQL As String
    Dim f As Variant
    Dim numRows As Integer
    Dim numFields As Integer
    Dim r As Integer                    ' row counter
    Dim c As Integer                    ' column counter

    Set conn = New ADODB.Connection
    Set rst = New ADODB.Recordset

    conn.Provider="Microsoft.Jet.OLEDB.4.0;" & _
        "Data Source=" & CurrentProject.Path & _
        "\Northwind.mdb"

    strSQL = "SELECT * From Shippers"

    conn.Open
    rst.Open strSQL, conn, adOpenStatic, _
        adLockReadOnly, adCmdText

    rst.MoveLast
    rst.MoveFirst

    numRows = rst.RecordCount
    numFields = rst.Fields.Count

    ' notice that the Word application is declared
    ' at the top of the module
    Set myWord = New Word.Application

    ' create a new Word document
    Set doc = myWord.Documents.Add

    ' insert table
    Set WordTbl = doc.Tables.Add _
        (doc.Range, numRows + 1, numFields)

    c = 1
    If numRows > 0 Then
        ' Create the column headings in table cells
        For Each f In rst.Fields
            With WordTbl
                .Cell(1, c).Range.Text = f.Name
                c = c + 1
            End With
```

```
        Next f
    End If

    r = 2
    Do While Not rst.EOF
        For c = 1 To numFields
            WordTbl.Cell(r, c).Range.Text = rst.Fields(c - 1).Value
        Next c
        r = r + 1
        rst.MoveNext
    Loop

    myWord.Visible = True

    rst.Close
    Set rst = Nothing
    Set myWord = Nothing
    Set conn = Nothing
End Sub
```

Copying Records to a Text File

To write records to a text file, save them as a string by using the recordset's GetString method. Next, create a text file with the CreateTextFile method of the FileSystemObject.

The procedure in Hands-On 14-8 demonstrates how to write the records from the Order Details table in the Northwind database to a text file named "testfile." Figures 14-3 and 14-4 show the generated text file after it has been opened in Notepad and in Microsoft Office Excel.

◉ Hands-On 14-8: Copy Records to a Text File

1. In the Code window, enter the WriteToFile procedure as shown below.

```
Sub WriteToFile()
    Dim conn As ADODB.Connection
    Dim rst As ADODB.Recordset
    Dim f As ADODB.Field
    Dim fso As Object
    Dim txtfile As Object

    Set conn = New ADODB.Connection
    conn.Open "Provider=Microsoft.Jet.OLEDB.4.0;" & _
        "Data Source=" & CurrentProject.Path & _
        "\Northwind.mdb"

    Set fso = CreateObject("Scripting.FileSystemObject")
    Set txtfile = fso.CreateTextFile("c:\testfile.txt", True)

    Set rst = New ADODB.Recordset
    rst.Open "[Order Details]", conn
    With rst
        For Each f In .Fields
            ' Write field name to the text file
```

```
            txtfile.Write (f.Name)
            txtfile.Write Chr(9)
         Next
         ' move to a new line
         txtfile.WriteLine
         ' write out all the records to the text file
         txtfile.Write rst.GetString(adClipString)
         .Close
      End With

      txtfile.Close
      Set rst = Nothing
      conn.Close
      Set conn = Nothing
   End Sub
```

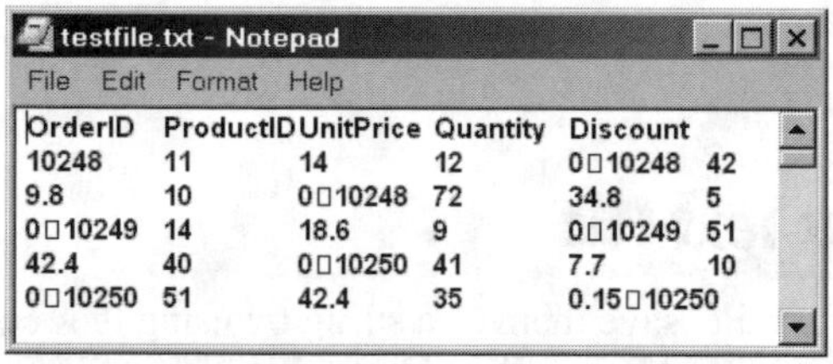

Figure 14-3: After running the WriteToFile procedure in Hands-On 14-8, the records from the Order Details table are placed in a text file.

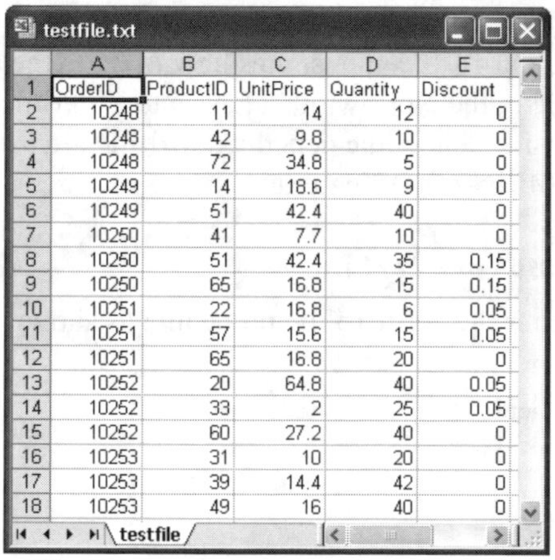

	A	B	C	D	E
1	OrderID	ProductID	UnitPrice	Quantity	Discount
2	10248	11	14	12	0
3	10248	42	9.8	10	0
4	10248	72	34.8	5	0
5	10249	14	18.6	9	0
6	10249	51	42.4	40	0
7	10250	41	7.7	10	0
8	10250	51	42.4	35	0.15
9	10250	65	16.8	15	0.15
10	10251	22	16.8	6	0.05
11	10251	57	15.6	15	0.05
12	10251	65	16.8	20	0
13	10252	20	64.8	40	0.05
14	10252	33	2	25	0.05
15	10252	60	27.2	40	0
16	10253	31	10	20	0
17	10253	39	14.4	42	0
18	10253	49	16	40	0

Figure 14-4: The Access-generated text file in Hands-On 14-8 is now opened in Excel.

Filtering Records with an SQL Clause

You can restrict the records returned in an open recordset to those matching the criteria specified in the SQL WHERE clause. If the expression contained in the WHERE clause is True, then the record is selected; otherwise, the record is excluded from the opened set of records.

The procedure in Hands-On 14-9 opens a recordset that contains only records having the value of Null in the Region field or an entry of "Mrs." in the TitleOfCourtesy field.

⊚ Hands-On 14-9: Filtering Records with an SQL Clause

1. In the Code window, enter the GetRecords_WithSQLWhere procedure as shown below.

```
Sub GetRecords_WithSQLWhere()
    Dim conn As ADODB.Connection
    Dim rst As ADODB.Recordset
    Dim strSQL As String

    strSQL = "Select * from Employees Where IsNull(Region)" & _
        " OR TitleOfCourtesy = 'Mrs.' "

    Set conn = New ADODB.Connection
    conn.Open "Provider=Microsoft.Jet.OLEDB.4.0;" & _
        "Data Source=" & CurrentProject.Path & _
        "\Northwind.mdb"

    Set rst = New ADODB.Recordset
    rst.Open strSQL, conn, adOpenKeyset, adLockOptimistic
    MsgBox "Selected " & rst.RecordCount & " records."

    rst.Close
    Set rst = Nothing
    conn.Close
    Set conn = Nothing
End Sub
```

Filtering Records Using the Filter Property

You can use the ADO Filter property to obtain a set of records that meet specific criteria. To remove the filter, set the Filter property to adFilterNone.

Use the Filter property as a workaround to the ADO Find method whenever you need to find records that meet more than one condition. If the specific set of records you want to obtain is located on the SQL Server, you should use stored procedures instead of the Filter property.

The FltrRecords procedure in Hands-On 14-10 creates a filtered view of customers listed in the Northwind database who are located in Madrid, Spain.

⊚ Hands-On 14-10: Filtering Records Using the Filter Property

1. In the Code window, enter the FltrRecords procedure as shown below.

```
Sub FltrRecords()
    Dim conn As ADODB.Connection
    Dim rst As ADODB.Recordset

    Set conn = New ADODB.Connection
    conn.Open "Provider=Microsoft.Jet.OLEDB.4.0;" & _
        "Data Source=" & CurrentProject.Path & _
        "\Northwind.mdb"

    Set rst = New ADODB.Recordset
    With rst
```

```
      .Open "Customers", conn, adOpenKeyset, adLockOptimistic
      .Filter = "City='Madrid' and Country='Spain'"
      MsgBox .RecordCount & " records meet the criteria.", _
          vbInformation, "Customers in Madrid (Spain)"
   End With

   Do Until rst.EOF
      Debug.Print rst.Fields(1).Value
      rst.MoveNext
   Loop

   rst.Filter = adFilterNone
   MsgBox "Filter was removed. " & vbCr _
      & "The table contains " & rst.RecordCount & " records."

   rst.Close
   Set rst = Nothing
   conn.Close
   Set conn = Nothing
End Sub
```

Sorting Records

You can use the recordset's Sort property to change the order in which records are displayed. The Sort property does not physically rearrange the records; it merely displays the records in the order specified by the index. If you are sorting on non-indexed fields, a temporary index is created for each field specified in the index. This index is removed automatically when you set the Sort property to an empty string. You can only use Sort on client-side cursors. If you use the server-side cursor, you will receive this error:

```
The operation requested by the application is not supported by the provider
```

The default sort order is ascending. To order a recordset by country in ascending order, then by city in descending order, you would use the following statement:

```
rst.Sort = "Country ASC, City DESC"
```

Although you can use the Sort property to sort your data, you will most likely get better performance by specifying an SQL ORDER BY clause in the SQL statement or query used to open the recordset.

The procedure in Hands-On 14-11 displays customer records from the Northwind database in ascending order by country.

⊚ Hands-On 14-11: Sorting Records

1. In the Code window, enter the SortRecords procedure as shown below.

```
Sub SortRecords()
   Dim conn As ADODB.Connection
   Dim rst As ADODB.Recordset

   Set conn = New ADODB.Connection
```

```
        conn.Open "Provider=Microsoft.Jet.OLEDB.4.0;" & _
            "Data Source=" & CurrentProject.Path & _
            "\Northwind.mdb"

    Set rst = New ADODB.Recordset

    ' sort on non-indexed field
    With rst
        .CursorLocation = adUseClient
        .Open "Customers", conn, adOpenKeyset, adLockOptimistic
        .Sort = "Country"
        Do Until rst.EOF
            Debug.Print rst.Fields("CompanyName").Value & ": " & _
                rst.Fields("Country").Value
            .MoveNext
        Loop
        Debug.Print "------------original sort"
        .Sort = ""
        Do Until .EOF
            Debug.Print rst.Fields("CompanyName").Value & ": " & _
                rst.Fields("Country").Value
            .MoveNext
        Loop
        .Close
    End With

    Set rst = Nothing
    conn.Close
    Set conn = Nothing
End Sub
```

Notice that after sorting records in the specified order, the Sort property is set to an empty string and records are displayed in the order in which they physically appear in the table.

Chapter Summary

This chapter demonstrated several methods of the ADO Recordset object you can use for working with records. You learned about the Add, Update, and Delete methods for performing such common database tasks as adding, modifying, and deleting records. These methods are suitable for handling a small number of records. Better performance can be achieved by using the SQL INSERT, UPDATE, and DELETE statements, as shown in Chapter 23.

This chapter also showed you how to render your database records into three popular formats: an Excel spreadsheet, a Word document, and a text file. Because working with large quantities of records can be difficult unless data is properly organized, this chapter also covered methods for filtering and sorting your records.

In the next chapter you will learn how to use ADO to create and run Access queries.

Chapter 15

Creating and Running Queries with ADO

Having worked with Microsoft Access for a while, you already know that to retrieve relevant information from your database and perform data-oriented tasks you need to write queries. Queries are SQL statements that are saved in the database and can be run at any time. Microsoft Office Access 2003 supports several types of queries.

The simplest queries allow you to select a set of records from a table. However, when you need to extract information from more than one table at a time, you must write a more complex query by using an SQL JOIN statement. Other queries perform specific actions on existing data, such as making a new table, appending rows to a table, updating the values in a table, or deleting rows from a table. Although Microsoft Office Access 2003 provides a friendly interface — the Query Design view — for creating queries manually, this chapter teaches you how to create and execute the same queries by using ActiveX Data Objects (ADO) and Data Manipulation Language (DML) SQL statements in VBA code.

Creating a Select Query Manually

Select queries retrieve a set of records from a database table. These queries are easily recognized by the SELECT and FROM keywords in their syntax. Let's take a look at a couple of examples:

`SELECT LastName FROM Employees`	Selects the LastName field from the Employees table. If there is a space in the field name, enclose the field name in square brackets: [Last Name].
`SELECT FirstName, LastName, PhoneNo FROM Employees`	Selects the FirstName, LastName, and PhoneNo fields from the Employees table.
`SELECT * FROM Employees`	Selects all fields for all records from the Employees table. The asterisk (*) is used to represent all fields.

Often the WHERE clause is used with Select queries to specify criteria that determine which records the query will affect. Some examples of using the WHERE clause to restrict records are shown below:

SELECT * FROM Employees WHERE City IN ('Redmond', 'London')	Selects from the Employees table all fields for all records that have the value Redmond or London in the City field.
SELECT * FROM Employees WHERE City IN ('Redmond', 'London') AND ReportsTo LIKE 'Buchanan, Steven'	Selects from the Employees table all fields for all records that have the value Redmond or London in the City field and have a value Buchanan, Steven in the ReportsTo field.
SELECT * FROM Employees WHERE ((Year([HireDate])<1993) OR (City='Redmond'))	Selects from the Employees table all fields for all records that have a value less than 1993 in the HireDate field or have the value Redmond in the City field.
Select * FROM Products WHERE UnitPrice Between 10 and 25	Selects from the Products table all fields for all records that have an amount in the UnitPrice field between $10 and $25.
Select * from Employees WHERE ReportsTo IS NULL	Select from the Employees table all fields for all records that do not have a value in the ReportsTo field.

You can use expressions in WHERE clauses to qualify SQL statements. An SQL expression is a string that is used in SQL statements. Expressions can contain literal values, constants, field names, operators, and functions. Several operators that are often used in expressions are shown in Table 15-1.

Table 15-1: Operators commonly used in expressions

Operator Name	Description/Usage
IN	The IN operator is used to determine whether the value of an expression is equal to any of several values in a specified list. If the expression is found in the list of values, the IN operator returns True; otherwise, it returns False. You can include the NOT logical operator to determine whether the expression is not in the list of values. For example, you can use NOT IN to determine which employees don't live in Redmond or London: SELECT * FROM Employees WHERE City NOT IN ('Redmond', 'London')
LIKE	The LIKE operator compares a string expression to a pattern in an SQL expression. For a pattern, you specify the complete value (for example, LIKE 'Buchanan, Steven'), or you can use wildcard characters to find a range of values (for example, LIKE 'B*'). You can use a number of wildcard characters in the LIKE operator pattern (see Table 15-2).

Operator Name	Description/Usage

BETWEEN...AND	The BETWEEN...AND operator is used to determine whether the value of an expression falls within a specified range of values. If the value of the expression is between value1 and value2 (inclusive), the BETWEEN...AND operator returns True; otherwise, it returns False. You can include the NOT logical operator to evaluate the opposite condition, that is, whether the expression falls outside the range defined by value1 and value2.
	
	For example, you can select all products with the amount in the UnitPrice field less than $10 and greater than $25:
	
	`Select * FROM Products`
	`WHERE UnitPrice NOT BETWEEN 10 and 25`

IS NULL	The IS NULL operator is used to determine whether the expression value is equal to the Null value. A Null value indicates missing or unknown data. You can include the NOT logical operator to return only records that have values in the specified field.
	
	For example, you can extract only the employee records that have a value in the ReportsTo field. Records where the ReportsTo field is blank will not be included:
	
	`Select * from Employees`
	`WHERE ReportsTo IS NOT NULL`

Table 15-2: Wildcard characters used in the LIKE operator patterns

Wildcard	Description
* (asterisk)	Matches any number of characters.
? (question mark)	Matches any single character.
% (percent sign)	Matches any number of characters (used only with the ADO and Jet OLE DB provider; not in the Access user interface).
_ (underscore)	Matches any single character (used only with the ADO and Jet OLE DB provider; not in the Access user interface).
# (number sign)	Matches any single digit.
[] (square brackets)	Match any single character within the list of characters enclosed within brackets.
! (exclamation point)	Matches any single character that is not found in the list enclosed within the square brackets.
- (hyphen)	Matches any one of the range of characters enclosed within the square brackets.

In addition to the WHERE clause, you can use predicates to further restrict the set of records to be retrieved. A *predicate* is an SQL statement that qualifies the SELECT statement, similar to the WHERE clause; however, the predicate must be placed before the column list. Several popular predicates are shown in Table 15-3.

Creating and Manipulating Databases with ADO

Table 15-3: Commonly used predicates in SQL SELECT statements

Predicate Name	Description/Usage

ALL	The ALL keyword is the default keyword and is used when no predicate is declared in the SQL statement.
	
	The following two examples are equivalent and return all records from the Employees table:
	
	`SELECT ALL *`
	`FROM Employees`
	`ORDER BY EmployeeID;`
	
	`SELECT *`
	`FROM Employees`
	`ORDER BY EmployeeID`

DISTINCT	The DISTINCT keyword eliminates duplicate values from the returned set of records. The values for each field listed in the SELECT statement must be unique.
	
	For example, to return a list of non-duplicate (unique) cities from the Employees table, you can write the following SELECT statement:
	
	`SELECT DISTINCT City`
	`FROM Employees`
	
	Note: The output of a query that uses DISTINCT isn't updatable (it's read-only).

DISTINCTROW	While the DISTINCT keyword is based on duplicate fields, the DISTINCTROW keyword is based on entire rows. It is used only with multiple tables.
	
	For example, if you join the Customers and Orders tables on the CustomerID field, you can find customers that have at least one order. The Customers table contains no duplicate CustomerID fields, but the Orders table does because each customer can have many orders.
	
	`SELECT DISTINCTROW CompanyName`
	`FROM Customers, Orders`
	`WHERE Customers.CustomerID =`
	`Orders.CustomerID`
	`ORDER BY CompanyName;`
	
	Note: If you omit DISTINCTROW, this SELECT statement will produce multiple rows for each company that has more than one order. DISTINCTROW has an effect only when you select fields from some, but not all, of the tables used in the query. DISTINCTROW is ignored if your query includes only one table or if you output fields from all tables.

Predicate Name	Description/Usage
TOP or PERCENT	The TOP keyword returns a certain number of records that fall at the top or bottom of a range specified by an ORDER BY clause.
	For example, suppose you want to select the five most expensive products:
	`SELECT TOP 5 * FROM Products` `ORDER BY UnitPrice DESC`
	The TOP predicate doesn't choose between equal values. If there are equal values present, the TOP keyword will return all rows that have the equal value.
	You can also use the PERCENT keyword to return a percentage of records that fall at the top or the bottom of a range specified by an ORDER BY clause.
	For example, to return the lowest 10 percent priced products, you can write the following statement:

	`SELECT TOP 10 PERCENT *`
	`FROM Products`
	`ORDER BY UnitPrice ASC;`

	Note: If you don't include the ORDER BY clause, the SELECT TOP statement will return a random set of rows.

If you'd like to sort records returned by the SELECT statement, use the ORDER BY clause with the ASC (ascending sort) or DESC (descending sort) keywords, as shown in the following example:

`SELECT * FROM Employees` `ORDER BY Country DESC`	Select all records from the Employees table and arrange them in descending order based on the Country field. If no order is specified, the order is ascending (ASC) by default.

By default, records are sorted in ascending order. The fields you want to sort by do not need to be enumerated in the SELECT statement's field list. Instead of sorting by field name, you can sort by field position. For example, the statement:

```
SELECT * FROM EMPLOYEES
ORDER BY 2
```

will sort the records in ascending order by the second field.

Creating a Select Query from a VBA Procedure

Now that we've reviewed the basics of using the most popular SQL statement (SELECT), let's get back to ADO and see how you can use the SELECT statement for retrieving records programmatically.

In ADO, queries, SQL statements, views, and stored procedures are represented by the Command object. This object is part of the ADOX Object Model (see Chapter 11, Figure 11-1). The Command object has many properties and methods that will allow you to return records or execute changes to your data (inserts, updates, and deletes). In this chapter you will get to know the properties of the Command object, including: ActiveConnection, CommandText, and

CommandType. These properties will be discussed as they appear in the example procedure code. You will also learn how to use the Command object's Execute method to run your queries.

The procedure in Hands-On 15-1 demonstrates how to create and save a Select query.

◎ Hands-On 15-1: Creating a Select Query with ActiveX Data Objects

1. Create a new Microsoft Office Access database or open the **Acc2003_ Chap15.mdb** file from the book's downloadable files.

2. In the Database window, press **Alt+F11** to switch to the Visual Basic Editor window.

3. In the Visual Basic Editor window, choose **Insert | Module**.

4. Choose **Tools | References** and select the following object libraries:

   Microsoft ADO Ext. 2.7 for DDL and Security Object Library
   Microsoft ActiveX Data Objects 2.7 Object Library

5. In the module's Code window, type the Create_SelectQuery procedure shown below.

6. Choose **Run | Run Sub/UserForm** to execute the procedure.

```
Sub Create_SelectQuery()
    Dim cat As ADOX.Catalog
    Dim cmd As ADODB.Command
    Dim strPath As String
    Dim strSQL As String
    Dim strQryName As String

    On Error GoTo ErrorHandler

    ' assign values to string variables
    strPath = CurrentProject.Path & "\Northwind.mdb"
    strSQL = "SELECT Employees.* FROM Employees WHERE " _
        & "Employees.City='London';"

    strQryName = "London Employees"

    ' open the Catalog
    Set cat = New ADOX.Catalog
    cat.ActiveConnection = "Provider=Microsoft.Jet.OLEDB.4.0;" & _
        "Data Source=" & strPath

    ' create a query based on the specified SELECT statement
    Set cmd = New ADODB.Command
    cmd.CommandText = strSQL

    ' add the new query to the database
    cat.Views.Append strQryName, cmd

ExitHere:
    Set cmd = Nothing
```

```
    Set cat = Nothing

    MsgBox "The procedure completed successfully.", _
        vbInformation, "Create Select Query"
    Exit Sub

ErrorHandler:
    If InStr(Err.Description, "already exists") Then
        cat.Views.Delete strQryName
        Resume
    Else
        MsgBox Err.Number & ": " & Err.Description
        Resume ExitHere
    End If
End Sub
```

The Create_SelectQuery procedure opens the Catalog object and sets its ActiveConnection property to the Northwind database:

```
Set cat = New ADOX.Catalog
cat.ActiveConnection="Provider=Microsoft.Jet.OLEDB.4.0;" & _
    "Data Source=" & strPath
```

As you may recall from Chapter 11, the Catalog object represents an entire database. It contains objects that represent all the elements of the database: tables, stored procedures, views, columns of tables, and indexes (see the ADOX Object Model in Chapter 11). The ActiveConnection property of the Catalog object indicates the ADO Connection object the Catalog belongs to. The value of this property can be a reference to the Connection object or a connection string containing the definition for a connection.

Next, the procedure defines a Command object and uses its CommandText property to set the SQL statement for the query:

```
Set cmd = New ADODB.Command
cmd.CommandText = strSQL
```

The CommandText property contains the text of a command you want to issue against a provider. In this procedure, we assigned the string variable's value (strSQL) to the CommandText property.

The ADO Command object always creates a temporary query. So, to create a stored (saved) query in a database, the procedure must append the Command object to the ADOX Views collection, like this:

```
cat.Views.Append strQryName, cmd
```

If you open the sample Northwind database after running the above procedure, you will find the London Employees query in the Queries section of the Database window.

Row-returning, Non-parameterized Queries

Queries that return records, such as Select queries, are known as row-returning, non-parameterized queries.

Use the ADOX View object to work with queries that return records and do not take parameters. All View objects are contained in the Views collection of the ADOX Catalog object. To save these queries in a database, append the ADO Command object to the ADOX Views collection as shown in Hands-On 15-1.

Executing a Select Query

There's more than one way of executing a row-returning query with ADO. This section demonstrates two procedures that run the Products by Category query located in the Northwind database.

The procedure in Hands-On 15-2 uses the Command and Recordset objects to perform this task.

◉ Hands-On 15-2: Executing a Select Query

1. In the Visual Basic Editor window, choose **Insert | Module**.

2. In the module's Code window, type the Execute_SelectQuery procedure shown below.

3. Choose **Run | Run Sub/UserForm** to execute the procedure.

```
Sub Execute_SelectQuery()
    Dim cmd As ADODB.Command
    Dim rst As ADODB.Recordset
    Dim strPath As String

    strPath = CurrentProject.Path & "\Northwind.mdb"

    Set cmd = New ADODB.Command
    With cmd
        .ActiveConnection = "Provider=Microsoft.Jet.OLEDB.4.0;" & _
            "Data Source=" & strPath
        .CommandText = "[Products by Category]"
        .CommandType = adCmdTable
    End With

    Set rst = New ADODB.Recordset
    Set rst = cmd.Execute

    Debug.Print rst.GetString

    rst.Close
    Set rst = Nothing
    Set cmd = Nothing
    MsgBox "View results in the Immediate window."
End Sub
```

In the Execute_Select Query procedure above, the connection to the database is opened by setting the ActiveConnection property of the Command object.

Next, the Command object's CommandText property specifies the name of the query you want to run. Notice that you need to place square brackets around the query's name because it contains spaces.

The query type is determined by setting the CommandType property of the Command object. Use the adCmdTable or adCmdStoredProc constants if the query string in the CommandText property is a query name.

Finally, the Execute method of the Command object executes the query. Notice that the resulting recordset is passed to the Recordset object variable so that you can access the records retrieved by the query. Instead of looping through the records to read the returned records, the procedure uses the Recordset object's GetString method to print all the recordset rows to the Immediate window. The GetString method returns the recordset as a string (for more information refer to Chapter 13).

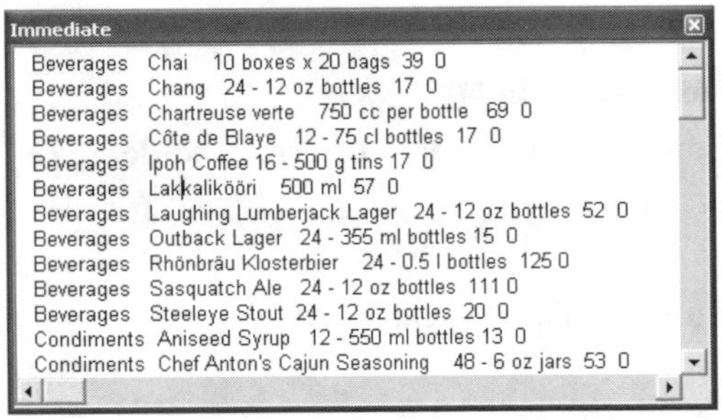

Figure 15-1: This is a sample result of records that were generated by executing a Select query (see Hands-On 15-2).

The next example procedure (Hands-On 15-3) demonstrates another method of running a row-returning query with ADO. Notice that in addition to the ADO Command and Recordset objects, this procedure uses the ADOX Catalog object. The connection to the database is established by setting the ActiveConnection of the Catalog object, and not the Command object, as was the case in the preceding example (Hands-On 15-2).

◉ Hands-On 15-3: Executing a Select Query with an ADO Catalog Object

1. In the Visual Basic Editor window, choose **Insert | Module**.

2. In the module's Code window, type the Execute_SelectQuery2 procedure shown below.

3. Choose **Run | Run Sub/UserForm** to execute the procedure.

```
Sub Execute_SelectQuery2()
    Dim cat As ADOX.Catalog
    Dim cmd As ADODB.Command
    Dim rst As ADODB.Recordset
    Dim strPath As String

    strPath = CurrentProject.Path & "\Northwind.mdb"
```

```
        Set cat = New ADOX.Catalog
        cat.ActiveConnection = "Provider=Microsoft.Jet.OLEDB.4.0;" & _
            "Data Source=" & strPath

        Set cmd = New ADODB.Command
        Set cmd = cat.Views("Products by Category").Command

        Set rst = New ADODB.Recordset
        rst.Open cmd, , adOpenStatic, adLockReadOnly, adCmdTable

        Debug.Print rst.GetString
        MsgBox "The query returned " & rst.RecordCount & vbCr & _
            " records to the Immediate window."
        rst.Close
        Set rst = Nothing
        Set cmd = Nothing
        Set cat = Nothing
    End Sub
```

Notice that the following line of code is used to indicate the name of the query to be executed:

```
    Set cmd = cat.Views("Products by Category").Command
```

This statement sets the cmd object variable to the desired query stored in the Views collection of the ADOX Catalog object.

Next, the Open method of the Recordset object is used to open the recordset based on the specified query:

```
    rst.Open cmd, , adOpenStatic, adLockReadOnly, adCmdTable
```

Notice that several optional arguments of the Open method are used to specify the data source: cmd, ActiveConnection (a comma appears in this spot because the existing connection is being used), CursorType (adOpenStatic), LockType (adLockReadOnly), and Options (adCmdTable). Refer to Chapter 13 for information about using these ADO constants.

Next, the procedure dumps the contents of the records into the Immediate window (just as the procedure in Hands-On 15-2 did) by using the recordset's GetString method. The MsgBox function contains a string that includes the information about the number of records retrieved. The RecordCount property of the Recordset object is used to get the record count. To get the correct record count you must set the CursorType argument of the recordset's Open method to adOpenStatic. If you set this argument to adOpenDynamic or adOpenForwardOnly, the RecordCount property will return –1. To learn more about these constants, refer to the sections on working with Recordset objects in ADO in Chapter 13.

Creating a Parameter Query

To create a row-returning, parameterized query, simply add the parameters to the query's SQL string. The parameters must be defined by using the Parameters keyword, as in the following:

```
strSQL = "Parameters [Type Country Name] Text;" & _
    "SELECT Customers.* FROM Customers WHERE " _
    & "Customers.Country=[Type Country Name];"
```

The above SQL statement begins by defining one parameter called Type Country Name. This parameter will be able to accept text entries. The second part of the SQL statement selects all the records from the Customers table that have an entry in the Country field equal to the provided parameter value.

The complete procedure is shown in Hands-On 15-4. Because the ADO Command object always creates a temporary query, you must append the Command object to the ADOX Procedures collection in order to save a parameterized query in a database.

⊚ Hands-On 15-4: Creating a Parameter Query

1. In the Visual Basic Editor window, choose **Insert | Module**.

2. In the module's Code window, type the Create_ParameterQuery procedure shown below.

3. Choose **Run | Run Sub/UserForm** to execute the procedure.

```
Sub Create_ParameterQuery()
    Dim cat As ADOX.Catalog
    Dim cmd As ADODB.Command
    Dim strPath As String
    Dim strSQL As String
    Dim strQryName As String

    On Error GoTo ErrorHandler

    strPath = CurrentProject.Path & "\Northwind.mdb"

    strSQL = "Parameters [Type Country Name] Text;" & _
        "SELECT Customers.* FROM Customers WHERE " _
        & "Customers.Country=[Type Country Name];"

    strQryName = "Customers by Country"

    Set cat = New ADOX.Catalog
    cat.ActiveConnection = "Provider=Microsoft.Jet.OLEDB.4.0;" & _
        "Data Source=" & strPath

    Set cmd = New ADODB.Command
    cmd.CommandText = strSQL
```

Creating and Running Queries with ADO | 275

Creating and Manipulating Databases with ADO

```
          cat.Procedures.Append strQryName, cmd
          Set cmd = Nothing
          Set cat = Nothing

          MsgBox "The procedure completed successfully.", _
              vbInformation, "Create Parameter Query"
          Exit Sub

    ErrorHandler:
          If InStr(Err.Description, "already exists") Then
              cat.Procedures.Delete strQryName
              Resume
          Else
              MsgBox Err.Number & ": " & Err.Description
          End If
    End Sub
```

Row-returning, Parameterized Queries

Queries that return records and take parameters are known as row-return-ing, parameterized queries.

Use the ADOX Procedure object to work with queries that return records and take parameters. All Procedure objects are contained in the Procedures collection of the ADOX Catalog object. To save these queries in a database, append the ADO Command object to the ADOX Procedures collection.

Executing a Parameter Query

Suppose you want to run a query named Invoices Filter that looks like the one shown in the Query grid in Figure 15-2.

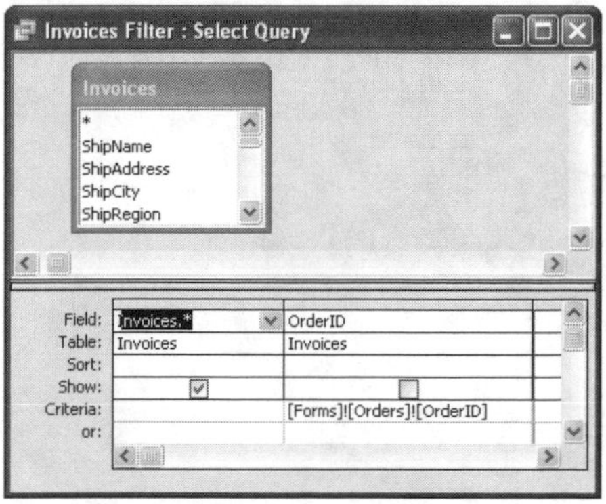

Figure 15-2: A parameter query can be based on a value supplied by a field placed on an Access form.

Because the query is linked to the OrderID field located on the Orders form and the Orders form is closed, you are prompted to enter the parameter value before the query can be executed.

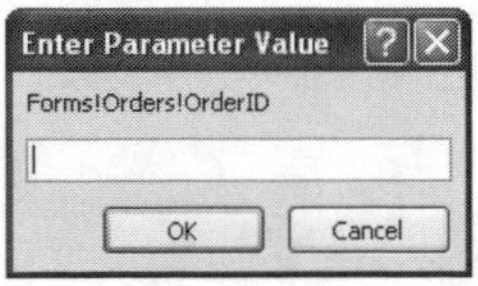

Figure 15-3: When you execute a parameter query, a dialog box displays an input box to enter the value of the required parameter.

The procedure in Hands-On 15-5 shows how to run this sort of a query by using ADO.

◉ Hands-On 15-5: Executing a Parameter Query

1. In the Visual Basic Editor window, choose **Insert | Module**.

2. In the module's Code window, type the Execute_ParamQuery procedure shown below.

3. Choose **Run | Run Sub/UserForm** to execute the procedure.

```
Sub Execute_ParamQuery()
    Dim cat As ADOX.Catalog
    Dim cmd As ADODB.Command
    Dim rst As ADODB.Recordset
    Dim strPath As String

    strPath = CurrentProject.Path & "\Northwind.mdb"

    Set cat = New ADOX.Catalog
    cat.ActiveConnection = "Provider=Microsoft.Jet.OLEDB.4.0;" & _
        "Data Source=" & strPath

    Set cmd = New ADODB.Command
    Set cmd = cat.Procedures("Invoices Filter").Command

    ' specify a parameter value
    cmd.Parameters("Forms!Orders!OrderID") = 10258
    ' use the Execute method of the Command object to open the recordset

    Set rst = cmd.Execute
    ' return product names to the Immediate window
    Do Until rst.EOF
        Debug.Print rst(20).Name & ": " & rst(20)
        rst.MoveNext
    Loop

    rst.Close
    Set rst = Nothing
    Set cmd = Nothing
    Set cat = Nothing
End Sub
```

The Execute_ParamQuery procedure shown above establishes the connection to the Northwind database. Next, the name of the query is supplied in the following statement:

```
Set cmd = cat.Procedures("Invoices Filter").Command
```

Because this is a parameter query, the parameter value is specified by using the Parameters collection of the Command object, like this:

```
cmd.Parameters("Forms!Orders!OrderID") = 10258
```

> **Note:** Instead of specifying the parameter values before the recordset is open, you can use the Parameters argument of the recordset's Open method to pass the parameter value, as shown below:
>
> ```
> Set rst = cmd.Execute(Parameters:=10258)
> ```

Then, the Recordset object is opened by using the Execute method of a Command object:

```
Set rst = cmd.Execute
```

Finally, the procedure loops through the recordset to retrieve the contents of each record's 20th field (ProductName) and print them to the Immediate window. After running this procedure, the following lines are returned to the Immediate window:

```
ProductName: Chang
ProductName: Chef Anton's Gumbo Mix
ProductName: Mascarpone Fabioli
```

Creating a Pass-Through Query

SQL pass-through queries are SQL statements that are sent directly to the database server for processing. To create a pass-through query manually, you need to activate the Query Design screen and choose Query | SQL Specific | Pass-Through. This will bring up a window where you can type a query statement like the one shown in Figure 15-4. The SQL statement must be in the format understood by the external data source from which you are retrieving data. Pass-through queries can also be used in lieu of Action queries when you need to bulk append, update, or delete data in remote databases.

Figure 15-4: A pass-through query used to access external data sources is a special type of query and can only be created via the SQL Pass-Through Query window or in a VBA procedure.

CustomerID	CompanyName	ContactName	ContactTitle	Address
BLONP	Blondesddsl père et fils	Frédérique Citeaux	Marketing Manager	24, place Kléber
BONAP	Bon app'	Laurence Lebihan	Owner	12, rue des Bouchers
DUMON	Du monde entier	Janine Labrune	Owner	67, rue des Cinquante Otages
FOLIG	Folies gourmandes	Martine Rancé	Assistant Sales Agent	184, chaussée de Tournai
FRANR	France restauration	Carine Schmitt	Marketing Manager	54, rue Royale
LACOR	La corne d'abondance	Daniel Tonini	Sales Representative	67, avenue de l'Europe
LAMAI	La maison d'Asie	Annette Roulet	Sales Manager	1 rue Alsace-Lorraine
PARIS	Paris spécialités	Marie Bertrand	Owner	265, boulevard Charonne
SPECD	Spécialités du monde	Dominique Perrier	Marketing Manager	25, rue Lauriston
VICTE	Victuailles en stock	Mary Saveley	Sales Agent	2, rue du Commerce
VINET	Vins et alcools Chevalier	Paul Henriot	Accounting Manager	59 rue de l'Abbaye

Record: 1 of 11

Figure 15-5: A pass-through query returns only the requested data from the remote data source. The returned data is read-only.

Pass-through queries can also be created using VBA procedures. In earlier versions of Microsoft Access, pass-through queries were used with Data Access Objects (DAO) to increase performance when accessing external ODBC data sources. In ADO, you can use the Microsoft OLE DB Provider for SQL Server to directly access the SQL Server. For this reason, you do not need to create pass-through queries. However, since it is possible to create a pass-through query using ADOX and Microsoft Jet Provider, the next hands-on demonstrates how to do this.

⊚ Hands-On 15-6: Creating a Pass-Through Query with ADOX

1. In the Visual Basic Editor window, choose **Insert | Module**.

2. In the module's Code window, type the Create_PassThroughQuery procedure shown below.

3. Choose **Run | Run Sub/UserForm** to execute the procedure.

```
Sub Create_PassThroughQuery()
    Dim cat As ADOX.Catalog
    Dim cmd As ADODB.Command
    Dim rst As ADODB.Recordset
    Dim strPath As String
    Dim strSQL As String
    Dim strQryName As String
    Dim strODBCConnect As String

    On Error GoTo ErrorHandle

    strSQL = "SELECT Customers.* FROM Customers WHERE " _
        & "Customers.Country='France';"

    strQryName = "French Customers"

    ' modify the following string to connect
    ' to your SQL Server
    strODBCConnect = "ODBC;Driver=SQL Server;" & _
        "Server=JULITTA733\JKDESKTOP1;" & _
        "Database=Northwind;" & _
```

```
            "UID=;" & _
            "PWD="

    ' strODBCConnect = "ODBC;DSN=ODBCNorth;UID=sa;PWD=;"

    Set cat = New ADOX.Catalog
    cat.ActiveConnection = CurrentProject.Connection

    Set cmd = New ADODB.Command
    With cmd
        .ActiveConnection = cat.ActiveConnection
        .CommandText = strSQL
        .Properties("Jet OLEDB:ODBC Pass-Through Statement") = True
        .Properties("Jet OLEDB:Pass-Through Query Connect String") = _
            strODBCConnect
    End With

    cat.Procedures.Append strQryName, cmd

    Set cmd = Nothing
    Set cat = Nothing
    MsgBox "The procedure completed successfully.", _
        vbInformation, "Create Pass-Through Query"
    Exit Sub

ErrorHandler:
    If InStr(Err.Description, "already exists") Then
        cat.Procedures.Delete strQryName
        Resume
    Else
        MsgBox Err.Number & ": " & Err.Description
    End If
End Sub
```

The above procedure creates a pass-through query named French Customers in
the current database. The SQL statement used to generate this query and the
output of this statement were illustrated earlier in Figures 15-4 and 15-5.
Notice that to connect to the SQL Server database, the following string is built
and later assigned to the CommandText property of the Command object:

```
strODBCConnect = "ODBC;Driver=SQL Server;" & _
    "Server=JULITTA733\JKDESKTOP1;" & _
    "Database=Northwind;" & _
    "UID=;" & _
    "PWD="
```

Needless to say, if you want to try this procedure, you must have access to a
remote data source (such as an SQL Server database) and you'll need to modify the above string to point to your server. The above string allows you to
connect via the DSN-less connection. You may build your connection string to
the remote data source using the Data Source Name (DSN) that you define in
the Control Panel via Administrative Tools (ODBC). Your connection string
could then look like this:

```
strODBCConnect = "ODBC;DSN=myDSN;UID=sa;PWD=;"
```

To create a pass-through query you must also set two provider-specific properties of the Command object: Jet OLEDB:ODBC Pass-Through Statement and
Jet OLEDB:Pass-Through Query Connect String.

To permanently store the pass-through query in your database, you need to
append it to the Catalog's Procedures collection, like this:

```
cat.Procedures.Append strQryName, cmd
```

After you run the Create_PassThroughQuery procedure, the query can be
viewed and accessed from the Queries screen in the Microsoft Access database
window.

Executing a Pass-Through Query

In Hands-On 15-6, you learned how to create a pass-through query in VBA
with ADO. This query retrieved the list of French customers from the
Northwind database located on the SQL Server. The pass-through query was
named French Customers and was saved permanently in the Acc2003_Chap15
database. Let's see how you can execute this query from a VBA procedure.

◉ Hands-On 15-7: Executing a Pass-Through Query Saved in Access

1. In the Visual Basic Editor window, choose **Insert | Module**.

2. In the module's Code window, type the Execute_PassThroughQuery procedure shown below.

3. Choose **Run | Run Sub/UserForm** to execute the procedure.

```
Sub Execute_PassThroughQuery()
    Dim cat As ADOX.Catalog
    Dim cmd As ADODB.Command
    Dim rst As ADODB.Recordset
    Dim strConnect As String

    strConnect = "Provider=SQLOLEDB;" & _
        "Data Source=Julitta733\JKDesktop1;" & _
        "Initial Catalog=Northwind;" & _
        "User Id=sa;" & _
        "Password="

    Set cat = New ADOX.Catalog
    cat.ActiveConnection = CurrentProject.Connection

    Set cmd = New ADODB.Command
    Set cmd = cat.Procedures("French Customers").Command
    Set rst = cmd.Execute

    Debug.Print "--French Customers Only--" & vbCrLf _
        & rst.GetString
```

```
      Set rst = Nothing
      Set cmd = Nothing
      Set cat = Nothing
   End Sub
```

The procedure begins by building a connection string to the SQL Server database. This is a standard connection that uses the native OLE DB SQL Server Provider (SQLOLEDB). This connection requires that you also provide the name of the SQL Server (Data Source), the name of the database from which to retrieve records (Initial Catalog), and the security context with which to log in (UserId, Password). If you connect to your SQL Server database using the NT integrated security, your connection string will look like this:

```
strConnect = "Provider=SQLOLEDB;" & _
    "Data Source=yourServerName;" & _
    "Integrated Security=SSPI;" & _
    "Initial Catalog=Northwind"
```

Because the pass-through query you want to execute has been saved in the Access database, you need to open the ADOX Catalog object to access its Procedures collection. The following line of code specifies the name of the query you want to execute and assigns it to the Command object:

```
Set cmd = cat.Procedures("French Customers").Command
```

To execute a pass-through query that returns records, you need to use the Recordset object in addition to the Command object. The following statement executes the pass-through query:

```
Set rst = cmd.Execute
```

The pass-through query executes on the server. To quickly view data on the client machine, we retrieve the contents of the recordset by using the GetString method:

```
Debug.Print "--French Customers Only--" & vbCrLf _
    & rst.GetString
```

Executing an Update Query

Executing bulk queries that update data is quite easy with ADO. You can use the Execute method of the Connection or Command object. The procedure in Hands-On 15-8 uses the Connection object's Execute method to update records in the Products table of the Northwind database where CategoryId is equal to 8. The UnitPrice of the records that match this condition will be increased by one dollar. Note that the number of updated records is returned by the Execute method in the NumOfRec variable.

⊚ Hands-On 15-8: Executing an Update Query

1. In the Visual Basic Editor window, choose **Insert | Module**.

2. In the module's Code window, type the Execute_UpdateQuery procedure shown below.

3. Choose **Run | Run Sub/UserForm** to execute the procedure.

```
Sub Execute_UpdateQuery()
    Dim conn As ADODB.Connection
    Dim NumOfRec As Integer
    Dim strPath As String

    strPath = CurrentProject.Path & "\Northwind.mdb"

    Set conn = New ADODB.Connection

    conn.Open "Provider=Microsoft.Jet.OLEDB.4.0;" & _
        "Data Source=" & strPath

    conn.Execute "UPDATE Products " & _
        "SET UnitPrice = UnitPrice + 1" & _
        "WHERE CategoryId = 8", _
        NumOfRec, adExecuteNoRecords

    MsgBox NumOfRec & " records were updated."
    conn.Close
    Set conn = Nothing
End Sub
```

The above procedure uses the Data Manipulation Language (DML) UPDATE statement to make a change in the UnitPrice field of the Products table. The Execute method of the Connection object allows the provider to return the number of records that were affected via the RecordsAffected parameter. This parameter applies only for Action queries or stored procedures. To get the number of records returned by a result-returning query or stored procedure, you must use the RecordCount property. In the procedure shown above, we store the number of records affected in the string variable NumOfRec.

Note that when a command does not return a recordset, you should include the value adExecuteNoRecords. The adExecuteNoRecords value can only be passed as an optional parameter to the Command or Connection Execute method.

The procedure in Hands-On 15-9 demonstrates how to execute an update query by using the ADO Command object instead of the Connection object used in the preceding example. By running the following example, the UnitPrice of all the records in the Products table will be increased by 10 percent.

⊚ Hands-On 15-9: Executing an Update Query using the Command Object

1. In the Visual Basic Editor window, choose **Insert | Module**.

2. In the module's Code window, type the Execute_UpdateQuery2 procedure shown below.

3. Choose **Run | Run Sub/UserForm** to execute the procedure.

```
Sub Execute_UpdateQuery2()
    Dim cmd As ADODB.Command
    Dim NumOfRec As Integer
    Dim strPath As String

    strPath = CurrentProject.Path & "\Northwind.mdb"

    Set cmd = New ADODB.Command
    With cmd
        .ActiveConnection = "Provider=Microsoft.Jet.OLEDB.4.0;" & _
            "Data Source=" & strPath
        .CommandText = "Update Products Set UnitPrice = UnitPrice *1.1"
        .Execute NumOfRec, adExecuteNoRecords
    End With
    MsgBox NumOfRec
    Set cmd = Nothing
End Sub
```

Non-row-returning Queries

Queries that do not return records, such as Action queries or Data Definition Language (DDL) queries, are known as non-row-returning queries.

- Action queries are Data Manipulation Language (DML) queries that perform bulk operations on a set of records. They allow you to add, update, or delete records.

- The DDL queries are used for creating database objects and altering the structure of a database.

Use the ADOX Procedure object to work with queries that don't return records. All Procedure objects are contained in the Procedures collection of the ADOX Catalog object. To save these types of queries in a database, append the ADO Command object to the ADOX Procedures collection.

Modifying a Stored Query

If you'd like to modify an existing, stored query, follow these steps:

1. Retrieve the query from the Views or Procedures collection of the Catalog object.

2. Set the CommandText property of the Command object to the new SQL statement.

3. Save the changes by setting the Procedure or View object's Command property to the modified Command object.

Earlier in this chapter you learned how to create a Select query named "London Employees" by using ADO (see Hands-On 15-1). Let's see how you can now modify this query so that it orders the employee records by date of birth.

⊚ Hands-On 15-10: Modifying a Select Query

1. In the Visual Basic Editor window, choose **Insert | Module**.

2. In the module's Code window, type the Modify_Query procedure shown below.

3. Choose **Run | Run Sub/UserForm** to execute the procedure.

```
Sub Modify_Query()
    Dim cat As ADOX.Catalog
    Dim cmd As ADODB.Command
    Dim strPath As String
    Dim newStrSQL As String
    Dim oldStrSQL As String
    Dim strQryName As String

    strPath = CurrentProject.Path & "\Northwind.mdb"
    newStrSQL = "SELECT Employees.* FROM Employees" & _
        " WHERE Employees.City='London'" & _
        " ORDER BY BirthDate;"
    strQryName = "London Employees"

    Set cat = New ADOX.Catalog
    cat.ActiveConnection = "Provider=Microsoft.Jet.OLEDB.4.0;" & _
        "Data Source=" & strPath

    Set cmd = New ADODB.Command
    Set cmd = cat.Views(strQryName).Command

    ' get the existing SQL statement for this query
    oldStrSQL = cmd.CommandText

    MsgBox oldStrSQL, vbInformation, _
        "Current SQL Statement"

    ' now update the query's SQL statement
    cmd.CommandText = newStrSQL
    MsgBox newStrSQL, vbInformation, _
        "New SQL Statement"

    ' save the modified query
    Set cat.Views(strQryName).Command = cmd

    Set cmd = Nothing
    Set cat = Nothing
End Sub
```

Listing Queries in a Database

The procedure in Hands-On 15-11 retrieves the names of all saved queries in the Northwind database by iterating through the View objects stored in the ADOX Catalog's Views collection.

⊚ Hands-On 15-11: Listing All Saved Queries in a Database

1. In the Visual Basic Editor window, choose **Insert | Module**.
2. In the module's Code window, type the List_SavedQueries procedure shown below.
3. Choose **Run | Run Sub/UserForm** to execute the procedure.

```
Sub List_SavedQueries()
    Dim cat As New ADOX.Catalog
    Dim v As ADOX.View
    Dim strPath As String

    strPath = CurrentProject.Path & "\Northwind.mdb"
    cat.ActiveConnection = "Provider=Microsoft.Jet.OleDb.4.0;" & _
        "Data Source= " & strPath

    For Each v In cat.Views
        Debug.Print v.Name
    Next
    Set cat - Nothing
End Sub
```

Deleting a Stored Query

To delete a query, use the Procedures or Views collection's Delete method. By running the procedure in Hands-On 15-12, you can quickly delete the London Employees query created earlier in this chapter.

⊚ Hands-On 15-12: Deleting a Stored Query

1. In the Visual Basic Editor window, choose **Insert | Module**.
2. In the module's Code window, type the Delete_Query procedure shown below.
3. Choose **Run | Run Sub/UserForm** to execute the procedure.

```
Sub Delete_Query()
    Dim cat As New ADOX.Catalog
    Dim strPath As String

    On Error GoTo ErrorHandler
```

```
        strPath = CurrentProject.Path & "\Northwind.mdb"
        cat.ActiveConnection = "Provider=Microsoft.Jet.OleDb.4.0;" & _
            "Data Source= " & strPath

        cat.Views.Delete "London Employees"

    ExitHere:
        Set cat = Nothing
        Exit Sub

    ErrorHandler:
        If Err.Number = 3265 Then
            MsgBox "Query does not exist."
        Else
            MsgBox Err.Number & ": " & Err.Description
        End If
        Resume ExitHere
    End Sub
```

Chapter Summary

Creating and executing queries are the most frequently performed database operations. This chapter has shown you how to create and run various types of queries using the ADO code.

In the next chapter, you will get to know more of the advanced features of the ADO Object Model.

Chapter 16

Using Advanced ADO Features

So far you should feel pretty comfortable using ADO in most of your Microsoft Office Access programming endeavors. What's more, using the knowledge acquired during the last few chapters, you can switch to any other Office application (Excel, Word, PowerPoint, or Outlook) and start programming. Because you already know the ADO methods of accessing databases and manipulating records, all you need to learn is the object model that the specific application is using. Learning a new type library is not very hard. Recall that VBA offers the Object Browser that lists all the application's objects, properties, methods, and intrinsic constants that you may need for writing code. However, if you'd like to accomplish more with ADO, this chapter will introduce you to a couple of more advanced ADO features that will set you apart from beginning programmers. You will learn about fabricating, persisting, disconnecting, cloning, and shaping recordsets. You will also learn how to process data modifications and additions by using ADO transactions.

Fabricating a Recordset

In previous chapters, you worked with recordsets that were created from data that came from a Microsoft Access database, a text or dBASE file, an Excel spreadsheet, or a Word document. You may have also practiced working with a recordset generated from an SQL Server database. In each of these circumstances, to get the necessary data, you needed to establish a connection to the appropriate data source. In other words, you worked with recordsets that had a live connection to the data source. These connected recordsets obtained their structure and data from a query to a data source to which they were connected. But what if you need to create a recordset with data that does not come from a data source? As you may recall from the introduction to ADO in Chapter 10, the ADO Object Model allows you to work with both relational and non-relational data stores.

To store non-relational data in an ADO recordset, you can create your recordset from scratch. This recordset will be defined programmatically in memory and will not be connected to any data source. For example, you can easily fabricate a custom recordset that holds non-relational data, such as the information about the files located in one of your hard drive's directories.

When you create your own recordset from scratch, you define the types of fields in the recordset and then populate the recordset with the information you want. The fields are defined using the Fields collection's Append method. You must specify the field name, the data type, and the length. The syntax for the Append method looks like this:

```
Fields.Append Name, DataType[, FieldSize], [Attribute]
```

Recall that arguments in square brackets are optional. FieldSize specifies the size in characters or bytes. Attribute specifies characteristics such as whether the field enables Null values or whether it is a primary key or an identity column.

Once you have defined the structure of your recordset, you should open it and proceed to populate it with the data. You can add data to your custom recordset in the same way you add data to a connected recordset: by using the Recordset object's AddNew method.

The procedure in Hands-On 16-1 demonstrates how to create an empty recordset containing three fields (Name, Size, and Modified) and then populate it with files located in a user-specified file folder.

◉ Hands-On 16-1: Creating a Custom Recordset

1. Create a new Microsoft Office Access database or open the **Acc2003_Chap16.mdb** file from the book's downloadable files.

2. In the Database window, press **Alt+F11** to switch to the Visual Basic Editor window.

3. In the Visual Basic Editor window, choose **Insert | Module**.

4. In the module's Code window, type the Custom_Recordset procedure shown below.

```
Sub Custom_Recordset()
    Dim rst As ADODB.Recordset
    Dim strFile As String
    Dim strPath As String
    Dim strFolder As String

    strPath = InputBox("Enter pathname, e.g., C:\My Folder")
    If Right(strPath, 1) <> "\" Then strPath = strPath & "\"

        strFolder = strPath
        strFile = Dir(strPath & "*.*")
        If strFile = "" Then
           MsgBox "This folder does not contain files."
           Exit Sub
        End If
        Set rst = New ADODB.Recordset
          ' Create an empty recordset with 3 fields
          With rst
                Set .ActiveConnection = Nothing
                .CursorLocation = adUseClient
                With .Fields
```

```
                    .Append "Name", adVarChar, 255
                    .Append "Size", adDouble
                    .Append "Modified", adDBTimeStamp
                End With
                .Open
                Do While strFile <> ""
                    If strFile = "" Then Exit Do
                        ' Add a new record to the recordset
                        .AddNew Array("Name", "Size", "Modified"), _
                                Array(strFile, FileLen(strFolder & strFile), _
                                FileDateTime(strFolder & strFile))
                        strFile = Dir
                Loop
                .MoveFirst
            ' Print the contents of the recordset to the Immediate window
                Do Until .EOF
                        Debug.Print !Name & vbTab & !Size & vbTab & !Modified
                        .MoveNext
                Loop
                .Close
            End With
        Set rst = Nothing
    End Sub
```

In the Custom_Recordset procedure shown above, we start by creating a
Recordset object variable. To tell ADO that your recordset is not connected to
any database, we set the ActiveConnection property of the Recordset object to
Nothing. We also set the CursorLocation property to adUseClient to indicate
that the processing will occur on the client machine as opposed to the database
server. Next, we determine what columns the recordset should contain and add
these columns to the recordset's Fields collection by using the Append method.
Once the structure of your recordset is defined, you can call the Open method
to actually open your custom recordset. Now you can populate the recordset
with the data you want. We obtain the data by looping through the folder the
user specified in the input box and read the information about each file. The
VBA FileLen function is used to retrieve the size of a file in bytes. Another
VBA function, FileDateTime, is used to retrieve the date and time a file was
last modified. To retrieve the date and time separately, use the FileDateTime
function as an argument of the DateValue or TimeValue functions.

Check the following statements in the Immediate window while stepping
through the Custom_Recordset procedure:

```
? DateValue(FileDateTime(myFolder & myFile))
? TimeValue(FileDateTime(myFolder & myFile))
```

Now that the recordset is fabricated and populated with the required data, you
can display its contents in the Immediate window or send the output to another
application. You can also save the recordset to a disk file as explained later in
this chapter.

Disconnected Recordsets

In the previous section, you learned how to create a recordset from scratch. This recordset had a structure custom-defined by you and was populated with data that did not come from a database. In other words, it was a disconnected recordset that was defined on the fly.

A *disconnected recordset* is a recordset that is not connected to a data source. A disconnected recordset can be defined programmatically (as you saw in Hands-On 16-1) or it can get its information from the data source (as shown in Hands-On 16-2).

Using disconnected recordsets allows you to connect to a database, retrieve some records, return the records to the client, and then disconnect from the database. By keeping your connection to a database open just long enough to obtain the required data, you can help conserve valuable server resources. You can work with the disconnected recordset offline and then connect to the database again to add your changes.

To get started using disconnected recordsets, perform Hands-On 16-2. The example procedure retrieves some data from the Orders table in the Northwind database, then disconnects from the database. While disconnected from the database, you manipulate and examine the content of the retrieved recordset.

◎ Hands-On 16-2: Creating a Disconnected Recordset

➔ **Note:** Because this hands-on retrieves data from the Northwind database, adjust the path found in the procedure code to point to the correct location of this file on your computer.

1. In the Visual Basic Editor window, choose **Insert | Module**.

2. In the module's Code window, type the Rst_Disconnected procedure shown below.

```
Sub Rst_Disconnected()
    Dim conn As ADODB.Connection
    Dim rst As ADODB.Recordset
    Dim strConn As String
    Dim strSQL As String
    Dim strRst As String

    strSQL = "Select * From Orders where CustomerID = 'VINET'"

    strConn = "Provider=Microsoft.Jet.OLEDB.4.0;"
    strConn = strConn & "Data Source = C:\Program Files\" & _
            "Microsoft Office\Office11\Samples\Northwind.mdb"

    Set conn = New ADODB.Connection
    conn.ConnectionString = strConn
    conn.Open

    Set rst = New ADODB.Recordset
    Set rst.ActiveConnection = conn
```

```
        ' retrieve the data
        rst.CursorLocation = adUseClient
        rst.LockType = adLockBatchOptimistic
        rst.CursorType = adOpenStatic
        rst.Open strSQL, , , , adCmdText

        ' disconnect the recordset
        Set rst.ActiveConnection = Nothing

        ' change the CustomerID in the first record to 'OCEAN'
        rst.MoveFirst
        Debug.Print rst.Fields(0) & " was " & rst.Fields(1) & " before."
        rst.Fields("CustomerID").Value = "OCEAN"
        rst.Update

        ' stream out the recordset as a comma-delimited string
        strRst = rst.GetString(adClipString, , ",")
        Debug.Print strRst
    End Sub
```

Notice that to create a disconnected recordset that gets its data from a data source, you need to set the CursorLocation, LockType, and CursorType properties of the Recordset object. CursorLocation should be set to adUseClient. This setting indicates that the cursor will reside on the client computer that is creating the recordset. Set LockType to adLockBatchOptimistic to enable multiple records to be updated. Finally, set CursorType to adOpenStatic to retrieve the snapshot of the data.

To disconnect a recordset, you must set the Recordset object's Active-Connection property to Nothing after you've called the recordset's Open method.

When the recordset is disconnected from the database, you can freely manipulate its data or pass it to another application or process. In the example procedure above, we manipulate our recordset by changing the value of the CustomerID field in the first retrieved record from VINET to OCEAN. Then we create a comma-delimited string using the Recordset object's GetString method. The content of the disconnected recordset is then printed out to the Immediate window, as shown here:

```
10274 was VINET before.
10274,OCEAN,6,8/6/1996,9/3/1996,8/16/1996,1,6.01,Vins et alcools Chevalier,59
rue de l'Abbaye,Reims,,51100,France
10295,VINET,2,9/2/1996,9/30/1996,9/10/1996,2,1.15,Vins et alcools Chevalier,59
rue de l'Abbaye,Reims,,51100,France
10737,VINET,2,11/11/1997,12/9/1997,11/18/1997,2,7.79,Vins et alcools
Chevalier,59 rue de l'Abbaye,Reims,,51100,France
10739,VINET,3,11/12/1997,12/10/1997,11/17/1997,3,11.08,Vins et alcools
Chevalier,59 rue de l'Abbaye,Reims,,51100,France
```

Saving a Recordset to Disk

The ADO has a Save method that allows you to save a recordset to disk and work with it from your VBA application. This method takes two parameters. You must specify a filename and one of the following two data formats:

- adPersistADTG — Advanced Data TableGram
- adPersistXML — Extensible Markup Language

A *saved* (or *persisted*) *recordset* is a recordset that is saved to a file. This file can later be reopened without an active connection.

In this section, you will persist a recordset into a file using the adPersistADTG format. You will work with the adPersistXML format in Part V of this book.

To save a recordset in a file, you must first open it. When you have applied a filter to a recordset and then decide to save this recordset, only the filtered records will be saved. Using the Save method does not close the recordset. You can continue to work with the recordset after it has been saved. However, always remember to close the recordset when you are done working with it.

The procedure in Hands-On 16-3 opens the recordset based on the Customers table. Once the recordset is open, the Save method is called to persist the customer records into a file.

⊚ Hands-On 16-3: Saving Records to a Disk File

➔ **Note:** Because this hands-on retrieves data from the Northwind database, adjust the path found in the procedure code to point to the correct location of this file on your computer.

1. In the Visual Basic Editor window, choose **Insert | Module**.

2. In the module's Code window, type the SaveRecordsToDisk procedure shown below.

```
Sub SaveRecordsToDisk()
    Dim conn As ADODB.Connection
    Dim rst As ADODB.Recordset
    Dim strFileName As String
    Dim strNorthPath As String

    strFileName = CurrentProject.Path & "\" & "Companies.rst"
    strNorthPath = "C:\Program Files\Microsoft Office\" & _
                    "Office11\Samples\Northwind.mdb"

    On Error GoTo ErrorHandle

    Set conn = New ADODB.Connection

    With conn
        .Provider = "Microsoft.Jet.OLEDB.4.0"
        .ConnectionString = "Data Source = " & strNorthPath
        .Mode = adModeReadWrite
```

```
            .Open
        End With

        Set rst = New ADODB.Recordset
        With rst
            .CursorLocation = adUseClient
            ' Retrieve the data
            .Open "Customers", conn, _
                    adOpenKeyset, adLockBatchOptimistic, adCmdTable

            ' Disconnect the recordset
            .ActiveConnection = Nothing

            ' Save the recordset to disk
            .Save strFileName, adPersistADTG
            .Close
        End With

        MsgBox "Records were saved in " & strFileName & "."

ExitHere:
        ' Cleanup
        Set rst = Nothing
        Exit Sub

ErrorHandle:
        If Not IsEmpty(Dir(strFileName)) Then
            Kill strFileName
            Resume
        Else
            MsgBox Err.Number & ": " & Err.Description
            Resume ExitHere
        End If
End Sub
```

3. Run the above procedure to save the recordset to a file.

The procedure shown in this example saves all the data located in the Customers table to a file with an .rst extension. We named this file Companies.rst, but you are free to choose any filename and extension while saving your recordset.

Persisted recordsets are very useful for populating combo boxes or list boxes, especially when the data is located on a server and does not change too often. You can update your data as needed by running a procedure that creates a new dump of the required records and deletes the old disk file. This way, your Access application can display the most recent data in its combo or list boxes without having to connect to a database. Let's look at how you can fill a combo box with a saved recordset by working with Custom Project 16-1.

Custom Project 16-1: Filling a Combo Box with a Disconnected Recordset

This custom project requires that you complete Hands-On 16-2.

1. Create a form as shown in Figure 16-1. Place a combo box control in the form. Change the Name property of this control to **cboCompany**. Set the Caption property of the label control to **Company:**.

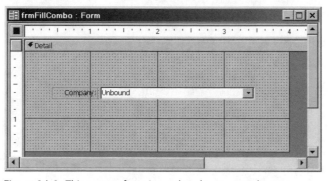

Figure 16-1: This custom form is used to demonstrate how you can fill the combo box control with a disconnected recordset.

2. Set the form's Caption property to **Disconnected Combo**.

3. Save the form as **frmFillCombo**.

4. In the form's properties sheet, activate the **Event** tab and click the button next to the **On Load** event name. In the Choose Builder dialog box, select **Code Builder** and click **OK**.

5. Complete the Form_Load procedure as shown below.

```
Private Sub Form_Load()
    Dim rst As ADODB.Recordset
    Dim strRowSource As String
    Dim strName As String

    strName = CurrentProject.Path & "\" & _
        "Companies.rst"

    Set rst = New ADODB.Recordset
        With rst
            .CursorLocation = adUseClient
            .Open strName, , , , adCmdFile
            Do Until .EOF
                strRowSource = strRowSource & rst!CompanyName & ";"
                .MoveNext
            Loop
            With Me.cboCompany
                .RowSourceType = "Value List"
                .RowSource = strRowSource
            End With
```

Creating and Manipulating Databases with ADO

```
            .Close
        End With
    Set rst = Nothing
End Sub
```

To populate a combo box with values, the code in the Form_Load procedure changes the RowSourceType property of the combo box control to Value List and sets the RowSource property to the string obtained by iterating though the recordset.

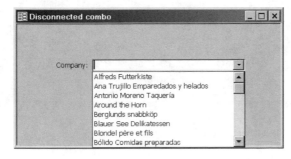

Figure 16-2: After opening the form prepared in Custom Project 16-1, the combo box is filled with the names of companies obtained via a persisted recordset.

Persisted recordsets are especially handy when you need to support disconnected users or when you want to take data on the road with you. You can save the required set of records to a disk file, send it to your users in remote locations, or take it with you. While disconnected from the database, you or your users can view or modify the records. The next time you connect to the database you can update the original data with your changes using the BatchUpdate method. Custom Project 16-2 demonstrates this scenario.

◎ Custom Project 16-2: Taking Persisted Data on the Road

This custom project requires that you complete Hands-On 16-2.

Part 1: Saving a Recordset to Disk

Before you can take a recordset on the road with you, you must save the records to a disk file. To create the data for this project, prepare and run the procedure in Hands-On 16-2. You should have the Companies.rst file available on your computer prior to going to Part 2.

Part 2: Creating an Unbound Access Form to View and Modify Data

Once you've saved the recordset to a disk file, the recordset becomes portable. You can take the file with you on the road or send it to someone else. But, before either one of you can view the data and modify it, you need some sort of a user interface. In this part, you will create an unbound Access form that will enable you to work with the file that contains the saved recordset.

1. Create a form as shown in Figure 16-3. Notice that this form contains only a couple of fields from the Customers table. This form serves only as an example. You can use as many fields as you have saved in the disk file.

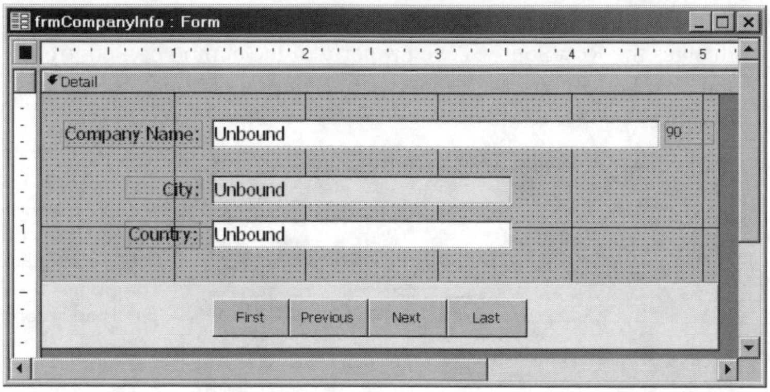

Figure 16-3: This custom form is used to demonstrate how you can use the saved recordset in an unbound form.

2. Set the following properties for the form's controls:

Object	Property	Setting
Label1	Caption	Company Name:
Text box next to the Company Name label	Name	txtCompany
Label2	Caption	City:
Text box next to the City label	Name Back Color	txtCity Select any color you like
Label3	Caption	Country:
Text box next to the Country label	Name	txtCountry
Label4	Caption Name	90 lbRecordNo
Command button 1	Caption Name	First cmdFirst
Command button 2	Caption Name	Previous cmdPrevious
Command button 3	Caption Name	Next cmdNext
Command button 4	Caption Name	Last cmdLast

Note: We have set the Back Color property of the txtCity text box in the example application to visually indicate that the user can update only this field's data.

3. To visually match the form in Figure 16-3, draw a rectangle control over the command buttons and set its Back Color property to any color you like. Select the rectangle and choose **Format | Send to Back** to move the rectangle behind the command buttons.

4. Select the form by choosing **Edit | Select Form** and activate the form's properties sheet to set the following properties:

Property Name	Setting
Scroll Bars	Neither
Record Selectors	No
Navigation Buttons	No

5. Save the form as **frmCompanyInfo**.

Part 3: Writing Procedures to Control the Form and Its Data

Now that you've designed the form for your data, you need to write a couple of VBA procedures. The first procedure you'll write is an event procedure for the Form_Load event. This procedure will load the form with data from the persisted file. You will start by declaring a module-level Recordset object variable called rst and a module-level Integer variable called counter. You will also write Click procedures for all the command buttons and a procedure to fill the text boxes with the data from the current record in the recordset. Let's get started!

1. In the form's properties sheet, activate the Event tab and click the **Build** button next to the **On Load** event name. In the Choose Builder dialog box, select **Code Builder** and click **OK**.

2. Enter the code for the Form_Load event procedure as shown below, starting with the declaration of module-level variables:

```
Option Compare Database
Dim rst As ADODB.Recordset
Dim counter As Integer

Private Sub Form_Load()
    Dim strFileName As String

    strFileName = CurrentProject.Path & "\" & "Companies.rst"
    On Error GoTo ErrorHandle

    Set rst = New ADODB.Recordset
    With rst
        .CursorLocation = adUseClient
        .Open strFileName, , adOpenKeyset, adLockBatchOptimistic, adCmdFile
    End With

    counter = 1
    Call FillTxtBoxes(rst, Me)
```

```
        Me.txtCompany.SetFocus
        Me.cmdFirst.Enabled = False
        Me.cmdPrevious.Enabled = False
        Me.lbRecordNo.Caption = counter
ExitHere:
    Exit Sub
ErrorHandle:
    MsgBox Err.Number & ": " & Err.Description
    Resume ExitHere
End Sub
```

3. The Form_Load event procedure loads Companies.rst from a disk file. To fill the text boxes with the data from the current record in the recordset, you need to write the following code:

```
Me.txtCompany = rst!CompanyName
Me.txtCity = rst!City
Me.txtCountry = rst!Country
```

Because the above code will need to be entered in several procedures in this application, you can save yourself a great deal of typing by placing this code in a subroutine and calling it like this:

```
Call FillTxtBoxes(rst, Me)
```

The above statement calls the subroutine named FillTxtBoxes and passes it two arguments: the Recordset object variable and the reference to the current form. The FillTxtBoxes subroutine is entered in a standard module and contains the code shown in the next step.

The counter variable, which was declared at the module level, is initialized to the value of 1. We will use this variable to control the display of command buttons on the form. The Form_Load event procedure ends by setting the focus to the first text box (Company) and disabling the first two command buttons. These buttons will not be required when the form first opens on the first record.

4. In the Visual Basic Editor Code window, choose **Insert | Module** and type the code of the FillTxtBoxes procedure as shown below:

```
Sub FillTxtBoxes(ByVal rst As ADODB.Recordset, frm As Form)
    With frm
        .txtCompany = rst!CompanyName
        .txtCity = rst!City
        .txtCountry = rst!Country
    End With
End Sub
```

The procedure above fills the three text boxes placed on the form with the data from the current record in the recordset. This procedure is called from the Form_Load event procedure and the Click event procedures for each command button.

5. Write the following Click event procedure for the First command button:

```
Private Sub cmdFirst_Click()
    On Error GoTo Err_cmdFirst_Click

    rst.Update "City", Me.txtCity
    rst.MoveFirst

    Call FillTxtBoxes(rst, Me)

    Me.txtCompany.SetFocus
    Me.cmdFirst.Enabled = False
    Me.cmdLast.Enabled = True
    Me.cmdPrevious.Enabled = False
    Me.cmdNext.Enabled = True

    counter = 1
    Me.lbRecordNo.Caption = counter
Exit_cmdFirst_Click:
    Exit Sub

Err_cmdFirst_Click:
    MsgBox Err.Description
    Resume Exit_cmdFirst_Click
End Sub
```

6. Write the following Click event procedure for the Next command button:

```
Private Sub cmdNext_Click()
    On Error GoTo Err_cmdNext_Click

    rst.Update "City", Me.txtCity
    rst.MoveNext
    counter = counter + 1

    Me.cmdFirst.Enabled = True

    Call FillTxtBoxes(rst, Me)

    Me.cmdPrevious.Enabled = True
    Me.lbRecordNo.Caption = counter
    Me.txtCompany.SetFocus
    If counter = rst.RecordCount Then
        Me.cmdNext.Enabled = False
        Me.cmdLast.Enabled = False
    End If

Exit_cmdNext_Click:
    Exit Sub

Err_cmdNext_Click:
    MsgBox Err.Description
    Resume Exit_cmdNext_Click
End Sub
```

7. Write the following Click event procedure for the Previous command button:

```
Private Sub cmdPrevious_Click()
    On Error GoTo Err_cmdPrevious_Click

    rst.Update "City", Me.txtCity

    rst.MovePrevious
    counter = counter - 1

    Call FillTxtBoxes(rst, Me)

    Me.txtCompany.SetFocus
    Me.cmdLast.Enabled = True
    Me.cmdNext.Enabled = True

    Me.lbRecordNo.Caption = counter
    If counter = 1 Then
        Me.cmdFirst.Enabled = False
        Me.cmdPrevious.Enabled = False
    End If

Exit_cmdPrevious_Click:
    Exit Sub

Err_cmdPrevious_Click:
    MsgBox Err.Description
    Resume Exit_cmdPrevious_Click
End Sub
```

8. Write the following Click event procedure for the Last command button:

```
Private Sub cmdLast_Click()
    On Error GoTo Err_cmdLast_Click

    rst.Update "City", Me.txtCity
    rst.MoveLast

    Call FillTxtBoxes(rst, Me)

    Me.txtCompany.SetFocus
    Me.cmdFirst.Enabled = True
    Me.cmdPrevious.Enabled = True
    Me.cmdLast.Enabled = False
    Me.cmdNext.Enabled = False

    counter = rst.RecordCount
    Me.lbRecordNo.Caption = counter
Exit_cmdLast_Click:
    Exit Sub

Err_cmdLast_Click:
    MsgBox Err.Description
    Resume Exit_cmdLast_Click
End Sub
```

Notice that all the Click event procedures you prepared in steps 5-8 above contain the following line of code:

```
rst.Update "City", Me.txtCity
```

This statement updates the value of the City field in the recordset with the current value found in the txtCity text box on the form as you move through the records. Although the user can enter data in other text boxes, all modifications are ignored as there is no code in the Click event procedures that will allow changes to fields other than City. Of course, you can easily change this behavior by adding the necessary lines of code.

Depending on which button was clicked, certain command buttons are disabled and others are enabled. This gives the user a visual clue of what actions are allowed at a particular moment.

To make the form work, we need to write one more event procedure. Before closing the form, we must make sure that the changes to the City field in the current record are saved and all changes in the City field we made while working with the form data are written back to the disk file. In other words, we must replace the Companies.rst disk file with a new file. This is done in the Form_Unload event procedure as shown in step 9.

9. Write the code of the Form_Unload event procedure as shown below:

```
Private Sub Form_Unload(Cancel As Integer)
    If rst.Fields("City").OriginalValue <> Me.txtCity Then
        rst.Update "City", Me.txtCity
    End If
    Kill (CurrentProject.Path & "\Companies.rst")
    rst.Save CurrentProject.Path & "\Companies.rst", _
        adPersistADTG
End Sub
```

The ADO recordsets have a special property called OriginalValue, which is used for storing original values that were retrieved from a database. These original values are left unchanged while you edit the recordset offline. Any changes to the data made locally are recorded using the Value property of the Recordset object. The OriginalValue property is updated with the values changed locally when you reconnect to the database and perform an UpdateBatch operation (see Part 5 of Custom Project 16-2).

The Form_Unload event occurs when you attempt to close a form, but before the form is actually removed from the screen. This is a good place to perform those operations that must be executed before the form is closed. In the Form_Unload procedure above, we use the recordset's OriginalValue property to check whether changes were made to the content of the City field in the current record. If OriginalValue is different from the value found in the current record's txtCity text box, we want to save the record by using the Update method of the recordset. Next, we delete the file containing the original recordset and save the current recordset to a file with the same name.

Part 4: Viewing and Editing Data Offline

Now that you've written all the procedures for the custom application, let's begin using the form to view and edit the data.

1. Open the **frmCompanyInfo** form.
2. In the first record, replace Berlin with **Drezden**.
3. Click the **Last** button, and replace Warszawa with **Opole**.
4. Click the **First** button and notice that the value of City is Drezden, just as you changed it in step 2.
5. Use the **Next** button to move to the fourth record and replace London with **Dover**.
6. Close the form and then reopen it. Check the values in the City text box in the first, fourth, and last records. You should see Drezden, Dover, and Opole.

Part 5: Connecting to a Database to Update the Original Data

After you've made changes to the data by using the custom form, you can send the file with the modified recordset to your database administrator so that he or she can update the underlying database with your changes. Let's proceed to write a procedure that will take care of this task.

Note: The procedure that you are about to write will modify the Customers table in the Northwind database. I recommend that you take few minutes now and create a copy of this database so that you can restore the original data later if necessary.

1. In the Visual Basic Editor window, choose **Insert | Module**.
2. In the module's Code window, type the UpdateDb procedure shown below.

```
Sub UpdateDb()
    Dim conn As ADODB.Connection
    Dim rst As ADODB.Recordset
    Dim strNorthPath As String
    Dim strRecStat As String

    On Error GoTo ErrorHandle
    strNorthPath = "C:\Program Files\Microsoft Office\" & _
                    "Office11\Samples\Northwind.mdb"

    ' Open the connection to the database
    Set conn = New ADODB.Connection
    With conn
        .Provider = "Microsoft.Jet.OLEDB.4.0"
        .ConnectionString = "Data Source = " & strNorthPath
        .Mode = adModeReadWrite
        .Open
    End With

    ' Open the recordset from the local file
```

```
' that was persisted to the hard drive
' and update the data source with the changes
Set rst = New ADODB.Recordset
With rst
    .CursorLocation = adUseClient
    .Open CurrentProject.Path & "\Companies.rst", conn, _
            adOpenKeyset, adLockBatchOptimistic, adCmdFile
    .UpdateBatch adAffectAll

    ' Check if there were records with conflicts
    ' during the update
    .Filter = adFilterAffectedRecords
        Do Until .EOF
            strRecStat = strRecStat & rst!City & ":" & rst.Status
            .MoveNext
        Loop
    .Close
    Debug.Print strRecStat
End With

ExitHere:
    Set rst = Nothing
    Set conn = Nothing
    Exit Sub

ErrorHandle:
        MsgBox Err.Number & ": " & Err.Description
        Resume ExitHere
End Sub
```

In the UpdateDb procedure shown above, we used the UpdateBatch method of the ADO Recordset object to update the underlying database with the changes we made to the data while working with it offline. The UpdateBatch method takes an optional parameter that determines how many records will be affected by the update. This parameter can be one of the constants shown in Table 16-1.

Table 16-1: Enumerated constants used with the UpdateBatch method

Constant	Value	Description
adAffectCurrent	1	Pending changes will be written only for the current record.
adAffectGroup	2	Pending changes will be written for the records that satisfy the current filter.
adAffectAll	3	Pending changes will be written for all the records in the recordset. This is the default.

When you update the data, your changes are compared with values that are currently in the database. The update will fail if the record was deleted or updated in the underlying database since the recordset was saved to disk. Therefore, after calling the UpdateBatch method, you should check the status of the records to locate records with conflicts. To do this, we must filter the recordset to see only the affected records:

```
rst.Filter = adFilterAffectedRecords
```

Next, we loop through the recordset and check the Status property of each record. This property can return different values, as shown in Table 16-2. You can locate these values in the Object Browser by typing RecordStatusEnum in the Search box.

Table 16-2: RecordStatusEnum constants returned by the Status property

Constant	Value	Description
adRecCanceled	0x100	The record was not saved because the operation was cancelled.
adRecCantRelease	0x400	The new record was not saved because the existing record was locked.
adRecConcurrencyViolation	0x800	The record was not saved because optimistic concurrency was in use.
adRecDBDeleted	0x40000	The record has already been deleted from the data source.
adRecDeleted	0x4	The record was deleted.
adRecIntegrityViolation	0x1000	The record was not saved because the user violated integrity constraints.
adRecInvalid	0x10	The record was not saved because its bookmark is invalid.
adRecMaxChangesExceeded	0x2000	The record was not saved because there were too many pending changes.
adRecModified	0x2	The record was modified.
adRecMultipleChanges	0x40	The record was not saved because it would have affected multiple records.
adRecNew	0x1	The record is new.
adRecObjectOpen	0x4000	The record was not saved because of a conflict with an open storage object.
adRecOK	0	The record was successfully updated.
adRecOutOfMemory	0x8000	The record was not saved because the computer has run out of memory.
adRecPendingChanges	0x80	The record was not saved because it refers to a pending insert.
adRecPermissionDenied	0x10000	The record was not saved because the user has insufficient permissions.
adRecSchemaViolation	0x20000	The record was not saved because it violates the structure of the underlying database.
adRecUnmodified	0x8	The record was not modified.

If the updates occurred without any conflict, the Status property will return the value of 8 (adRecUnmodified). While iterating through the recordset you can add additional code to resolve any encountered conflicts or check, for example, the original value and the updated value of the fields in updated records. As mentioned earlier, the OriginalValue property returns the field value that existed prior to any changes (since the last Update method was called). You can cancel all pending updates by using the CancelBatch method.

3. Run the UpdateDb procedure to write your changes to the database.

4. Open the Northwind database and review the content of the City field in the Customers table. You should see Drezden, Dover, and Opole in the first, fourth, and last record.

5. Close the Northwind database.

This completes Custom Project 16-2 in which you learned how to:

- Save the recordset to disk with the Save method
- Create a custom form to view and edit the recordset data in the disk file
- Open the recordset from disk with the Open method
- Work with the recordset offline (view and edit data)
- Reopen the connection to the original database and write your changes with the UpdateBatch method

> **Note:** Refer to Part V of this book to find out how you can save a recordset in XML format using the adPersistXML format.

Cloning a Recordset

Sometimes you may want to manipulate a recordset without losing the current position in the recordset. You can do this by *cloning* your original recordset. Use the ADO Clone method to create a recordset that is a copy of another recordset. You can create a recordset clone like this:

```
Dim rstOrg As ADODB.Recordset        ' your original recordset
Dim rstClone As ADODB.Recordset      ' cloned recordset

Set rstCone = myOrgRst.Clone
```

As you can see from the assignment statement above, a *clone* is an object variable containing a reference to the original recordset. After you've used the Clone method, you end up with two copies of the recordset that contain the same records but can be filtered and manipulated separately. You can create more than one clone of the original recordset.

Use the Clone method when you want to perform an operation on a recordset that requires multiple current records. The Clone object and the original Recordset object each have their own current records; therefore, the record pointers in the original and cloned recordsets can move independently of one another. And, because the clone points to the same set of data as the original, any changes made using either the original recordset or any of its clones will be visible in the original and its clones. However, the original recordset and its clones can get out of sync if you requery the original recordset against the database.

When you close the original recordset, the clones remain open until you close them. Closing any of the clones does not close the original recordset.

Because the Clone method does not create another copy of the data (it only points to the data), cloning a recordset is faster and more efficient than opening a second recordset based on the same criteria. A recordset created by a method other than cloning will have a different set of bookmarks than the original recordset, even when it is based on the same SQL statement.

You can make a clone read-only by using an optional parameter like this:

```
Set rstCone = myOrgRst.Clone(adLockReadOnly)
```

It's worth mentioning that you can only clone bookmarkable recordsets. Use the Recordset object's Supports method to find out if the recordset supports bookmarks (see the section called "Using Bookmarks" in Chapter 13). If you try to clone a non-bookmarkable recordset, you will receive a run-time error.

The clone and the original recordset have the same bookmarks, which you can share. A bookmark reference from one Recordset object refers to the same record in any of its clones.

In Access, the Combo Box Wizard uses the Clone method in the combo box's AfterUpdate event. You will examine this code while building Custom Project 16-3. This project demonstrates how the Clone method can be used to create a single form for displaying the current and previous record side by side (see Figure 16-4).

◎ Custom Project 16-3: Displaying the Contents of the Current and Previous Record by Using the Clone Method

1. In the Northwind database, create a form in Design view based on the Customers table (see Figure 16-4). Follow the steps below to set up the form and its control properties.

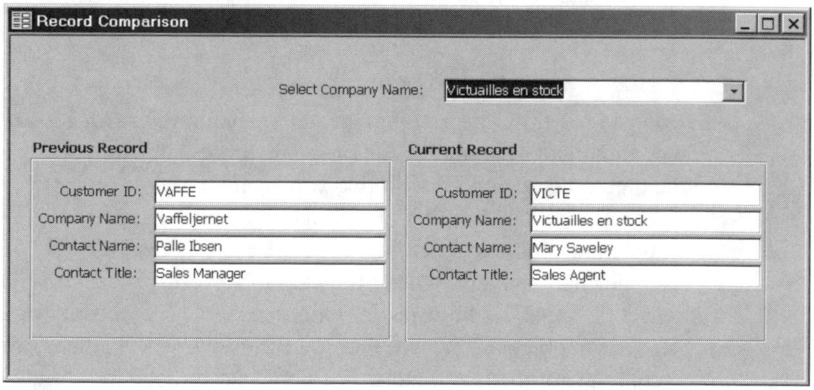

Figure 16-4: This custom form is used to demonstrate how you can use recordset cloning to read the contents of the previous record.

2. Use the Combo Box Wizard to add an unbound combo box to your form. In the Combo Box Wizard's first screen, choose the third option button: **Find a record on my form based on the value I selected in my combo box**, and click **Next**. The fields available in the Customers table should appear. Select **CustomerId** and **CompanyName** and click **Next**. In the next Wizard dialog, adjust the width of the combo box column to fit the company name and click **Finish**. Now you should see the combo box placed on your form.

3. Set the following properties for the form's controls (properties of controls that are not listed below do not need to be set for this application to work):

Object	Property	Setting
Label1 (in front of the combo box)	Caption Tag	Select Company Name cbo
Combo0 (created by the Combo Box Wizard)	Name Tag	CboCompany cbo
Label2	Caption Tag	Previous Record PrevRec
Label3	Caption	Current Record
Rectangle: Box1	Tag	PrevRec
Label4 (in front of Text box 1)	Caption Tag	Customer ID: PrevRec
Text box 1	Name Tag Control Source	CustIdPrev PrevRec should be blank
Label5 (in front of Text box 2)	Caption Tag	Company Name: PrevRec
Text box 2	Name Tag Control Source	CompanyPrev PrevRec should be blank
Label6 (in front of Text box 3)	Caption Tag	Contact Name: PrevRec
Text box 3	Name Tag Control Source	ContactPrev PrevRec should be blank
Label7 (in front of Text box 4)	Caption Tag	Contact Title: PrevRec
Text box 4	Name Tag Control Source	TitlePrev PrevRec should be blank
Label8 (in front of Text box 5)	Caption	Customer ID:
Text box 5	Name Control Source	CustomerID CustomerID
Label9 (in front of Text box 6)	Caption	Company Name:
Text box 6	Name Control Source	CompanyName CompanyName
Label10 (in front of Text box 7)	Caption	Contact Name:
Text box 7	Name Control Source	ContactName ContactName
Label11 (in front of Text box 8)	Caption	Contact Title:
Text box 8	Name Control Source	ContactTitle ContactTitle

4. Select the form by choosing **Edit | Select Form** and activate the form's properties sheet to set the following properties:

Property Name	Setting
Caption	Record Comparison
Scroll Bars	Neither
Record Selectors	No
Navigation Buttons	No

5. Save the form as **frmCompare**.

6. Click the Combo Box control on the form to select it. Activate the Event tab in the properties sheet and notice that the entry [Event Procedure] appears next to the AfterUpdate event name. Click on this entry and then click the **Ellipsis** button (with three dots) to activate the Code window. Take a look at the procedure that the Combo Box Wizard has written:

```
Private Sub Combo0_AfterUpdate()
    ' Find the record that matches the control.
    Dim rs As Object

    Set rs = Me.Recordset.Clone
    rs.FindFirst "[CustomerID] = '" & Me![Combo0] & "'"
    If Not rs.EOF Then Me.Bookmark = rs.Bookmark
End Sub
```

Notice that the wizard has created a clone of the form's recordset before calling the FindFirst method to locate the customer record based on the entry selected in the combo box. To ensure that the form's record is in sync with the entry selected in the combo box, the last line of code moves the form's bookmark to the same location as the recordset clone's bookmark as long as we are not at the end of file (EOF). If you comment out this last line of code, you will notice that selecting an entry in the combo box does not move the record to the selected company.

Notice that because we changed the properties of the combo box after we used the Combo Box Wizard, this code will not work.

7. Replace the references to Combo0 in the code prepared by the Combo Box Wizard with the name you assigned to the combo box's Name property. After the modification, your code should look like this:

```
Private Sub cboCompany_AfterUpdate()
    ' Find the record that matches the control.
    Dim rs As Object

    Set rs = Me.Recordset.Clone
    rs.FindFirst "[CustomerID] = '" & Me![cboCompany] & "'"
    If Not rs.EOF Then Me.Bookmark = rs.Bookmark
End Sub
```

8. After making the change in step 7, activate the combo box's properties sheet and ensure that the entry [Event Procedure] is displayed on the Event tab next to the AfterUpdate event of the combo box.

9. Save the current changes to the form.

10. Test your form by opening it in Form view. Selecting a company name from the combo box should fill the text boxes placed under the Current Record label with the selected company's data.

11. Revise the cboCompany_AfterUpdate() event procedure as shown below to have the form also display the data from the previous record.

```
Private Sub cboCompany_AfterUpdate()
' Find the record that matches the control.
    Dim rs As Object
    Dim c As Control

    On Error GoTo ErrHandle

    Set rs = Me.Recordset.Clone
    rs.FindFirst "[CustomerID] = '" & Me![cboCompany] & "'"
    If Not rs.EOF Then Me.Bookmark = rs.Bookmark
    ' Move to the previous record in the clone
    ' so that we can load the previous records'
    ' data in the form's text boxes
    rs.MovePrevious
    If Not rs.BOF Then
        For Each c In Me.Controls
                c.Visible = True
        Next
        Me.CustIdPrev = rs.Fields(0).Value
        Me.CompanyPrev = rs.Fields(1)
        Me.ContactPrev = rs.Fields(2)
        Me.TitlePrev = rs.Fields(3)
    Else
        For Each c In Me.Controls
            If c.Tag = "PrevRec" Then
                c.Visible = False
            End If
        Next
    End If
ExitHere:
    Exit Sub
ErrHandle:
    MsgBox Err.Number & ":" & Err.Description
    Resume ExitHere
End Sub
```

The revised cboCompany_AfterUpdate procedure ensures that the controls used to display the contents of the previous record are visible whenever the selected record is not the first record. The procedure uses the controls' Tag property to allow easy selection of controls that need to be hidden or made visible.

Before we start working with this custom project, let's write a Form_Load event procedure to ensure that only the combo box and its label are visible when the form is opened.

12. In the Form Design view, choose **Edit | Select Form**. In the form's properties sheet activate the Event tab, and click the **Build** button next to the **On Load** event name. In the Choose Builder dialog box, select **Code Builder** and click **OK**.

13. Enter the code for the Form_Load event procedure as shown below:

```
Private Sub Form_Load()
    Dim c As Control

    For Each c In Me.Controls
        If c.Tag <> "cbo" Then
            c.Visible = False
        End If
    Next
End Sub
```

14. Compile your VBA project by choosing the first option in the Debug menu.

15. Save and close your form.

16. Reopen the frmCompare form and test it by choosing various company names from the combo box.

Think of other ways to improve this form. For example, add a set of controls and write additional code to display the next record.

Introduction to Data Shaping

Designing database applications often requires that you pull information from multiple tables. For instance, to obtain a listing of customers and their orders, you must link the required tables with SQL join statements as demonstrated below:

```
SELECT Customers.CustomerID AS [Cust Id],
    Customers.CompanyName,
    Orders.OrderDate,
    [Order Details].OrderID,
    Products.ProductName,
    [Order Details].UnitPrice,
    [Order Details].Discount,
    CCur([Order Details].[UnitPrice]*[Quantity]*(1-[Discount])/100)*100 AS
        [Extended Price]
FROM Products
    INNER JOIN ((Customers
    INNER JOIN Orders ON Customers.CustomerID = Orders.CustomerID)
    INNER JOIN [Order Details] ON Orders.OrderID = [Order Details].OrderID)
    ON Products.ProductID = [Order Details].ProductID
ORDER BY Customers.CustomerID, Orders.OrderDate DESC;
```

Creating and Manipulating Databases with ADO

When you execute the above SQL statement, your output will match Figure 16-5.

Figure 16-5: When you use SQL join statements you get a flat recordset with a lot of duplicate information.

When you output your data in a standard way by using the SQL Join syntax, you get a lot of duplicate information. You can eliminate this redundant information by using an advanced feature of the ADO known as a *shaped* (or *hierarchical*) *recordset*.

Data shaping allows you to create recordsets within recordsets with a single ADO object. This sort of hierarchical data arrangement is often seen as a *parent-child relationship*. The parent recordset contains the child recordset. A child recordset can contain another child recordset, a grandchild of the original recordset. A parent-child relationship can be placed in an easy-to-read tree structure. You will produce such a structure in Custom Project 16-4 later in this chapter. For now, let's focus on learning a couple of new concepts that will enable you to present your data in a format that's easy to view and navigate.

Writing a Simple SHAPE statement

You can easily create a hierarchy of data by using a *data shaping language*. All you need to know is how to use the following three commands: SHAPE, APPEND, and RELATE. The basic data SHAPE syntax looks like this:

```
SHAPE {parent-command}
APPEND ({child-command} [[AS] table-alias]
RELATE (parent-column TO child-column)
```

The parent-command and child-command are often SQL SELECT statements that pull the data from the required tables. Let's look at the following example that uses the above syntax:

```
SHAPE {SELECT CustomerID as [Cust Id], CompanyName as [Company] FROM Customers}
APPEND ({SELECT CustomerId, OrderDate, OrderId, Freight FROM Orders} AS custOrders
RELATE (CustomerID TO CustomerID)
```

The statement above is a shaped recordset. This statement selects two fields from the Customers table and four fields from the Orders table. By using this

SHAPE statement, you can list all orders for each of the customers in the Customers table without returning any redundant information.

Notice that there are two SELECT statements in this recordset:

■ The first SELECT statement is the parent recordset. This recordset retrieves the data from the Customers table. Notice this SELECT statement is surrounded by curly braces and preceded by the SHAPE command, which defines a recordset.

■ The second SELECT statement is the child recordset. It gets the data from the Orders table. Notice that this SELECT statement is also surrounded by curly braces; however, it is preceded by the APPEND clause and an opening parenthesis. The APPEND clause will add the child recordset to the parent.

Note: When you append a child recordset to the parent recordset, a new field (column) is created in a parent recordset. This field is called a chapter column and has a data type called adChapter. You can use the AS clause to assign a name to the chapter column. If the appended column has no chapter-alias, a name will be generated for it automatically. In our example, the chapter column is called custOrders. Always specify an alias for your child recordset if you are planning to refer to it later in your code.

After specifying the SELECT statement for the child recordset, you must also indicate how you want the two recordsets to be linked. You do this with the RELATE clause. The column (CustomerID) from the parent recordset is related to the column (CustomerID) of the child recordset. Notice that you don't have to specify table names in the RELATE clause. Always specify the name of the parent column first.

Note: The fields you use to relate parent and child recordsets must be in both recordsets. For example, you could not relate both recordsets if you did not select CustomerID from the Orders table.

Finally, remember to place a closing parenthesis at the end of the statement.

Working with Data Shaping

To work with data shaping in your VBA procedure, you need two providers: one for the data shaping functionality and the other one for the data itself. Therefore, before you can create shaped (hierachical) recordsets in your programs, you will need to specify:

■ The name of a service provider

The data shaping functionality is provided by the Data Shaping Service for OLE DB. The name of this service provider is MSDataShape and it is specified as the value of the Connection object's Provider property like this:

```
conn.Provider = "MSDataShape"
```

or can be a connection string like this:

```
"Provider=MSDataShape"
```

■ The name of a data provider

Because a shaped recordset needs to be populated with rows of data, you must specify the name of a data provider as the value of the Data Provider property of the Connection object:

```
conn.DataProvider = "Microsoft.Jet.OLEDB.4.0;"
```

or the connection string like this:

```
"Data Provider=Microsoft.Jet.OLEDB.4.0;"
```

The following is a code fragment from the procedure in Hands-On 16-4 that demonstrates how to specify the names of the data and service providers:

```
' define database connection string
' using the OLE DB provider
' and Northwind database as Data Source
strConn = "Data Provider=Microsoft.Jet.OLEDB.4.0;"
strConn = strConn & "Data Source = C:\Program Files\" & _
    "Microsoft Office\Office11\Samples\Northwind.mdb"

' specify Data Shaping provider
' and open connection to the database
Set conn = New ADODB.Connection
With conn
    .ConnectionString = strConn
    .Provider = "MSDataShape"
    .Open
End With
```

Data Shaping with Other Databases

The data shaping service creates a shaped (hierarchical) recordset from any data supplied by a data provider. In order to provide shaped data from a database other than Microsoft Access, let's say, SQL Server database, a connection string might look like this:

```
Dim conn As ADODB.Connection
Set conn = New ADODB.Connection
conn.Open = "Provider = MSDataShape;" & _
    "Data Provider = SQLOLEDB;" & _
    "Server=myServerName;" & _
    "Initial Catalog = Northwind;" & _
    "User ID = myId; Password="
```

or like this:

```
Dim conn As ADODB.Connection
Set conn = New ADODB.Connection
conn.Provider = "MSDataShape"
conn.Open "Data Provider=SQLOLEDB; Integrated Security=SSPI; Database=Northwind"
```

The following hands-on creates a shaped recordset in a VBA procedure and displays hierarchical data in the Immediate window.

Hands-On 16-4: Creating a Shaped Recordset

Note: Because this hands-on retrieves data from the Northwind database, adjust the path found in the procedure code to point to the correct location of this file on your computer.

1. Insert a new module and, in the module's Code window, enter the ShapeDemo procedure as shown below.

```
Sub ShapeDemo()
    Dim conn As ADODB.Connection
    Dim rst As ADODB.Recordset
    Dim rstChapter As Variant
    Dim strConn As String
    Dim shpCmd As String

    ' define database connection string
    ' using the OLE DB provider
    ' and Northwind database as Data Source
    strConn = "Data Provider=Microsoft.Jet.OLEDB.4.0;"
    strConn = strConn & "Data Source = C:\Program Files\" & _
        "Microsoft Office\Office11\Samples\Northwind.mdb"

    ' specify Data Shaping provider
    ' and open connection to the database
    Set conn = New ADODB.Connection
    With conn
        .ConnectionString = strConn
        .Provider = "MSDataShape"
        .Open
    End With

    ' define the SHAPE command for the shaped recordset
    shpCmd = "SHAPE {SELECT CustomerID as [Cust Id], " & _
        " CompanyName as Company FROM Customers}" & _
        " APPEND ({SELECT CustomerID, OrderDate," & _
        " OrderID, Freight FROM Orders} AS custOrders" & _
        " RELATE [Cust Id] To CustomerID)"

    ' create and open the parent recordset
    ' using the open connection
    Set rst = New ADODB.Recordset
    rst.Open shpCmd, conn

    ' output data from the parent recordset
    Do While Not rst.EOF
        Debug.Print rst("Cust Id"); _
            Tab; rst("Company")
        rstChapter = rst("custOrders")
        ' write out column headings
        ' for the child recordset
```

```
                    Debug.Print Tab; _
                        "OrderDate", "Order #", "Freight"
                    ' output data from the child recordset
                    Do While Not rstChapter.EOF
                        Debug.Print Tab; _
                            rstChapter("OrderDate"), _
                            rstChapter("OrderID"), _
                            Format(rstChapter("Freight"), "$ #.##")
                        rstChapter.MoveNext
                    Loop
                rst.MoveNext
            Loop

            ' Cleanup
            rst.Close
            Set rst = Nothing
            Set conn = Nothing
        End Sub
```

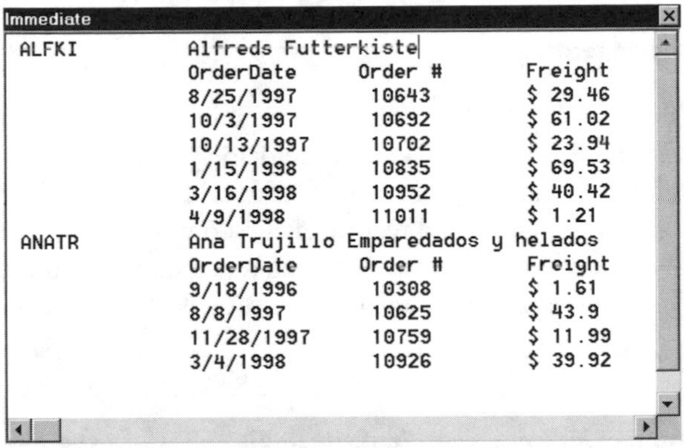

Immediate			
ALFKI	Alfreds Futterkiste		
	OrderDate	Order #	Freight
	8/25/1997	10643	$ 29.46
	10/3/1997	10692	$ 61.02
	10/13/1997	10702	$ 23.94
	1/15/1998	10835	$ 69.53
	3/16/1998	10952	$ 40.42
	4/9/1998	11011	$ 1.21
ANATR	Ana Trujillo Emparedados y helados		
	OrderDate	Order #	Freight
	9/18/1996	10308	$ 1.61
	8/8/1997	10625	$ 43.9
	11/28/1997	10759	$ 11.99
	3/4/1998	10926	$ 39.92

Figure 16-6: After running the ShapeDemo procedure in Hands-On 16-4, you can see the contents of the hierarchical recordset in the Immediate window.

Let's take a few minutes to examine the ShapeDemo procedure in Hands-On 16-4. This procedure begins by specifying the data provider and data source name in the strConn variable. Next, we define a new ADO connection object and set the ConnectionString property of this object to the strConn variable. Now that we have the data provider name and also know which database we need to pull the data from, we go on to specify the data shaping service provider. This is done by using the Provider property of the Connection object. We set this property to MSDataShape, which is the name of the service provider for the hierarchical recordsets. Now we are ready to actually open a connection to the database. Before we can pull the required data from the database, we define the shaped recordset statement and store it in the ShpCmd String variable. Next, we create a new Recordset object and open it using the open database connection. Then, we populate it with the content of the ShpCmd variable like this:

```
Set rst = New ADODB.Recordset
rst.Open shpCmd, conn
```

Now that we have filled the hierarchical recordset, we begin to loop through the parent recordset. The first statement in the loop

```
Debug.Print rst("Cust Id"); Tab; rst("Company")
```

will write out the customer ID (Cust Id) and the company name (Company) to the Immediate window.

In the second statement in the loop

```
rstChapter = rst("custOrders")
```

we create a Recordset object variable based on the value of the custOrders field.

As you recall from an earlier discussion, custOrders is an alias for the child recordset. The Object variable (rstChapter) can be any name you like as long as it's not a VBA keyword.

➔ **Note:** Because a child recordset is simply a field in a parent recordset, when you retrieve the value of that field you will get the entire recordset filtered to include only the related records.

Before iterating through the child recordset, the column headings are output to the Immediate window for the fields we want to display. This way it is much easier to understand the meaning of the data in the child recordset. The next block of code loops through the child recordset and dumps the data to the Immediate window under the appropriate column heading. Once the data is retrieved for each parent record, we can close the recordset and release the memory.

How to Determine If a Recordset Contains a Field Pointing to Another Recordset

To find out if a certain recordset contains another recordset, you can use the following conditional statement:

```
Dim rst as New ADODB.Recordset

If rst.Fields("custOrders").Type = adChapter then
    Debug.Print "This is a child recordset"
End If
```

Note: custOrders is the chapter column alias you created with the AS clause while appending a child recordset to the parent.

Writing a Complex SHAPE Statement

In the previous section, you worked with a simple SHAPE statement that displayed order information for each customer in the Northwind database in the Immediate window. You learned how to nest a child recordset within a parent recordset and access the fields in both.

In the following sections, you will learn how to write more complex SHAPE statements that include multiple child and grandchild recordsets.

Shaped Recordsets with Multiple Children

Data shaping does not limit you to having just one child recordset within a parent recordset. You can specify as many children as you want. For example, to display a parent with two children, use the following syntax:

```
SHAPE {SELECT * FROM Parent}
APPEND ({SELECT * FROM Child1}
            RELATE parent-column TO child1-column) AS child1-alias,
        ({SELECT * FROM Child2}
            RELATE parent-column TO child2-column) AS child2-alias
```

Notice that additional children (siblings) are added to the end of the APPEND clause.

Suppose you want to display both the orders and products for a customer in the Northwind database. Using the syntax provided earlier, you can shape your hierarchical recordset as demonstrated in the ShapeMultiChildren procedure shown in Hands-On 16-5.

Hands-On 16-5: Creating a Shaped Recordset with Multiple Children

Note: Because this hands-on retrieves data from the Northwind database, adjust the path found in the procedure code to point to the correct location of this file on your computer.

1. Insert a new module and, in the module's Code window, enter the ShapeMultiChildren procedure as shown below.

```
Sub ShapeMultiChildren()
    Dim conn As ADODB.Connection
    Dim rst As ADODB.Recordset
    Dim rstChapter1 As Variant
    Dim rstChapter2 As Variant
    Dim strConn As String
    Dim shpCmd As String
    Dim strParent As String
    Dim strChild1 As String
    Dim strChild2 As String
    Dim strLink As String
    Dim str1stChildName As String
    Dim str2ndChildName As String

    ' define database connection string
    ' using the OLE DB provider
    ' and Northwind database as Data Source
    strConn = "Data Provider=Microsoft.Jet.OLEDB.4.0;"
    strConn = strConn & "Data Source = " & _
            CurrentProject.Path & "\Northwind.mdb"

    ' specify Data Shaping provider
```

```
' and open connection to the database
Set conn = New ADODB.Connection
With conn
    .ConnectionString = strConn
    .Provider = "MSDataShape"
    .Open
End With

' define the SHAPE command for the shaped recordset

strParent = "SELECT CustomerID as [Cust Id], " & _
    "CompanyName as Company FROM Customers"

strChild1 = "SELECT CustomerID, OrderDate," & _
    "OrderID, Freight FROM Orders"

strChild2 = "SELECT Customers.CustomerID," & _
    "Products.ProductName FROM Products " & _
    "INNER JOIN ((Customers INNER JOIN Orders ON " & _
    "Customers.CustomerID = Orders.CustomerID) " & _
    "INNER JOIN [Order Details] ON " & _
    "Orders.OrderID = [Order Details].OrderID) ON " & _
    "Products.ProductID = [Order Details].ProductID " & _
    "Order By Products.ProductName"

str1stChildName = "custOrders"
str2ndChildName = "custProducts"

strLink = "RELATE [Cust Id] To CustomerID"

shpCmd = "SHAPE {"
shpCmd = shpCmd & strParent
shpCmd = shpCmd & "}"
shpCmd = shpCmd & " APPEND ({"
shpCmd = shpCmd & strChild1
shpCmd = shpCmd & "}"
shpCmd = shpCmd & strLink
shpCmd = shpCmd & ")"
shpCmd = shpCmd & " AS " & str1stChildName
shpCmd = shpCmd & ", ({"
shpCmd = shpCmd & strChild2
shpCmd = shpCmd & "} "
shpCmd = shpCmd & strLink
shpCmd = shpCmd & ")"
shpCmd = shpCmd & " AS " & str2ndChildName

' create and open the parent recordset
' using the open connection
Set rst = New ADODB.Recordset
rst.Open shpCmd, conn

' output data from the parent recordset
Do While Not rst.EOF
```

```
                    Debug.Print rst("Cust Id"); Tab; rst("Company")
                    rstChapter1 = rst("custOrders")

                    ' write out column headings
                    ' for the 1st child recordset
                    Debug.Print Tab(4); " (" & rst("Cust Id") & " Orders)"
                    Debug.Print Tab; "OrderDate", "Order #", "Freight"

                    ' output data from the 1st child recordset
                    Do While Not rstChapter1.EOF
                        Debug.Print Tab; _
                            rstChapter1("OrderDate"), _
                            rstChapter1("OrderID"), _
                            Format(rstChapter1("Freight"), "$ #,#0.00")
                        rstChapter1.MoveNext
                    Loop

                    rstChapter2 = rst("custProducts")
                    ' write out column headings
                    ' for the 2nd child recordset
                    Debug.Print Tab(4); " (" & rst("Cust Id") & " Products)"

                    ' output data from the 2nd child recordset
                    Do While Not rstChapter2.EOF
                        Debug.Print Tab; _
                            rstChapter2("ProductName")
                        rstChapter2.MoveNext
                    Loop
                rst.MoveNext
            Loop

            ' Cleanup
            rst.Close
            Set rst = Nothing
            Set conn = Nothing
        End Sub
```

The SHAPE statement in the above procedure has been specially formatted so that you can easily create any shaped recordset containing multiple children by replacing SELECT statements with your own. This procedure produces the output in the Immediate window as shown in Figure 16-7. Notice that each customer has two child records: Orders and Products.

```
┌─Immediate────────────────────────────────────────────────────────[×]─┐
│ ALFKI      Alfreds Futterkiste                                    [▲]│
│   (ALFKI Orders)                                                     │
│             OrderDate      Order #        Freight                    │
│             8/25/1997      10643         $ 29.46                     │
│             10/3/1997      10692         $ 61.02                     │
│             10/13/1997     10702         $ 23.94                     │
│             1/15/1998      10835         $ 69.53                     │
│             3/16/1998      10952         $ 40.42                     │
│             4/9/1998       11011         $ 1.21                      │
│     (ALFKI Products)                                                 │
│             Aniseed Syrup                                            │
│             Chartreuse verte                                         │
│             Escargots de Bourgogne                                   │
│             Fløtemysost                                              │
│             Grandma's Boysenberry Spread                             │
│             Lakkalikööri                                             │
│             Original Frankfurter grüne Soße                          │
│             Raclette Courdavault                                     │
│             Rössle Sauerkraut                                        │
│             Rössle Sauerkraut                                        │
│             Spegesild                                                │
│             Vegie-spread                                             │
│  ANATR      Ana Trujillo Emparedados y helados                       │
│   (ANATR Orders)                                                     │
│             OrderDate      Order #        Freight                    │
│             9/18/1996      10308         $ 1.61                   [▼]│
│ [◄][       ]                                                    [►] │
└───────────────────────────────────────────────────────────────────┘
```

Figure 16-7: After running the ShapeMultiChildren procedure in Hands-On 16-5, you can see the output of the hierarchical recordset with multiple children in the Immediate window.

Shaped Recordsets with Grandchildren

In addition to the parent recordset having multiple children, the child recordset can contain a child of its own. Simply put, your hierarchical recordset can contain grandchildren. Creating such a hierarchy is a bit harder, but it can be tackled in no time if you take a step-by-step approach. The SHAPE syntax that includes grandchildren looks like this:

```
SHAPE {SELECT * FROM Parent}
APPEND (( SHAPE {SELECT * FROM Child}
    APPEND ({SELECT * FROM Grandchild}
    RELATE child-column TO grandchild-column) AS grandchild-alias)
RELATE parent-column TO child-column) as child-alias
```

Notice that when grandchildren are present, the child recordset is appended with another SHAPE command.

Although you can have as many children or grandchildren as you want, it will be more difficult to write a SHAPE statement that uses more than three or four levels.

Quickly Generate SHAPE Commands

If you happen to have a copy of Visual Basic 6.0, you can use the Data Environment Designer to visually create SHAPE commands. Using this tool can save you time, especially when you need to create complex shapes containing grandchildren and aggregations. You can also use the hierarchical FlexGrid ActiveX control to quickly display your shaped recordset.

Now it's time for a special project. In Custom Project 16-4 you will create a shaped recordset that contains both children and grandchildren. Next, you will display this recordset on the Access form in the ActiveX TreeView control (see

Figure 16-12 for the final output). This project will also introduce you to using aggregate functions within your shaped recordsets.

◎ Custom Project 16-4: Using Hierarchical Recordsets

Part 1: Creating a Form with a TreeView Control

1. In the left pane of the Database window, click the **Forms** object button, and click the **New** button.

2. In the New Form window, choose **Design View** and click **OK**. The Form design window opens.

3. Choose **Insert | ActiveX Control**.

4. In the ActiveX Control box, choose **Microsoft TreeView Control 6.0** as shown in Figure 16-8, and click **OK** to place a TreeView control on the form.

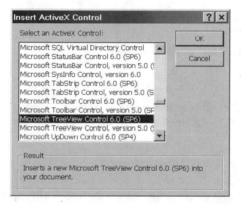

Figure 16-8: The Microsoft TreeView control provides an excellent way to display shaped recordsets in an Access form.

5. Resize the TreeView control and the form to match Figure 16-9.

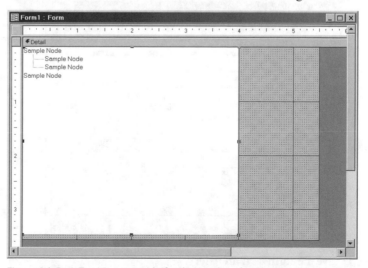

Figure 16-9: A TreeView control after being placed and resized on the Access form.

6. Click the TreeView control to select it and choose **View | Properties**.

7. In the ActiveX Control properties sheet, change the Name property of the TreeView control to **myTreeCtrl**, as shown in Figure 16-10.

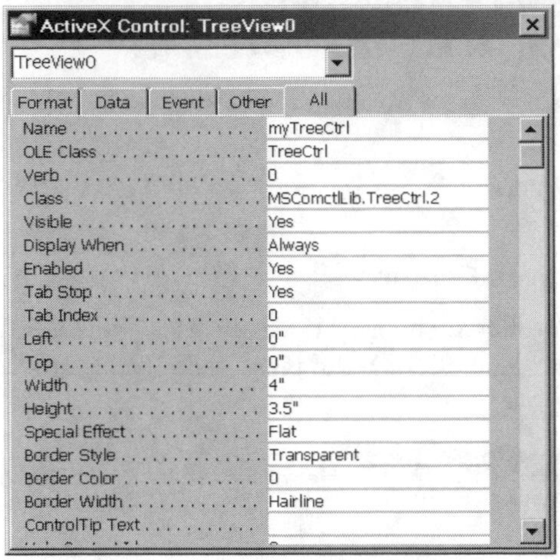

Figure 16-10: You can set the standard properties of the TreeView control by right-clicking the control in the form's Design view and choosing Properties.

8. Close the properties sheet. You should be back in Design view.

9. Choose **Edit | TreeCtrl Object** and click **Properties**. Adjust the custom properties of the TreeView control as listed on the General tab in Figure 16-11.

   Notice that in addition to the properties access via the Access properties sheet (see Figure 16-10), the ActiveX TreeView control exposes a number of custom properties that can be adjusted via the TreeCtrl Properties window as shown in Figure 16-11.

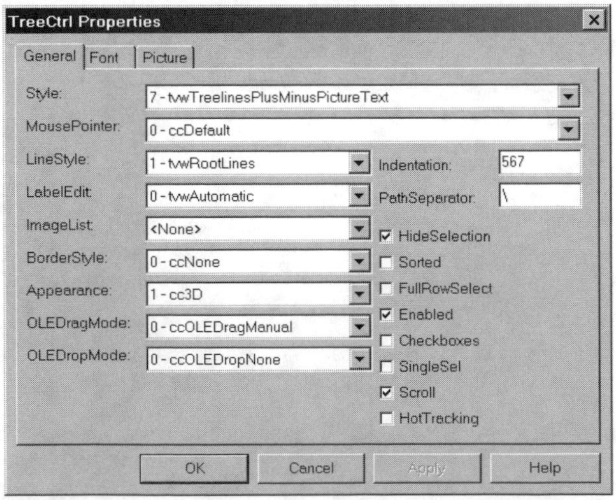

Figure 16-11: You can set custom properties of the TreeView control in the TreeCtrl Properties window by choosing Edit | TreeCtrl Object.

10. Save the form as **frmOrders**.

Part 2: Writing an Event Procedure for the Form Load Event

1. In the Form Design view where you placed the TreeView control, choose **Edit | Select Form**.

2. Choose **View | Properties** to display the Properties window for the selected form.

3. In the Form window, select the Event tab, and click next to the **On Load** event property.

4. Click the **Build** button (…) next to the OnLoad property to display the Choose Builder window.

5. In the Choose Builder window, select **Code Builder** and click **OK**. The form module window appears with the following Form_Load event procedure stub:

```
Private Sub Form_Load()

End Sub
```

6. Write the code for the Form_Load event procedure as shown below:

```
Private Sub Form_Load()
    Dim conn As ADODB.Connection
    Dim rstCustomers As ADODB.Recordset
    Dim rstOrders As ADODB.Recordset
    Dim rstOrderDetails As ADODB.Recordset
    Dim fld As Field
    Dim objNode1 As Node
    Dim objNode2 As Node
    Dim strConn As String
    Dim strSQL As String

    Dim strSQLCustomers As String
    Dim strSQLOrders As String
    Dim strSQLOrderDetails As String
    Dim strSQLRelParentToChild As String
    Dim strSQLRelGParentToParent As String

    ' Create the ADO Connection object
    Set conn = New ADODB.Connection

    ' Specify a valid connection string
    strConn = "Data Provider=Microsoft.Jet.OLEDB.4.0;"
    strConn = strConn & "Data Source = " & _
            CurrentProject.Path & "\Northwind.mdb"
    conn.ConnectionString = strConn

    ' Specify the Data Shaping provider
    conn.Provider = "MSDataShape"

    ' Open the connection
    conn.Open
```

```
' Specify SELECT statement for the Grandparent
strSQLCustomers = "SELECT CustomerID AS [Cust #]," & _
                  "CompanyName AS [Customer] " & _
                  "FROM Customers"

' Specify SELECT statement for the Parent
strSQLOrders = "SELECT OrderID AS [Order #]," & _
               "OrderDate AS [Order Date]," & _
               "Orders.CustomerID AS [Cust #] " & _
               "FROM Orders ORDER BY OrderDate DESC"

' Specify SELECT statement for the Child
strSQLOrderDetails = "SELECT od.OrderID AS [Order #]," & _
                     "p.CategoryId AS [Category]," & _
                     "p.ProductName AS [Product]," & _
                     "od.Quantity," & _
                     "od.ProductId," & _
                     "od.UnitPrice AS [Unit Price]," & _
                     "(od.UnitPrice * od.Quantity) " & _
                     "AS [Extended Price] " & _
                     "FROM [Order Details] od " & _
                     "INNER JOIN Products p " & _
                     "ON od.ProductID = p.ProductID " & _
                     "ORDER BY p.CategoryId, p.ProductName"

' Specify RELATE clause to link Parent to Child
strSQLRelParentToChild = "RELATE [Order #] TO [Order #]"

' Specify RELATE clause to link Grandparent to Parent
strSQLRelGParentToParent = "RELATE [Cust #] TO [Cust #]"

' Build complete SQL statement for the shaped recordset
' adding aggregate functions for the Grandparent and Parent
strSQL = "SHAPE(SHAPE{" & strSQLCustomers & "}"
strSQL = strSQL & "APPEND((SHAPE{" & strSQLOrders & "} "
strSQL = strSQL & "APPEND({" & strSQLOrderDetails & "} "
strSQL = strSQL & strSQLRelParentToChild & ") AS rstOrderDetails,"
strSQL = strSQL & "COUNT(rstOrderDetails.Product) "
strSQL = strSQL & "        AS [Items On Order],"
strSQL = strSQL & "SUM(rstOrderDetails.[Extended Price]) "
strSQL = strSQL & "        AS [Order Total])"
strSQL = strSQL & strSQLRelGParentToParent & ") AS [rstOrders],"
strSQL = strSQL & "SUM(rstOrders.[Order Total]) "
strSQL = strSQL & "        AS [Cust Grand Total]"
strSQL = strSQL & ") AS rstCustomers"

' Create and open the Grandparent recordset
Set rstCustomers = New ADODB.Recordset
rstCustomers.Open strSQL, conn

' Fill the TreeView control
Do While Not rstCustomers.EOF
```

```
    Set objNode1 = myTreeCtrl.Nodes.Add _
        (Text:=rstCustomers.Fields(0) & _
        "   " & rstCustomers.Fields(1) & _
        "   ($ " & rstCustomers.Fields(3) & ")")
    Set rstOrders = rstCustomers.Fields("rstOrders").Value
        Do While Not rstOrders.EOF
            Set objNode2 = myTreeCtrl.Nodes.Add _
                (relative:=objNode1.Index, _
                relationship:=tvwChild, _
                Text:=rstOrders.Fields(0) & _
                "   " & rstOrders.Fields(1) & _
                "   " & rstOrders.Fields(4) & " (items)" & _
                "     $" & rstOrders.Fields(5) & _
                " (Order Total)")
            Set rstOrderDetails = _
                rstOrders.Fields("rstOrderDetails").Value
                Do While Not rstOrderDetails.EOF
                    myTreeCtrl.Nodes.Add _
                        relative:=objNode2.Index, _
                        relationship:=tvwChild, _
                        Text:=rstOrderDetails.Fields(3) & _
                        "   " & rstOrderDetails.Fields(2) & _
                        "   $" & rstOrderDetails.Fields(6) & _
                        "   (" & rstOrderDetails.Fields(3) & _
                        " x $" & rstOrderDetails.Fields(5) & ")"
                    rstOrderDetails.MoveNext
                Loop
            rstOrders.MoveNext
        Loop
        rstCustomers.MoveNext
    Loop

    ' Cleanup
        rstCustomers.Close
        Set rstCustomers = Nothing
        Set conn = Nothing
End Sub
```

When you open the frmOrders form, the Form_Load procedure shown in step 6 populates the TreeView control with the data from the Northwind database. As you can see from Figure 16-12, the results are quite impressive. Clicking on the nodes in the TreeView control expands and collapses the details underneath the node. You can quickly create such hierarchical views of your own data by modifying the Form_Load procedure's SQL statements.

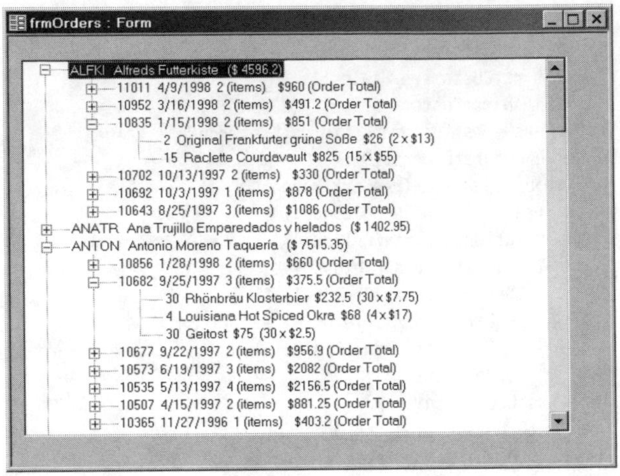

Figure 16-12: The TreeView control is filled with the data from the Northwind database when the user opens the form.

Prior to populating the TreeView control with the data, we connect to the database and enlist the services of the Data Shaping provider:

```
conn.Provider = "MSDataShape"
```

Because a TreeView control displays data as a hierachy, we need to build a complex SQL statement using the SHAPE syntax we learned in preceding sections.

To make things easier for ourselves, we start by defining SQL statements with fields we want to display for parent, child, and grandchild recordsets. Notice that we renamed some fields using the AS clause. We also defined separate statements to allow us to link grandparent to parent and parent to child.

The structure we need to create can be illustrated like this:

```
Grandparent
      Parent
            Child
```

Now that we've defined the relationship and the fields for our data hierachy, we use the SHAPE commands to build the complete SHAPE statement:

```
strSQL = "SHAPE(SHAPE{" & strSQLCustomers & "}"
strSQL = strSQL & "APPEND((SHAPE{" & strSQLOrders & "} "
strSQL = strSQL & "APPEND({" & strSQLOrderDetails & "} "
strSQL = strSQL & strSQLRelParentToChild & ") AS rstOrderDetails,"
strSQL = strSQL & "COUNT(rstOrderDetails.Product) "
strSQL = strSQL & "          AS [Items On Order],"
strSQL = strSQL & "SUM(rstOrderDetails.[Extended Price]) "
strSQL = strSQL & "          AS [Order Total])"
strSQL = strSQL & strSQLRelGParentToParent & ") AS [rstOrders],"
strSQL = strSQL & "SUM(rstOrders.[Order Total]) "
strSQL = strSQL & "          AS [Cust Grand Total]"
strSQL = strSQL & ") AS rstCustomers"
```

Creating and Manipulating Databases with ADO

While creating the SHAPE statement, we added additional calculated fields using the aggregate functions. For instance, in the parent recordset (rstOrders) we calculated the number of items ordered using the COUNT function,

```
COUNT(rstOrderDetails.Product) AS [Items On Order]
```

and used the SUM function to obtain the total amount of the order:

```
SUM(rstOrderDetails.[Extended Price]) AS [Order Total]
```

In the grandparent recordset (rstCustomers) we used the SUM function to calculate the total amount owed by a customer.

When expanded, the complete SHAPE statement will look as follows:

```
strSQL = "SHAPE(SHAPE{"
strSQL = strSQL & "SELECT CustomerID AS [Cust #],"
strSQL = strSQL & "CompanyName AS [Customer]"
strSQL = strSQL & "FROM Customers"
strSQL = strSQL & "}"
strSQL = strSQL & "APPEND((SHAPE{"
strSQL = strSQL & "SELECT OrderID AS [Order #],"
strSQL = strSQL & "OrderDate AS [Order Date],"
strSQL = strSQL & "Orders.CustomerID AS [Cust #]"
strSQL = strSQL & "FROM Orders "
strSQL = strSQL & "ORDER BY OrderDate DESC"
strSQL = strSQL & "}"
strSQL = strSQL & "APPEND({"
strSQL = strSQL & "SELECT od.OrderID AS [Order #],"
strSQL = strSQL & "p.CategoryId AS [Category],"
strSQL = strSQL & "p.ProductName AS [Product],"
strSQL = strSQL & "od.Quantity,"
strSQL = strSQL & "od.ProductId,"
strSQL = strSQL & "od.UnitPrice AS [Unit Price],"
strSQL = strSQL & "(od.UnitPrice * od.Quantity) "
strSQL = strSQL & "AS [Extended Price] "
strSQL = strSQL & "FROM [Order Details] od INNER JOIN Products p "
strSQL = strSQL & "ON od.ProductID = p.ProductID "
strSQL = strSQL & "ORDER BY p.CategoryId, p.ProductName"
strSQL = strSQL & "}"
strSQL = strSQL & "RELATE [Order #] TO [Order #]"
strSQL = strSQL & ")"
strSQL = strSQL & "AS rstOrderDetails,"
strSQL = strSQL & "COUNT(rstOrderDetails.Product) "
strSQL = strSQL & "AS [Items On Order],"
strSQL = strSQL & "SUM(rstOrderDetails.[Extended Price]) "
strSQL = strSQL & "AS [Order Total])"
strSQL = strSQL & "RELATE [Cust #] TO [Cust #]"
strSQL = strSQL & ") "
strSQL = strSQL & "AS [rstOrders],"
strSQL = strSQL & "SUM(rstOrders.[Order Total]) "
strSQL = strSQL & "AS [Cust Grand Total]) AS rstCustomers"
```

Notice that the SHAPE statement we built contains standard fields pulled from the database tables and child recordsets (rstOrders, rstOrderDetails), as well as calculated columns. The rstOrders recordset is a field in the rstCustomers recordset. This field contains order information for a customer. rstOrderDetails is a field within the rstOrders recordset. This field contains the order details information for a customer's order.

Now that we've completed the SHAPE statement, we can open the grandparent recordset and begin populating the TreeView control with our data.

A TreeView control consists of Node objects, which you can expand or collapse to display or hide child nodes. Nodes that have child nodes are referred to as *parent* nodes. The nodes located at the top of the tree control are referred to as *root* nodes. Root nodes can have *sibling* nodes that are located on the same level. For example, customer ALFKI (see Figure 16-12) is a root node, and so is the customer ANATR, ANTON, and so on. They are also siblings of one another.

To populate a TreeView control, we use the Add method of the Nodes collection like this:

```
Set objNode1 = myTreeCtrl.Nodes.Add
```

The objNode1 above is an object variable representing the Node object. The first node added to a tree view is a root node.

The Add method of the Nodes collection uses the following syntax:

```
object.Add([relative,] [relationship,] [key], text[, image,] [selectedimage])
```

In the syntax above, the only required arguments are object and text. The object is the Object variable (myTreeCtrl) representing the TreeView control. The text is a string that appears in the node. Now, looking at the complete statement

```
Set objNode1 = myTreeCtrl.Nodes.Add _
        (Text:=rstCustomers.Fields(0) & _
    "    " & rstCustomers.Fields(1) & _
    "    ($ " & rstCustomers.Fields(3) & ")")
```

we have created a root node to display the following information:

```
Cust # (rstCustomers.Fields(0))
Customer (rstCustomers.Fields(1))
Cust Grand Total (rstCustomers.Fields(3))
```

Because the above statement appears inside a looping structure, the TreeView control will display all the customers at their root level.

Now that we've taken care of the root node, we go on to add children and grandchildren. A child node has a relationship to a parent node that has already been added. To define a child node, in addition to the required text argument, we will use two optional arguments of the Add method as described below:

■ relative — This is the index number or key of a preexisting Node object. In our example, we used the index of the parent node that we just created (relative:=objNode1.Index).

➡ **Note:** When a Node object is created, it is automatically assigned an index number. This number is stored in the Node object's Index property.

■ relationship — Specifies the type of relationship you are creating. Use the tvwChild setting to create a child node of the node named in the relative argument (see above).

The statement that creates a child node looks like this:

```
Set objNode2 = myTreeCtrl.Nodes.Add _
        (relative:=objNode1.Index, _
        relationship:=tvwChild, _
        Text:=rstOrders.Fields(0) & _
    "  " & rstOrders.Fields(1) & _
    "  " & rstOrders.Fields(4) & " (items)" & _
    "     $" & rstOrders.Fields(5) & _
    " (Order Total)")
```

The above statement displays order information for a customer. The child node text argument is set to display:

```
Order # (rstOrders.Fields(0))
Order Date (rstOrders.Fields(1))
Items On Order (rstOrders.Fields(4))
Order Total (rstOrders.Fields(5))
```

Because the statement above appears inside a looping structure, the TreeView control will display the order information for each customer.

Finally, we add grandchildren using the following statement:

```
myTreeCtrl.Nodes.Add _
        relative:=objNode2.Index, _
        relationship:=tvwChild, _
        Text:=rstOrderDetails.Fields(3) & _
    "  " & rstOrderDetails.Fields(2) & _
    "  $" & rstOrderDetails.Fields(6) & _
    "  (" & rstOrderDetails.Fields(3) & _
    " x $" & rstOrderDetails.Fields(5) & ")"
```

The above statement displays order details for a customer's order. Notice that this Node object references the index number of the child object that has just been added (relative:=objNode2.Index).

The grandchild node text argument is set to display:

```
Quantity (rstOrderDetails.Fields(3))
Product (rstOrderDetails.Fields(2))
Extended Price (rstOrderDetails.Fields(6))
Quantity x Unit Price (rstOrderDetails.Fields(3) & "x $" &
rstOrderDetails.Fields(5))
```

The looping structure ensures that the order details above are listed for all customers' orders.

Now that you are done with this custom project, you should be able to provide your own hierarchical data in a pretty neat user interface.

Transaction Processing

To improve your application's performance and to ensure that database activities can be recovered in case an unexpected hardware or software error occurs, consider grouping sets of database activities into a transaction. A *transaction* is a set of operations that are performed together as as a single unit. If you use an automatic teller machine (ATM), you are already familiar with transaction processing. When you go to the bank to get cash, your account must be debited. In other words, the cash withdrawal must be deducted from your savings or checking account. A transaction is a two-sided operation. If anything goes wrong during the transaction, the entire transaction is cancelled. If both operations succeed, that is, you get the cash and the bank debits your account, the transaction's work is saved (or committed).

Database transactions often involve modifications and additions of one or more records in a single table or in several tables. When a transaction has to be undone or cancelled, the transaction is rolled back. Often, when you perform batch updates to database tables and an error occurs, updates to all tables must be cancelled or the database could be left in an inconsistent state.

Transactions are extremely important for maintaining data integrity and consistency. If you don't use transactions for operations that should be performed together, the database could be left in an inconsistent state, resulting not only in loss of important information but also in a number of other headaches.

In ADO, the Connection object offers three methods (BeginTrans, CommitTrans, and RollbackTrans) for managing transaction processing. You should use these methods to save or cancel a series of changes made to the data as a single unit.

- BeginTrans — Begins a new transaction.
- CommitTrans — Saves any changes and ends the current transaction.
- RollbackTrans — Cancels any changes made during the current transaction and ends the transaction.

Please note that in ADO a transaction is limited to one database because the Connection object can only point to one database.

Creating a Simple Transaction

Use the BeginTrans method to specify the beginning of a transaction. Use the CommitTran method to save the changes. BeginTrans and CommitTrans are used in pairs. The data-modifying instructions you place between these keywords are stored in memory until Visual Basic encounters the CommitTrans statement. After reaching CommitTrans, Access writes the changes that have occurred since the BeginTrans statement to the disk; therefore, any changes you've done in the tables become permanent.

If an error is generated during the transaction process, the RollbackTrans statement placed further down in your procedure will undo all changes made since the BeginTrans statement. The rollback ensures that the data is returned to the state it was in before you started the transaction.

Using transaction processing helps improve database performance since the operations carried out during a transaction are run in memory. If the transaction succeeds, the results are written to the disk in a single operation. If any operation included in a transaction fails, the transaction is simply aborted and no changes are written to the database. If you don't use transactions, the results of each operation must be written to the disk separately — a process that consumes more database resources.

The procedure in Hands-On 16-6 assumes that you want to enter an order for a new customer. Because this customer does not exist in the database, you will use a transaction to ensure that the new order is entered only after the customer record has been created in the Customers table.

◎ Hands-On 16-6: Using a Database Transaction to Insert Records

1. Insert a new module and, in the module's Code window, enter the Create_ Transaction procedure as shown below.

```
Sub Create_Transaction()
    Dim conn As ADODB.Connection

    On Error GoTo ErrorHandler

    Set conn = New ADODB.Connection

    With conn
        .Provider = "Microsoft.Jet.OLEDB.4.0"
        .ConnectionString = "Data Source = " & _
                    CurrentProject.Path & "\Northwind.mdb"
        .Open
        .BeginTrans

            ' insert a new customer record
            .Execute "INSERT INTO Customers " & _
                    "Values ('GWIPO','Gwiazda Polarna'," & _
                    "'Marcin Garnia', 'Sales Manager', 'ul.Majewskiego 10'," & _
                    "'Warszawa', Null, '02-106', 'Poland', '0114822230445', Null)"

            ' insert the order for that customer
            .Execute "INSERT INTO Orders " & _
                    " (CustomerId, EmployeeId, OrderDate, RequiredDate) " & _
                    " Values ('GWIPO', 1, Date(), Date()+5)"
        .CommitTrans
        .Close
        MsgBox "Both inserts completed."
    End With

ExitHere:
    Set conn = Nothing
    Exit Sub
ErrorHandler:
    If Err.Number = -2147467259 Then
```

```
            MsgBox Err.Description
            Resume ExitHere
        Else
            MsgBox Err.Description
            With conn
                .RollbackTrans
                .Close
            End With
            Resume ExitHere
        End If
    End Sub
```

The first SQL INSERT INTO statement inserts the customer data into the Customers table in the Northwind database. Before the customer can actually order specific products, a record must be added to the Orders table. The second SQL INSERT INTO statement takes care of this task. Because both inserts must occur prior to filling in order details, they are treated as a single transaction. If an error occurs anywhere (for example, the Orders table is open in the Design view), the entire transaction is rolled back.

Notice how the INSERT INTO statement is used in this procedure. If you do not specify the field names, you will need to include values for each field in the table.

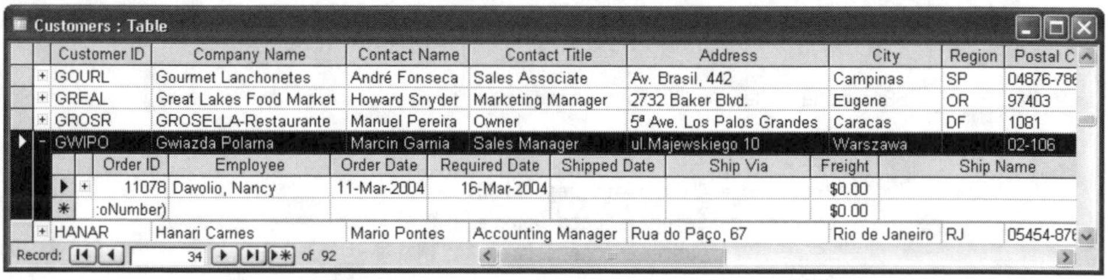

Figure 16-13: After running the procedure in Hands-On 16-6, a record for a new customer, "GWIPO," is added to the Customers and Orders tables.

Try using transaction processing for archiving historical data. For instance, write a VBA procedure that selects orders that were placed prior to a specific date, append them to your archive table, and delete them from the current Orders table.

Chapter Summary

This chapter covered quite a bit of advanced ADO material you will find useful in developing professional applications in Microsoft Access.

You started by creating your own recordset from scratch and using it for storing non-relational data. Next, you learned how to disconnect a recordset from a database and work with it offline. You also learned that a recordset can be saved to a disk file and later reopened without an active connection to the database. Next, you discovered how you can use the Clone method of the Recordset object to create a recordset that is a copy of another recordset. Finally, you familiarized yourself with the concepts of data shaping and learned statements that make it possible to create impressive, hierarchical views of your data. You also learned how transactions are used to ensure that certain database operations are always performed as a single unit.

In the next chapter, you will learn how to use ADO to handle database security.

Chapter 17

Implementing Database Security with ADOX and JRO

In addition to managing objects and modifying the design of your database, you can use the ADOX Object Model to handle database security issues by creating user and group accounts and assigning permissions to users, groups, or both.

- Use the Users and Groups collections of the ADOX Catalog object to create and manage security user accounts.
- Use the GetPermissions and SetPermissions methods of the ADOX User and Group objects to retrieve and set permissions on database objects.
- Use the ChangePassword method of the ADOX User object to change the user's password.
- Use the CompactDatabase method of the JRO JetEngine object to set a database password.

To use ADOX, you must set a reference to the Microsoft ADO Ext. 2.7 for DDL and Security Object Library (choose Tools | References in the Visual Basic application window).

To use JRO, you must set a reference to the Microsoft Jet and Replication Objects (JRO) Library (choose Tools | References in the Visual Basic application window).

The following sections of this chapter will walk you through the steps required to manage database security in your VBA procedures. You will work with objects and methods available in the Groups and Users collections in the ADOX Object Model.

Two Types of Security in Microsoft Access

Depending on your requirements, Microsoft Office Access allows you to implement *share-level* or *user-level* security to protect and secure your Access database.

Share-Level Security

Using passwords to secure the database or objects in the database is known as *share-level security*. When you set a password on the database, users will be required to enter a password in order to gain access to the data and database objects. Because you cannot assign permissions to users or groups with this option, anyone with the password has unrestricted access to all Access data and database objects.

To manually change the database password, choose Tools | Security | Set Database Password. Refer to the section titled "Setting a Database Password" later in this chapter to set a database password from within a VBA program.

User-Level Security

User-level security is a relatively complex process that secures the code and objects in your database so that users can't accidentally modify or change them. With this type of security you can provide the most restrictive access over the database and objects it contains. When you use user-level security, the Microsoft Jet Engine uses a *workgroup information file* to determine who can open a database and to secure its objects.

The workgroup information file holds group and user information, including passwords. The information contained in this file determines not only who can open the database, but also the permissions users/groups have on the objects in the database. The workgroup information file contains built-in groups (Admins and Users) and a generic user account (Admin) with unlimited privileges on the database and the objects it contains. For more information on the workgroup information file, refer to the following two sections of this chapter.

The Microsoft Office Access user interface provides four commands on the Tools | Security menu that allow you to manually implement user-level security. You can also define user and group accounts and their passwords from your VBA procedures by using ADO code, as demonstrated later in this chapter.

Understanding Workgroup Information Files

To successfully run the procedures demonstrated in this chapter, you need to know the location of the workgroup information file on your computer. This file, also known as system database (System.mdw), is created automatically when you install Microsoft Office Access 2003 and open a database for the first time. You will find a System.mdw file in the Application Data folder in the user profile in the following path:

C:\Documents and Settings\<user name>\Application Data\Microsoft\
Access\System.mdw

The Application Data folder is a hidden folder. To browse this folder, switch to Microsoft Windows Explorer and choose Tools | Folder Options. In the Folder Options window, click the View tab, click the option button next to Show hidden files and folders, and click OK. Now you should be able to access the above path, where <user name> is the name of your user profile. Take a few minutes right now to locate the System.mdw file on your machine.

Table 17-1: The workgroup information file in different versions of Access

Access Version	Default Workgroup Information Filename	Workgroup Information File Location
2.0	System.mda	C:\Access
95	System.mdw	C:\MSOffice\Access
97	System.mdw	C:\Windows\System
2000	System.mdw	C:\Program Files\Common Files\System
2002/2003	System.mdw	C:\Documents and Settings\<user name>\Application Data\Microsoft\Access

In Microsoft Access 2003, you can also find out the location and name of the workgroup information file using the following methods:

■ Start Microsoft Access without opening a specific database. Choose Tools | Security, and click the Workgroup Administrator. The dialog box that appears displays the path of your workgroup information file.

■ Start Microsoft Access and open any database. Switch to the Visual Basic Editor window and activate the Immediate window. Type the following statement and press Enter:

```
? CurrentProject.Connection.Properties("Jet OLEDB:System Database").Value
```

When you press Enter, Access displays the full path of the workgroup information file that the currently open database uses for its security information. The Jet OLEDB:System Database is a provider-specific property of the Microsoft OLE DB provider for Jet in the ADO Properties collection of the Connection object.

Access uses the workgroup information file to store the following information:

■ The name of each user and group
■ The list of users who belong to each group
■ The encrypted logon password for each workgroup user
■ The Security Identifier (SID) of each user and group in a binary format

Once you add user and group accounts to your database, the workgroup information file will contain vital security information. YOU DON'T WANT TO LOSE THIS INFORMATION. Always take time to make a backup copy of the System.mdw file and store it in a safe location. This way, if the original file gets corrupted, you'll be able to quickly restore your backup file and avoid having to recreate user and group accounts.

The workgroup information file is like any other Access database except that it contains hidden system tables with information regarding user and group accounts and their actual permissions. However, you cannot change the security information by opening this file directly. All the security data stored in hidden system tables is encrypted and protected. Changes to the workgroup information file are done automatically by the Jet Engine when you use the built-in Access commands to manage security or execute ADO/JRO code in your VBA procedures.

You can use the same workgroup information file for more than one database or you can create a separate workgroup information file for each database you are securing. You can also give this file a name other than the default System.mdw. I find the best way is to use the same name as the database file. For example, if my secured database file is named Assets.mdb, I would create a workgroup information file called Assets.mdw and put it in the same folder as the database file. This way I'd know right away that these two files are associated with one another even after many weeks or months have passed since I created them. Keeping track of which workgroup information file goes with which database can be quite challenging, especially if you are managing more than a couple of secured Access databases.

➡ **Note:** If you try to open a secured database while another workgroup information file is active, Access displays the following message:

You do not have the necessary permissions to use the <name> object. Have your system administrator or the person who created this object establish the appropriate permissions for you.

If you receive the above message while opening an Access database, you should look for the accompanying workgroup information file and perform one of the following:
- Start Access without opening a specific database. Use Tools | Security | Workgroup Administrator and click the Join button. Specify the correct workgroup information file for the database you wish to open. When the Workgroup Administrator has confirmed joining the specified workgroup, start the Access database (see the Access online help on using the Workgroup Administrator Security menu option).
- Set up a shortcut to the database file that uses the /WKGRP command-line switch to load the specified workgroup information file when the database is opened (see Part 3 in Custom Project 17-1).

Creating and Joining Workgroup Information Files

When you open a database, Microsoft Access reads the workgroup information file to find out who is allowed to access the database. If security was put into place, you will be prompted for the user ID and password. The first hands-on in this chapter will walk you through the steps required to create and join a new workgroup information file. Once you join the workgroup, you will create a new Access database and set up a password for the Admin user. This information will be saved in the workgroup information file that you've just joined.

The workgroup information file is created using the Workgroup Administrator. This option is available from the Tools menu after you launch the Microsoft Access application and before you open a specific database file. To work with this chapter's example procedures, you will create a new workgroup information file in Hands-On 17-1.

For more information on using Workgroup Administrator, workgroup information files, and securing Microsoft Access databases using the built-in user interface, start Microsoft Access and choose Help | Show Office Assistant.

Type Workgroup Adminstrator in the search box and click Search. You can also type this search string after pressing F1 in the Database window.

Our first project in this chapter will create a secured Microsoft Access database. Securing a database is a complex process that can be achieved in more than one way. You can use the options available on the Tools | Security menu to manually secure your database or you can run a User-Level Security Wizard as demonstrated in Custom Project 17-1. Securing a database boils down to creating a new workgroup information file, adding a new member to the Admins group, and removing the default Admin user from that group. You also need to remove permissions from the Admin user and from the Users group, and assign permissions to your own groups that you create.

Don't be discouraged if you need to go over the security steps more than once. Access security is complex and can be approached from many different angles. Books of several hundred pages have been written to explain its inner workings. The approach presented here will simply provide us with a secured Access database file we will use to perform the programming exercises in this chapter. Although you could learn how to use the ADOX commands for managing security using the currently open unsecured Access database, I think this particular approach will give you a better set of skills to begin with. So let's begin.

◉ Custom Project 17-1: Securing a Microsoft Access Database

You must complete this custom project in order to work with the hands-ons in this chapter.

Part 1: Creating a New Database

1. Create a new folder on your computer and name it **BookProject**.

2. Start Microsoft Office Access and create a new blank database called **SpecialDb.mdb**. Save this database in the BookProject folder you created in step 1. Keep this database open and proceed to Part 2 below.

Part 2: Establishing User-Level Security

We will use the built-in User-Level Security Wizard to secure the blank Access database we created in Part 1.

1. Choose **Tools | Security | User-Level Security Wizard**.

2. Click **Yes** in response to the message that the database should be opened in the shared mode to run the Security Wizard.

3. Microsoft Access closes the database and reopens it in the shared mode. If the Security Warning message appears, click **Open**.

4. Microsoft Access automatically activates the Security Wizard (Figure 17-1). Click **Next** to continue.

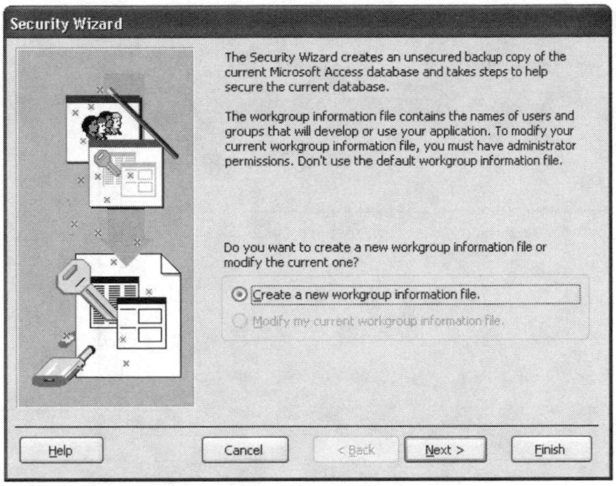

Figure 17-1

5. Another Security Wizard window appears (Figure 17-2). Do not make any changes in this screen. Click **Next** to continue.

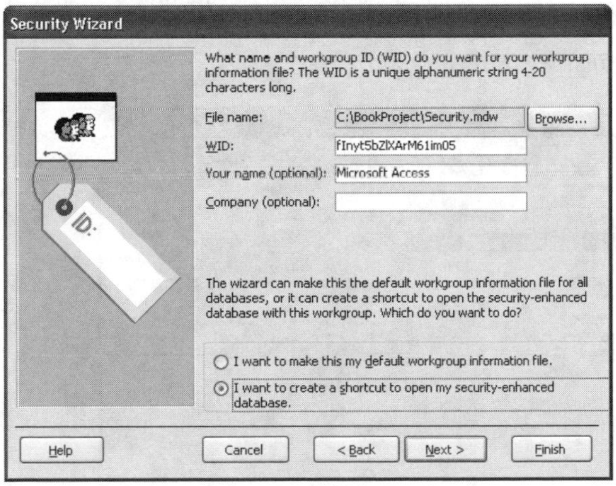

Figure 17-2

6. The Security Wizard window now shows an empty tabbed screen that normally displays database objects (Figure 17-3). Because our database does not contain any tables, queries, reports, etc., there's nothing you can do in this screen. Press **Next** to continue.

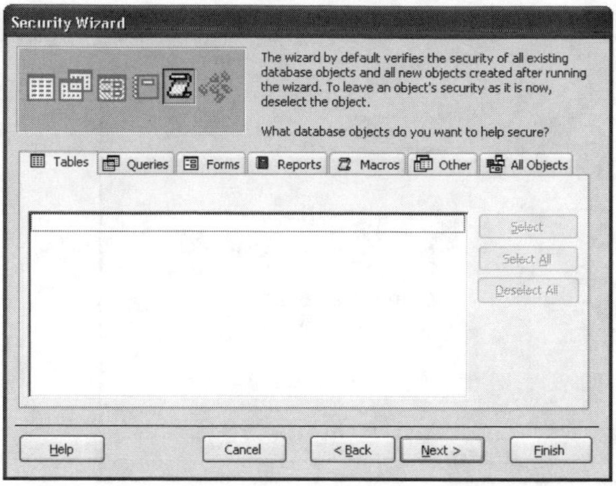

Figure 17-3

7. The Security Wizard window now goes on to display a list of optional security accounts that you could include in your new workgroup information file (Figure 17-4). Because we will define our accounts in programming code later in this chapter, do not make any selections in this screen. Press **Next** to continue.

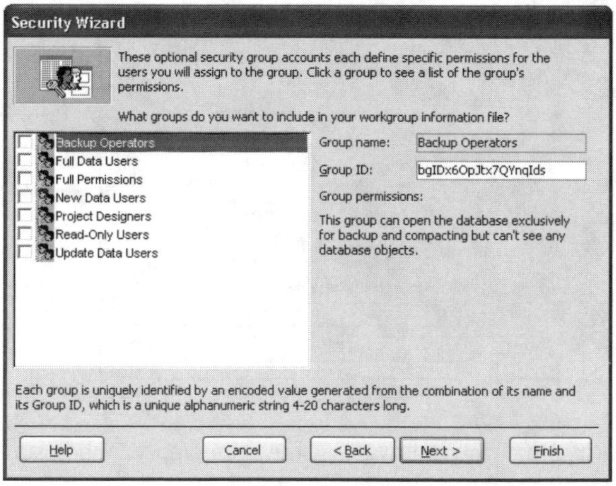

Figure 17-4

8. Now the Security Wizard asks you whether you want to grant permissions to Users group (Figure 17-5). Do not make any changes in this screen. The Users group will have no permissions. We will work with permissions in our VBA procedures later. Press **Next** to continue.

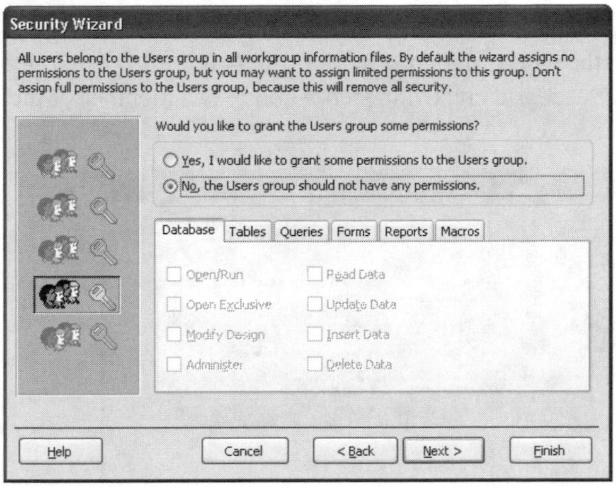

Figure 17-5

9. Now the Security Wizard shows a screen where we finally can do a little bit of work. We need to define a new user in our database. This user will function as a new Admin. We'll call our new user a **Developer** and allow him to log into the database using **chapter17** as a password. Fill in the User name and the Password boxes as shown in Figure 17-6 and click the **Add This User to the List** button. The Developer now appears in the users list. Do not leave this screen yet.

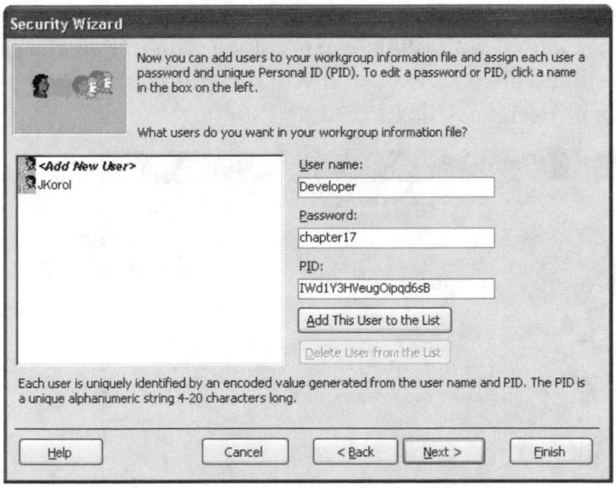

Figure 17-6

10. Now we will remove the user account with which we have logged into Access to start this custom project. In the list of users, select the user name you logged in with (I selected JKorol) and click the **Delete User from the List** button. Now the Developer is the only user in our database. Click **Next** to continue.

11. The Security Wizard shows the screen where you can assign users to groups in the workgroup information file (Figure 17-7). Notice that the Developer user you created in step 9 above is a member of the Admins group. Press **Next** to continue.

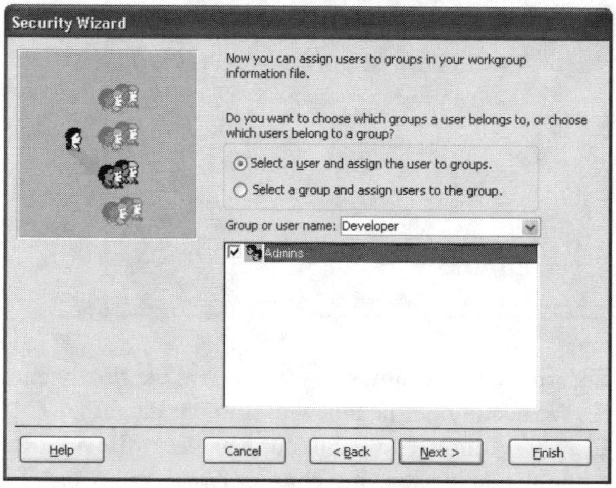

Figure 17-7

12. The Security Wizard has now collected all the required information. As a final step it suggests the name for the backup copy of the unsecured database (Figure 17-8). The unsecured database is, in this case, the blank database we started with. When we are done with this final step, our database will still be blank; however, it will be secured. Do not make any changes in this screen. Click **Finish**.

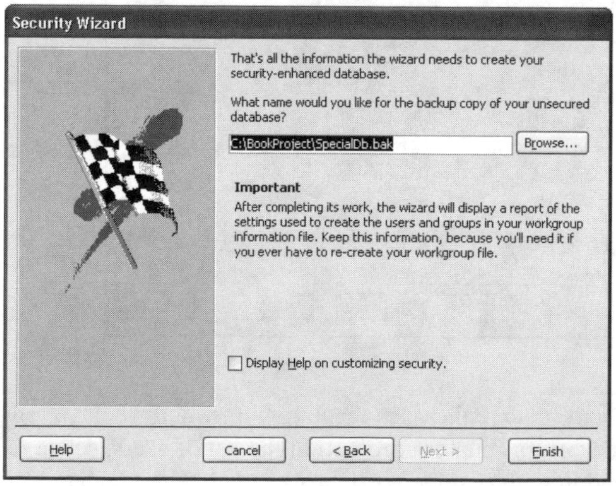

Figure 17-8

13. Access performs its final tasks of securing your database and displays the Security Wizard report. If you are connected to the printer, it's a good idea to take a minute now to print this report. You can also magnify the report to

read it on screen. When you are done, close the Security Wizard report window. Upon closing the window, the Security Wizard displays a warning message that asks whether you would like to save the report as a Snapshot (.snp) file that you can view later. For this exercise, click **No** in response to this question. You should see the confirmation message that the Security Wizard has encoded your database and to reopen the database you must use the new workgroup file you have created by closing Access and reopening it. We'll do as suggested in the next step. Click **OK** to this message.

14. Close the Microsoft Access application window.

Part 3: Opening a Secured Database

After completing the previous two parts of this custom project, the BookProject folder on your computer contains three files:

- A database file named SpecialDb.mdb
- A workgroup information file named Security.mdb that stores user and group account information for the SpecialDb database
- A backup copy of the SpecialDb database named SpecialDb.bak

Also, there is a shortcut on your desktop (created by the Security Wizard) that allows you to quickly start the SpecialDb database using the new workgroup information file (Security.mdb). If you right-click that desktop shortcut and choose Properties, you will see in the Target box the following path:

```
"C:\Program Files\Microsoft Office\OFFICE11\MSACCESS.EXE"
    "C:\BookProject\SpecialDb.mdb" /WRKGRP "C:\BookProject\Security.mdw"
```

Because this path is very long, I have split it into two lines. Notice that the first part of this path is the location of the Microsoft Access executable program on your disk surrounded by quotation marks. The path to the Access .exe is then followed by a space and the full path of the database file (also in quotation marks). Because this database file is secured, we must also include a space and a command-line switch, /WKGRP, followed by a space and the name of the accompanying workgroup information file (also in quotation marks).

The /WKGRP command-line switch tells Access that you want to start a database with a specific workgroup. If you know what user account you want to log on with, you can use the /User and /Pwd command-line switches to avoid being prompted by Access for the user name and password:

```
"C:\Program Files\Microsoft Office\OFFICE11\MSACCESS.EXE"
    "C:\BookProject\SpecialDb.mdb" /WRKGRP "C:\BookProject\Security.mdw"
        /User "Developer"  /Pwd "chapter17"
```

The information about the user name and password follows the name of the workgroup information file and a single space.

Now that you know how the path to a secured database is built, you can create similar shortcuts to other secured databases if they use different workgroup information files.

1. On your desktop, double-click the shortcut to **SpecialDb.mdb** to open this database. Because this database is protected, a logon box appears. Enter

Developer in the Name box and **chapter17** in the Password box and click **OK**. If the Security Warning message appears, click **Open**.

2. Now that your secured database file is open, we will take a look at the changes the Security Wizard has made in the Users and Groups accounts. Choose **Tools | Security | User and Group Accounts**. Notice that the Admin user is a member of the Users group (Figure 17-9). The Security Wizard removed the Admin account from the Admins group. If you open the drop-down list in the User area of this screen and select Developer, you will see that Developer is a member of two groups: Admins and Users. Click **Cancel** to exit the User and Group Accounts window.

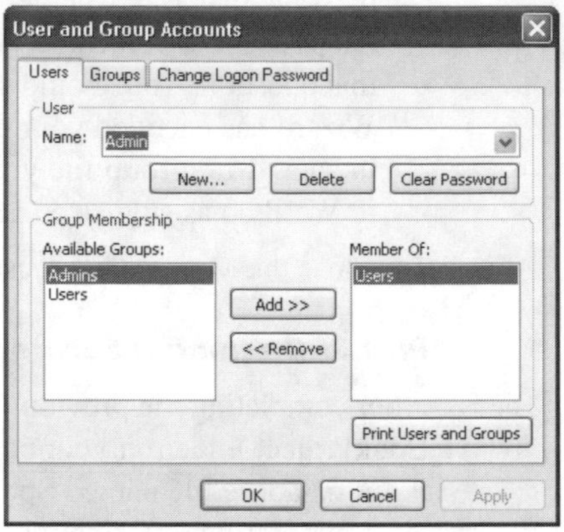

Figure 17-9: In Custom Project 17-1, we removed the default Admin user from the Admins group while running the built-in User-Level Security Wizard.

3. Having checked the Users and Groups accounts, you can also examine the changes made by the Security Wizard in the group permissions. Choose **Tools | Security | User and Group Permissions**. The Developer and Admin users don't have permissions on any new objects (Figure 17-10). To view group permissions, click the **Groups** option button. The Admins group has all the necessary permissions to administer the database while the Users group has no permissions at all. We will learn how to grant and revoke permissions to database objects in the example procedures in this chapter. Now click **Cancel** to exit the User and Group Permissions window.

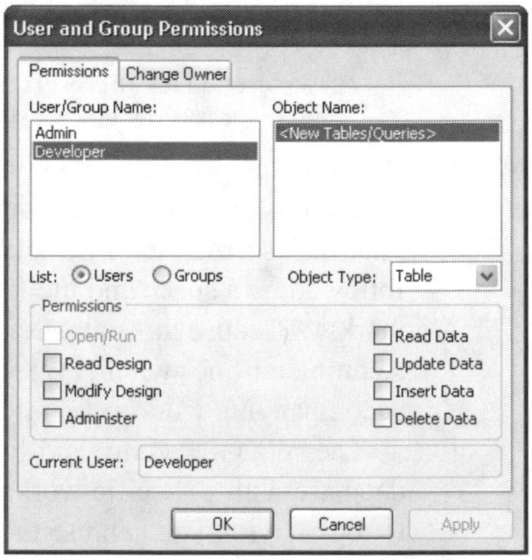

Figure 17-10: Use the User and Group Permissions window to check current permissions for the Admin and Developer users after running the User-Level Security Wizard in Custom Project 17-1.

4. Now let's import some objects to our still empty database. Later in this chapter when we learn to handle permissions to database objects we will need a couple of objects available in this database for our tests. In the Database window, choose **File | Get External Data | Import**. In the Import

dialog box, switch to the folder that contains the Northwind sample database, highlight **Northwind.mdb**, and click **Import**.

5. In the Import Objects window, click **Select All** to select all the tables. Click the **Queries** tab, and then **Select All** to select all the queries. Finally, click **OK** to begin importing.

6. The objects you selected in step 5 have now been added to your database. Close the SpecialDb database and close the Access application. This step concludes the special project of creating a secured Access database. Now, let's proceed to the programming part.

Working with Accounts

The following sections explain how to create and work with group and user accounts.

Creating a Group Account

To create a new group account from a VBA procedure, you need to open the ADOX Catalog object by specifying the connection to the appropriate database and use the Append method of the Catalog object's Groups collection to add a new group account.

The procedure in Hands-On 17-1 illustrates how to create a new group account named Masters in the secured database (SpecialDb.mdb) that you created in Custom Project 17-1. If the group with the specified name already exists, the error trap will detect it, and you will be notified with a message.

◎ Hands-On 17-1: Creating a Group Account

This hands-on requires that you have completed Custom Project 17-1.

1. Start Microsoft Access without opening a database.

2. Choose **Tools | Security | Workgroup Administrator**. Access displays the Workgroup Administrator dialog box where you can check the path to the workgroup information file that is currently used. Perform one of the following steps:

   a. If System.mdw appears in the Workgroup path, click **OK** to exit the Workgroup Administrator dialog box and proceed with step 3 below.

   b. If the Workgroup path includes the Security.mdw file that was created in Custom Project 17-1, click the **Join** button to join another workgroup. Use the **Browse** button in the Workgroup Information File dialog box to select and open **System.mdw**. Refer to the beginning of this chapter for information on the default location of this file. Once you select the correct file, the dialog box should display its full path. Click **OK** to exit this dialog box. Access will display a message box saying you successfully joined the workgroup defined by the selected information file. Click **OK** to the message and click **OK** in the Workgroup Administrator dialog box to exit.

3. Open the **Acc2003_Chap17.mdb** file from the downloadable files, or create this file from scratch using the Microsoft Office Access user interface.

4. Switch to the Visual Basic Editor window and insert a new module.

5. Because you will be programming using the ADOX and JRO Object Models, you need to set up the reference to these libraries. Choose **Tools | References** and click the check box next to **Microsoft ADO Ext. 2.7 for DDL and Security** and **Microsoft Jet and Replication Objects Library**. After making these selections, click **OK** to exit the References dialog box.

6. In the module's Code window, enter the Create_Group procedure as shown below.

```
Sub Create_Group()
    Dim cat As ADOX.Catalog
    Dim conn As ADODB.Connection
    Dim strDB As String
    Dim strSysDb As String
    Dim strName As String

    On Error GoTo ErrorHandle

    strDB = "C:\BookProject\SpecialDb.mdb"
    strSysDb = "C:\BookProject\Security.mdw"
    strName = "Masters"

    ' Open connection to the database using the specified system database
    Set conn = New ADODB.Connection
        With conn
            .Provider = "Microsoft.Jet.OLEDB.4.0"
            .Properties("Jet OLEDB:System Database") = strSysDb
            .Properties("User ID") = "Developer"
            .Properties("Password") = "chapter17"
            .Open strDB
        End With

    ' Open the catalog and create a group account
    Set cat = New ADOX.Catalog
    With cat
        .ActiveConnection = conn
        .Groups.Append strName
    End With
    MsgBox "Successfully created " & strName & " group account."

ExitHere:
    Set cat = Nothing
    conn.Close
    Set conn = Nothing
    Exit Sub
ErrorHandle:
    If Err.Number = -2147467259 Then
        MsgBox strName & " group already exists."
```

```
        Else
            MsgBox Err.Description
        End If
        Resume ExitHere
    End Sub
```

Upon executing the above procedure, a new group account named Masters will be established in the database that you created in Custom Project 17-1. Notice that before opening the database we need to set the Jet OLEDB:System Database property in the Properties collection of the ADO Connection object to specify the path and name of the workgroup information file that should be active when the database is opened. We also set the User ID and Password properties to log onto the database. After opening the database, we open the Catalog object and use the Append method of the Catalog's Groups collection to add a new group account. The Groups collection contains all groups in the specified workgroup information file. You can verify that the Masters group account was indeed created by opening the SpecialDb.mdb file. If you'd like to take a moment now, open this database using the shortcut on your desktop. Once the database is open choose Tools | Security | User and Group Accounts (Figure 17-11). Notice that the database contains the Masters group in addition to the default Admins and Users groups. Close the SpecialDb database and the Access application window in which it was displayed. Be careful not to close the Acc2003_Chap17 database you are working with.

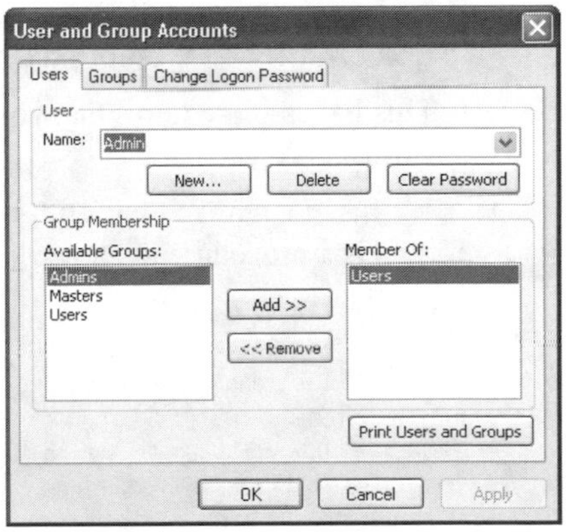

Figure 17-11: Running the procedure in Hands-On 17-1 adds a new group account named Masters.

To create a new group account in the current database, your VBA procedure will look like this:

```
Sub Create_Group2()
    Dim cat As ADOX.Catalog

    On Error GoTo ErrorHandle

    ' Open the catalog and create a new group account
    Set cat = New ADOX.Catalog
    With cat
        .ActiveConnection = CurrentProject.Connection
        .Groups.Append "Masters"
    End With

ExitHere:
    Set cat = Nothing
    Exit Sub
ErrorHandle:
```

```
            If Err.Number = -2147467259 Then
                MsgBox "This group already exists."
            Else
                MsgBox Err.Description
            End If
            Resume ExitHere
        End Sub
```

Creating a User Account

With ADOX you can create a new user simply by passing the name and pass-word to the Append method of the Users collection.

The procedure in Hands-On 17-2 creates a new user account named PowerUser and designates "star" as the password. Specifying a password at this time is optional. You can assign a password later with the Change-Password method for the User object.

◉ Hands-On 17-2: Creating a User Account

This hands-on requires that you have performed all the steps listed under Custom Project 17-1.

1. Insert a new module and, in the module's Code window, enter the Create_ User procedure as shown below.

```
Sub Create_User()
    Dim cat As ADOX.Catalog
    Dim conn As ADODB.Connection
    Dim strDB As String
    Dim strSysDb As String
    Dim strName As String

    On Error GoTo ErrorHandle

    strDB = "C:\BookProject\SpecialDb.mdb"
    strSysDb = "C:\BookProject\Security.mdw"
    strName = "PowerUser"

    ' Open connection to the database using the specified system database
    Set conn = New ADODB.Connection
        With conn
            .Provider = "Microsoft.Jet.OLEDB.4.0"
            .Properties("Jet OLEDB:System Database") = strSysDb
            .Properties("User ID") = "Developer"
            .Properties("Password") = "chapter17"
            .Open strDB
        End With

    ' Open the catalog
    Set cat = New ADOX.Catalog
    With cat
        .ActiveConnection = conn
        ' Create a new user and append it to
        ' the Users collection
```

```
        .Users.Append strName, "star"
    End With
        MsgBox "Successfully created " & strName & " user account."

ExitHere:
    Set cat = Nothing
    conn.Close
    Set conn = Nothing
    Exit Sub
ErrorHandle:
    If Err.Number = -2147467259 Then
        MsgBox strName & " user already exists."
    Else
        MsgBox Err.Description
    End If
    Resume ExitHere
End Sub
```

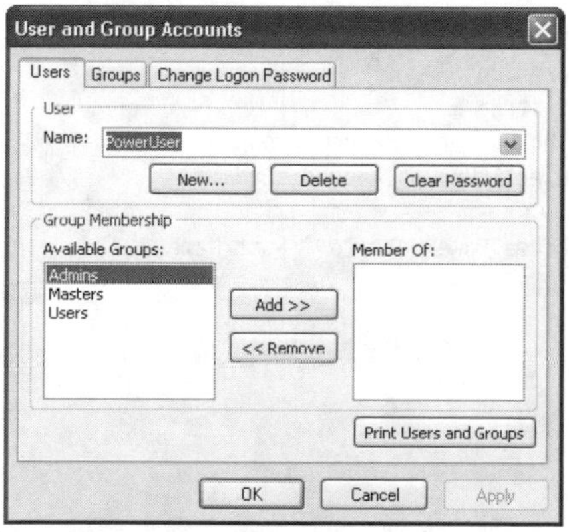

Figure 17-12: Running the procedure in Hands-On 17-2 creates the PowerUser account. This user's group membership has not yet been established. To access this window, double-click the shortcut to the SpecialDb database on your desktop. Log in as Developer and type chapter17 for the password. Once the database opens, choose Tools | Security | User and Group Accounts.

Adding a User to a New Group

The procedure in Hands-On 17-3 creates a new group named Elite, and then appends the user account named PowerUser to this group.

Hands-On 17-3: Adding a User to a New Group

This hands-on requires that you have performed all the steps listed under Custom Project 17-1 and Hands-On 17-2.

1. Insert a new module and, in the module's Code window, enter the AddUser_ToNewGroup procedure as shown below.

```
Sub AddUser_ToNewGroup()
    Dim cat As ADOX.Catalog
    Dim conn As ADODB.Connection
    Dim strDB As String
    Dim strSysDb As String
    Dim strName As String

    On Error GoTo ErrorHandle
```

```vb
    strDB = "C:\BookProject\SpecialDb.mdb"
    strSysDb = "C:\BookProject\Security.mdw"
    strName = "Elite"

    ' Open connection to the database using
    ' the specified system database
    Set conn = New ADODB.Connection
        With conn
            .Provider = "Microsoft.Jet.OLEDB.4.0"
            .Properties("Jet OLEDB:System Database") = strSysDb
            .Properties("User ID") = "Developer"
            .Properties("Password") = "chapter17"
            .Open strDB
        End With

    ' Open the catalog
    Set cat = New ADOX.Catalog
        With cat
            .ActiveConnection = conn
            ' Create a new group
            .Groups.Append strName
            ' Add an exising user to the new group
            .Users("PowerUser").Groups.Append strName
        End With
    MsgBox "Successfully added PowerUser to " & strName & _
           " group account."
ExitHere:
    Set cat = Nothing
    conn.Close
    Set conn = Nothing
    Exit Sub
ErrorHandle:
    Set cat = Nothing
    If Err.Number = -2147467259 Then
        MsgBox strName & " account already exists."
    Else
        MsgBox Err.Description
    End If
    Resume ExitHere
End Sub
```

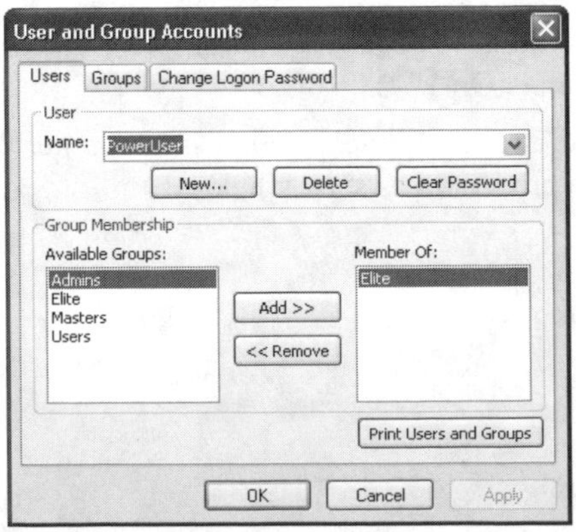

Figure 17-13: Running the procedure in Hands-On 17-3 creates the new group named Elite and appends the PowerUser account to the group.

Deleting a User Account

Use the Delete method of the Catalog object's Users collection to delete a user account. The procedure in Hands-On 17-4 deletes the PowerUser account created by a procedure in Hands-On 17-2.

⊚ Hands-On 17-4: Deleting a User Account

1. Insert a new module and, in the module's Code window, enter the Delete_ User procedure as shown below. Notice that this procedure takes as an argument the name of the user account you want to delete.

```
Sub Delete_User(UserName As String)
    Dim cat As ADOX.Catalog
    Dim conn As ADODB.Connection
    Dim strDB As String
    Dim strSysDb As String

    On Error GoTo ErrorHandle

    strDB = "C:\BookProject\SpecialDb.mdb"
    strSysDb = "C:\BookProject\Security.mdw"

    ' Open connection to the database using
    ' the specified system database
    Set conn = New ADODB.Connection
        With conn
            .Provider = "Microsoft.Jet.OLEDB.4.0"
            .Properties("Jet OLEDB:System Database") = strSysDb
            .Properties("User ID") = "Developer"
            .Properties("Password") = "chapter17"
            .Open strDB
        End With

    ' Open the catalog
    Set cat = New ADOX.Catalog
    With cat
        .ActiveConnection = conn
        ' Delete user
        .Users.Delete UserName
    End With
    MsgBox "The " & UserName & " was deleted."

ExitHere:
    Set cat = Nothing
    conn.Close
    Set conn = Nothing
    Exit Sub
ErrorHandle:
    If Err.Number = 3265 Then
        cat.Users.Append UserName, "star"
        Resume
    Else
        MsgBox Err.Description
        Resume ExitHere
```

```
        End If
End Sub
```

2. To run the Delete_User procedure shown above, enter the following state-
    ment in the Immediate window and press **Enter** to execute it:

```
Delete_User "PowerUser"
```

Deleting a Group Account

Use the Delete method of the Catalog object's Groups collection to delete a
group account. The procedure in Hands-On 17-5 deletes the Masters group
account created by a procedure in an earlier section.

◉ Hands-On 17-5: Deleting a Group Account

1. Insert a new module and, in the module's Code window, enter the
    Delete_Group procedure as shown below. Notice that this procedure takes
    as an argument the name of the group account you want to delete.

```
Sub Delete_Group(GroupName As String)
    Dim conn As ADODB.Connection
    Dim cat As ADOX.Catalog
    Dim strDB As String
    Dim strSysDb As String

    On Error GoTo ErrorHandle

    strDB = "C:\BookProject\SpecialDb.mdb"
    strSysDb = "C:\BookProject\Security.mdw"

    ' Open connection to the database using
    ' the specified system database
    Set conn = New ADODB.Connection
        With conn
            .Provider = "Microsoft.Jet.OLEDB.4.0"
            .Properties("Jet OLEDB:System Database") = strSysDb
            .Properties("User ID") = "Developer"
            .Properties("Password") = "chapter17"
            .Open strDB
        End With

    ' Open the catalog
    Set cat = New ADOX.Catalog
    With cat
        .ActiveConnection = conn
        ' Delete group
        .Groups.Delete GroupName
    End With
    MsgBox "The " & GroupName & " group was deleted."

ExitHere:
    Set cat = Nothing
    conn.Close
    Set conn = Nothing
```

```
        Exit Sub
    ErrorHandle:
        If Err.Number = 3265 Then
            cat.Groups.Append "Masters"
            Resume
        Else
            MsgBox Err.Description
            Resume ExitHere
        End If
    End Sub
```

2. To run the Delete_ Group procedure shown above, enter the following statement in the Immediate window and press **Enter** to execute it:

```
Delete_Group "Masters"
```

Listing All Group Accounts

The procedure in Hands-On 17-6 demonstrates how to retrieve the names of all defined group accounts from the Groups collection of the Catalog object.

◎ Hands-On 17-6: Listing All Group Accounts

1. Insert a new module and, in the module's Code window, enter the List_Groups procedure as shown below.

```
Sub List_Groups()
    Dim conn As ADODB.Connection
    Dim cat As ADOX.Catalog
    Dim grp As New ADOX.Group
    Dim strDB As String
    Dim strSysDb As String

    strDB = "C:\BookProject\SpecialDb.mdb"
    strSysDb = "C:\BookProject\Security.mdw"

    ' Open connection to the database using
    ' the specified system database
    Set conn = New ADODB.Connection
        With conn
            .Provider = "Microsoft.Jet.OLEDB.4.0"
            .Properties("Jet OLEDB:System Database") = strSysDb
            .Properties("User ID") = "Developer"
            .Properties("Password") = "chapter17"
            .Open strDB
        End With

    ' Open the catalog
    Set cat = New ADOX.Catalog
    cat.ActiveConnection = conn
    For Each grp In cat.Groups
        Debug.Print grp.Name
    Next
    Set cat = Nothing
```

```
        conn.Close
        Set conn = Nothing

        MsgBox "See groups listing in the Immediate window."
    End Sub
```

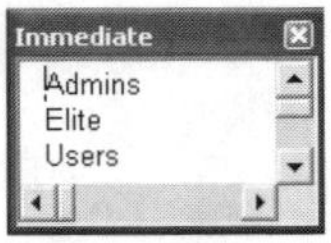

Figure 17-14: The names of existing security group accounts are written to the Immediate window by the List_Groups procedure in Hands-On 17-6.

Listing All User Accounts

The procedure in Hands-On 17-7 demonstrates how to retrieve the names of all defined security user accounts from the Users collection of the Catalog object.

◎ Hands-On 17-7: Listing All User Accounts

1. Insert a new module and, in the module's Code window, enter the List_Users procedure as shown below.

```
Sub List_Users()
    Dim conn As ADODB.Connection
    Dim cat As ADOX.Catalog
    Dim myUser As New ADOX.User
    Dim strDB As String
    Dim strSysDb As String

    strDB = "C:\BookProject\SpecialDb.mdb"
    strSysDb = "C:\BookProject\Security.mdw"

    ' Open connection to the database using
    ' the specified system database
    Set conn = New ADODB.Connection
        With conn
            .Provider = "Microsoft.Jet.OLEDB.4.0"
            .Properties("Jet OLEDB:System Database") = strSysDb
            .Properties("User ID") = "Developer"
            .Properties("Password") = "chapter17"
            .Open strDB
        End With

    ' Open the catalog
    Set cat = New ADOX.Catalog
    cat.ActiveConnection = conn
    For Each myUser In cat.Users
        Debug.Print myUser.Name
    Next
    Set cat = Nothing
    conn.Close
    Set conn = Nothing

    MsgBox "Users are listed in the Immediate window."
End Sub
```

Creating and Manipulating Databases with ADO

Figure 17-15: The names of existing security user accounts are written to the Immediate window by the List_Users procedure in Hands-On 17-7. In addition to the user accounts that you have defined, Access reveals the names of its two built-in users: Creator and Engine. To keep these built-in users from showing up in your users listing, use the following conditional statement:

```
If myUser.Name <>"Creator" And _
    myUser.Name <> "Engine" Then
        Debug.Print myUser.Name
End If
```

Listing Users in Groups

Sometimes you will need to know what users belong to what groups. The procedure in Hands-On 17-8 demonstrates how to obtain such a list.

◉ Hands-On 17-8: Listing Users in Groups

1. Insert a new module and, in the module's Code window, enter the List_UsersInGroups procedure as shown below.

```
Sub List_UsersInGroups()
    Dim conn As ADODB.Connection
    Dim cat As ADOX.Catalog
    Dim grp As New ADOX.Group
    Dim myUser As New ADOX.User
    Dim strDB As String
    Dim strSysDb As String

    strDB = "C:\BookProject\SpecialDb.mdb"
    strSysDb = "C:\BookProject\Security.mdw"

    ' Open connection to the database using
    ' the specified system database
    Set conn = New ADODB.Connection
        With conn
            .Provider = "Microsoft.Jet.OLEDB.4.0"
            .Properties("Jet OLEDB:System Database") = strSysDb
            .Properties("User ID") = "Developer"
            .Properties("Password") = "chapter17"
            .Open strDB
        End With

    ' Open the catalog
    Set cat = New ADOX.Catalog
    cat.ActiveConnection = conn
    For Each grp In cat.Groups
        Debug.Print "Group Name: " & grp.Name
        If cat.Groups(grp.Name).Users.Count = 0 Then
            Debug.Print vbTab & "There are no users in the " & _
                grp & " group."
        End If
        For Each myUser In cat.Groups(grp.Name).Users
            Debug.Print vbTab & "User Name: " & myUser.Name
```

```
        Next myUser
    Next grp

    Set cat = Nothing
    conn.Close
    Set conn = Nothing
    MsgBox "Groups and Users are listed in the Immediate window."
End Sub
```

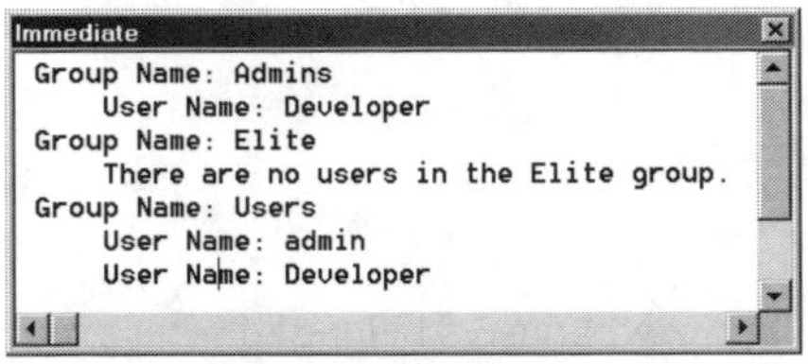

Figure 17-16: After running the List_UsersInGroup procedure in Hands-On 17-8, security group account names and the corresponding user accounts are listed in the Immediate window.

Setting and Retrieving User and Group Permissions

Users and groups of users can be granted specific permissions to database objects. For example, a user or an entire group of users can be authorized to only read an object's contents while other users or groups can have less restrictive access to a database, allowing them to modify or delete objects.

It is important to understand that when you set permissions for a group, every user in that group automatically inherits those permissions. Also, keep in mind that while the user and group accounts are stored in the workgroup information file, the permissions that those users/groups have to specific objects are stored in system tables in your database.

The following sections of this chapter will familiarize you with using ADOX to retrieve, list, and set permissions for various database objects.

Determining the Object Owner

The database, and every object in the database, has an owner. The owner is the user that created that particular object. The object owner has special privileges. He or she can always assign or revoke permissions for that object. To retrieve the name of the object owner, use the GetObjectOwner method of a Catalog object. This method takes two parameters: the object's name and type. For example, to determine the owner of a table, use the following syntax

```
cat.GetObjectOwner(myObjName, adPermObjTable)
```

where cat is an object variable representing the ADOX Catalog object, myObjName is the name of a database table, and adPermObjTable is a built-in ADOX constant specifying the type of object. The constants for the Type parameter can be looked up in the Object Browser, as shown in Figure 17-17.

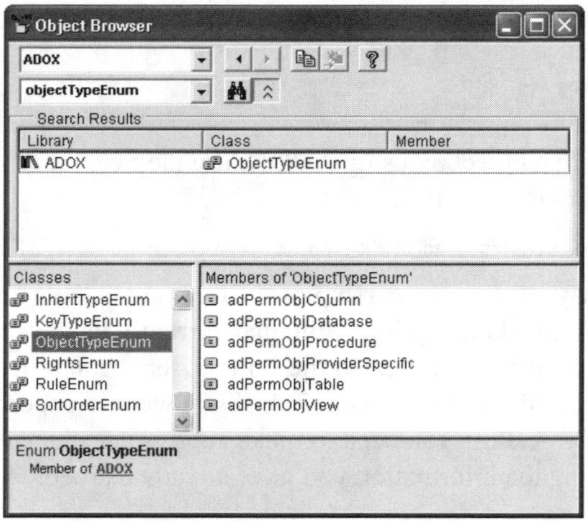

Creating and Manipulating Databases with ADO

Figure 17-17: The Object Browser displays the required constants for the Type parameter of the GetObjectOwner method.

◉ Hands-On 17-9: Retrieving the Name of the Object Owner

1. Insert a new module and, in the module's Code window, enter the Get_ObjectOwner procedure as shown below.

```
Sub Get_ObjectOwner()
    Dim conn As ADODB.Connection
    Dim cat As ADOX.Catalog
    Dim strObjName As Variant
    Dim strDB As String
    Dim strSysDb As String

    strDB = "C:\BookProject\SpecialDb.mdb"
    strSysDb = "C:\BookProject\Security.mdw"
    strObjName = "Customers"

    ' Open connection to the database using
    ' the specified system database
    Set conn = New ADODB.Connection
        With conn
            .Provider = "Microsoft.Jet.OLEDB.4.0"
            .Properties("Jet OLEDB:System Database") = strSysDb
            .Properties("User ID") = "Developer"
            .Properties("Password") = "chapter17"
            .Open strDB
        End With

    ' Open the catalog
    Set cat = New ADOX.Catalog
    cat.ActiveConnection = conn

    ' Display the name of the table owner
    MsgBox "The owner of the " & strObjName & " table is " & vbCr _
        & cat.GetObjectOwner(strObjName, adPermObjTable) & "."
```

```
        Set cat = Nothing
        conn.Close
        Set conn = Nothing
    End Sub
```

To set the ownership of an object by using ADOX, use the SetObjectOwner method of the Catalog object like this:

```
cat.SetObjectOwner("Customers", adPermObjTable, "PowerUser")
```

The above statement says that the ownership of the Customers table is to be transferred to the user named PowerUser. Note that currently there is no such user in the SpecialDb database. We created the PowerUser account in Hands-On 17-2 and deleted it in Hands-On 17-4. If you want to experiment with changing object ownership, you need to make appropriate changes in the example procedure using the information you have already learned.

Setting User Permissions for an Object

With ADOX, you set permissions on an object by using the SetPermissions method. User-level security can be easier to manage if you set permissions only for groups, and then assign users to the appropriate groups. Recall that permissions set for the group are automatically inherited by all users in that group. The SetPermissions method, which can be used for setting both user and group permissions, has the following syntax:

```
GroupOrUser.SetPermissions(Name, ObjectType, Action, Rights[, Inherit]
[,ObjectTypeID])
```

- Name — The name of the object to set permissions on.
- ObjectType — The type of object the permissions are set for. (See Figure 17-17 for the names of the ADOX built-in constants that can be used to specify the Type parameter.)
- Action — The type of action to perform when setting permissions. Use the adAccessSet constant for Microsoft Access databases to specify that the group of users will have exactly the requested permissions.
- Rights —A Long value containing a bitmask indicating the permissions to set. The Rights argument can consist of a single permissions constant or several constants combined by using the OR operator. See Figure 17-18 for the names of the ADOX built-in constants that can be used in the Rights argument to specify the type of permissions to set.

➔ **Note:** A *bitmask* is a numeric value intended for a bit-by-bit value comparison with other numeric values, usually to flag options in parameters or return values. In Visual Basic, this comparison is done with bitwise logical operators, such as AND and OR. The ADOX GetPermissions and SetPermissions methods use the bitwise logical operator OR to retrieve the bitmask for the existing permissions and to add new permissions to the bitmask.

The example procedure in Hands-On 17-10 grants a user the permission to read (adRightRead), insert (adRightInsert), update (adRightUpdate), and delete (adRightDelete) records.

The last two arguments (those in square brackets) are optional:

- Inherit — A Long value that specifies how objects will inherit these permissions. The default value is adInheritNone.
- ObjectTypeId — A Variant value that specifies the GUID (global unique identifier) for a provider object type not defined by OLE DB. This parameter is required if ObjectType is set to adPermObjProviderSpecific (which is used for setting permissions for forms, reports, and macros); otherwise, it is not used.

Table 17-2: GUIDs for provider objects

Object	GUID
Form	{c49c842e-9dcb-11d1-9f0a-00c04fc2c2e0}
Report	{c49c8430-9dcb-11d1-9f0a-00c04fc2c2e0}
Macro	{c49c842f-9dcb-11d1-9f0a-00c04fc2c2e0}

Classes	Members of 'RightsEnum'
Procedures	adRightCreate
Properties	adRightDelete
Property	adRightDrop
Table	adRightExclusive
Tables	adRightExecute
User	adRightFull
Users	adRightInsert
View	adRightMaximumAllowed
Views	adRightNone
ActionEnum	adRightRead
AllowNullsEnum	adRightReadDesign
ColumnAttributesEn	adRightReadPermissions
DataTypeEnum	adRightReference
InheritTypeEnum	adRightUpdate
KeyTypeEnum	adRightWithGrant
ObjectTypeEnum	adRightWriteDesign
RightsEnum	adRightWriteOwner
RuleEnum	adRightWritePermissions
SortOrderEnum	

Figure 17-18: In ADOX, you can use a great many security constants for setting permissions to database objects.

◉ Hands-On 17-10: Setting User Permissions for an Object

1. Insert a new module and, in the module's Code window, enter the Set_UserObjectPermissions procedure as shown below.

```
Sub Set_UserObjectPermissions()
    Dim conn As ADODB.Connection
    Dim cat As ADOX.Catalog
    Dim strDB As String
    Dim strSysDb As String

    On Error GoTo ErrorHandle

    strDB = "C:\BookProject\SpecialDb.mdb"
    strSysDb = "C:\BookProject\Security.mdw"

    ' Open connection to the database using
    ' the specified system database
    Set conn = New ADODB.Connection
```

```
    With conn
        .Provider = "Microsoft.Jet.OLEDB.4.0"
        .Properties("Jet OLEDB:System Database") = strSysDb
        .Properties("User ID") = "Developer"
        .Properties("Password") = "chapter17"
        .Open strDB
    End With


' Open the catalog
Set cat = New ADOX.Catalog
cat.ActiveConnection = conn
' add a user account
cat.Users.Append "PowerUser", "star"

' Set permissions for PowerUser on the Customers table
cat.Users("PowerUser").SetPermissions "Customers", _
    adPermObjTable, _
    adAccessSet, _
    adRightRead Or _
    adRightInsert Or _
    adRightUpdate Or _
    adRightDelete
MsgBox "Read, Insert, Update and Delete permissions " & _
    vbCrLf & " were set on Customers table " & _
    "for PowerUser."
ExitHere:
    Set cat = Nothing
    conn.Close
    Set conn = Nothing
    Exit Sub
ErrorHandle:
    If Err.Number = -2147467259 Then
        MsgBox "PowerUser user already exists."
        Resume Next
    Else
        MsgBox Err.Description
        Resume ExitHere
    End If
End Sub
```

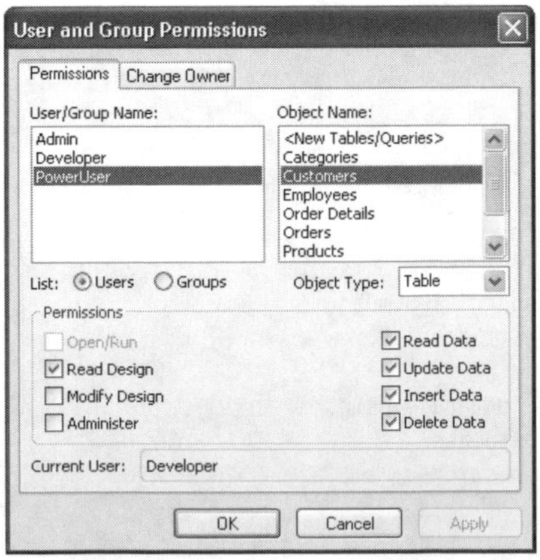

Figure 17-19: The settings in the User and Group Permissions window for the SpecialDb database were set by the Set_ UserObjectPermissions procedure in Hands-On 17-10.

Setting User Permissions for a Database

To specify permissions for the database, specify an empty string (" ") as the name of the database:

```
cat.Users("PowerUser").SetPermissions " ", _
    adPermObjDatabase, _
    adAccessSet, adRightExclusive
```

The above statement gives the user named PowerUser the right to open the database exclusively.

◉ Hands-On 17-11: Setting User Permissions for a Database

1. Insert a new module and, in the module's Code window, enter the Set_UserDbPermissions procedure as shown below.

```
Sub Set_UserDbPermissions()
    Dim conn As ADODB.Connection
    Dim cat As ADOX.Catalog
    Dim strDB As String
    Dim strSysDb As String

    On Error GoTo ErrorHandle

    strDB = "C:\BookProject\SpecialDb.mdb"
    strSysDb = "C:\BookProject\Security.mdw"

    ' Open connection to the database using
    ' the specified system database
    Set conn = New ADODB.Connection
        With conn
            .Provider = "Microsoft.Jet.OLEDB.4.0"
            .Properties("Jet OLEDB:System Database") = strSysDb
            .Properties("User ID") = "Developer"
            .Properties("Password") = "chapter17"
            .Open strDB
        End With

    ' Open the catalog
    Set cat = New ADOX.Catalog
    cat.ActiveConnection = conn

    ' add a user account
    cat.Users.Append "PowerUser", "star"

    ' Set permissions for PowerUser
    cat.Users("PowerUser").SetPermissions " ", adPermObjDatabase, _
            adAccessSet, adRightExclusive
    MsgBox "PowerUser has been granted permission to " & vbCrLf & _
            "open the database exclusively."
ExitHere:
    Set cat = Nothing
    conn.Close
    Set conn = Nothing
    Exit Sub
```

```
ErrorHandle:
    If Err.Number = -2147467259 Then
        ' because PowerUser user already exists
        ' we ignore this statement
        Resume Next
    Else
        MsgBox Err.Description
        Resume ExitHere
    End If
End Sub
```

Figure 17-20: The following settings are found in the User and Group Permissions window for the SpecialDb database after running the Set_UserDbPermissions procedure in Hands-On 17-11.

Setting User Permissions for Containers

Now that you've learned how to grant permissions to a user for a specific object such as a table or query, you may want to know how to specify permissions for a whole set of objects such as tables, queries, forms, reports, and macros.

Each Database object has a Containers collection consisting of built-in Container objects. A Container object groups together similar types of Document objects. You can use the Containers collection to set security for all Document objects of a given type. You can set the permissions that users and groups will receive by default on all newly created objects in a database by passing in Null for the object name argument of the ADOX SetPermissions method, as shown in the example procedure in Hands-On 17-12. The code of this procedure gives the PowerUser account (recall that this account was created in Hands-On 17-2) the permission to design, read, update, insert, and delete data for all newly created tables and queries. Notice that Null is passed as the first argument of the SetPermissions method to indicate that permissions are to be set only on new objects of the type specified by the second argument of this method.

◎ Hands-On 17-12: Setting User Permissions for Containers

1. Insert a new module and, in the module's Code window, enter the Set_UserContainerPermissions procedure as shown below.

```
Sub Set_UserContainerPermissions()
    Dim conn As ADODB.Connection
    Dim cat As ADOX.Catalog
    Dim strDB As String
    Dim strSysDb As String

    On Error GoTo ErrorHandle

    strDB = "C:\BookProject\SpecialDb.mdb"
    strSysDb = "C:\BookProject\Security.mdw"

    ' Open connection to the database using
    ' the specified system database
    Set conn = New ADODB.Connection
        With conn
            .Provider = "Microsoft.Jet.OLEDB.4.0"
            .Properties("Jet OLEDB:System Database") = strSysDb
            .Properties("User ID") = "Developer"
            .Properties("Password") = "chapter17"
            .Open strDB
        End With

    ' Open the catalog
    Set cat = New ADOX.Catalog
    cat.ActiveConnection = conn

    ' add a user account
    cat.Users.Append "PowerUser", "star"

    ' Set permissions for PowerUser on the Tables Container
    cat.Users("PowerUser").SetPermissions Null, _
        adPermObjTable, _
        adAccessSet, _
        adRightRead Or _
        adRightInsert Or _
        adRightUpdate Or _
        adRightDelete, adInheritNone
    MsgBox "You have successfully granted permissions " & vbCrLf & _
            "to PowerUser on the Tables Container."
ExitHere:
    Set cat = Nothing
    conn.Close
    Set conn = Nothing
    Exit Sub
ErrorHandle:
    If Err.Number = -2147467259 Then
        ' because PowerUser user already exists
        ' we ignore this statement
        Resume Next
```

```
    Else
        MsgBox Err.Description
        Resume ExitHere
    End If
End Sub
```

After executing the procedure above, the user account PowerUser has the permissions listed in Figure 17-21 on all newly created Table and Query objects.

Figure 17-21: The following settings are found in the User and Group Permissions window after running the Set_UserContainerPermissions procedure in Hands-On 17-12.

Checking Permissions for Objects

You can retrieve the permissions for a particular user or group on a particular object with the ADOX GetPermissions method. Because this method returns a numeric permission value for the specified object, if you want to display the names of constants representing permissions, you must write more code to decipher the returned value. The procedure in Hands-On 17-13 demonstrates how to retrieve the permissions set for the PowerUser on the Customers table in a sample database.

Hands-On 17-13: Checking Permissions for a Specific Object

1. Insert a new module and, in the module's Code window, enter the GetObjectPermissions procedure as shown below.

```
Sub GetObjectPermissions(strUserName As String, _
            varObjName As Variant, _
            lngObjType As ADOX.ObjectTypeEnum)

    Dim conn As ADODB.Connection
    Dim cat As ADOX.Catalog
    Dim strDB As String
    Dim strSysDb As String
    Dim listPerms As Long
    Dim strPermsTypes As String
```

```
        On Error GoTo ErrorHandle

        strDB = "C:\BookProject\SpecialDb.mdb"
        strSysDb = "C:\BookProject\Security.mdw"

        ' Open connection to the database using
        ' the specified system database
        Set conn = New ADODB.Connection
            With conn
                .Provider = "Microsoft.Jet.OLEDB.4.0"
                .Properties("Jet OLEDB:System Database") = strSysDb
                .Properties("User ID") = "Developer"
                .Properties("Password") = "chapter17"
                .Open strDB
            End With

        ' Open the catalog
        Set cat = New ADOX.Catalog
        cat.ActiveConnection = conn
        ' add a user account
        cat.Users.Append "PowerUser", "star"

        listPerms = cat.Users(strUserName) _
            .GetPermissions(varObjName, lngObjType)
        Debug.Print listPerms

        If (listPerms And ADOX.RightsEnum.adRightCreate) = adRightCreate Then
            strPermsTypes = strPermsTypes & "adRightCreate" & vbCr
        End If
        If (listPerms And RightsEnum.adRightRead) = adRightRead Then
            strPermsTypes = strPermsTypes & "adRightRead" & vbCr
        End If
        If (listPerms And RightsEnum.adRightUpdate) = adRightUpdate Then
            strPermsTypes = strPermsTypes & "adRightUpdate" & vbCr
        End If
        If (listPerms And RightsEnum.adRightDelete) = adRightDelete Then
            strPermsTypes = strPermsTypes & "adRightDelete" & vbCr
        End If
        If (listPerms And RightsEnum.adRightInsert) = adRightInsert Then
            strPermsTypes = strPermsTypes & "adRightInsert" & vbCr
        End If
        If (listPerms And RightsEnum.adRightReadDesign) = adRightReadDesign Then
            strPermsTypes = strPermsTypes & "adRightReadDesign" & vbCr
        End If

        Debug.Print strPermsTypes
        MsgBox "Permissions are listed in the Immediate window."
ExitHere:
        Set cat = Nothing
        conn.Close
        Set conn = Nothing
        Exit Sub
ErrorHandle:
        If Err.Number = -2147467259 Then
            ' because PowerUser user already exists
            ' we ignore this statement
```

```
            Resume Next
        Else
            MsgBox Err.Description
            Resume ExitHere
        End If
    End Sub
```

2. To run the GetObjectPermissions procedure shown above, enter the follow-
    ing statement in the Immediate window and press **Enter** to execute it:

```
GetObjectPermissions "PowerUser", "Customers", adPermObjTable
```

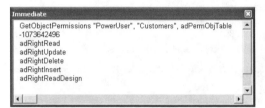

Figure 17-22: The procedure
in Hands-On 17-13 writes the
permissions found for
PowerUser to the Customers
table to the Immediate
window.

Setting a Database Password

You can implement *share-level* security by setting a database password. When
you set a database password, the password dialog box will appear when you
open the database. Only users with a valid password can open the database.

To set a database password you cannot use ADOX objects. Instead, you
have to use the objects from the Microsoft Jet and Replication Objects (JRO)
Library. Use the CompactDatabase method of the JRO JetEngine object and
specify the Password parameter.

The following procedure sets the sample database password to "welcome."
Prior to running the procedure in Hands-On 17-14, set a reference to the JRO
Objects Library as shown in Figure 17-23.

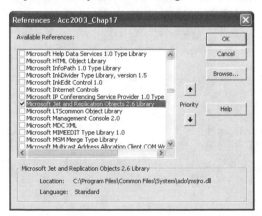

Figure 17-23: Before writing
procedures that set or change
the database password, you
must set a reference to the
Microsoft Jet and Replication
Objects Library. To do this,
choose Tools | References in
the Visual Basic Editor window
and select the required library
in the list of Available
References.

◉ Hands-On 17-14: Setting a Database Password

While this hands-on uses the sample database that you prepared in Chapter 1 of this book, you can use any unsecured Access database for this password changing exercise.

1. Insert a new module and, in the module's Code window, enter the Change_DBPassword procedure as shown below.

```
Sub Change_DBPassword()
    Dim jetEng As JRO.JetEngine
    Dim strCompactFrom As String
    Dim strCompactTo As String
    Dim strPath As String

    On Error GoTo ErrHandle
    strPath = CurrentProject.Path & "\"

    strCompactFrom = "Acc2003_Chap01.mdb"
    strCompactTo = "Acc2003_Chap01A.mdb"

    Set jetEng = New JRO.JetEngine
    ' Compact the database specifying the new database password
    jetEng.CompactDatabase "Data Source=" & strPath & strCompactFrom & ";", _
                           "Data Source=" & strPath & strCompactTo & ";" & _
                           "Jet OLEDB:Database Password=welcome"

ExitHere:
    Set jetEng = Nothing
    Exit Sub
ErrHandle:
    If Err.Number = -2147217897 Then
        Kill strPath & strCompactTo
        Resume
    Else
        MsgBox Err.Number & ": " & Err.Description
        Resume ExitHere
    End If
End Sub
```

2. After you run the procedure in Hands-On 17-14, open the **Acc2003_ Chap01A.mdb** file. You should be prompted for the password. Type **welcome** to log in.

Changing a User Password

User passwords are stored in the workgroup information file. To change a user's password from your VBA code, use the ADOX User object's ChangePassword method. This method takes as parameters the user's current password and the new password. If a user does not yet have a password, use an empty string (" ") for the user's current password.

The procedure in Hands-On 17-15 demonstrates how to change a password for the Admin user. Recall that Admin is the default user account that has a blank password. In an unsecured Access database, all users are automatically logged on using the Admin account. When establishing user-level security you should start by changing the password for the Admin user. Changing an Admin password activates the Logon dialog box the next time you start Microsoft Access. Only users with a valid user name and password will be able to log onto the database. Although users are permitted to change their own passwords, only a user that belongs to the Admins account can clear a password that another user has forgotten.

◉ Hands-On 17-15: Changing a User Password

While this hands-on uses the sample database that you prepared in Chapter 1 of this book, you can use any unsecured Access database for this password changing exercise.

1. Insert a new module and, in the module's Code window, enter the Change_UserPassword procedure as shown below.

```
Sub Change_UserPassword()
    Dim cat As ADOX.Catalog
    Dim strDB As String
    Dim strSysDb As String

    On Error GoTo ErrorHandle

    strDB = CurrentProject.Path & "\Acc2003_Chap01.mdb"
    ' change the path to use the default workgroup information file
    ' on your computer
    strSysDb = "C:\Documents and Settings\JKorol\" & _
                "Application Data\Microsoft\Access\System.mdw"

    ' Open the catalog, specifying the system database to use
    Set cat = New ADOX.Catalog
    With cat
        .ActiveConnection = "Provider='Microsoft.Jet.OLEDB.4.0';" & _
                            "Data Source='" & strDB & "';" & _
                            "Jet OLEDB:System Database='" & strSysDb & "';" & _
                            "User Id=Admin;Password=;"

        ' Change the password for the Admin user
        .Users("Admin").ChangePassword " ", "secret"
    End With

ExitHere:
    Set cat = Nothing
    Exit Sub
ErrorHandle:
    MsgBox Err.Description
    GoTo ExitHere
End Sub
```

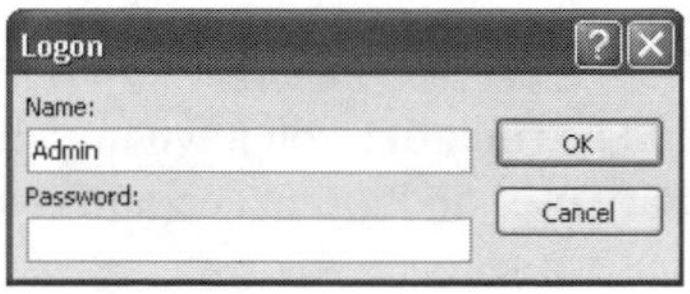

Creating and Manipulating Databases with ADO

Figure 17-24: When you open the Acc2003_Chap01.mdb database after running the procedure in Hands-On 17-15, a Logon dialog will appear. Enter Admin in the Name text box and secret for the Admin password.

2. Remove the Admin password by choosing **Tools | Security**. Click the **Change Logon Password** tab and type the old password (**secret**). Click the **Apply** button, and click **OK** to exit the window (Figure 17-25).

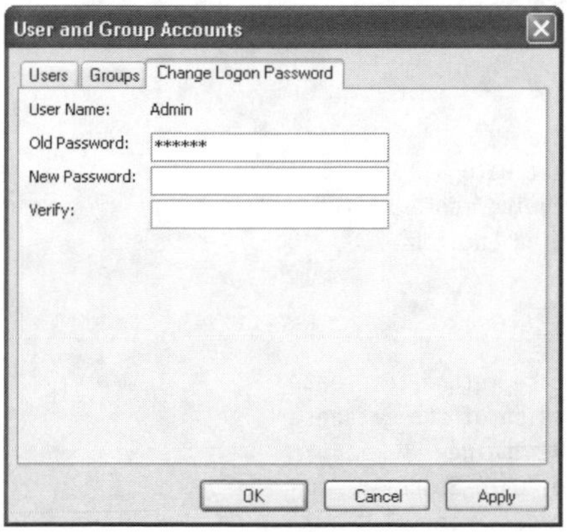

Figure 17-25: You can remove the Admin password manually via the Change Logon Password tab in the User and Group Accounts window, or by modifying the VBA code shown in Hands-On 17-15.

3. After removing the Admin password set in Hands-On 17-15, reopen the **Acc2003_Chap01.mdb** file. The database should open without prompting you to enter a password.

Encrypting a Database

To achieve a higher level of security and protect your database from unauthorized access, you can encrypt it. Prior to encrypting, secure your database by setting user and group permissions on database objects. To encrypt a database you must be the owner or the creator of the database, or a member of the Admins group in the workgroup information file (System.mdw) that was in use when the database was created.

Use the CompactDatabase method of the Microsoft Jet and Replication Objects (JRO) JetEngine object to encrypt or decrypt a database. To use the JRO JetEngine object, you must set a reference to the Microsoft Jet and Replication Objects Library. To encrypt the database, set the Jet OLEDB:Encrypt Database property to True in the connection string destination argument of the CompactDatabase method.

After a database has been encrypted it cannot be read or written to directly by using any utility program or word processor. The procedure in Hands-On 17-16 creates an encrypted version of the Northwind sample database.

◉ Hands-On 17-16: Encrypting a Database

The procedure in this hands-on should be run after you have initially secured your database by creating the necessary user and group accounts and assigned user and group permissions on database objects.

1. Insert a new module and, in the module's Code window, enter the EncryptDb procedure as shown below.

```
Sub EncryptDb()
    Dim jetEng As JRO.JetEngine
    Dim strCompactFrom As String
    Dim strCompactTo As String
    Dim strPath As String

    strPath = CurrentProject.Path & "\"
    strCompactFrom = "Northwind.mdb"
    strCompactTo = "Northwind_Enc.mdb"

    On Error GoTo HandleErr

    ' Use the CompactDatabase method to create
    ' a new, encrypted version of the database
    Set jetEng = New JRO.JetEngine
    jetEng.CompactDatabase "Data Source=" & _
            strPath & strCompactFrom & ";", _
            "Data Source=" & strPath & strCompactTo & ";" & _
            "Jet OLEDB:Encrypt Database=True"
ExitHere:
    Set jetEng = Nothing
    Exit Sub
HandleErr:
    MsgBox Err.Number & ": " & Err.Description
    Resume ExitHere
End Sub
```

Chapter Summary

In this chapter, you learned how to secure a Microsoft Office Access database from VBA procedures by using various objects and methods that are available in the ADOX and JRO object libraries. You practiced creating and modifying user and group accounts for a sample database, and granted and revoked permissions on objects. You also learned how to secure an Access database with a password and wrote a VBA procedure that encrypts the entire database.

In the next chapter, you discover how you can make the database available to users in remote locations via database replication.

Chapter 18

Database Replication

To make your database available to users in various geographical locations, you can provide them with a full or partial copy of the database. Mobile or remote users can maintain a local copy of a database, make changes to data offline, and synchronize with the main database on a regular basis. All this can be achieved via the technology known as *database replication*. When you replicate a database you simply create multiple copies (replicas) of your application and distribute them to users in remote locations so that they can easily share the changes they are making to a database. Database replication also offers other advantages, such as:

- Convenient distribution of updates to existing applications — Changes made to queries, forms, reports, and other application components can be automatically updated in remote copies of the database during the next synchronization.
- Reduction of network traffic — Database replicas can be placed on different servers serving different groups of users, thus reducing the network load.
- Data backup — You don't need to make a separate backup copy of your database as each member of the replica set can serve as a backup. If the Design Master is corrupted, you can always make another member of the replica set the Design Master. You learn about creating the Design Master and replicas later in this chapter.

Although you can create a replica of your database via the Microsoft Office Access 2003 user interface (see the Replication command in the Tools menu), in the following sections of this chapter, you will learn how to perform the replication tasks by using ADO.

Before beginning your experiments with database replication by writing code, set a reference to the Microsoft Jet and Replication Objects Library (JRO) by choosing Tools | References in the Microsoft Visual Basic Editor screen.

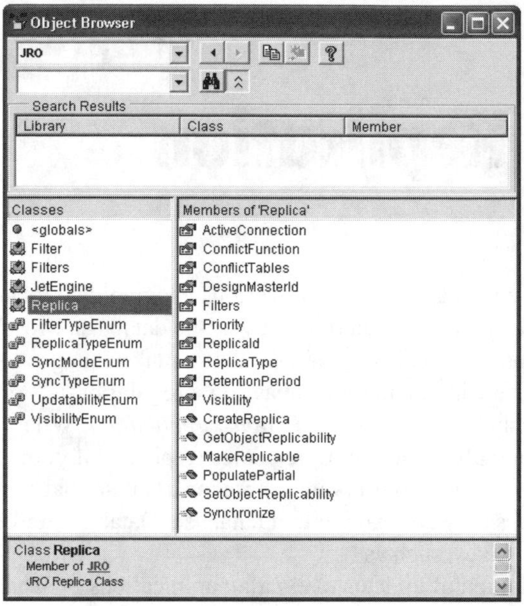

Figure 18-1: After setting the reference to the Microsoft Jet and Replication Objects Library (JRO) you can use the Object Browser to view available objects, properties, and methods.

The Replica object has methods for determining if an object is replicable (GetObjectReplicability method), creating a replica (CreateReplica method), converting a database to a Design Master (MakeReplicable method), populating a partial replica (PopulatePartial method), setting an object's replicability (SetObjectReplicability method), and synchronizing replicas (Synchronize method). In addition to methods, there are quite a few Replica properties that allow you to set or retrieve various characteristics such as DesignMasterId, ReplicaId, Visibility, RetentionPeriod, and ConflictTables. The VBA procedures in this section will give you a head start in database replication.

➜ **Note:** This chapter requires that you complete all hands-on exercises in order.

Creating a Design Master

A *replica* is a copy of a database. There are three types of replicas: Design Master, full replica, and partial replica. To work with replication, start by creating a backup copy of your database. You will need it in case there is a problem with the replicated database. Next, create a replica of your database by using the Replica object's MakeReplicable method. This method requires that you provide a full path to your database and indicate whether you want column-level tracking. With column-level tracking, changing different columns in the same row of a table in two replicas doesn't cause a conflict. The Make-Replicable method converts a normal Access database into a Design Master.

This is a master replica from which you can create additional replicas with the CreateReplica method.

The Design Master is the first member of a replica set. When you create a Design Master, new system tables are added to a database and new fields are added to the existing tables. Only the Design Master can accept changes to the database structure. If the Design Master is damaged, you can promote one of the replicas to become the Design Master. Hands-On 18-1 below demonstrates how to make a backup copy of the original database and create a Design Master.

◎ Hands-On 18-1: Creating a Design Master

1. Open the **Acc2003_Chap18.mdb** file from the book's downloadable files or create this file from scratch using the Access user interface.

2. Make sure you have a copy of the Northwind database in the same folder as the Acc2003_Chap18.mdb file.

3. Switch to the Visual Basic Editor window and insert a new module.

4. Choose **Tools | References** and add the following two libraries: **Microsoft Jet and Replication Objects Library** and **Microsoft Scripting Runtime Library**.

5. In the module's Code window, enter the Create_DesignMaster procedure as shown below.

```
Sub Create_DesignMaster(dbName As String, strPath As String)
    Dim repDesignMaster As New JRO.Replica
    Dim fso As Scripting.FileSystemObject
    Dim strDb As String

    ' create a new instance of the FileSystemObject
    Set fso = New FileSystemObject

    ' store a file name for the Design Master in a variable
    strDb = strPath & "DM_" & dbName

    ' create a copy of the sample Northwind database
    If Not fso.FileExists(strDb) Then
        fso.CopyFile strPath & dbName, strDb
    Else
        MsgBox "The " & strDb & " database file already exists."
        Exit Sub
    End If

    ' make the database replicable
    repDesignMaster.MakeReplicable strDb, True
    MsgBox "Your Design Master was successfully created." _
            , , "DM_Northwind"

    Set repDesignMaster = Nothing
    Set fso = Nothing
End Sub
```

To access your computer's file system, the above procedure uses the FileSystemObject from the Microsoft Scripting Runtime Library. The FileSystemObject gives you access to numerous methods and properties for working with drives, folders, and files. Notice how we use the FileExists method of FileSystemObject to find out if a file named DM_Northwind.mdb already exists in the specified folder. If the file does not exist, we use another method (CopyFile) of the FileSystemObject to create a copy of the Northwind database and name it DM_Northwind.mdb. Next, we use the MakeReplicable method of the JRO Replica object to create a master replica (Design Master).

6. To execute the Create_DesignMaster procedure, type the following statement in the Immediate window and press **Enter**:

```
Create_DesignMaster "Northwind.mdb", CurrentProject.Path & "\"
```

For the above statement to work you must ensure that the Northwind.mdb file is located in the same folder as the Acc2003_Chap18.mdb file you are currently working with.

After running the Create_DesignMaster procedure, the current folder should contain a database file named DM_Northwind.mdb, which is a Design Master.

Creating a Full Replica

After you've created your Design Master you can create additional replicas from it by using the CreateReplica method. This method takes two required arguments. The first one is replicaName, which specifies the name and path of the full or partial replica to be created. The second argument is description, a string value describing the replica to be created.

The CreateReplica method can also take several optional arguments that let you specify the type of replica and its visibility, priority, and updatability. By omitting additional arguments, a full replica is created. This replica will have global visibility and will be fully updatable.

Hands-On 18-2 demonstrates how to create a full replica without optional arguments.

⊙ Hands-On 18-2: Creating a Full Replica

1. Switch to the Visual Basic Editor window and insert a new module.

2. In the module's Code window, enter the Make_FullReplica procedure as shown below.

```
Sub Make_FullReplica(DesignMasterName As String, _
            NewRepName As String)
    Dim repDesignMaster As New JRO.Replica

    On Error GoTo ErrorHandle

    With repDesignMaster
        .ActiveConnection = DesignMasterName
```

```
                    .CreateReplica CurrentProject.Path & "\" & NewRepName, _
                        "Replica of " & DesignMasterName
              End With

              MsgBox "Full replica named " & NewRepName & " was created."

      ExitHere:
          Set repDesignMaster = Nothing
          Exit Sub
      ErrorHandle:
          If Err.Number = -2147217897 Then
              Kill CurrentProject.Path & "\" & NewRepName
              Resume
          Else
              MsgBox Err.Number & ": " & Err.Description
              Resume ExitHere
          End If
      End Sub
```

3. Execute the Make_FullReplica procedure by typing the following statement in the Immediate window and pressing **Enter**:

```
Make_FullReplica CurrentProject.Path & "\DM_Northwind.mdb", "Replica_North.mdb"
```

When you run the Make_FullReplica procedure, a new file named
Replica_North.mdb is created. This file is a full replica of the
DM_Northwind.mdb database.

You can create as many replicas of the original database (Design Master) as
you want. All replicas created from the same Design Master belong to the
same replica set, and only replicas from the same set can synchronize and
exchange data with each other.

Creating a Partial Replica

A partial replica is a replica that does not contain all the data of the original
object. This type of replica is useful for those who only need to see or work
with certain data. A partial replica is created by setting an expression-based or
relationship-based filter on tables or queries. A partial replica contains all the
tables that exist in the full replica; however, the user only sees the data as
allowed by the specified filter. Therefore, some of the tables in a partial replica
are empty. Because partial replicas have fewer records, they can synchronize
quicker than full replicas.

You can create a partial replica by using the CreateReplica method and
specifying two required arguments (the partial replica's name and description)
and an enumeration constant of jrRepTypePartial for the optional argument.
For instance, in Hands-On 18-3 you use the following statement to create a
partial replica to display records for only Spanish customers:

```
repDesignMaster.CreateReplica repPartialName, _
    "Partial Replica (Spanish Customers)", _
    jrRepTypePartial
```

The above statement creates a partial replica. Next, you must specify which records the partial replica will contain by defining filters. Each replica can have one or more filters.

There are two types of filters in JRO:

■ An *expression-based filter* is a criterion that a record in the partial replica table must satisfy in order to be replicated from the full replica. This criterion is like the SQL WHERE clause without the WHERE keyword. For example, the procedure that follows uses a criterion to allow access only to customer records from the specified country:

```
"[Country] ='Spain'"
```

■ The second type of filter, *a relationship-based filter*, restricts the records based on relationships between tables. In Hands-On 18-3 below, only information related to Spanish customers will be accessible to the user.

After setting the filters, use the PopulatePartial method to add records to a partial replica based on the specified filter. For instance:

```
repPartial.PopulatePartial repMasterName
```

In the statement above, repPartial is an object variable that points to the partial replica. repMasterName is a string variable that denotes the path and filename for the full replica set.

The PopulatePartial method will first clear all records in the partial replica, then repopulate the replica based on the specified filters. This type of operation requires that the partial replica be opened with exclusive access.

◎ Hands-On 18-3: Creating a Partial Replica

1. Switch to the Visual Basic Editor window and insert a new module.

2. In the module's Code window, enter the Make_PartialReplica procedure as shown below.

```
Sub Make_PartialReplica(FilterOption As Integer)
    Dim repDesignMaster As New JRO.Replica
    Dim repPartial As New JRO.Replica
    Dim flt As JRO.Filter
    Dim repMasterName As String
    Dim repPartialName As String
    Dim strFilterType As String

    On Error GoTo ErrorHandle

    repMasterName = CurrentProject.Path & "\DM_Northwind.mdb"
    repPartialName = CurrentProject.Path & "\Spanish.mdb"

    ' Create partial replica
    repDesignMaster.ActiveConnection = repMasterName
    repDesignMaster.CreateReplica repPartialName, _
        "Partial Replica (Spanish Customers)", _
        jrRepTypePartial
```

```
        Set repDesignMaster = Nothing

        ' open an exclusive connection to the partial replica
        repPartial.ActiveConnection = "Provider=Microsoft.Jet.OLEDB.4.0;" & _
            "Data Source= " & repPartialName & ";Mode=Share Exclusive"

        If FilterOption = 1 Then
            ' Create an expression-based filter in the partial replica
            repPartial.Filters.Append "Customers", jrFilterTypeTable, "[Country]
                ='Spain'"

        ElseIf FilterOption = 2 Then
            ' Create a relationship-based filter in the partial replica
            repPartial.Filters.Append "Customers", jrFilterTypeTable, "[Country]
                ='Spain'"
            repPartial.Filters.Append "Orders", jrFilterTypeRelationship,
                "CustomersOrders"
        End If

        ' Populate the partial replica based on the specified filter
        repPartial.PopulatePartial repMasterName

        MsgBox "Partial replica named " & repPartialName & vbCrLf _
            & "was created based on the selected filter type." & vbCrLf _
            & "Please view filter information in the Immediate window."

        ' Print filter information to the Immediate window
        For Each flt In repPartial.Filters
            If flt.FilterType = jrFilterTypeTable Then
                strFilterType = "Table Filter"
            Else
                strFilterType = "Relationship Filter"
            End If
            Debug.Print "Table Name: " & flt.TableName & vbCr _
                ; vbTab & "Filter Type: " & strFilterType & vbCr _
                ; vbTab & "Filter Criteria: " & flt.FilterCriteria
        Next

ExitHere:
    Set repPartial = Nothing
    Exit Sub
ErrorHandle:
    If Err.Number = -2147217897 Then
        Kill repPartialName
        Resume
    Else
        MsgBox Err.Number & ": " & Err.Description
        Resume ExitHere
    End If
End Sub
```

3. Execute the Make_PartialReplica procedure by typing the following statement in the Immediate window and pressing **Enter**:

```
Make_PartialReplica 1
```

The above statement specifies that the Make_PartialReplica procedure should use the expression-based filter (1) when repopulating the partial replica. The filter information is printed to the Immediate window:

```
Table Name: MSysCmdbars
      Filter Type: Table Filter
      Filter Criteria: TRUE
Table Name: MSysIMEXColumns
      Filter Type: Table Filter
      Filter Criteria: TRUE
Table Name: MSysIMEXSpecs
      Filter Type: Table Filter
      Filter Criteria: TRUE
Table Name: MSysAccessObjects
      Filter Type: Table Filter
      Filter Criteria: TRUE
Table Name: Customers
      Filter Type: Table Filter
      Filter Criteria: [Country] ='Spain'
```

4. Execute the Make_PartialReplica procedure again by typing the following statement in the Immediate window and pressing **Enter**:

```
Make_PartialReplica 2
```

The above statement specifies that the Make_PartialReplica procedure should use the relationship-based filter (2) when repopulating the partial replica.

Replicating Objects

When you create additional replicas from your Design Master you may choose to replicate all objects or keep some objects local and prevent them from being replicated. You can set object replicability with the SetObjectReplicability method. This method requires three arguments: a string indicating the name of a table or query, the string "Tables," and a Boolean value of True if the object is to be replicable, or False otherwise.

⊚ Hands-On 18-4: Checking If an Object is Replicable

1. Open the Design Master named **DM_Northwind.mdb**. (This Design Master was created by the procedure in Hands-On 18-1.)

2. In the DM_Northwind Design Master database, create a new query named **SampleQuery** based on any available tables. For example, you can use the following SQL statement to create the sample for this hands-on:

```
SELECT Employees.LastName,
       Employees.FirstName,
       Orders.OrderDate,
       Orders.ShipCity,
       Orders.ShipCountry
FROM Employees
       INNER JOIN Orders ON Employees.EmployeeID = Orders.EmployeeID;
```

Upon creation, the SampleQuery object is local to your database. To confirm this, right-click the query name in the Database window and choose Properties from the shortcut menu. Notice that the Replicable check box is not checked.

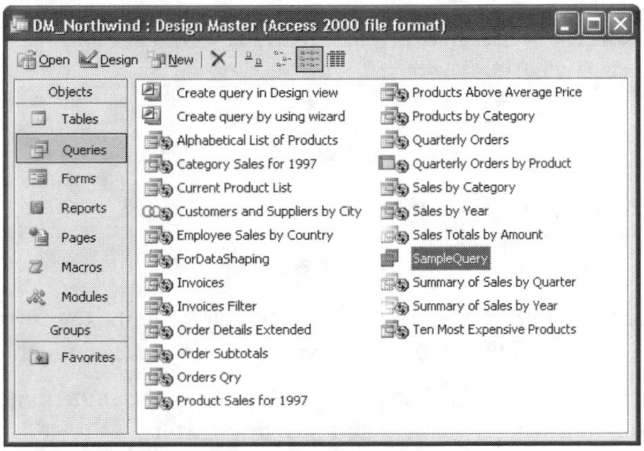

Figure 18-2: When you open the Design Master file you will notice different icons in front of object names that are replicable. The local query you created in step 2 is highlighted in this screen shot.

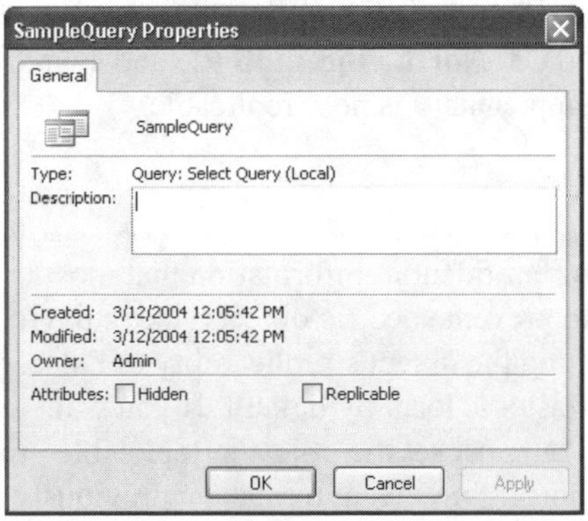

Figure 18-3: You can determine whether a certain database object is replicable or not by checking the object's properties. The Replicable check box is not checked for local objects.

If at this time you create an additional replica from the Design Master or try to synchronize with an existing replica, this new query object will not be replicated. To ensure the new object is replicated, you can check the Replicable property in the Properties box (Figure 18-3 above) or set the object's replicability in VBA code by using the SetObjectReplicability method. We will set the replicability of the SampleQuery object in the procedure code in Hands-On 18-5.

3. Close the DM_Northwind database without checking the Replicable property for the SampleQuery object.

⊚ Hands-On 18-5: Making an Object Replicable

1. Switch to the Visual Basic Editor window and insert a new module.

2. In the module's Code window, enter the MakeObject_Replicable procedure as shown below.

```
Sub MakeObject_Replicable(repName As String, objName As String)
    Dim repDesignMaster As New JRO.Replica
    With repDesignMaster
        .ActiveConnection = repName
        .SetObjectReplicability objName, "Tables", True
    End With
    Set repDesignMaster = Nothing
    MsgBox objName & " is now replicable."
End Sub
```

The procedure in Hands-On 18-5 takes two arguments: the full path of your Design Master and the object name you want to make replicable.

3. Run the MakeObject_Replicable procedure from the Immediate window by typing the following statement and pressing **Enter**:

```
MakeObject_Replicable CurrentProject.Path & "\DM_Northwind.mdb", "SampleQuery"
```

4. Open the Design Master **DM_Northwind.mdb** file and switch to the queries pane. Notice that SampleQuery is now replicable.

Keeping Objects Local

When your database contains confidential information that most users do not need to see, you may want to prevent specific objects (like a payroll table) from being replicated by setting the object's replicability to False. A newly created object in a Design Master is local by default. If you want this object to be seen by another replica, you must set the object's Replicable property to True (see the preceding section). If you want to make a previously replicated object local, make sure to synchronize first to avoid losing any changes that could have been made to this object in another replica. When you make a replicated object local in the Design Master and then synchronize, the object will be deleted from the replica.

The next hands-on prevents a previously replicated object from being replicated by setting its Replicable property to False using the SetObject-Replicability method that was introduced in the preceding section.

Creating and Manipulating Databases with ADO

 Hands-On 18-6: Preventing an Object from Being Replicated

1. Switch to the Visual Basic Editor window and insert a new module.

2. In the module's Code window, enter the MakeObjectLocal_ InDesignMaster procedure as shown below.

```
Sub MakeObjectLocal_InDesignMaster(myDb As String, _
        objName As String, _
        objType As String)
    Dim repDesignMaster As New JRO.Replica

    With repDesignMaster
        .ActiveConnection = myDb
        .SetObjectReplicability objName, objType, False
    End With

    Set repDesignMaster = Nothing

    MsgBox "The object named " & objName & _
        " in the collection of " & _
        objType & vbCr & "will not be replicated. " & _
        "It has been set as local.", vbInformation, _
        "Operation Completed"
End Sub
```

Notice that the above procedure takes three arguments: the full path of your Design Master, the object name, and the object type.

5. Run the MakeObjectLocal_InDesignMaster procedure from the Immediate window by typing the following statement and pressing **Enter**:

```
MakeObjectLocal_InDesignMaster CurrentProject.Path & "\DM_Northwind.mdb", _
    "Current Product List", "Tables"
```

Note: You must type the above statement on one line in the Immediate window.

When you execute this statement, the Current Product List query will no longer be replicable. You can confirm this by opening your Design Master (DM_Northwind.mdb) and switching to the queries pane.

Synchronizing Replicas

Synchronization allows reconciliation of all changes between replicas. This means that any changes, additions, or deletions can be exchanged between replicas, thus keeping all the copies current and up to date. In JRO, there are three types of synchronization, as shown in Table 18-1.

Table 18-1: Replica synchronization types

Synchronization Type	Constant	Description
Bi-directional, import/export	jrSyncTypeImpExp	Updates are mutual; they flow from the target replica to the source replica and from the source replica to the target replica.
Import only	jrSyncTypeImport	Updates will flow only from the target replica to the source replica.
Export only	jrSyncTypeExport	Updates will flow only from the source replica to the target replica.

In addition to the type of synchronization, you can specify the synchronization mode (Table 18-2).

Table 18-2: Replica synchronization modes

Synchronization Mode	Constant	Description
Direct (default setting)	jrSyncModeDirect	Both replicas must reside on computers connected to a common local area network (LAN) or wide area network (WAN).
Indirect	jrSyncModeIndirect	When a replica resides on a computer disconnected from a network, updates are placed in a dropbox folder and are automatically synchronized when the user connects to the network. This process requires synchronizers to be installed both on the network and on the disconnected computer.
Internet	jrSyncModeInternet	Used for synchronizing with a database connected to a web server.

To synchronize one replica with another, both database files must belong to the same replica set. Each replica set is identified by a unique replica set ID. For two replicas to belong to the same replica set, they must be created from the same Design Master. It is not sufficient to create replicas from the same nonreplicable original database. If you created two replicas that belong to different replica sets and want to bring data from one replica set to another, you can copy and paste or import the data. You cannot use synchronization to reconcile the changes between two replicas from different replica sets.

Hands-On 18-7 demonstrates how to use direct, bidirectional (two-way) synchronization.

Hands-On 18-7: Synchronizing Replicas

1. Switch to the Visual Basic Editor window and insert a new module.

2. In the module's Code window, enter the Sync_Replicas procedure as shown below.

```
Sub Sync_Replicas(strRep As String, strReplica As String, _
                Optional sncType As SyncTypeEnum, _
                Optional sncMode As SyncModeEnum)
    Dim repDesignMaster As New JRO.Replica


    repDesignMaster.ActiveConnection = strRep

    ' exchange data and design changes between replicas
    repDesignMaster.Synchronize strReplica, sncType, sncMode
    Set repDesignMaster = Nothing
    MsgBox strRep & vbCrLf & _
        "and " & vbCrLf & _
        strReplica & vbCrLf & _
        "were synchronized."
End Sub
```

Notice that the Sync_Replicas procedure takes two required and two optional arguments.

3. Run the Sync_Replicas procedure from the Immediate window by typing the following statement and pressing **Enter**:

```
Sync_Replicas CurrentProject.Path & "\DM_Northwind.mdb",
    CurrentProject.Path & "\Replica_North.mdb",
    jrSyncTypeImpExp, jrSyncModeDirect
```

➔ **Note:** The above statement must be entered on one line in the Immediate window.

When you execute this statement the full replica named Replica_North.mdb (see Hands-On 18-2) will be synchronized with the Design Master named DM_Northwind.mdb (see Hands-On 18-1).

Retrieving Replica Properties

The procedure in Hands-On 18-8 examines Microsoft Office Access database files in the specified path and lists their replication properties to the Immediate window.

Table 18-3: List of replica properties checked in Hands-On 18-8

Property	Description
ReplicaType	Specifies the type of replica — Full, Partial, Design Master, or database is not replicable. Use the following enumerators: jrReplicaTypeFull jrReplicaTypePartial jrRepTypeDesignMaster jrRepTypeNotReplicable
DesignMasterId	Unique ID for the Design Master in a replica set.
RetentionPeriod	Number of days that the replica set retains details of deleted records, schema changes, and other information. The default RetentionPeriod is 60 days.
Priority	Determines who wins and who loses in case of a synchronization conflict. The priority values range from 0 to 100. The Design Master has a default priority of 90. The maximum value for priority of any replica is 90 percent of its parent.
Visibility	Ability to synchronize with other replicas.
ReplicaID	Unique ID for each replica in the replica set.

◉ Hands-On 18-8: Retrieving Replica Properties

1. Switch to the Visual Basic Editor window and insert a new module.

2. In the module's Code window, enter the Get_ReplicaProperties procedure as shown below.

```
Sub Get_ReplicaProperties(strPath As String)
    Dim fso As Object
    Dim mdbFile As Object
    Dim myFolder As Object
    Dim typeNum As Integer
    Dim repName As String
    Dim repMaster As New JRO.Replica

    On Error Resume Next

    Set fso = CreateObject("Scripting.FileSystemObject")
    Set myFolder = fso.GetFolder(strPath)
        For Each mdbFile In myFolder.Files
            If InStr(mdbFile.Name, ".mdb") Then
                repName = strPath & mdbFile.Name
                repMaster.ActiveConnection = repName

            Select Case repMaster.ReplicaType
                Case jrRepTypeNotReplicable
                    Debug.Print repName & " is not replicable."
```

```
                    Case jrRepTypeDesignMaster
                        Debug.Print repName & " is a Design Master."
                        Debug.Print "Design Master Id: " & _
                            repMaster.DesignMasterID
                        Debug.Print "Retention Period: " & _
                            repMaster.RetentionPeriod
                        Debug.Print "Priority: " & repMaster.Priority
                        Debug.Print "Visibility: " & repMaster.Visibility
                    Case jrRepTypeFull
                        Debug.Print repName & " is a Full Replica."
                        Debug.Print "Replica Id: " & repMaster.ReplicaID
                        Debug.Print "Retention Period: " & _
                            repMaster.RetentionPeriod
                        Debug.Print "Priority: " & repMaster.Priority
                        Debug.Print "Visibility: " & repMaster.Visibility
                    Case jrRepTypePartial
                        Debug.Print repName & " is a Partial Replica."
                        Debug.Print "Retention Period: " & _
                                repMaster.RetentionPeriod
                        Debug.Print "Priority: " & repMaster.Priority
                        Debug.Print "Visibility: " & repMaster.Visibility
                End Select
            End If
        Next mdbFile
        MsgBox "View Replica Properties in the Immediate window."
    End Sub
```

To retrieve replica properties, the above procedure must be able to access your computer's file system. This is done by using the FileSystemObject from the Microsoft Scripting Runtime Library (see Hands-On 18-1). We use the GetFolder method of the FileSystemObject object to return a Folder object corresponding to the folder in a specified path. Then we look at all the .mdb files in this folder and, if the file is replicable, we check the properties listed in Table 18-3.

Notice that the Get_ReplicaProperties procedure takes two required and two optional arguments.

3. Run the Get_ReplicaProperties procedure from the Immediate window by typing the following statement and pressing **Enter**:

```
Get_ReplicaProperties currentProject.Path & "\"
```

Synchronization Conflicts

During the synchronization of replicas errors may occur. An error may be caused when the same record is updated in two members of the replica set and Microsoft Jet attempts to synchronize the two versions.

The following custom project illustrates how you can use the Replication command on the Tools menu in the Microsoft Office Access user interface to create and synchronize replicas. To learn about conflicts during the synchronization of replicas, we will create two replicas, Replica_England.mdb and Replica_France.mdb, and enter some conflicting data into the same record in both of these replicas.

◎ Custom Project 18-1: Replication via Microsoft Access User Interface

Part 1: Creating a Replica Named Replica_England.mdb

1. Open another copy of Microsoft Access with the Design Master **DM_Northwind.mdb** file that you created in Hands-On 18-1.

2. Choose **Tools | Replication | Create Replica**. In the Filename text box, enter **Replica_England.mdb** as the name of the new replica and click **OK**.

3. Microsoft Access displays a Creating Replica message box. When the process of creating a new replica is finished, you are asked whether you want to close and reopen the database. Click **Yes** in response to this message. Access reloads the Design Master DM_Northwind database. You may need to click **Open** in the Security Warning message to complete the loading process.

Part 2: Creating a Replica Named Replica_France.mdb

1. Choose **Tools | Replication | Create Replica**. In the Filename text box, enter **Replica_France.mdb** as the name of the new replica and click **OK**.

2. Microsoft Access displays a Creating Replica message box. When the process of creating a new replica is finished, you are asked whether you want to close and reopen the database. Click **Yes** in response to this message. Access reloads the Design Master DM_Northwind database. You may need to click **Open** in the Security Warning message to complete the loading process.

Part 3: Making Changes in the Replica_England Database

1. Exit Access, closing the Design Master DM_Northwind database.

2. Switch to Windows Explorer. Locate the **Replica_England.mdb** database file that you created in step 2 of Part 1 above. Double-click this file to open it.

3. In the Customers table, locate the customer record **Around the Horn**. Type **98051** in the Postal Code field for this record. Click on any other record to ensure that the data you entered is saved.

4. Close the Customers table.

5. Exit Access, closing the Replica_England.mdb database file.

Part 4: Making Changes in the Replica_France Database

1. Switch to Windows Explorer. Locate the **Replica_France.mdb** database file that you created in Part 2, step 1 above. Double-click this file to open it.

2. In the Customers table, locate the customer record **Around the Horn**. Type **98053** in the Postal Code field for this record. Click on any other record to ensure that the data you entered is saved.

3. Close the Customers table.

4. Exit Access, closing the Replica_France.mdb database file.

Part 5: Synchronizing Replicas

1. Start Access and load the Design Master **DM_Northwind** database.

2. Choose **Tools | Replication | Synchronize Now**.

3. When the Synchronize Database dialog box appears (see Figure 18-4), select the **Replica_England.mdb** file and click **OK**.

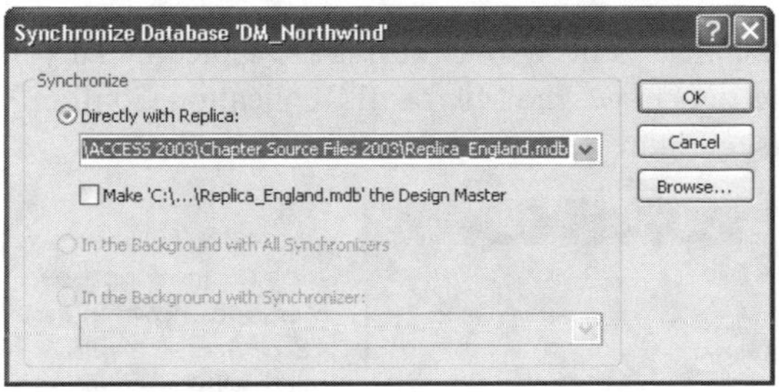

Figure 18-4: To synchronize the Design Master directly with the replica, use the Browse button to find the Replica_England.mdb file on your computer.

4. Click **Yes** in response to the message that the database must be closed prior to synchronization. Access reloads the Design Master DM_Northwind database. If the Security Warning message appears, click **Open**.

5. Click **OK** to confirm the completion of the synchronization process.

6. In the Design Master DM_Northwind database, choose **Tools | Replication | Synchronize Now**.

7. When the Synchronize Database dialog box appears (see Figure 18-5), select the **Replica_France.mdb** file and click **OK**.

Figure 18-5: To synchronize the Design Master directly with the second replica that you created in this custom project, use the Browse button to find the Replica_France.mdb file on your computer.

8. Click **Yes** in response to the message that the database must be closed prior to synchronization. Access reloads the Design Master DM_Northwind database. If the Security Warning message appears, click **Open**.

9. Click **OK** to confirm the completion of the synchronization process.

10. Microsoft Access displays a message indicating a synchronization problem (see Figure 18-6).

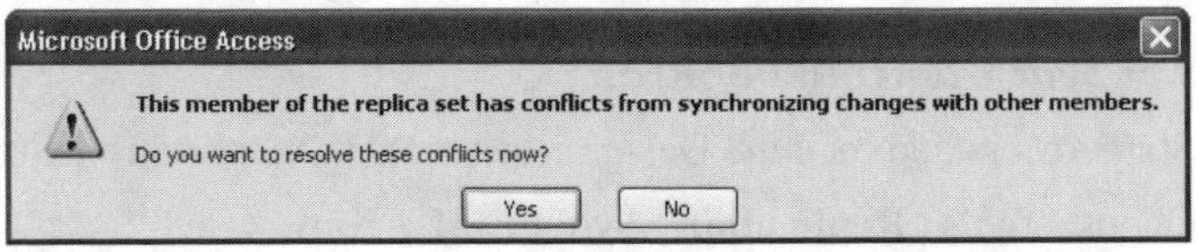

Figure 18-6: This message appears when Access finds out that a member of the replica set has a conflict with another member of the same replica set.

11. Click **Yes** in response to the above message to indicate that you want to resolve the conflicts now. The Microsoft Replication Conflict Viewer window appears (see Figure 18-7).

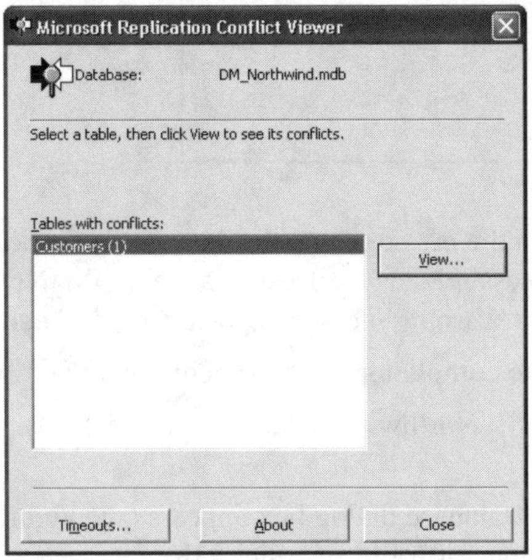

Figure 18-7: When you click Yes in response to the message shown in Figure 18-6, Access displays the Microsoft Replication Conflict Viewer, listing tables with conflicts.

12. In the Microsoft Replication Conflict Viewer window, click the **View** button. Microsoft Access now displays a window specifying the reason for conflict (see Figure 18-8) and allows you to resolve the conflict.

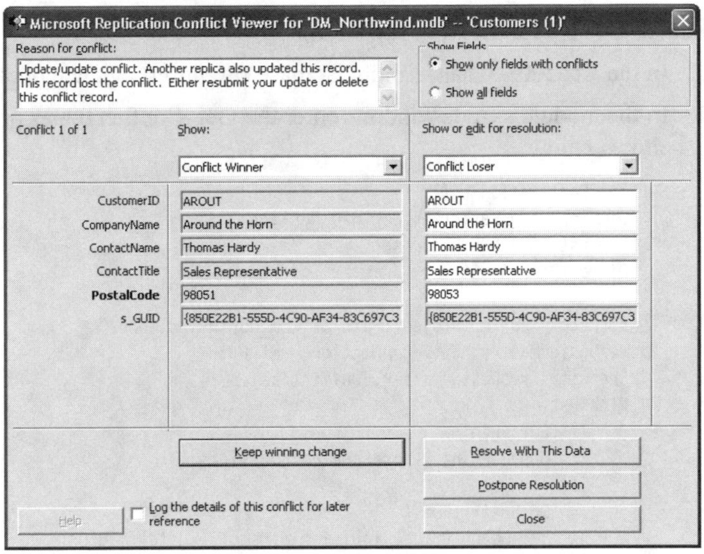

Figure 18-8: This window with conflict details appears when you click the View button in the Microsoft Replication Conflict Viewer window (see Figure 18-7).

13. For this example, click **Close** to exit the Microsoft Replication Conflict Viewer for DM_Northwind.mdb – Customers (1) window without making any changes. Click **Close** again to close the Microsoft Replication Conflict Viewer (shown in Figure 18-7).

14. Close the Design Master DM_Northwind.mdb database file.

The steps you've just completed demonstrate how to create and synchronize replicas using the Microsoft Access user interface. By entering conflicting data in the same field of the same record you were able to see how Access can locate the problem area during the synchronization process and how you can resolve the data conflict using the Microsoft Replication Conflict Viewer window.

Hands-On 18-9 illustrates how you can use the ConflictTables property to find out whether any conflicts occurred during the synchronization of replicas. This property returns the name of the conflict table that contains the database records that conflicted during synchronization.

The conflict table has two columns. The first column contains the names of the tables where conflicts occurred and the second one lists the associated conflict table names. If there is no conflict table (or the database is nonreplicable), the ConflictTables property returns a zero-length string (" "). If you find out that the conflict occurred during synchronization, you should write a custom conflict-resolution procedure to handle the conflicts depending on your needs.

◎ Hands-On 18-9: Retrieving the Name of the Conflict Table

1. In the Acc2003_Chap18.mdb database file, insert a new module.

2. In the module's Code window, enter the Get_ConflictTables procedure as shown below.

```
Sub Get_ConflictTables()
    Dim repDesignMaster As New JRO.Replica
    Dim rst As ADODB.Recordset
    Dim strPath As String

    strPath = CurrentProject.Path & "\DM_Northwind.mdb"
    repDesignMaster.ActiveConnection = strPath
    Set rst = repDesignMaster.ConflictTables
    With rst
        If .EOF Then
            Debug.Print "There are no conflicts."
        Else
            Do Until .EOF
                Debug.Print "Table: " & rst.Fields(0) & vbCr _
                ; "Conflict Table: " & .Fields(1) & vbCrLf
                .MoveNext
            Loop
            .Close
        End If
    End With
    Set repDesignMaster = Nothing
    Set rst = Nothing
End Sub
```

3. Run the Get_ConflictTables procedure to find out the name of the conflict table.

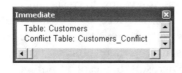

Figure 18-9: The procedure in Hands-On 18-9 prints the location of the synchronization conflict table and the name of the table in which conflict has occurred.

Figure 18-10: The conflict table is hidden in the database window of the Design Master. To unhide it, choose Tools | Options. On the View tab, click the check box next to Hidden Objects.

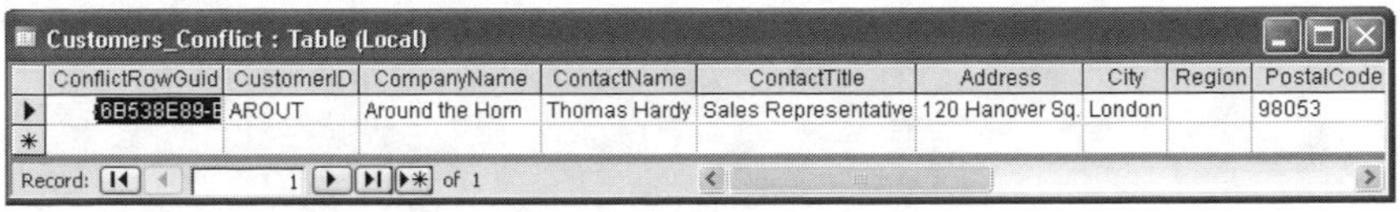

Creating and Manipulating Databases with ADO

Figure 18-11: The conflict table lists the conflicting record.

Chapter Summary

This chapter introduced you to numerous objects, properties, and methods available in the Microsoft Jet and Replication Objects Library (JRO) for programmatic control and management of database replication tasks. You learned how to convert a normal Access database file into a Design Master and used the new Design Master to create both full and partial replicas and learned how to ensure that a database object is replicable as well as how to avoid replicating some of the objects by keeping them local. You also tried out basic replication tasks, such as synchronization and conflict resolution.

This chapter concludes Part II of this book in which you learned how to use ADO for performing important database tasks by writing VBA code.

PART III

Programming with the Jet Data Definition Language

The Data Definition Language (DDL) is a component of the Structured Query Language (SQL), which is used for defining database objects (tables, views, stored procedures, primary keys, indexes, and constraints) and managing database security.

In this part of the book, you learn how to use the DDL statements with Jet databases, ADO, and the Jet OLE DB provider.

Chapter 19

Creating, Modifying, and Deleting Tables and Fields

In Part II of this book, you learned about the ADO Object Model and tried out different methods that are available in Microsoft Office Access 2003 for creating and manipulating databases via programming code. In particular, you've learned how to create new databases from scratch, add tables and indexes, set up relationships between tables, secure a database with a password, define user and group security accounts, and handle object permissions. In addition to ADO, you can perform many of the mentioned database tasks by using the Data Definition Language (DDL), which is a component of the Structured Query Language (SQL).

SQL is a widely used language for data retrieval and manipulation in databases. The SQL specification (known as ANSI SQL-89) was first published in 1989 by the American National Standards Institute (ANSI). The ANSI SQL standard was revised in 1992 and this version is referred to as ANSI SQL-92 or SQL-2. This revised specification is supported by the major database vendors, many of whom have created their own extensions of the SQL language.

Microsoft Office Access 2003 supports both SQL specifications and refers to them as *ANSI-SQL query modes*. While the ANSI-89 SQL query mode (also called *Microsoft Jet SQL* and *ANSI SQL*) uses the traditional Jet SQL syntax, the ANSI-92 SQL mode uses syntax that is more compliant with SQL-92 and Microsoft SQL Server. For example, ANSI-92 uses the percent sign (%) and the underscore character (_) for its wildcards instead of the asterisk (*) and the question mark (?), which are commonly used in VBA. Microsoft Access Jet Engine does not implement the complete ANSI SQL-92 standard and provides its own Jet 4.0 ANSI SQL-92 extensions to support new features of Access. For more information about syntax differences see the topic "Comparison of Microsoft Jet SQL and ANSI SQL" in the Microsoft Office Access built-in help.

You can use the ANSI-92 syntax in your VBA procedures with the Microsoft OLE DB Provider for Jet or with the Data Definition Language, which we cover in this part of the book. ANSI-89 is the default setting for a new Microsoft Access database in Access 2002-2003 and 2000 file format.

Because the two ANSI SQL query modes are not compatible, you must decide which query mode you are going to use for the current database. This can easily be done in the Microsoft Access user interface as outlined in Hands-On 19-1.

⊚ Hands-On 19-1: Setting the ANSI SQL Query Mode

1. Create a new Microsoft Access database named **Test of Query Mode.mdb**.

2. In the Database window, choose **Tools | Options**, and click the **Tables/Queries** tab (Figure 19-1).

3. In the SQL Server Compatible Syntax (ANSI 92) area, set the query mode to ANSI-92 SQL by clicking the **This database** check box. (You can set the query mode to ANSI-89 SQL by clearing the This database check box.)

4. Click the **Apply** button.

5. Click **OK** to exit the Options window. Microsoft Access displays a message as shown in Figure 19-2.

6. Click the **Help** button to read more information about the ANSI SQL query mode.

7. Return to the message and click **OK**. Microsoft Access database will close and reopen with the new settings in effect.

8. Close the Test of Query Mode database file.

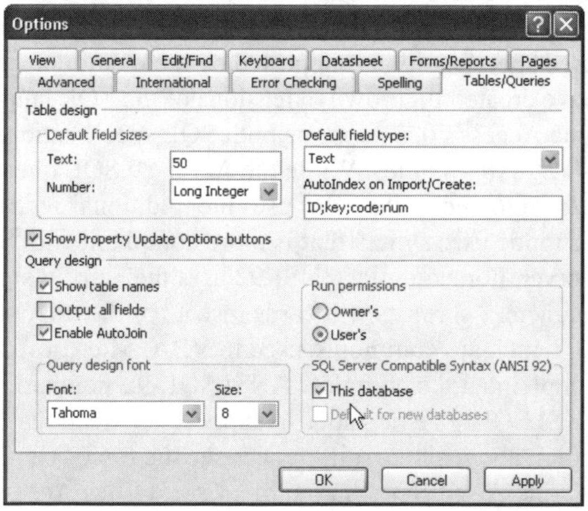

Figure 19-1: Use the Options window to set the ANSI SQL query mode for the current database or all new databases.

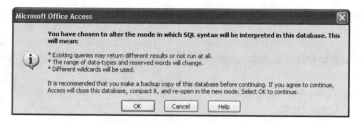

Figure 19-2: When you change the query mode to ANSI-92, Microsoft Access displays an informational message alerting you to possible problems.

There are two areas of Microsoft Access Jet 4.0 Engine's version of SQL:

■ Data Definition Language (DDL) offers a number of SQL statements to manage database security and to create and alter database components (such as tables, indexes, relationships, views, and stored procedures). These statements are: CREATE TABLE, DROP TABLE, ALTER TABLE, CREATE INDEX, DROP INDEX, CHECK CONSTRAINT, CREATE VIEW, DROP VIEW, CREATE PROCEDURE, DROP PROCEDURE, EXECUTE, ADD USER, ALTER DATABASE, ALTER USER, CREATE GROUP, CREATE USER, DROP GROUP, DROP USER, GRANT, and REVOKE.

■ Data Manipulation Language (DML) offers SQL statements that allow you to retrieve and manipulate data contained in the database tables as well as perform transactions. These statements are: SELECT, UNION, UPDATE, DELETE, INSERT INTO, SELECT INTO, TRANSFORM, PARAMETER, BEGIN TRANSACTION, COMMIT, and ROLLBACK.

This chapter and the remaining chapters of Part III focus on using the DDL language for creating and changing the underlying structure of a database. To get the most out of these chapters, you should be familiar with using ADO, which was discussed in Part II.

Creating Tables

Using the Microsoft Jet 4.0 CREATE TABLE statement, you can easily create a table in a database. This statement can only be used with Microsoft Jet database engine databases. The two examples that follow illustrate how to create and delete a table named tblSchools in the currently open database and in a new database.

⊚ Hands-On 19-2: Creating a Table in the Current Database

1. Open the **Acc2003_Chap19.mdb** file from the book's downloadable files or create this file from scratch using the Microsoft Office Access user interface.

2. Make sure that the ANSI SQL query mode is set to ANSI-92 (see Hands-On 19-1).

3. Switch to the Visual Basic Editor window and insert a new module.

4. In the module's Code window, enter the CreateTable procedure as shown below.

```
Sub CreateTable()
' you must set up a reference to
' the Microsoft ActiveX Data Objects Library
' in the References dialog box
    Dim conn As ADODB.Connection
    Dim strTable As String

    On Error GoTo ErrorHandler
    Set conn = CurrentProject.Connection

    strTable = "tblSchools"
    conn.Execute "CREATE TABLE " & strTable & _
        "(SchoolId AUTOINCREMENT(100, 5), " & _
        "SchoolName CHAR," & _
        "City Char (25), District Char (35), " & _
        "YearEstablished Date);"

    Application.RefreshDatabaseWindow
ExitHere:
    conn.Close
    Set conn = Nothing
    Exit Sub
ErrorHandler:
    MsgBox Err.Number & ":" & Err.Description
    Resume ExitHere
End Sub
```

The procedure above specifies the seed and increment values of AutoNumber columns by using the following syntax:

```
Column_name AUTOINCREMENT (seed, increment)
```

Notice that the table, tblSchools, has an AutoNumber column with a seed of 100 and an increment of 5. When you switch to a Database window and open this table in the Datasheet view, the SchoolId for the first record will be 100, the second will be 105, the third will be 110, and so on.

When you examine the code of the CreateTable procedure and compare the resultant table in Figure 19-3, you will notice that Access SQL uses different data types than those available in the Table Design window. Table 19-1 presents the equivalent SQL data types.

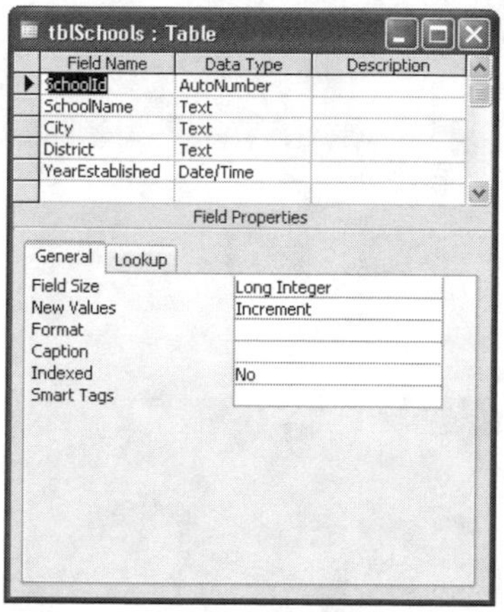

Figure 19-3: The tblSchools table was generated by the CreateTable procedure in Hands-On 19-2 using the SQL statement CREATE TABLE.

Table 19-1: Table Design data types and their Access SQL equivalents

Table Design Data Types	Access SQL Data Types
Text	TEXT, ALPHANUMERIC, CHAR, CHARACTER, STRING, or VARCHAR
Memo	LONGTEXT, MEMO, LONGCHAR, or NOTE
Number (Field Size = Byte)	BYTE or INTEGER1
Number (Field Size = Integer)	SHORT, INTEGER2, or SMALLINT
Number (Field Size = Long Integer)	COUNTER, INTEGER, INT, or AUTOINCREMENT
Number (Field Size = Single)	SINGLE, FLOAT4, or REAL
Number (Field Size = Double)	DOUBLE, FLOAT, or NUMBER
Date/Time	DATETIME, DATE, TIME, or TIMESTAMP
Currency	CURRENCY or MONEY
AutoNumber (Field Size = Long Integer)	AUTOINCREMENT or COUNTER
AutoNumber (Field Size = Replication Id)	GUID
Yes/No	BOOLEAN, BIT, LOGICAL, LOGICAL1, or YESNO
OLE Object	LONGBINARY, OLEOBJECT, or GENERAL

The procedure in Hands-On 19-3 demonstrates how to create a table in a brand new database.

⦿ Hands-On 19-3: Creating a Table in a New Database

1. Switch to the Visual Basic Editor window and insert a new module.

2. In the module's Code window, enter the CreateTableInNewDb procedure as shown below.

```
Sub CreateTableInNewDb()
' use the References dialog box to set up a reference to
' Microsoft ADO Ext. for DDL and Security Object Library
' and Microsoft ActiveX Data Objects Library
```

```
Dim cat As ADOX.Catalog
Dim conn As ADODB.Connection
Dim strDb As String
Dim strTable As String
Dim strConnect As String

On Error GoTo ErrorHandler

Set cat = New ADOX.Catalog
strDb = CurrentProject.Path & "\Sites.mdb"
strConnect = "Provider=Microsoft.Jet.OLEDB.4.0;" & _
             "Data Source=" & strDb

' create a new database file
cat.Create strConnect
MsgBox "The database was created (" & strDb & ")."

' set connection to currently open catalog
Set conn = cat.ActiveConnection

strTable = "tblSchools"
conn.Execute "CREATE TABLE " & strTable & _
    "(SchoolId AUTOINCREMENT(100, 5), " & _
    "SchoolName CHAR," & _
    "City Char (25), District Char (35), " & _
    "YearEstablished Date);"
ExitHere:
    Set cat = Nothing
    Set conn = Nothing
    Exit Sub
ErrorHandler:
    If Err.Number = -2147217897 Then
        ' delete the database file if it exists
        Kill strDb
        ' start from statement that caused this error
        Resume 0
    Else
        MsgBox Err.Number & ": " & Err.Description
        GoTo ExitHere
    End If
End Sub
```

The CreateTableInNewDb procedure shown above creates a new database named Sites.mdb in the current folder. As you recall from Chapter 10, you can create a new Microsoft Access database by using the Create method of the ADOX Catalog object. Before we can create a table in this new database we must set the conn object variable to the currently open catalog, like this:

```
Set conn = cat.ActiveConnection
```

Next, we use the Connection object's Execute method to create a new table named tblSchools in the Sites.mdb file. Notice that this table will contain an AutoNumber field with a sequence starting at 100 that will be incremented by 5 as new columns are added.

Deleting Tables

Use the DROP TABLE statement to delete an existing table from a database. Note that a table must be closed before it can be deleted. The procedure in Hands-On 19-4 demonstrates how to use the DROP TABLE statement inside a VBA procedure. We will delete the tblSchool table that was created in Hands-On 19-2.

⊚ Hands-On 19-4: Deleting a Table

This hands-on requires the prior completion of Hands-On 19-2.

1. In the Visual Basic Editor window, insert a new module.
2. In the module's Code window, enter the DeleteTable procedure as shown below.

```
Sub DeleteTable()
    Dim conn As ADODB.Connection
    Dim strTable As String

    On Error GoTo ErrorHandler
    Set conn = CurrentProject.Connection

    strTable = "tblSchools"
    conn.Execute "DROP TABLE " & strTable
    Application.RefreshDatabaseWindow
ExitHere:
    conn.Close
    Set conn = Nothing
    Exit Sub
ErrorHandler:
    If Err.Number = -2147217900 Then
        DoCmd.Close acTable, strTable, acSavePrompt
        Resume 0
    Else
        MsgBox Err.Number & ":" & Err.Description
        Resume ExitHere
    End If
End Sub
```

You can also execute the DROP TABLE statement directly in the Microsoft Office Access user interface's Data Definition Query window by following these steps:

- Create a new query.
- Click the **Close** button in the Show Table dialog box.
- From the Query menu, choose **SQL Specific | Data Definition**.
- Enter the following statement in the query window:

```
Drop Table tblSchools;
```

- Run the query by selecting **Run** from the Query menu.

Deleting Database Files

There is no SQL statement that allows deleting entire database files. However, if you need to delete a database file, you can use the VBA Kill statement (as shown in Hands-On 19-5).

◎ Hands-On 19-5: Deleting a Database File

This hands-on requires prior completion of Hands-On 19-3.

1. In the Visual Basic Editor window, insert a new module.

2. In the module's Code window, enter the DeleteDbFile procedure as shown below.

```
Sub DeleteDbFile()
    Dim strFile As String

    strFile = CurrentProject.Path & "\Sites.mdb"

    If Dir(strFile) <> "" Then
        Kill strFile
        MsgBox "The database file " & strFile & _
            " was successfully deleted."
    End If
End Sub
```

Modifying Tables with DDL

You can modify a table definition by altering, adding, or dropping columns and constraints. *Constraints* allow you to enforce integrity by creating rules for a table. The procedures in the following sections illustrate how to use Jet 4.0 SQL DDL statements to:

- Add new columns to a table
- Change the column's data type
- Change the size of a text column
- Delete a field from a table
- Add a primary key to an existing table
- Add a unique, multiple-field index to an existing table
- Delete an index
- Delete an indexed column
- Set a default value for a column in a table
- Change the seed and increment value of AutoNumber columns

Adding New Fields to a Table

Use the ALTER TABLE statement followed by a table name to modify the design of a table after it has been created with the CREATE TABLE statement. Prior to modifying the structure of an existing table, it's recommended that you make a backup copy of the table.

The ALTER TABLE statement can be used with the ADD COLUMN clause to add a new field to the table. For example, the procedure in Hands-On 19-6 adds a Currency field called Budget2004 to the tblSchools table with the following statement:

```
ALTER TABLE tblSchools ADD COLUMN Budget2004 MONEY
```

When you add a new field to a table you should specify the name of the field, its data type and, for Text and Binary fields, the size of the data type.

Hands-On 19-6: Adding a New Field to an Existing Table

1. Run the procedure in Hands-On 19-2 to create the tblSchools table in the current database.

2. In the Visual Basic Editor window, insert a new module.

3. In the module's Code window, enter the AddNewField procedure as shown below.

```
Sub AddNewField()
    Dim conn As ADODB.Connection
    Dim strTable As String
    Dim strCol As String

    On Error GoTo ErrorHandler
    Set conn = CurrentProject.Connection

    strTable = "tblSchools"
    strCol = "Budget2004"

    conn.Execute "ALTER TABLE " & strTable & _
        " ADD COLUMN " & strCol & " MONEY;"
ExitHere:
    conn.Close
    Set conn = Nothing
    Exit Sub
ErrorHandler:
    MsgBox Err.Number & ":" & Err.Description
    Resume ExitHere
End Sub
```

Changing the Data Type of a Table Column

You can use the ALTER COLUMN clause in the ALTER TABLE statement to change the data type of a table column. You must specify the name of the field, the desired data type, and the size of the data type, if required. The procedure in Hands-On 19-7 changes the data type of the SchoolId field in the tblSchools table from AutoNumber to a 15-character Text field.

⊚ Hands-On 19-7: Changing the Field Data Type

This hands-on uses the tblSchools table created in Hands-On 19-2.

1. In the Visual Basic Editor window, insert a new module.

2. In the module's Code window, enter the ChangeFieldType procedure as shown below.

```
Sub ChangeFieldType()
    Dim conn As ADODB.Connection
    Dim strTable As String
    Dim strCol As String

    On Error GoTo ErrorHandler
    Set conn = CurrentProject.Connection

    strTable = "tblSchools"
    strCol = "SchoolId"
    conn.Execute "ALTER TABLE " & strTable & _
        " ALTER COLUMN " & strCol & " CHAR(15);"
ExitHere:
    conn.Close
    Set conn = Nothing
    Exit Sub
ErrorHandler:
    MsgBox Err.Number & ":" & Err.Description
    Resume ExitHere
End Sub
```

Changing the Size of a Text Column

It's easy to increase or decrease the size of a Text column. Simply use the ALTER TABLE statement followed by the name of the table, and the ALTER COLUMN clause followed by the name of the column whose size you want to modify. Next, specify the data type of the column and the new column size. Hands-On 19-8 modifies the size of the SchoolName field from the default 255 characters to 40.

⊚ Hands-On 19-8: Changing the Size of a Field

This hands-on uses the tblSchools table created in Hands-On 19-2.

1. In the Visual Basic Editor window, insert a new module.

2. In the module's Code window, enter the ChangeFieldSize procedure as shown below.

```
Sub ChangeFieldSize()
    Dim conn As ADODB.Connection
    Dim strTable As String
    Dim strCol As String

    On Error GoTo ErrorHandler
    Set conn = CurrentProject.Connection
```

```
        strTable = "tblSchools"
        strCol = "SchoolName"

    conn.Execute "ALTER TABLE " & strTable & _
        " ALTER COLUMN " & strCol & " CHAR(40);"
ExitHere:
        conn.Close
        Set conn = Nothing
        Exit Sub
ErrorHandler:
        MsgBox Err.Number & ":" & Err.Description
        Resume ExitHere
End Sub
```

Deleting a Column from a Table

Use the DROP COLUMN clause in the ALTER TABLE statement to delete a column from a table. You only need to specify the name of the field you want to remove. The example procedure in Hands-On 19-9 deletes the Budget2004 column from the tblSchools table.

⊚ Hands-On 19-9: Deleting a Field from a Table

This hands-on uses the tblSchools table created in Hands-On 19-2. Make sure this table contains the Budget2004 column, which was added in Hands-On 19-6.

1. In the Visual Basic Editor window, insert a new module.

2. In the module's Code window, enter the DeleteField procedure as shown below.

```
Sub DeleteField()
    Dim conn As ADODB.Connection
    Dim strTable As String
    Dim strCol As String

    On Error GoTo ErrorHandler
    Set conn = CurrentProject.Connection

    strTable = "tblSchools"
    strCol = "Budget2004"

    conn.Execute "ALTER TABLE " & strTable & _
        " DROP COLUMN " & strCol & ";"
ExitHere:
        conn.Close
        Set conn = Nothing
        Exit Sub
ErrorHandler:
        MsgBox Err.Number & ":" & Err.Description
        Resume ExitHere
End Sub
```

Adding a Primary Key to a Table

You can use the ADD CONSTRAINT clause in the ALTER TABLE statement to define one or more columns as a primary key. Hands-On 19-10 defines a primary key for the tblSchools table created in Hands-On 19-2.

◎ Hands-On 19-10: Adding a Primary Key to a Table

This hands-on uses the tblSchools table created in Hands-On 19-2.

1. In the Visual Basic Editor window, insert a new module.

2. In the module's Code window, enter the AddPrimaryKey procedure as shown below.

```
Sub AddPrimaryKey()
    Dim conn As ADODB.Connection
    Dim strTable As String
    Dim strCol As String

    On Error GoTo ErrorHandler
    Set conn = CurrentProject.Connection

    strTable = "tblSchools"
    strCol = "SchoolId"

conn.Execute "ALTER TABLE " & strTable & _
    " ADD CONSTRAINT pKey PRIMARY KEY " & _
    "(" & strCol & ");"
ExitHere:
    conn.Close
    Set conn = Nothing
    Exit Sub
ErrorHandler:
    MsgBox Err.Number & ":" & Err.Description
    Resume ExitHere
End Sub
```

Adding a Multiple-Field Index to a Table

Use the ADD CONSTRAINT clause and the UNIQUE keyword in the ALTER TABLE statement to add a multiple-field index. The UNIQUE keyword prevents duplicate values in the index.

◎ Hands-On 19-11: Adding a Unique Index Based on Two Fields to an Existing Table

This hands-on uses the tblSchools table created in Hands-On 19-2.

1. In the Visual Basic Editor window, insert a new module.

2. In the module's Code window, enter the AddMulti_UniqueIndex procedure as shown below.

```
Sub AddMulti_UniqueIndex()
    Dim conn As ADODB.Connection
    Dim strTable As String
    Dim strCol As String

    On Error GoTo ErrorHandler
    Set conn = CurrentProject.Connection

    strTable = "tblSchools"
    strCol = "SchoolId, District"

    conn.Execute "ALTER TABLE " & strTable & _
        " ADD CONSTRAINT multiIdx UNIQUE " & _
        "(" & strCol & ");"
ExitHere:
    conn.Close
    Set conn = Nothing
    Exit Sub
ErrorHandler:
    MsgBox Err.Number & ":" & Err.Description
    Resume ExitHere
End Sub
```

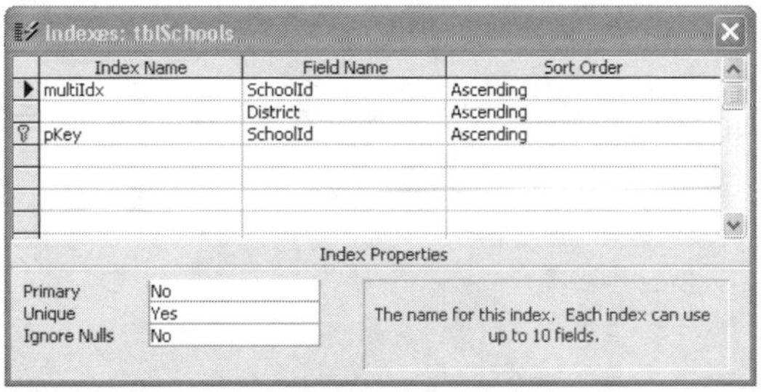

Figure 19-4: After running the procedures in Hands-On 19-10 and 19-11, the tblSchools table contains a primary key and a unique index based on two fields.

Deleting an Indexed Column

Deleting an index field is a two-step process:

1. Use the DROP CONSTRAINT clause to delete an index. You must specify the index name.

2. Use the DROP COLUMN clause to delete the desired column. You must specify the column name.

Both clauses must be used in the ALTER TABLE statement. The following procedure deletes the District column from the tblSchools table. Recall that the procedure in Hands-On 19-11 added a multiple-field index based on the SchoolId and District columns.

⊚ Hands-On 19-12: Deleting a Field that is a Part of an Index

This hands-on uses the tblSchools table created in Hands-On 19-2. You must perform Hands-On 19-11 prior to running this procedure.

1. In the Visual Basic Editor window, insert a new module.

2. In the module's Code window, enter the DeleteIdxField procedure as shown below.

```
Sub DeleteIdxField()
    Dim conn As ADODB.Connection
    Dim strTable As String
    Dim strCol As String
    Dim strIdx As String

    On Error GoTo ErrorHandler
    Set conn = CurrentProject.Connection

    strTable = "tblSchools"
    strCol = "District"
    strIdx = "multiIdx"

conn.Execute "ALTER TABLE " & strTable & _
    " DROP CONSTRAINT " & strIdx & ";"

conn.Execute "ALTER TABLE " & strTable & _
    " DROP COLUMN " & strCol & ";"

ExitHere:
    conn.Close
    Set conn = Nothing
    Exit Sub
ErrorHandler:
    MsgBox Err.Number & ":" & Err.Description
    Resume ExitHere
End Sub
```

Deleting an Index

Use the DROP CONSTRAINT clause to delete an index. You must specify the index name. The following procedure deletes a primary key index from the tblSchools table.

⊚ Hands-On 19-13: Deleting an Index

This hands-on uses the tblSchools table created in Hands-On 19-2. You must perform Hands-On 19-11 prior to running this procedure.

1. In the Visual Basic Editor window, insert a new module.

2. In the module's Code window, enter the DeleteIndex procedure as shown below.

```
Sub DeleteIndex()
    Dim conn As ADODB.Connection
    Dim strTable As String
    Dim strIdx As String

    On Error GoTo ErrorHandler
    Set conn = CurrentProject.Connection

    strTable = "tblSchools"
    strIdx = "pKey"

conn.Execute "ALTER TABLE " & strTable & _
    " DROP CONSTRAINT " & strIdx & ";"

ExitHere:
    conn.Close
    Set conn = Nothing
    Exit Sub
ErrorHandler:
    MsgBox Err.Number & ":" & Err.Description
    Resume ExitHere
End Sub
```

After running the procedures in Hands-On 19-12 and 19-13, the Indexes window (see Figure 19-4 earlier) should be empty.

Setting a Default Value for a Table Column

Specifying a default value for a field automatically enters that value in the field each time a new record is added to a table unless the user provides a value for the field. Using DDL, you can add a default value for an existing column with the SET DEFAULT clause. The required syntax is as follows:

```
ALTER TABLE table_name ALTER [COLUMN] column_name SET DEFAULT default-value;
```

Notice that [COLUMN] in the above syntax is optional.

⊚ Hands-On 19-14: Setting a Default Value for a Field

This hands-on uses the tblSchools table created in Hands-On 19-2.

1. In the Visual Basic Editor window, insert a new module.

2. In the module's Code window, enter the SetDefaultFieldValue procedure as shown below.

```
Sub SetDefaultFieldValue()
    Dim conn As ADODB.Connection
    Dim strTable As String
    Dim strCol As String
    Dim strDefVal As String
    Dim strSQL As String

    On Error GoTo ErrorHandler
    Set conn = CurrentProject.Connection
```

```
        strTable = "tblSchools"
        strCol = "City"
        strDefVal = "Boston"
        strSQL = "ALTER TABLE " & strTable & _
            " ALTER " & strCol & " SET DEFAULT " & strDefVal

        conn.Execute strSQL

ExitHere:
        conn.Close
        Set conn = Nothing
        Exit Sub
ErrorHandler:
        MsgBox Err.Number & ":" & Err.Description
        Resume ExitHere
End Sub
```

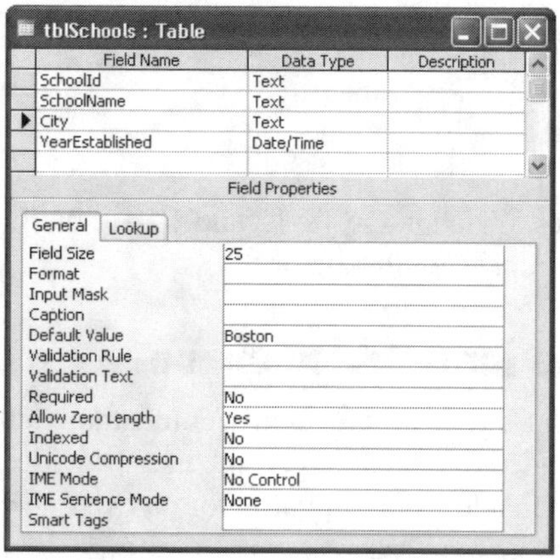

Figure 19-5: After running the procedure in Hands-On 19-14, the Default Value property in the Table Design window is set to Boston.

Changing the Seed and Increment Value of AutoNumber Columns

When a table contains a field with an AutoNumber data type, you can set a seed value and an increment value. The seed value is the initial value for the column, and the increment value is the number added to the seed value to obtain a new counter value for the next record. If not specified, both seed and increment values default to 1. You can use the DDL to change the seed and increment values of AutoNumber columns by using one of the following three statements:

```
ALTER TABLE Table_name ALTER COLUMN Column_name AUTOINCREMENT (seed, increment)

ALTER TABLE Table_name ALTER COLUMN Column_name COUNTER (seed, increment)

ALTER TABLE Table_name ALTER COLUMN Column_name IDENTITY (seed, increment)
```

The example procedure in Hands-On 19-15 modifies the seed value of the existing AutoNumber column in the SchoolId column to start at 1000. Because we changed the SchoolId column's data type to the Text data type in one of the earlier hands-on exercises, you will modify the SchoolId column in the Sites.mdb file you created in Hands-On 19-3 at the beginning of this chapter.

Hands-On 19-15: Changing the Start (Seed) Value of the AutoNumber Field

This hands-on uses the Sites.mdb database file and tblSchools table created in Hands-On 19-3.

1. In the Visual Basic Editor window, insert a new module.
2. In the module's Code window, enter the ChangeAutoNumber procedure as shown below.
3. Run the ChangeAutoNumber procedure.
4. Launch Microsoft Office Access with the Sites.mdb database and open the tblSchools table.
5. Enter a couple of new records in this table. In the YearEstablished field enter the date in the format mm/dd/yyyy. Note that the first new record is numbered 1000, the second 1001, the third 1002, and so on.

```
Sub ChangeAutoNumber()
    Dim conn As ADODB.Connection
    Dim strDb As String
    Dim strConnect As String
    Dim strTable As String
    Dim strCol As String
    Dim intSeed As Integer

    On Error GoTo ErrorHandler

    strDb = CurrentProject.Path & "\" & "Sites.mdb"
    strConnect = "Provider=Microsoft.Jet.OLEDB.4.0;" & _
                "Data Source=" & strDb

    strTable = "tblSchools"
    strCol = "SchoolId"
    intSeed = 1000

    Set conn = New ADODB.Connection
    conn.Open strConnect
    conn.Execute "ALTER TABLE " & strTable & _
        " ALTER COLUMN " & strCol & _
        " COUNTER (" & intSeed & ");"
ExitHere:
    conn.Close
    Set conn = Nothing
    Exit Sub
ErrorHandler:
    If Err.Number = -2147467259 Then
        MsgBox "The database file cannot be located.", _
            vbCritical, strDb
        Exit Sub
    Else
        MsgBox Err.Number & ":" & Err.Description
```

```
        Resume ExitHere
    End If
End Sub
```

Chapter Summary

In this chapter, you learned various Data Definition Language (DDL) commands for creating a new Access database, as well as creating, modifying, and deleting tables. You also learned how to add, modify, and delete fields and indexes, how to change the seed and increment values for AutoNumber fields, and how to change a field's data type. You also practiced assigning default values to table fields.

In the next chapter, you will get to know several DDL commands used for establishing relationships between tables and controlling referential integrity.

Chapter 20

Enforcing Data Integrity and Relationships between Tables

When creating tables in a database, you often need to define rules regarding the values allowed in columns (fields). As mentioned in Chapter 19, *constraints* allow you to enforce integrity by creating rules for a table. The five types of constraints are listed below.

Table 20-1: Table constraints

Constraint Name	Usage
PRIMARY KEY	Identifies the column or set of columns whose values uniquely identify a row in a table.
FOREIGN KEY	Defines the relationship between tables and maintains data integrity when records are being added, changed, or deleted in a table.
UNIQUE	Ensures that no duplicate values are entered in a specific column or combination of columns that is not a table's primary key.
NOT NULL	Specifies that a column cannot contain a Null value. Primary key columns are automatically defined as NOT NULL.
	Note: A Null value is not the same as zero (0), blank, or a zero-length character string (" "). A Null value indicates that no entry has been made. You can determine if a field contains a Null value by using the IsNull function.
CHECK	Enforces integrity by limiting the values that can be placed in a column.

When constraints are added, all existing data is verified for constraint violations.

Using Check Constraints

Tables and columns can contain multiple CHECK constraints. A *CHECK constraint* can validate a column value against a logical expression or another column in the same or another table. What you can't do with the CHECK constraint is specify the custom validation message, as is possible to do in the Access user interface.

The procedure in Hands-On 20-1 uses a PRIMARY KEY constraint explicitly named PrimaryKey to identify the Id column as a primary key. The CHECK constraint used in this procedure ensures that only numbers within the specified range are entered in the YearsWorked table column. You can apply CHECK constraints to a single column or to multiple columns. When a table is deleted, CHECK constraints are also dropped.

⊚ **Hands-On 20-1: Using a CHECK Constraint to Specify a Condition for All Values Entered for the Column**

1. Open the **Acc2003_Chap20.mdb** file from the book's downloadable files, or create this file from scratch using the Access user interface.

2. Switch to the Visual Basic Editor window and insert a new module.

3. In the module's Code window, enter the CheckColumnValue procedure as shown below.

```
Sub CheckColumnValue()
    Dim conn As ADODB.Connection
    Dim strTable As String

    On Error GoTo ErrorHandler

    Set conn = CurrentProject.Connection
    strTable = "tblAwards"
    conn.Execute "CREATE TABLE " & strTable & _
        "(Id AUTOINCREMENT CONSTRAINT PrimaryKey PRIMARY KEY," & _
        "YearsWorked INT, CONSTRAINT FromTo " & _
        "CHECK (YearsWorked BETWEEN 1 AND 30));"

ExitHere:
    conn.Close
    Set conn = Nothing
    Exit Sub
ErrorHandler:
    MsgBox Err.Number & ":" & Err.Description
    Resume ExitHere
End Sub
```

4. Run the above procedure to create the tblAwards table with the CHECK constraint.

5. Open the tblAwards table and enter a value that does not fall between 1 and 30 in the YearsWorked column. You should receive the message shown in Figure 20-1.

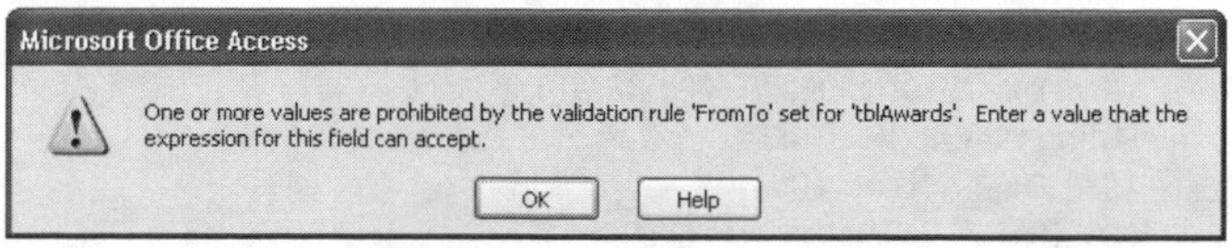

Figure 20-1: This message appears when you attempt to enter a value in the YearsWorked column that is not within the range specified by the FromTo constraint (see Hands-On 20-1).

The next hands-on procedure demonstrates how to create a CHECK constraint to ensure that the values of the Items column in the tblBookOrders table is less than the value of the MaxUnits column in the tblSupplies table for the specified ISBN number. This hands-on also illustrates using the SQL Data Manipulation Language (DML) statements INSERT INTO, BEGIN TRANSACTION, COMMIT TRANSACTION, and ROLLBACK TRANSACTION.

◉ Hands-On 20-2: Creating a Table with a Validation Rule Referencing a Column in Another Table

1. In the Visual Basic Editor window, insert a new module.

2. In the module's Code window, enter the ValidateAgainstCol_InAnotherTbl procedure as shown below.

```
Sub ValidateAgainstCol_InAnotherTbl()
    Dim conn As ADODB.Connection
    Dim strTable1 As String
    Dim strTable2 As String
    Dim InTrans As Boolean

    On Error GoTo ErrorHandler

    Set conn = CurrentProject.Connection
    strTable1 = "tblSupplies"
    strTable2 = "tblBookOrders"

    conn.Execute "BEGIN TRANSACTION"
    InTrans = True
    conn.Execute "CREATE TABLE " & strTable1 & _
        "(ISBN CHAR CONSTRAINT " & _
        "PrimaryKey PRIMARY KEY, " & _
        "MaxUnits LONG);", adExecuteNoRecords

    conn.Execute "Insert INTO " & strTable1 & _
        " (ISBN,MaxUnits) " & _
        " Values ('158-76609-09', 5);", _
        adExecuteNoRecords

    conn.Execute "INSERT INTO " & strTable1 & _
        " (ISBN,MaxUnits) " & _
        " Values ('167-23455-69', 7);", _
        adExecuteNoRecords
```

```
        conn.Execute "CREATE TABLE " & strTable2 & _
            "(OrderNo AUTOINCREMENT CONSTRAINT " & _
            "PrimaryKey PRIMARY KEY, " & _
            "ISBN CHAR, Items LONG, " & _
            "CONSTRAINT OnHandConstr CHECK " & _
            "(Items <(Select MaxUnits from " & strTable1 & _
            " WHERE ISBN = " & strTable2 & ".ISBN)));", _
            adExecuteNoRecords
        conn.Execute "COMMIT TRANSACTION"
        InTrans = False
    Application.RefreshDatabaseWindow
ExitHere:
    conn.Close
    Set conn = Nothing
    Exit Sub
ErrorHandler:
    If InTrans Then
        conn.Execute "ROLLBACK TRANSACTION"
        Resume ExitHere
    Else
        MsgBox Err.Number & ":" & Err.Description
        Exit Sub
    End If
End Sub
```

The procedure above creates two tables. Because the Items column in the tblBookOrders table needs to be validated against the contents of the MaxUnits column in the tblSupplies table, we wrapped the process of creating these tables and entering data in the tblSupplies table into a transaction. Because various errors could occur during the procedure execution, we declared a Boolean variable named InTrans to help us determine whether an error occurred during the transaction. Therefore, if the value of the InTrans variable is True, we will cancel the transaction. Notice that in Jet SQL syntax we use the BEGIN TRANSACTION statement to start the transaction, the COMMIT TRANSACTION statement to save the results of the transaction, and the ROLLBACK TRANSACTION statement to cancel any changes. Note that these transaction statements can only be used through the Jet OLE DB provider and ADO. They will cause an error when used with the Access user interface or DAO (Data Access Objects).

Notice that in this example procedure we used the adExecuteNoRecords option to specify that no rows should be returned. You can use this setting with the Connection or Command object's Execute method to improve performance when no rows are returned or when you don't plan to access the returned rows in your procedure code. If you omit this setting, your ADO code will still execute successfully, but the ADO will unnecessarily create a Recordset object as the return value for the Execute method. Using the adExecuteNoRecords setting is one of several techniques of optimizing data access using ADO.

3. Run the above procedure to create the tblBookOrders table.

4. Open the tblBookOrders table and enter the record shown at the top of Figure 20-2.

5. When you try to save this record or move to the next data row, Access will display a message informing you that the value you are trying to enter is prohibited.

6. Enter the value of **4** in the Items column. This time Access approves of the entry and no error message is displayed.

7. Close the tblBookOrders table.

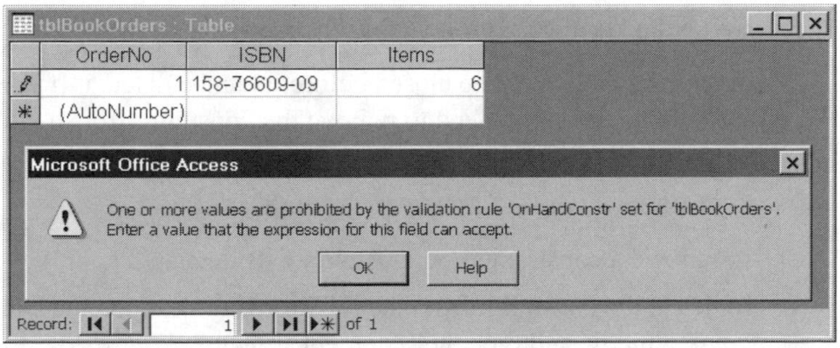

Figure 20-2: When you attempt to enter a value that does not meet the validation rule, Microsoft Office Access displays an error message.

8. In the Database window, right-click the **tblBookOrders** table and choose **Delete**. Click **Yes** to confirm the deletion.

9. Access will respond with the error message shown in Figure 20-3.

Figure 20-3: If you try to manually delete a table referenced by the CHECK constraint, Microsoft Office Access will display an error message.

Now, let's see how you can use the Access user interface to issue commands that delete tables and CHECK constraints.

◉ Hands-On 20-3: Deleting Tables and Constraints Using the Access User Interface

This hands-on requires that you have the tblBookOrders and tblAwards tables created in Hands-On 20-1 and 20-2.

1. In the Database window, select the **Queries** object and click the **New** button.

2. In the New Query dialog box, select **Design View** and click **OK**.

3. In the Show Table dialog box, click the **Close** button.

4. Choose **Query | SQL Specific | Data Definition** from the menu bar.

5. In the Data Definition Query window, enter the statement shown in Figure 20-4.

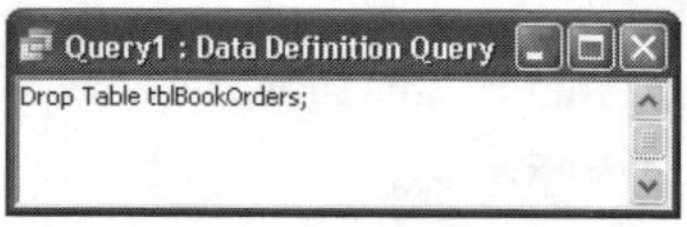

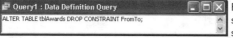

Figure 20-4: To delete a table that contains a CHECK constraint, type the DROP TABLE statement in the Data Definition Query window and choose Query | Run.

6. To run the Data Definition Query, choose **Query | Run**.

   Note that a table must be closed before it can be deleted. If you don't want to delete the table but need to remove the constraint from a table, use the following syntax:

   ```
   ALTER TABLE table_name DROP CONSTRAINT constraint_name
   ```

   To remove a constraint, you must know its name.

7. To delete the constraint from the tblAwards table, open the Data Definition Query window and type the statement shown in Figure 20-5.

Figure 20-5: To remove a table constraint use the DROP CONSTRAINT statement with ALTER TABLE.

Note: Before using ALTER TABLE, it is a good idea to make a backup copy of the table.

8. Choose **Query | Run** to execute the statement to delete the constraint.

9. On your own, delete the tblSupplies table using the Data Definition Query.

Establishing Relationships between Tables

To establish a link between the data in two tables, you add one or more columns that hold one table's primary key values to the other table. This column becomes a *foreign key* in the second table. In SQL DDL, you can use a FOREIGN KEY constraint to reference another table. Foreign keys can be single- or multi-column.

A *FOREIGN KEY constraint* enforces referential integrity by ensuring that changes made to data in the primary key table do not break the link to data in the foreign key table. For example, you cannot delete a record in a primary key table or change a primary key value if the deleted or changed primary key value corresponds to a value in the FOREIGN KEY constraint of another table. The REFERENCES clause identifies the parent table of the relation.

To create a brand new table and relate it to an existing table, the following steps are required:

1. Use the CREATE TABLE statement followed by a table name.

   Example: CREATE TABLE tblOrder_Details

2. Follow the table name with one or more column definitions. A *column definition* consists of ColumnName followed by the data type and column size (if required).

   Example: InvoiceID CHAR, ProductId CHAR, Units LONG, PRICE MONEY

3. To designate a primary key, use the CONSTRAINT clause followed by the constraint name, the PRIMARY KEY clause, and the name of the column or columns to be designated as the primary key.

   Example: CONSTRAINT PrimaryKey PRIMARY KEY(InvoiceId, ProductId)

4. To designate a foreign key, use the CONSTRAINT clause followed by the constraint name, the FOREIGN KEY clause, and the name of the column to be designated as foreign key.

   Example: CONSTRAINT fkInvoiceId FOREIGN KEY (InvoiceId)

5. Use the REFERENCES clause to specify the parent table to which a relationship is established.

   Example: REFERENCES tblProduct_Orders

6. If required, specify ON UPDATE CASCADE and/or ON DELETE CASCADE to enable referential integrity rules with cascading updates or deletes.

   Example: ON UPDATE CASCADE ON DELETE CASCADE

> **Note:** You may choose not to enforce referential integrity rules by specifying ON UPDATE NO ACTION or ON DELETE NO ACTION, or skipping the ON UPDATE or ON DELETE keywords. If you choose this path, you will not be able to change the value of a primary key if matching records exist in the foreign table.

Refer to the procedure in Hands-On 20-4 to find out how to correctly combine the above example statements into a single SQL statement.

Hands-On 20-4: Relating Two Tables and Setting up Cascading Referential Integrity Rules

1. In the Visual Basic Editor window, insert a new module.

2. In the module's Code window, enter the RelateTables procedure as shown below.

```
Sub RelateTables()
    Dim conn As ADODB.Connection
    Dim strPrimaryTbl As String
```

```
    Dim strForeignTbl As String

    On Error GoTo ErrorHandler

    Set conn = CurrentProject.Connection
    strPrimaryTbl = "tblProduct_Orders"
    strForeignTbl = "tblOrder_Details"

    conn.Execute "CREATE TABLE " & strPrimaryTbl & _
        "(InvoiceId CHAR(15), PaymentType CHAR(20), " & _
        " PaymentTerms CHAR(25), Discount LONG, " & _
        " CONSTRAINT PrimaryKey PRIMARY KEY (InvoiceId));", _
        adExecuteNoRecords

    conn.Execute "CREATE TABLE " & strForeignTbl & _
        "(InvoiceId CHAR(15), ProductId CHAR(15), " & _
        " Units LONG, Price MONEY, " & _
        "CONSTRAINT PrimaryKey PRIMARY KEY (InvoiceId, ProductId), " & _
        "CONSTRAINT fkInvoiceId FOREIGN KEY (InvoiceId) " & _
        "REFERENCES " & strPrimaryTbl & _
        " ON UPDATE CASCADE ON DELETE CASCADE);", _
        adExecuteNoRecords

    Application.RefreshDatabaseWindow
ExitHere:
    conn.Close
    Set conn = Nothing
    Exit Sub
ErrorHandler:
    MsgBox Err.Number & ":" & Err.Description
    Resume ExitHere
End Sub
```

The RelateTables procedure in Hands-On 20-4 creates and joins two tables. A Primary Key table named tblProduct_Orders is created with a primary key on the InvoiceId field. The Foreign Key table named tblOrder_Details is created with a multi-field primary key index based on the ProductId and InvoiceId fields. The REFERENCES clause specifies the tblProduct_Orders table as the parent table. The created relationship has the referential integrity rules enforced via the ON UPDATE CASCADE and ON DELETE CASCADE statements.

The outcome of the RelateTables procedure in Hands-On 20-4 is illustrated in the following figures. Figure 20-6 displays the one-to-many relationship between tblProduct_Orders and tblOrder_Details. Figure 20-7 presents the Edit Relationships window in which both cascading updates and deletes are selected.

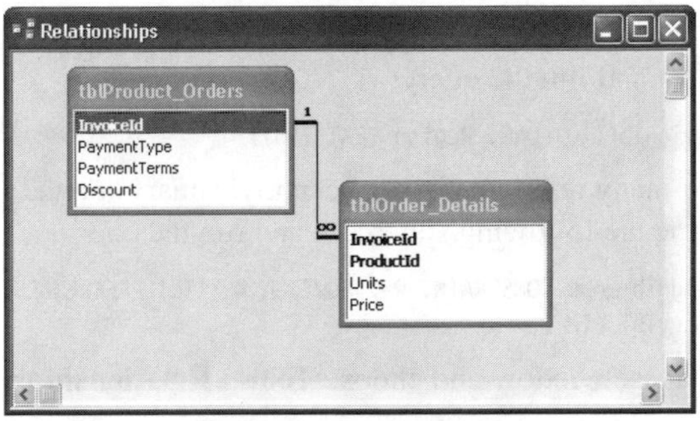

Programming with the Jet Data Definition Language

Figure 20-6: To access the Relationships window, choose Tools | Relationships.

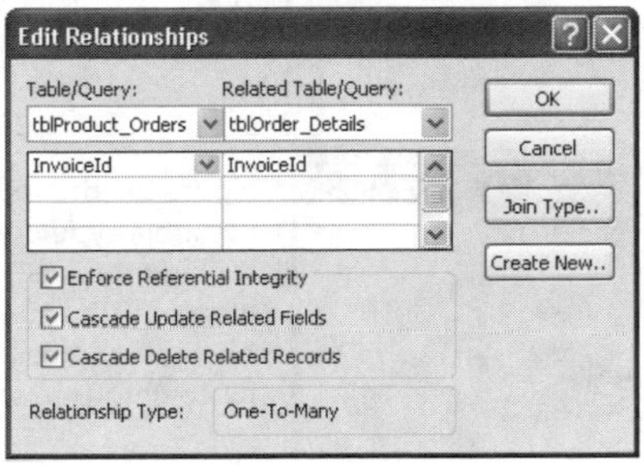

Figure 20-7: To access the Edit Relationships window, choose Relationships | Edit Relationship.

Using the Data Definition Query Window

To enhance your understanding about creating tables and relationships with the Data Definition Language, you may want to perform Hands-On 20-5 using the Data Definition Query window.

◉ Hands-On 20-5: Running Data Definition Statements in the Microsoft Access User Interface

Each of the statements in this hands-on can be executed by selecting Run from the Query menu.

To access the Data Definition Query window, perform the following steps:

1. In the Database window, select the **Queries** object and click the **New** button.

2. In the New Query dialog box, select **Design View** and click **OK**.

3. In the Show Table dialog box, click the **Close** button.

4. Choose **Query | SQL Specific | Data Definition** from the menu bar.

5. To create a table on the Primary (one) side of the relationship, type the following statement and run the query:

```
CREATE TABLE myPrimaryTbl(ID COUNTER CONSTRAINT pKey PRIMARY KEY, COUNTRY
    TEXT(15));
```

6. To create a table on the Foreign (many) side of the relationship, type the following statement and run the query:

```
CREATE TABLE myForeignTbl(ID LONG, Region TEXT (15));
```

7. To create a one-to-many relationship between myPrimaryTbl and myForeignTbl, type the following statement and run the query:

```
ALTER TABLE myForeignTbl ADD CONSTRAINT Rel FOREIGN KEY(Id) REFERENCES
            myPrimaryTbl (Id);
```

8. Switch to the Database window and choose **Tools | Relationships**.

9. In the Relationships window, choose **Relationships | ShowAll**. This will add both tables (myPrimaryTbl and myForeignTbl) to the Relationships window (Figure 20-8).

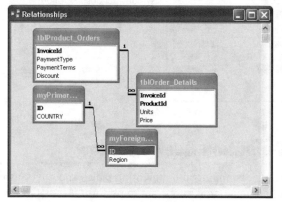

Figure 20-8: Notice that the tables you created by running the DDL statements in steps 5 and 6 above are joined on the ID column (see step 7).

10. Double-click the joining line between the two tables (myPrimaryTbl and myForeignTbl) to display the Edit Relationships window.

Figure 20-9: You can edit relationships between tables via the Edit Relationships window.

11. To delete the relationship between the tables, type the following statement and run the query:

```
ALTER TABLE myForeignTbl DROP CONSTRAINT Rel;
```

12. To delete the table on the one side (myPrimaryTbl), type the following statement and run the query:

```
DROP TABLE myPrimaryTbl;
```

13. To delete the table on the many side (myForeignTbl), type the following statement and run the query:

```
DROP TABLE myForeignTbl;
```

Chapter Summary

In this chapter, you learned how to enforce data integrity by creating rules for tables with constraints. You learned how to validate data against another column in the same table or a column located in another table. You also learned how to use the Access Data Definition Query window to delete tables that have constraints and remove constraints from a table. Finally, you saw how you can establish relationships between tables using the DDL commands inside your VBA procedures.

In addition, one of the procedures in this chapter introduced you to a couple of advanced Data Manipulation Language (DML) statements used for inserting data into tables and executing transactions.

The next chapter focuses on ways to use DDL for defining and removing indexes and primary keys.

Chapter 21

Defining Indexes and Primary Keys

Indexes speed the processes of finding and sorting records. You should create indexes for fields that are frequently used in searches and in sorting. You can create an index on a new or existing table. An index can be made of one or more fields. This chapter presents a number of procedures that use Data Definition Language statements to define indexes and primary keys.

Creating Tables with Indexes

You can create an index while creating a table by using the CONSTRAINT clause with the CREATE TABLE statement. The procedure in Hands-On 21-1 creates a new table called Supplier1 with a unique index called idxSupplierName based on the SupplierName field.

◎ Hands-On 21-1: Creating a Table with a Single-Field Index

1. Open the **Acc2003_Chap21.mdb** file from the book's downloadable files, or create a new blank Access database to use for this chapter's procedures.

2. Switch to the Visual Basic Editor window and insert a new module.

3. In the module's Code window, enter the SingleField_Index procedure as shown below.

```
Sub SingleField_Index()
    Dim conn As ADODB.Connection
    Dim strTable As String

    On Error GoTo ErrorHandler

    Set conn = CurrentProject.Connection

    strTable = "Supplier1"

    conn.Execute "CREATE TABLE " & strTable _
        & "(SupplierId INTEGER, " _
        & "SupplierName CHAR (30), " _
        & "SupplierPhone CHAR (12), " _
        & "SupplierCity CHAR (19), " _
        & "CONSTRAINT idxSupplierName UNIQUE " _
```

```
            & "(SupplierName));"
    Application.RefreshDatabaseWindow
ExitHere:
        conn.Close
        Set conn = Nothing
        Exit Sub
ErrorHandler:
        MsgBox Err.Number & ":" & Err.Description
        Resume ExitHere
End Sub
```

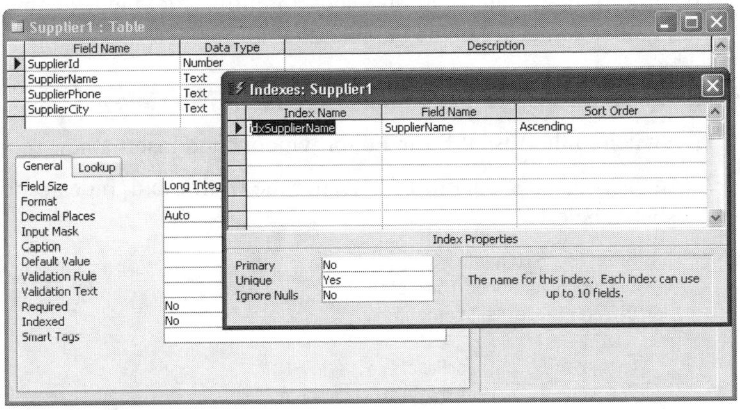

Figure 21-1: The idxSupplierName index was created by running the procedure in Hands-On 21-1.

Adding an Index to an Existing Table

To add an index to an existing table, use the CREATE INDEX statement. You can add an index based on one or more fields. The procedure in Hands-On 21-2 demonstrates how to add an index named idxCity to the Supplier1 table.

⊚ Hands-On 21-2: Adding a Single-Field Index to an Existing Table

1. Switch to the Visual Basic Editor window and insert a new module.

2. In the module's Code window, enter the SingleField_Index2 procedure as shown below.

```
Sub SingleField_Index2()
    Dim conn As ADODB.Connection
    Dim strTable As String

    On Error GoTo ErrorHandler

    Set conn = CurrentProject.Connection
        strTable = "Supplier1"
```

```
conn.Execute "CREATE INDEX idxCity ON " & strTable & _
              "(SupplierCity) ;"
ExitHere:
    conn.Close
    Set conn = Nothing
    Exit Sub
ErrorHandler:
    MsgBox Err.Number & ":" & Err.Description
    Resume ExitHere
End Sub
```

The procedure in Hands-On 21-3 adds a multiple-field index named idxSupplierNameCity to the Supplier2 table.

Hands-On 21-3: Creating an Index Based on Two Fields

1. Switch to the Visual Basic Editor window and insert a new module.

2. In the module's Code window, enter the MultiField_Index procedure as shown below.

```
Sub MultiField_Index()
    Dim conn As ADODB.Connection
    Dim strTable As String

    On Error GoTo ErrorHandler
    Set conn = CurrentProject.Connection

    strTable = "Supplier2"

    conn.Execute "CREATE TABLE " & strTable _
        & "(SupplierId INTEGER, " _
        & "SupplierName CHAR (30), " _
        & "SupplierPhone CHAR (12), " _
        & "SupplierCity CHAR (19), " _
        & "CONSTRAINT idxSupplierNameCity UNIQUE " _
        & "(SupplierName, SupplierCity));"

    Application.RefreshDatabaseWindow
ExitHere:
    conn.Close
    Set conn = Nothing
    Exit Sub
ErrorHandler:
    MsgBox Err.Number & ":" & Err.Description
    Resume ExitHere
End Sub
```

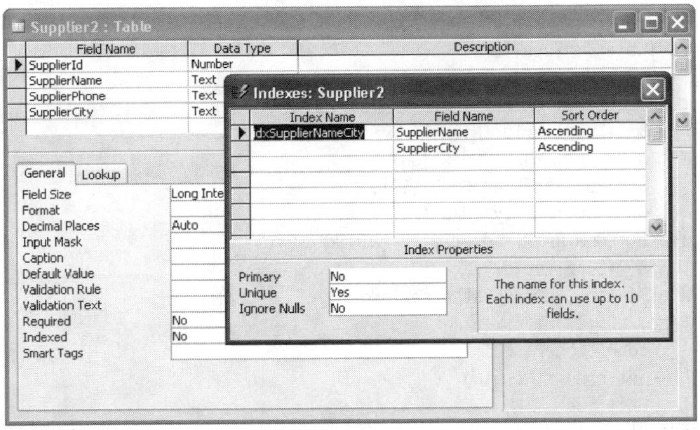

Programming with the Jet Data Definition Language

Figure 21-2: The procedure in Hands-On 21-3 adds an index based on two fields to the existing Supplier2 table.

Creating a Table with a Primary Key

When you create a database table you should define a primary key to uniquely identify rows within the table. A *primary key* allows you to relate a particular table with other tables in the database (for procedure examples, refer to the previous chapter). A table can have only one primary key; however, a primary key can consist of more than one column.

To create a table with a primary key, use the CONSTRAINT clause with the CREATE TABLE statement. The procedure in Hands-On 21-4 uses the following CONSTRAINT clause to create a single-field primary key based on the SupplierId field:

```
CONSTRAINT idxPrimary PRIMARY KEY(SupplierId)
```

To create a table with a primary key based on two or more columns, specify column names in parentheses following the PRIMARY KEY keyword. For example, the following CONSTRAINT clause will create a primary key based on the SupplierId and SupplierName columns:

```
CONSTRAINT idxPrimary PRIMARY KEY (SupplierId, SupplierName)
```

Hands-On 21-4: Creating a Single-Field Primary Key

1. Switch to the Visual Basic Editor window and insert a new module.

2. In the module's Code window, enter the SingleField_PKey procedure as shown below.

```
Sub SingleField_PKey()
    Dim conn As ADODB.Connection
    Dim strTable As String

    On Error GoTo ErrorHandler
```

```
        Set conn = CurrentProject.Connection
        strTable = "Supplier3"

        conn.Execute "CREATE TABLE " & strTable _
            & "(SupplierId INTEGER, " _
            & "SupplierName CHAR (30), " _
            & "SupplierPhone CHAR (12), " _
            & "SupplierCity CHAR (19), " _
            & "CONSTRAINT idxPrimary PRIMARY KEY " _
            & "(SupplierId));"
        Application.RefreshDatabaseWindow
ExitHere:
        conn.Close
        Set conn = Nothing
        Exit Sub
ErrorHandler:
        MsgBox Err.Number & ":" & Err.Description
        Resume ExitHere
End Sub
```

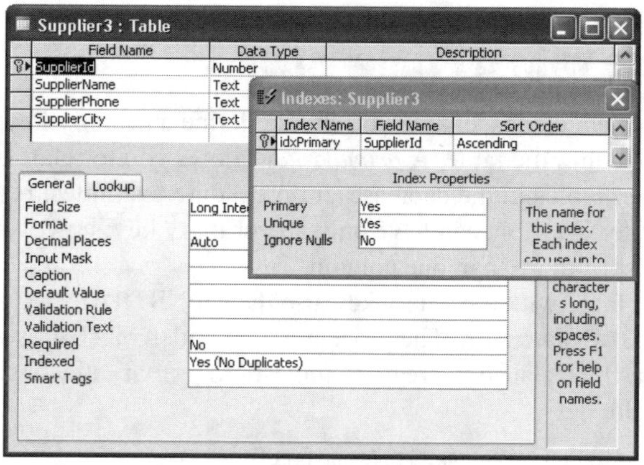

Figure 21-3: The result of running the SingleField_PKey procedure in Hands-On 21-4 is a primary key index named idxPrimary based on the SupplierID column.

Creating Indexes with Restrictions

You can use the CREATE INDEX statement to add an index to an existing table. The CREATE INDEX statement can be used with the following options:

- PRIMARY option — Creates a primary key index that does not allow duplicate values in the key.
- DISALLOW NULL option — Creates an index that does not allow adding records with Null values in the indexed field.
- IGNORE NULL option — Creates and index that does not include records with Null values in the key.

Use the WITH keyword to declare the above index options.

The procedure in Hands-On 21-5 designates the SupplierId field as the primary key by using the PRIMARY option.

◎ Hands-On 21-5: Creating a Primary Key Index with Restrictions

1. Switch to the Visual Basic Editor window and insert a new module.

2. In the module's Code window, enter the Index_WithPrimaryOption procedure as shown below.

```
Sub Index_WithPrimaryOption()
    Dim conn As ADODB.Connection
    Dim strTable As String

    On Error GoTo ErrorHandler

    Set conn = CurrentProject.Connection
    strTable = "Supplier1"

    conn.Execute "CREATE INDEX idxPrimary1 ON " & strTable _
        & "(SupplierId) WITH PRIMARY ;"
ExitHere:
    conn.Close
    Set conn = Nothing
    Exit Sub
ErrorHandler:
    MsgBox Err.Number & ":" & Err.Description
    Resume ExitHere
End Sub
```

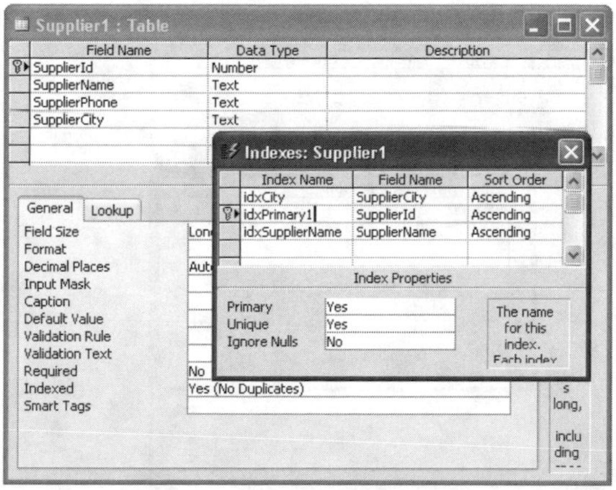

Figure 21-4: The index created by the procedure in Hands-On 21-5 has the Unique and Primary properties set to Yes, which means that this index is a primary key and every value in this index must be unique.

➲ **Note:** Primary key indexes are automatically created as unique indexes.

You can prohibit the entry of Null values in the indexed fields by using the DISALLOW NULL option as shown in the example procedure in Hands-On 21-6.

◎ Hands-On 21-6: Creating an Index that Disallows Null Values in the Key

1. Switch to the Visual Basic Editor window and insert a new module.

2. In the module's Code window, enter the Index_WithDisallowNullOption procedure as shown below.

```
Sub Index_WithDisallowNullOption()
    Dim conn As ADODB.Connection
    Dim strTable As String

    On Error GoTo ErrorHandler
    Set conn = CurrentProject.Connection

    strTable = "Supplier3"
    conn.Execute "CREATE INDEX idxSupplierCity ON " & strTable _
        & "(SupplierCity) WITH DISALLOW NULL ;"
ExitHere:
    conn.Close
    Set conn = Nothing
    Exit Sub
ErrorHandler:
    MsgBox Err.Number & ":" & Err.Description
    Resume ExitHere
End Sub
```

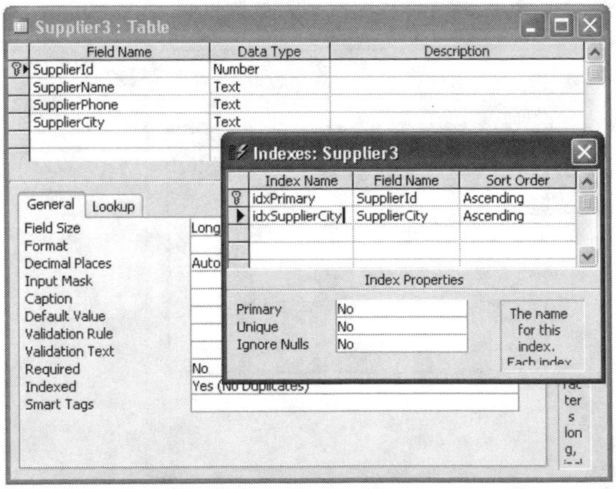

Figure 21-5: The result of running the procedure in Hands-On 21-6 is an index called idxSupplierCity that does not allow Null values.

You can prevent records with Null values in the indexed fields from being included in the index by using the IGNORE NULL option, as illustrated in Hands-On 21-7.

◎ Hands-On 21-7: Creating an Index with the Ignore Null Option

1. Switch to the Visual Basic Editor window and insert a new module.
2. In the module's Code window, enter the Index_WithIgnoreNullOption procedure as shown below.

```
Sub Index_WithIgnoreNullOption()
    Dim conn As ADODB.Connection
    Dim strTable As String

    On Error GoTo ErrorHandler

    Set conn = CurrentProject.Connection

    strTable = "Supplier3"

    conn.Execute "CREATE INDEX idxSupplierPhone ON " & strTable _
        & "(SupplierPhone) WITH IGNORE NULL ;"
ExitHere:
    conn.Close
    Set conn = Nothing
    Exit Sub
ErrorHandler:
    MsgBox Err.Number & ":" & Err.Description
    Resume ExitHere
End Sub
```

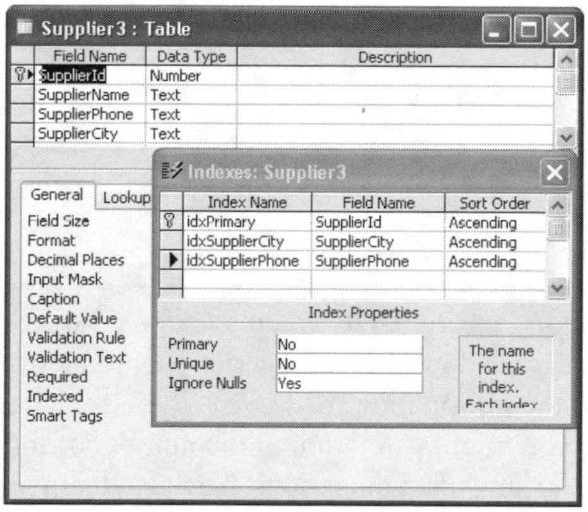

Figure 21-6: The result of running the procedure in Hands-On 21-7 is an index called idxSupplierPhone that allows Null values in the key. However, records containing Null values will be excluded from any searches that use that index.

Deleting Indexes

Use the DROP INDEX statement to remove an index. Note that anytime you want to delete a column that is part of an index, you must first remove the index using the DROP CONSTRAINT or DROP INDEX statement. Before removing the index, make sure that the table containing the index is closed.

⊚ Hands-On 21-8: Deleting an Index

1. Switch to the Visual Basic Editor window and insert a new module.

2. In the module's Code window, enter the DeleteIndex procedure as shown below.

```
Sub DeleteIndex()
    Dim conn As ADODB.Connection
    Dim strTable As String

    On Error GoTo ErrorHandler

    Set conn = CurrentProject.Connection
    strTable = "Supplier1"

    conn.Execute "DROP INDEX idxSupplierName ON " & strTable & ";"
ExitHere:
    conn.Close
    Set conn = Nothing
    Exit Sub
ErrorHandler:
    MsgBox Err.Number & ":" & Err.Description
    Resume ExitHere
End Sub
```

Chapter Summary

This chapter introduced you to using DDL statements for creating indexes. Columns that are frequently used in database queries should be indexed to allow for faster access to the information. However, if you frequently add, delete, and update rows, you might want to limit the number of indexes, as they take up disk space and slow data operations. You also learned that a primary key is a special type of index that allows you to uniquely identify rows in a table as well as create a relationship between two tables, as demonstrated in the previous chapter.

The next chapter shows you a number of DDL statements that are used to manage database security.

Chapter 22

Database Security

The Jet 4.0 ANSI SQL-92 extensions support a number of security features that allow you to easily manage database and user passwords, create or delete user and group accounts, and grant or delete permissions for database objects. The procedures in this chapter demonstrate how to use simple Data Definition Language statements to manage database security.

Setting the Database Password

Database security can be handled at share level or user level. Share-level security is the easiest to implement, as it only requires that you set a password on the database. You can use the ALTER DATABASE statement to set a new database password or change an existing password. The syntax looks like this:

```
ALTER DATABASE PASSWORD newPassword oldPassword
```

When setting the password for the first time, use Null for the old password (see the example procedure in Hands-On 22-1). The Access database must be opened in exclusive mode to perform password operations. Therefore, set the ADO Connection object's Mode property to adModeShareExclusive before opening a database.

⊚ Hands-On 22-1: Setting a Database Password

This hands-on requires the prior completion of Hands-On 19-3 in Chapter 19.

1. Prior to running this procedure, run the procedure in Hands-On 19-3 (Chapter 19) to create the Sites.mdb file. As a workaround, you can also create a blank database in the Microsoft Access user interface, close it, and then run the SetDbPassword procedure.

2. Open the **Acc2003_Chap22.mdb** file from the book's downloadable files, or create this file from scratch using the Microsoft Office Access user interface.

3. Switch to the Visual Basic Editor window and insert a new module.

4. In the module's Code window, enter the SetDbPassword procedure as shown below.

```
Sub SetDbPassword()
    Dim conn As ADODB.Connection
    Dim strPath As String
```

```
        On Error GoTo ErrorHandler
        strPath = CurrentProject.Path

        Set conn = New ADODB.Connection
        With conn
            .Mode = adModeShareExclusive
            .Open "Provider = Microsoft.Jet.OLEDB.4.0;" & _
                        "Data Source=" & strPath & "\Sites.mdb;"
            .Execute "ALTER DATABASE PASSWORD secret null  "
        End With
ExitHere:
        If Not conn Is Nothing Then
            If conn.State = adStateOpen Then conn.Close
        End If
        Set conn = Nothing
        Exit Sub
ErrorHandler:
        MsgBox Err.Number & ":" & Err.Description
        Resume ExitHere
End Sub
```

After opening a database in exclusive mode, the above procedure changes the database password from Null to "secret." Notice that the new password is listed first, followed by the old password. Notice also how the above procedure uses the State property of the ADO Connection object to determine whether the connection to the database is open. State returns adStateOpen if the Connection object is open and adStateClosed if it is not.

Removing the Database Password

To remove a database password, replace the existing password with Null. The password can be removed by using the ALTER DATABASE PASSWORD statement as illustrated in the preceding section. When the database is secured with a password, you will need to use the Jet OLEDB:Database Password property to specify the password to open the database. This is a Microsoft Jet 4.0 OLE DB Provider-specific property of the Connection object. The following procedure shows how to remove the password "secret" from the Sites.mdb database that was set by the SetDbPassword procedure in Hands-On 22-1.

◉ Hands-On 22-2: Deleting a Database Password

This procedure requires prior completion of Hands-On 22-1 and 19-3 (Chapter 19).

1. Switch to the Visual Basic Editor window and insert a new module.

2. In the module's Code window, enter the DeleteDbPassword procedure as shown below.

```
Sub DeleteDbPassword()
    Dim conn As ADODB.Connection
    Dim strPath As String
```

```
                Dim strPass As String

                On Error GoTo ErrorHandler

                strPath = CurrentProject.Path
                strPass = "secret"

                Set conn = New ADODB.Connection

                With conn
                    .Mode = adModeShareExclusive
                    .Open "Provider = Microsoft.Jet.OleDb.4.0;" & _
                        "Data Source=" & strPath & "\Sites.mdb;" _
                        & "Jet OLEDB:Database Password = " & strPass
                    .Execute "ALTER DATABASE PASSWORD null secret"
                End With
            ExitHere:
                If Not conn Is Nothing Then
                    If conn.State = adStateOpen Then conn.Close
                End If
                Set conn = Nothing
                Exit Sub
            ErrorHandler:
                MsgBox Err.Number & ":" & Err.Description
                Resume ExitHere
            End Sub
```

Creating a User Account

Establishing database security at a user level is more involved than setting a database password. It requires that you create group and user accounts and assign permissions to groups and users to perform operations on various database objects. Use the CREATE USER statement to create a new user account. Specify the user name to log in to the account followed by the required password and a personal identifier (PID) to make the account unique. The syntax of creating a user account looks like this:

```
CREATE USER userLoginName password PID
```

You can create more than one user account at a time by separating the user names with a comma.

The procedure in Hands-On 22-3 sets up a new user account for GeorgeM with "fisherman" as the login password and "0302" as the PID. While this example procedure uses a simple PID number, in the production environment, the PID number you choose should be from 4 to 20 characters long (preferably a combination of numbers and uppercase and lowercase characters that are difficult for someone to guess).

⊚ Hands-On 22-3: Creating a User Account

1. Switch to the Visual Basic Editor window and insert a new module.

2. In the module's Code window, enter the CreateUserAccount procedure as shown below.

```
Sub CreateUserAccount()
    Dim conn As ADODB.Connection

    On Error GoTo ErrorHandler

    Set conn = CurrentProject.Connection

    conn.Execute "CREATE USER GeorgeM fisherman 0302"
ExitHere:
    If Not conn Is Nothing Then
        If conn.State = adStateOpen Then conn.Close
    End If
    Set conn = Nothing
    Exit Sub
ErrorHandler:
    MsgBox Err.Number & ":" & Err.Description
    Resume ExitHere
End Sub
```

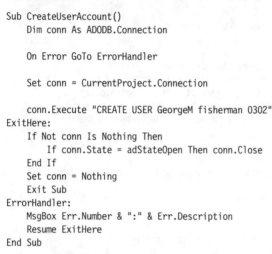

Figure 22-1: After running the CreateUserAccount procedure in Hands-On 22-3, you should see a listing for the GeorgeM user account in the User and Group Accounts window (choose Tools | Security | User and Group Accounts).

Changing a User Password

A user account password can be changed by using the ALTER USER statement in the following form:

```
ALTER USER userAccountName PASSWORD newPassword oldPassword
```

The procedure in Hands-On 22-4 changes the GeorgeM account's user password from "fisherman" to "primate."

Hands-On 22-4: Changing a User Password

This hands-on requires prior completion of Hands-On 22-3.

1. Switch to the Visual Basic Editor window and insert a new module.
2. In the module's Code window, enter the ChangeUserPassword procedure as shown below.

```
Sub ChangeUserPassword()
    Dim conn As ADODB.Connection

    On Error GoTo ErrorHandler

    Set conn = CurrentProject.Connection

    conn.Execute "ALTER USER GeorgeM PASSWORD primate fisherman"
ExitHere:
    If Not conn Is Nothing Then
        If conn.State = adStateOpen Then conn.Close
    End If
    Set conn = Nothing
    Exit Sub
ErrorHandler:
    MsgBox Err.Number & ":" & Err.Description
    Resume ExitHere
End Sub
```

Creating a Group Account

Use the CREATE GROUP statement to create a new group account. You must specify the group name followed by a unique PID (personal identifier):

```
CREATE GROUP groupName PID
```

You can create more than one group at a time by separating the group names with a comma. The procedure in Hands-On 22-5 creates a new group account called "Mozart" with "2001Best" as the PID.

Hands-On 22-5: Creating a Group Account

1. Switch to the Visual Basic Editor window and insert a new module.
2. In the module's Code window, enter the CreateGroupAccount procedure as shown below.

```
Sub CreateGroupAccount()
    Dim conn As ADODB.Connection

    On Error GoTo ErrorHandler

    Set conn = CurrentProject.Connection

    conn.Execute "CREATE GROUP Mozart 2001Best"
ExitHere:
    If Not conn Is Nothing Then
        If conn.State = adStateOpen Then conn.Close
```

```
    End If
    Set conn = Nothing
    Exit Sub
ErrorHandler:
    MsgBox Err.Number & ":" & Err.Description
    Resume ExitHere
End Sub
```

Adding Users to Groups

Use the ADD USER statement to make a user account a member of a group.
Specify the user account name followed by the TO keyword and a group name:

```
ADD USER userAccountName TO groupName
```

⊚ Hands-On 22-6: Making a User Account a Member of a Group

This hands-on requires prior completion of Hands-On procedures 22-3 and
22-5.

1. Switch to the Visual Basic Editor window and insert a new module.

2. In the module's Code window, enter the AddUserToGroup procedure as
   shown below.

```
Sub AddUserToGroup()
    Dim conn As ADODB.Connection

    On Error GoTo ErrorHandler

    Set conn = CurrentProject.Connection

    conn.Execute "ADD USER GeorgeM TO Mozart"
ExitHere:
    If Not conn Is Nothing Then
        If conn.State = adStateOpen Then conn.Close
    End If
    Set conn = Nothing
    Exit Sub
ErrorHandler:
    MsgBox Err.Number & ":" & Err.Description
    Resume ExitHere
End Sub
```

Removing a User from a Group

To delete a user from a group, use the DROP USER statement followed by the
username, the FROM keyword, and the group name. For example, to delete the
GeorgeM account from the Mozart group, you should use the following
statement:

```
DROP USER GeorgeM FROM Mozart
```

Hands-On 22-7: Removing a User Account from a Group

This hands-on requires prior completion of Hands-On procedures 22-5 and 22-6.

1. Switch to the Visual Basic Editor window and insert a new module.

2. In the module's Code window, enter the RemoveUserFromGroup procedure as shown below.

```
Sub RemoveUserFromGroup()
    Dim conn As ADODB.Connection

    On Error GoTo ErrorHandler

    Set conn = CurrentProject.Connection

    conn.Execute "DROP USER GeorgeM FROM Mozart"
ExitHere:
        If Not conn Is Nothing Then
            If conn.State = adStateOpen Then conn.Close
        End If
        Set conn = Nothing
        Exit Sub
ErrorHandler:
        MsgBox Err.Number & ":" & Err.Description
        Resume ExitHere
End Sub
```

Deleting a User Account

To delete a user account, use the DROP USER statement followed by the user account name, as demonstrated by the DeleteUserAccount procedure in Hands-On 22-8.

Hands-On 22-8: Deleting a User Account

This procedure requires prior completion of Hands-On 22-3.

1. Switch to the Visual Basic Editor window and insert a new module.

2. In the module's Code window, enter the DeleteUserAccount procedure as shown below.

```
Sub DeleteUserAccount()
    Dim conn As ADODB.Connection

    On Error GoTo ErrorHandler

    Set conn = CurrentProject.Connection

    conn.Execute "DROP USER GeorgeM"
ExitHere:
        If Not conn Is Nothing Then
            If conn.State = adStateOpen Then conn.Close
        End If
```

```
        Set conn = Nothing
        Exit Sub
    ErrorHandler:
        MsgBox Err.Number & ":" & Err.Description
        Resume ExitHere
    End Sub
```

Granting Permissions for an Object

Use the GRANT statement to assign security permissions for an object in a database to an existing user or group account. The procedure in Hands-On 22-9 grants the SELECT, DELETE, INSERT, and UPDATE permissions on all tables to the Mozart group.

The GRANT statement requires the following:

- A list of privileges to be granted
- The keyword ON followed by the name of a table, a non-table object, or an object container (e.g., Tables, Forms, Reports, Modules, Scripts)
- The keyword TO followed by the user or group name

```
GRANT listOfPermissions ON tableName | objectName | containerName TO accountName
```

Please note that in addition to tables, the Tables container contains queries, views, and procedures, and the Scripts container includes macros.

⊚ Hands-On 22-9: Granting Permissions for Tables to an Existing Group

This hands-on requires prior completion of Hands-On 22-5.

1. Switch to the Visual Basic Editor window and insert a new module.

2. In the module's Code window, enter the SetTblPermissions procedure as shown below.

```
Sub SetTblPermissions()
    Dim conn As ADODB.Connection

    On Error GoTo ErrorHandler

    Set conn = CurrentProject.Connection

    conn.Execute "GRANT SELECT, DELETE, INSERT, " _
        & "UPDATE ON CONTAINER TABLES TO Mozart"
ExitHere:
    If Not conn Is Nothing Then
        If conn.State = adStateOpen Then conn.Close
    End If
    Set conn = Nothing
    Exit Sub
ErrorHandler:
    MsgBox Err.Number & ":" & Err.Description
    Resume ExitHere
End Sub
```

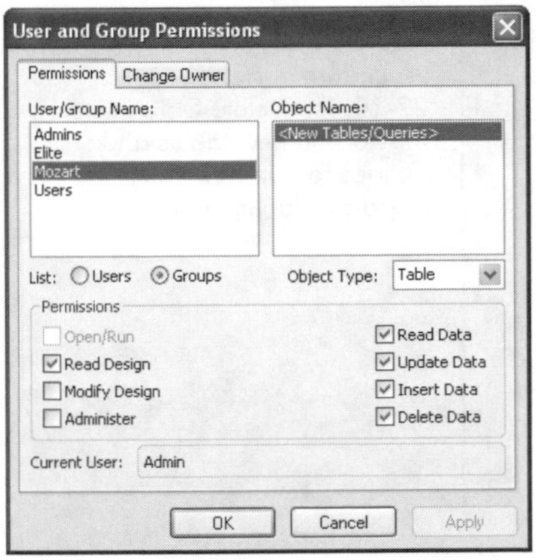

Programming with the Jet Data Definition Language

Figure 22-2: You can open the User and Group Permissions window (choose Tools | Security | User and Group Permissions) to check out the privileges granted to the members of the Mozart group by the SetTblPermissions procedure in Hands-On 22-9.

Revoking Security Permissions

Use the REVOKE statement to revoke security permissions for an object from an existing user or group account. This statement has the following form:

```
REVOKE listOfPermissions ON tableName | objectName | containerName FROM
accountName
```

The procedure in Hands-On 22-10 removes the privilege of deleting tables from the members of the Mozart group.

◎ Hands-On 22-10: Revoking Security Permissions

This hands-on requires prior completion of Hands-On procedures 22-5 and 22-9.

1. Switch to the Visual Basic Editor window and insert a new module.

2. In the module's Code window, enter the RevokePermission procedure as shown below.

```
Sub RevokePermission()
    Dim conn As ADODB.Connection

    On Error GoTo ErrorHandler

    Set conn = CurrentProject.Connection

    conn.Execute "REVOKE DELETE ON CONTAINER TABLES FROM Mozart"
ExitHere:
    If Not conn Is Nothing Then
        If conn.State = adStateOpen Then conn.Close
    End If
    Set conn = Nothing
    Exit Sub
ErrorHandler:
    MsgBox Err.Number & ":" & Err.Description
    Resume ExitHere
End Sub
```

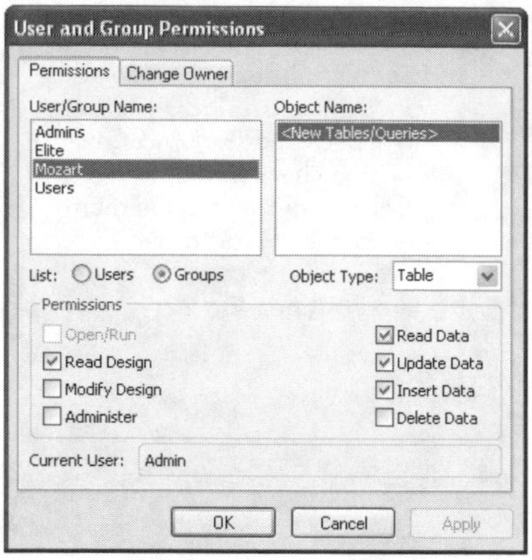

Figure 22-3: After running the procedure in Hands-On 22-10, the Delete Data permission on new tables and queries for the members of the Mozart group is turned off.

Deleting a Group Account

Use the DROP GROUP statement to delete a group account. You only need to specify the name of the group account you want to delete. If you'd like to delete more than one account, separate each group name with a comma.

Hands-On 22-11: Deleting a Group Account

This hands-on requires prior completion of Hands-On 22-5.

1. Switch to the Visual Basic Editor window and insert a new module.

2. In the module's Code window, enter the DeleteGroupAccount procedure as shown below.

```
Sub DeleteGroupAccount()
    Dim conn As ADODB.Connection

    On Error GoTo ErrorHandler

    Set conn = CurrentProject.Connection

    conn.Execute "DROP GROUP Mozart"
ExitHere:
    If Not conn Is Nothing Then
        If conn.State = adStateOpen Then conn.Close
    End If
    Set conn = Nothing
    Exit Sub
ErrorHandler:
    MsgBox Err.Number & ":" & Err.Description
    Resume ExitHere
End Sub
```

Chapter Summary

This chapter showed you how to use Jet DDL statements to manage security in the Microsoft Access database. You used the ALTER DATABASE statement to create, modify, and remove the database password and managed the user-level accounts with the CREATE, ADD, ALTER, and DROP statements. You learned how to use the GRANT and REVOKE statements to establish and remove permissions on database objects for user and group accounts.

In the next chapter, you learn how to organize your data using structures known as views, and how to use stored procedures in lieu of Access Action and Parameter queries.

Chapter 23

Views and Stored Procedures

In this chapter, we will work with advanced Data Definition Language statements that are used for creating, altering, and deleting two special objects known as views and stored procedures. These objects are used to perform various query operations. *Views* are like Access Select queries, however you can't use the ORDER BY clause to sort your data or use parameters to filter records. *Stored procedures* perform the same operations as Access Action and Parameter queries. They can also be used for creating sorted Select queries. Stored procedures are saved precompiled so that at run time the procedure executes much faster than standard SQL. Learning how to create and use views and stored procedures will give you more control over your database.

Creating a View

If you want users to view and update data in a table or set of tables, but you do not want them to open the underlying tables directly, you can create a view. An SQL *view* is like a virtual table. Similar to an Access Select query, a view can display data from one or more tables. Instead of providing all the available data in your tables, you decide exactly what fields you'd like to include for viewing.

To create a view, use a SELECT statement to select the columns you want to include in a view. Next, associate the SELECT statement with a CREATE VIEW statement. The syntax looks like this:

```
CREATE VIEW viewName [(columnNames)]
AS
    SELECT (columnNames)
    FROM tableName;
```

Views must have unique names in the database. The name of the View cannot be the same as the name of an existing table. Specifying the names of columns following the name of the view is optional (note the square brackets in the syntax above). Column names must be specified in the SELECT statement. Use the asterisk (*) to select all columns.

Let's put more meaning into the above syntax. The example statement below creates a view that lists only orders with a Freight amount less than $20.

```
CREATE VIEW cheapFreight
AS
     SELECT      Orders.OrderID,
                 Orders.Freight,
                 Orders.ShipCountry
     FROM  Orders
     WHERE Orders.Freight < 20;
```

The SELECT statement that defines the view cannot contain any parameters and cannot be typed directly in the SQL pane of the Query window. It must be used through the ADO's Execute method after establishing connection to a database, as illustrated below:

```
Sub Create_View_CheapFreight()
    Dim conn As ADODB.Connection
    Set conn = CurrentProject.Connection
    conn.Execute "CREATE VIEW CheapFreight AS " & _
                 "SELECT Orders.OrderID, Orders.Freight, " & _
                 "Orders.ShipCountry " & _
                 "FROM Orders WHERE Orders.Freight < 20;"
    Application.RefreshDatabaseWindow
    conn.Close
    Set conn = Nothing
End Sub
```

The Application.RefreshDatabaseWindow statement ensures that after the view is created it is immediately listed in the Queries pane of the Database window. If you omit this statement, you will need to refresh the Database window manually by pressing F5 or choosing View | Refresh.

A view can be used as if it were a table. To return data from the CheapFreight view, double-click its name, or perform the following steps:

1. In the Access Database window, click the **Queries** object button.

2. Click the **New** button to display the New Query dialog box.

3. Choose **Design View** and click **OK**.

4. Click **Close** in the Choose Table dialog box.

5. Choose **View | SQL View**.

6. Type the following statement: **SELECT * FROM CheapFreight;**

7. Choose **Query | Run**.

After performing the above steps, the Query window displays all the records as returned from the CheapFreight view. Remember that a view never stores any data; it simply returns the data as stated in the SELECT statement used in the view definition.

Because a view is like a Select query, you can use the OpenQuery method of the Access DoCmd object to open it from your VBA code:

```
Sub OpenView()
    DoCmd.OpenQuery "CheapFreight", acViewNormal
End Sub
```

The OpenQuery method is used to carry out the OpenQuery action in Visual Basic.

To get working experience with the views, let's proceed to the hands-on section. We will start by creating a view called vw_Employees. This view is based on the Employees and Orders tables, and contains five columns (Employee Id, Full Name, Title, ReportsTo, and Order Id).

⊚ Hands-On 23-1: Creating a View Based on a Table

➔ **Note:** The Acc2003_Chap23.mdb file contains the tables from the Northwind database that will be used in this chapter's exercises.

1. Open the **Acc2003_Chap23.mdb** file from the book's downloadable files, or create this file from scratch using the Microsoft Office Access user interface. (Be sure to import the Employees and Orders tables from Northwind.mdb.)

2. Switch to the Visual Basic Editor window and insert a new module.

3. In the module's Code window, enter the Create_View procedure as shown below.

```
' Don't forget to set up a reference to the
' Microsoft ActiveX Data Objects Library
' in the References dialog box

Sub Create_View()
    Dim conn As ADODB.Connection

    Set conn = CurrentProject.Connection

    On Error GoTo ErrorHandler

    conn.Execute "CREATE VIEW vw_Employees AS " & _
                 "SELECT Employees.EmployeeId as [Employee Id], " & _
                 "FirstName & chr(32) & LastName as [Full Name], " & _
                 "Title, ReportsTo, Orders.OrderId as [Order Id] " & _
                 "FROM Employees " & _
                 "INNER JOIN Orders ON " & _
                 "Orders.EmployeeId = Employees.EmployeeId;"

    Application.RefreshDatabaseWindow
ExitHere:
    If Not conn Is Nothing Then
        If conn.State = adStateOpen Then conn.Close
    End If
    Set conn = Nothing
    Exit Sub
ErrorHandler:
    If Err.Number = -2147217900 Then
        conn.Execute "DROP VIEW vw_Employees"
        Resume
```

```
        Else
            MsgBox Err.Number & ":" & Err.Description
            Resume ExitHere
        End If
    End Sub
```

The procedure above creates a view named vw_Employees. If the view already exists, it will be deleted using the DROP VIEW statement. The Chr(32) statement will insert a space between the first and last name.

Views are visible in Microsoft Access 2003 after selecting the Queries object in the left pane of the Database window. Notice that views don't differ much from a saved query. When you open the view created by the Create_View procedure in Design view, you will notice that this view is simply a Select query. Because the query defined by the SELECT statement is updatable, the vw_Employees view is also updatable. If the query was not updatable, the view would be read-only.

Views cannot contain the ORDER BY clause. To return the records in a specific order, you might want to use the view in a stored procedure, as discussed later in this chapter.

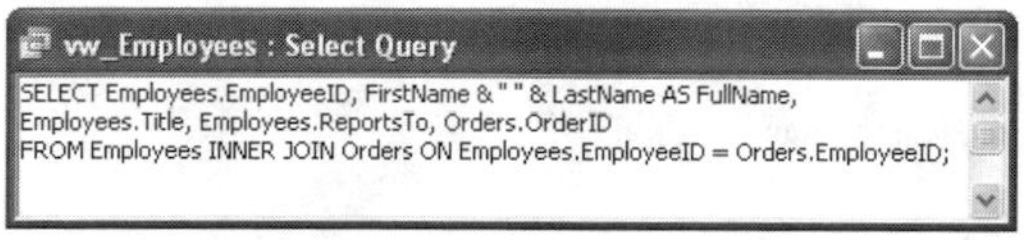

Figure 23-1: The statement used to select records for the view (see Hands-On 23-1) is shown here in the SQL view window.

Enumerating Views

You can find out the names of the views by iterating through the Views collection of the ADOX Catalog object, as illustrated in Hands-On 23-2. (Refer to Chapter 10 for more information about using the ADO Object Model and ADOX objects.)

Hands-On 23-2: Generating a List of Saved Views

1. Switch to the Visual Basic Editor window and insert a new module.

2. In the module's Code window, enter the List_Views procedure as shown below.

```
' Don't forget to set up a reference to the
' Microsoft ADO Ext. 2.7 for DDL and Security

Sub List_Views()
    Dim cat As New ADOX.Catalog
    Dim myView As ADOX.View

    cat.ActiveConnection = CurrentProject.Connection

    For Each myView In cat.Views
        Debug.Print myView.Name
    Next myView
End Sub
```

The List_Views procedure illustrated above writes the names of the existing views to the Immediate window.

Deleting a View

Use the DROP VIEW statement to delete a particular view from the database. You must specify the names of the views you want to delete. The example procedure below deletes a view named vw_Employees created by the procedure in Hands-On 23-1.

Note that both the CREATE VIEW and DROP VIEW statements can only be executed using the Execute method of the ADO Connection object.

◉ Hands-On 23-3: Deleting a View

1. Switch to the Visual Basic Editor window and insert a new module.

2. In the module's Code window, enter the Delete_View procedure as shown below.

```
Sub Delete_View()
    Dim conn As ADODB.Connection

    Set conn = CurrentProject.Connection

    On Error GoTo ErrorHandler
    conn.Execute "DROP VIEW vw_Employees"
ExitHere:
    If Not conn Is Nothing Then
        If conn.State = adStateOpen Then conn.Close
    End If
    Set conn = Nothing
    Exit Sub
ErrorHandler:
    If Err.Number = -2147217865 Then
        MsgBox "The view was already deleted."
    Exit Sub
    Else
        MsgBox Err.Number & ":" & Err.Description
        Resume ExitHere
    End If
End Sub
```

Creating a Stored Procedure

Stored procedures allow you to perform bulk operations that delete, update, or append records. Unlike views, stored procedures allow the ORDER BY clause and parameters. Use the CREATE PROCEDURE (or CREATE PROC) statement to create a stored procedure. You must specify the name of the stored procedure and the AS keyword followed by the desired SQL statement that performs the required database operation. The syntax is as follows:

```
CREATE PROC[EDURE] procName
[(param1 datatype1 [, param2 datatype2 [, ...] ])]
AS
sqlStatement;
```

The name of the stored procedure must be different from the name of an existing table. If you want to pass values to a stored procedure, then the procedure name must be followed by one or more parameters. Parameter names are followed by a data type and separated by commas. The parameter list must be enclosed in parentheses (see Hands-On 23-4 in the next section). Up to 255 parameters can be specified in the parameter list. If your stored procedure does not require parameters, the AS keyword immediately follows the name of the stored procedure.

The SQL statement can be prepared using the Access Query Design tool and then copied to the VBA procedure from the SQL view and appropriately formatted.

Suppose you want to return the employee records from the vw_Employees view (see Hands-On 23-1) ordered by Full Name. You can write the following stored procedure:

```
CREATE PROCEDURE usp_EmpByFullName
AS
Select * From vw_Employees
ORDER BY [Full Name];
```

The stored procedure above selects all columns that exist in the vw_Employees view and orders the returned data by the employee's Full Name. Notice that this procedure does not require any parameters. You might want to precede the stored procedure name with a prefix indicating the type of stored procedure. The "usp" prefix is often used to indicate a user-defined stored procedure.

Like views, stored procedures are created via the ADO Execute method after establishing a connection to the database. Therefore, we can use the following VBA code to create the usp_EmpByFullName stored procedure:

```
Sub Create_StoredProc()
    Dim conn As ADODB.Connection

    Set conn = CurrentProject.Connection
    conn.Execute "CREATE PROCEDURE usp_EmpByFullName AS " & _
             "SELECT * FROM vw_Employees " & _
             "ORDER BY [Full Name];"
    Application.RefreshDatabaseWindow
    conn.Close
    Set conn = Nothing
End Sub
```

Once created, stored procedures are visible in Microsoft Access 2003 after selecting the Queries object in the left pane of the Database window. They can be executed in the Access user interface by double-clicking the stored procedure name, or from VBA code by calling the EXECUTE statement with the ADO Execute method (see Hands-On 23-5).

Creating a Parameterized Stored Procedure

Most advanced stored procedures require one or more parameters. The parameters are then used as part of the SQL statement, usually the WHERE clause. When creating a parameterized stored procedure, Access allows you to specify up to 255 parameters in the parameters list. The stored procedure parameters must be separated by commas and enclosed in parentheses.

The procedure in Hands-On 23-4 creates a stored procedure that allows you to insert a new record into the Shippers table on the fly by supplying the required parameter values. Note that the SQL Data Manipulation Language (DML) INSERT INTO statement is used for adding new records to a table.

◉ Hands-On 23-4: Creating a Stored Procedure that Accepts Parameters

1. Import the Shippers table from the Northwind database.

2. Switch to the Visual Basic Editor window and insert a new module.

3. In the module's Code window, enter the Create_SpWithParam procedure as shown below.

```
Sub Create_SpWithParam()
    Dim conn As ADODB.Connection

    On Error GoTo ErrorHandler

    Set conn = CurrentProject.Connection

    conn.Execute "CREATE PROCEDURE procEnterData " & _
        "(@Company TEXT (40), " & _
        "@Tel TEXT (24)) AS " & _
        "INSERT INTO Shippers (CompanyName, Phone) " & _
        "VALUES (@Company, @Tel);"
ExitHere:
    If Not conn Is Nothing Then
        If conn.State = adStateOpen Then conn.Close
    End If
    Set conn = Nothing
    Exit Sub
ErrorHandler:
    If InStr(1, Err.Description, "procEnterData") Then
        conn.Execute "DROP PROC procEnterData"
        Resume
    Else
        MsgBox Err.Number & ":" & Err.Description
        Resume ExitHere
    End If
End Sub
```

The stored procedure above will require two values to be entered at run time. The first value is passed by the @Company parameter and the second one by the parameter named @Tel. In this example, the names of the parameters have been preceded with the @ sign for easy migration of the stored procedure into the SQL Server environment. If you omit the @ sign, the procedure will still execute correctly in Microsoft Access. If the procedure already exists, it will be dropped using the DROP PROC statement.

Similar to views, stored procedures appear in the Database window in the Queries view. Because we used the SQL INSERT INTO statement, Microsoft Office Access is treating this stored procedure as a parameterized Append query.

To execute the stored procedure named procEnterData created by the VBA procedure in Hands-On 23-4, double-click the stored procedure name in the Queries pane of the Access Database window. Figures 23-2 through 23-7 outline the process of running this stored procedure.

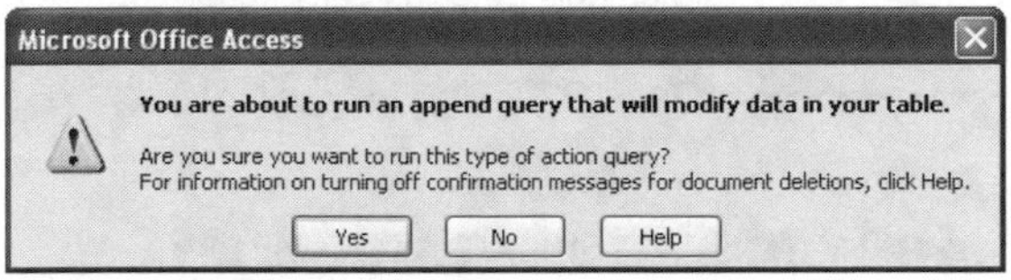

Figure 23-2: When you double-click a stored procedure name in the Queries pane of the Access Database window, Access displays this message when the stored procedure expects parameters and its SQL statement attempts to insert data into a table.

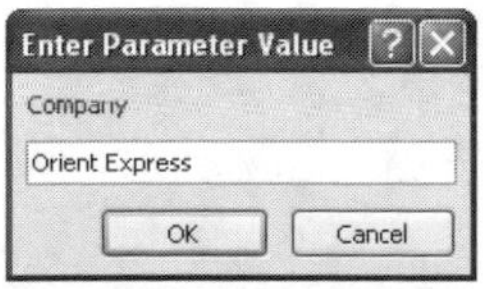

Figure 23-3: Since the stored procedure expects some input, you are being prompted for the first parameter value.

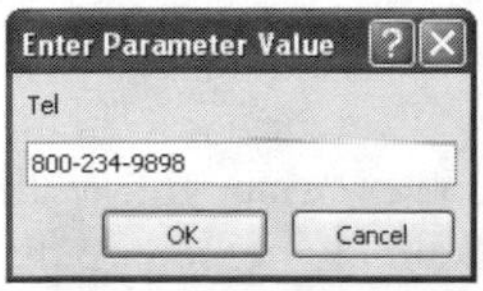

Figure 23-4: Here you are being prompted to enter the phone number for the second stored procedure parameter.

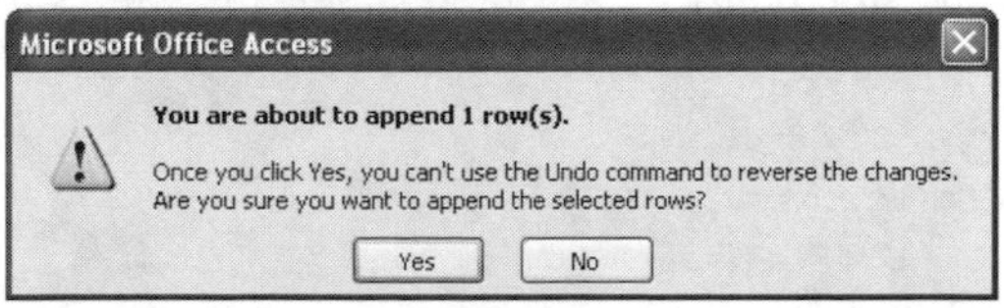

Figure 23-5: Once all input has been gathered via the parameters, Access informs you about the action that is to be performed. Click Yes to execute the stored procedure or No to cancel.

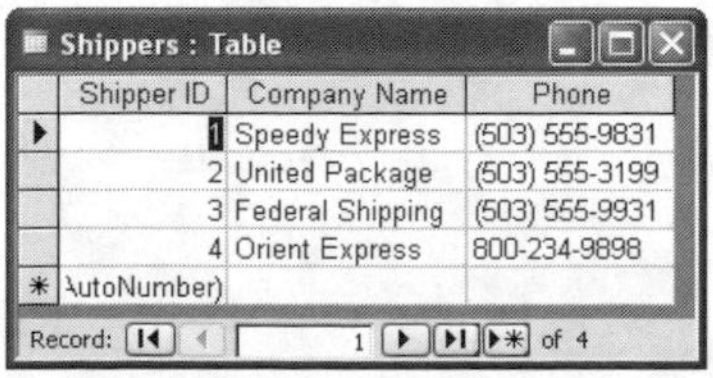

Shippers : Table

	Shipper ID	Company Name	Phone
▶	1	Speedy Express	(503) 555-9831
	2	United Package	(503) 555-3199
	3	Federal Shipping	(503) 555-9931
	4	Orient Express	800-234-9898
*	\utoNumber)		

Record: 1 of 4

Figure 23-6: Once you click Yes, Access displays the result of the operation. Notice that a new record (Orient Express) was added to the Shippers table.

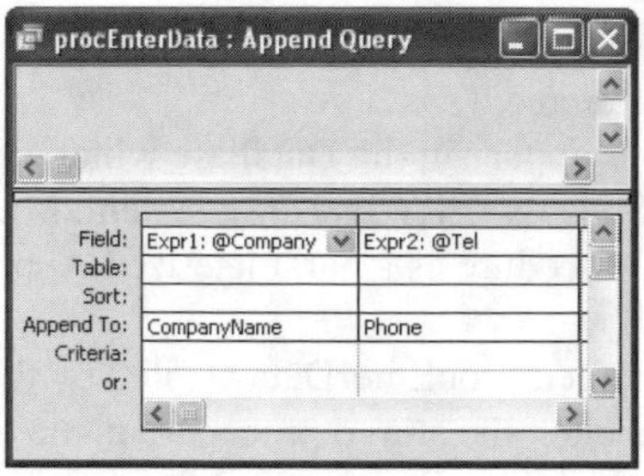

Figure 23-7: You can examine the contents of the stored procedure in the Design view (choose View | Design View). This example displays the Design view of the Append query. Other stored procedures that you create may be presented as different Action queries.

Figure 23-8: You can examine the SQL statements used by Access to execute your stored procedure by switching to SQL view (choose View | SQL View).

Executing a Parameterized Stored Procedure

In the preceding section, you learned how to run a parameterized stored procedure from the Access user interface. To execute an existing stored procedure from VBA code, you can use the Execute method of the ADO Connection or Command object. Here's how:

■ With the Execute method of the Connection object:

```
conn.Execute "procName"
```

■ With the Execute method of the Command object:

```
cmd.CommandText = "procName"
cmd.CommandType = adCmdStoredProc
cmd.Execute
rst. Open cmd
```

If the stored procedure requires parameters, parameter values follow the procedure name as a comma-separated list. Here's an example procedure that executes the procEnterData stored procedure and contains the values for its two parameters:

```
Sub RunProc_WithParam()
    Dim conn As ADODB.Connection

    Set conn = CurrentProject.Connection
    conn.Execute "procEnterData ""My Company2"", ""(234) 334-3344"""
    conn.Close
    Set conn = Nothing
End Sub
```

Instead of surrounding parameters with sets of double quotes, you can use single quotes like this:

```
conn.Execute "procEnterData 'My Company2', '(234) 334-3344'"
```

The procedure in Hands-On 23-5 runs the stored procedure named procEnterData created in Hands-On 23-4. Notice how this procedure uses the InputBox function to obtain the parameter values from the user instead of hard-coding them in the Execute method of the Connection object (as shown above). Still another way of providing parameter values to a stored procedure would be via an Access form. I will leave this idea for you to try on your own.

◎ Hands-On 23-5: Executing a Parameterized Stored Procedure

1. Switch to the Visual Basic Editor window and insert a new module.

2. In the module's Code window, enter the Execute_StoredProcWithParam procedure as shown below.

```
Sub Execute_StoredProcWithParam()
    Dim conn As ADODB.Connection
    Dim strCompany As String
    Dim strPhone As String

    On Error GoTo ErrorHandler

    Set conn = CurrentProject.Connection

    strCompany = InputBox("Please enter company name;", "Input Company")

    strPhone = InputBox("Please enter the phone number:", "Input Phone")

    If strCompany <> "" And strPhone <> "" Then
        conn.Execute "procEnterData " & strCompany & ", " & strPhone
    End If

ExitHere:
    If Not conn Is Nothing Then
        If conn.State = adStateOpen Then conn.Close
    End If
    Set conn = Nothing
    Exit Sub
ErrorHandler:
    MsgBox Err.Number & ":" & Err.Description
    Resume ExitHere
End Sub
```

When you run the parameterized stored procedure in Hands-On 23-5, Access displays an input box for each parameter where you can type in the value you want to insert. After you have supplied both required parameters, a new record is entered into the Shippers table.

Another way to write a statement to execute a stored procedure is by using the SQL EXECUTE command (or its shortened version — EXEC) like this:

```
conn.Execute "EXECUTE procEnterData " & strCompany & ", " & strPhone
```

or

```
conn.Execute "EXEC procEnterData " & strCompany & ", " & strPhone
```

Deleting a Stored Procedure

Use the DROP PROCEDURE (or DROP PROC) statement to delete a stored procedure. The syntax looks like this:

```
DROP PROCEDURE procedureName
```

The example procedure below deletes the stored procedure named procEnterData from the current database.

◉ Hands-On 23-6: Deleting a Stored Procedure

1. Switch to the Visual Basic Editor window and insert a new module.
2. In the module's Code window, enter the Delete_StoredProc procedure as shown below.

```
Sub Delete_StoredProc()
    Dim conn As ADODB.Connection

    On Error GoTo ErrorHandler

    Set conn = CurrentProject.Connection

    conn.Execute "DROP PROCEDURE procEnterData; "
ExitHere:
    If Not conn Is Nothing Then
        If conn.State = adStateOpen Then conn.Close
    End If
    Set conn = Nothing
    Exit Sub
ErrorHandler:
    If InStr(1, Err.Description, "cannot find") Then
        MsgBox "The procedure you want to delete " & _
                "does not exist.", _
                vbDefaultButton1 + vbInformation, "Request failed"
    Else
        MsgBox Err.Number & ":" & Err.Description
    End If
    Resume ExitHere
End Sub
```

Changing Database Records with Stored Procedures

Stored procedures can perform various actions similar to what Access Action queries and Select queries with parameters can do. For example, here's how you would write a statement to create a stored procedure that, when executed, deletes a record from the Shippers table:

```
conn.Execute "CREATE PROCEDURE usp_DeleteRec " & _
                "(Id INTEGER) " & _
                "AS " & _
                "DELETE * FROM Shippers WHERE ShipperId = Id;"
```

To update a phone number in a specified record in the Shippers table, you may want to create a stored procedure that performs the specified record update with the following statement:

```
conn.Execute "CREATE PROCEDURE usp_UpdatePhone " & _
             "(Id Integer, tel text (24)) " & _
             "AS " & _
             "UPDATE Shippers SET Phone = tel " & _
             "WHERE ShipperId = Id;"
```

Chapter Summary

This chapter introduced you to two powerful database objects you can use in Access: views and stored procedures. You learned how views are used as virtual tables to make specific rows and columns from one or more tables available to your Access users. Remember that views are similar to SELECT statements, except they cannot contain the ORDER BY clause to sort the data and they do not allow parameters. Views can be used in queries to hide from users the complexity of joins between the tables. Converting your Access queries into views and stored procedures will help migrate your Access applications to the SQL Server environment in the future.

This chapter concludes Part III of this book, which presented numerous examples of using SQL DDL statements inside VBA procedures and in the Access SQL Query Design window. In particular, you learned how DDL statements are used to create tables, views, stored procedures, primary keys, indexes, and constraints that define the database. You also learned a couple of advanced Data Manipulation Language (DML) statements. Although there is more to Access SQL than this part has covered, this should be quite sufficient to get you started using SQL in your own applications.

PART IV

Event Programming in Forms and Reports

The behavior of Microsoft Access objects such as forms, reports, and controls can be modified by writing programming code known as an event procedure or an event handler.

In this part of the book you learn how you can make your forms, reports, and controls do useful things by writing event procedures in class modules.

Chapter 24

Using Form Events

In Chapter 1, you got a quick introduction to events, event properties, and event procedures. I walked you through an event procedure that changed the background color of a text box control placed on a form. Now is a good time to go back to the beginning of this book and review these topics. Here's a rundown of the terms you need to be familiar with:

Event — Events are things that happen to an object. Events occur when you move a mouse; press a key; make changes to data; open a form; add, modify, or delete a record; etc. An event can be triggered by the user or by the operating system.

Event property — Forms, reports, and controls have various event properties you can use to trigger desired actions. When an event occurs, Microsoft Access runs a procedure assigned to an event property. Event properties are listed in the Event tab of the object's property sheet. The name of the event property begins with the word On followed by the event's name. Therefore, the On Click event property corresponds to the Click event, and the On Got Focus event property is used for responding to the GotFocus event.

Event procedure — This is programming code you write to specify how a form, report, or control should respond to a particular event. By writing event procedures you can modify the application's built-in response to an event.

Event trapping — When you assign a program to an event property, you set an event trap. When you trap an event you interrupt the default processing that Access would normally carry out in response to the user's keypress or mouse click.

Sequence of events — Events occur in a predefined order. For example, the Click event occurs before the DoubleClick event. When you perform an action, several events occur, one after the other. For instance, the following form and control events occur when you open a form:

> Open - Load - Resize - Activate - Current - Enter (control) - GotFocus (control)

Closing the form triggers the following control and form events:

> Exit (control) - LostFocus (control) - Unload - Deactivate - Close

To find out whether a particular event is triggered in response to a user action, you may want to place the MsgBox statement inside the event procedure for the event you want to test. Microsoft Access forms, reports, and controls recognize numerous events.

Events can be organized by object (form, report, control) or by cause (what caused the event to happen). This chapter is filled with numerous examples of event procedures you can write to make your forms and reports dynamic. You can also experiment with various events in the data entry/lookup application located in the downloadable AssetDataEntry.mdb file. You will find several examples from this application discussed in Chapter 26.

Microsoft Access forms can respond to a variety of events. These events allow you to manage entire records and respond to changes in the data. You can determine what happens when records are added, changed, or deleted, or when a different record becomes current. You can decide how the form appears to the user when it is first displayed on the screen and what happens when the form is closed. You can also manage problems that occur when the data is unavailable. As you design your custom forms, you will find that some form events are used more frequently than others. The following sections show numerous hands-on examples of event procedures you can write for Access forms.

Data Events

Data events occur when you change the data in a control or record placed on a form, or when you move the focus from one record to another.

Current

The Current event occurs when the form is opened or requeried and when the focus moves to a different record. Use the Current event to synchronize data among forms or move focus to a specific control.

The event procedure in Hands-On 24-1 sets the BackColor property of the form's header (Section 1) to red (255) for each discontinued product. The Form_Current event will occur each time you move to a new record if the specified condition is true.

◎ Hands-On 24-1: Writing the Form_Current Event Procedure

1. Open the **Acc2003_Chap24.mdb** file from the book's downloadable files or, if you'd like to start from scratch, create a new Microsoft Office Access database. This database should contain tables, queries, forms, and reports from the sample Northwind database. You can import these objects by choosing **File | Get External Data | Import** or you can create a copy of the Northwind database to be used for this chapter's hands-on exercises.

2. In the Database window of the Acc2003_Chap24 database, select the **Products** form and click the **Design** button.

3. Choose **View | Properties** or click the **Properties** button on the toolbar to display the Form properties sheet.

4. Click the **Event** tab. Click next to the **On Current** event property and choose **[Event Procedure]** from the drop-down box. Click the **Build** button (…).

5. Access opens the Visual Basic Editor window and writes the stub of the Form_Current event procedure. Complete the code of the Form_Current event procedure as shown below.

```
Private Sub Form_Current()
    If Discontinued = True Then
        Me.Section(1).BackColor = 255
        Me.Picture = ""
    Else
        Me.Picture = "C:\Program Files\" & _
            "Microsoft Office\Office11\" & _
            "Bitmaps\Styles\Stone.bmp"
    End If
End Sub
```

6. To test the above event procedure, activate the **Products** form that is currently open in the background in the Design view. Choose **View | Form View**. Use the record selectors to move to record 5. Because this record is marked as Discontinued, the code in the Form_Current event will change the header section's color to red.

BeforeInsert

This event occurs when the first character is typed in a new record but before the new record is created. Use this event to verify that the data is valid or to display information about data being added. You can use this event to place default values in the fields at run time. The BeforeInsert event can be cancelled if the data being added does not meet specific criteria.

The event procedure in Hands-On 24-2 demonstrates how to enter a default value in the Country field when a user begins to enter data in the form.

⦿ Hands-On 24-2: Writing the Form_BeforeInsert Event Procedure

1. Use the Form Wizard to create a new form based on the Northwind Customers table.

2. Select the following fields: **CustomerId**, **CompanyName**, **Address**, **City**, **Region**, **PostalCode**, and **Country**. Step through the Form Wizard screen, pressing the **Next** button until you get to the screen where you are asked for the form's title. Type **New Customers** for the form's title and click **Finish**.

3. Access opens the New Customers form in Form view. Choose **View | Design View** and click the **Properties** button to activate the Form properties sheet.

4. In the Form properties sheet, click the **Data** tab and set the Data Entry property to **Yes**.

5. In the Form properties sheet, click the **Event** tab. Click next to the **Before Insert** event property and choose **[Event Procedure]** from the drop-down box. Click the **Build** button (…).

6. Access opens the Visual Basic Editor window and writes the stub of the Form_BeforeInsert event procedure. Complete the code of the Form_ BeforeInsert event procedure as shown below.

```
Private Sub Form_BeforeInsert(Cancel As Integer)
    Me.Country = "USA"
End Sub
```

7. Switch to the New Customers form currently open in the Design view.

8. Choose **View | Form View**. As soon as you start filling in the form's text boxes, the text "USA" appears in the Country field.

9. Close the New Customers form without saving it.

AfterInsert

The AfterInsert event occurs when a new record has been inserted. Use this event to requery the recordset when a new record is added or to display other information.

The event procedure in Hands-On 24-3 retrieves the total number of records in the Customers table after a new record has been inserted.

⊚ Hands-On 24-3: Writing the Form_AfterInsert Event Procedure

This hands-on uses the New Customers form created in Hands-On 24-2.

1. In the Visual Basic Editor window, double-click **Form_New Customers**.

2. In the Code window, you will see the event procedure prepared in Hands-On 24-2. Below this procedure code, enter the Form_AfterInsert event procedure as shown below.

```
Private Sub Form_AfterInsert()
    Dim conn As New ADODB.Connection
    Dim rst As New ADODB.Recordset
    Set conn = CurrentProject.Connection

    rst.CursorType = adOpenKeyset
    rst.Open "Customers", conn
    MsgBox "Added " & rst.RecordCount & _
        "th customer."

    rst.Close
    Set rst = Nothing
    conn.Close
    Set conn = Nothing
End Sub
```

3. To test the above event procedure, open the New Customers form in Form view. Type **TRYIT** in the Customer ID text box. Type **Test Events** in the Company Name text box. Use the record selector to move to the next

record. Access executes the code in the Form_AfterInsert event procedure and displays the total number of records.

BeforeUpdate

This event occurs after a record has been edited but before it is written to the table. This event is triggered by moving to another record or attempting to save the current record. The BeforeUpdate event takes place after the BeforeInsert event. Use this event to validate the entire record and display a message to confirm the change. The BeforeUpdate event can be cancelled if the record cannot be accepted.

The event procedure in Hands-On 24-4 will supply the value for the EmployeeId index field before the newly entered record is saved.

◉ Hands-On 24-4: Writing the Form_BeforeUpdate Event Procedure

This hands-on uses the New Customers form created in Hands-On 24-2.

1. In the Visual Basic Editor window, double-click **Form_New Customers**.

2. In the Code window, other procedures prepared in Hands-On 24-2 and 24-3 will be listed. Enter the following Form_BeforeUpdate event procedure below the last procedure code.

```
Private Sub Form_BeforeUpdate(Cancel As Integer)
    If Not IsNull(Me.CompanyName) Then
        Me.CustomerID = Left(CompanyName, 3) & _
            Right(CompanyName, 2)
        MsgBox "You just added Customer ID: " & _
            Me.CustomerID
    Else
        MsgBox "Please enter Company Name.", _
            vbOKOnly, "Missing Data"
        Me.CompanyName.SetFocus
        Cancel = True
    End If
End Sub
```

3. To test the above event procedure, open the New Customers form and switch to Form view. Type **Event Enterprises** in the Company Name box. Click the record selector to move to the next record. The BeforeUpdate event procedure code will run at this point and you will see a message box that displays the custom-generated Customer ID. Click **OK** to the message. Another message will appear with the number of total records. This message box is generated by the AfterInsert event procedure that was prepared in Hands-On 24-3.

4. Close the New Customers form.

AfterUpdate

This event occurs after the record changes have been saved in the database. It is also invoked when a control loses focus and after the data in the control has changed. Use the AfterUpdate event to update data in other controls on the form or to move focus to a different record or a control.

The event procedure in Hands-On 24-5 creates an audit trail for all newly added records, as illustrated in Figure 24-1.

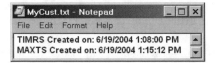

Figure 24-1: The Form_AfterUpdate event procedure is used here to store information about newly added records in a text file.

◎ Hands-On 24-5: Writing the Form_AfterUpdate Event Procedure

This hands-on uses the New Customers form that was created in Hands-On 24-2.

1. In the Visual Basic Editor window, double-click **Form_New Customers**.

2. Other procedures that were prepared in Hands-On 24-2 and 24-3 will be listed in the Code window. Enter the following Form_AfterUpdate event procedure below the last procedure code.

3. For this code to work you must set the reference to **Microsoft Scripting Runtime** in the References dialog box. Choose **Tools | References** in the Visual Basic Editor window.

```
Private Sub Form_AfterUpdate()
    Dim fso As FileSystemObject
    Dim myFile As Object
    On Error Resume Next

    Set fso = New FileSystemObject
    Set myFile = fso.GetFile("C:\MyCust.txt")

    If Err.Number = 0 Then
        ' open text file
        Set myFile = fso.OpenTextFile("C:\MyCust.txt", 8)
    Else
        ' create a text file
        Set myFile = fso.CreateTextFile("C:\MyCust.txt")
    End If
    myFile.writeLine UCase(Me.CustomerID) & _
        " Created on: " & Date & " " & Time

    myFile.Close
Set fso = Nothing

    End Sub
```

The procedure first checks whether the text file named C:\MyCust.txt exists on your computer. If the file is found, then the Err.Number statement returns zero. At this point you want to open the file. The "8" represents the open mode for appending. You would use "2" if you wanted to replace the contents of a file with the new data.

4. To test the above event procedure, switch to the New Customers form and open it in Form view. Type **Time Organizers** in the Company Name box. Click the record selector to move to the next record. The BeforeUpdate event procedure code you prepared in Hands-On 24-4 will run at this point and you should see a message box that displays the custom-generated Customer ID. Click **OK** to the message. The next message box notifies you about the location of the audit trail (the result of the AfterUpdate event procedure prepared in this hands-on). Click **OK** to the message. Another message will appear with the number of total records. This message box is generated by the AfterInsert event procedure that was prepared in Hands-On 24-3.

As you enter more customer records using the New Customers form, events are executed in the following order:

BeforeInsert (Hands-On 24-2)
BeforeUpdate (Hands-On 24-4)
AfterUpdate (Hands-On 24-5)
AfterInsert (Hands-On 24-3)

5. Close the New Customers form.

Dirty

The Dirty event occurs when the contents of a form or the text portion of a combo box changes. This event will be triggered by an attempt to enter a character directly in the form's text box or combo box. Use this event to determine if the record can be changed.

The event procedure in Hands-On 24-6 disallows changes to form data when the CategoryID is less than or equal to 4.

⊚ Hands-On 24-6: Writing the Form_Dirty Event Procedure

1. Use the Form Wizard to create a new form based on the Northwind database Categories table. Add all the fields as listed in the Categories table and use the **Columnar** option in the New Form dialog box. Type **Product Categories** for the form's title and click **Finish**.

2. Access opens the Product Categories form in Form view. Choose **View | Design View** and click the **Properties** button to activate the Form properties sheet.

3. In the Form properties sheet, click the **Event** tab. Click next to the **On Dirty** event property and choose **[Event Procedure]** from the drop-down box. Click the **Build** button (...).

4. Access opens the Visual Basic Editor window and writes the stub of the Form_Dirty event procedure. Complete the code of the Form_Dirty event procedure as shown below.

```
Private Sub Form_Dirty(Cancel As Integer)
    If CategoryID <= 4 Then
        MsgBox "You cannot make changes in this record."
        Cancel = True
    End If
End Sub
```

5. Open the **Product Categories** form in Form view. Try to make any changes to the original records. You will not be able to make changes to the data if the product's CategoryID is less than or equal to 4.

OnUndo

The OnUndo event occurs when the user undoes a change to a combo box control, form, or text box control. By setting the Cancel argument to True, you can cancel the undo operation and leave the control or form in its edited state. The Undo event for forms is triggered when the user clicks the Undo button on the toolbar, presses the Esc key, or calls the Undo method.

Delete

The Delete event occurs when you select one or more records for deletion and before the records are actually removed from the table. Use this event to place restrictions on the data that can be deleted. When deleting multiple records, the Delete event occurs for each record. This enables you to confirm or cancel each deletion in your event procedure code. You can cancel the deletion in the Delete or BeforeDelConfirm events by setting the Cancel argument to True.

After the record is deleted, the focus moves to the next record and the Current event for that record occurs.

The event procedure in Hands-On 24-7 demonstrates how to disallow deletion of records when CategoryID is less than or equal to 8 and ask the user to confirm the deletion for other records.

⊚ Hands-On 24-7: Writing the Form_Delete Event Procedure

This hands-on uses the Product Categories form created in Hands-On 24-6.

1. In the Visual Basic Editor window, double-click **Form_Product Categories**, which was created in Hands-On 24-6.

2. Enter the following Form_Delete event procedure below the Form_Dirty event procedure prepared in Hands-On 24-6.

```
Private Sub Form_Delete(Cancel As Integer)
    If CategoryID <= 8 Then
        MsgBox "You can't delete the original categories."
        Cancel = True
    Else
```

```
            If MsgBox("Do you really want to delete " & _
                "this record?", vbOKCancel, _
                "Delete Verification") = vbCancel Then
                    Cancel = True
            End If
        End If
    End Sub
```

3. To test the above event procedure, open the **Product Categories** form in Form view.

4. Click on the record selector to the left of the first record and press the **Delete** key. You can also click the **Delete Record** button (🗙) on the toolbar. At this point Access will execute the code of the Form_Delete event procedure. You should see the message that you cannot delete original product categories.

5. Add a new category and try to delete it. If there is no code in the Form_BeforeDelConfirm event procedure (see Hands-On 24-8), you will be prompted twice to confirm the deletion.

6. Close the Product Categories form.

BeforeDelConfirm

This event occurs after the Delete event, before the Delete Confirm dialog box is displayed. If you don't write your own BeforeDelConfirm event, Access will display a standard delete confirmation message. You can use this event to write a custom deletion confirmation message.

The event procedure in Hands-On 24-8 demonstrates how to eliminate the Access default delete confirmation message.

◎ Hands-On 24-8: Writing the Form_BeforeDelConfirm Event Procedure

This hands-on uses the Product Categories form created in Hands-On 24-6.

1. In the Visual Basic Editor window, double-click **Form_Product Categories**, which was created in Hands-On 24-6 and modified in Hands-On 24-7.

2. In the Code window, two event procedures are shown that were prepared in Hands-On 24-6 and 24-7. Enter the following Form_BeforeDelConfirm event procedure below the last procedure code.

```
Private Sub Form_BeforeDelConfirm(Cancel _
        As Integer, Response As Integer)
    Response = acDataErrContinue
End Sub
```

In the procedure code above, this statement

```
Response = acDataErrContinue
```

will suppress the default dialog box that Microsoft Access normally displays when you attempt to delete a record.

3. To test the above event procedure, activate the **Product Categories** form and open it in Form view.

4. Add a new record, save it, and then delete it. The Form_Delete event procedure prepared in Hands-On 24-7 will be executed at this point, and you will see a dialog with your custom prompt to confirm the deletion. Click **Yes**. Notice that Access does not display its default message asking you to confirm the deletion of the specified number of records.

Note: Instead of writing your custom confirmation message in the Form_Delete event procedure, you can place it in the Form_BeforeDelConfirm event procedure as shown below:

```
Private Sub Form_BeforeDelConfirm(Cancel As Integer, _
                                   Response As Integer)
    ' remove the default Access dialog box that prompts to confirm deletion
    Response = acDataErrContinue
    If MsgBox("Do you really want to delete this record?", _
            vbOKCancel) = vbCancel Then
        Cancel = True
    End If
End Sub
```

AfterDelConfirm

This event occurs after the record is actually deleted or after deletion is cancelled in the BeforeDelConfirm event procedure. Use the AfterDelConfirm event to move to another record or to display a message indicating whether the deletion was successful.

The Status argument allows you to check whether deletion progressed normally or was cancelled by the user or Visual Basic. The following constants can be used for the Status argument in the AfterDelConfirm event procedure: acDelete(6), acDeleteCancel(1), acDeleteOK(0), or acDeleteUserCancel(2).

The event procedure in Hands-On 24-9 displays a message when a record is successfully deleted.

Hands-On 24-9: Writing the Form_AfterDelConfirm Event Procedure

This hands-on uses the Product Categories form created in Hands-On 24-6.

1. In the Visual Basic Editor window, double-click **Form_Product Categories**.

2. The Code window appears with several event procedures that were prepared in previous hands-on exercises. Enter the following Form_After-DelConfirm event procedure below the last procedure code.

```
Private Sub Form_AfterDelConfirm(Status As Integer)
    MsgBox "The selected record was deleted."
    Debug.Print "Status = " & Status
End Sub
```

3. To test the above event procedure, switch to the **Product Categories** form and open it in Form view.

4. Add a new record, save it, and delete it. Access will execute the code in the Form_Delete event procedure (Hands-On 24-7) that displays a message box asking you whether you want to delete the record. Click **Yes**. Access will then check the code in Form_BeforeDelConfirm (Hands-On 24-8). The statement Response = acDataErrContinue will cause Access to suppress its default Delete Confirm dialog box and you will not be prompted again to reconfirm the deletion. Finally, Form_AfterDelConfirm will run and you will see a message about the successful deletion.

5. Close the Product Categories form.

Focus Events

Focus events occur when a form becomes active or inactive and when a form or form control loses or gains the focus.

Activate

The Activate event occurs whenever the form gets focus and becomes the active window. This situation occurs when the form is first opened, and when the user activates the form again by clicking on the form or one of its controls. Use this event to display or hide supporting forms or toolbars.

The event procedure in Hands-On 24-10 will hide the tab labeled Personal Information when the Employees form is displayed. Notice that the tabs are numbered beginning with 0, hence the second tab in the tab control placed on the form has an index value of 1.

⊙ Hands-On 24-10: Writing the Form_Activate Event Procedure

1. In the Visual Basic Editor window, double-click **Form_Employees.**

2. In the Code window there are a number of event procedures and functions already written for this form. Enter the following Form_Activate event procedure below the last procedure code.

```
Private Sub Form_Activate()
    Me.TabCtl0.Pages(1).Visible = False
End Sub
```

3. To test the above event procedure, activate the **Employees** form in Form view. Notice that only the tab labeled Company Info is shown.

4. Close the Employees form.

Deactivate

The Deactivate event occurs when the user switches to another form or closes the form. Use this event to display or hide supporting forms or toolbars.

The event procedure in Hands-On 24-11 shows how to display a Print Preview toolbar when the focus moves to a different window.

◉ Hands-On 24-11: Writing the Form_Deactivate Event Procedure

1. In the Visual Basic Editor window, double-click **Form_Employees**.

2. In the Code window there are a number of event procedures and functions already written for this form. Enter the following Form_Deactivate event procedure below the last procedure code.

```
Private Sub Form_Deactivate()
    DoCmd.ShowToolbar "Print Preview", acToolbarYes
End Sub
```

3. To test the above event procedure, activate the **Employees** form in Form view. Now switch to the Database window. Notice that the Print Preview toolbar is visible.

4. Turn off the Print Preview toolbar by choosing **View | Toolbars | Print Preview**.

5. Close the Employees form.

GotFocus

This event happens when a form receives the focus, provided that there are no visible or enabled controls on the form. The GotFocus event is frequently used for controls placed on the form and hardly ever used for the form itself.

LostFocus

The LostFocus event happens when a form loses focus, provided there are no visible or enabled controls on the form. This event is frequently used for controls placed on the form and rarely used for a form.

Mouse Events

Mouse events occur when you move a mouse or click any of the available mouse buttons.

Click

The Click event occurs when you click a mouse button on a blank area of a form, a form's record selector, or a control placed on the form.

The event procedure in Hands-On 24-12 will cause a text box control to move one inch to the right when you click the record selector.

◉ Hands-On 24-12: Writing the Form_Click Event Procedure

1. Create a new form with two text boxes. Position both text boxes starting at 1 inch on the horizontal ruler. Save the form as **Mouse Test**.

2. Click the **Properties** button to activate the Form properties sheet, if it is not already open.

3. In the Form properties sheet, click the **Event** tab. Click next to the **On Click** event property and choose **[Event Procedure]** from the drop-down box. Click the **Build** button (…).

4. Access opens the Visual Basic Editor window and writes the stub of the Form_Click event procedure. Complete the code of the Form_Click event procedure as shown below.

```
Private Sub Form_Click()
    MsgBox "Form Click Event Occurred."
    Me.Text0.Left = Text0.Left + 1440
End Sub
```

The first text box control placed on the form is automatically named Text0. The Left property is used to specify an object's location on a form or report. The above procedure moves a text box control one inch to the right. Screen measurements are expressed in units called twips and there are 1440 twips per inch. Thus, to calculate the new position of the text box, you must add 1440 to the current position.

5. To test the above event procedure, open the **Mouse Test** form in Form view. Click on the record selector (a small box or bar to the left of a record). This will cause the Form_Click event procedure code to execute and you will see a message box. After clicking **OK** in response to the message, the first text box control will move one inch to the right.

DblClick

The DblClick event occurs when you double-click on a blank area of the form, the form's record selector, or a control placed on the form.

MouseDown

The MouseDown event occurs when you click on a blank area of the form, the form's record selector, or a control placed on the form. This event occurs before the Click event. The MouseDown event has four arguments:

- **Button** — Identifies the state of the mouse buttons. Use acLeftButton to check for the left mouse button, acRightButton to check for the right mouse button, and acMiddleButton to check for the middle mouse button.
- **Shift** — Specifies the state of the Shift, Ctrl, and Alt keys when the button specified by the Button argument was pressed or released. Use acShiftMask(1) to test for the Shift key, acCtrlMask(2) to test for the Ctrl key, and acAltMask(4) to test for the Alt key. You can test for any combination of buttons. For example, to specify that Ctrl and Alt were pressed, use the value of 6 (2+4) as the Shift argument.
- **X** — Specifies the horizontal (x) position from the left edge of the form or control.
- **Y** — Specifies the vertical (y) position from the top edge of the form or control.

The event procedure in Hands-On 24-13 displays two messages when the form's MouseDown event is fired. The first message tells whether you pressed the Alt, Ctrl, or Shift key, and the second one announces which mouse button was used.

◉ Hands-On 24-13: Writing the Form_MouseDown Event Procedure

1. Create a new form based on the Products table. Add all the available fields to the form. Save this form as **Products Test**.

2. Click the **Properties** button to activate the Form properties sheet.

3. In the Form properties sheet, click the **Event** tab. Click next to the **On Mouse Down** event property and choose **[Event Procedure]** from the drop-down box. Click the **Build** button (...).

4. Place the code shown below in the Form_MouseDown event.

```
Private Sub Form_MouseDown(Button As Integer, _
                           Shift As Integer, _
                           X As Single, _
                           Y As Single)
    Debug.Print "Mouse Down"

    Select Case Shift
        Case 0
            MsgBox "You did not press a key."
        Case 1 ' or acShiftMask
            MsgBox "You pressed SHIFT."
        Case 2 ' or acCtrlMask
            MsgBox "You pressed CTRL."
        Case 3
            MsgBox "You pressed CTRL and SHIFT."
        Case 4 ' or acAltMask
            MsgBox "You pressed ALT."
        Case 5
            MsgBox "You pressed ALT and SHIFT."
        Case 6
            MsgBox "You pressed CTRL and ALT."
        Case 7
            MsgBox "You pressed CTRL, ALT, and SHIFT."
    End Select

    If Button = 1 Then ' acLeftButton
        MsgBox "You pressed the left button."
    ElseIf Button = 2 Then 'acRightButton
        MsgBox "You pressed the right button."
    ElseIf Button = 4 Then 'acMiddleButton
        MsgBox "You pressed the middle button."
    End If
End Sub
```

5. To test the above event procedure, switch to the **Products Test** form and open it in Form view. Click on the record selector while holding down any mouse button and pressing the Shift, Ctrl, or Alt keys or their combinations.

6.   Close the Products Test form.

MouseMove

The MouseMove event occurs when you move the mouse over the blank area of the form, the form's record selector, or a control placed on the form. The MouseMove event occurs before the Click event and has the same arguments as the MouseDown event.

MouseUp

The MouseUp event occurs when you release the mouse button. It occurs before the Click event and uses the same arguments as the MouseDown and MouseMove events.

MouseWheel

The MouseWheel event occurs in Form view, Datasheet view, PivotChart view, or PivotTable view when the user rotates the mouse wheel on a mouse device that has a wheel. This event takes the following two arguments:

■   **Page** — Returns True if the page was changed.
■   **Count** — Specifies the number of lines that were scrolled with the mouse wheel.

➡ **Note:**   Because there is no Cancel argument, you cannot use the MouseWheel event to prevent users from using the mouse wheel to scroll through records on a form. If your application requires this feature, search the web for the Microsoft Knowledge-Base article Q278379.

Keyboard Events

Keyboard events occur when you press a key on the keyboard or send a keystroke using the SendKeys method.

KeyDown

The KeyDown event occurs when there are no controls on the form or if the form's KeyPreview property is set to Yes. A form's KeyPreview property determines whether form keyboard events are invoked before control keyboard events.

The KeyDown event takes the following two arguments:

■   **KeyCode** — Determines which key was pressed. To specify key codes, use members of the KeyCodeConstants class in the VBA Object Library in the Object Browser.
■   **Shift** — Determines if the Shift, Ctrl, or Alt key was pressed. Use acShiftMask(1) to test for the Shift key, acCtrlMask(2) to test for the Ctrl key, and acAltMask(4) to test for the Alt key. You can test for any

combination of buttons. For example, to specify that Ctrl and Alt were pressed, use the value of 6 (2+4) as the Shift argument.

The event procedure in Hands-On 24-14 displays a message when you press one of the following keys: F1, Home, Tab, Shift, Ctrl, or Alt.

⊚ Hands-On 24-14: Writing the Form_KeyDown Event Procedure

1. Open the **Suppliers** form in Design view.

2. Click the **Properties** button and, in the Form properties sheet, click the **Event** tab.

3. Set the Key Preview property to **Yes**.

4. Save the Suppliers form.

5. In the Code window there are a couple of event procedures already written for this form. Enter the following Form_KeyDown event procedure below the last procedure code.

```
Private Sub Form_KeyDown _
        (KeyCode As Integer, Shift As Integer)
    Select Case KeyCode
        Case vbKeyF1
            MsgBox "You pressed the F1 key."
        Case vbKeyHome
            MsgBox "You pressed the Home key."
        Case vbKeyTab
            MsgBox "You pressed the Tab key."
    End Select
    Select Case Shift
        Case acShiftMask
            MsgBox "You pressed the SHIFT key."
        Case acCtrlMask
            MsgBox "You pressed the CTRL key."
        Case acAltMask
            MsgBox "You pressed the ALT key."
    End Select
End Sub
```

6. To test the above event procedure, open the **Suppliers** form in Form view. Press one of the following keys: **F1**, **Home**, **Tab**, **Shift**, **Ctrl**, or **Alt**.

7. Close the Suppliers form.

KeyUp

The KeyUp event occurs when there are no controls on the form or if the form's KeyPreview property is set to Yes. This event can be cancelled by setting the KeyCode argument to zero (0).

The event procedure in Hands-On 24-15 will print the code and the value of the key that was released in the Immediate window.

◎ Hands-On 24-15: Writing the Form_KeyUp Event Procedure

1. Open the **Suppliers** form in Design view.

2. Click the **Properties** button and, in the Form properties sheet, click the **Event** tab.

3. Set the Key Preview property to **Yes**.

4. Save the Suppliers form.

5. In the Code window there are a couple of event procedures already written for this form. Enter the following Form_KeyUp event procedure below the last procedure code.

```
Private Sub Form_KeyUp(KeyCode As Integer, _
                    Shift As Integer)
    Debug.Print "You released " & _
        KeyCode & Space(1) & Chr(KeyCode)
End Sub
```

6. To test the above event procedure, open the **Suppliers** form in Form view. Press the **Down Arrow** key three times to move to the Address field. Press the **End** key to move to the Home Page field. Type **www.exotliq.com**. Use the **Backspace** key to delete what you have just typed.

7. Switch to the Visual Basic Editor window and activate the Immediate window. You should see a listing of the keys that were released while performing step 6 above.

8. Close the Suppliers form.

KeyPress

The KeyPress event occurs when you press and release a key or a key combination. The KeyPress event happens when there are no controls on the form or if the form's KeyPreview property is set to Yes. The KeyPress event responds only to the ANSI characters generated by the keyboard. This event can be cancelled by setting the KeyAscii argument to zero (0).

The event procedure in Hands-On 24-16 prints the ASCII code and the value of the pressed key in the Immediate window. Upon pressing the Escape key (KeyAscii 27), the form will close.

◎ Hands-On 24-16: Writing the Form_KeyPress Event Procedure

1. In the Database window, right-click the **Suppliers** form and choose **Copy**.

2. Right-click in a blank area of the Database window and choose **Paste**.

3. Type **Suppliers KeyPress** as the name of the form and press **OK**.

4. Open the **Suppliers KeyPress** form in Design view.

5. Click the **Properties** button and, in the Form properties sheet, click the **Event** tab.

6. Set the Key Preview property to **Yes**.

7. Set the On Key Press property to **[Event Procedure]** and press the **Build** button (...).

8. Access will create the event procedure stub. Enter the following Form_ KeyPress event procedure.

```
Private Sub Form_KeyPress(KeyAscii As Integer)
    Debug.Print "KeyAscii = " & KeyAscii & _
        Space(1) & "= " & Chr(KeyAscii)
    If KeyAscii = 27 Then
        DoCmd.Close
    Else
        KeyAscii = 0
    End If
End Sub
```

The statement KeyAscii = 0 will disable any input to all the controls on the form. Recall that a form's KeyPreview property determines whether form keyboard events are invoked before control keyboard events. To prevent keystrokes from going to the form's controls, the KeyPreview property must be set to Yes.

9. To test the above event procedure, open the **Suppliers KeyPress** form in Form view. Try to edit a field by typing some text. Because the input to all the controls on the form has been disabled by the Form_KeyPress event procedure, you cannot see any input. However, when you switch to the Immediate window, you will see the complete listing of keys that you pressed. Switch back to the Suppliers KeyPress form and press the **Escape** key to close this form.

Error Events

The Error event is triggered by run-time errors generated either in the Microsoft Access interface or by the Microsoft Jet database engine. The Error event does not trap VBA errors.

Error

The Error event occurs when there is a problem accessing data for the form. Use this event to suppress the standard error messages and display a custom error message instead.

The Error event takes the following two arguments:

▪ **DataErr** — Contains the number of the Microsoft Access error that occurred.

▪ **Response** — Determines whether or not error messages should be displayed. It may be one of the following constants:

  ▪ *acDataErrContinue* — Ignore the error and continue without displaying the default Microsoft Access error message.

  ▪ *acDataErrDisplay* — Display the default Microsoft Access error message. This is the default.

The event procedure in Hands-On 24-17 displays a custom message when an attempt is made to add a new record with a customer ID that already exists. The standard Microsoft Access error message is not displayed.

◎ Hands-On 24-17: Writing the Form_Error Event Procedure

1. Create a new form based on the **Customers** table. Add all the fields from the Customers table and save the new form as **Customers Data Entry**.

2. In the Design view of the Customers Data Entry form, choose **Edit | Select Form**.

3. Choose **View | Properties** to activate the Form properties sheet.

4. Click the **Data** tab and set the form's DataEntry property to **Yes**.

5. Click the **Event** tab, set the On Error property to **[Event Procedure]**, and press the **Build** button (...).

6. Access will create the event procedure stub. Enter the following Form_Error event procedure

```
Private Sub Form_Error(DataErr As Integer, Response As Integer)
    Dim strMsg As String
    Dim custId As String

    Const conDuplicateKey = 3022
    custId = Me.CustomerID

    If DataErr = conDuplicateKey Then
        ' Don't show built-in error messages
        Response = acDataErrContinue
        strMsg = "Customer " & custId & " already exists."
        ' Show a custom error message
        MsgBox strMsg, vbCritical, "Duplicate Value"
    End If
End Sub
```

7. Open the **Customers Data Entry** form in Form view mode.

8. Enter **ALFKI** in the CustomerId field and **Alfred Fiki** in the Company Name field. When you try to save this record, the Form_Error event procedure code will cause a message box to appear, saying that the customer already exists. Click **OK** to the message. Press **Esc** to cancel the changes to this record.

9. Close the Customers Data Entry form.

Filter Events

Filter events are triggered by opening or closing a filter window or when you are applying or removing a filter.

Filter

The Filter event occurs when you design a filter to limit the form's records to those matching specified criteria. This event takes place when you select the Filter By Form or Advanced Filter/Sort options. Use this event to remove the filter that was previously set, to enter initial settings for the filter, or to call your own custom filter dialog box. To cancel the filtering command, set the Cancel argument for the event procedure to True.

The event procedure in Hands-On 24-18 allows the user to use the Filter by Form option but disallows the use of the Advanced Filter/Sort option.

⊚ Hands-On 24-18: Writing the Form_Filter Event Procedure

This hands-on uses the Product Categories form created in Hands-On 24-6.

1. In the Visual Basic Editor window, open the **Product Categories** form.

2. The Code window shows other event procedures already written for this form. Enter the following Form_Filter event procedure below the last procedure code.

```
Private Sub Form_Filter(Cancel As Integer, _
            FilterType As Integer)
    Select Case FilterType
        Case acFilterByForm
            MsgBox "You selected to filter records " & _
                "by form.", vbOKOnly + vbInformation, _
                "Filter By Form"
            Me.CategoryName.SetFocus
            Me.CategoryID.Enabled = False
        Case acFilterAdvanced
            MsgBox "You are not authorized to use " & _
                " Advanced Filter/Sort.", _
                vbOKOnly + vbInformation, _
                "Advanced Filter By Form"
            Cancel = True
    End Select
End Sub
```

3. To test the above event procedure, open the **Product Categories** form in Form view.

4. Choose **Records | Filter | Filter by Form** (or click the **Filter by Form** button on the toolbar).

5. The code in the Form_Filter event procedure runs and you will see a message box. Click **OK**. The Filter by Form dialog box appears with the Category ID text box disabled. You can disable certain controls on the form if you don't want the user to filter by them.

6. Filter the form to display only records for **Seafood** and **Meat/Poultry**.

7. Remove the filter by clicking the **Remove Filter** button (🗹) on the toolbar or by choosing **Records | Remove Filter/Sort**.

8. Choose **Records | Filter | Advanced Filter/Sort**. You will not be able to use the advanced filter for this form because the form's Filter event has disabled this action.

9. Close the Product Categories form.

ApplyFilter

The ApplyFilter event occurs when you apply the filter to restrict the records. This event takes place when you select the Apply Filter/Sort, Filter by Selection, or Remove Filter/Sort options. Use this event to change the form display before the filter is applied or undo any changes made when the Filter event occurred.

The ApplyType argument can be one of the predefined constants shown in Table 24-1.

Table 24-1: ApplyType argument constants

Constant Name	Constant Value
acShowAllRecords	0
acApplyFilter	1
acCloseFilterWindow	2
acApplyServerFilter	3
acCloseServerFilterWindow	4

The event procedure in Hands-On 24-19 displays a different message depending on whether or not the user has made a selection in the Filter by Form window.

◎ Hands-On 24-19: Writing the Form_ApplyFilter Event Procedure

This hands-on uses the Product Categories form created in Hands-On 24-6.

1. In the Visual Basic Editor window, open the **Product Categories** form.

2. The Code window shows other event procedures already written for this form. Enter the following Form_ApplyFilter event procedure below the last procedure code.

```
Private Sub Form_ApplyFilter(Cancel As Integer, _
            ApplyType As Integer)
    Dim Response As Integer
    If ApplyType = acApplyFilter Then
        If Me.Filter = "" Then
            MsgBox "You did not select any criteria.", _
                vbOKOnly + vbCritical, "No Selection"
            GoTo ExitHere
        End If
        Response = MsgBox("The selected criteria " & _
```

```
                    "is as follows:" & vbCrLf & _
                    Me.Filter, vbOKCancel + vbQuestion, _
                    "Filter Criteria")
            End If
            If Response = vbCancel Then
                Cancel = True
            End If
            If ApplyType = acShowAllRecords Then
                Me.Filter = ""
                MsgBox "Filter was removed."
            End If
            If ApplyType = acCloseFilterWindow Then
                Response = MsgBox("Are you sure you " & _
                    "want to close the Filter window?", vbYesNo)
                If Response = vbNo Then
                    Cancel = True
                End If
            End If
    ExitHere:
        With Me.CategoryID
            .Enabled = True
            .SetFocus
        End With
    End Sub
```

3. To test the above event procedure, open the **Product Categories** form in Form view.

4. Choose **Records | Filter | Filter by Form** (or click the **Filter by Form** button on the toolbar). The Form_Filter event will be triggered (see Hands-On 24-18). Click **OK** to the message box.

5. Select a category from the Category Name combo box and click the **Apply Filter** button on the toolbar. This action will trigger the Form_ApplyFilter event procedure. Experiment with the form filter, testing other situations such as clicking the Apply Filter button when the filtering criteria were not specified or closing the Filter by Form window.

6. To test the condition that removes the filter, choose the filtering criteria and press **OK** to limit the records. Next, click the **Remove Filter** button. Notice that the name of this button changes to Remove Filter or Apply Filter depending on the situation.

7. Close the Product Categories form.

Timing Events

Timing events occur in response to a specified amount of time passing.

Timer

The Timer event occurs when the form is opened. The duration of this event is determined by the value (milliseconds) entered in the TimerInterval property located on the Event tab of the form's property sheet. Use this event to display a splash screen when the database is opened. The Timer event is helpful in limiting the time the record remains locked in multi-user applications.

The event procedure in Hands-On 24-20 will flash the button's text, "Preview Product List" (or the entire button if you use the commented code instead). For the code to work you must start the timer by changing the TimerInterval property from 0 (stopped) to the desired interval. A timer interval of 1,000 will invoke a timer event every second. The form's Load event procedure sets the form's TimerInterval property to 250, so the button text (or the entire button) is toggled once every quarter second.

You may change the timer interval manually by typing the value next to the form's TimerInterval property in the properties sheet or by placing the following statement in the Form_Load event:

```
Me.TimerInterval = 250
```

◎ Hands-On 24-20: Writing the Form_Timer Event Procedure

1. In the Visual Basic Editor window, open the **Products** form.

2. The Code window shows other event procedures already written for this form. Enter the following Form_Timer event procedure below the last procedure code.

```
Private Sub Form_Timer()
    Static OnOff As Integer
    If OnOff Then
        Me.PreviewReport.Caption = "Preview Product List"
        ' Me.PreviewReport.Visible = True
    Else
        Me.PreviewReport.Caption = ""
        ' Me.PreviewReport.Visible = False
    End If
    OnOff = Not OnOff
End Sub
```

3. Activate the **Product Categories** form in Design view.

4. Choose **Edit | Select Form** and click the **Properties** button on the toolbar.

5. In the Form properties sheet, click the **Event** tab.

6. Enter **250** in the TimerInterval property.

7. Choose **View | Form View**. Notice the flashing effect of the Preview Product List button's text.

8. Close the Products form.

➔ **Note:** To make the entire button flash, uncomment the commented lines of code and comment the original lines. Next, open the Products form in Form view and notice that the entire button is now flashing.

PivotTable/PivotChart Events

Beginning with Access 2002, table and query data can be presented in an
Access form in a PivotTable or PivotChart view, allowing users to perform
interactive data analysis. PivotTable and PivotChart views can be built programmatically in a Microsoft Access form by using the Office Web
Components Object Model. To give programmers enhanced control over
PivotTable and PivotChart views, Access forms offer a number of events that
are available when the form is displayed in one of these views. These events
are organized in five categories, as shown in Table 24-2.

Table 24-2: PivotTable/PivotChart events

Category Name	Event Name	PivotTable Event	PivotChart Event
Data Source Events	OnConnect	Yes	No
	OnDisconnect	Yes	No
	BeforeQuery	Yes	No
	Query	Yes	No
Display Events	BeforeScreenTip	Yes	Yes
	AfterLayout	No	Yes
	BeforeRender	No	Yes
	AfterRender	No	Yes
	AfterFinalRender	No	Yes
Change Events	DataChange	Yes	No
	DataSetChange	No	Yes
	PivotTableChange	Yes	No
	SelectionChange	Yes	Yes
	ViewChange	Yes	Yes
Command Events	CommandEnabled	Yes	Yes
	CommandChecked	Yes	Yes
	CommandBeforeExecute	Yes	Yes
	CommandExecute	Yes	Yes
Keyboard and Mouse Events	KeyDown	Yes	Yes
	KeyPress	Yes	Yes
	KeyUp	Yes	Yes
	MouseDown	Yes	Yes
	MouseMove	Yes	Yes
	MouseUp	Yes	Yes
	MouseWheel	Yes	Yes
	Click	Yes	Yes
	DblClick	Yes	Yes

> **Note:** Microsoft Office Web Components (OWC) is a set of ActiveX controls installed with Microsoft Office 2003. You can find detailed documentation about using and programming these components in the help files (OWCVBA11.CHM, OWCDCH11.CHM, OWCDPL11.CHM) installed on your computer's system drive in the following folder:
>
>   \Program Files\Common Files\Microsoft Shared\Web Components\11\1033

Referencing the Microsoft Office Web Components Object Library

The next several sections of this chapter demonstrate event procedures for PivotTable and PivotChart views. To successfully work with these events, follow the steps below to add a reference to the Microsoft Office Web Components 11 Object Library:

1. In the Acc2003_Chap24 Database window, choose **Tools** | **Macro** | **Visual Basic Editor**.

2. In the Visual Basic Editor window, choose **Tools** | **References**.

3. Click the **Browse** button and locate the following file:

   C:\Program Files\Common Files\Microsoft Shared\WebComponents\ 11\OWC11.DLL

4. Click the **OWC11.DLL** file and then click **Open**. A reference to Microsoft Office Web Components 11.0 should appear in the Available References list.

5. Click **OK** to close the References dialog box.

After you add a reference to the Microsoft Office Web Components Object Library, you can use the Object Browser to view the properties, methods, events, and constants for each class of a web component. To see the available classes of a web component, select OWC11 in the Project/Library box in the Object Browser.

Data Source Events

Data Source events occur when the PivotTable connects to or disconnects from its data source or when the data source is queried.

OnConnect

The OnConnect event occurs when the PivotTable report connects to its data source. Use this event to perform the required operations once the PivotTable has connected to the data source.

The procedure in Hands-On 24-21 notifies the user that the connection to the data source has been established and displays the SELECT statement that provides the dataset for the PivotTable view.

◎ Hands-On 24-21: Writing the Form_OnConnect Event Procedure

1. In the Database window, select the **Sales Analysis Subform 1** and click the **Design** button. This is one of the forms included with the Northwind sample database.

2. Choose **Edit | Select Form**.

3. Choose **View | Properties** to activate the Form properties sheet.

4. Click the **Event** tab, set the **On Connect** property to **[Event Procedure]**, and press the **Build** button (…).

5. Access will create the event procedure stub. Enter the following Form_OnConnect event procedure:

```
Private Sub Form_OnConnect()
    MsgBox "You have successfully connected to the data source." & vbCrLf _
        & "The following SELECT statement will be used for the PivotTable: " _
        & vbCrLf & Me.RecordSource
End Sub
```

6. Switch to the **Sales Analysis Subform 1** form and close it. Click **Yes** when asked to save the design changes.

7. In the Database window, double-click the **Sales Analysis Subform 1** form. The Form_OnConnect event procedure will run and you should see the message as coded in step 5 above. Click **OK** to the message to open the form.

OnDisconnect

The OnDisconnect event occurs when the PivotTable report disconnects from its data source or the connection to the data source is changed. Use this event to notify the user that the connection to the data source has been lost. This event does not occur when you close the form.

BeforeQuery

The BeforeQuery event occurs before the PivotTable queries its data source. Actions such as adding new fields to the PivotTable report, moving fields, and sorting and filtering data will trigger this event. Because running a complex query could take longer than expected, you may want to let the user know that a query is in progress by changing the mouse pointer to an hourglass and turning it off during the Query event (see Hands-On 24-22). There is no way to determine what type of query is going to be performed.

Query

The Query event occurs after a PivotTable view sends a query to its data source. Actions such as adding new fields to the PivotTable report, moving fields, and sorting and filtering data will trigger this event. There is no way to determine what type of query has been performed.

The procedure in Hands-On 24-22 demonstrates how to change the mouse pointer to an hourglass before the query is sent to the data source and how to turn off the hourglass pointer after the query has run. Prior to sending the query, we also ask the user to specify the background color of the detail rows.

⊚ Hands-On 24-22: Writing the Form_BeforeQuery and Form_Query Event Procedures

1. In the Visual Basic Editor window, double-click **Form_Sales Analysis Subform 1**.

2. The Code window shows the Form_OnConnect event procedure you prepared in Hands-On 24-21. Enter the following Form_BeforeQuery and Form_Query event procedures below the last procedure code.

```
Private Sub Form_BeforeQuery()
    Dim strColor As String
    strColor = InputBox("Type 1 for Red, 2 for Yellow, " & _
            "or 3 for Green", "Specify Background Color for " & _
            "Detail Rows")

    Select Case strColor
        Case 1
            strColor = "Red"
        Case 2
            strColor = "Yellow"
        Case 3
            strColor = "Green"
        Case Else
            strColor = "White"
    End Select

    DoCmd.Hourglass True
    Me.PivotTable.ActiveView.DataAxis.FieldSets(0). _
        Fields(0).DetailBackColor = strColor
    Debug.Print "Executing the BeforeQuery event"
    Debug.Print "(Changed detail color to: " & strColor & ")"

End Sub

Private Sub Form_Query()
    Debug.Print "Executing the Query event"
    DoCmd.Hourglass False
    Debug.Print "(Turned off the hourglass mouse pointer)"
End Sub
```

3. To test the above event procedures, double-click the **Sales Analysis Subform 1** form in the Database window.

4. You should first see the message as coded in the Form_OnConnect event procedure (see Hands-On 24-21). Click **OK** to the message to open the form. You should then be prompted for the color of the detail rows as coded in the Form_BeforeQuery event procedure. Type your selection and

click **OK**. The hourglass should disappear when the form loading process is completed.

5. Open the Visual Basic Editor window and examine the Immediate window.

Let's examine the two event procedures that you wrote in this hands-on. Notice that to display the hourglass pointer, we used the statement DoCmd.Hourglass True in the Form_BeforeQuery event procedure. To turn off the hourglass, we put the statement DoCmd.Hourglass False in the Form_Query event procedure.

Also, notice the following statement that sets the background color for the PivotTable detail rows in the Form_BeforeQuery event procedure:

```
Me.PivotTable.ActiveView.DataAxis.FieldSets(0).Fields(0).DetailBackColor
    = strColor
```

In the above statement, the PivotTable property is used to access the PivotTable object exposed by a form. The ActiveView property represents the layout of the PivotTable report. The DataAxis property refers to one of the four areas of the PivotTable where you can drop fields of data. The DataAxis property contains the Totals and Details fields, which are displayed at the intersection of each row and column. Other areas of a PivotTable are used to display row fields (RowAxis), column fields (ColumnAxis), and filter fields (FilterAxis).

In addition to axes, a PivotTable contains a field list that shows which fields are available for use in the PivotTable report based on the form's RecordSource. The field list displays expandable nodes listing fields available on the form (see Figure 24-2).

The PivotTable field list contains two types of nodes: Totals and Fieldsets. A Totals node near the top of the field list shows all aggregate functions, or calculations used in the PivotTable report. Other expandable nodes in the PivotTable field list are known as Fieldsets, and can include one or more fields.

To manipulate a particular PivotField object in the PivotTable report via VBA code you need to access the Fieldset object in the Fieldsets collection of the ActiveView object. Each Fieldset object (a top-level node in the field list) contains a Fields collection, which contains PivotField objects. If you look at the expanded nodes in Figure 24-2 you will notice the Country Fieldset with one PivotField (Country), the Last Name Fieldset with a LastName PivotField, and the Shipped Date By Week Fieldset with six PivotField objects representing different time intervals (Years, Weeks, Days, Hours, Minutes, and Seconds).

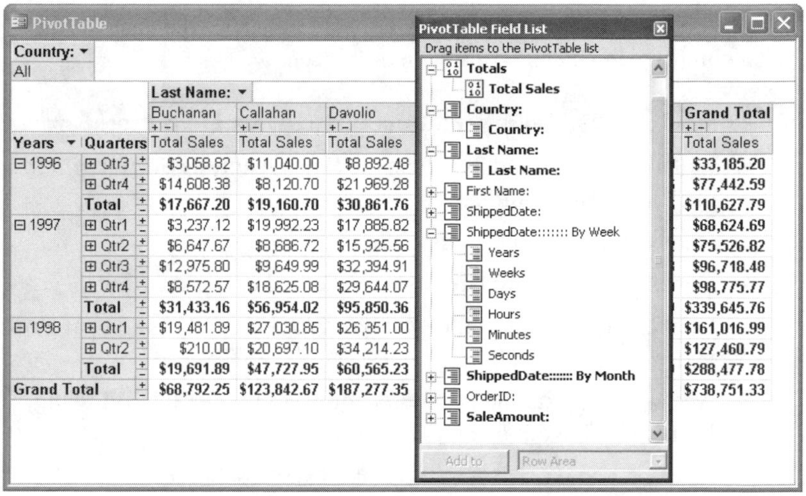

Figure 24-2: PivotTable report and its field list.

Display Events

Display events are used to draw custom lines, text, and drawings in a
PivotChart view before or after a PivotChart has been rendered.

BeforeScreenTip

The BeforeScreenTip event occurs before a ScreenTip is displayed for an element in a PivotChart view or PivotTable view. This event takes the following
two arguments:

■ **TipText** — Specifies the default text of the ScreenTip. By setting this argument to an empty string (TipText = "") you can hide the ScreenTip. Set this
argument to any other text to display the required text in the ScreenTip.

■ **SourceObject** — Specifies the object that generates the ScreenTip.

AfterLayout

The AfterLayout event occurs after the chart in the PivotChart view has been
laid out but before the chart elements have been drawn on screen. Use this
event to draw custom lines, text, and various drawings on the chart.

The drawObject parameter in the AfterLayout event represents a
chChartDraw object. The DrawEllipse, DrawLine, DrawPolyLine, and
DrawPolygon methods of the chChartDraw object can be used to add drawing
objects to a chart. The DrawText method can be used to add text to a chart. The
Border, Font, Interior, and Line properties can be used to format each drawing
object before it is added to the chart.

The AfterLayout event can also be used to reposition the chTitle, chLegend,
chChart, and chAxis objects of each PivotChart view by changing their Left
and Top properties. You can reposition the chPlotArea object by changing its
Left, Top, Right, and Bottom properties.

The event procedure in Hands-On 24-23 changes the chart legend and its accompanying label's position on the screen.

⦿ Hands-On 24-23: Writing the Form_AfterLayout Event Procedure

1. In the Database window, select the **Sales Analysis Subform 2** form and click the **Design** button.
2. Choose **Edit | Select Form**.
3. Choose **View | Properties** to activate the Form properties sheet.
4. Click the **Event** tab, set the **After Layout** property to **[Event Procedure]**, and press the **Build** button (…).
5. Access will create the event procedure stub. Enter the following Form_AfterLayout event procedure:

```
Private Sub Form_AfterLayout(ByVal drawObject As Object)
    Dim oSeriesDropZ As Object

    Me.ChartSpace.ChartSpaceLegend.Top = 50
    Set oSeriesDropZ = Me.ChartSpace.DropZones(chDropZoneSeries)
    oSeriesDropZ.Top = 30
End Sub
```

In the procedure above, the ChartSpace object represents the chart workspace. The ChartSpaceLegend property of the ChartSpace object returns a chLegend object that represents the chart workspace legend. To reposition the chart legend on the screen, its Top property was set to 50 pixels. Along with the chart legend, the procedure repositions the Last Name button in the series drop zone by using the DropZones method of the ChartSpace object. This method takes one required argument, ChartDrop-ZonesEnum, which represents the drop zone you want to format.

ChartDropZonesEnum can be one of the following constants:

chDropZoneCategories = 2
chDropZoneCharts = 4
chDropZoneData = 3
chDropZoneFilter = 0
chDropZoneSeries = 1

6. Switch to the **Sales Analysis Subform 2** form and choose **View | PivotChart View**. When the form opens you should see the chart legend and the Last Name button positioned in the top area of the PivotChart view.

BeforeRender

The BeforeRender event occurs before elements of a PivotChart view are drawn on the screen. Use this event to draw lines, text, and drawings on the chart before a specific chart element is drawn or to change the position and properties of the chart element before it is drawn on the screen. You can use the TypeName function to determine what type of object is about to be rendered.

The procedure in Hands-On 24-24 draws a red ellipse around each legend entry and cancels drawing of the gridlines.

◎ Hands-On 24-24: Writing the Form_BeforeRender Event Procedure

1. In the Visual Basic Editor window, double-click **Form_Sales Analysis Subform 2**.

2. The Code window shows the Form_AfterLayout event procedure you prepared in Hands-On 24-23. Enter the following Form_BeforeRender event procedure below the last procedure code.

```
Private Sub Form_BeforeRender(ByVal drawObject As Object, _
                             ByVal chartObject As Object, _
                             ByVal Cancel As Object)

    If TypeName(chartObject) = " ChLegendEntry " Then
        drawObject.Border.Color = "red"
        drawObject.DrawEllipse chartObject.Left, _
                               chartObject.Bottom, _
                               chartObject.Right, _
                               chartObject.Top
    End If

    If TypeName(chartObject) - "ChGridlines" Then
        Cancel.Value = True
    End If

End Sub
```

3. Switch to the **Sales Analysis Subform 2** form and choose **View | PivotChart View**. When the form opens you should see the PivotChart formatted as shown in Figure 24-3.

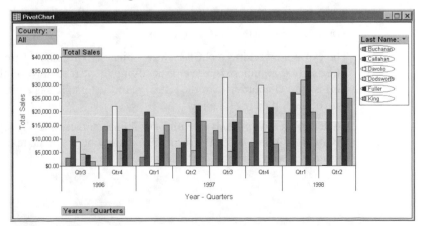

Figure 24-3: This PivotChart view has been altered in the BeforeRender event (see Hands-On 24-24).

AfterRender

The AfterRender event occurs after elements of a PivotChart view have been drawn on the screen. Use this event to draw custom lines, text, and various shapes/drawings on the chart after a specific chart element is drawn. You can use the TypeName function to determine what type of object has just been rendered.

The procedure in Hands-On 24-25 adds text in the chart's plot area after the chart legend (chLegend) object has been rendered on the screen.

◎ Hands-On 24-25: Writing the Form_AfterRender Event Procedure

1. In the Visual Basic Editor window, double-click **Form_Sales Analysis Subform 2**.

2. The Code window shows the procedures created in the previous hands-on exercises for this chapter. Enter the following Form_AfterRender event procedure below the last procedure code.

```
Private Sub Form_AfterRender(ByVal drawObject As Object, _
                    ByVal chartObject As Object)

    Dim oChart As Object
    Set oChart = Me.ChartSpace.Charts.Item(0)

    If TypeName(chartObject) = "ChLegend" Then

      drawObject.DrawText "Chart legend has been rendered", _
              oChart.PlotArea.Left + 15, _
              oChart.PlotArea.Top

    End If
End Sub
```

The DrawText method is used to draw a text string on a chart. This method uses the following syntax:

```
expression.DrawText(bstrText, Left, Top)
```

The expression returns a chChartDraw object. All arguments are required. The bstrText argument is a string specifying the text to draw on the chart. Left is a pixel coordinate of the left edge of the text. Top is a pixel coordinate of the top edge of the text.

3. Switch to the **Sales Analysis Subform 2** form and choose **View | PivotChart View**. When the form opens you should see the text "Chart legend has been rendered" in the chart's plot area.

AfterFinalRender

The AfterFinalRender event occurs after all elements of a PivotChart view have been drawn on the screen. Use this event to draw custom lines, text, and drawings on the topmost layer of the chart after all the chart elements have been drawn.

The procedure in Hands-On 24-26 adds a text message to the chart space, specifying the total number of data points used in the chart.

⊚ Hands-On 24-26: Writing the Form_AfterFinalRender Event Procedure

1. In the Visual Basic Editor window, double-click **Form_Sales Analysis Subform 2**.

2. The Code window shows the procedures created in the previous hands-on exercises for this chapter. Enter the following Form_AfterFinalRender event procedure below the last procedure code.

```
Private Sub Form_AfterFinalRender(ByVal drawObject As Object)
    Dim oChart As Object
    Dim s As Object
    Dim p As Object
    Dim strText As String
    Dim num As Integer

    Set oChart = Me.ChartSpace.Charts(0)

    For Each s In oChart.SeriesCollection
        For Each p In s.Points
            num = num + 1
            Debug.Print num
        Next
    Next

    strText = "This chart contains " & num & " data points."

    With drawObject.Font
        .Size = 9
        .Color = "blue"
        .Italic = True
    End With
    drawObject.DrawText strText, 200, 20
End Sub
```

3. Switch to the **Sales Analysis Subform 2** form and choose **View | Pivot-Chart View**. When the form opens you should see the PivotChart formatted as shown in Figure 24-4.

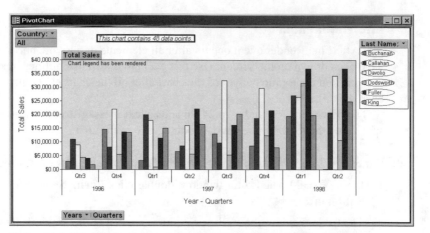

Figure 24-4: After all the elements of the PivotChart have been drawn on the screen, the procedure in Hands-On 24-26 calculates the total number of data points in the chart and places this information in the text message in the PivotChart view.

Change Events

When the user views and manipulates the data in the PivotTable and PivotChart views, various events are bound to happen. For example, data underlying a PivotChart view may have changed, or the user may have selected, added, removed, or filtered data in the PivotTable or PivotChart view. You can determine specific changes that occurred and take appropriate action by using one of the events discussed below.

DataChange

The DataChange event occurs when certain properties of the PivotTable view are changed or when certain methods are executed from a PivotTable view. You can find out what sort of change occurred by evaluating the Reason argument. This argument contains a value from the PivotDataReasonEnum enumeration. For example, you can use Reason to determine if the user added or removed columns from the PivotTable view.

The event procedure in Hands-On 24-27 evaluates whether a change occurred in the PivotTable Last Name drop-down list. For all other changes in the PivotTable view, the procedure writes the Reason code to the Immediate window. To find out the meaning of the returned Reason codes, search for the PivotDataReasonEnum constant in the Object Browser.

◎ Hands-On 24-27: Writing the Form_DataChange Event Procedure

1. In the Visual Basic Editor window, double-click **Form_Sales Analysis Subform 1**.

2. The Code window shows several event procedures you prepared earlier in this chapter. Enter the following Form_DataChange event procedure below the last procedure code.

```
Private Sub Form_DataChange(ByVal Reason As Long)
    Select Case Reason
        Case OWC11.plDataReasonAllIncludeExcludeChange
            Debug.Print "Change in the included/excluded members."
        Case OWC11.plDataReasonIncludedMembersChange
            Debug.Print "Included Members Change"
        Case OWC11.plDataReasonExcludedMembersChange
            Debug.Print "Excluded Members Change"
        Case Else
            Debug.Print "Reason code: " & Reason
    End Select
End Sub
```

3. To test the above event procedure, open **Sales Analysis Subform 1** in Form view. Because you've already created several event procedures for this form, various events will be triggered as the form is being loaded. Respond to all the prompts and, once the form opens, click the drop-down arrow next to the Last Name button and choose to add or remove an employee. Then switch to the **Immediate** window in the Visual Basic screen to see the captured Reason codes and changes in the included /excluded members.

DataSetChange

The DataSetChange event occurs whenever the dataset for a PivotChart view changes. This happens when a query supplying the underlying data for the PivotChart has changed or the data displayed in the current PivotChart view has been changed by the addition or removal of a data series. You cannot use this event to find out the reason for a change to the dataset. You must use the display events introduced earlier to trap for specific changes to the PivotChart view.

PivotTableChange

The PivotTableChange event occurs when you add or delete a field, fieldset, or total from the PivotTable field list. Use the Reason argument to determine which operation type has occurred. This argument contains a value from the PivotDataReasonEnum enumeration.

The event procedure in Hands-On 24-28 evaluates the Reason argument to determine if the Total was added in the Totals area in the field list.

Hands-On 24-28: Writing the Form_PivotTableChange Event Procedure

1. In the Visual Basic Editor window, double-click **Form_Sales Analysis Subform 1**.

2. The Code window shows several event procedures you prepared earlier in this chapter. Enter the following Form_PivotTableChange event procedure below the last procedure code.

```
Private Sub Form_PivotTableChange(ByVal Reason As Long)
    If Reason = OWC11.plPivotTableReasonTotalAdded Then
      MsgBox "Just added a Total."
    End If
End Sub
```

3. To test the above event procedure, open **Sales Analysis Subform 1** in Form view. Because you've already created several event procedures for this form, various events will be triggered. Respond appropriately to the prompts. During the course of events, you should see the message informing you that a Total field has just been added.

SelectionChange

The SelectionChange event occurs whenever the user makes a new selection within the PivotTable or PivotChart object. Use the SelectionType property to determine the object type of the current selection.

The event procedure in Hands-On 24-29 prints the name of the selected object to the Immediate window.

⊚ Hands-On 24-29: Writing the Form_SelectionChange Event Procedure

1. In the Visual Basic Editor window, double-click **Form_Sales Analysis Subform 1**.

2. The Code window shows several event procedures you prepared earlier in this chapter. Enter the following Form_SelectionChange event procedure below the last procedure code.

```
Private Sub Form_SelectionChange()
    Debug.Print "Selection Type: " & Me.PivotTable.SelectionType
End Sub
```

3. To test the above event procedure, open **Sales Analysis Subform 1** in Form view. Because you've already created several event procedures for this form, various events will be triggered. Respond appropriately to the prompts. Once the form opens in the PivotTable view, click on various areas of the PivotTable and open the **Immediate** window to see the names of the selected objects. Notice that the SelectionType values are always returned in plural:

```
Selection Type: PivotColumnMembers
Selection Type: PivotFields
Selection Type: PivotRowMembers
Selection Type: PivotAggregates
```

ViewChange

The ViewChange event occurs whenever the PivotTable or ChartSpace objects are redrawn. This event may occur multiple times for a single operation. For PivotTable views, you can use the Reason argument to determine how the view was changed. This argument contains a value from the PivotDataReasonEnum enumeration. Do not use the Reason argument with a ChartSpace.

The event procedure in Hands-On 24-30 displays a message when the user clicks the Show/Hide Details button in PivotTable view.

⦿ Hands-On 24-30: Writing the Form_ViewChange Event Procedure

1. In the Visual Basic Editor window, double-click **Form_Sales Analysis Subform 1**.

2. The Code window shows several event procedures you prepared earlier in this chapter. Enter the following Form_ViewChange event procedure below the last procedure code.

```
Private Sub Form_ViewChange(ByVal Reason As Long)
    Select Case Reason
        Case OWC11.plViewReasonHideDetails
            MsgBox "You selected to hide the details."
        Case OWC11.plViewReasonShowDetails
            MsgBox "You selected to show the details."
    End Select
End Sub
```

3. To test the above event procedure, open **Sales Analysis Subform 1** in Form view. Because you've already created several event procedures for this form, various events will be triggered. Respond appropriately to the prompts. Once the form opens in the PivotTable view, click the **Show/Hide Details** (+ /–) button below any employee name.

Command Events

CommandEnabled

The CommandEnabled event occurs whenever the enabled state of a menu bar or toolbar command changes. Because the same command can be accessed from multiple locations (toolbar, menu bar, shortcut menu), this event will fire for each command. This event takes two arguments:

■ **Command** — Returns a PivotCommandId constant and allows you to determine which command has been enabled or disabled. You can use the Object Browser to view the list of commands for this constant.

■ **Enabled** — An object whose Value property indicates whether the command is enabled or disabled.

The event procedure in Hands-On 24-31 checks whether the Copy command has been enabled or disabled.

⦿ Hands-On 24-31: Writing the Form_CommandEnabled Event Procedure

1. In the Visual Basic Editor window, double-click **Form_Sales Analysis Subform 1**.

2. The Code window shows several event procedures you prepared earlier in this chapter. Enter the following Form_CommandEnabled event procedure below the last procedure code.

```
Private Sub Form_CommandEnabled(ByVal Command As Variant, _
                                ByVal Enabled As Object)

    If Command = OWC11.plCommandCopy Then
        If Enabled.Value = True Then
            Debug.Print "Copy command enabled."
        Else
            Debug.Print "Copy command disabled."
        End If
    End If
End Sub
```

3. To test the above event procedure, open **Sales Analysis Subform 1** in Form view. Because you've already created several event procedures for this form, various events will be triggered. Respond appropriately to the prompts. Once the form opens, switch to the **Immediate** window and examine the results of the events that were executed.

CommandChecked

The CommandChecked event occurs whenever a menu bar command becomes checked or unchecked or a toolbar command's state changes from pressed to not pressed and vice versa. Because the same command can be accessed from multiple locations (toolbar, menu bar, shortcut menu), this event will fire for each command. The CommandChecked event takes the following two arguments:

■ **Command** — Returns a PivotCommandId constant and allows you to determine which command has been checked or unchecked. You can use the Object Browser to view the list of commands for this constant.

■ **Checked** — An object whose Value property indicates whether the command is checked or unchecked.

For example, the Sort Ascending command is available on the menu bar, toolbar, and shortcut menu of the form. Whenever the Sort Ascending command becomes checked or unchecked, the CommandChecked event will fire at least three times.

The event procedure in Hands-On 24-32 checks whether the SortAscending command has been checked or unchecked.

◉ Hands-On 24-32: Writing the Form_CommandChecked Event Procedure

1. In the Visual Basic Editor window, double-click **Form_Sales Analysis Subform 1**.

2. The Code window shows several event procedures you prepared earlier in this chapter. Enter the following Form_CommandChecked event procedure below the last procedure code.

```
Private Sub Form_CommandChecked(ByVal Command As Variant, _
                                ByVal Checked As Object)

    If Command = OWC11.plCommandSortAsc Then
        If Checked.Value = True Then
```

```
            Debug.Print "Sort Ascending command is checked."
        Else
            Debug.Print "Sort Ascending command unchecked."
        End If
    End If
End Sub
```

3. To test the above event procedure, clear the Immediate window by select-ing all the text and pressing **Delete**. Next, open **Sales Analysis Subform 1** in Form view. Because you've already created several event procedures for this form, various events will be triggered. Respond appropriately to the prompts. Once the form opens, click the **SortDescending** button on the toolbar. Switch to the **Immediate** window to see the results of the events that were executed.

CommandBeforeExecute

The CommandBeforeExecute event occurs when a user selects a command from the menu bar or toolbar but before the action associated with the com-mand takes place. You can use this event to cancel the command selected or to impose certain restrictions before a command is executed. This event takes the following two arguments:

■ **Command** — Returns a PivotCommandId constant and allows you to determine which command the user wishes to execute. You can use the Object Browser to view the list of commands for this constant.

■ **Cancel** — Returns an object. By setting the Value property of this argu-ment to True, the specified command will not be executed.

The event procedure in Hands-On 24-33 demonstrates how to prevent the user from executing the AutoFilter command.

◉ Hands-On 24-33: Writing the Form_CommandBeforeExecute Event Procedure

1. In the Visual Basic Editor window, double-click **Form_Sales Analysis Subform 1**.

2. The Code window shows several event procedures you prepared earlier in this chapter. Enter the following Form_CommandBeforeExecute event pro-cedure below the last procedure code.

```
Private Sub Form_CommandBeforeExecute(ByVal Command As _
                    Variant, ByVal Cancel As Object)

    If Command = OWC11.plCommandAutoFilter Then
        MsgBox "Auto filtering is not allowed."
        Cancel.Value = True
    End If
End Sub
```

3. To test the above event procedure, open **Sales Analysis Subform 1** in Form view. Because you've already created several event procedures for this form, various events will be triggered. Respond appropriately to the

prompts. Once the form is opened, right-click anywhere in the PivotTable and choose the **AutoFilter** command from the shortcut menu. The Form_ CommandBeforeExecute event procedure will fire and you will see the message informing you that this command is disallowed.

CommandExecute

The CommandExecute event occurs after a user selects a command from the menu bar or toolbar. You can use this event when you want to execute a set of commands after a particular command is executed. This event takes the Command argument that returns a PivotCommandId constant, which allows you to determine which command the user executed. You can use the Object Browser to view the list of commands for this constant.

The event procedure in Hands-On 24-34 checks whether the user used the Copy command. If the Copy command was executed, the procedure displays a message.

⊚ Hands-On 24-34: Writing the Form_CommandExecute Event Procedure

1. In the Visual Basic Editor window, double-click **Form_Sales Analysis Subform 1**.

2. The Code window shows several event procedures you prepared earlier in this chapter. Enter the following Form_CommandExecute event procedure below the last procedure code.

```
Private Sub Form_CommandExecute(ByVal Command As Variant)
    If Command = OWC11.plCommandCopy Then
            MsgBox "You just copied some data to the clipboard."
    End If
End Sub
```

3. To test the above event procedure, open **Sales Analysis Subform 1** in Form view. Because you've already created several event procedures for this form, various events will be triggered. Respond appropriately to the prompts. Once the form is opened, right-click any amount in the detail rows in the PivotTable and choose **Copy** from the shortcut menu. After choosing the Copy command you should see the message informing you that the text was copied to the clipboard.

Keyboard and Mouse Events

PivotTable and PivotChart views in Access can also respond to the following events: KeyDown, KeyPress, KeyUp, MouseDown, MouseMove, MouseUp, MouseWheel, Click, and DblClick. These events are the same as the form's keyboard and mouse events discussed earlier in this chapter.

Events Recognized by Form Sections

In addition to trapping events for the entire form, you can write event procedures for the following form sections: Detail, FormHeader, FormFooter, PageHeader, and PageFooter. Form sections respond to the following events: Click, DblClick, MouseDown, MouseUp, and MouseMove.

DblClick (Form Section Event)

The DblClick event occurs when you double-click inside the form's header or footer section.

The example procedure in Hands-On 24-35 demonstrates how to randomly change the background color for each of the form's sections every time you double-click anywhere within the form's Detail section.

⊚ Hands-On 24-35: Writing the Detail_DblClick Event Procedure

1. In the Database window, open the **Product Categories** form in Design view. Recall that you created this form in Hands-On 24-6.

2. Turn on the header and footer by choosing **View | Form Header/Footer**.

3. Increase the size of the header and footer so that they are visible when you run the form.

4. Click the **Form Detail** to select it, and then click the **Properties** button on the toolbar.

5. In the Section Detail properties sheet, click the **Event** tab and select **[Event Procedure]** next to the DblClick property name. Click the **Build** button (...) to move directly to the event procedure.

6. In the Code window, you should have the stub of the Detail_DblClick event procedure already written for you. Complete this procedure as shown below.

```
Private Sub Detail_DblClick(Cancel As Integer)
    With Me
        .Section(acHeader).BackColor = _
            RGB(Rnd * 128, _
            Rnd * 256, _
            Rnd * 255)
        .Section(acDetail).BackColor = _
            RGB(Rnd * 128, _
            Rnd * 256, _
            Rnd * 255)
        .Section(acFooter).BackColor = _
            RGB(Rnd * 128, _
            Rnd * 256, _
            Rnd * 255)
    End With
End Sub
```

7. To test the above event procedure, open the **Product Categories** form in Form view. Double-click anywhere in the **Detail** section of the form and see the colors of the Detail, Header, and Footer sections change.

Chapter Summary

In this chapter, you learned that many events can occur on a Microsoft Access form and that you can react to a specific form event by writing an event procedure. If you don't write your own code to handle a particular form event, Access will handle this event in its default way.

After trying out the 35 hands-on examples presented in this chapter, you should have a good understanding of how to write event procedures for an Access form. You should also be able to recognize the importance of form events in an Access application. You will find more examples of using form events in a custom application introduced in Chapter 26.

For more hands-on experience with event programming, proceed to the next chapter, which discusses the events recognized by an Access report and its sections.

Chapter 25

Using Report Events

When an Access report is run, a number of events can occur. The following examples demonstrate how to control what happens not only when the report is opened, activated, deactivated, or closed, but also when there are no records for the report to display or the report record source simply does not exist.

Open

The Open event for a report occurs when the report is opened. Use this event to display support forms or custom toolbars, or to change the record source for the report.

The event procedure in Hands-On 25-1 demonstrates how to change a report's record source on the fly.

◎ Hands-On 25-1: Writing the Report_Open Event Procedure

1. Open the **Acc2003_Chap25.mdb** file from the book's downloadable files or, if you'd like to start from scratch, create a new Microsoft Office Access database. This database should contain tables, queries, forms, and reports from the sample Northwind database. You can import these objects by choosing **File | Get External Data | Import**, or you can create a copy of the Northwind database to be used for this chapter's hands-on exercises.

2. Create a tabular report based on the Northwind database's **Customers** table. Save this report as **rptCustomers**.

3. Choose **View | Design View** to switch to the Design view of the rptCustomers report. In the Report Header area, click the report title (label control) to select it.

4. If the Report properties sheet does not appear on the screen, click the **Properties** button on the toolbar. Click the **All** tab and type **lblCustomers** as the Name property and enter **Customers** as the Caption property for the selected label control.

5. In the Report properties sheet, click the **Event** tab. Click next to the **On Open** event property and choose **[Event Procedure]** from the drop-down box. Click the **Build** button (…).

6. Access opens the Visual Basic Editor window and writes the stub of the Report_Open event procedure. Complete the code of the Report_Open event procedure as shown below.

```
Private Sub Report_Open(Cancel As Integer)
    Dim strCustName As String
    Dim strSQL As String
    Dim strWHERE As String

    On Error GoTo ErrHandler
    strSQL = "SELECT * from Customers"

    strCustName = InputBox("Type the first letter of " & _
        " the Company Name or type an asterisk (*) to view" & _
        " all companies.", "Show All /Or Filter")

    If strCustName = "" Then
        Cancel = True
    ElseIf strCustName = "*" Then
        Me.RecordSource = strSQL
        Me.lblCustomers.Caption = "All Customers"
    Else
      strCustName = "'" & Trim(strCustName) & "*" & "'"
      strWHERE = " WHERE CompanyName Like " _
            & strCustName & ""
      Debug.Print strSQL
      Debug.Print strWHERE
      Me.RecordSource = strSQL & strWHERE
      Me.lblCustomers.Caption = "Selected Customers" & _
            " (" & UCase(strCustName) & ")"
    End If
    Exit Sub
ErrHandler:
        MsgBox Err.Description
End Sub
```

7. Switch to the **rptCustomers** report's Design view and choose **File | Print Preview**. A message box will appear where you can enter an asterisk (*) to view all customers or the first letter of a company name if you'd like to limit your records. To cancel the report, click **Cancel** or press the **Esc** key.

Close

The Close event occurs when you close the report. Use this event to close support forms or custom toolbars, or to perform other cleanup operations. You cannot cancel the Close event.

When viewing reports in the Print Preview window, users often click the Maximize button to look at the report in full screen view. The event procedure in Hands-On 25-2 ensures that upon closing the report, the Database window is always returned to its previous size.

◉ Hands-On 25-2: Writing the Report_Close Event Procedure

This hands-on uses the rptCustomers report created in Hands-On 25-1.

1. In the Visual Basic Editor Code window for the rptCustomers report, type the following Report_Close event procedure:

```
Private Sub Report_Close()
    DoCmd.Restore
End Sub
```

2. Switch to the **rptCustomers** report's Design view and choose **File | Print Preview**. A message box will appear where you can enter an asterisk (*) to view all customers, or a first letter of a company name if you'd like to limit your records. When the report comes up, click the Maximize button to make the report window cover the entire screen. Now, close the report window. When the report closes, the Database window appears in its previous size. Without the DoCmd.Restore statement, the Database window would have been maximized.

Activate

The Activate event occurs when the report is opened right after the Open event but before the event for the first section of the report. Use this event to display a custom toolbar.

◉ Hands-On 25-3: Writing the Report_Activate Event Procedure

This hands-on uses the rptCustomers report created in Hands-On 25-1.

1. Create a custom toolbar named **Printing Reports** with the buttons as shown in Figure 25-1 below. (Refer to the online help for detailed instructions on how to design Access toolbars.)

➦ **Note:** Some of the toolbar buttons that you can see in Figure 25-1 do not appear in the Customize dialog box. However, you can steal them from the built-in Print Preview toolbar. Design your custom Printing Reports toolbar while in the Report Print Preview screen where the Print Preview toolbar is visible by default. Then, use the Customize dialog box to create a new toolbar named Printing Reports. Hold down the Ctrl key while dragging the required button from the Print Preview toolbar to your Printing Reports toolbar. Other buttons can be found on the Commands tab in the Customize dialog box.

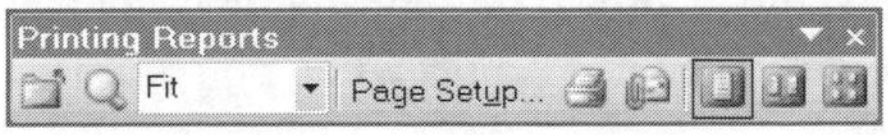

Figure 25-1: When a report is activated you may want to display a custom toolbar like this one.

2. In the Visual Basic Editor Code window for the **rptCustomers** report, type the following Report_Activate event procedure:

```
Private Sub Report_Activate()
    DoCmd.ShowToolbar "Print Preview", _
        acToolbarNo
    DoCmd.ShowToolbar "Printing Reports", _
        acToolbarYes
End Sub
```

3. Open the **rptCustomers** report and type your criteria when prompted. Upon activation of the report, the code you placed in the Report_Activate event procedure will run, causing the default Print Preview toolbar that Microsoft Access normally displays to be hidden and your custom toolbar to appear.

Deactivate

The Deactivate event occurs before the Close event for the report. You can use this event to hide a custom toolbar.

The procedure in Hands-On 25-4 hides a custom report toolbar when the report is deactivated.

⊚ Hands-On 25-4: Writing the Report_Deactivate Event Procedure

This hands-on uses the rptCustomers report created in Hands-On 25-1.

1. In the Visual Basic Editor Code window for the **rptCustomers** report, type the following Report_Deactivate event procedure:

```
Private Sub Report_Deactivate()
    DoCmd.ShowToolbar "Printing Reports", _
        acToolbarNo
End Sub
```

2. Open the **rptCustomers** report and type your criteria when prompted. Upon deactivation of the report, the code you placed in the Report_Deactivate event procedure will run, causing the default Print Preview toolbar that Microsoft Access normally displays to be restored and your custom toolbar to be hidden.

NoData

The NoData event occurs when the record source for the report contains no records. This event allows you to cancel the report when no records are available.

The event procedure in Hands-On 25-5 displays a message when the user enters criteria that are not met.

⊚ Hands-On 25-5: Writing the Report_NoData Event Procedure

This hands-on uses the rptCustomers report created in Hands-On 25-1.

1. In the Visual Basic Editor Code window for the **rptCustomers** report, type the following Report_NoData event procedure:

```
Private Sub Report_NoData(Cancel As Integer)
    MsgBox "There is no data for the criteria " & _
        "you entered."
    Cancel = True
End Sub
```

2. Open the **rptCustomers** report and request to see customers with a company name starting with the letter "X." Because there aren't any company names beginning with "X," a message box will be displayed, saying that there is no data for the criteria entered, and the report will be cancelled.

Page

The Page event occurs after a page is formatted but before it is printed. Use the Page event to customize the appearance of your printed reports by adding lines, circles, and graphics.

The event procedure in Hands-On 25-6 will draw a thick red border around the report pages. Notice that the DrawWidth method specifies the thickness of the line and the Line method draws a line with an upper-left corner at (0, 0) and the lower-right corner at (Me.ScaleWidth, MeScaleHeight). The ScaleWidth and ScaleHeight properties specify the width and height of the report.

⊚ Hands-On 25-6: Writing the Report_Page Event Procedure

This hands-on uses the rptCustomers report created in Hands-On 25-1.

1. In the Visual Basic Editor Code window for the **rptCustomers** report, type the following Report_Page event procedure:

```
Private Sub Report_Page()
    Me.DrawWidth = 25 ' pixels
    Me.Line (0, 0)-(Me.ScaleWidth, _
        Me.ScaleHeight), vbRed, B
End Sub
```

2. Open the **rptCustomers** report and type your criteria. Notice that when the report appears on the screen, a thick red border surrounds the pages (see Figure 25-2).

All Customers

Customer ID	Company Name	ContactName	ContactTitle	Address	City	Region	PostalCode	Country	Phone	Fax
ALFKI	Alfreds Futterkiste	Maria Anders	Sales Represent	Obere Str. 57	Berlin		12209	Germany	030-0074	030-00765
ANATR	Ana Trujillo Empareda	Ana Trujillo	Owner	Avda. de la Constituci	México D.F.		05021	Mexico	(5) 555-47	(5) 555-37
ANTON	Antonio Moreno Taque	Antonio Moreno	Owner	Mataderos 2312	México D.F.		05023	Mexico	(5) 555-39	
AROUT	Around the Horn	Thomas Hardy	Sales Represent	120 Hanover Sq.	London		WA1 1DP	UK	(171) 555-	(171) 555-
BERGS	Berglunds snabbköp	Christina Berglund	Order Administra	Berguvsvägen 8	Luleå		S-958 22	Sweden	0921-12 3	0921-12 3
BLAUS	Blauer See Delikatess	Hanna Moos	Sales Represent	Forsterstr. 57	Mannheim		68306	Germany	0621-084	0621-0892
BLONP	Blondel père et fils	Frédérique Citeau	Marketing Mana	24, place Kléber	Strasbourg		67000	France	88.60.15.	88.60.153
BOLID	Bólido Comidas prepar	Martín Sommer	Owner	C/ Araquil, 67	Madrid		28023	Spain	(91) 555 2	(91) 555 9
BONAP	Bon app'	Laurence Lebihan	Owner	12, rue des Bouchers	Marseille		13008	France	91.24.45.	91.24.45.4
BOTTM	Bottom-Dollar Markets	Elizabeth Lincoln	Accounting Man	23 Tsawassen Blvd.	Tsawassen	BC	T2F 8M4	Canada	(604) 555-	(604) 555-
BSBEV	B's Beverages	Victoria Ashworth	Sales Represent	Fauntleroy Circus	London		EC2 5NT	UK	(171) 555-	
CACTU	Cactus Comidas para l	Patricio Simpson	Sales Agent	Cerrito 333	Buenos Aires		1010	Argentina	(1) 135-55	(1) 135-48
CENTC	Centro comercial Moct	Francisco Chang	Marketing Mana	Sierras de Granada 99	México D.F.		05022	Mexico	(5) 555-33	(5) 555-72
CHOPS	Chop-suey Chinese	Yang Wang	Owner	Hauptstr. 29	Bern		3012	Switzerland	0452-076	
COMMI	Comércio Mineiro	Pedro Afonso	Sales Associate	Av. dos Lusíadas, 23	São Paulo	SP	05432-043	Brazil	(11) 555-7	
CONSH	Consolidated Holdings	Elizabeth Brown	Sales Represent	Berkeley Gardens	London		WX1 6LT	UK	(171) 555-	(171) 555-
DRACD	Drachenblut Delikates	Sven Ottlieb	Order Administra	Walserweg 21	Aachen		52066	Germany	0241-039	0241-0594
DUMON	Du monde entier	Janine Labrune	Owner	67, rue des Cinquante	Nantes		44000	France	40.67.88.	40.67.898

Saturday, July 31, 2004 — *Page 1 of 5*

Figure 25.2: You can frame your Access report pages with a thick red line by implementing the Report_Page event procedure as shown in Hands-On 25-6.

Error

The Error event is triggered by errors in accessing the data for the report. Use this event to replace the default error message with your custom message. The Error event takes the following two arguments:

- **DataErr** — Contains the number of the Microsoft Access error that occurred.
- **Response** — Determines whether or not error messages should be displayed. It may be one of the following constants:
  - ***acDataErrContinue*** — Ignore the error and continue without displaying the default Microsoft Access error message.
  - ***AcDataErrDisplay*** — Display the default Microsoft Access error message. This is the default.

The Report_Error event procedure in Hands-On 25-7 illustrates how to use the value of the DataErr argument together with the AccessError method to determine the error number and its descriptive string.

The statement

```
Response = acDataErrContinue
```

will prevent the standard Microsoft Access error message from appearing. The Error event for reports works the same as the Error event for forms — but only the Microsoft Access or the Jet Engine errors can be trapped here.

To trap errors in your VBA code, use the On Error GoTo statement to direct the procedure flow to the location of the error-handling statements within your procedure.

◎ Hands-On 25-7: Writing the Report_Error Event Procedure

1. In the Database window, rename the Customers table to **Customers2**.

2. Open the **rptCustomers** report you created in Hands-On 25-1 in Design view.

3. In the Visual Basic Editor Code window for the **rptCustomers** report, type the following Report_Error event procedure:

```
Private Sub Report_Error(DataErr As Integer, _
        Response As Integer)
    ' obtain information about the error
    MsgBox Application.AccessError(DataErr), _
        vbOKOnly, "Error Number: " & DataErr
    If DataErr = 3078 Then
        MsgBox "Your custom error message goes here."
    End If
    Response = acDataErrContinue
End Sub
```

4. Run the **rptCustomers** report. When the input box appears prompting you for the criteria, type any letter and press **OK**. At this point the Report_ Error event will fire because the underlying data for the rptCustomers report does not exist. Because you renamed the Customers table that this report uses for its data source, Microsoft Access cannot locate the data, which generates the error.

5. In the Database window, rename the Customers2 table back to **Customers** and run the **rptCustomers** report to ensure that it does not produce unexpected errors.

Events Recognized by Report Sections

A Microsoft Access report can contain as many as 25 sections. These include Report Header/Footer, Page Header/Footer, the Detail section, and ten Group Headers/Footers. All report sections can respond to the Format and Print events. These events occur when you print or preview a report. In addition, the Report Header/Footer and the Detail section recognize the Retreat event that occurs when Access returns to a previous section during report formatting.

Format (Report Section Event)

A Format event occurs for each section in a report before Microsoft Access formats the section for previewing or printing. This event takes the following two arguments:

■ **Cancel** — Determines if the formatting of the section occurs. To cancel the section formatting, set this argument to True.

■ **FormatCount** — An integer that specifies whether the Format event has occurred more than once for a section. If a section does not fit on one page and the rest of the section needs to be moved to the next page of the report, the FormatCount argument is set to 2.

Use the Format event in the appropriate report section for changes that affect page layout. For changes that don't affect page layout, use the Print event for the report section (see Hands-On 25-10 later in this chapter).

Table 25-1: Effect of format event on report sections

Report Sections	Description of Format Event
Detail	The Format event occurs for each record in the section just before Microsoft Access formats the data in the record. You can access the data in the current record using the event procedure.
Group Headers	The Format event occurs for each new group. You can access the data in the group header and the data in the first record in the Detail section using the event procedure.
Group Footers	The Format event occurs for each new group. You can access the data in the Group Footer and the data in the last record in the Detail section via an event procedure.

The event procedure in Hands-On 25-8 demonstrates how to make reports easier to read by shading alternate rows.

◎ Hands-On 25-8: Writing the Detail_Format Event Procedure

1. Use the **rptCustomers** report you created in Hands-On 25-1.

2. In the Visual Basic Editor Code window for the **rptCustomers** report, type the following Detail_Format event procedure. Do not type the Option Compare Database and Option Explicit statements if they are already at the top of the Code window.

```
Option Compare Database
Option Explicit

Dim shaded As Boolean

Private Sub Detail_Format(Cancel As Integer, _
        FormatCount As Integer)
    If shaded Then
        Me.Detail.BackColor = vbYellow
    Else
        Me.Detail.BackColor = vbWhite
    End If
        shaded = Not shaded
End Sub
```

Notice that at the top of the module sheet (in the module's Declarations area) we have placed the following statement:

```
Dim shaded As Boolean
```

The above statement declares the global variable of the Boolean type to keep track of the alternate rows.

When you run the report, upon printing the Detail section, Access will check the value of the shaded variable. If the value is True, it will change the background of the formatted row to yellow (which produces a light gray background when printed on a laser printer). The shaded value will then be set to False for the next row by using the following statement:

```
shaded = Not shaded
```

The above statement works as a toggle. If shaded was True, it will be False now, and so on.

3. Run the **rptCustomers** report. When the input box appears prompting you for the criteria, type an asterisk (*) and press **OK**.

All Customers

Customer ID	Company Name	ContactName	ContactTitle	Address	City	Region	Postal Code	Country	Phone	Fax
ALFKI	Alfreds Futterkiste	Maria Anders	Sales Represent	Obere Str. 57	Berlin		12209	Germany	030-0074	030-00765
ANATR	Ana Trujillo Empareda	Ana Trujillo	Owner	Avda. de la Constitucí	México D.F.		05021	Mexico	(5) 555-47	(5) 555-37
ANTON	Antonio Moreno Taque	Antonio Moreno	Owner	Mataderos 2312	México D.F.		05023	Mexico	(5) 555-39	
AROUT	Around the Horn	Thomas Hardy	Sales Represent	120 Hanover Sq.	London		WA1 1DP	UK	(171) 555-	(171) 555-
BERGS	Berglunds snabbköp	Christina Berglund	Order Administra	Berguvsvägen 8	Luleå		S-958 22	Sweden	0921-123	0921-123
BLAUS	Blauer See Delikatess	Hanna Moos	Sales Represent	Forsterstr. 57	Mannheim		68306	Germany	0621-084	0621-0892
BLONP	Blondel père et fils	Frédérique Citeau	Marketing Mana	24, place Kléber	Strasbourg		67000	France	88.60.15.	88.60.15.3
BOLID	Bólido Comidas prepar	Martín Sommer	Owner	C/ Araquil, 67	Madrid		28023	Spain	(91) 555 2	(91) 555 9
BONAP	Bon app'	Laurence Lebihan	Owner	12, rue des Bouchers	Marseille		13008	France	91.24.45.	91.24.45.4
BOTTM	Bottom-Dollar Markets	Elizabeth Lincoln	Accounting Man	23 Tsawassen Blvd.	Tsawassen	BC	T2F 8M4	Canada	(604) 555-	(604) 555-
BSBEV	B's Beverages	Victoria Ashworth	Sales Represent	Fauntleroy Circus	London		EC2 5NT	UK	(171) 555-	
CACTU	Cactus Comidas para l	Patricio Simpson	Sales Agent	Cerrito 333	Buenos Aires		1010	Argentina	(1) 135-55	(1) 135-48
CENTC	Centro comercial Moct	Francisco Chang	Marketing Mana	Sierras de Granada 99	México D.F.		05022	Mexico	(5) 555-33	(5) 555-72
CHOPS	Chop-suey Chinese	Yang Wang	Owner	Hauptstr. 29	Bern		3012	Switzerland	0452-076	
COMMI	Comércio Mineiro	Pedro Afonso	Sales Associate	Av. dos Lusíadas, 23	São Paulo	SP	05432-043	Brazil	(11) 555-7	
CONSH	Consolidated Holdings	Elizabeth Brown	Sales Represent	Berkeley Gardens	London		WX1 6LT	UK	(171) 555-	(171) 555-
DRACD	Drachenblut Delikates	Sven Ottlieb	Order Administra	Walserweg 21	Aachen		52066	Germany	0241-039	0241-0594
DUMON	Du monde entier	Janine Labrune	Owner	67, rue des Cinquante	Nantes		44000	France	40.67.88.	40.67.89.8

Saturday, July 31, 2004 *Page 1 of 5*

Figure 25-3: The formatting result after implementing the Detail_Format event in Hands-On 25-8 is illustrated here.

The next hands-on demonstrates how to suppress the Page Footer on the first page of your report by placing code in the PageFooterSection_Format event procedure.

Hands-On 25-9: Writing the PageFooterSection_Format Event Procedure

1. Using the Report Wizard, create a report called **rptProducts** based on the Products table. Choose the following fields for this report: **ProductId**, **ProductName**, **UnitPrice**, and **UnitsInStock**.
2. In the Design view of the rptProducts report, click on the **Page Footer** section heading and choose **View | Properties**. In the PageFooterSection properties sheet, click the **Event** tab. Click next to the **OnFormat** property and select **[Event Procedure]** from the drop-down list. Click the **Build** button (...) to activate the Code window.

3. In the Code window for Report_rptProducts, enter the following PageFooterSection_Format event procedure:

```
Private Sub PageFooterSection_Format(Cancel As Integer, _
    FormatCount As Integer)
    Dim ctrl As Control

    For Each ctrl In Me.PageFooterSection.Controls
        If Me.Page = 1 Then
            ctrl.Visible = False
        Else
            ctrl.Visible = True
        End If
    Next ctrl
End Sub
```

4. Switch to the rptProducts report in Design view and click the **Print Preview** button. Notice that the footer does not appear on the first page of the report.

Print (Report Section Event)

The Print event occurs after the data in a report section has been formatted but before the data is printed. The Print event occurs only for sections that are actually printed. To access data from sections that are not printed, use the Format event.

You can use the PrintCount argument to check whether the Print event has occurred more than once for a record. If part of a record is printed on one page and the rest is printed on the next page, the Print event will occur twice, and the PrintCount argument will be set to 2. You can use the Cancel argument to cancel the printing of a section.

Table 25-2: Effect of Print event on report sections

Report Section	Description of Event
Detail	The Print event occurs for each record in the Detail section just before Microsoft Access prints the data in the record.
Group Headers	The Print event occurs for each new group.
Group Footers	The Print event occurs for each new group.

The event procedure in Hands-On 25-10 demonstrates how to print a record range indicator in the report's footer. This indicator will display the range of records printed on each page. You can easily modify this example procedure to print the first and last customer ID on the page (see the discussion before Figure 25-5).

⊚ Hands-On 25-10: Writing the Detail_Print Event Procedure

This hands-on uses the rptCustomers report you created in Hands-On 25-1.

1. Open the **rptCustomers** report in the Design view and place two unbound text boxes in the report's page footer.
   - ▦ Change the Name property of the first box to **txtPage** and set its Visible property to **No**. Delete the label control in front of this text box.
   - ▦ Name the second text box **txtRange** and set the Caption property of its label control to **Records:**.

2. Click in the **Detail** section of the report and activate the properties sheet. Set the **On Print** property of the Detail section to **[Event Procedure]** and write the code for the Detail_Print event as shown below.

```
Private Sub Detail_Print(Cancel As Integer, _
        PrintCount As Integer)
    Static rCount As Integer
    Static start As Integer
    Static firstId As String
    Static lastId As String

    If Me.Page <> Me.txtPage Then
        start = Me.CurrentRecord
        firstId = CustomerID
        Me.txtPage = Me.Page
        rCount = 0
    End If
        rCount = rCount + 1
        lastId = CustomerID
    If start <= rCount Then
        Me.txtRange = start & "-" & rCount
      ' Me.txtRange = UCase(firstId) & "-" & UCase(lastId)
    Else
        rCount = Me.CurrentRecord
        lastId = CustomerID
    End If
End Sub
```

The Detail_Print event procedure occurs for each record. It uses the start and rCount variables to keep track of the first and last item on the page.

3. In the Code window, enter the PageHeaderSection_Print event procedure as shown below.

```
Private Sub PageHeaderSection_Print(Cancel As Integer, _
                    PrintCount As Integer)
    Me.txtPage = 0
End Sub
```

4. To test the above event procedure, open **rptCustomers** and click the **Print Preview** button on the toolbar. Notice the record range indicator at the bottom of the report page.

The PageHeaderSection_Print event procedure will set the value of the unbound txtPage text box to zero (0) whenever the Print event occurs for a new page.

BOLID	Bólido Comidas prepar	Martín Sommer	Owner	C/ Araquil, 67	Madrid
BONAP	Bon app'	Laurence Lebihan	Owner	12, rue des Bouchers	Marseille
BOTTM	Bottom-Dollar Markets	Elizabeth Lincoln	Accounting Man	23 Tsawassen Blvd.	Tsawassen
BSBEV	B's Beverages	Victoria Ashworth	Sales Represent	Fauntleroy Circus	London
CACTU	Cactus Comidas para l	Patricio Simpson	Sales Agent	Cerrito 333	Buenos Aires
CENTC	Centro comercial Moct	Francisco Chang	Marketing Mana	Sierras de Granada 99	México D.F.
CHOPS	Chop-suey Chinese	Yang Wang	Owner	Hauptstr. 29	Bern
COMMI	Comércio Mineiro	Pedro Afonso	Sales Associate	Av. dos Lusíadas, 23	São Paulo
CONSH	Consolidated Holdings	Elizabeth Brown	Sales Represent	Berkeley Gardens	London
DRACD	Drachenblut Delikates	Sven Ottlieb	Order Administra	Walserweg 21	Aachen
DUMON	Du monde entier	Janine Labrune	Owner	67, rue des Cinquante	Nantes

Saturday, July 31, 2004   **Records:** 1-18

Page: |◄ ◄   1   ► ►| ◄

Figure 25-4: This report displays the record range indicator at the bottom of the page (see Hands-On 25-10).

You can modify the event procedure in Hands-On 25-10 to print the first and last customer ID on the page as shown in Figure 25-5. Simply replace the following statement in the Detail_Print event procedure

```
Me.txtRange = start & "-" & rCount
```

with the following line of code

```
Me.txtRange = UCase(firstId) & "-" & UCase(lastId)
```

BOLID	Bólido Comidas prepar	Martín Sommer	Owner	C/ Araquil, 67	Madrid
BONAP	Bon app'	Laurence Lebihan	Owner	12, rue des Bouchers	Marseille
BOTTM	Bottom-Dollar Markets	Elizabeth Lincoln	Accounting Man	23 Tsawassen Blvd.	Tsawassen
BSBEV	B's Beverages	Victoria Ashworth	Sales Represent	Fauntleroy Circus	London
CACTU	Cactus Comidas para l	Patricio Simpson	Sales Agent	Cerrito 333	Buenos Aires
CENTC	Centro comercial Moct	Francisco Chang	Marketing Mana	Sierras de Granada 99	México D.F.
CHOPS	Chop-suey Chinese	Yang Wang	Owner	Hauptstr. 29	Bern
COMMI	Comércio Mineiro	Pedro Afonso	Sales Associate	Av. dos Lusíadas, 23	São Paulo
CONSH	Consolidated Holdings	Elizabeth Brown	Sales Represent	Berkeley Gardens	London
DRACD	Drachenblut Delikates	Sven Ottlieb	Order Administra	Walserweg 21	Aachen
DUMON	Du monde entier	Janine Labrune	Owner	67, rue des Cinquante	Nantes

Saturday, July 31, 2004   **Records:** ALFKI-DUMON

Page: |◄ ◄   1   ► ►| ◄

Figure 25-5: This report displays the first and last customer ID for a specific page at the bottom of each printed page.

Retreat

The Retreat event occurs when Microsoft Access returns to previous sections of the report during report formatting. For example, after formatting a report section, if Access discovers that the data will not fit on the page, it will go back to the necessary location in the report to ensure that the section can properly begin on the next page.

The Retreat event occurs after the Format event but before the Print event. This event applies to all report sections except page headers and footers. The Retreat event occurs for group headers and footers whose KeepTogether property has been set to Whole Group or With First Detail. This report is also triggered in subreports whose CanGrow or CanShrink properies have been set to True.

The Retreat event makes it possible to undo any changes made during the Format event for the section.

The Retreat event is demonstrated in the sample Northwind database's Sales by Year report as shown in Figure 25-6.

```
Northwind - Report_Sales by Year (Code)
GroupFooter1              Retreat

    Private Sub GroupFooter1_Retreat()
    ' If ShowDetails check box on Sales by Year Dialog form is checked,
    ' set value of Show text box to True so that page header will print on
    ' next page.

        If Forms![Sales by Year Dialog]!ShowDetails Then Me!Show.Value = True

    End Sub
```

Figure 25-6: The Sales by Year report in the Northwind database uses the GroupFooter1_Retreat event procedure to control printing of a page header.

Chapter Summary

In this chapter you learned about many events that fire when the Access report is run. By writing your own event procedures you can specify what happens when the report is opened, activated/deactivated, or closed. You can also display a custom message when an error occurs or the report does not contain any data; or you can make last-minute changes to the report layout before it is printed or previewed.

In the next chapter, you will learn about events recognized by various form controls while working with a custom application.

Chapter 26

Events Recognized by Controls

In addition to the events for forms and reports introduced in Chapters 24 and 25, you can control a great many events that occur for labels, text boxes, combo and list boxes, option buttons, check boxes, and other controls installed by default with an Access application. These events make it possible to manage what happens on a field level.

The best way to learn about events that a form, report, and/or control can respond to is to develop an application that addresses a specific problem. The downloadable files for this book contain a form that is used for data entry and lookup purposes. The subject of the Asset Management form is keeping track of computer assets in numerous schools within a school district. We will use this form to further experiment with event programming. The form is divided into four easy-to-maintain sections as illustrated in Figure 26-1.

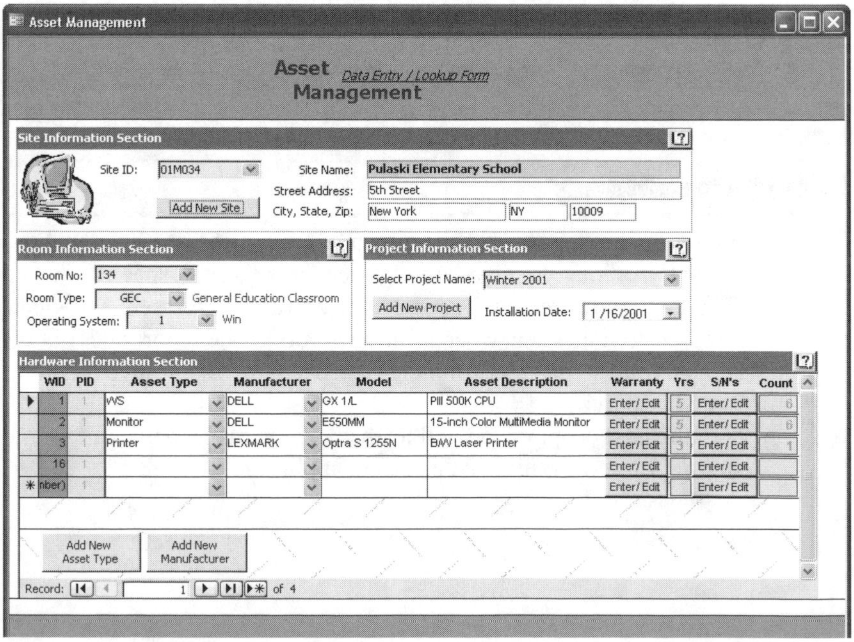

Figure 26-1: Custom data entry form.

◎ Hands-On 26-1: Launching the Custom Access Application

1. Copy the **AssetsDataEntry.mdb** file from the downloadable files to your local disk.

2. To gain access to the database source code, open the **AssetsDataEntry.mdb** file while holding down the **Shift** key.

3. Open the **frmDataEntryMain** form in Design view.

Now that the main data entry form is open, we will proceed to examine the events that this form's controls respond to.

Enter (Control)

The Enter event occurs before a control actually receives the focus from another control on the same form. The Enter event applies to text boxes, combo and list boxes, option buttons, check boxes, option groups, command buttons, toggle buttons, bound and unbound object frames, and subform and subreport controls. You can use the Enter event to display a message directing the user to first fill in another control on the form.

For example, when a user attempts to make a selection from the combo box controls located in the Room Information and Project Information sections of the Asset Management sample form when he or she hasn't yet selected a Site ID from the Site ID combo box, the following Enter event procedures may be triggered: cboRooms_Enter, cboRoomType_Enter, cboOS_Enter, and cboProject_Enter.

◎ Hands-On 26-2: Using the Enter Event Procedure for the Combo Box Control

1. Open the **frmDataEntryMain** form in Form view.

2. Click inside the combo box control located to the right of the **Room No:** label. This action will fire the following Enter event procedure:

```
Private Sub cboRooms_Enter()
    If Me.cboSiteId = "" Or IsNull(Me.cboSiteId) Then
        MsgBox "Site ID must be specified.", _
            vbInformation + vbOKOnly, _
            "Missing Site ID"
        Me.cboSiteId.SetFocus
        Exit Sub
    End If
End Sub
```

3. Click **OK** to the information message generated by the cboRooms_Enter event procedure and notice that the cursor has been positioned inside the combo box control containing Site IDs. Don't make any selections from the Site ID combo box at this time.

4. Click on the combo box control next to the **Room Type** label. This action will fire the following Enter event procedure:

```
Private Sub cboRoomType_Enter()
    If Me.cboSiteId = "" Or IsNull(Me.cboSiteId) Then
        MsgBox "Site ID must be specified.", _
            vbInformation + vbOKOnly, "Missing Site ID"
        Me.cboSiteId.SetFocus
        Exit Sub
    End If
    If Me.cboRooms = "" Or IsNull(Me.cboRooms) Then
        MsgBox "Room number must be specified.", _
            vbInformation + vbOKOnly, "Missing Room Number"
        Me.cboRooms.SetFocus
        Exit Sub
    End If
End Sub
```

When the user clicks the cboRoomType combo box control, the Enter event checks whether the cboSiteId combo box control or cboRoom combo box control is empty. If the user did not make a selection in these controls, a message box is displayed and the focus is moved to the appropriate combo box control.

5. Click **OK** to the information message generated by the cboRoomType_ Enter event procedure and notice that the cursor has again been positioned inside the Site ID combo box control.

BeforeUpdate (Control)

The BeforeUpdate event occurs when you attempt to save the record or leave the control after making changes. This event applies to text boxes, combo and list boxes, option buttons, check boxes, and bound object frames. Use this event to validate the entry.

For example, the combo box control in the Site Information section of the Asset Management sample form causes Microsoft Access to display a custom message if the value of the cboSiteId combo box control is Null. To cancel the Update event, the Cancel argument has been set to True.

⊚ Hands-On 26-3: Using the BeforeUpdate Event Procedure for the Combo Box Control

1. Make sure that the frmDataEntryMain form is open in Design view.

2. Right-click the list box control to the right of the **Site ID** label and choose **Build Event** from the shortcut menu.

3. The Microsoft Visual Basic Editor window will appear with the cursor positioned inside the following event procedure:

```
Private Sub cboSiteId_BeforeUpdate(Cancel As Integer)
    Dim strMsg As String, strTitle As String
    Dim intStyle As Integer

    If IsNull(Me!cboSiteId) Or Me!cboSiteId = "" Then
        strMsg = "You must pick a value from the Site ID list."
        strTitle = "Site ID Required"
        intStyle = vbOKOnly
        MsgBox strMsg, intStyle, strTitle
        Cancel = True
    End If
End Sub
```

4. Position the cursor inside the **If** statement, then press **F9** or choose **Debug |
   Toggle Breakpoint**.

5. Activate the **frmDataEntryMain** form in Form view and make a selection
   from the Site ID combo box.

   When you make your selection, the BeforeUpdate event procedure is fired
   and the Code window appears in Break mode. Press **F8** to step through the
   code line by line. Because you have not set up more breakpoints, you cannot see that two other events (cboSiteId_AfterUpdate and cboRooms_
   Enter) were triggered when you made a selection from the Site ID combo
   box.

6. When the procedure finishes executing, activate the **frmDataEntryMain**
   form. You should see the text boxes filled with a school name and address
   and the cursor positioned inside the Room No combo box and ready for the
   next selection or data entry.

AfterUpdate (Control)

The AfterUpdate event occurs after the data in the control has been modified.
It applies to text boxes, combo and list boxes, option buttons, check boxes, and
bound object frames. Unlike the BeforeUpdate event, the AfterUpdate event
cannot be cancelled. Use this event to fill in other controls on the form based
on the newly entered or selected value.

For example, after updating the cboSiteId combo box in the Site Information section of the Asset Management sample form, the following event
procedure is executed:

```
Private Sub cboSiteId_AfterUpdate()
    With Me
        .txtSchoolName = Me.[cboSiteId].Column(1)
        .txtStreet = Me.cboSiteId.Column(2)
        .txtCity = Me.cboSiteId.Column(3)
        .txtState = Me.cboSiteId.Column(4)
        .txtZip = Me.cboSiteId.Column(5)
        .cboRooms.Value = vbNullString
        .cboRooms.Requery
        .txtRoomDescription = vbNullString
        .cboRoomType = vbNullString
```

```
            .cboOS = vbNullString
            .txtOperatingSystem = vbNullString
            .cboProject = vbNullString
            .txtPID = vbNullString
        End With
        If Me.cboRooms.ListCount = 0 Then
            ' do not display column headings
            Me.cboRooms.ColumnHeads = False
        Else
            Me.cboRooms.ColumnHeads = True
        End If
        Me.cboRooms.SetFocus
    End Sub
```

In the procedure shown above, the school address information is filled in based on the contents of the cboSiteId columns. For example, to fill in the street address, you can read the value of the Columns() property of the cboSiteId control, even though this column is not visible when you view the combo box:

```
    Me.txtStreet = Me.cboSiteId.Column(2)
```

Note that because the combo box column numbering begins with zero (0), the above statement actually reads the contents of the third column. Next, the combo box labeled "Room No" is requeried and a number of other controls on the form are cleared.

Also, note how the intrinsic constant named vbNullString is used here instead of an empty string ("") to clear text boxes or combo boxes on a form. The final code segment above contains the If...Then...Else statement that sets the ColumnHeads property of the cboRooms control to False if there are no rooms associated with the selected Site ID.

The last line of the code

```
    Me.cboRooms.SetFocus
```

moves the focus to the combo box control with the room numbers. When this code is executed, the cboRoom_Enter event procedure will be triggered.

◎ Hands-On 26-4: Using the AfterUpdate Event Procedure for the Combo Box Control

1. Make sure that the frmDataEntryMain form is open in Design view.

2. Right-click the list box control to the right of the **Site ID** label and choose **Build Event** from the shortcut menu.

3. In the Code window, choose the **AfterUpdate** event from the Procedure drop-down box and set a breakpoint on the first line of this procedure.

4. Switch to Form view of the **frmDataEntryMain** form and make another selection from the Site ID combo box. When the Code window appears in Break mode, step through the code line by line by pressing **F8**. Notice that the following three event procedures are run:

```
cboSiteId_BeforeUpdate
cboSiteId_AfterUpdate
cboRoom_Enter
```

5. When the procedure finishes executing, activate the **frmDataEntryMain** form.

NotInList (Control)

The NotInList event is triggered if the user enters a value that is not in the list when the LimitToList property of a combo box control is set to True. The NotInList event procedure can take the following two arguments:

- **NewData** — A string that Access uses for passing to the event procedure the text that the user entered.
- **Response** — An integer specifying what Access should do after the procedure executes. This argument can be set to one of the following constants:
  - *acDataErrAdded* — Set the Response argument to acDataErrAdded if the event procedure enters a new value in the combo box. This constant tells Access to requery the combo box, adding the new value to the list.
  - *acDataErrDisplay* — Set the Response argument to acDataErrDisplay if you want Access to display the default error message when a user attempts to add a new value to the combo box. The default Access message requires the user to enter a valid value from the list.
  - *acDataErrContinue* — Set the Response argument to acDataErr-Continue if you display your own message in the event procedure. Access will forego displaying its default error message.

The NotInList event applies only to combo boxes. Use this event to display a custom warning message or trigger a custom function that allows the user to add a new item to the list.

For example, after attempting to enter a nonexisting value in the combo box labeled Room Type in the Room Information section of the Asset Management sample form, the following event procedure is executed:

```
Private Sub cboRoomType_NotInList(NewData As String, _
                                  Response As Integer)
    MsgBox "Please select a value from the list.", _
           vbInformation + vbOKOnly, "Invalid entry"
    ' Continue without displaying default error message.
    Response = acDataErrContinue
End Sub
```

The code above displays a custom message if a user attempts to type an invalid entry in the cboRoomType combo box control on the form.

1. Open the **frmDataEntryMain** form in Form view.

2. Select the **Site ID** from the combo box.

3. Select the **Room No** from the combo box or type your own room number value in this box.

4. Type any value in the Room Type combo box and click on the **Operating System** combo box. This will trigger the cboRoomType_NotInList event procedure code to run. Your custom error message should appear. Click **OK** to the message box. Notice that Access does not display its own default message because you set the Response argument to acDataErrContinue.

5. Select the **Room Type** value from the combo box.

Click (Control)

The Click event occurs when the user clicks a control with the left mouse button or presses an Enter key when a command button placed on a form has its Default property set to Yes. The Click event applies only to forms, form sections, and controls on a form. The Asset Management data entry form contains several command buttons that allow the user to add new values to appropriate combo box selections. For example, when the user clicks a button labeled "Add New School," the following Click event procedure is triggered:

```
Private Sub cmdNewSite_Click()
On Error GoTo Err_cmdNewSite_Click

    Dim stDocName As String

    stDocName = "frmAddSite"
    DoCmd.OpenForm stDocName

Exit_cmdNewSite_Click:
    Exit Sub
Err_cmdNewSite_Click:
    MsgBox Err.Description
    Resume Exit_cmdNewSite_Click
End Sub
```

The above event procedure opens the New Site Data Entry Screen dialog (Figure 26-2) where the user can enter new school information.

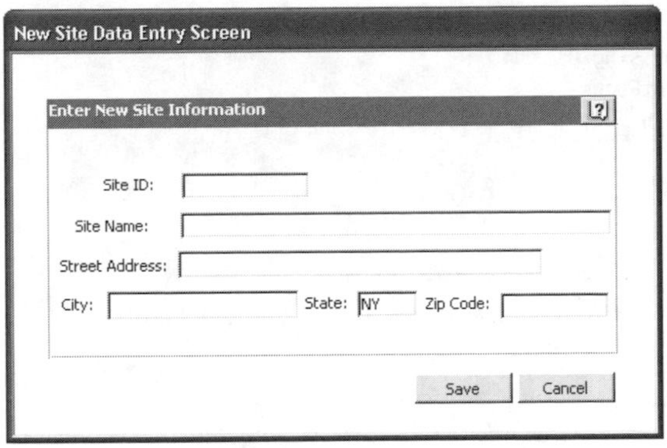

Event Programming in Forms and Reports

Figure 26-2: This data entry form is used for adding new schools to the database.

When the user clicks the Save button on the New Site Data Entry Screen, the Click event procedure attached to this button ensures that:

- All text boxes have been filled in
- The Site ID does not contain more than six characters
- The third character in the Site ID text box is one of the following letters: K, M, R, Q, or X
- The Zip Code text box contains a five-digit zip code
- The Site ID does not already exist in the table

Notice that the New Site Data Entry Screen form is unbound (it isn't connected to a record source such as a table, query, or SQL statement). Because all the text boxes placed on this form are unbound, after successful data validation, the procedure uses the ADO AddNew method to create a new record. This record is added to the tblSites table that provides the recordsource for the Site ID combo box control on the Asset Management data entry form. Next, the cboSiteId combo box control on the Asset Management form is requeried so that the new Site ID can be accessed from the drop-down list when the user returns to the form.

```
Private Sub cmdSaveSiteInfo_Click()
    Dim conn As ADODB.Connection
    Dim rst As New ADODB.Recordset
    Dim ctrl As Control
    Dim count As Integer

    On Error GoTo Err_cmdSaveSiteInfo_Click

    ' validate data prior to save

    For Each ctrl In Me.Controls
      If ctrl.ControlType = acTextBox And IsNull(ctrl) _
                Or IsEmpty(ctrl) Then
        count = count + 1
        If count > 0 Then
          MsgBox "All text fields must be filled in.", _
```

```
                        vbInformation + vbOKOnly, _
                        "Missing Data"
                ctrl.SetFocus
                Exit Sub
            End If
        End If
    Next

    If Len(Me.txtAddSiteId) <> 6 Then
      MsgBox "There must be 6 characters in the Site ID field."
      Me.txtAddSiteId.SetFocus
      Exit Sub
    End If

    If Not ((Me.txtAddSiteId)) Like "##[KMRQX]###" Then
      MsgBox "The 3rd character must be a letter: " _
            & vbCr & vbCr _
            & "K = Brooklyn" & vbCr _
            & "M = Manhattan" & vbCr _
            & "R = Staten Island" & vbCr _
            & "Q = Queens" & vbCr _
            & "X = Bronx", _
        vbInformation + vbOKOnly, "Invalid Borough Designation"
      Me.txtAddSiteId.SetFocus
      Exit Sub
    End If


    ' check the zip code field
    If Len(Me.txtAddZip) <> 5 Then
        MsgBox "Zip codes must be 5 characters " _
            & "in length. " & vbCr & vbCr _
            & "Please re-enter the zip code.", _
            vbInformation + vbOKOnly, "Invalid Zip Code"
        Me.txtAddZip.SetFocus
        Exit Sub
    End If


    ' are any alphabetic characters in zip code?
    If Not IsNumeric(Me.txtAddZip) Then
      MsgBox "You can't have letters in Zip Code.", _
         vbInformation + vbOKOnly, "Invalid Zip Code"
      Me.txtAddZip.SetFocus
      Exit Sub
    End If
    ' save the data
    Set conn = CurrentProject.Connection
        With rst
          .Open "Select * from tblSites", _
             conn, adOpenKeyset, adLockOptimistic
          ' check if the SiteID is not a duplicate
          .Find "SiteID='" & Me.txtAddSiteId & "'"
          ' if site already exists then get out
          If Not rst.EOF Then
            MsgBox "This Site is already in the list : " _
                & rst("SiteID"), _
                vbInformation + vbOKOnly, "Duplicate Site Id"
```

Event Programming in Forms and Reports

```
                Me.txtAddSiteId.SetFocus
        Exit Sub
        End If
            .AddNew
                !SiteID = Me.txtAddSiteId
                !SchoolName = Me.txtAddSchoolName
                !Street = Me.txtAddStreet
                !City = Me.txtAddCity
                !State = Me.txtAddState
                !ZipCode = Me.txtAddZip
            .Update
            .Close
        End With
    Set rst = Nothing
    conn.Close
    Set conn = Nothing

    ' requery the combo box on the main form
    Forms!frmDataEntryMain.cboSiteId.Requery
    ' close the form
    DoCmd.Close

Exit_cmdSaveSiteInfo_Click:
        Exit Sub
Err_cmdSaveSiteInfo_Click:
        MsgBox Err.Description
        Resume Exit_cmdSaveSiteInfo_Click
End Sub
```

◉ Hands-On 26-6: Using the Click Event Procedure for the Command Button Control

1. Open the **frmDataEntryMain** form in Form view.

2. Click the **Add New Site** command button.

3. When the New Site Data Entry Screen window appears, enter the information as shown in Figure 26-3 below.

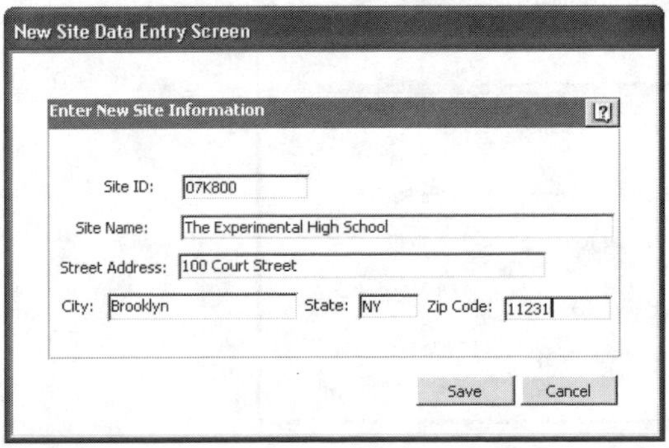

Figure 26-3: After saving the new school information, the Site ID will appear in the Site ID combo box on the main form.

4. Click the **Save** button to save the site information. Access will run the cmdSaveSiteInfo_Click event procedure, as shown earlier. If you have not entered data according to the criteria listed inside this event procedure, Access will not allow you to save data until you correct the problem.

5. Back on the main form, select the newly added site (**07K800**) from the Site ID combo box.

The Asset Management data entry form also displays a number of icons with a question mark. Each icon is actually a command button with a Click event attached to it. When you click on the question mark button you will get a simple form with help information pertaining to the form's section or the data entry screen.

For example, the following Click event procedure is executed upon clicking the question mark button in the Room Information section on the Asset Management data entry form:

```
Private Sub cmdRoomInfoSec_Click()
    Dim stDocName As String
    Dim stLinkCriteria As String

    On Error GoTo Err_cmdRoomInfoSec_Click

    stDocName = "frmHelpMe"
    stLinkCriteria = "HelpId = 2"
    DoCmd.OpenForm stDocName, , , stLinkCriteria

Exit_cmdRoomInfoSec_Click:
        Exit Sub
Err_cmdRoomInfoSec_Click:
        MsgBox Err.Description
        Resume Exit_cmdRoomInfoSec_Click
    End Sub
```

The above procedure loads the appropriate help topic into the text box control, as illustrated in Figure 26-4 below.

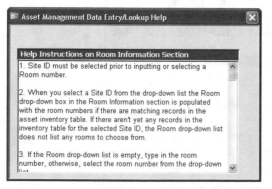

Figure 26-4: By clicking the question mark button in each section of the data entry form, users can get detailed guidelines on how to work with the section.

DblClick (Control)

The DblClick event occurs when the user double-clicks the form or control. This event applies only to forms, form sections, and controls on a form, not controls on a report.

For example, Hands-On 26-7 demonstrates how the user of the Asset Management application can delete an asset by double-clicking on its name.

⊚ Hands-On 26-7: Using the DblClick Event Procedure for the List Box Control

1. Open the **frmDataEntryMain** form in Form view.

2. Make appropriate selections on the Asset Management data entry form.

3. Click the **Add New Asset Type** button in the Hardware Information section. If this button cannot be clicked, you have not made all the necessary selections in the upper part of the form.

4. The Add New Asset Type Data Entry Screen window will appear as shown in Figure 26-5.

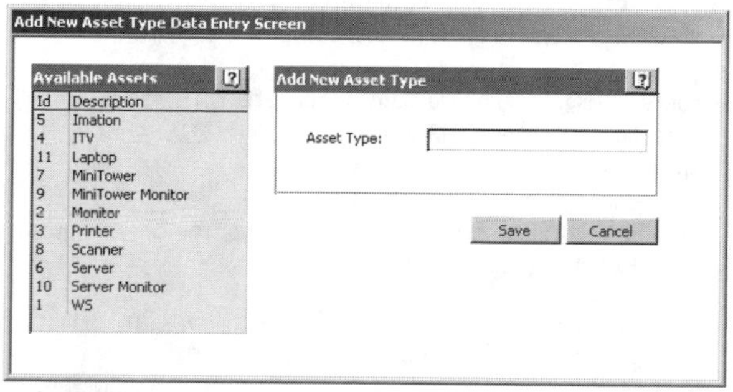

Figure 26-5: This form allows the user to add a new entry to the Asset Type column in the Hardware Information section of the Asset Management form or delete the Asset entry by double-clicking on the entry in the Available Assets list box.

5. In the Add New Asset Type Data Entry Screen window, enter **Zip Drive** in the Asset Type text box and click the **Save** button.

6. In the main form, open the combo box in the **Asset Type** column and scroll down to view the newly added asset type — Zip Drive. Do not make any selection in this combo box.

7. Click the **Add New Asset Type** button in the Hardware Information section to return to the Add New Asset Type Data Entry Screen window.

The left-hand side of the data entry screen (see Figure 26-5) displays a list box with the currently available assets. The user can double-click any item in the list and the DblClick event procedure shown below will determine whether the item can be deleted or not.

```
Private Sub lboxCategories_DblClick(Cancel As Integer)
    Dim conn As ADODB.Connection
    Dim myAsset  As String
    Dim myAssetDesc As String
    Dim Response As String
    Dim strSQL As String

    myAsset = Me.lboxCategories.Value
    myAssetDesc = Me.lboxCategories.Column(1)

      If myAsset >= 1 And myAsset <= 11 Then
        MsgBox "Cannot Delete - This item is being used.", _
            vbOKOnly + vbCritical, "Asset Type: " & myAsset
        Exit Sub
      End If

      If (Not IsNull(DLookup("[AssetType]", "tblProjectDetails", _
          "[AssetType] = " & myAsset))) Or _
          Not IsNull(DLookup("[EquipCategoryId]", "tblEquipInventory", _
          "[EquipCategoryId] = " & myAsset)) Then

        MsgBox "This item cannot be deleted.", _
            vbOKOnly + vbCritical, "Asset Type: " & myAsset
      Else
        Response = MsgBox("Do you want to delete this Asset?", _
            vbYesNo, "Delete - " & myAssetDesc & " ?")
      If Response = 6 Then
          Set conn = CurrentProject.Connection
          strSQL = "DELETE * FROM tblEquipCategories Where EquipCategoryId = "
          conn.Execute (strSQL & myAsset)
          conn.Close
          Set conn = Nothing
          Me.lboxCategories.Requery
        End If
      End If
      DoCmd.Close

    ' requery the combo box on the subform
    Forms!frmDataEntryMain.frmSubProjectDetails.Form.EquipCatId.Requery
End Sub
```

8. Double-click on **Zip Drive** in the Available Assets list box. The DblClick event procedure attached to the list box will ask you whether you want to delete this asset. Click **Yes** to the message.

Notice that the Zip Drive entry disappears from the Available Assets list box.

9. Click the **Cancel** button to exit the Add New Asset Type Data Entry Screen window.

Chapter Summary

In this chapter you worked with a custom Microsoft Access application and learned how to write event procedures for various controls placed on an Access form. There are a number of other event procedures not discussed here that control how the Asset Management form and its controls respond to the user's actions. As you explore this application on your own you will start noticing the areas where writing additional event handlers would prove beneficial to the application's users. So get to it. Tear this sample application apart. Rebuild it. Add new features. Change the user interface if you want. Learn how to handle whatever event may come your way. And be prepared, because events happen frequently in an Access application, and sooner or later you'll need to respond to them.

In the next chapter you learn how to handle an object's events from classes other than the form classes, as well as how to program and raise your own events.

Chapter 27

More about Event Programming

So far in this book you've worked with event procedures that executed from the form or report class module when a certain event occurred for a form, report, or a control. You probably noticed that event programming, as you've seen it implemented in the form and report class modules, require that you copy and paste your existing event code into new form or report events in order to obtain exactly the same functionality. For instance, say you added certain features to a text box on one form and now you'd like to have a text box on other forms behave in the same way. You could react to the text box's events in the same way on all your forms by entering the same event procedure code in a form class module for each form, or you could save keystrokes by learning how to centralize and reuse your event code.

You can avoid typing the same event procedure code again and again by using classes. Recall that we've already used classes in this book — in Chapter 8 you learned how you can design your own objects in VBA by writing code in a standalone class module. You worked with property procedures that allowed data to be read or written to the object. You also learned how to create functions in a class module that worked as object methods. In this chapter you learn how to react to an object's events from a standalone class module. The following new VBA terms will be introduced:

- **Event Sink** — A class that implements an event. Only classes can sink events.
- **Event Source** — An object that raises events. An event source can have multiple event sinks. Note: Source and sink terminology is derived from electronics. A device that outputs current when active is said to be sourcing current. A device that draws current into it when active is said to be sinking current.
- **WithEvents** — A keyword that allows you to handle an object's events inside classes other than form or report classes. The variable that you declare for the WithEvents keyword is used to handle an object's events.
- **Event** — A statement used to declare a user-defined event. The Event declaration must appear in a class module.
- **RaiseEvent** — A statement used to call a custom event. The custom event must first be declared using the Event statement.

Sinking Events in Standalone Class Modules

Instead of writing your event procedures in the form and report class modules, you can make the maintenance of your Microsoft Access applications much simpler by writing the event code in standalone class modules.

Recall that a *standalone class module* is a special type of a class module that is not associated with any particular form or a report. This class module can be inserted in the Visual Basic Editor window by choosing Insert | Class Module. In addition to creating custom objects (see examples in Chapter 8), standalone class modules can implement object events.

The process of listening to an object's events is called *sinking the event*. To sink (handle) events in a standalone class module you must use the WithEvents keyword. This keyword will tell the class that you want to sink some or all of the object's events in the class module. You determine which events you want to sink by writing appropriate event code (see Custom Project 27-1). Only classes can sink events. Therefore, the WithEvents keyword can only be used in classes. You can use the WithEvents keyword to declare as many individual variables as you need; however, you cannot create arrays using WithEvents.

An object that generates events is called an *event source*. The process of broadcasting an event is called *sourcing the event*. To handle events raised by an event source you must declare an object variable using the WithEvents keyword. For example, to react to form events in a standalone class module, you would need to enter the following module-level variable declaration in the class module:

```
Private WithEvents m_frm As Access.Form
```

In the above statement, m_frm is the name of the object variable that references the Form object. While you can use any variable name you want, this variable cannot be a generic object. That means you cannot declare it as Object. If the variable were declared as Object, Visual Basic wouldn't know what type library should be used. Therefore, it would not be able to provide you with the names of events that you can write code for.

Now, let's walk through these new concepts step by step. Custom Project 27-1 demonstrates how to create a record logger class that handles a form's AfterUpdate event. Each time the AfterUpdate event occurs, this class will enter information about the newly created record into a text file. With minor modifications, this class will use the same event code that was introduced in Hands-On 24-5 (Chapter 24).

◎ Custom Project 27-1: Sinking Events in a Standalone Class Module

Part 1: File Preparation

1. Open the **Acc2003_Chap27.mdb** file from the book's downloadable files or, if you'd like to start from scratch, create a new Microsoft Office Access database. This database should contain the Customers, Products, Suppliers, and Categories tables from the sample Northwind database. You can import these objects by choosing **File | Get External Data | Import**.

2. In the Database window, click the **Forms** object button and double-click **Create form by using wizard**. Use the Form Wizard dialogs to create a new form based on the Customers table. Select all the fields from the **Customers** table and specify **Columnar** layout, **Blueprint** style, and **frmCustomers** as the form's title. After you click **Finish**, the newly designed frmCustomers form will appear in the Form view as shown in Figure 27-1.

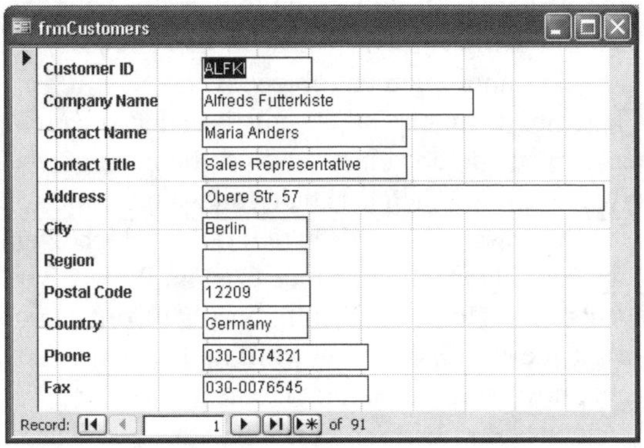

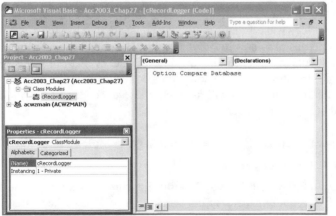

Figure 27-1: The frmCustomers form is used in Custom Project 27-1 to demonstrate how an object's event can be handled outside of the form class module.

3. Close the frmCustomers form created in step 2 above.

Part 2: Creating the cRecordLogger Class

1. In the Database window, press **Alt+F11** to activate the Visual Basic Editor window.

2. Insert a new class module by choosing **Insert | Class Module**. A new class called Class1 will appear in the Project Explorer window. Use the Properties window to change the name of the class to **cRecordLogger** (Figure 27-2).

Figure 27-2: Use the Name property in the Properties window to change the name of the class module.

3. In the cRecordLogger class module's Code window, enter the following module-level variable declaration, just below the Option Compare Database statement:

```
Private WithEvents m_frm As Access.Form
```

Now that you've declared the object variable WithEvents, the variable name m_frm appears in the Object box in your class module (Figure 27-3). When you select this variable from the drop-down list, the valid events for that object will appear in the Procedure box (Figure 27-4). By choosing an event from the Procedure drop-down list, an empty procedure stub will be added to the class module where you can write your code for handling the selected event. By default, Access adds the Load event procedure stub after selecting an object from the Object drop-down list.

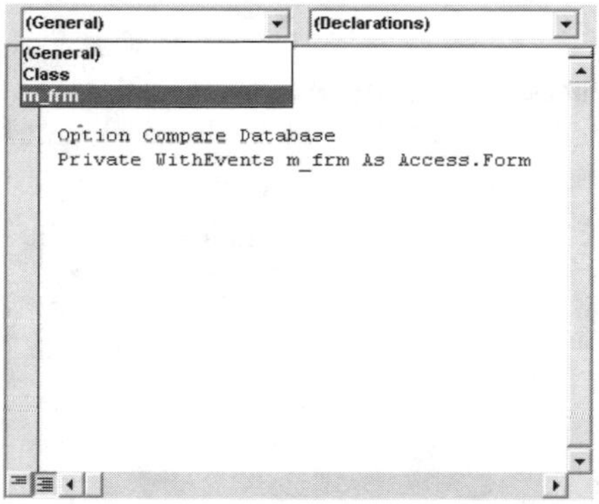

Figure 27-3: The Object drop-down list in the cRecordLogger's Code window lists the m_frm object variable that was declared using the WithEvents keyword.

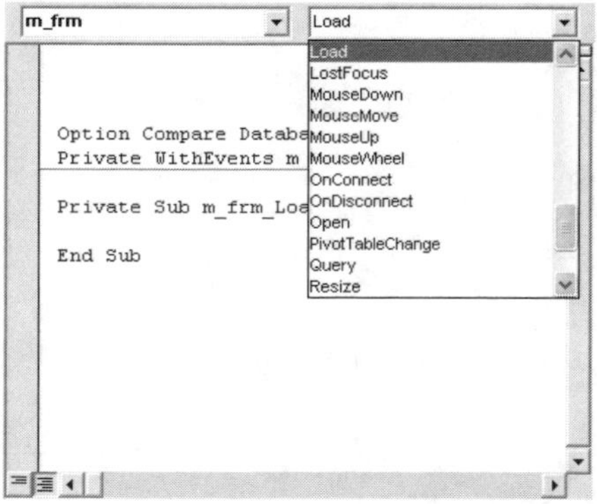

Figure 27-4: The Procedure drop-down list in the cRecordLogger's Code window lists the valid events for the object declared with the WithEvents keyword.

4. In the cRecordLogger class module's Code window, enter the following Property procedure just below the variable declaration:

```
Public Property Set Form(cur_frm As Form)
    Set m_frm = cur_frm
    m_frm.AfterUpdate = "[Event Procedure]"
End Property
```

In order to sink events in the class module, you must tell the class which specific form's events the class should be responding to. You do this by writing the Property Set procedure. Recall from Chapter 8 that Property Set procedures are used to assign a reference to an object. Therefore, the statement

```
Set m_frm = cur_frm
```

will assign the current form (passed in the cur_frm variable) to the m_frm object variable declared in step 3 above.

Pointing the object variable (m_frm) at the object (cur_frm) isn't enough. Access will not raise the event unless the object's Event property is set to "[Event Procedure]". Therefore, the second statement in the procedure above

```
m_frm.AfterUpdate = "[Event Procedure]"
```

will ensure that Access knows that it must raise the form's AfterUpdate event.

5. Choose **Tools | References** and add the **Microsoft Scripting Runtime Library** to the class module. You will need this library to gain access to the File System in the next step.

6. In the cRecordLogger class module's Code window, enter the following event procedure:

```
Private Sub m_frm_AfterUpdate()
    Dim fso As FileSystemObject
    Dim myFile As Object
    Dim strFileN As String
    On Error Resume Next

    Set fso = New FileSystemObject
    strFileN = "C:\MyCust.txt"
    Set myFile = fso.GetFile(strFileN)

    If Err.number = 0 Then
        ' open text file
        Set myFile = fso.OpenTextFile(strFileN, 8)
    Else
        ' create a text file
        Set myFile = fso.CreateTextFile(strFileN)
    End If

    myFile.WriteLine UCase(m_frm.Controls(0)) & _
        " Created on: " & Date & " " & Time & _
        " (Form: " & m_frm.Name & ")"

    myFile.Close
    Set fso = Nothing
    MsgBox "See the audit trail in " & strFileN & "."
End Sub
```

The code inside the m_frm_AfterUpdate event procedure will be executed after Access finds that the form's AfterUpdate property is set to "[Event Procedure]". This code tells Access to open or create a text file named

C:\MyCust.txt and write a line consisting of the value of the first control on the form (m_frm.Controls(0)), the date and time the record was inserted or modified, and the name of the form.

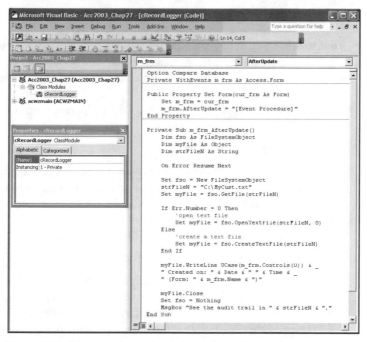

Figure 27-5: A custom cRecordLogger class is used to handle a form's AfterUpdate event.

7. Save the code that you wrote in the class module by clicking the **Save** button on the toolbar or choosing **File | Save**. When the Save As dialog box appears with cRecordLogger in the text box, click **OK**.

For the events to actually fire now that you've written the code to handle the event in the standalone class module, you need to instantiate the class and pass it the object whose events you want to track. This requires that you write a couple of lines of code in your form's class module.

Part 3: Creating an Instance of the Custom Class in the Form's Class Module

1. In the Database window, select the **frmCustomers** form you created in step 2 of Part 1 and click the **Design** button.

2. While frmCustomers is in Design view, choose **View | Code**.

3. In the frmCustomers Code window, enter the following code:

```
Private clsRecordLogger As cRecordLogger

Private Sub Form_Open(Cancel As Integer)
    Set clsRecordLogger = New cRecordLogger
```

```
        Set clsRecordLogger.Form = Me
End Sub

Private Sub Form_Close()
    Set clsRecordLogger = Nothing
End Sub
```

To instantiate a custom class module, we begin by declaring a module-level object variable, clsRecordLogger, as the name of our custom class, cRecordLogger. You can choose any name you wish for your variable name.

Next, we instantiate the class in the Form_Open event procedure by using the following Set statement:

```
Set clsRecordLogger = New cRecordLogger
```

Notice that you must use the New keyword to create a new object of a particular class. By setting the reference to an actual instance of the object when the form first opens, we ensure that the object refers to an actual object by the time the event is first fired.

The second statement in the Form_Open event procedure

```
Set clsRecordLogger.Form = Me
```

sets the Form property defined by the Property procedure in the class module (see step 4 of Part 2) to the Form object whose events we want to sink. The Me keyword represents the current instance of the Form class.

When you are done pointing the object variable to the instance of the custom class, it is a good idea to release the variable reference. We've done this by setting the object variable clsRecordLogger to Nothing in the Form_Close event procedure. The complete code entered in the frmCustomers form class module is shown in Figure 27-6.

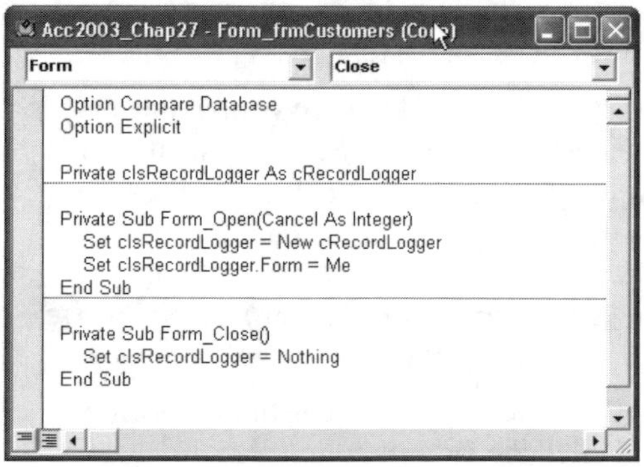

Figure 27-6: To sink form events in a custom class module, you must enter some code in the form class module.

4. Save the code you entered in step 3 above by clicking the **Save** button on the toolbar.

5. Close the frmCustomers form.

Now that all the code has been written in the standalone class module and in the form class module, it's time to test our project.

Part 4: Testing the cRecordLogger Custom Class

1. Open the **frmCustomers** form in Form view.
2. Choose **Records | Data Entry**.
3. Enter **MARSK** in the Customer ID text box and **Marski Enterprises** in the Company Name text box (Figure 27-7). Press the record selector on the left side of the form to save the record.

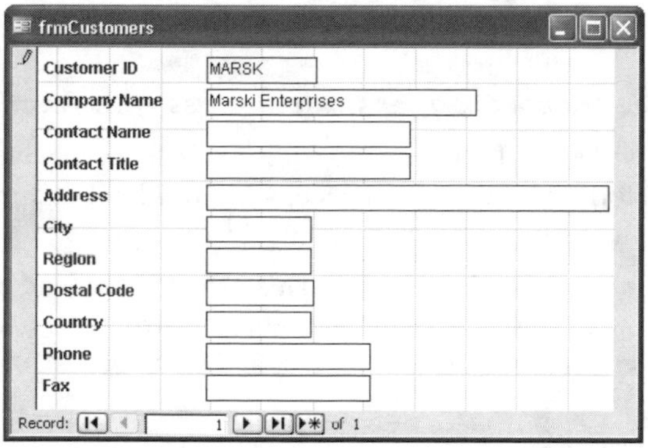

Figure 27-7: The frmCustomers form in the Data Entry mode is used for testing out the custom cRecordLogger class.

When you save the newly entered record, a message box appears with the text, "See the audit trail in C:\MyCust.txt." Recall that this message was programmed inside the m_frm_AfterUpdate() event procedure in the cRecordLogger class module. It looks like our custom class has success-fully sunk the AfterUpdate event. The form's AfterUpdate event was prop-agated to the custom class module.

4. Click **OK** to close the message box.
5. Activate Windows Explorer and open the **C:\MyCust.txt** file.

The MyCust.txt file (Figure 27-8) displays the record log. You may want to revise the m_frm_AfterUpdate() event procedure so that you can track whether a record was created or modified.

Figure 27-8: The MyCust.txt file is used by the cRecordLogger custom class for track-ing record additions.

6. Close the C:\MyCust.txt file.

7. Add few more records to the frmCustomers form and check out the MyCust.txt file.

8. Close the frmCustomers form.

Now that you know how to sink the form's AfterUpdate event outside the form class module, you can use the same idea to sink other form events in a class module and make your code easier to implement and maintenance free. Just remember that if you want to sink events in a standalone class module, you must write code in two places: in your class module and in your form or report class module. The class module must contain a module-level WithEvents variable declaration and you must set the reference to an actual instance of the object in the form or report module.

Part 5: Using the cRecordLogger Custom Class with Another Form

The code you've written so far in this project is ready for reuse in another Microsoft Access form. In the remaining steps, we will hook it up to the frmProducts form. Let's begin by creating this form.

1. In the Database window, choose the **Forms** object button and click the **New** button. In the New Form window, choose **AutoForm: Columnar**, choose **Products** from the drop-down list, and click **OK** to complete your selections.

2. When the Products form appears, click the **Save** button on the toolbar. In the Save As dialog box, type **frmProducts** for the form name and click **OK**.

3. Choose **View | Design View** to open frmProducts in Design view.

4. Choose **View | Code** to activate the frmProducts Code window.

5. Copy the code from the **frmCustomers** Code window to the **frmProducts** Code window. The code in the frmProducts Code window should match Figure 27-6 shown earlier.

6. In the frmProducts Code window, replace all the references to the object variable clsRecordLogger with **clsRecordLogger2**.

➔ **Note:** To quickly perform this operation, position the cursor inside the first clsRecordLogger variable name and choose Edit | Replace. The Find What text box should automatically display the name of the variable you want to replace. Type clsRecordLogger2 in the Replace With text box and click the Replace All button. Click OK to confirm the replacement of four variable names. Click Cancel to exit the Replace dialog box.

7. Save and close the frmProducts form.

8. Open the **frmProducts** form in Form view.

9. Choose **Records | Data Entry**.

10. Enter **Delicious Raisins** in the Product Name text box and press the record selector on the left side of the form to save the record.

At this point you should receive the custom message about the audit trail that you defined in the AfterUpdate event procedure within the custom cRecordLogger class module. This indicates that the AfterUpdate event that was raised by the form when you saved the newly entered record was successfully propagated to the custom class module.

11. Click **OK** to close the message box.

12. Close the frmProducts form.

13. Open the **C:\MyCust.txt** file to view the record log. You may want to choose a more generic name for your record log text file since it will be tracking various types of information.

Writing Event Procedure Code in Two Places

If you write event procedure code for the same event both in the form module and the class module, the code defined in the form class module will run first, followed by the code in the custom class module. You can easily test this by entering the following Form_AfterUpdate event procedure code in the form class module of the frmCustomers or frmProducts forms prepared in Custom Project 27-1:

```
Private Sub Form_AfterUpdate()
    MsgBox "Transferring control to the custom class."
    ' when you click OK to this message, the code
    ' inside the AfterUpdate procedure in the custom
    ' class module will run
End Sub
```

When you open the form and add and save a new record, the Form_ AfterUpdate event will fire and you will see the message about transferring control to the custom class. Next, the AfterUpdate event procedure will run in the custom class, and you will see a message informing you that you can view the audit trail in the specified text file.

Responding to Control Events in a Class

Everyone designing Microsoft Access forms sooner or later realizes that it takes a long time to customize some of the controls placed on the form. It's no wonder then that once the control is working correctly, if another form requires a control equipped with the same functionality, there is a tendency toward copying the control and its event procedures to a new form. If you followed this chapter carefully you already know a better (and a neater) solution. By using the WithEvents keyword you can create an object variable that points to the control raising the events. Instead of responding to control events in the form module, you will react to these events in a different location: a standalone class module. This lets you write centralized code that is easy to implement in other form controls of the same type.

Suppose you need a text box that converts lowercase letters to uppercase and disallows numbers. Hands-On 27-1 demonstrates how to create a text box with these features and hook it up with any Microsoft Access form.

Hands-On 27-1: Responding to Control Events in a Class

This hands-on requires prior completion of Custom Project 27-1.

1. Activate the **Visual Basic Editor** window and choose **Insert | Class Module**. A new class named Class1 will appear in the Project Explorer window.

2. In the Properties window, click the **(Name)** property and type **UCaseBox** as the new name of Class1. Click again on the **(Name)** property to save the new name. You should see the UCaseBox entry under the Class Modules folder in the Project Explorer.

3. In the UCaseBox class module's Code window, enter the following code:

```
Private WithEvents txtBox As Access.TextBox

Public Function InitializeMe(myTxt As TextBox)
    Set txtBox = myTxt
    txtBox.OnKeyPress = "[Event Procedure]"
End Function

Private Sub txtBox_KeyPress(KeyAscii As Integer)
    Select Case KeyAscii
        Case 48 To 57
          MsgBox "Numbers are not allowed!"
          KeyAscii = 0
        Case Else
        ' convert to uppercase
          KeyAscii = Asc(UCase(Chr(KeyAscii)))
    End Select

    txtBox.FontBold = True
    txtBox.FontItalic = True
    txtBox.BackColor = vbYellow
End Sub
```

Notice that to respond to a control's events in a class module you start by declaring a module-level object variable using the WithEvents keyword. In our text box example, we declared the object variable txtBox as an Access text box control.

Because the form can contain more than one text box control, we should tell the class which text box it needs to respond to. We do this by creating a Property Set procedure (similar to the one created in Custom Project 27-1) or a function procedure like the one shown above. We called this function InitializeMe, but you can use any name you wish. Recall from Chapter 8 that a function entered in a class module serves as an object's method. We will call the InitializeMe method later from a form class module and pass it the actual control we want it to respond to (see step 8). The

InitializeMe method will assign the passed control to the WithEvents object variable like this:

```
Set txtBox = myTxt
```

Next, we set the text box KeyPress property to "[Event Procedure]" to tell the class that we are interested in tracking this particular event.

Finally, we write the event procedure code for the text box control's KeyPress event. This code begins by checking the value of the key that was pressed by the user. If a number was entered, the user is advised that numbers aren't allowed and the digit is removed from the text box by setting the value of KeyAscii to zero (0). Otherwise, if the user typed a lowercase letter, the character is converted to uppercase using the following statement:

```
KeyAscii = Asc(UCase(Chr(KeyAscii)))
```

KeyAscii is an integer that returns a numerical ANSI keycode. To convert the KeyAscii argument into a character, we use the Chr function:

```
Chr(KeyAscii)
```

Once we've converted a key into a character we use the UCase function to convert it to uppercase:

```
UCase(Chr(KeyAscii))
```

Finally, we translate the character back to an ANSI number by using the Asc function:

```
Asc(UCase(Chr(KeyAscii)))
```

The txtBox_KeyPress event procedure ends by adding some visual enhancements to the text box. The text entered in it will appear in italics and bold type on a yellow background.

4. Save the code you entered in the UCaseBox class module's Code window by pressing the **Save** button on the toolbar.

5. In Design view, open the **frmProducts** form you created in Custom Project 27-1 earlier in this chapter.

6. Choose **View | Code** to switch to the frmProducts form's Code window.

The Form_frmProducts class module's Code window should already contain code you entered while working with Part 4 of Custom Project 27-1 earlier in this chapter. To connect the UCaseBox class module with the actual text box on any Access form, you would need to enter the code as shown below in a form's class module (do not enter it yet):

```
' module-level variable declaration
Private clsTextBox1 As UCaseBox
```

```
Private Sub Form_Open(Cancel As Integer)
    Set clsTextBox1 = New UCaseBox
    clsTextBox1.InitializeMe Me.Controls("ProductName")
End Sub

Private Sub Form_Close()
    Set clsTextBox1 = Nothing
End Sub
```

Since the frmProducts form already contains a call to the cRecordLogger class created earlier, all of the procedures we need are already in place; therefore, we will simply add the appropriate lines of code to the existing procedures. So let's proceed.

7. In the Form_frmProducts Code window, enter the following module-level variable declaration just above the Form_Open event procedure (see Figure 27-9):

```
Private clsTextBox1 As UCaseBox
```

The above statement declares the clsTextBox1 class variable. This variable is used in instantiating the UCaseBox object and connecting it with the actual text box control on the form (see step 8 below).

8. Enter the following lines of code before the End Sub of the Form_Open event procedure (see Figure 27-9):

```
Set clsTextBox1 = New UCaseBox
clsTextBox1.InitializeMe Me.Controls("ProductName")
```

Before our UCaseBox class can respond to a text box's events you need these two lines of code; the first one sets the class variable clsTxtBox1 to a new instance of the UCaseBox class, and the second one calls the class InitializeMe method and supplies it with the name of the text box control.

9. Enter the following line of code before the End Sub of the Form_Close event procedure (see Figure 27-9):

```
Set clsTextBox1 = Nothing
```

When we are done with the object variable, we set it to Nothing to release the resources that have been assigned to it.

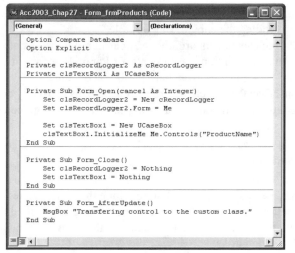

Figure 27-9: The form class module shows code that instantiates and hooks up objects created in the cRecordLogger and UCaseBox class modules with the form and text box control.

10. Save the changes made in the Code window by clicking the **Save** button on the toolbar.

11. Open the **frmProducts** form in Form view and choose **Records | Data Entry**.

12. Enter **prune butter** in the Product Name text box. Notice that as you type, the characters you enter are converted to uppercase. They are also made bold and italics, and appear on a yellow background. If you happen to press a number key that is disallowed by your custom KeyPress event, you receive an error message.

13. Close the frmProducts form. Because this form also responds to the AfterUpdate event that we programmed in Custom Project 27-1, you should see two message boxes as you exit this form.

Declaring and Raising Events

Standalone class modules automatically support two events: Initialize and Terminate. Use the Initialize event to give the variables in your classes initial values. The Initialize event is called when you make a new instance of a class. The Terminate event is called when you set the instance to Nothing.

In addition to these default events, you can define custom events for your class module. To create a custom event, use the Event statement in the declaration section of a class module. For example, the following statement declares an event named SendFlowers that requires two arguments:

```
Public Event SendFlowers(ByVal strName As String, cancel As Boolean)
```

The Event statement declares a user-defined event. This statement is followed by the name of the event and any arguments that will be passed to the event procedure. Arguments are separated by commas. An event can have ByVal and ByRef arguments. Recall that when passing the variable ByRef, you are actually passing the memory location of the variable. If you pass a variable ByVal, you are sending the copy of the variable.

When declaring events with arguments, bear in mind that events cannot have named arguments, optional arguments, or ParamArray arguments. The Public keyword is optional as events are public by default.

Use the RaiseEvent statement to fire the event. This is usually done by creating a method in a class module. For example, here's how you could trigger the SendFlowers event:

```
Public Sub Dispatch(ByVal toWhom As String, cancel As Boolean)
    RaiseEvent SendFlowers(toWhom, True)
End Sub
```

Events can only be raised in the module in which they are declared using the Event statement. After declaring the event and writing the method that will be used for raising the event, you need to switch to the form class module and perform the following tasks:

- Declare a module-level variable of the class type using the WithEvents keyword
- Assign an instance of the class containing the event to the object defined using the WithEvents statement
- Write a procedure that calls the class method
- Write the event handler code

The next hands-on demonstrates how a user-defined event can be used in a class. We will learn how to raise the SendFlowers event from a Microsoft Access form.

⊙ Hands-On 27-2: Declaring and Raising Events

1. Activate the **Visual Basic Editor** window and choose **Insert | Class Module**. A new class named Class1 will appear in the Project Explorer window.

2. In the Properties window, click the **(Name)** property and type **cDispatch** as the new name of Class1. Click again on the **(Name)** property to save the new name. You should see the cDispatch entry under the Class Modules folder in the Project Explorer.

3. In the cDispatch class module's Code window, enter the following code:

```
Public Event SendFlowers(ByVal strName As String, _
                         cancel As Boolean)

Sub Dispatch(ByVal ToWhom As String, cancel As Boolean)
    If ToWhom = "Julitta" Then
        cancel = True
        MsgBox "Dispatch to " & ToWhom & " was cancelled.", _
            vbInformation + vbOKOnly, "Reason Unknown"
    Else
        RaiseEvent SendFlowers(ToWhom, True)
    End If
End Sub
```

The first statement in the code above declares a custom event called SendFlowers. This event will accept two arguments: the name of the person to whom flowers should be sent and a Boolean value of True or False that will allow you to cancel the event if necessary.

Next, the Dispatch procedure is used as a class method. The code states that the flowers should be sent to the person whose name is passed in the ToWhom argument as long as the person's name is not "Julitta." The RaiseEvent statement will call the event handler that we will write in a form module in a later step.

4. Create a new form as shown in Figure 27-10. Notice that this form isn't bound to any data source. Set the Name property of the text box control to **Recipient** and the Name property of the command button to **cmdFlowers**. Save this form as **frmFlowers**.

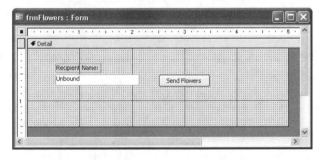

Figure 27-10: The frmFlowers form is used in Hands-On 27-2 to demonstrate the process of raising and handling custom events.

5. While the frmFlowers form is in Design view, choose **View | Code**.

6. Enter the following code in the Form_frmFlowers Code window:

```
Private WithEvents clsDispatch As cDispatch

Private Sub Form_Load()
    Set clsDispatch = New cDispatch
End Sub

Private Sub Form_Close()
    Set clsDispatch = Nothing
End Sub
```

Our form class can only respond to events from an object if it has a reference to that object. Therefore, at the top of the form class module we declare the object variable clsDispatch by using the WithEvents keyword. This means that from now on the instance of the cDispatch class is associated with events.

The next step involves setting the object variable to an object. In the Form_Load event procedure we create a class object with the Set statement and the New keyword.

When the object variable is no longer needed, we release the reference to the object by setting the object variable to Nothing (see the Form_Close event procedure above).

Now that we are done with declaring, setting, and resetting the object variable, let's proceed to write some code that will allow us to raise the SendFlowers event when we click on the Send Flowers button.

7. In the Form_frmFlowers Code window, enter the following Click event procedure for the cmdFlowers command button that you placed on the frmFlowers form:

```
Private Sub cmdFlowers_Click()
    If Len(Me.Recipient) > 0 Then
        clsDispatch.Dispatch Me.Recipient, False
    Else
        MsgBox "Please specify the recipient name."
        Me.Recipient.SetFocus
        Exit Sub
    End If
End Sub
```

Notice that the above event procedure begins by checking whether the user has entered data in the Recipient text box. If the data exists, the Dispatch method is called; otherwise, the user is asked to enter data in the text box. When calling the Dispatch method we must provide two arguments that this method expects: the name of the recipient and the value for the Boolean variable Cancel. Recall that the Dispatch method has the necessary code that raises the SendFlowers event (see step 3 earlier). Now what's left to do is to write an event handler for the SendFlowers event.

8. Select the **clsDispatch** variable from the object drop-down list in the upper-left corner of the Form_frmFlowers Code window. As you make this selection, a template of the event procedure will be inserted into the Code window as shown below:

```
Private Sub clsDispatch_SendFlowers(ByVal strName As String, cancel As Boolean)

End Sub
```

The code that you write within the above procedure stub will be executed when the event is generated by the object.

9. Enter the following statement inside the clsDispatch_SendFlowers procedure stub:

```
MsgBox "Flowers will be sent to " & strName & ".", , "Order taken"
```

Our custom event is not overly exciting but should give you an understanding of how custom events are declared and raised in a standalone class module and how they are consumed in a client application (form class module).

The complete code we entered in the form class module is pictured in Figure 27-11.

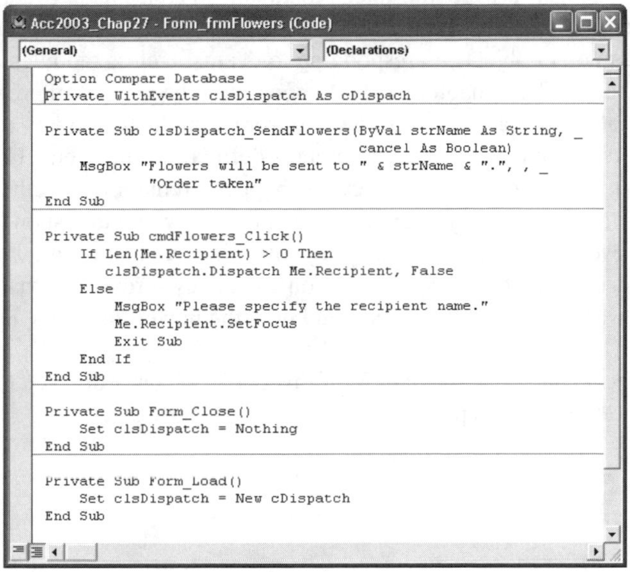

Figure 27-11: The form class module shows code that uses a custom object with its events.

10. To test the code, open the **frmFlowers** form in Form view, type any name in the Recipient text box, and click the **Send Flowers** button. You should see the message generated by the SendFlowers custom event. Also see what happens when you type my name (Julitta) in the text box.

➡ **Note:** If you need more practice declaring and raising custom events, there's an additional example in the Acc2003Chap_27 database. You will find there the default Class1 class module with the Splash event that displays a splash screen when a form is loaded. Also, be sure to try out the example provided in the online help in the RaiseEvent statement topic. The quickest way to find this example is by positioning the cursor in the RaiseEvent statement (located in the cDispatch class module) and pressing F1.

Chapter Summary

In this chapter, you were introduced to advanced concepts in event-driven programming. You learned how you can make your code more manageable and portable to other objects by responding to events in class modules other than form modules. This chapter has also shown you the process of creating your own events for a class and raising them from a public method by calling the RaiseEvent statement with the arguments defined for the event. The important thing to understand is that while events happen all the time whether you respond to them or not, you are the one to decide where to respond to the built-in events. And, if you ever find yourself short of an event, with the knowledge acquired in this chapter, you can always create one that does exactly what you need. Now that you know the power tools, it's up to you to use them.

The next chapter begins Part V of this book, which is devoted to working with Access from web pages.

Taking Your VBA Programming Skills to the Web

Gone are the times when working with Access required the presence of the Microsoft Access application on a user's desktop. Thanks to the development of Internet technologies, you can now publish both static and dynamic Access data to the web.

In this part of the book you learn how Active Server Pages (ASP) and Extensible Markup Language (XML) are used with Microsoft Access to develop database solutions for the World Wide Web.

Access and Active Server Pages

In today's world, everyone wants to be able to access data via the company intranet or the World Wide Web. This book would not be complete without showing you how to take your skills where the demand is. So, how can you make the information stored in your Access database available for others to view or query in a web browser? By adding some HyperText Markup Language (HTML) and Microsoft Visual Basic Scripting Edition (VBScript) to your current VBA skill set, you can start making your applications web-ready. Microsoft Access 2003 continues to offer the File menu's Export command, which you can use to save tables, queries, and forms to the web in one of the following formats: HTML documents (*.html; *htm), Microsoft Active Server Pages (*.asp), Microsoft IIS 1-2 (*.htx; *.idc), and XML (*.xml).

The following hands-on exercise demonstrates how to use the Export command to save a table in the Microsoft Active Server Pages format and later view the file in a web browser.

◎ Hands-On 28-1: Generating an Active Server Page from an Access Table

1. Create a new folder named **Learn_ASP** for this chapter's files.

2. Open the **Acc2003_Chap28.mdb** file from the downloadable files, or create a new Microsoft Access database named Acc2003_Chap28.mdb. If you are creating this file from scratch, use the **File | Get External Data | Import** command and import all the tables from the Northwind sample database.

3. Select the **Employees** table in the Database window and choose **File | Export**.

4. In the Export Table 'Employees' As window (Figure 28-1), use the Save in drop-down list to switch to the **Learn_ASP** folder that you created in step 1 above. Choose **Microsoft Active Server Pages (*.asp)** from the Save as type drop-down list, and click **Export**.

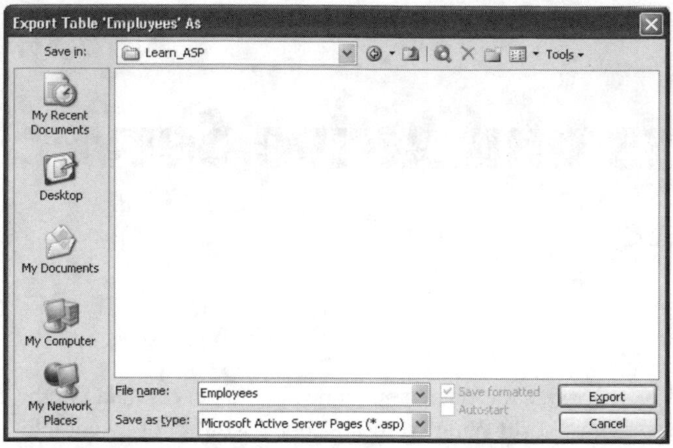

Figure 28-1: This window appears when you choose the Export command on the File menu. To create a dynamic HTML page, type the filename and select Microsoft Active Server Pages from the Save as type drop-down list.

After clicking the Export button, the Microsoft Active Server Pages Output Options window appears (Figure 28-2).

5. Enter the following information in the Microsoft Active Server Pages Output Options window:

Data Source Name: **Northwind**
User to Connect As: **Admin**
Server URL: **http://localhost**

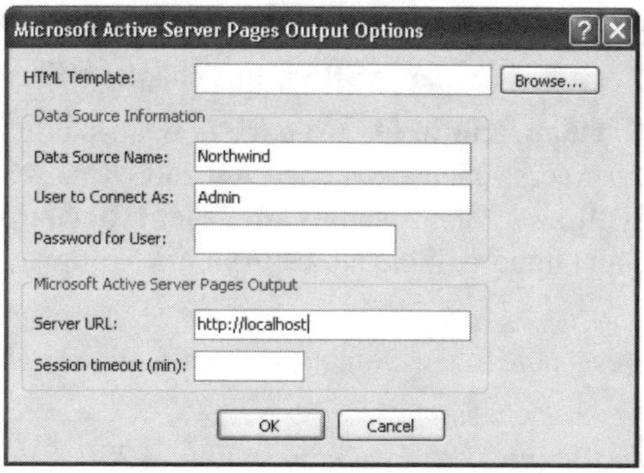

Figure 28-2: The Microsoft Active Server Pages Output Options window allows you to specify the details of your ASP pages.

The Microsoft Active Server Pages Output Options window (Figure 28-2) consists of the following three sections:

■ The top section allows you to specify the formatting of your data. This is done via the HTML Template text box. You can find some sample templates in the \Program Files\Microsoft Office\Templates\1033 folder. Notice that we did not use a template in this hands-on exercise.

■ The middle section is Data Source Information. You must specify the data source name in the text box. The data source name defines the connection that will be used by the server to connect to the Access database to retrieve data. You can use any name you wish. Do not forget what you've called your data source, as the name you entered here will be needed later for setting up the connection. For this hands-on, we've named our data source "Northwind." If the database you'll be connecting to is secured, you will need to specify a username and password to access the database. For this hands-on, we kept the default setting, Admin, and left the password box blank.

■ The bottom section is Microsoft Active Server Pages Output. Here you specify the URL and timeout values for the ASP. Server URL is the network name of the web server. We entered the value "http://localhost" to indicate that the web server is on our computer. The Session timeout value allows you to specify how long a connection will be left open for an idle user. Here we left the text box blank to accept the default value of 5 minutes. However, in a real-life situation, if you find that users are complaining about their sessions timing out, you may want to increase this timeout value.

6. After entering the data in step 5 above, click **OK**. Clicking OK in the window creates the Active Server Pages file named Employees.asp in the Learn_ASP folder. This ASP file is dynamically linked to the Employees table. Because you selected the ASP format, this page will immediately reflect any changes in the underlying data. We will look at the contents of the Employees.asp file in Hands-On 28-2. If you try to access this page now, you'll get an ODBC error because you have not defined the data source.

Before you can actually display this ASP page in your browser, there are extra steps involved that you will perform later in this chapter after you've learned more about Active Server Pages and have taken a look at the contents of the ASP page in Hands-On 28-2:

■ Set up and configure your web server so that the Server URL you indicated in the dialog box above can be accessed (see Hands-On 28-3 and 28-4).

■ Create an ODBC Data Source with the exact name as indicated in the Data Source Name box in the Microsoft Active Server Pages Output Options window (see Hands-On 28-5).

Using the Access built-in Export command to create dynamic web content (as demonstrated in Hands-On 28-1) can get you up and running quickly. However, this chapter's focus is on showing you how you can create your own ASP files from scratch so that you will feel comfortable when displaying, querying, inserting, updating, and deleting data stored in a Microsoft Access database from any web browser.

Introduction to Active Server Pages

With Active Server Pages (ASP), a technology developed by Microsoft, you can design and program powerful and dynamic web applications. The current version of ASP is 3.0, and it is available with Internet Information Services (IIS) 5.0. Active Server Pages are text files with the .asp extension. These files contain standard HTML formatting tags and embedded scripting statements. Because the default scripting language for ASP is VBScript, a subset of Visual Basic and Visual Basic for Applications, you already have many of the skills required to web-enable your Access applications. In addition, the tools you need to make Access work with the intranet or Internet are within your reach. Although most of the examples in this chapter have been prepared using Microsoft Visual InterDev 6.0, you can use Windows Notepad or any other text editor to write your code. So, where do you start? You can start by acquiring some working knowledge of the HyperText Markup Language (HTML). A good place to start is the Internet. For easy, step-by-step tutorials, check out the following web sites: http://www.htmlgoodies.com or http://www.html-tutorials.ca/. Because Active Server Pages are a mix of HTML with a programming language such as VBScript or JavaScript, you should learn as much as you can about each component.

To better understand this chapter's topics, here are some terms to get acquainted with:

■ **HyperText Markup Language (HTML)** — A simple, text-based language that uses special commands known as *tags* to create a document that can be viewed in a browser. HTML tags begin with a less-than sign (<) and end with a greater-than sign (>). For example, to indicate that the text should be displayed in bold letters, you simply type your text between the <B> and </B> tags like this:

```
<B>This text will appear in bold letters</B>
```

Using plain HTML you can produce static web pages with text, images, and hyperlinks to other web pages.

■ **Dynamic HTML (DHTML)** — Allows the HTML tags to be changed programmatically via scripting. Use DHTML to add interactivity to your web pages.

■ **VBScript** — A scripting language based on Microsoft Visual Basic for Applications (VBA). Because this is just a subset of VBA, some of the VBA features have been removed. For example, VBScript does not support data types — every variable is a variant. Like VBA, VBScript is an event-driven language — the VBScript code is executed in response to an event caused by a user action or the web browser itself.

■ **JavaScript** — A compact, object-oriented scripting language invented by Netscape and used for developing client and server Internet applications. This is a cross-platform language that can be embedded in other products and applications, such as web browsers.

■ **Active Server Pages (ASP)** — An Internet technology that enables you to combine HTML, scripts, and reusable ActiveX server components to create dynamic and powerful web-based applications and business solutions. ASP is not limited to a particular language. To create ASP pages, you can use VBScript, JavaScript, or any language for which you have a third-party ActiveX scripting engine.

While HTML pages store the actual data, Active Server Pages only store the information on how to obtain the data. How does this work? Suppose you typed the address of the ASP page in your web browser's address bar and pressed Enter or clicked the Go button. The web server will read the VBScript instructions contained in the ASP page and access the specified database. Once the data is obtained, the web server will put this information into an HTML page and return that page to you in the web browser in plain HTML code. Users never see the instructions contained in your ASP file unless they have access to the web server and have been given the appropriate permissions to open these files. You can rest assured that with ASP your development ideas and intellectual property are well protected.

Because the web server reads and processes the instructions in the ASP page every time your browser requests the page, the information you receive is highly dynamic. ASP allows the page to be built or customized on the fly before the page is returned to the browser. ASP is platform independent. This means that you can view ASP pages in any browser. The two most popular browsers are Internet Explorer and Netscape Navigator.

Hands-on 28-2 shows and describes the contents of the Employees.asp file you created earlier.

◎ Hands-On 28-2: Viewing the Contents of an ASP Page

This hands-on uses the Employees.asp file that was created in Hands-On 28-1.

1. Click the **Start** menu button and choose **Run**. In the Run dialog box, type **notepad C:\Learn_ASP\Employees.asp** (substitute the correct path if necessary) and click **OK** to open the Employees.asp file. When the text editor opens, you will see the Active Server Pages code, as shown in Figure 28-3.

2. Scroll down in Notepad and take a look at the structure of this file. Notice the many tags between the angle brackets: <HTML>, <HEAD>, </HEAD>, <TITLE>, </TITLE>, <BODY>, <B>, </B>, <TR>, and so on.

The tags tell the browser how to display the file. The <HTML> tag at the beginning of the file tells the browser that what follows is an HTML document. The closing </HTML> tag at the end of the file tells the browser that the HTML document is completed. The closing tags are denoted by placing the forward slash before the tag name (for example, </TITLE>, </BODY>, </HTML>). Closing tags cancel the effect of the tag. Refer to the web sites mentioned at the beginning of this section to learn the meaning of all the HTML tags used in the Employees.asp file.

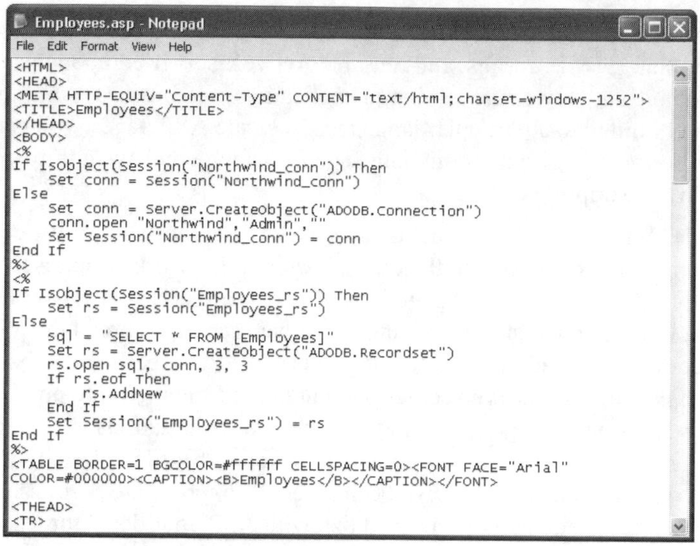

Figure 28-3: You can explore the contents of the Employees.asp file created by the Microsoft Access Export command in Hands-On 28-1 by opening it in Notepad.

In addition to HTML tags that are interpreted by the browser when the page is viewed, the Employees.asp file contains the <% and %> symbols. The <% says that what follows is a server-side script, not HTML. The %> indicates the end of a script segment. The script code between the <% and %> delimiters is executed on the web server as the page is processed. Any values you want returned by the script are placed between the <%= and %> delimiters.

Active Server Pages (ASP) is a form of server-side scripting. A *server-side script* is the script code that runs on the web server before the page comes down to the client (the user's machine). This script begins to run when a browser requests an .asp file from your web server. The web server then calls the ASP Interpreter (ASP.dll), which processes the blocks of code between the <% and %> delimiter tags. After the script commands are executed, the web page is sent to the browser. Server-side scripts cannot be readily copied because only the result of the script is returned to the browser. Users cannot view the script commands that created the page they are viewing. All they can see is the HTML source code for the page.

In addition to server-side scripts, an .asp file can contain client scripts. A *client script* is the script code that is processed by a browser on the user's machine while the page is viewed. Client scripts are enclosed between <SCRIPT> and </SCRIPT> tags. When a browser encounters a <SCRIPT> tag, it sends the script that follows this tag to a scripting engine. A scripting engine is the part of the web browser that processes the scripts. Because not all browsers can process client scripts, comment tags (<!-- and -->) are often used to make browsers that do not recognize the <SCRIPT> tag ignore it.

When you scroll down in the Employees.asp file, you will notice several VBScript lines that output data to a web page. The output appears between the <%= and %> delimiters (notice the highlighted statement in Figure 28-4).

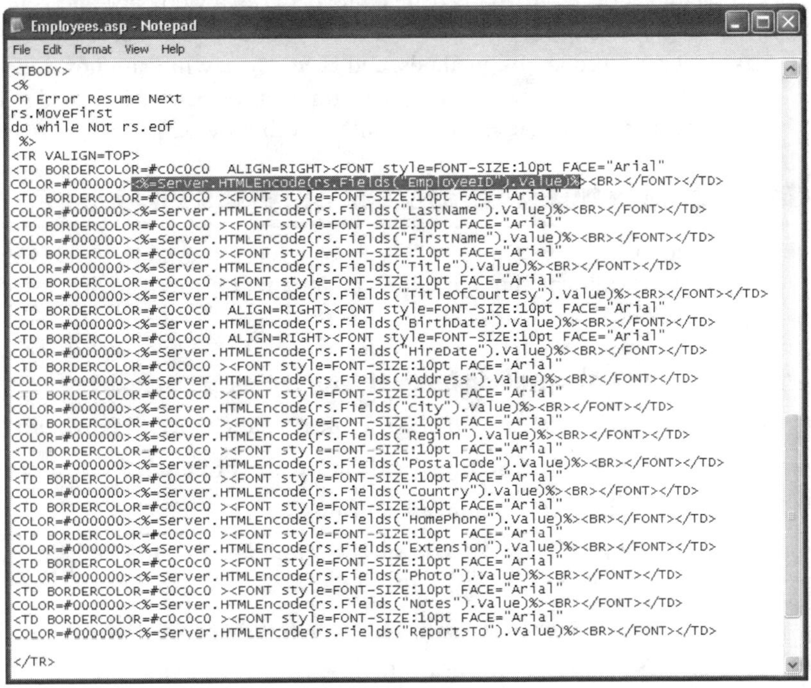

Figure 28-4: The contents of an ASP page as displayed in the Windows Notepad application. The highlighted statement will cause the value of the Employee field to appear on the web page when the page is viewed in the browser.

By using the equals sign inside these delimiters, you can write a VBScript variable value to a web page.

3. Close the Employees.asp file and exit Notepad.

The ASP Object Model

ASP has its own object model consisting of the objects shown in Table 28-1.

Table 28-1: The ASP Object Model

ASP Object Name	Object Description
Request	Obtains information from a user
Response	Sends the information to the client browser
Application	Shares information for all the users of an application
Server	Creates server components and server settings
Session	Stores information pertaining to a particular visitor

The ASP objects have methods, properties, and events that can be called to manipulate various features. For example, the Response object's Write method allows you to write text to the client browser. The CreateObject method of the Server object is required to create a link between a web page and your Access database. Although this chapter does not introduce you to all of the available ASP objects, properties, methods, and events, you will learn how to use the objects and methods required for performing a specific task related to displaying or manipulating Access data from the web browser.

Installing Internet Information Services (IIS)

To perform all the examples in this chapter, let's proceed to Hands-On 28-3, which will walk you through setting up Internet Information Services 5.0 on your computer.

⊙ Hands-On 28-3: Installing Internet Information Services 5.0

1. Insert the Windows 2000 or XP Professional CD-ROM into a drive.
2. Click **Start**, select **Settings**, and click **Control Panel**.
3. Double-click **Add/Remove Programs**.
4. Click the **Add/Remove Windows Components** button in the left-hand panel.
5. Click the box beside **Internet Information Services (IIS)**.
6. Click **Next** to start the installation.
7. When the installation is complete, click **Finish** to close the wizard.

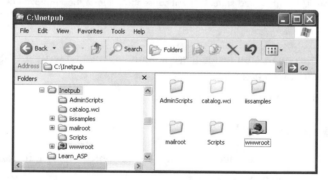

Figure 28-5: After completing the Internet Information Services installation steps in Hands-On 28-3, you should see the Inetpub folder on your computer. The \Inetpub\wwwroot folder is automatically set as the home directory for IIS 5.0.

Creating a Virtual Directory

The default home directory for the World Wide Web service is \Inetpub\ wwwroot. Files located in the home directory and its subdirectories are automatically available to visitors to your site. You can create virtual directories to make web pages that are not stored in the home directory or its subdirectories available for viewing. A virtual directory appears to client browsers as if it were physically contained in the home directory.

For the purposes of this chapter, you created a directory called Learn_ASP on your computer (see Hands-On 28-1). In Hands-On 28-4 we will set up the Learn_ASP folder as a virtual directory.

⊚ Hands-On 28-4: Creating a Virtual Directory

1. Open **Windows Explorer** and right-click the **Learn_ASP** folder you created in Hands-On 28-1. Select **Properties** from the shortcut menu.

2. In the Learn_ASP Properties window, click the **Web Sharing** tab (Figure 28-6). This window may look slightly different if you are using Windows 2000.

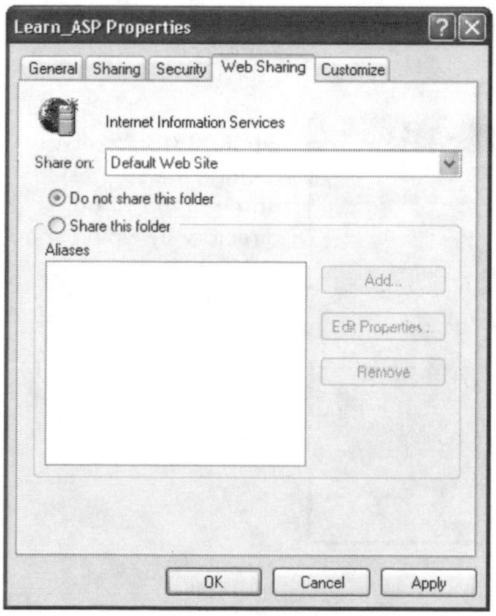

Figure 28-6: You can use the Learn_ASP Properties window to quickly set up an alias users will use to access pages in the specified directory.

3. Click the **Share this folder** option button. The Edit Alias window will appear, as shown in Figure 28-7.

    A virtual directory has an *alias*, a name that client browsers use to access that directory. An alias is often used to shorten a long directory name. In addition, an alias provides increased security. Because users do not know where your files are physically located on the server, they cannot modify them.

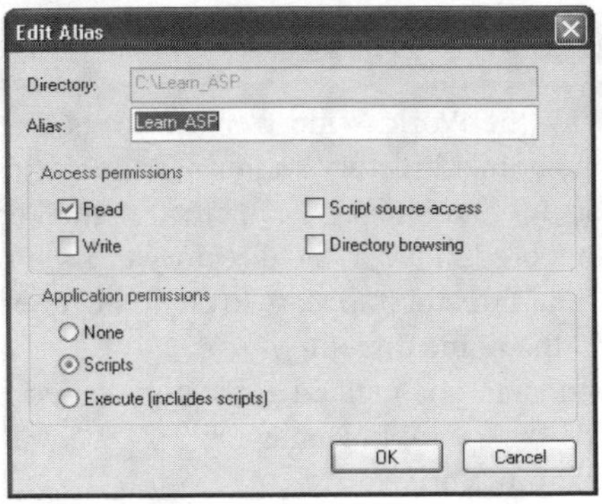

Figure 28-7: The Edit Alias window can be accessed from the Properties window by choosing the Share this folder button (see Figure 28-6). The directory name is automatically entered as the suggested name for the virtual directory (alias).

4. Enter **NorthDB** in the Alias box, as shown in Figure 28-8. In the Access permissions area, make sure that the **Read** permission is selected. In the Application permissions area, make sure that the **Scripts** option button is selected. Click **OK** to close the window.

   When you set up a virtual directory, it is important to specify the access permissions for that directory. The Read permission allows users to access web pages. The Read permission is turned on by default. In addition, the Scripts permission should be turned on for virtual directories that will contain ASP pages.

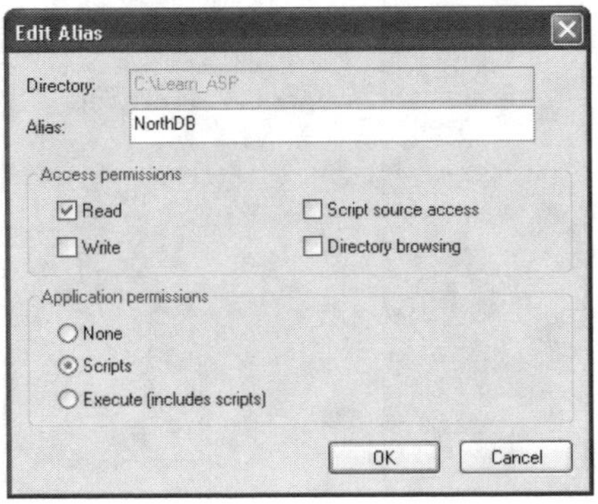

Figure 28-8: You can change the suggested name of the virtual directory by typing your own entry in the Alias box.

5. When you click **OK**, you will see the alias NorthDB listed in the Aliases box (see Figure 28-9).

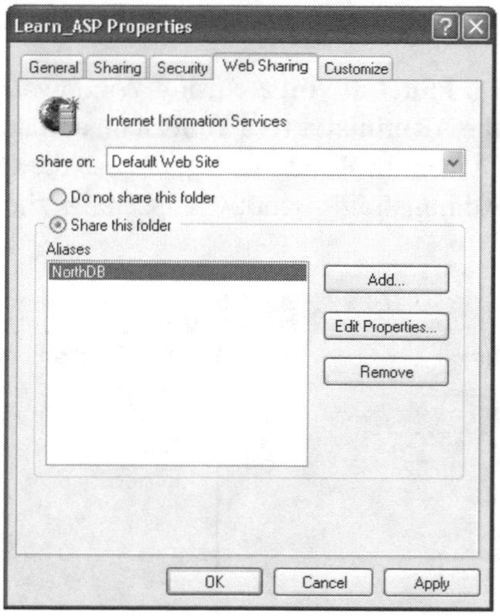

Figure 28-9: NorthDB is the name your browser will use to access files in the Learn_ASP folder while working with this chapter.

6. Click **OK** to close the Learn_ASP Properties window.

7. To ensure that all the components you need for the exercises in this chapter can be quickly accessed, copy the sample **Northwind.mdb** database file from the \Program Files\Microsoft Office\Office11\Samples folder to your Learn_ASP folder.

8. Ensure that the Employees.asp file you created at the beginning of this chapter is also located in the Learn_ASP folder.

Now that you have a place for storing the necessary files, let's proceed to the next section where we establish a connection with our Microsoft Access sample database.

Connecting to a Microsoft Access Database via DSN

For the web server to access a database, you need to define an ODBC data source. A *data source* contains the information required to connect to a data provider, in this case, a Microsoft Access database. Earlier in this book you learned about three types of data sources: User DSN, File DSN, and System DSN. File DSNs offer the most flexibility for web work. Because the information required to connect to the data source is stored in a text file, file DSNs can be readily shared with other users and even easily moved to another web server if needed.

The following hands-on exercise will walk you through the steps required to set up a File DSN on your computer.

⊚ Hands-On 28-5: Creating a File DSN

1. Open the Windows **Control Panel**. If you are using Windows XP or Windows 2000, double-click the **Administrative Tools** icon and double-click the **Data Sources (ODBC)** icon. In Windows NT, choose the **ODBC** icon. The ODBC Data Source Administrator window appears, as shown in Figure 28-10.

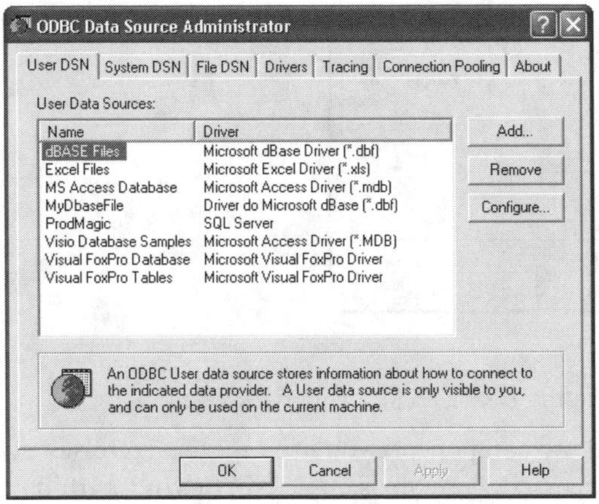

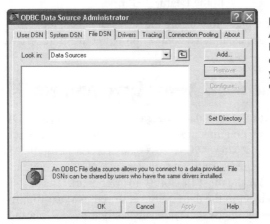

Figure 28-10: Use the ODBC Data Source Administrator window to set up the required connection to your database.

2. In the ODBC Data Source Administrator window, select the **File DSN** tab and click the **Add** button (Figure 28-11).

Figure 28-11: Use the Add button on the File DSN tab to add a file data source name for your database connection.

3. The Create New Data Source window opens. Select the **Microsoft Access Driver** as shown in Figure 28-12 and click **Next**.

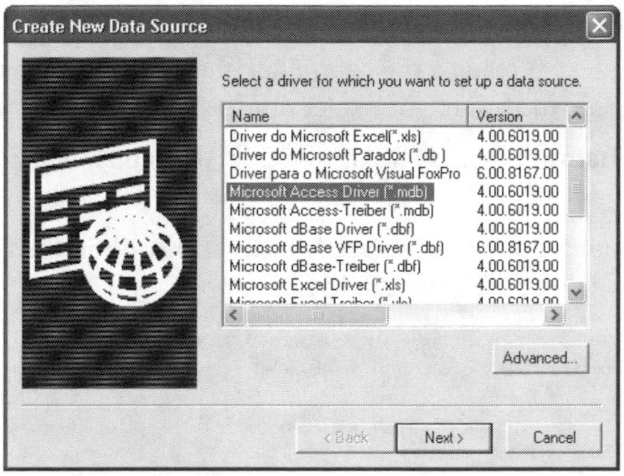

Figure 28-12: The first step in creating a new data source is to specify a driver that will enable you to connect to the required data provider.

4. Type **Northwind** for the name for the DSN, and click **Next**.

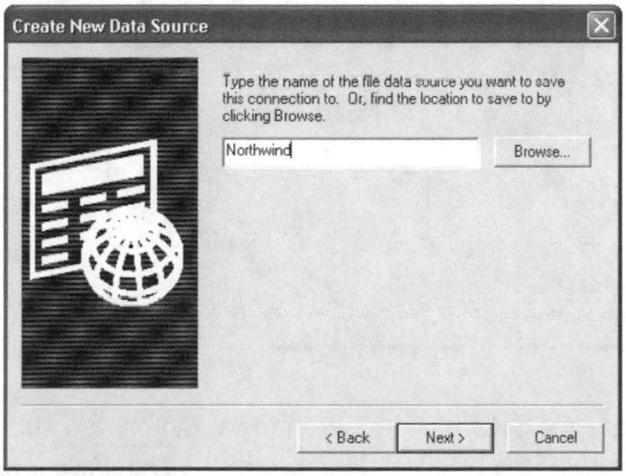

Figure 28-13: Use the Create New Data Source window to specify the name of the data source.

The second Create New Data Source dialog box will appear as shown in Figure 28-14.

Figure 28-14: Access displays the information you selected during the ODBC DSN setup so that you can revise it, if necessary, by clicking the Back button.

5. After ensuring that your information matches Figure 28-14, click the **Finish** button. If you have made a mistake, click the Back button and move to the appropriate step to correct your selections.

6. In the ODBC Microsoft Access Setup window that appears, click the **Select** button.

7. In the Select Database window, select **Northwind.mdb** in the Learn_ASP folder, and click **OK** (see Figure 28-15).

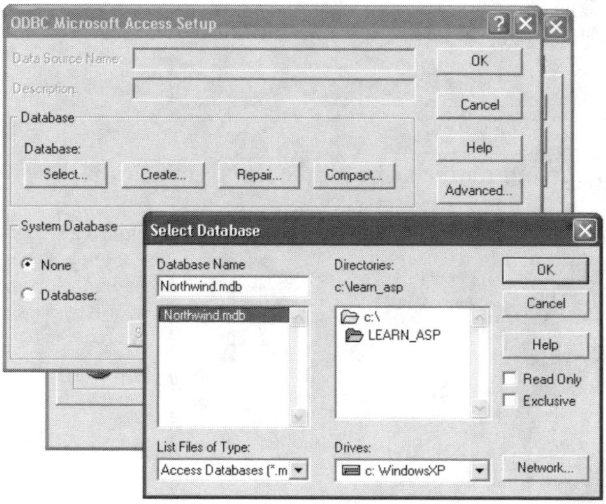

Figure 28-15: Use the ODBC Microsoft Access Setup window to specify the name of the database you want to connect to.

8. Click **OK** to close the Select Database window. When you click OK you should see the path of the selected database in the Database area of the ODBC Microsoft Access Setup window (Figure 28-16).

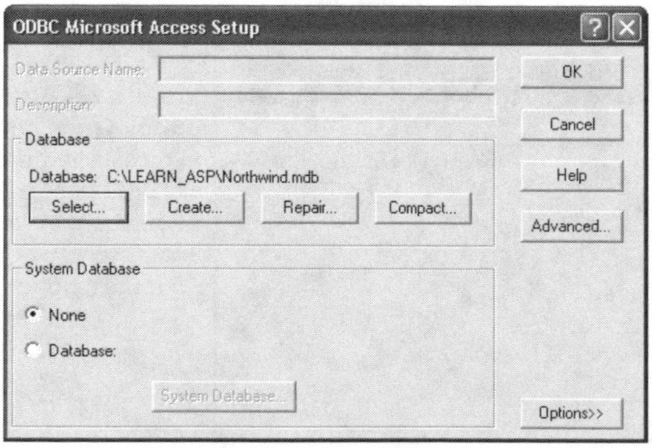

Figure 28-16: After choosing the database name using the Select button, the ODBC Microsoft Access Setup window displays the full path of the selected database.

9. Click **OK** to close the ODBC Microsoft Access Setup window. The ODBC Data Source Administrator window appears with the name of your new data source, Northwind (Figure 28-17).

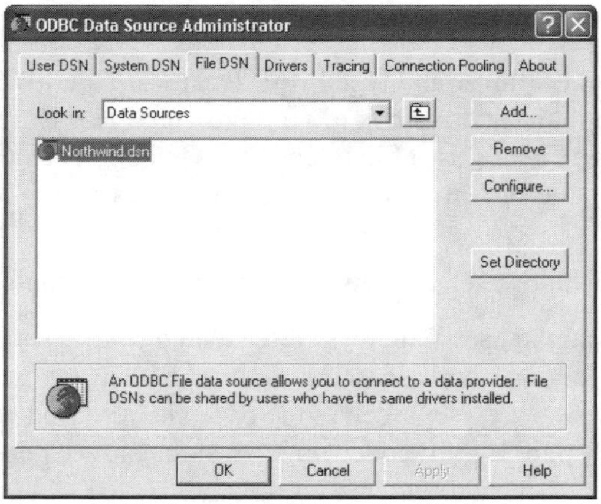

Figure 28-17: The ODBC Data Source Administrator window displays the file data source named Northwind.dsn created in Hands-on 28-5.

By default, the File DSN is stored in the \Program Files\Common Files\ODBC\Data Sources folder.

10. Click **OK** to close the ODBC Data Source Administrator window.

11. Open **Windows Explorer** and copy **Northwind.dsn** from the \Program Files\Common Files\ODBC\Data Sources folder to your Learn_ASP folder.

The following hands-on exercise demonstrates how you should edit the Employees.asp file created in Hands-On 28-1 so that it uses the Northwind data source name that was set up in Hands-On 28-5.

⊚ Hands-On 28-6: Modifying the ASP File to Use the File DSN

1. Start Notepad and open the **Employees.asp** file located in the Learn_ASP folder.

2. Find the following statement in the Employees.asp file:

```
conn.open "Northwind","Admin",""
```

and replace it with:

```
conn.open "FILEDSN=C:\Learn_ASP\Northwind.dsn","Admin",""
```

Change the drive letter in the above statement, if necessary, to match the setup of the Learn_ASP folder on your computer. The modified code fragment should look as follows:

```
<BODY>
<%
If IsObject(Session("Northwind_conn")) Then
    Set conn = Session("Northwind_conn")
Else
    Set conn = Server.CreateObject("ADODB.Connection")
    conn.open "FILEDSN=C:\Learn_ASP\Northwind.dsn","Admin",""
    Set Session("Northwind_conn") = conn
End If
%>
```

3. Save the Employees.asp file and exit Notepad.

4. Launch **Internet Explorer** and type **http://localhost/NorthDB/ Employees.asp** in the address box of your browser. Press **Enter** to execute the Active Server Pages (.asp) file or click the **Go** button. The contents of the Employees table should appear in your browser as shown in Figure 28-18.

5. In the browser window, select **View | Source** to view the source code.

The Source command uses Windows Notepad to display a source file. Because the script commands contained in the ASP file are evaluated on the server before the browser receives the page, the resulting page in the browser is 100% pure HTML code. Notice that the browser does not display any of your ASP code.

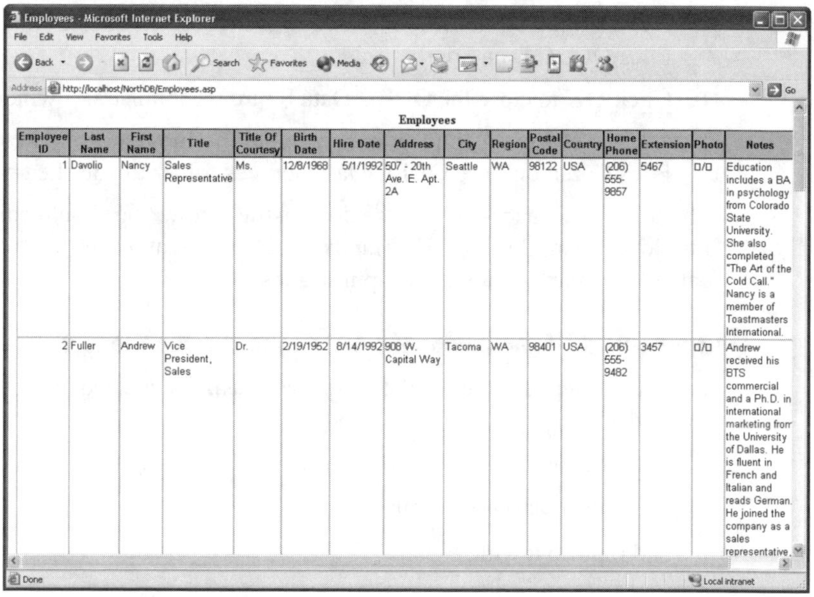

Figure 28-18: After adjusting the connection setting in the Employees.asp file (see step 2 above), you can request the ASP page by typing its URL in the web browser's address bar.

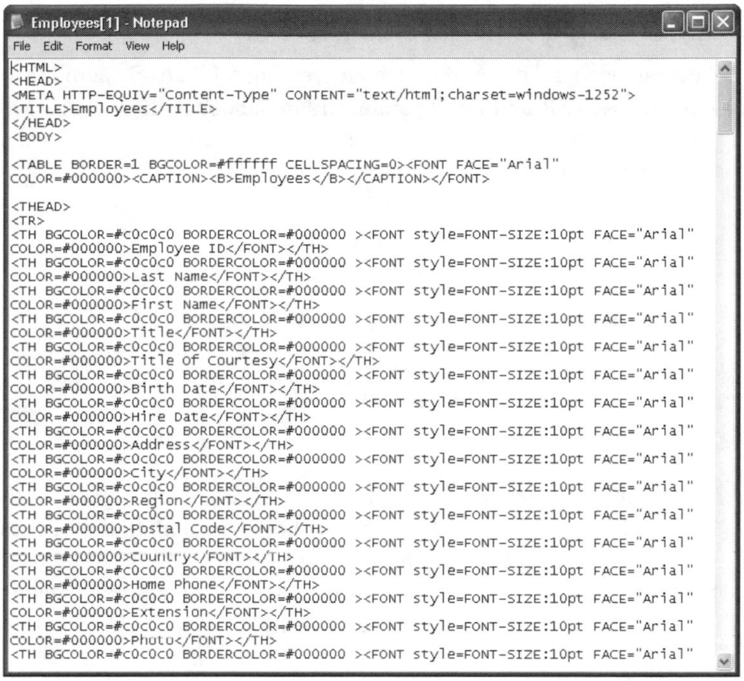

Figure 28-19: When you examine the source code of an ASP page (as instructed in step 5 of Hands-On 28-6), you will only see the HTML code. The scripting code is evaluated on the server and only the resulting HTML is passed to the browser!

6. Close Notepad and Internet Explorer.

Other Methods of Connecting to a Microsoft Access Database

Recall that earlier in this chapter (see Hands-On 28-5) we created a File DSN in order to connect to the Northwind sample database. The following sections demonstrate other methods of establishing a connection to your database:

- A DSN-less connection
- A connection via OLE DB Provider

The above connection methods were already discussed in Part II of this book. They are mentioned here again so that you feel comfortable using them in the context of the ASP files.

Establishing a DSN-less Connection

You can open a data source without creating a File or System DSN by specifying the DRIVER and DBQ parameters in the connection string.

For example, if you want to use a DSN-less connection, you should revise the Employees.asp file like this:

```
<%
If IsObject(Session("Northwind_conn")) Then
    Set conn = Session("Northwind_conn")
Else
    Set conn = Server.CreateObject("ADODB.Connection")
    conn.Open "DRIVER=Microsoft Access Driver (*.mdb);DBQ=" & _
            "C:\Learn_ASP\Northwind.mdb"
    Set Session("Northwind_conn") = conn
End If
%>
```

In the above connection string, the DRIVER parameter specifies the Microsoft Access driver, and the DBQ parameter holds the path to the Microsoft Access database file. The above script creates an instance of the ADO Connection object and opens a connection to the Northwind database located in the Learn_ASP folder on the C: drive by using a Microsoft Access driver.

Connecting to a Microsoft Access Database Using OLE DB

You can also connect to an Access database by using a native OLE DB provider for Microsoft Access — Microsoft.Jet.OLEDB.4.0. When using an OLE DB connection, you must specify the provider name in the Provider parameter and provide the path to the Access database in the Data Source parameter.

For example, if you want to use the OLE DB provider, you should revise the Employees.asp file like this:

```
<%
If IsObject(Session("Northwind_conn")) Then
    Set conn = Session("Northwind_conn")
Else
    Set conn = Server.CreateObject("ADODB.Connection")
    conn.Open "Provider=Microsoft.Jet.OLEDB.4.0;Data Source=" & _
            "C:\Learn_ASP\Northwind.mdb"
    Set Session("Northwind_conn") = conn
End If
%>
```

The above script creates an instance of the ADO Connection object and opens a connection to the Northwind database by using an OLE DB connection string.

Retrieving Records

Now that you know several ways of connecting to an Access database in an ASP page, you will learn how to create an ASP page from scratch and execute a simple SQL statement to return some data from a table. The example ASP code in Hands-On 28-7 retrieves only customer names from the Customers table.

◎ Hands-On 28-7: Creating an ASP File to Retrieve Records

If you don't feel like typing, locate the GetCustomers.asp file from the downloadable files and copy it to your Learn_ASP folder.

1. Start **Windows Notepad** and enter the ASP code as shown below.

```
<%@ Language=VBScript %>
<HTML>
<HEAD>
<TITLE>Retrieving a Recordset</TITLE>
</HEAD>
<BODY>

<%
    Set conn = Server.CreateObject("ADODB.Connection")
    conn.Open "DRIVER=Microsoft Access Driver (*.mdb);DBQ=" & _
        "C:\Learn_ASP\Northwind.mdb"
    Set rst = conn.Execute("SELECT CompanyName FROM Customers")
    Do While Not rst.EOF
        Response.Write rst("CompanyName") & "<BR>"
        rst.MoveNext
    Loop
%>
</BODY>
</HTML>
```

2. Save the file as **GetCustomers.asp** in your Learn_ASP folder, and close Notepad.

The GetCustomers.asp file shown above begins by specifying a scripting language for the page by using the ASP directive <%@ LANGUAGE= VBScript %>. The script contained in the <% and %> is Visual Basic script. This script performs the following actions:

■ Creates an instance of the ADO Connection object
■ Opens the connection to the Northwind database using the Microsoft Access driver (this is the DSN-less connection that was discussed earlier)

The SQL SELECT statement retrieves the values in the CompanyName field from the table named Customers into a Recordset object named rst. The SELECT statement is executed with the Execute method of the Server Connection object. Notice that the instance of the Recordset object is created implicitly when the SQL statement is executed.

The Do While loop is used to output all the rows from the recordset to the browser.

The Write method of the Response object outputs the value of a specific string or expression to the browser. Here, the value of the CompanyName field is written to the browser with the Response.Write statement like this:

```
Response.Write rst("CompanyName") & "<BR>"
```

The rst("CompanyName") retrieves the value of the CompanyName field from the Recordset object. You can output the values from the Recordset object by using any of the following statements:

```
Response.Write rst.Fields("CompanyName")
Response.Write rst.Fields("CompanyName").Value
Response.Write rst.Fields(1)
Response.Write rst.Fields(1).Value
Response.Write rst(1)
Response.Write rst("CompanyName")
```

Because the Fields collection is the default collection of the Recordset object, you can omit the word Fields.

The HTML <BR> tag is used to produce a carriage return effect after the value of the CompanyName field is output to the browser. Thanks to this tag, all company names are displayed on separate lines. The MoveNext method moves to the next record in the Recordset.

Now that you know what the code does, let's proceed and request this page in the browser.

3. Open your web browser and type **http://localhost/NorthDB/ GetCustomers.asp** in the address bar.

4. Press **Enter** or click **Go**. When you request the GetCustomers.asp file in the browser, you get the results shown in Figure 28-20.

Figure 28-20: The ASP page created in Hands-On 28-7 displays the names of customers from the Customers table in the Northwind database.

Taking Your VBA Programming Skills to the Web

Breaking Up a Recordset When Retrieving Records

In the preceding section, you worked with the ASP pge that retrieved 91 records from the Customers table in the Northwind database. When you need to display more than a few records, it is a good idea to break up the recordset by dividing the list into multiple pages. This allows the user of your application to view a limited number of records at a time.

In Hands-on 28-8 you will create an ASP page that displays 12 customer names per page. The user will be able to move between the pages of data by clicking on the appropriate page number listed at the bottom of the page. To make the ASP page more useful, you will display the customer names as hyperlinks. Clicking on the customer name will call another ASP page displaying the customer's address as listed in the Customers table.

◉ Hands-On 28-8: Creating a Multi-Page ASP File

If you don't feel like typing, locate the PageMe.asp file from the downloadable files and copy it to your Learn_ASP folder.

1. Start **Windows Notepad** and enter the ASP code as shown below.

```
<%@ Language=VBScript %>
<HTML>
<HEAD>
<TITLE>View Few at a Time</TITLE>
</HEAD>
<BODY>
<%
    Dim conn, rst, mySQL, currPage, rows, counter
    Set conn = Server.CreateObject("ADODB.Connection")
    conn.Open "DRIVER=Microsoft Access Driver (*.mdb);DBQ=" & _
        "c:\Learn_ASP\Northwind.mdb"
    Set rst = Server.CreateObject("ADODB.Recordset")

    rst.CursorType = 3 'adOpenStatic
    rst.PageSize = 12

    mySQL= "SELECT * FROM Customers ORDER BY CompanyName"
    rst.Open mySQL, conn
    If Request.QueryString("CurrPage")="" Then
        currPage=1
    Else
        currPage=Request.QueryString("currPage")
    End If

    rst.AbsolutePage=currPage
    rows = 0

    Response.Write "<H2>Northwind Customers</H2>"
    Response.Write "<I>Displaying page" & currPage & " of "
    Response.Write rst.PageCount & "</I>"
    Response.Write "<HR>"
```

```
Do While Not rst.EOF And rows < rst.PageSize
    Response.Write "<A HREF="""Address.asp?CustomerId=" & _
                    rst("CustomerId") & """>"
    Response.Write rst("CompanyName") & "</A><BR>"
    rows = rows + 1
rst.MoveNext
Loop

Response.Write "<HR>"
Response.Write "<B>Result Pages: </B>"

For counter = 1 To rst.PageCount
    Response.Write "<A HREF="""PageMe.asp?currPage=" & counter & """>"
    Response.Write counter & "</A>"
    Response.Write Chr(32)
Next
rst.close
Set rst = Nothing
conn.Close
Set conn = Nothing
%>
</BODY>
</HTML>
```

2. Save the file as **PageMe.asp** in the Learn_ASP folder.

The PageMe.asp file scripting section begins with the declaration of variables. Because all variables are variants in Active Server Pages, it is convenient to list them on one line:

```
Dim conn, rst, mySQL, currPage, rows, counter
```

Following the declaration of variables, the Connection object is created and the connection to the Northwind database is opened using the Microsoft Access driver.

Next, the Recordset object is created. For Recordset paging to work properly, the CursorType must be set to adOpenStatic. Notice that the script uses the literal value (3) instead of the constant name adOpenStatic. By default, ADO enumerated constants are not defined in VBScript. However, a list of constants used with ADO is defined in the Adovbs.inc file (for VBScript) or in the Adojavas.inc file (for JScript). These files are installed in the \Program Files\Common Files\System\ado folder. To use constant names instead of their values, you can add a reference to the Adovbs.inc file at the top of your ASP page by using the #INCLUDE FILE directive, as shown below:

```
<%@ Language=VBScript %>
<!-- #INCLUDE FILE="adovbs.inc" -->
<HTML>
```

For the #INCLUDE FILE directive to work, you must copy the Adovbs.inc file to the Learn_ASP folder. When you add the above directive, you will be able to use the ADO constants instead of literal values in your VBScript. Using the enumerated constants will make your code easier to understand.

Use the PageSize property of the Recordset object to specify how many records are to be displayed on a page. The page is set to display 12 records:

```
rst.PageSize = 12
```

The SQL SELECT statement retrieves all the records in the Customers table into the recordset. We store this statement in the mySQL variable and proceed to open the recordset using the connection that we set up earlier:

```
rst.Open mySQL, conn
```

Next, the script retrieves the page you are currently on. If the contents of the currPage variable is an empty string (" "), then you are on the first page.

The AbsolutePage property of the Recordset object is used to move to a particular page after opening the recordset. The AbsolutePage property identifies the page number on which the current record is located. AbsolutePage equals 1 when the current record is the first record in the recordset.

Next, the rows variable is initialized to zero (0). This variable limits the number of records that are displayed on a particular page.

Next, we use the Write method of the Response object to write a little HTML code that formats the page. For example, to format the page title we use the HTML second level heading tag <H2> and its ending companion tag </H2> like this:

```
Response.Write "<H2>Northwind Customers</H2>"
```

The next two Response.Write statements will inform the user about the page number being displayed and the total number of available pages:

```
Response.Write "<I>Displaying page" & currPage & " of "
Response.Write rst.PageCount & "</I>"
```

The HTML <I> tag will cause the text to appear in italics. You get the page number from the currPage variable and obtain the total number of pages from the PageCount property of the Recordset object.

Before we display the data, we want to draw a horizontal line on the page. This is done with the HTML <HR> tag.

Now comes the Do While loop that iterates through the recordset, counting the rows (records) as they are being retrieved and making sure that the number of records displayed per page is less than the specified page size. Company names are written to each page as hyperlinks using the HTML <A> anchor tag. The anchor tag uses the HREF attribute to designate a target page and forwards data to the target page when the user clicks the company name link:

```
Response.Write "<A HREF=""Address.asp?CustomerId=" & rst("CustomerId") & """>"
Response.Write rst("CompanyName") & "</A><BR>"
```

The target page (Address.asp) is created in the next hands-on in this chapter. A question mark (?) separates the target page from the data. The data attached to the hyperlink is a field name followed by an equals sign and the field value. When you use Response.Write to write the links you must pay attention to the quotes. Notice the pairs of double quotes inside the string. Each pair of double quotes ("") can be replaced with a single quote (') to make it easier to read, like this:

```
Response.Write "<A HREF='Address.asp?CustomerId='" & rst("CustomerId") & ">"
Response.Write rst("CompanyName") & "</A><BR>"
```

The HTML <BR> tag ensures that each company name appears on a separate line.

When the value of the rows variable is greater than the page size, the records are output to the next page.

After all records are retrieved and placed on appropriate pages, a horizontal line is placed on the page using the HTML <HR> tag. Following the horizontal line, a list of links to the individual pages appears with the text "Result Pages:" formatted in bold (see the <B> and </B> HTML tags). Again, to write those page links we use the HTML <A> tag with the HREF attribute:

```
Response.Write "<A HREF=""PageMe.asp?currPage=" & counter & """>"
Response.Write counter & "</A>"
```

The next statement uses the Chr(32) function to put a space between the page links:

```
Response.Write Chr(32)
```

Finally, the script segment ends by closing all objects and releasing the memory used. We announce the end of the file by writing two ending HTML tags:

```
</BODY>
</HTML>
```

Now that you know what the code does, let's proceed to request this page in the browser.

3. Open your browser and type **http://localhost/NorthDB/PageMe.asp** in the address bar.

4. Press **Enter** or click **Go**. You should see the listing of Northwind customers spanning multiple pages (Figure 28-21).

5. Navigate to different pages by clicking on a page link.

Note: Clicking on the company name does not work yet. You must create another ASP page to display the selected customer's address (see Hands-On 28-9).

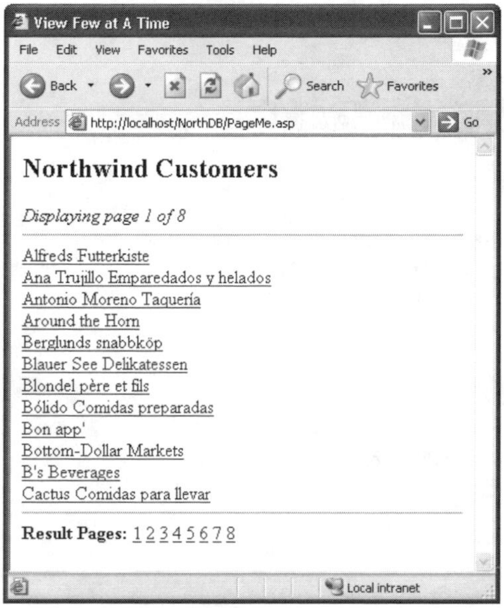

Figure 28-21: The result of running the ASP page titled PageMe.asp is a list of Northwind customers that is both easy to examine and use.

⊚ Hands-On 28-9: Creating an ASP File for Loading from a Hyperlink

This hands-on is required for using the company name hyperlinks in the PageMe.asp file created in Hands-On 28-8. If you don't feel like typing, locate the Address.asp file from the downloadable files and copy it to your Learn_ASP folder.

1. Start **Windows Notepad** and enter the ASP code as shown below.

```
<%@ Language=VBScript %>
<HTML>
<HEAD><TITLE>Lookup Results</TITLE></HEAD>
<BODY>
<%
    Dim mySQL, myPath
    CustomerId = TRIM(Request.QueryString("CustomerId"))
    myPath = "C:\Learn_ASP\Northwind.mdb"
    Set conn = Server.CreateObject("ADODB.Connection")
    conn.Open "Provider=Microsoft.Jet.OLEDB.4.0;Data Source=" & myPath
    Set rst = Server.CreateObject("ADODB.Recordset")
    rst.CursorType = 3 'adOpenStatic
    mySQL= "SELECT * FROM Customers WHERE CustomerId='" & CustomerId & "'"
    rst.Open mySQL,conn
%>
    <H1>Address Lookup</H1>
    <I>Displaying address for <B><%=rst("CompanyName")%></B></I>
    <HR>
    <TABLE colspan=2 align="Center">
    <TR>
        <TD>Customer Id:</TD>
        <TD><input type="text" name="CustomerId"
            value="<%=rst("CustomerId")%>" size="5">
        </TD>
```

```
            </TR>
            <TR>
                <TD>Street:</TD>
                <TD><input type="text" name="Address"
                    value="<%=rst("Address")%>" size="60">
                </TD>
            </TR>
            <TR>
                <TD>City:</TD>
                <TD><input type="text" name="City"
                    value="<%=rst("City")%>" size="15">
                </TD>
            </TR>
            <TR>
                <TD>Region:</TD>
                <TD><input type="text" name="Region"
                    value="<%=rst("Region")%>" size="15">
                </TD>
            </TR>
            <TR>
                <TD>Country:</TD>
                <TD><input type="text" name="Country"
                    value="<%=rst("Country")%>" size="15">
                </TD>
            </TR>
            <TR>
                <TD>Zip:</TD>
                <TD><input type="text" name="PostalCode"
                    value="<%=rst("PostalCode")%>" size="10">
                </TD>
            </TR>
            <TR>
                <TD>Phone:</TD>
                <TD><input type="text" name="Phone"
                    value="<%=rst("Phone")%>" size="24">
                </TD><BR>
            </TR>
            <TR>
                <TD>Fax:</TD>
                <TD><input type="text" name="Fax"
                    value="<%=rst("Fax")%>" size="24">
                </TD><BR>
            </TR>
            </TABLE>
            <BR>
            <BR>
            <CENTER>[  <A HREF="VBScript:history.back(1)">Go Back </A>  ]</CENTER>
<%
    rst.close
    Set rst = Nothing
    conn.Close
    Set conn = Nothing
%>
</BODY>
</HTML>
```

2. Save the file as **Address.asp** in the Learn_ASP folder.

The first VBScript code segment between the <% and %> delimiters connects to the sample Northwind database using the native OLE DB Provider. The SQL SELECT statement retrieves the record for the selected customer, and the information is output to the page. First, the internal title is written out and formatted using the HTML level 1 heading tag <H1>. The user is informed about the name of the customer whose information he or she is viewing. Next follows the horizontal line (see the <HR> tag) and the table structure that displays the customer information. The HTML tag <TABLE> denotes the beginning of a table. <TR> starts a new row, and <TD> indicates the table cell (where the data is displayed). Each of these tags is closed with an ending tag (</TD>, </TR>, and </TABLE>). Using a table to format the results is more pleasing to the eye.

Once the data is written to the page, you should provide the user with a way to return to the previous page so that another customer record can be requested. The Go Back hyperlink at the bottom of the page performs the same action as clicking the Back button in the browser's toolbar:

```
<CENTER>[ <A HREF="VBScript:history.back(1)">Go Back </A> ]</CENTER>
```

The HTML <CENTER> tag positions the hyperlink centered between the page margins.

Now that you know what the code does, let's proceed to request this page in the browser.

3. Open your browser and type **http://localhost/NorthDB/PageMe.asp** in the address bar.

4. Press **Enter** or click **Go**. You should see the listing of Northwind customers spanning multiple pages.

5. Click a company name of your choice to view its address information. When you click a company name in the browser, the Address Lookup screen appears as illustrated in Figure 28-22.

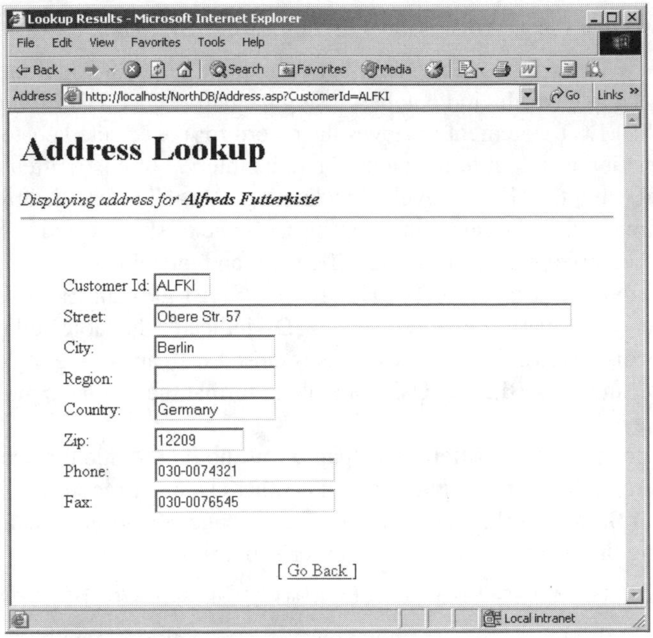

Figure 28-22: When you click the company name on the PageMe.asp page (see Figure 28-21), you are presented with the web page that displays the selected company's address.

Retrieving Records with the GetRows Method

Instead of looping through a recordset to retrieve records, you can use the GetRows method of the Recordset object to retrieve records into a two-dimensional array. You've already seen examples of using the GetRows method earlier in this book. Hands-On 28-10 uses the GetRows method to move the records from the Shippers table into an array. Once in the array, the records are written out to a table and displayed in a client browser. When you place records into an array, you can free up the Recordset and Connection objects earlier than in a loop, thus releasing valuable server resources.

⊚ Hands-On 28-10: Quick Data Retrieval

If you don't feel like typing, locate the FastRetrieve.asp file from the downloadable files and copy it to your Learn_ASP folder.

1. Start **Windows Notepad** and enter the ASP code as shown below.

```
<%@ Language=VBScript %>
<HTML>
<HEAD><TITLE>Fast Retrieve</TITLE></HEAD>
<BODY>
<%
    Dim conn, rst, strSQL, myPath, fld, allShippers, RowCounter, ColCounter
    Dim NumOfCols, NumOfRows, currField
```

Taking Your VBA Programming Skills to the Web

```
strSQL = "SELECT * FROM Shippers ORDER BY ShipperId"
myPath = "C:\Learn_ASP\Northwind.mdb"
Set conn = Server.CreateObject("ADODB.Connection")
conn.open "Provider=Microsoft.Jet.OLEDB.4.0;Data Source=" & myPath
Set rst = conn.Execute(strSQL)

Response.Write "<TABLE Border=1><TR>" & VbCrLf
    For Each fld In rst.Fields
        Response.Write "<TD><B>" & fld.name & "</B></TD>" & VbCrLf
    Next
Response.Write "</TR>" & VbCrLf
allShippers = rst.GetRows

rst.Close
Set rst = Nothing
conn.Close
Set conn = Nothing

NumOfCols = UBound(allShippers, 1) 'columns returned
NumOfRows = UBound(allShippers, 2) 'rows returned
For RowCounter = 0 To NumofRows
    Response.Write "<TR>"& VbCrLf
    For ColCounter = 0 To NumOfCols
        currField = allShippers(ColCounter, RowCounter)
        If IsNull(currField) Then
            currField = currField & "<BR>"
        ElseIf currField= "" Then
            currField="."
        End If
        Response.Write "<TD Valign=Top>"
        Response.Write currField
        Response.Write "</TD>" & VbCrLf
    Next
    Response.Write "<TR>" & VbCrLf
Next
Response.Write "</TABLE>"
%>
</BODY>
</HTML>
```

2. Save the file as **FastRetrieve.asp** in the Learn_ASP folder.

The VBScript code above uses the OLE DB Provider to connect to the Northwind database. After executing the SQL statement, the Write method of the Response object is used to create a table:

```
Response.Write "<TABLE Border=1><TR>" & VbCrLf
```

The VbCrLf constant denotes a carriage return/linefeed combination. Because this constant is built into VBScript, you don't need to define it before using it. The HTML <TR> tag is used for adding a table row.

Next, the For Each…Next loop retrieves the fields from the recordset and places the field names as table headings in the first table row. Notice how the HTML tags are embedded within the VBScript code segment. After the headings are filled in, the procedure uses the GetRows method of the Recordset object and places all the fetched records in the variable named allShippers.

Because we already have all the data that we need, we close the recordset and the connection to the database.

At this point the records are in a two-dimensional array. Prior to writing them into table cells, you can use the VBA UBound function to check how many rows and columns were retrieved. The data is placed into table cells by using the For…Next loop.

Because some fields in a retrieved recordset may not have any data in them, you can end up with some missing HTML table cells. To avoid blank spaces in a table, the VBScript code places the HTML
 (break) tag in a table cell if the field contains a Null value:

```
currField = currField & "<BR>"
```

You can also use a non-breaking space (nbsp;) for this purpose:

```
currField = currField & " "
```

The above statement will make the cell border show up when the cell is empty. You can also write the following statement to ensure that there are no gaps in your table:

```
Response.Write "<TD>" & currField & " </TD>"
```

In addition, if a field contains a zero-length string (" "), the VBScript procedure places a dot in a table cell, so that you not only keep the structure of the table intact but also differentiate between information that does not exist (zero-length) and information that may exist (Null). Recall that by setting the AllowZeroLength property of a table field to Yes and the Required property to No, you can enter two double quotation marks to indicate that the information does not exist. Leaving the field blank by not entering any data in it indicates that the information may exist, but it is not known at the time of entry.

3. Open your browser and type **http://localhost/NorthDB/FastRetrieve.asp** in the address bar.

4. Press **Enter** or click **Go**. You should see the listing of three shipping companies placed in a table (Figure 28-23).

Figure 28-23: The FastRetrieve ASP page fetches records from the Shippers table using the fast GetRows method.

5. Open the **Northwind** database located in the Learn_ASP folder and open the **Shippers** table in Design view. Click in the **Phone** field and change the Required property of this field to **No** and the Allow Zero Length property to **Yes**.

6. Save the **Shippers** table and open it in Datasheet view. Add **Airborne Express** as a new shipping company. Leave the Phone field for Airborne Express empty. Add **DHL** as a new shipping company. Enter two double quotation marks and a space (" ") in the Phone field for DHL. Upon saving the record, the quotation marks will disappear.

7. Close the Shippers table and exit Microsoft Access.

8. Return to your browser and press **F5** to refresh the window or click the **Go** button to update the display.

Notice that the Phone cell is empty for Airborne Express and there is a dot in the Phone cell for DHL.

Database Lookup Using Drop-Down Lists

Access forms often use a combo box to look up information in a database. When you use a drop-down box, the available choices are limited, so you don't need to worry that the user will enter incorrect information. Hands-On 28-11 illustrates how you can display a drop-down list box in a browser, load it with the product names, and return product information formatted in a table.

◎ Hands-On 28-11: Creating a Web Page with a Drop-down List Box

If you don't feel like typing, locate the ProductLookup.asp file from the downloadable files and copy it to your Learn_ASP folder.

1. Start **Windows Notepad** and enter the ASP code as shown below.

```
<%@ Language=VBScript %>

<%
Dim conn, rst, strSQL
Set conn = Server.CreateObject("ADODB.Connection")
conn.ConnectionTimeout = 15
conn.CommandTimeout = 30
conn.Open "Driver={Microsoft Access Driver (*.mdb)}; DBQ=" & _
    Server.MapPath("Northwind.mdb") & ";"
Set rst = Server.CreateObject("ADODB.Recordset")
If Len(Request.QueryString("ProductID")) <> 0 Then
    strSQL="SELECT * FROM Products WHERE ProductId="
    rst.Open(strSQL & Request.QueryString("ProductId")), conn, 0, 1
    If Not rst.EOF Then
        rst.MoveFirst
        Response.Write "<TABLE Border=1>"
        Response.Write "<TR>"
        Response.Write "<TD><B>Product Id</B></TD>"
        Response.Write "<TD><B>Product Name</B></TD>"
        Response.Write "<TD><B>Quantity Per Unit</B></TD>"
        Response.Write "<TD><B>Units in Stock</B></TD>"
```

```
            Response.Write "<TD><B>Unit Price</B></TD>"
            Response.Write "</TR>"
            Response.Write "<TR>"
            Response.Write "<TD Align='Center'>"
            Response.Write rst.Fields("ProductId") & "</TD>"
            Response.Write "<TD Align='Left'>"
            Response.Write rst.Fields("ProductName") & "</TD>"
            Response.Write "<TD Align='Left'>"
            Response.Write rst.Fields("QuantityPerUnit") & "</TD>"
            Response.Write "<TD Align='Center'>"
            Response.Write rst.Fields("UnitsInStock") & "</TD>"
            Response.Write "<TD Align='Right'>"
            Response.Write FormatCurrency(rst.Fields("UnitPrice"),2) & "</TD>"
            Response.Write "</TR>"
            Response.Write "</TABLE>"
        End If
        rst.Close
    End If
    rst.Open "Products", conn, 0, 1
    If Not rst.EOF Then
        rst.MoveFirst
        Response.Write "<FORM Action='./ProductLookup.asp' Method='get'>"
        Response.Write "<B>Select a Product:</B><BR>"
        Response.Write "<SELECT Name='ProductId'>"
        Response.Write "<OPTION></OPTION>"
        Do While Not rst.EOF
            Response.Write "<OPTION value=" & rst.Fields("ProductId") & ">"
            Response.Write rst.Fields("ProductName") & "</OPTION>"
            rst.MoveNext
        Loop
        Response.Write "</SELECT>"
        Response.Write "<INPUT Type='Submit' Value='Get Product Details'>"
        Response.Write "</FORM>"
    End If
    rst.Close
    Set rst = Nothing
    conn.Close
    Set conn = Nothing
%>
```

2. Save the file as **ProductLookup.asp** in the Learn_ASP folder.

The VBScript code segment above begins with establishing a connection with the data source. Instead of using a fully qualified path to the Northwind database, the code shows you how to use the MapPath method of the ASP Server object to retrieve the path to the database. The statement Server.MapPath("Northwind.mdb") will return the following path: Learn_ASP\Northwind.mdb. In fact, if you add Response.Write Server.MapPath("Northwind") to the code above, the filename with its path will appear in the browser. It is not difficult to guess that using Server.MapPath generates an additional request for the server to process. Therefore, when deploying your web site, you should replace Server.MapPath with a fully qualified path to get a better performance (see the previous hands-on examples for how this is done).

Notice that before the connection to the database is opened, the following statements are used:

```
conn.ConnectionTimeout = 15
conn.CommandTimeout = 30
```

The first statement instructs the Connection object's ConnectionTimeout property to wait 15 seconds before abandoning a connection attempt and issuing an error message. In the second statement above, the CommandTimeout property of the Connection object specifies how long to wait while executing a command before terminating the attempt and generating an error. The default for the ConnectionTimeout and CommandTimeout properties is 30 seconds. Using ConnectionTimeout and CommandTimeout in this example procedure is optional. Before utilizing these properties in your own database applications, make sure that the data source and the provider you are using support them.

Next, the script above instantiates a Recordset object and opens it using the open connection. The Recordset is opened as forward-only (0 = adOpenForwardOnly) and read-only (1 = adLockReadOnly). As mentioned earlier in this chapter, to use enumerated ADO constants, you need to add the #INCLUDE FILE directive at the beginning of the Active Server Pages file.

The SQL SELECT statement contains the WHERE clause that will pull only the record for a selected product ID if the user makes a selection from the drop-down box. The data available for the selected record is then placed in a table. In this example, the table headings are hard-coded. If you don't want to hard-code the headings, you could loop through the recordset to read the field names (see the FastRetrieve.asp file created earlier for an example).

After writing out table headings, the procedure fills the table cells with data. The table will contain only one row of data because the recordset is limited to one product selected from the drop-down list. After the data is presented in a table, the Recordset object is closed.

Next, another recordset is opened. This time the code opens the entire Products table. We loop through the recordset to build a drop-down list box. For each record, an <OPTION> tag is created, its value is set to the ProductId field, and the text is set to the ProductName. The first entry in the drop-down list is a blank line. This effect is achieved by omitting the value and text attributes inside the HTML <OPTION> tag:

```
<OPTION></OPTION>
```

The drop-down list box is part of a form. The <FORM> tag is used to generate an HTML form.

Forms allow user input into the browser and act as a container for ActiveX controls. There are two types of forms: GET and POST. This example uses the GET method to send information. (See Hands-On 28-13 for an example of processing form input with the POST method.) Within a <FORM> and </FORM> block, you can insert tags representing various HTML controls. In this example, the form contains the list box produced by the <SELECT> tag and a command button produced by the <INPUT> tag. When the user clicks a submit form button labeled "Get Product Details," the data gathered from the drop-down list box is passed to the Active Server Pages file specified within the <FORM> statement by the ACTION parameter.

3. Open your browser and type **http://localhost/NorthDB/ProductLookup.asp** in the address bar.

4. Press **Enter** or click **Go**. The web page displays a drop-down box and a button as shown in Figure 28-24.

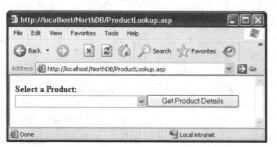

Figure 28-24: By using a drop-down box in a web page, you can provide a user-friendly interface for selecting records.

5. Open the drop-down list. When you open a drop-down list box, the list of products appears. Notice that the first entry in the list is a blank line.

6. Select a product from the drop-down list and click the **Get Product Details** button. The product details appear in a table, as shown in Figure 28-25.

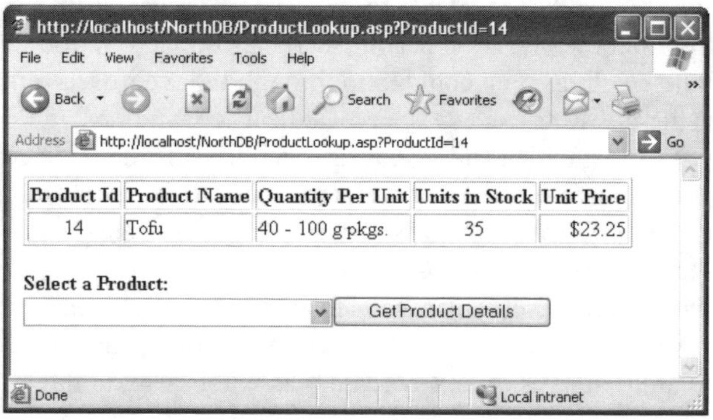

Figure 28-25: When you select a product from the drop-down list and click the Get Product Details button, the selected product information is presented at the top of the web page.

When you use the form with the GET method to send the information, the data is appended to the request for the processing page. The data being passed is visible in the address bar in your browser (see the figure above). Because the data is visible, you can easily troubleshoot any problems by looking at the address bar. The drawback of using the GET method for sending information is that the data is not secure and it is limited in size to the maximum length of the request string.

Database Lookup Using a Multiple Selection List Box

In the previous section, you've seen an example of looking up product information by selecting a product name from a drop-down list. At times, however, a user may want to view several products at once. To meet this requirement, you will need to create a multiple selection list box and process the user's selections.

Hands-On 28-12 illustrates how you can display a multiple selection list box in a browser, load it with the product names, and return product information formatted in a table.

◉ Hands-On 28-12: Creating a Web Page with a List Box

If you don't feel like typing, locate the MultiProductLookup.asp file from the downloadable files and copy it to your Learn_ASP folder.

1. Start **Windows Notepad** and enter the ASP code as shown below.

```
<%@ Language=VBScript %>
<HTML>
<HEAD><TITLE>Select Multiple Products</TITLE></HEAD>
<BODY>
<%
    Dim conn, rst, strSelect, strWhere, strSQL, totalItems, fld

    Set conn = Server.CreateObject("ADODB.Connection")
    conn.ConnectionTimeout = 15
    conn.CommandTimeout = 30

    conn.Open "Driver={Microsoft Access Driver (*.mdb)}; DBQ=" & _
        Server.MapPath("Northwind.mdb") & ";"
    Set rst = Server.CreateObject("ADODB.Recordset")

If Len(Request.QueryString("ProductID")) <> 0 Then
    strSelect="SELECT ProductId as [ID], ProductName as [Product Name], " & _
            "QuantityPerUnit as [Qty/Unit], UnitsInStock as Stock, " & _
            "UnitPrice as [Unit Price] FROM Products "
    strWhere = "WHERE ProductId="
    strSQL = strSelect & strWhere

    totalItems = Request.QueryString("ProductId").Count
    myValues = Request.QueryString("ProductId").Item

    Response.Write "<P><H5><I>The following SQL statement was used:</I>"

    If totalItems = 1 Then
        rst.Open(strSQL & Request.QueryString("ProductId")), conn, 0, 1
        %>
            <PRE><%= strSQL & Request.QueryString("ProductId") %></PRE>
        <%
Else
        strWhere = "WHERE ProductId IN ("
```

```
            strSQL = strSelect & strWhere
            rst.Open(strSQL & myValues & ")"), conn, 0, 1
            %>
                <PRE><%= strSQL & myValues & ")" %></PRE>
            <%
        End if


        ' get table headings
        Response.Write "</H5><P><TABLE Border=1>"
        Response.Write "<TR>"
        For Each fld in rst.Fields
            Response.Write "<TH>" & fld.Name & "</TH>"
        Next
        Response.Write "</TR>"

        ' get the data
        Do While not rst.EOF
        Response.Write "<TR>"

            For Each fld in rst.Fields
                Response.Write "<TD>"
                If fld.Name = "UnitPrice" Then
                    Response.Write FormatCurrency(fld.value,2)
                Else
                    Response.Write fld.value
                End If
                    Response.Write "</TD>"
            Next
            Response.Write "</TR>"
            rst.MoveNext
        Loop
        Response.Write "</TABLE>"
        rst.Close
End If

rst.Open "Products", conn, 0, 1
If Not rst.EOF Then
    rst.MoveFirst
%>
    <FORM Action="MultiProductLookup.asp" Method="get">
    <B><I><FONT Size=2 Face=Tahoma>Hold down CTRL or SHIFT <BR>
        to select multiple products:</FONT></I></B><BR>
    <SELECT Name="ProductId" MULTIPLE Size=8>
<%
    Do While Not rst.EOF
%>
    <OPTION Value="<%=rst.Fields("ProductId")%>">
    <%=rst.Fields("ProductName")%></OPTION>
<%
    rst.MoveNext
    Loop
%>
    </SELECT>
    <INPUT Type="Submit" Value="Get Product(s) Details">
    </FORM>
<%
```

```
End If
rst.Close
Set rst = Nothing
conn.Close
Set conn = Nothing
%>
</BODY>
</HTML>
```

2. Save the file as **MultiProductLookup.asp** in the Learn_ASP folder.

The VBScript code segment above establishes a DSN-less connection to the Northwind database by using the Microsoft Access driver and instantiates a Recordset object. Refer to the previous hands-on exercise for an explanation of the Connection object's ConnectionTimeout and CommandTimeout properties and the Server object's MapPath method.

The code proceeds to check whether the user has selected any items in the list box. If at least one product was picked from the list, the procedure defines the SQL SELECT statement and uses the QueryString method of the Request object to retrieve the total number of selected products. This number is then stored in the totalItems variable.

The next Request.QueryString statement retrieves the IDs of the selected items and places them in the myValues variable.

The next statement announces that the line that follows is the SQL statement the user has selected. This statement is formatted with the HTML <H5> and <I> tags. This will make the enclosed text an italicized heading of size 5 (the largest heading is 1 and the smallest 6). The <P> tag designates the text as a plain paragraph. The ending </P> tag is optional.

If one product was selected in the list box, a recordset is opened using the following statement:

```
rst.Open(strSQL & Request.QueryString("ProductId")), conn, 0, 1
```

Recall that 0 and 1 at the end of this statement indicate a forward-only and read-only recordset.

The statement

```
<PRE><%=strSQL & Request.QueryString("ProductId") %></PRE>
```

will write the complete SQL statement to the browser for the user to see. When you use the HTML <PRE> and </PRE> tags, the text between these tags is formatted exactly as it is typed. Spaces and carriage returns are preserved.

If more than one product was selected in the list box, we need to change the contents of the strWhere variable to include the IN keyword in the WHERE clause. The IN keyword restricts the rows being selected to those rows where the column values are in the list presented in the SQL statement.

Assuming that the user selected products with IDs of 1, 3, and 6 in the list box, the following SQL statement will be generated:

```
SELECT ProductId as [ID], ProductName as [Product Name], QuantityPerUnit as
    [Qty/Unit], UnitsInStock as Stock, UnitPrice as [Unit Price] FROM Products
    WHERE ProductId IN (1, 3, 6)
```

The remaining code segment in the code above creates a table in a browser. We use the For Each...Next loop to write out the column names to the browser:

```
For Each fld in rst.Fields
    Response.Write "<TH>" & fld.Name & "</TH>"
Next
```

The <TH> tag makes a cell a table heading. This automatically makes the text bold.

After populating the table with the headings, we use the Do While loop to write out the table rows until the end of the recordset is encountered. We must obtain field values for each column in a row. This is done with the For Each... Next loop like this:

```
For Each fld in rst.Fields
    Response.Write "<TD>"
    If fld.Name = "UnitPrice" Then
        Response.Write FormatCurrency(fld.value,2)
    Else
        Response.Write fld.value
    End If
        Response.Write "</TD>"
Next
```

Notice the conditional statement within the above code segment. We use it to perform an additional operation on the UnitPrice field. We format this field as currency using the FormatCurrency function.

When all the table rows are written to the browser, the table is closed with the HTML table close tag </TABLE>, and the recordset itself is closed.

Next, the VBScript code continues by opening the recordset based on the Products table and cycling through this recordset to retrieve the product IDs and product names for inclusion in the list box. The HTML form section contains the MULTIPLE keyword in the <SELECT> tag to indicate that the list box should be created. The size of the list box is set to display eight products like this:

```
<FORM Action="MultiProductLookup2.asp" Method="get">
    <B><I><FONT Size=2 Face=Tahoma>Hold down CTRL or SHIFT <BR>
        to select multiple products:</FONT></I></B><BR>
    <SELECT Name="ProductId" MULTIPLE Size=8>
```

Notice that the above code is a client-side script. This code appears outside the VBScript <% and %> delimiters. To make this code a part of the VBScript you may want to rewrite it as follows:

```
Response.Write "<FORM Action=""./MultiProductLookup3.asp"" Method=""get"">"
Response.Write "<B><I><FONT Size=2 Face=Tahoma>Hold down CTRL or SHIFT <BR>"
Response.Write "to select multiple products:</FONT></I></B><BR>"
Response.Write "<SELECT Name=""ProductId"" MULTIPLE Size=8>"
```

Once we have defined the list box we can populate it with product names using a Do While loop. We use the <OPTION> tag with the value attribute <OPTION value=" "> to specify items in the list:

Taking Your VBA Programming Skills to the Web

```
Do While Not rst.EOF
%>
    <OPTION Value="<%=rst.Fields("ProductId")%>">
    <%=rst.Fields("ProductName")%></OPTION>
<%
    rst.MoveNext
Loop
```

Notice again that we set the list values outside the VBScript. For better understanding, and to practice various methods of coding, you can rewrite this code like this:

```
Do While Not rst.EOF
    Response.Write "<OPTION Value="
    Response.Write rst.Fields("ProductId") & ">"
    Response.Write rst.Fields("ProductName") & "</OPTION>"
    rst.MoveNext
Loop
```

To allow the user to submit selections to the server, the form contains the submit button titled "Get Product(s) Details." When the user presses this button, the form data will be submitted using the GET method.

The procedure ends by closing both the Recordset and Connection objects and freeing up memory.

Let's go on to test our work in the browser.

3. Open your browser and type **http://localhost/NorthDB/MultiProduct-Lookup.asp** in the address bar.

4. Press **Enter** or click **Go**.

5. The browser will display a list box. Select the items as shown in Figure 28-26 and press the **Get Product(s) Details** button.

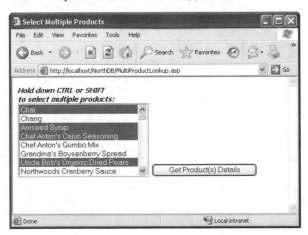

Figure 28-26: You can allow users to filter the data by using a multiple selection list box.

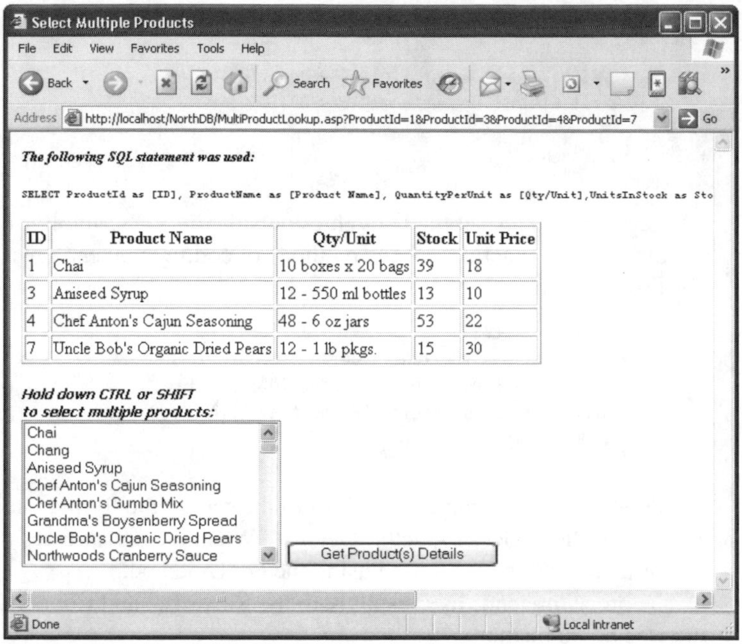

Figure 28-27: After selecting the products in the list box (see Figure 28-26) and clicking on the Get Product(s) Details button, your browser displays data as shown here.

Adding Data into a Table

You may want to use a web page to collect data from a user and save it in a Microsoft Access form. The following hands-on example creates a simple data entry form that contains two fields. The purpose of this form is to allow users to enter new shippers into the Northwind database Shippers table.

◎ Hands-On 28-13: Creating a Data Input Page

If you don't feel like typing, locate the NWDataEntry.asp file from the downloadable files and copy it to your Learn_ASP folder.

1. Start **Windows Notepad** and enter the ASP code as shown below.

```
<%@ Language=VBScript %>
<%
Dim conn, strConn, strSQL, name, phone, goAhead
name=Request("txtCompanyName")
phone=Request("txtPhone")

For Each key In Request.Form
    If Request.Form(key) = "" Then
    If key = "txtCompanyName" Then
        Response.Write "<FONT Color = 'Blue'>Please enter the Shipper _
                    name.</Font>"
    Else
```

```
                    Response.Write "<FONT Color = 'Red'>Please enter the Phone _
                               number.</Font>"
        End If
        goAhead = False
        Exit For
        End If
        GoAhead=True
    Next
    If goAhead = True Then
        name=Replace(Request("txtCompanyName"),"'","''")
            If Len(name)<> 0 Or _
                        Len(phone)<>0 Then
                Set conn = Server.CreateObject("ADODB.Connection")
                strConn="Provider=Microsoft.Jet.OLEDB.4.0;Data Source="
                strConn=strConn & server.MapPath("Northwind.mdb") & ";"
                strConn=strConn & "User ID=; Password=;"

                strSQL = "INSERT INTO Shippers (CompanyName, Phone)"
                strSQL = strSQL & "Values ('" & name & "'"
                strSQL = strSQL & ",'" & Phone & "')"
                With conn
                .Mode = 3
                .Open strConn
                .Execute(strSQL)
                End With
            Response.Write "<I><FONT Color = 'Green'>" & _
                        "Successfully added the following data:</I></FONT><HR>"

             ' get the ShipperId (the autonumber field in the Shippers table)
             strSQL = "SELECT MAX(ShipperId) AS lastId From Shippers;"

             Set rst = conn.Execute(strSQL)
             Response.Write "Shipper Id: <B>" & rst("lastId")& "</B><P>"

             rst.close
             Set rst = Nothing
             conn.Close
             Set conn = Nothing

             Response.Write "Company Name: <B>" & Request("txtCompanyName") & _
                        "</B></P>"
             Response.Write "Phone Number: <B>" & phone & "</B>"

             ' clear the Shipper Name and Phone input boxes
             name = ""
             phone = ""
        End If
    End If
%>
<HTML>
<HEAD>
<TITLE>Data Entry Screen</TITLE>
</HEAD>
<BODY>
<FORM Name="form1" Action="NWdataentry.asp" Method="POST" >
    <P>
```

```
Shipper Name: <INPUT Type="text" Name="txtCompanyName"
    Value="<%=name%>" Size= "30" > 
Phone: <INPUT Type="text" Name="txtPhone" Value="<%=phone%>"></P>
    <P>
<INPUT Type="Submit" Name="cmdSubmit" Value="Add Data"></P>
</FORM>
</BODY>
</HTML>
```

2. Save the file as **NWDataEntry.asp** in the Learn_ASP folder.

The VBScript segment shown above assigns values to the name and phone variables. These values are collected from the text fields located on the HTML form. To collect information from a form, use the Request.Form("name") command, where name is the name of the form field (text box, check box, etc.).

The VBScript above uses the abbreviated form of the Request.Form command:

```
Request("txtCompanyName")
```

To remove leading and trailing spaces that users often enter in text fields, use the TRIM function as follows:

```
name =TRIM(Request("txtCompanyName")
```

The For Each…Next loop validates user input prior to sending information to the server. It's a good idea to write validation scripts to check for such things as whether the user entered a valid number or whether a text box was left empty. This example only checks if any of the text fields are empty. Data validation should be performed on the client side to reduce server loads and improve response time. Notice how we check the values of the form elements with the For Each…Loop:

```
For Each key In Request.Form
    If Request.Form(key)= "" Then
    If key = "txtCompanyName" Then
        Response.Write "<FONT Color = 'Blue'>Please enter the Shipper _
                        name.</Font>"
    Else
        Response.Write "<FONT Color = 'Red'>Please enter the Phone _
                        number.</Font>"
    End If
    goAhead = False
    Exit For
    End If
    GoAhead=True
Next
```

The code above iterates through the Forms collection to check whether the user has entered any data in the CompanyName and Phone fields and displays a message in a different color if any of the text fields were left blank.

If both text fields were filled in, the goAhead variable is set to True, and the procedure continues.

Because the company name that the user entered may contain an apostrophe, an error could occur when the value is inserted into the SQL statement. To avoid the error, the procedure uses the Replace function to replace one apostrophe with two apostrophes in the user-supplied text:

```
name=Replace(Request("txtCompanyName"),"'","''")
```

Provided that the length of the strings contained in the name or phone variables is not equal to zero (0), the connection is established to the Northwind database, and the SQL INSERT INTO statement is executed. This statement inserts a new record into the Shippers table and places the contents of the name or phone variables into the CompanyName and Phone fields.

Next, the procedure uses the green font color to inform the user about the successful addition of the data. Another SQL statement is executed to retrieve the ID of the newly added record, and the Response.Write statement displays the ShipperId for the user to see in the browser.

After retrieving the value of the ShipperId field, the Recordset and Connection objects are closed. Next, we write out the user-supplied shipper name and phone number to the browser, and clear the name and phone variables so that the form's input boxes display no data.

The remaining section of the ASP page contains HTML tags that generate a form where the user can enter the shipping company and phone number, and includes a button for submitting information to a web server. Notice that the form's ACTION argument refers to the file named NWDataEntry.asp. When the user submits data that he or she entered in the form's text fields by clicking the Add Data button, the browser will use the POST method to send the information to the .asp file on the server, in this case NWDataEntry.asp. An .asp file can create a form that posts information to itself (as shown in this example), to another .asp file, or by using the POST method you can send an almost unlimited number of characters to the web server. The POST method is also more secure than the GET method because the information passed to the server does not appear in the browser's address bar. (Refer to the previous hands-on exercise for an example of processing form input with the GET method.)

Notice how the values of the name and phone variables are retrieved:

```
Value = "<%=name%>">
Value = "<%=phone%>">
```

Now let's request this data entry page from the browser.

3. Open your browser and type **http://localhost/NorthDB/NWData-Entry.asp** in the address bar.

4. Press **Enter** or click **Go**.

5. Enter the data as shown in Figure 28-28 and press the **Add Data** button.

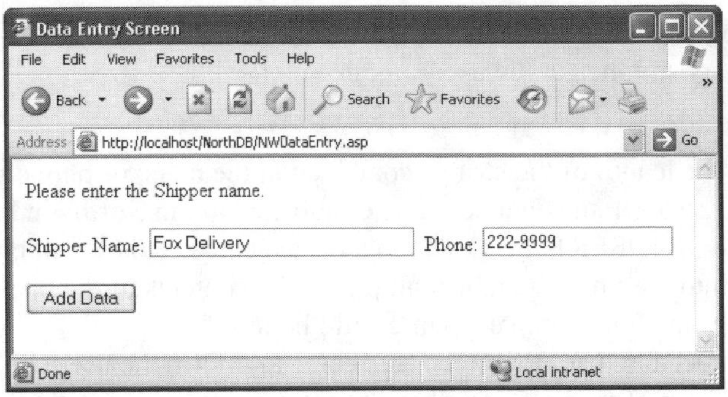

Figure 28-28: When you request the ASP page prepared in Hands-On 28-13, you are presented with the data entry screen for the Northwind database Shippers table.

When you enter data in the Shipper Name text box and click the Add Data button, the browser displays the data that was inserted into the Shippers table and allows you to make more additions by clearing out previous values from input boxes.

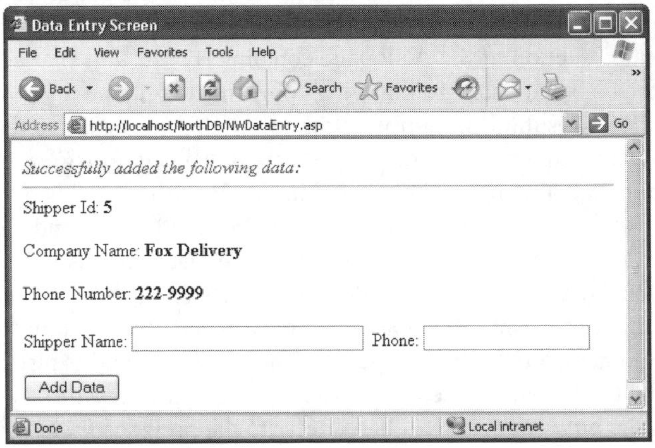

Figure 28-29: Notice that the browser displays the Shipper ID of the newly added record as well as the data entered in the text boxes prior to pressing the Add Data button (see Figure 28-28). You can continue adding new data by typing new values into the text boxes and clicking the Add Data button.

Modifying a Record

You can display a record in a browser and allow the user to edit the data. Changes made to the data can then be submitted to the server for processing. The easiest and quickest way to modify a record is by executing the SQL UPDATE statement.

The following hands-on exercise creates an ASP page where the user can select a product to update from a drop-down list. After clicking on the Retrieve Data button, the selected product's current price and units in stock are retrieved from the Products table. The retrieved data is placed in text boxes inside a table structure. The user can edit the data in the retrieved fields and insert the changes to the database table by clicking the Update Data button.

◉ Hands-On 28-14: Creating a Page for Data Modification

If you don't feel like typing, locate the UpdateProduct.asp file from the downloadable files and copy it to your Learn_ASP folder.

1. Start **Windows Notepad** and enter the ASP code as shown below.

```
<%@ Language=VBScript %>
<HTML>
<HEAD><TITLE>Update Product Information</TITLE></HEAD>
<%
Set conn = Server.CreateObject("ADODB.Connection")
    conn.Open "DRIVER=Microsoft Access Driver (*.mdb);DBQ=" & _
        "c:\Learn_ASP\northwind.mdb"
set rst = Server.CreateObject("ADODB.Recordset")
If Len(Request.QueryString("ProductId")) <> 0 Then
    strSQL="SELECT * FROM Products WHERE ProductId="
    rst.Open(strSQL & Request.QueryString("ProductId")), conn, 0, 1
    If Not rst.EOF Then
        rst.MoveFirst
%>
<BODY>
<FORM ACTION="UpdateProduct.asp" METHOD="POST" id=form2 name=form2>
<Input Type=hidden Name=txtProductId Value="<% =rst("ProductId") %>">
<Input Type=hidden Name=txtProductName Value="<% =rst("ProductName") %>">

<CENTER><H4><% =rst("ProductName") %>
     (Product Id=<%=rst("ProductId")%>)</H></CENTER><P>
<TABLE BORDER=0 CELLSPACING=4 CELLPADDING=4>
    <TR>
        <TD WIDTH=200 COLSPAN="2"><FONT COLOR=Blue>Unit Price ($):</FONT></TD>
        <TD BGCOLOR="#00FF00">
        <INPUT TYPE="text" NAME="UnitPrice" VALUE="<% =rst("UnitPrice") %>"></TD>
    </TR>
    <TR>
        <TD COLSPAN="2"><FONT COLOR=Blue>Units In Stock:</FONT></TD>
        <TD BGCOLOR=#00FF00>
        <INPUT TYPE="text" NAME="UnitsInStock" VALUE="<% _
                            =rst("UnitsInStock") %>"></TD>
    </TR>
    <TR>
        <TD COLSPAN="2"></TD>
        <TD><INPUT type="submit" value="Update Data" id=submit2 _
                name=submit2></TD>
    </TR>
</TABLE><HR>
</FORM>
<%
    End If
    rst.Close
End If
If Not IsEmpty(Request.Form("submit2")) Then
    If Request.Form("UnitPrice")= "" or _
        Request.Form("UnitsInStock") = "" Then
        Response.Write "<B><Font Color=Red>You cannot leave any fields blank." _
            & "Please Try Again</B></FONT>"
```

```
    Else
        strSQL = "UPDATE Products SET " _
            & "UnitPrice = '" & Request.Form("UnitPrice")& "', " _
            & "UnitsInStock = '" & Request.Form("UnitsInStock")& "' " _
            & "WHERE ProductId = " & Request.Form("txtProductId")
        conn.Execute strSQL
        Response.Write "The following Update statement was executed for <B>" _
            & Request.Form("txtProductName") &"</B><BR>"
        Response.Write "<PRE>" & strSQL & "</PRE><BR>"
        End If
    End If
        strSql = "SELECT * FROM [Products] ORDER BY [ProductName]"
        Set rst = conn.Execute (strSql)
        If Not rst.EOF Then
            rst.MoveFirst
%>
<FORM ACTION="UpdateProduct.asp" METHOD="Get" >
<TABLE>
<TR>
    <TD><B>Select a Product to Update</B></TD>
    <TD><SELECT Name="ProductId">
    <OPTION></OPTION>
<%
    Do While Not rst.EOF
    Response.Write "<OPTION Value='" & rst("ProductID") & "'> " & _
        rst("ProductName") & "</OPTION>"
    rst.MoveNext
    Loop
    End If
    rst.Close
    set rst = Nothing
    conn.Close
    set conn = Nothing
%>
<TD><INPUT type="submit" value="Retrieve Data" id=submit1 name=submit1></TD>
</SELECT></TD>
</TR>
</TABLE><HR>
</FORM></BODY>
</HTML>
```

2. Save the file as **UpdateProduct.asp** in the Learn_ASP folder.

Notice that the ASP page shown above contains two HTML forms: Form1 and Form2.

Form1 (whose code appears at the bottom of the ASP page) displays a drop-down list of products for the user to select. This form uses the GET method to send data to the server. This means that you will see the query string in the browser's address bar once you click the Retrieve Data button (see Figures 28-30 and 28-31).

Form2 (whose code appears higher in the ASP page) displays two text boxes with Unit Price and Units in Stock values for the product that was selected from the drop-down list on Form1. The user can modify the data in these text boxes. This form uses the POST method to send the information to the server. The submitted information will not be visible in the browser's address bar. This form will be submitted to itself after the user clicks the Update Data button. Two hidden text fields are placed on Form2 to store information about the retrieved Product ID and Product Name:

```
<Input Type=hidden Name=txtProductId Value="<% =rst("ProductId") %>">
<Input Type=hidden Name=txtProductName Value="<% =rst("ProductName") %>">
```

In this example, the information stored in hidden fields is used by the VBScript code further in the .asp file to create an SQL UPDATE statement and write an information message in the browser. Hidden form fields are often used with the POST method to hide information from the user.

The first VBScript code segment establishes a connection to the Northwind database and creates an instance of the Recordset object. Next, we check if a selection was made from the drop-down list. If the user made a product selection and clicked the Retrieve Data button, we open the recordset:

```
rst.Open(strSQL & Request.QueryString("ProductId")), conn, 0, 1
```

The Open method of the Recordset object is used to issue an SQL SELECT statement with the WHERE clause that specifies which record should be retrieved. We placed the SELECT statement in the strSQL variable. The Open method also specifies the connection to the database (conn), the cursor type (adOpenForwardOnly = 0), and the lock type (adLockReadOnly = 1). The recordset is opened to retrieve only the data that the user is allowed to modify. The data is placed in a table (see the HTML code segment). Once the data is retrieved, the recordset is closed.

The next VBScript code segment runs after the user clicks the Update Data button on Form2. When the form is posted, all controls, including the command buttons, are posted with it. Using the IsEmpty function you can find out if the user clicked the command button:

```
If Not IsEmpty(Request.Form("submit2")) Then
```

Prior to submitting the data to the server for insertion into the Products table, the code checks whether the Unit Price and Units in Stock text boxes contain any data. If either of these fields is empty (the user may have erased the data completely), a validation message is sent to the browser and the user must request the product again from the drop-down list if he or she wants to continue. On the other hand, if there is data in both text fields (even if the user has not made any changes to the original data), clicking the Update button on the form will send the SQL UPDATE statement to the server. As a result, the user will see the name of the product he or she updated together with the SQL UPDATE statement that was executed.

The last code segment creates a recordset to populate a drop-down list with product names. You should already be familiar with this code as it was demonstrated in the previous hands-on exercise.

3. Open your browser and type **http://localhost/NorthDB/UpdateProduct.asp** in the address bar.

4. Press **Enter** or click **Go**.

5. Select the product as shown in Figure 28-30 and click the **Retrieve Data** button.

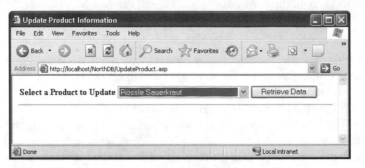

Figure 28-30: When you request the UpdateProduct.asp file in your browser, a screen appears with a drop-down list where you can select a product you want to update.

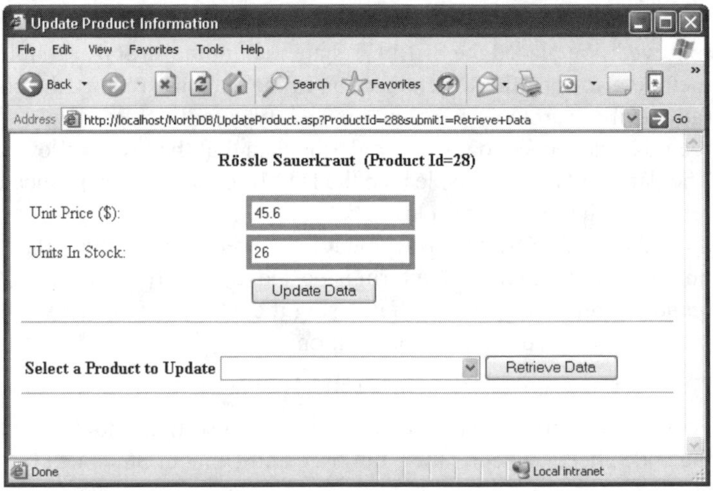

Figure 28-31: When you select a product from the drop-down list and click the Retrieve Data button, the selected product's unit price and units in stock data are retrieved from the Products table and placed at the top of the page.

The user can modify the original data in the text boxes and click the Update Data button. If the user clicks the Update Data button when information in missing in the Unit Price or Units in Stock text boxes, he is advised to enter the data and try again.

If the user clicks the Update Data button while the Unit Price and Units in Stock text boxes are not empty, the UPDATE statement is executed on the server and the submitted changes are inserted in the Products table. The user sees the page shown in Figure 28-32 in confirmation of the update request.

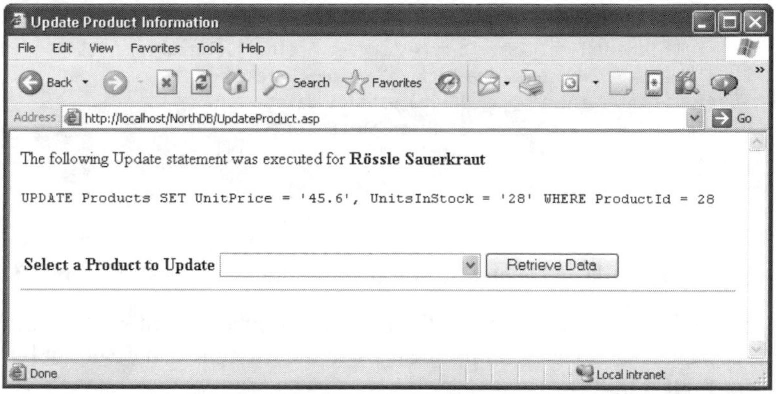

Figure 28-32: After submitting the product modification, the user sees the confirmation page with the UPDATE statement that was executed and is given an opportunity to continue by retrieving other products for modification.

Deleting a Record

When you need to delete a record, you can use the SQL DELETE statement. When writing a VBScript to handle the delete request, it's always a good idea to check for the following conditions:

- Did the user specify a record to delete? The user may have pressed the submit button without typing the record ID in the provided text box.
- Does the provided record ID exist in the table? This question is particularly important when the user is expected to type the record ID in a text box instead of selecting it from the drop-down list.
- What happens when the record the user wants to delete has related records in other tables? As you know, Microsoft Access will not allow you to delete records when the referential integrity rules are enforced.

The next hands-on exercise demonstrates how to delete a shipper from the Shippers table.

Hands-On 28-15: Creating Pages that Allow Record Deletions

This hands-on uses two files for performing the delete operation. The first file is the HTML form that will submit the data to the second file, which is the ASP page.

If you don't feel like typing, both files (DeleteShipper.html and DeleteShipper.asp) are available in the downloadable files and should be copied to your Learn_ASP folder.

1. Start **Windows Notepad** and enter the ASP code as shown below.

```
<HTML>
<HEAD>
<TITLE>DELETE DEMO</TITLE>
</HEAD>
```

```
<BODY>
<FORM Name=DeleteShipperForm Method=Get Action="DeleteShipper.asp"
<INPUT Type="Hidden" Name="Action" Value="Delete">
Please enter the Shipper ID you want to delete
<Input Type="Text" Size="6" Name="ShipperId">
<INPUT Type="Submit" Name="Delete" Value="Submit">
</FORM>
</BODY>
</HTML>
```

2. Save the file as **DeleteShipper.html** in the Learn_ASP folder.

    In the above HTML page, the form's Action argument will call the ASP
    page named DeleteShipper.asp when the user clicks the Submit button (see
    Figure 28-33).

3. Start **Windows Notepad** and enter the ASP code shown below.

```
<%@ Language=VBScript %>
<%
    Set conn = Server.CreateObject("ADODB.Connection")
    mydbFile=Server.MapPath("Northwind.mdb")
    conn.Open "Driver={Microsoft Access Driver (*.mdb)}; DBQ=" & mydbFile & ";"
    myShipper = Cstr(Request.QueryString("ShipperID"))
        If myShipper <>"" Then
            Set rst = Server.CreateObject("ADODB.Recordset")
            rst.Open "Shippers", conn, 3
            rst.Find "ShipperID = " & myShipper
            If rst.EOF Then
                Response.Write "The Shipper ID" & myShipper & " does not exist."
            Else
                On Error Resume Next
                conn.Execute "DELETE * FROM Shippers WHERE ShipperId = " & _
                             myShipper
                If conn.Errors.Count > 0 Then
                    Response.Write "Error Number: " & err.Number & "<P>"
                    Response.Write "Error Description: " & err.Description _
                                    & "<P>"
                Else
                    Response.Write "<H2>The Shipper ID " & myShipper & " _
                                    was deleted.</H2>"
                End If
                rst.close
                Set rst = Nothing
            End If
        Else
            Response.Write "The Shipper ID was not supplied. Cannot Delete."
    End If
%>
<HTML>
<HEAD><TITLE>DELETE SHIPPER</TITLE></HEAD>
<BODY>
<HR>
<A HREF="DeleteShipper.html">Please click here to return.</A>
</BODY>
</HTML>
```

4. Save the file as **DeleteShipper.asp** in the Learn_ASP folder.

The VBScript code segment shown above establishes a connection to the data source and stores the ShipperId value in the myShipper variable. If the variable is not empty, then the code proceeds to create an instance of the Recordset object and opens the Shippers table. The recordset is opened using the static cursor (adOpenStatic) represented by the value of 3 in the following statement:

```
rst.Open "Shippers", conn, 3
```

Recall that the static cursor retrieves all the data as it was at a point in time and is particularly desirable when you need to find data. The next statement uses the Find method to check if the supplied ShipperId exists in the Shippers table:

```
rst.Find "ShipperId = " & myShipper
```

Next, the If...Then...Else statement decides what information should be returned to the browser. When the EOF property of the Recordset object is True, the recordset contains no records. In this situation you want to tell the user that there is no such record in the table. However, if the record is found in the Shippers table, the SQL DELETE statement is executed:

```
conn.Execute "DELETE * FROM Shippers WHERE ShipperId = " & myShipper
```

As noted at the beginning of this section, a user may enter a ShipperId that has related records in other tables. Because this situation will certainly result in an error, the VBScript is instructed to ignore the error and continue with the next line of code:

```
On Error Resume Next
```

The next line of code is another If...Then...Else block statement that sends a different text message to the browser depending on whether the error was generated or not. You will know this by checking the contents of the Errors collection of the Connection object. The code displays the error number and error description if the user picked a Shipper ID that cannot be deleted. You may want to replace this code section with a more user-friendly message. If there is no error, then the browser will display a message that the record was deleted. The text of this message is formatted in large letters using the HTML level 2 heading tag <H2>.

Next, the Recordset object is closed. And now we are back at the first If...Then...Else statement block where the Else part is executed if the user happened to click the Submit button without first typing in the Shipper ID to delete.

The final part of the ASP page shown above creates a hyperlink to allow the user to navigate back to the HTML form (DeleteShipper.html). To create a hyperlink, use the following format:

```
<A HREF="address">displaytext</A>
```

where *address* is the name of the HTML file you want to activate and *displaytext* is the text that the user should click on.

Now let's proceed to actually performing the delete operation.

5. Open your browser and type **http://localhost/NorthDB/DeleteShipper.html** in the address bar.

6. Press **Enter** or click **Go**. Your screen should resemble Figure 28-33.

Figure 28-33: This HTML page is used for submitting information to an ASP page.

7. Click the **Submit** button without typing anything in the provided text box. You should see a message informing you that the Shipper ID was not supplied. Also, there is a link to allow you to return to the previous page.

8. Click the hyperlink to return to the previous page and enter **999** in the text box, then click the **Submit** button. Because this Shipper ID does not exist in the Shippers table, you are again informed about the problem and provided a way to return to the previous page.

9. Click the hyperlink to return to the previous page. Enter the Shipper ID that you inserted into the Shippers table in Hands-On 28-13 and click the **Submit** button. If you don't have any shipper record to delete, add a new record to the Shippers table and delete it using this process. When you type in a Shipper ID that exists in the Shippers table but is not referenced in other tables, you get the screen that confirms the deletion (Figure 28-34).

Figure 28-34: This screen announces a deletion of the shipper record having the ID of 5.

When you enter a Shipper ID that is referenced in other tables, Access will not allow you to delete that Shipper's record:

Error Number: –2147467259

Error Description: [Microsoft][ODBC Microsoft Access Driver] The record cannot be deleted or changed because table 'Orders' includes related records.

To see this error in action, try to delete the shipper with an ID of 1.

You can trap the error −2147467259 in your VBScript code to display a user-friendly message.

Creating a Web User Interface for Database Access

Now that we've developed some sample ASP pages, let's see how you can put them together so that they can be easily accessed from a web browser. Instead of typing the appropriate ASP filename in the browser's address bar every time you want to perform a particular operation, you can use hyperlinks and frames to organize the data. For example, take a look at Figure 28-35, which displays the Internet Explorer window divided into three areas. You can navigate between individual hands-on examples created in this chapter by clicking on the text in the left pane. When you click the hyperlink, the main portion of the window on the right-hand side will fill with the data retrieved from a database or display an interface to obtain the data (see Figure 28-36).

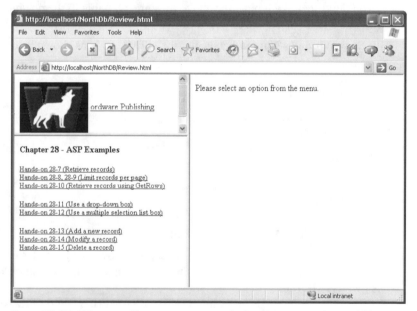

Figure 28-35: This page allows easy access to the hands-on examples on ASP programming introduced in this chapter.

Hands-On 28-16 walks you through the steps required to create the user interface shown in Figure 28-35.

◎ Hands-On 28-16: Providing Easy Access to Data with Frames

This hands-on uses the following four HTML files: Review.html, Logo.html, Examples.html, and Results.html.

Table 28-2: HTML files

File Name	Purpose
Review.html	Creates a page containing two frames and breaks one frame into two rows (resulting in three areas visible on the screen). Specifies what should be displayed within each frame and tells browsers that do not support frames to ignore them.
Logo.html	Places a company logo and a hyperlink to navigate to the company web site.
Examples.html	Creates jumps to this chapter's hands-on examples.
Results.html	Used for dumping information from the database or displaying the interface to obtain the data. Displays an information message to the user when the page is first opened.

If you don't feel like typing, the above files are available in the downloadable files and should be copied to your Learn_ASP folder.

1. Start **Windows Notepad** and enter the HTML code as shown below.

```
<HTML>
<FRAMESET COLS="290,*">
    <FRAMESET ROWS="110,*">
        <FRAME SRC="Logo.html">
        <FRAME SRC="Examples.html">
    </FRAMESET>
    <FRAME SRC="Results.html" Name="myDisplay">
</FRAMESET>
<NOFRAMES>
This page requires frames to be viewed.
</NOFRAMES>
</HTML>
```

2. Save the file as **Review.html** in the Learn_ASP folder.

The HTML code in the Review.html file shown above demonstrates how to divide a page into several areas by using frames. Each frame is controlled by its own HTML file.

You create a frame by using the HTML <FRAMESET> and <FRAME> tags with various parameters. A frame can contain other frames. The page shown in Figure 28-35 has two frames. The left frame is broken into two rows.

The statement

```
<FRAMESET COLS="290",*">
```

divides the page into two columns. The left-hand column is 290 pixels wide, and the right-hand column occupies the remainder of the screen (denoted by the asterisk). A frameset can contain both frames and other framesets.

Next, the left-hand column is divided into two rows, like this:

```
<FRAMESET ROWS="110", *">
```

The top row is 110 pixels high, and the bottom row occupies the remaining portion of the frame. The top frame points to the Logo.html file. The source file for the lower frame is Examples.html:

```
<FRAME SRC="Logo.html">
<FRAME SRC="Examples.html">
```

The two <FRAME> tags provide the information about each frame. The SRC attribute defines the source data for the frame.

Next, we define the source data for the frame on the right-hand side:

```
<FRAME SRC="Results.html" Name="myDisplay">
```

The Results.html file is created later in this hands-on exercise. We use the Name attribute to define the frame's name so that we can refer to this frame later.

Each frameset ends with the </FRAMESET> tag. Browsers that do not support frames will display an information message located between the <NOFRAMES> and </NOFRAMES> tags:

```
<NOFRAMES>
    This page requires frames to be viewed.
</NOFRAMES>
```

3. Choose **File | New** to create a new document in Notepad.

4. Enter the HTML code as shown below.

```
<HTML>
<BODY>
<IMG ALIGN="Middle" WIDTH="127" HEIGHT="99" ALT="Visit us today!"
SRC="Wordware.gif">
    <Font Color="Blue"><A HREF="http://www.wordware.com">ordware
    Publishing</A></Font>
</BODY>
</HTML>
```

5. Save the file as **Logo.html** in the Learn_ASP folder.

The HTML code above places an image (Wordware.gif, available in the downloadable files) in the top row of the frame on the left-hand side using the <IMG> tag. The ALIGN parameter tells the browser to position the text that follows in the middle. The WIDTH and HEIGHT parameters determine the size of the image in pixels. These measurements can be easily obtained by opening the image in the Windows Paint program and choosing Attributes from the Image menu. The text placed to the right of the image is a hyperlink. Clicking on it will jump to the Wordware Publishing web site.

6. Choose **File | New** to create a new document in Notepad.

7. Enter the HTML code as shown below.

```
<HTML><HEAD>
<BASE TARGET ="myDisplay">
</HEAD>
<BODY>
<H4>Chapter 28 - ASP Examples</H4>
<P>
<FONT Size="-1">
<A HREF="GetCustomers.asp" target=myDisplay>Hands-On 28-7 (Retrieve _
      records)</A><BR>
<A HREF="PageMe.asp">Hands-On 28-8, 28-9 (Limit records per page)</A><BR>
<A HREF="FastRetrieve.asp">Hands-On 28-10 (Retrieve records using _
      GetRows)</A><BR><P>
<A HREF="ProductLookup.asp">Hands-On 28-11 (Use a drop-down box)</A><BR>
<A HREF="MultiProductLookup.asp">Hands-On 28-12 (Use a multiple selection _
      list box)</A><BR><P>
<A HREF="NWDataEntry.asp">Hands-On 28-13 (Add a new record)</A><BR>
<A HREF="UpdateProduct.asp">Hands-On 28-14 (Modify a record)</A><BR>
<A HREF="DeleteShipper.html">Hands-On 28-15 (Delete a record)</A>
</FONT></P></BODY>
</HTML>
```

8. Save the file as **Examples.html** in the Learn_ASP folder.

The code in the Examples.html file is straightforward. It contains a set of jumps to different hands-on examples. Each of these examples has a corresponding .asp file in the Learn_ASP folder. To control where the requested information should be displayed, use the <BASE> tag:

```
<BASE Target="myDisplay">
```

The Target attribute is set to the name of the frame where the information should appear. When you place the BASE Target tag at the beginning of the file, all of the links will display in the same frame.

Here's how we create the first hyperlink:

```
<A href="GetCustomers.asp" target=myDisplay>Hands-On 28-7 (Retrieve _
      records)</A><BR>
```

The A tag defines a hypertext link. The href attribute specifies the associated URL. In other words, when the user clicks on the "Hands-On 28-7 (Retrieve records)" hyperlink, the GetCustomers.asp file will be requested and its output will be placed in the specified target (right-hand frame).

9. Choose **File | New** to create a new document in Notepad.

10. Enter the HTML code as shown below.

```
<HTML>
Please select an option from the menu.
</HTML>
```

11. Save the file as **Results.html** in the Learn_ASP folder. The Results.html file will display the information text when the Review.html file is first opened in the browser (refer to Figure 28-35 at the beginning of this section).

12. Exit Notepad. You now should have four HTML files as outlined at the beginning of this hands-on exercise. Let's test out our user interface.

13. Open your browser and type **http://localhost/NorthDB/Review.html** in the address bar. Your screen should resemble Figure 28-35 earlier in this chapter.

14. Verify the results of each hands-on by clicking on its link.

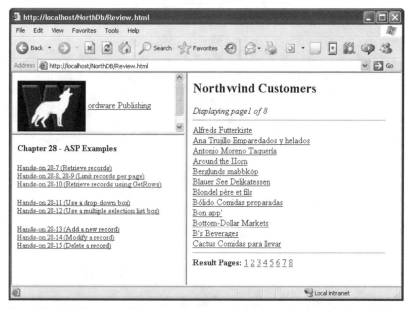

Figure 28-36: When you click a hyperlink on the left-hand side, the right-hand frame will display the requested information as illustrated here.

Chapter Summary

This chapter has introduced you to the world of web development by using a server-side scripting technology from Microsoft known as Active Server Pages (ASP). You learned how by using a subset of VBA, VBScript, you can quickly extract data from a database and present it to a user in a standard HTML page. You also learned how to submit Action queries to insert, update, and delete a database record. You've seen two coding styles: one that mixes HTML and script commands, and one that returns HTML text to the browser by using the ASP built-in object Response and its Write method. By working through several hands-on examples, you've seen that making your application web-ready is not rocket science. ASP scripts are quite easy to write if you understand VBA statements and have already worked with ActiveX Data Objects (ADO). Although it was easy to get started, this chapter did not attempt to teach you all there is to know about HTML, ASP, or VBScript. If you decide to move into the lucrative world of web development, you should learn more about these subjects. Numerous books and articles have been written on the topics we've only touched on in this chapter, as well as many other topics that are necessary to create truly functional Internet applications.

In the next chapter, you explore another Internet technology known as Extensible Markup Language (XML) and learn how it is integrated with Microsoft Office Access 2003.

Chapter 29

XML Features in Access 2003

If you need to deliver information over the World Wide Web or you want to store, share, and exchange data between different applications regardless of the operating system or programming language used, you need to become familiar with the Extensible Markup Language (XML).

Imagine these two scenarios where your combined knowledge of Access and XML will come in handy:

- You have just received a file in XML format and you need to merge its data with an existing Access table, or perhaps create a new table.
- You have been asked to provide a data dump from your Access database in XML format.

XML is a complex language that cannot be covered within the pages of one chapter; however, this single chapter will get you started using XML with Access 2003.

What Is XML?

In the previous chapter you learned how HTML (HyperText Markup Language) uses tags to format data in a web page. Like HTML, Extensible Markup Language uses markup tags; however, its tags serve a different purpose — they are used to describe data content. HTML uses fixed, non-customizable tags to provide formatting instructions that should be applied to the data. XML is *extensible*, which means that it is not restricted to a set of predefined tags. XML allows you to invent your own tags in order to define and describe data stored in a wide range of documents. The XML parser does not care what tags you use; it only needs to be able to find the tags and confirm that the XML document is well formed. When a document is well formed, it follows the formatting rules for XML (see "What Is a Well-Formed XML Document?" below).

What Is a Parser?

If you want to read, update, create, or manipulate any XML document, you will need an XML parser. A parser is a software engine, usually a dynamic-link library (DLL), which can read and extract data from XML. Microsoft Internet Explorer 5 or higher has a built-in XML parser (MSXML.DLL, MSXML2.DLL, and MSXML3.DLL) that is capable of reading well-formed documents and detecting those that are not. MSXML has its own object model, known as DOM (Document Object Model), that you can use from VBA to quickly and easily extract information from an XML document. To ensure that you are working with the most recent XML parser, check out the following link: http://www.microsoft.com/downloads/details.aspx?familyid=4a3ad088-a893-4f0b-a932-5e024e74519f&displaylang=en

An XML document must also be valid. When a document is valid, it follows the predefined rules for valid data. These rules are defined in a Document Type Definition (DTD) or a schema. Schemas are written in XML and define the rules that make an XML document valid. DTD is an old method of data validation. Later in this chapter you will see how Access uses a schema to determine the type of elements and attributes an XML document should contain, how these elements and attributes should be named, whether they're optional or required, their data types and default values, and the relationship between the elements.

Because of its extensibility, XML makes it easy to describe any data structure (structured or unstructured) and send it anywhere across the web using common protocols such as HTTP (HyperText Transfer Protocol) or FTP (File Transfer Protocol). Although XML was designed specifically for delivering information over the World Wide Web, it is being utilized in other areas, such as storing, sharing, and exchanging data. Because XML is stored in plain text files, it can be read by many types of applications, independent of the operating system or hardware.

What Is a Well-Formed XML Document?

An XML document must have one root element. While in HTML the root element is always <HTML>, in the XML document you can name your root element anything you want. Element names must begin with a letter or underscore character. The root element must enclose all other elements, and elements must be properly nested. The XML data must be hierarchical; the beginning and ending tags cannot overlap.

```
<Employee>
    <Employee Id>090909</Employee Id>
</Employee>
```

All element tags must be closed. A begin tag must be followed by an end tag:

```
<Sessions>5</Sessions>
```
You can use shortcuts, such as a single slash (/), to end the tag so you don't have to type the full tag name. For example, if the current Sessions element is empty (does not have value), you could use the following tag:

```
<Sesssions />.
```
Tag names are case-sensitive: The tags <Title> and </Title> aren't equivalent to <TITLE> and </TITLE>.

For example, the following line:

```
<Title>Beginning VBA Programming</Title>
```
is not the same as:

```
<TITLE>Beginning VBA Programming</TITLE>
```
All attributes must be in quotation marks:

```
<Course Id="VBAEX1"/>
```
You cannot have more than one attribute with the same name within the same element. If the <Course> element has two Id attributes, they must be written separately, as shown below:

```
<Course Id="VBAEX1"/>
<Course Id="VBAEX2"/>
```

The main goals of XML are the separation of content from presentation, and the portability of the data.

It is important to understand that XML was designed to address the limitations of HTML and not to replace it. One of these limitations is the inability of HTML to identify data. By using XML tags you can give meaning to the data in the document and provide a consistent way of identifying each item of data. By separating content from presentation and structuring data based on its meaning, we are finally able to create documents that are easy to reuse, manipulate, and search.

So, let's get started with XML in Access.

XML Support in Access 2003

Microsoft Access has supported XML since its 2002 version. You can export and import XML data using the built-in menu commands (File | Export, File | Import) or you can do this programmatically with VBA. Additionally, Access 2003 has the capability to export related tables to a single XML file. When importing XML data, you can create multiple tables from a single XML document and schema. Unfortunately, the parent-child relationships between the tables are not maintained; you must create them yourself. You can also specify a custom schema during the export or import of XML data.

Exporting XML Data

You can export tables, queries, forms, and/or reports to XML files from an Access database (.mdb) file or an Access project (.adp) file. There is no XML support for macros and modules. When you export a form or report, you actually export the data from the form or report's underlying table or query.

Access uses a special XML vocabulary known as ReportML for representing its objects as XML data. *ReportML* is an XML file that contains tags describing properties, methods, events, and attributes of the Access object being exported. This file is generated automatically by Access when you begin the export process and is used by Access to generate the final output files.

To allow XML data to be viewed in browsers in a user-friendly format, ReportML relies on the RPT2HTML4.xsl file, which is located in the \Program Files\Microsoft Office\Office11\AccessWeb folder. This file is a rather complicated stylesheet that contains formatting instructions. We examine stylesheets later in this chapter. After the formatting instructions contained in the stylesheet have been applied to the XML file, the ReportML file is automatically deleted.

> **Note:** If you'd like to take a look at the content of the ReportML file, you must tell Access not to delete it by default. This requires that you add the following entry to the Windows registry:
>
> HKEY_CURRENT_USER\Software\Microsoft\Office\11.0\Access\ReportML
>
> Unless you are very familiar with using RegEdit to edit registry settings, do not attempt this task on your own. Once you make the registry setting and complete the export to XML, you can open the ReportML file and look at its contents. This file should have the name of the Access object you exported, followed by an underscore and the word "report." For example, if you exported the Shippers table to an XML file, the ReportML name is Shippers_report.xml.

No matter what Access object you need to export to XML, you always follow the same procedure:

- To export all the data, select the appropriate object (table, query, report, or form) in the Database window and choose File | Export, or right-click the object and select Export from the shortcut menu.
- To export a single record or a filtered or sorted set of records, open the appropriate object and follow the steps as outlined below:

You want to...	Step 1	Step 2
Export a single record	Select that record	Choose File | Export
Export filtered records	Apply a filter to the records	Choose File | Export
Export records in a predefined order	Arrange records in the order you want	Choose File | Export

The following hands-on exercise demonstrates how to use the Export command to save the Access Shippers table in XML format.

◎ Hands-On 29-1: Exporting an Access Table to an XML File

1. Use Windows Explorer to create a new folder named **Learn_XML** for this chapter's practice files.

2. Open the sample **Northwind** database that comes with Access.

3. In the Northwind database window, select **Tables** in the Objects bar, highlight the **Shippers** table, and choose **File | Export**.

4. In the Save in drop-down list in the Export Table window, switch to the **Learn_XML** folder that you created in step 1 above. In the Save as type drop-down list, select **XML**. Access will enter Shippers into the File name drop-down list. Having specified the file format and its destination, click **Export** (see Figure 29-1).

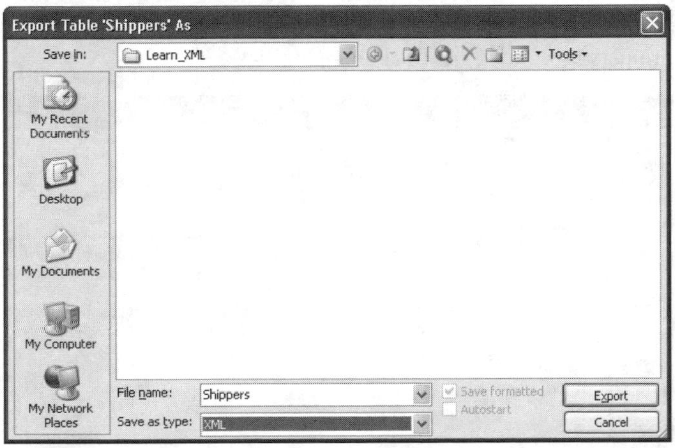

Figure 29-1: To save Access data in the XML format, choose XML from the Save as type drop-down list and click the Export button. Notice that Access automatically fills in the File name box. You can change the filename to any name you like.

In the Export XML dialog box that appears, two check boxes — Data (XML) and Schema of the data (XSD) — are already selected (see Figure 29-2). These options will create two files: an XML file that will contain the data from the Shippers table and an XSD file that will contain the definition of the data.

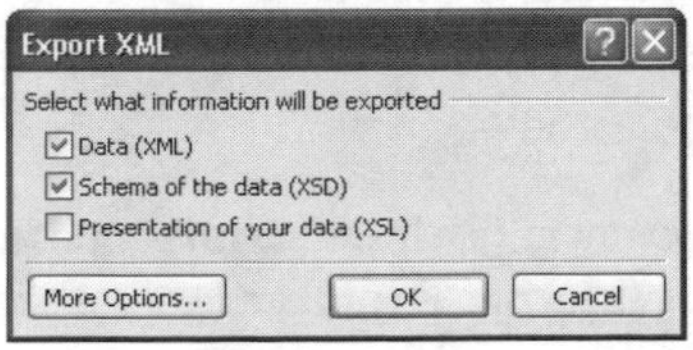

Figure 29-2: The Export XML dialog box displays three check boxes; the first two are selected by default. The More Options button allows for more customization.

5. Select the **Presentation of your data (XSL)** check box to tell Access to generate HTML and XSL files for presentation of the data in the web browser. With all three check boxes selected in the Export XML dialog box, click **OK** to proceed with the export.

Understanding the XML Data File

When Access completes the export operation, it returns you to the Database window. Switch to Windows Explorer and examine the contents of our Learn_XML folder.

⊙ Hands-On 29-2: Examining the Contents of an XML Data File

1. Open **Windows Explorer** and switch to the **Learn_XML** folder. Figure 29-3 displays the contents of the Learn_XML folder after exporting the Shippers table to XML in Hands-On 29-1.

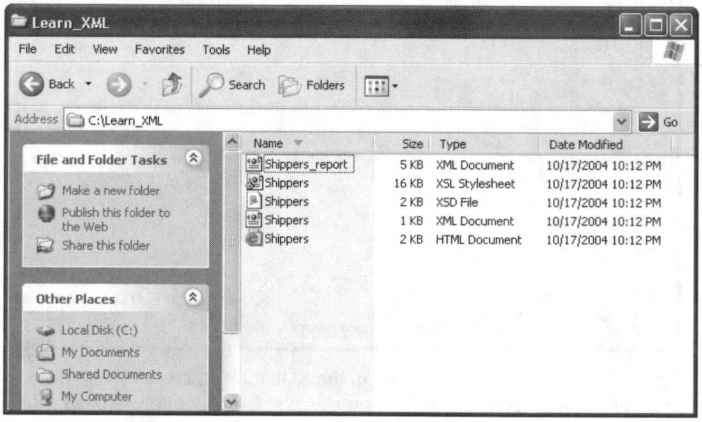

Figure 29-3: After exporting the Shippers table to XML with all three check boxes selected in the Export XML dialog box (see Figure 29-2), Access creates four files. The fifth file (shown first in this screen shot) is the ReportML file. If you didn't make changes in the registry as mentioned at the beginning of this section, your Learn_XML directory listing will not contain the Shippers_report file.

➔ **Note:** To have the file extensions displayed, choose Tools | Folder Options, click the View tab, and clear the check box next to Hide extensions for known file types.

2. Highlight the Shippers XML document (**Shippers.xml**) and choose **Open With** from the File menu. Select **Internet Explorer**. Access displays the Shippers data in XML format as shown in Figure 29-4.

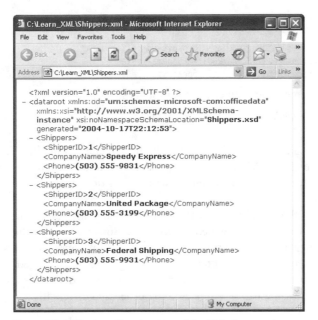

Figure 29-4: The tree-like structure of the XML document.

When you open an XML file in Internet Explorer, you can see the hierarchical layout of an XML document very clearly. The plus/minus (+ / –) signs make it possible to display the document as a collapsible tree.

The first line in the XML file is a processing instruction. Processing instructions begin with <? and end with ?>. The XML document begins with a processing instruction that contains an XML declaration:

```
<?xml version="1.0" encoding="UTF-8" ?>
```

The version attribute (version="1.0") tells the XML processor that the document conforms to version 1.0 of the XML specification. The encoding attribute (encoding="UTF-8") is used to indicate character sets to web browsers. By default, XML documents use the UTF-8 encoding of Unicode.

Character Encodings in XML

The encoding declaration in the XML document identifies which encoding is used to represent the characters in the document. UTF-8 encoding allows the use of non-ASCII characters, regardless of the language of the user's operating system and browser or the language version of Office. When you use UFT-8 or UTF-16 character encoding, an encoding declaration is optional. XML parsers can determine automatically if a document uses UTF-8 or UTF-16 Unicode encoding.

The second line in the XML document is a dataroot element:

```
<dataroot xmlns:od="urn:schemas-microsoft-com:officedata"
xmlns:xsi="http://www.w3.org/2001/XMLSchema-instance"
xsi:noNamespaceSchemaLocation="Shippers.xsd" generated="2004-10-17T22:12:53">
```

The dataroot element tag defines two namespaces:

```
xmlns:od="urn:schemas-microsoft-com:officedata"
xmlns:xsi="http://www.w3.org/2001/XMLSchema-instance"
```

A *namespace* is a collection of names in which each name is unique. The XML namespaces are used in XML documents to ensure that element names do not conflict with one another and are unique within a particular set of names (a namespace).

For example, the <TITLE> tag will certainly have a different meaning and content in an XML document generated from the Books table than the <TITLE> element used to describe the courtesy titles of your customers. If the two XML documents containing the <TITLE> tag were to be merged, there would be an element name conflict. Therefore, in order to distinguish between tags that have the same names but need to be processed differently, namespaces are used.

The attribute "xmlns" is an XML keyword for a namespace declaration. The namespace is identified by a Uniform Resource Identifier (URI) — either a Uniform Resource Locator (URL) or a Uniform Resource Name (URN). The URI used as an XML namespace name is simply an identifier; it is not guaranteed to point to anything. Most namespaces use URIs for the namespace names because URIs are guaranteed to be unique. The use of a namespace is identified via a name prefix. The prefix is mapped to a URI to select a namespace.

For example, in the context of the Shippers.xml document, the *od* prefix is associated with the "urn:schemas-microsoft-com:officedata" namespace and the *xsi* prefix identifies the "http://www.w3.org/2001/XMLSchema-instance" namespace. These prefixes may be associated with other namespaces outside of this particular XML document.

Notice that the prefix is separated from the xmlns attribute with a colon and the URI is used as the value of the attribute.

In addition to namespaces, the dataroot element specifies where to find the schema. This is done by using two attributes: the location of a schema file that defines the rules of an XML document and the date the file was generated.

```
xsi:noNamespaceSchemaLocation="Shippers.xsd" generated="2004-10-17T22:12:53"
```

An XML document's data is contained in elements. An element consists of the following three parts:

- Start tag — Contains the element's name (e.g., <ShipperID>)
- Element data — The representation of actual data (e.g., 1)
- End tag — Contains the element's name preceded by a slash (e.g., </ShipperID>)

If you click on the minus sign in front of the data root element, you will notice that the dataroot element encloses all the elements in the Access XML file. Each element in a tree structure is called a *node*.

The dataroot node contains child nodes for each row of the Shippers table. Notice that the table name is used for each element representing a row. You can expand or collapse any row element by clicking on the plus/or minus sign (+/–) in front of the element tag name.

Within row elements, there is a separate element for each column (ShipperID, CompanyName, and Phone). Notice that each XML element contains a start tag, the element data, and the end tag:

```
<Shippers>
    <ShipperID>1</ShipperID>
    <CompanyName>Speedy Express</CompanyName>
    <Phone>(503) 555-9831</Phone>
</Shippers>
```

The ShipperID, CompanyName, and Phone elements are children of the Shippers element. In turn, each Shippers element is a child of the dataroot element. XML documents can be nested to any depth as long as each inner node is entirely contained within the outer node.

3. Close the browser containing the Shippers.xml file.

Understanding the XML Schema File

Now that you have familiarized yourself with the structure of an XML document, let's look at another type of XML file that was created by Access during the export to XML process — the XML schema file (XSD).

Schema files describe XML data using the XML Schema Definition (XSD) language and allow the XML parser to validate the XML document. An XML document that conforms to the structure of the schema is said to be *valid*.

Here are some examples of the type of information that can be found in an XML schema file:

- Elements that are allowed in a given XML document
- Data types of allowed elements
- Number of allowed occurrences of a given element
- Attributes that can be associated with a given element
- Default values for attributes
- Child elements of other elements
- The sequence and number of child elements

⊚ Hands-On 29-3: Examining the Contents of an XML Schema File

1. Open **Windows Explorer** and switch to the **Learn_XML** folder containing the files generated in Hands-On 29-1 (see Figure 29-3).

2. Use **Windows Notepad** to open the **Shippers.xsd** file located in the Learn_XML folder. Access displays the contents of the Shippers.xsd file as shown in Figure 29-5.

```
Shippers - Notepad
File  Edit  Format  View  Help
<?xml version="1.0" encoding="UTF-8"?>
<xsd:schema xmlns:xsd="http://www.w3.org/2001/XMLSchema"
xmlns:od="urn:schemas-microsoft-com:officedata">
<xsd:element name="dataroot">
<xsd:complexType>
<xsd:sequence>
<xsd:element ref="Shippers" minOccurs="0" maxOccurs="unbounded"/>
</xsd:sequence>
<xsd:attribute name="generated" type="xsd:dateTime"/>
</xsd:complexType>
</xsd:element>
<xsd:element name="Shippers">
<xsd:annotation>
<xsd:appinfo>
<od:index index-name="PrimaryKey" index-key="ShipperID " primary="yes"
unique="yes" clustered="no"/>
</xsd:appinfo>
</xsd:annotation>
<xsd:complexType>
<xsd:sequence>
<xsd:element name="ShipperID" minOccurs="1" od:jetType="autonumber"
od:sqlSType="int" od:autounique="yes" od:nonNullable="yes" type="xsd:int"/>
<xsd:element name="CompanyName" minOccurs="1" od:jetType="text"
od:sqlSType="nvarchar" od:nonNullable="yes">
<xsd:simpleType>
<xsd:restriction base="xsd:string">
<xsd:maxLength value="40"/>
</xsd:restriction>
</xsd:simpleType>
</xsd:element>
<xsd:element name="Phone" minOccurs="0" od:jetType="text" od:sqlSType="nvarchar">
<xsd:simpleType>
<xsd:restriction base="xsd:string">
<xsd:maxLength value="24"/>
</xsd:restriction>
</xsd:simpleType>
</xsd:element>
</xsd:sequence>
</xsd:complexType>
</xsd:element>
</xsd:schema>
```

Figure 29-5: The schema file shown here defines the data in the Shippers.xml document.

If you take a look at the Shippers.xsd file currently open in Notepad, you will notice a number of XSD declarations and commands that begin with the <xsd> tag followed by a colon and the name of the command. You will also notice the names of the elements and attributes that are allowed in the Shippers.xml file as well as the data types for each element.

The names of the data types are preceded with the od prefix followed by a colon. For example:

od:jetType="text"	Defines the JetData type for an element
od:sqlSType="nvarchar"	Defines the Microsoft SQL Server data type for an element
od:autounique="yes"	Defines a Boolean data type for an auto-incremented identity column
od:nonNullable="yes"	Indicates whether or not a column can contain a Null value.

The schema file also specifies the number of times an element can be used in a document based on the schema. This is done via the minOccurs and maxOccurs attributes.

3. Close Notepad and the Shippers.xsd file.

> **Note:** To find out more about XML schemas, check out the following links:
> http://www.w3.org/TR/2004/REC-xmlschema-0-20041028/
> http://www.w3.org/TR/2004/REC-xmlschema-1-20041028/
> http://www.w3.org/TR/2004/REC-xmlschema-2-20041028/

Understanding the XSL Transformation Files

When you examined the contents of the Shippers.xml document earlier in this chapter you may have noticed that the file did not contain any formatting instructions. Although it is easy to display the XML file in the browser, end users expect to see documents nicely formatted. To meet their expectations, the raw XML data is formatted with the Extensible Stylesheet Language (XSL).

When you exported the Shippers table to XML and selected the Presentation of your data (XSL) check box in the Export XML dialog box (see Figure 29-2 earlier and step 5 in Hands-On 29-1), Access generated an XSL file. Extensible Stylesheet Language is a transformation style language that uses XSL Transformations (XSLT) to create templates that are applied to the source document data to create the target document. The target document can be another XML document, an HTML page, or even a text-based file.

XSL files include all the XSLT transforms that are needed to define how the data is to be presented. Transformations allow you to change the order of elements and selectively process elements. Later in this chapter you will learn how to create XSL files with XSLT transforms to display only selected fields from the Access-generated XML documents. There is no limit to the number of stylesheets that can be used with a particular XML document. By creating more than one XSL file, you can present different formats of the same XML document to various users.

Hands-On 29-4: Examining the Contents of an XSL File

1. Use Internet Explorer to open the **Shippers.xsl** file located in the Learn_XML folder. Access displays the contents of the Shippers.xsl file as shown in Figure 29-6.

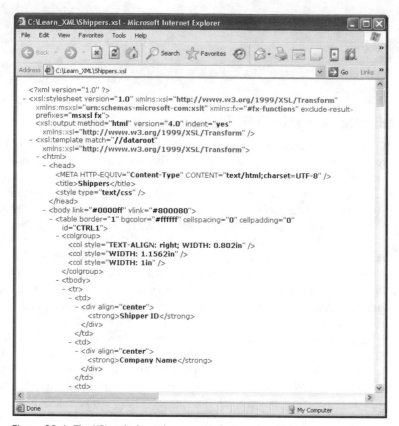

Figure 29-6: The XSL stylesheet document is just another XML document that contains HTML formatting instructions and XSLT formatting elements for transforming raw XML data into HTML.

When you take a look at the contents of the Shippers.xsl file you will notice a number of XSLT formatting elements such as <xsl:template>, <xsl:for-each>, and <xsl:value of>. You will also find in it many HTML formatting instructions such as <head>, <title>, <body>, <table>, <colgroup>, <col>, <tbody>, <tr>, <td>, <div>, and <strong>.

The first line of the stylesheet code declares that this is an XML document that follows the XML 1.0 standard (version). An XSL document is a type of XML document. While XML documents store data, XSL documents specify how the data should be displayed.

The second line declares the namespace to be used to identify the tags in the XSL document. (See the "Understanding the XML Data File" section earlier in this chapter for more information about namespaces). The third line specifies that HTML should be used to display the data.

The next line is the beginning of the formatting section. Before we look at the XSLT tags, you need to know that XSL documents use templates to perform transformations of XML documents. The XSL stylesheet can contain one or more XSLT templates. You can think of templates as special blocks of code that apply to one or more XML tags. Templates contain rules for displaying a particular branch of elements in the XML document. The use of templates is made possible via special formatting tags.

Notice that the Shippers.xsl file contains the <xsl:template> tag to define a template for the entire document. The <xsl:template> element has a match attribute. The value of the match attribute indicates the nodes (elements) for which this template is appropriate.

For example, the special pattern "//" in the match attribute tells the XSL processor that this is the template for the document root:

```
<xsl:template match="//dataroot"
xmlns:xsl="http://www.w3.org/1999/XSL/Transform">
```

The template ends with the </template> closing tag.

Following the definition of the template, standard HTML tags are used to format the document. Next, the XSLT formatting instruction <xsl:for-each> tells the XSL processor to do something every time it finds a pattern. The pattern follows the select attribute.

For example,

```
<xsl:for-each select="Shippers">
```

tells the XML processor to loop through the <Shippers> elements. The loop is closed with a closing loop tag:

```
</xsl:for-each>
```

The XSLT formatting instruction <xsl:value-of> tells the XSL processor to retrieve the value of the tag specified in the select attribute.

For example,

```
<xsl:value-of select="ShipperID">
```

tells the XML processor to select the ShipperID column. Because this formatting instruction is located below the <xsl:for-each> tag, the XSL processor will retrieve the value of the ShipperID column for each Shippers element.

The select attribute uses the XML Path language (XPath) expression to locate the child elements to be processed.

What Exactly Is XPath?

XPath is a query language used to create expressions for finding data in the XML data file. These expressions can manipulate strings, numbers, and Boolean values. They can also be used to navigate an XML tree structure and process its elements with XSLT instructions. XPath is designed to be used by XSL Transformations (XSLT). With XPath expressions, you can easily identify and extract from the XML document specific elements (nodes) based on their type, name, values, or the relationship of a node to other nodes. When preparing stylesheets for transforming your XML documents into HTML, you will often use various XPath expressions in the select attribute.

If you scroll down the Shippers.xsl file, you will also notice that Access has generated a number of VBScript functions to evaluate expressions. To prevent the XSL processor from parsing these functions, the function section is placed within the CDATA directive.

2. Close the browser containing the Shippers.xsl file.

Note: For more information about Extensible Stylesheet Language (XSL), visit the following link: http://www.w3.org/TR/2001/REC-xsl-20011015/Over-view.html#contents.

Viewing XML Documents Formatted with Stylesheets

When you exported the Shippers table to XML format, Access applied XSLT transforms to turn the XML data into an HTML file so that you can view formatted data in the browser (see Figure 29-7).

Figure 29-7: This HTML file was created from XML data by using XSLT.

Advanced XML Export Options

When you exported the Shippers table to XML format, you may have noticed the More Options button in the Export XML dialog box (see Figure 29-2 at the beginning of this chapter). Pressing this button opens a window with three tabs as shown in Figure 29-8. Each tab groups options for the types of XML objects that you can export. The Data tab contains options for the XML document, the Schema tab list options for the XSD document, and the Presentation tab provides options for generating the XSL document.

Data Export Options

The options shown on the Data tab (see Figure 29-8) control the data that is exported to the XML documents. These options are grouped into three main areas.

The Export Data section displays data that you may want to export. In this particular scenario I requested to export the Customers table. Because this table is directly related to the Orders table in the Northwind database, the Orders table is displayed as a child node of Customers. The Orders table is related to the Order Details table and so on. If you click on the plus sign in front of the [Lookup Data] node, you will see the names of tables that provide lookup information for the main tables. By clicking on the check box you may export just the table that you originally requested or you can export the customers' data along with all the orders, and perhaps include lookup information.

Below the Export Data section is the Export Location area that shows the filename for the XML document that will be created when you click the OK button. You can change the location of this document by using the Browse button. Simply navigate to the folder where you want to save the XML file. You can also change the name of the document by replacing the name shown in the text box with another name.

The area to the right of the Export Data section allows you to specify which records you want to export. This area contains three option buttons that allow you to export all records, filtered records, or the current record. Notice that only two options are enabled in Figure 29-8.

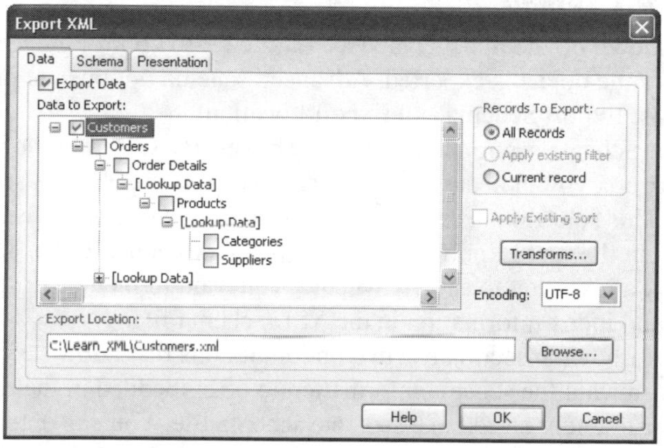

Figure 29-8: Use the Data tab in the Export XML window to set advanced data options.

If you highlight the table to export in the Database window and then choose the Export command on the File menu, only the All Records option button will be enabled in the Records To Export section. Opening the table prior to choosing the Export command tells Access to enable the All Records and Current record option buttons. And if you open the table and apply a filter to the data, then select the Export command, Access will enable the Apply existing filter option button in addition to the other two buttons.

The other options on the Data tab are Apply Existing Sort, Transforms, and Encoding. The Apply Existing Sort check box is enabled if the exported object is open and a sort is applied. Access will export the data in the specified order. By clicking on the Transforms button you can select a custom XSL transform file to apply to the data during export. You can choose from the transforms you have written or received with the XML data. Use the Encoding drop-down list to select UTF-8 or UTF-16 encoding for the exported XML. The default is UTF-8.

When you export an object from an Access .mdb file, Access exports static data. This means that the exported object is not automatically updated when the data changes. If the data in the Access database has changed since you exported an Access object to an XML data file, you will need to re-export the object so the new data is available to the client application.

Exporting live data is supported by Access data projects. If the underlying data in the database changes, the client application will receive the updated data automatically when it connects to the SQL Server database. If you are exporting an object from an Access Data Project (.adp) file that connects to the SQL Server database, the Data tab will contain the Live Data check box and the Virtual Directory text box above the Export Location section. The Virtual Directory text box holds the URL of the folder on the server that the export process should use. When exporting live data you must export the entire Access object (you cannot select individual records). The Live Data option also does not allow you to apply a transform during the export.

Schema Export Options

The options shown on the Schema tab (see Figure 29-9) control the way the schema file for the object is exported. Advanced schema options are presented in two sections: Export Schema and Export Location.

The Export Schema section has two check boxes. By selecting the Export Schema check box you indicate that you want to export the object's schema as an XSD file. This selection is the same as choosing the Schema of the data (XSD) option in the first Export XML dialog box (see Figure 29-2). The second check box allows you to specify whether you want to include or ignore primary key and index information in the XSD schema file.

The Export Location section has two option buttons that allow you to specify whether you want the schema information to be embedded in the exported XML data document or stored in a separate schema file. You can enter the filename in the provided text box and specify the location of the schema file by clicking the Browse button.

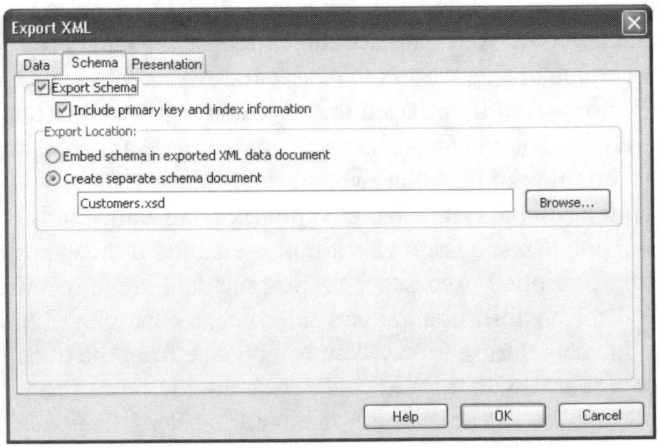

Figure 29-9: Use the Schema tab in the Export XML dialog box to set advanced schema options.

Presentation Export Options

The selections on the Presentation tab (see Figure 29-10) specify available options for the XSL files. The Export Presentation (HTML 4.0 Sample XSL) check box allows you to indicate whether you want to export the object's presentation. Choose the Client (HTML) option in the Run from section if you want the presentation to run on the client. Access will create an HTML file with the script necessary to perform the transform. The script will be executed on the client machine. While this selection reduces the load on the server, a client application will need to download a couple of files (HTML document, XML data file, and XSD schema file) to present the data in the browser. If the XSL file is going to be placed on the web server and called from an ASP page, choose the Server (ASP) option. By choosing this option, only the final HTML is downloaded to the client.

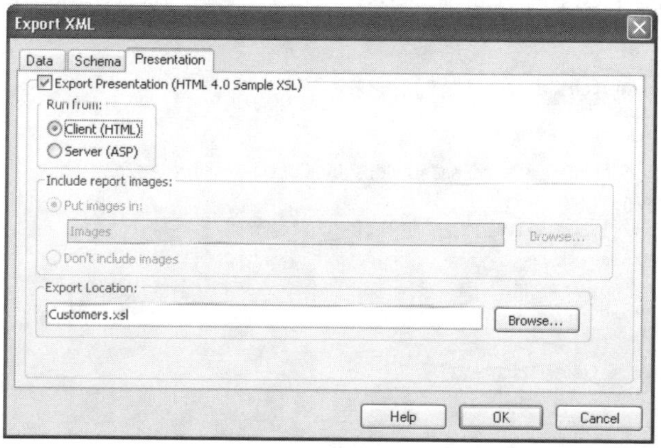

Figure 29-10: Use the Presentation tab in the Export XML dialog box to set advanced presentation options.

If the exported presentation includes pictures, you can indicate whether to include them in the output by clicking the appropriate option button in the Include report images section. If you choose to include the images, Access will create separate image files and link them with the HTML file. By default, the image files are stored in the Images folder of the main export folder. To place them in another location, click the Browse button to specify the folder name.

The Export Location section allows you to specify the name and location of the export files. When you export a presentation file, Access creates two files: an XSL file that includes all the XSLT transforms needed to define how the data is presented and a simple HTML file that contains properly formatted data from the exported object and not the raw data with XML tags. The HTML file contains a snapshot of the data as it existed during the export process.

Applying XSLT Transforms to Exported Data

When exporting Access data to XML format, you can use custom transformation files (XSL) to modify the data after you export it. Hands-On 29-5 demonstrates how to create a custom stylesheet for use after export. This stylesheet assumes that for each customer in the Customers table we want to display only selected columns from the Orders table. You learn how to apply this custom stylesheet in Hands-On 29-6. Take a quick look at Figure 29-13 later in this chapter to see the final outcome.

⊚ Hands-On 29-5: Creating a Custom Transformation File

1. Open **Notepad** and enter the statements as shown below.

```
<?xml version="1.0" encoding="UTF-8"?>
<xsl:stylesheet version="1.0" xmlns:xsl="http://www.w3.org/1999/XSL/Transform">
<xsl:output method="html" version="4.0" indent="yes"/>

<xsl:template match="dataroot">
    <html>
    <body>
        <h2><font name="Verdana">Orders by Customer</font></h2>
        <p></p>
            <xsl:apply-templates select="Customers"/>
    </body>
    </html>
</xsl:template>

<xsl:template match="Customers">
<table>
    <tr>
        <td BgColor="#FFCC33">
            <font color="#000000">
                <xsl:value-of select="CustomerID"/>
            </font>
        </td>
        <td><b>
            <xsl:value-of select="CompanyName"/>
        </b></td>
    </tr>
</table>
<table cellpadding="5" cellspacing="5">
    <tr BgColor="black">
        <td bgcolor="black" width="10px"></td>
        <td><font color="white" size="1">Order ID</font></td>
        <td><font color="white" size="1">Order Date</font></td>
        <td><font color="white" size="1">Shipped Date</font></td>
        <td><font color="white" size="1">Required Date</font></td>
        <td><font color="white" size="1">Freight</font></td>
    </tr>
    <xsl:apply-templates select="Orders"/>
</table>
</xsl:template>
```

```
<xsl:template match="Orders">
    <tr>
        <td bgcolor="black" width="10px"></td>
        <td><xsl:value-of select="OrderID"/></td>
        <td><xsl:value-of select="substring(OrderDate, 1, 10)"/></td>
        <td><xsl:value-of select="substring(ShippedDate, 1, 10)"/></td>
        <td><xsl:value-of select="substring(RequiredDate, 1, 10)"/></td>
        <td>$<xsl:value-of select="format-number(Freight,'####0.00')"/></td>
    </tr>
</xsl:template>

</xsl:stylesheet>
```

2. Save the file as **ListCustOrders.xsl** in the Learn_XML folder. You must type the file extension to ensure that the file is not saved as text.

3. Close Notepad.

Let's now proceed to analyze the contents of the ListCustOrders.xsl file that will be used to transform XML to HTML in our next hands-on exercise. Notice that because the XSLT stylesheet is an XML document, we started out with a standard XML declaration:

```
<?xml version="1.0" encoding="UTF-8"?>
```

Next, we defined the namespace for the stylesheet and declared its prefix like this:

```
<xsl:stylesheet version="1.0" xmlns:xsl="http://www.w3.org/1999/XSL/Transform">
```

On the third line we indicated that XSLT should transform the XML into HTML by using the <xsl:output> tag as follows:

```
<xsl:output method="html" version="4.0" indent="yes"/>
```

Notice that because the <xsl:output> tag is always empty, it must be terminated with a forward slash (/). This tag has two attributes: method and indent. The *method* attribute specifies the format of the output. This can be XML, HTML, or text. The *indent* attribute, which is set to "yes" in this example, indicates that the XML should be indented. This will make the final XML document more readable when viewed in the browser.

The remaining part of the XSL file contains transformation instructions for the XML document element nodes. We begin by creating the root template. The <xsl:template> tag initiates a template within a stylesheet. Because a template must indicate which nodes you want to use, we supplied the node information by using the tag's match attribute, like this:

```
<xsl:template match="dataroot">
```

This tells the XSLT processor to extract the XML document's root node. The root node provides a base node upon which we will build our web page. Notice that in the root template we included the <html> and <body> tags to create the structure of the final document and used HTML tags such as <h2>, <font>, and <p> to add the required formatting to our web page. In the root template we are also telling the XSLT processor that it should apply the template rules found in the Customers template (defined further down):

```
<xsl:apply-templates select="Customers"/>
```

Notice that the above instruction is placed within the <table> and </table> tags because we want to lay out the customer information using the table structure. When the XSLT processor encounters the <xsl:apply-templates> instruction, it will proceed to the following line:

```
<xsl:template match="Customers">
```

This line marks the beginning of the Customers template rule. Within it there are HTML tags as well other XSLT processing instructions. For example, to output the CustomerID we use the <xsl:value-of> tag with the select attribute like this:

```
<xsl:value-of select="CustomerID"/>
```

Because the <xsl:value-of> tag does not have any content, you must end it with the forward slash (/). Notice that we placed the value of the CustomerID field in a table cell. Using the same approach we output the CompanyName:

```
<xsl:value-of select="CompanyName"/>
```

Next, we defined the column headings for the Orders table. For a special effect, we added to the output a 10-pixel-wide dummy column with a black background:

```
<td bgcolor="black" width="10px"></td>
```

We also told the XSLT processor to apply the Orders template:

```
<xsl:apply-templates select="Orders"/>
```

The Orders template rules indicate how to extract values for each of the defined column headings. This is done by using the <xsl:value-of> tag with the select attribute, like this:

```
<td><xsl:value-of select="OrderID"/></td>
<td><xsl:value-of select="substring(OrderDate, 1, 10)"/></td>
<td><xsl:value-of select="substring(ShippedDate, 1, 10)"/></td>
<td><xsl:value-of select="substring(RequiredDate, 1, 10)"/></td>
<td>$<xsl:value-of select="format-number(Freight,'####0.00')"/></td>
```

To obtain only the date portion from the OrderDate, ShippedDate, and RequiredDate columns we use the XPath substring function in the select attribute. This function has the same syntax as the VBA Mid function, allowing you to extract a specified number of characters from a string starting at a specific position. The format of the substring function is shown below:

```
substring(string, startpos, length)
```

startpos is the position of the first character to extract, and *length* represents the number of characters to be returned from *string*. Therefore, the expression

```
<xsl:value-of select="substring(OrderDate, 1, 10)"/>
```

tells the XSLT processor to retrieve only the first 10 characters from the value found in the OrderDate column.

Notice also that to correctly format the Freight column we used the format-number XPath expression like this:

```
<xsl:value-of select="format-number(Freight,'####0.00')"/>
```

This tells the XSLT processor to format the value found in the Freight column as a number using two decimal places. Notice that the dollar sign cannot be a part of the XPath expression. It is appended to the final output as shown below:

```
<td>$<xsl:value-of select="format-number(Freight,'####0.00')"/></td>
```

Notice that each of the defined template rules ends with the </xsl:template> ending tag and the stylesheet itself ends with the </xsl:stylesheet> tag.

This concludes our hands-on example of how you can make your own custom stylesheets. While this is a basic stylesheet to get you started, in real life you will probably want to create stylesheets that allow:

- Batch-processing nodes (<xsl:for-each> tag with the select attribute)
- Conditional processing of nodes (<xsl:if> tag with the test attribute)
- Decisions based on conditions (<xsl:choose> tag and <xsl:when> tag with the test attribute)
- Sorting nodes before processing (<xsl:sort> tag with the select attribute).

Note: For more information about XSL Transformations (XSLT), visit the following link: http://www.w3.org/TR/xslt#section-Applying-Template-Rules

Now that you have a custom stylesheet, what do you do with it? Hands-On 29-6 demonstrates how to export data from an Access table directly to an HTML file and apply a custom transform so that only certain columns are displayed in the browser.

Hands-On 29-6: Exporting Data and Applying a Custom XSL File

1. Open the **Customers** table in the Northwind database and choose **File | Export**.

2. In the Export Table 'Customers' To window perform the following:
   - Select the **Learn_XML** folder from the Save in drop-down list.
   - Enter **ListCustOrders** in the File name box.
   - Select **XML** from the Save as type drop-down list.
   - Click **Export All**.

3. In the Export XML dialog box, the first two check boxes should be selected. Click the **More Options** button.

4. In the Data to Export area, the Customers table is automatically selected. Click the check box next to the **Orders** table to include it in the export.

5. Click the **Transforms** button.

6. In the Export Transforms window that appears, click the **Add** button.

7. Access displays the Add New Transform window. Switch to the Learn_XML folder and select the **ListCustOrders.xsl** file that you created in the previous hands-on exercise. Click the **Add** button to add this file to the list of transforms. The transformation file appears in the list as shown in Figure 29-11.

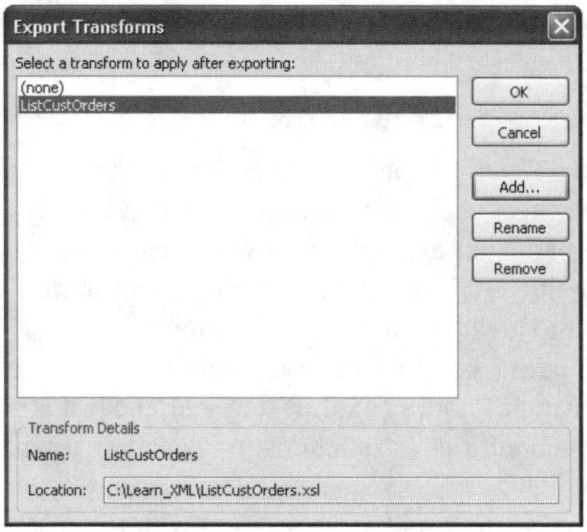

Figure 29-11: Use this window to indicate a transformation file (stylesheet) to be used after export.

8. In the Export Transforms window, click **OK**.

9. Back in the Export XML dialog box, change the file extension from xml to **html** as shown in Figure 29-12.

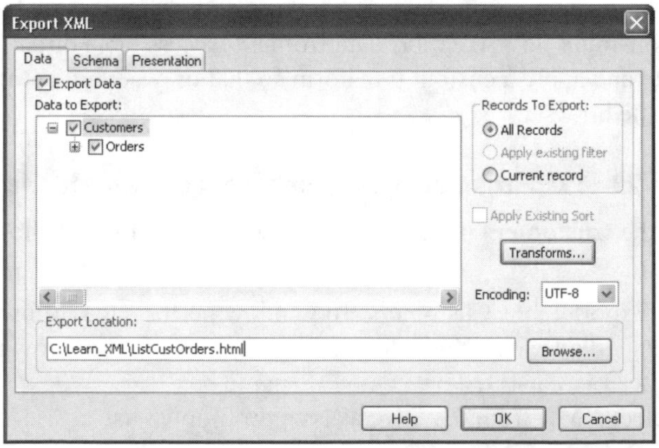

Figure 29-12: To export XML data directly to the HTML file, you must choose the transformation file using the Transforms button, and change the file extension from xml to html.

10. Click the **OK** button to begin the export.

> **Note:** If the selected transformation file is invalid, you will see an error message. Access will prompt you to save the data for troubleshooting and will bring up the Export XML dialog box. At this time you may want to open the transformation file in Notepad and make appropriate corrections. Once you save the corrected XSL file you should return to the Export XML dialog to try the export again. Before you click the OK button in the Export XML dialog box, ensure that the appropriate tables are selected.

11. Activate **Windows Explorer** and open the **ListCustOrders.html** file. The final result of applying the custom transformation file is shown in Figure 29-13.

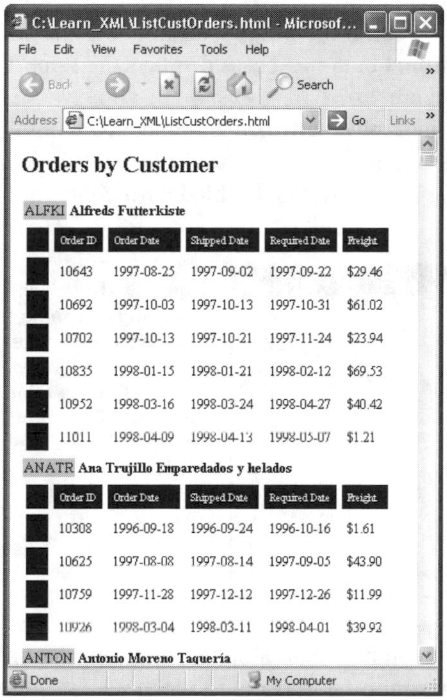

Figure 29-13: XML data can be formatted any way you like by applying a custom transform (see Hands-On 29-11 and 29-12).

12. Close the browser.

Importing XML Data

You can use the Access built-in Import command to import an XML data or XML schema document to a database. When you import structure or data from an XML file, Access assigns the Text data type to all the fields in a table. However, when you import structure from an XSD schema file, each field is assigned a data type that closely matches the data type specified in the schema. You can change the data types after importing data or a table structure as long as the fields' data allows such a change.

When you import a schema, Access creates a new empty table with the structure of the imported schema. Earlier in this chapter, when you exported the Shippers table to XML format, Access also created the schema of that table. Hands-On 29-7 shows how to import this schema document to a new Access database.

⊚ Hands-On 29-7: Importing a Schema File (XSD) to an Access Database

1. Create a new Access database named **Acc2003_Chap29.mdb**.

2. In the Database window, choose **File | Get External Data | Import**.

3. In the Import dialog box, select the **Shippers.xsd** file in the Learn_XML folder and click the **Import** button. Access displays the Import XML dialog box as shown in Figure 29-14.

   Notice that you cannot indicate which columns you would like to import. Access always imports the entire XSD file. The Options button in the Import XML dialog box is always disabled during the import of a schema file.

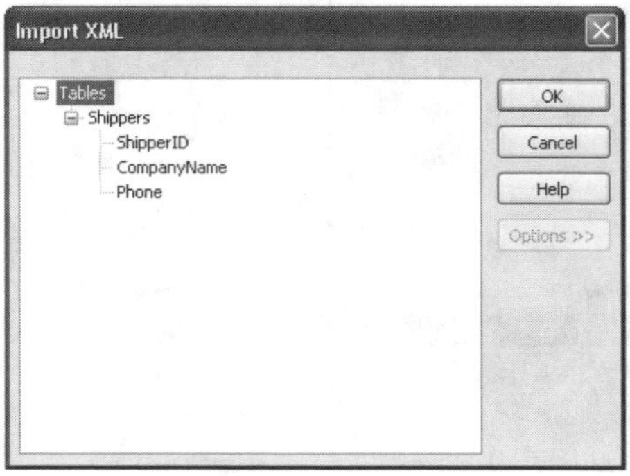

Figure 29-14: When importing a schema file to an Access database, the Import XML dialog box displays the table name and its columns as defined in the schema.

4. Click **OK** to perform the import. The Shippers table appears in the Database window. If you open this table you will see the three columns as shown in Figure 29-14. The first column is a primary key.

➔ **Note:** A schema file can also be imported to an Access database from the XML data file by choosing the Options button in the Import XML dialog box.

5. Close the Acc2003_Chap29.mdb database.

When importing an XML data file to an Access database, the Import XML dialog box's Options button allows you to specify whether you want to import structure only, structure and data, or append data to existing table (see Figure 29-15). When you append data to an existing table, Access compares the structure of the imported table with the table structures that are already in the database. If Access cannot find a table structure matching the imported table, the data is placed in a new table; otherwise, it is appended to the existing table.

   You can also click the Transform button in the Import XML dialog box to specify a transformation file that you want to apply when XML data is imported.

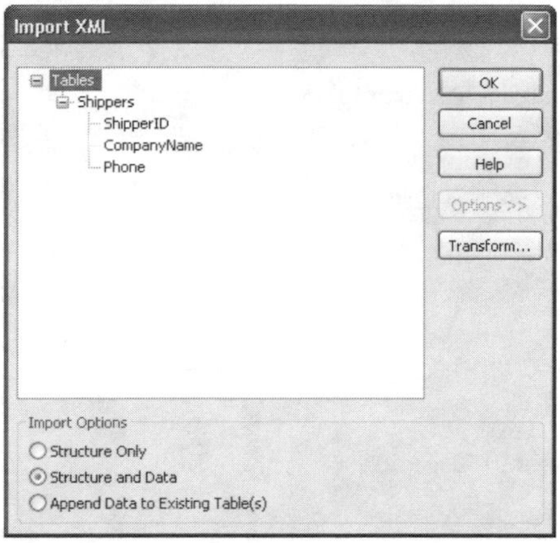

Figure 29-15: When importing an XML data file, you can use the Options button in the Import XML dialog to specify the import options. Use the Transform button to apply a transform to the data when it is imported.

It is important to point out that when XML data is imported to an Access database, it is not linked with the original XML file. This means that to refresh the data in the table, you need to repeat the import process.

The following project demonstrates how to import XML data to an Access database and modify the data before import using a transformation file. We will perform the tasks as outlined below:

1. Create a custom transformation file to be used after the XML data import

2. Export the Customers table and the related Orders table to an XML file

3. Import to an Access database only two columns from the Customers table and five columns from the Orders table.

⊚ Custom Project 29-1: Importing XML Data to an Access Database and Applying a Transform

Part 1: Create a Custom Transformation File to be Used After the XML Data Import

1. Open **Notepad** and enter the statements as shown below.

```
<?xml version="1.0" encoding="UTF-8"?>
<xsl:stylesheet version="1.0" xmlns:xsl="http://www.w3.org/1999/XSL/Transform">
<xsl:output method="html" version="4.0" indent="yes"/>

<xsl:template match="dataroot">
    <html>
        <body>
            <table>
                <xsl:apply-templates select="Customers"/>
            </table>
            <table>
                <xsl:apply-templates select="Customers/Orders"/>
            </table>
        </body>
    </html>
</xsl:template>
<xsl:template match="Customers">
```

```
        <Customer>
            <CustomerID>
                <xsl:value-of select="CustomerID"/>
            </CustomerID>
            <CompanyName>
                <xsl:value-of select="CompanyName"/>
            </CompanyName>
        </Customer>
    </xsl:template>

    <xsl:template match="Customers/Orders">
        <Order>
            <OrderID>
                <xsl:value-of select="OrderID"/>
            </OrderID>
            <OrderDate>
                <xsl:value-of select="substring(OrderDate, 1, 10)"/>
            </OrderDate>
            <ShippedDate>
                <xsl:value-of select="substring(ShippedDate, 1, 10)"/>
            </ShippedDate>
            <RequiredDate>
                <xsl:value-of select="substring(RequiredDate, 1, 10)"/>
            </RequiredDate>
            <Freight>
                <xsl:value-of select="format-number(Freight,'####0.00')"/>
            </Freight>
        </Order>
    </xsl:template>

</xsl:stylesheet>
```

2. Save the file as **CustomerOrders.xsl** in the Learn_XML folder. You must type the file extension to ensure that the file is not saved as text.

3. Close Notepad.

Since you've already created a similar stylesheet in Hands-On 29-5, the contents of the CustomerOrders.xsl file should be recognizable. All that's different here are the <Customer> and <Order> tags that specify the names of Access tables where we want to place our XML data. When importing data, tables are named according to the name of the XML element being imported. If the Access database already has a table with the specified name, a number is appended to the name.

Part 2: Export the Customers Table and the Related Orders Table to an XML File

1. In the Northwind Database window, highlight the **Customers** table and choose **File | Export**.

2. In the Export Table 'Customers' To window perform the following:
   ■ Select the **Learn_XML** folder in the Save in drop-down list.
   ■ Enter **CustomerOrders** in the File name box.

- Select **XML** from the Save as type drop-down box.
- Click **Export**.

3. In the Export XML dialog box, the first two check boxes should be selected. Click the **More Options** button.

4. In the Data to Export area of the Export XML dialog, select the check box next to the **Orders** table. Both Customers and Orders tables should be selected.

5. Click **OK** to perform the export of all the records in the selected tables.

Part 3: Import to an Access Database Only Two Columns from the Customers Table and Five Columns from the Orders Table

1. Open the **Acc2003_Chap29.mdb** database file that you created in Hands-On 29-7.

2. In the Database window, choose **File | Get External Data | Import**.

3. In the Import window, select the **CustomerOrders.xml** file in the Learn_XML folder and click the **Import** button.

    Access displays the Import XML window with the file's Customers and Orders tables listed. By expanding nodes in the tree structure you can see the columns in each table, but you cannot indicate which columns to import, as Access always imports the entire file by default. You can, however, tell Access to perform a custom XSLT transform to import only the columns needed.

4. In the Import XML window, click the **Options** button.

5. Click the **Transform** button.

6. In the Import Transforms window that appears, click the **Add** button to apply a transform before importing.

7. Access displays the Add New Transform window. Switch to the **Learn_XML** folder and select the **CustomerOrders.xsl** file that you created in Part 1 of this project. Click the **Add** button to add this file to the list of transforms.

8. In the Import Transforms window, click **OK**.

9. Back in the Import XML window make sure that the **Structure and Data** option button is selected under Import Options and click **OK**. Access imports the data and displays a message when the process is completed.

10. Click **OK** to clear the confirmation message.

11. In the Database window notice the appearance of two new tables: Customer and Order. Open both tables and check their contents.

    As you can see, Access has applied the custom stylesheet before importing the data and only the columns specified in the stylesheet were imported (Figure 29-16).

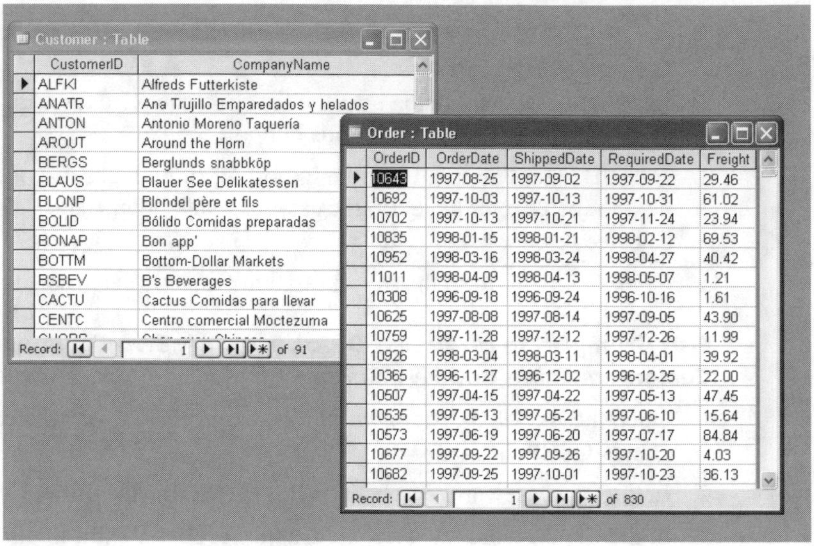

Customer : Table

CustomerID	CompanyName
ALFKI	Alfreds Futterkiste
ANATR	Ana Trujillo Emparedados y helados
ANTON	Antonio Moreno Taquería
AROUT	Around the Horn
BERGS	Berglunds snabbköp
BLAUS	Blauer See Delikatessen
BLONP	Blondel père et fils
BOLID	Bólido Comidas preparadas
BONAP	Bon app'
BOTTM	Bottom-Dollar Markets
BSBEV	B's Beverages
CACTU	Cactus Comidas para llevar
CENTC	Centro comercial Moctezuma

Record: 1 of 91

Order : Table

OrderID	OrderDate	ShippedDate	RequiredDate	Freight
10643	1997-08-25	1997-09-02	1997-09-22	29.46
10692	1997-10-03	1997-10-13	1997-10-31	61.02
10702	1997-10-13	1997-10-21	1997-11-24	23.94
10835	1998-01-15	1998-01-21	1998-02-12	69.53
10952	1998-03-16	1998-03-24	1998-04-27	40.42
11011	1998-04-09	1998-04-13	1998-05-07	1.21
10308	1996-09-18	1996-09-24	1996-10-16	1.61
10625	1997-08-08	1997-08-14	1997-09-05	43.90
10759	1997-11-28	1997-12-12	1997-12-26	11.99
10926	1998-03-04	1998-03-11	1998-04-01	39.92
10365	1996-11-27	1996-12-02	1996-12-25	22.00
10507	1997-04-15	1997-04-22	1997-05-13	47.45
10535	1997-05-13	1997-05-21	1997-06-10	15.64
10573	1997-06-19	1997-06-20	1997-07-17	84.84
10677	1997-09-22	1997-09-26	1997-10-20	4.03
10682	1997-09-25	1997-10-01	1997-10-23	36.13

Record: 1 of 830

Figure 29-16: Applying a custom transformation file before XML data import limits the data imported to an Access database.

12. Open the **Order** table in Design view. Notice that all the fields in this table have been assigned the Text data type. After importing data or table structure you can change the data type of fields.
13. Change the data type of the OrderDate, ShippedDate, and RequiredDate columns to **Date/Time** and the Freight column's data type to **Currency** to match the original Orders table.
14. Save the modified Order table.
15. Close the Acc2003_Chap29.mdb database file.

Exporting to and Importing from XML Programmatically

Now that you've mastered the use of Microsoft Office Access 2003 built-in commands for exporting and importing XML data, let's look at what tools are available for programmers who want to perform XML export and import operations via code. In the following sections of this chapter you will learn how to work with XML using:

- ExportXML and ImportXML methods from the Microsoft Office Access 11.0 Object Library
- TransformXML method

Exporting to XML Using the ExportXML Method

Use the Microsoft Office Access 11.0 Object Library ExportXML method of the Application object to export XML data, schemas (XSD), and presentation information (XSL) from a Microsoft Access database (.mdb), Microsoft SQL Server 2000 Desktop Engine (MSDE 2000), or Microsoft SQL Server 6.5 or later.

The ExportXML method takes a number of arguments that are shown in Table 29-1.

Table 29-1: Arguments of the ExportXML method (in order of appearance)

Argument Type	Data Type	Description
ObjectType (required)	AcExportXMLObjectType Use one of the following constants: Constant Value acExportDataAccessPage 6 acExportForm 2 acExportFunction 10 acExportQuery 1 acExportReport 3 acExportServerView 7 acExportStoredProcedure 9 acExportTable 0	Specifies the type of Access object to export.
DataSource (required)	String	Indicates the name of the Access object specified in the ObjectType argument.
DataTarget (optional)	String	Specifies the path and filename for the exported data. Omit this argument only if you don't want the data to be exported.
SchemaTarget (optional)	String	Specifies the path and filename for the exported schema information. Omit this argument only if you don't want the schema to be exported to a separate file.
PresentationTarget (optional)	String	Specifies the path and filename for the exported presentation information. Omit this argument only if you don't want the presentation information to be exported.
ImageTarget (optional)	String	Specifies the path for the exported images. Omit this argument if you don't want to export images.
Encoding (optional)	AcExportXMLEncoding Use one of the following constants: Constant Value acUTF16 1 acUTF8 0 The default is acUTF8.	Specifies the text encoding for the exported data.

Argument Type	Data Type	Description
OtherFlags (optional)	AcExportXMLOtherFlags Use one or more of the following constants: | Constant	Value
acEmbedSchema	1
acExcludePrimary-KeyAndIndexes	2
acLiveReportSource	8
acPersistReportML	16
acRunFromServer	4		Specifies behaviors associated with exporting to XML. Values can be added to specify a combination of behaviors. Here is the meaning of the constants: (1) Write schema information into a separate document specified by the DataTarget argument. This value takes precedence over the SchemaTarget argument. (2) Does not export primary key and index schema properties. (8) Used only when exporting reports bound to SQL Server 2000. Will create a live link to a Microsoft SQL Server database. (16) Persists the exported object's ReportML file. (4) Used only when exporting reports. Creates an Active Server Pages (ASP) or HTML wrapper. The default is HTML.
WhereCondition (optional)	String	Specifies subset of records to export.
AdditionalData (optional)	AdditionalData AdditionalData is an Access object that represents the collection of tables and queries that will be included with the parent table that is exported by the ExportXML method (see Hands-On 29-8).	Specifies additional tables to export. This argument is ignored if the OtherFlags argument is set to acLiveReportSource (8).

In its simplest form, the ExportXML method looks like this:

```
Application.ExportXML ObjectType:=acExportTable, _
        DataSource:="Customers", _
        DataTarget:= "C:\Learn_XML\Northwind_Customers.xml"
```

The above statement, when typed in the Visual Basic Editor's Immediate window or in a Visual Basic module (inside a VBA procedure stub), will render the Customers table in the XML format in the Northwind_Customers.xml file.

Using Table 29-1 you can easily write the command to export the XML Products table with its schema and presentation information placed in separate files:

```
Application.ExportXML ObjectType:=acExportTable, _
        DataSource:="Products", _
        DataTarget:= "C:\Learn_XML\Northwind_Products.xml", _
        SchemaTarget:= "C:\Learn_XML\Northwind_ProdSchema.xsd", _
        PresentationTarget:= "C:\Learn_XML\Northwind_ProdReport.xsl"
```

To export a specific customer's data to an XML data file, use the following statement:

```
Application.ExportXML ObjectType:=acExportTable, _
            DataSource:="Customers", _
            DataTarget:="C:\Learn_XML\OneCustomer.xml", _
            WhereCondition:="CustomerID = 'GROSR'"
```

➡ **Note:** You can try the above statements in the Immediate window. Recall that you must not type the underscore character (type the entire statement on one line with arguments separated by commas).

Hands-On 29-8 demonstrates how to export to XML three tables: Customers, Orders, and Order Details.

◎ Hands-On 29-8: Exporting Multiple Tables to an XML Data File

1. Make a copy of the Microsoft Access Northwind sample database and open it in Access.

2. In the Database window, choose **Tools | Macro | Visual Basic Editor**.

3. In the Visual Basic Editor window, choose **Insert | Module** to add a standard module to the current VBA project.

4. In the module's Code window, enter the Export_CustomerOrderDetails procedure as shown below.

```
Sub Export_CustomerOderDetails()
    Dim objOtherTbls As AdditionalData

    On Error GoTo ErrorHandle
    Set objOtherTbls = Application.CreateAdditionalData

    ' include the Orders and OrderDetails tables in export
    objOtherTbls.Add "Orders"
    objOtherTbls.Add "Order Details"

    ' export Customers, Orders, and Order Details table into one XML data file
    Application.ExportXML ObjectType:=acExportTable, _
            DataSource:="Customers", _
            DataTarget:="C:\Learn_XML\CustomerOrdersDetails.xml", _
            AdditionalData:=objOtherTbls

    MsgBox "Export operation completed successfully."

Exit_Here:
        Exit Sub
ErrorHandle:
        MsgBox Err.Number & ": " & Err.Description
        Resume Exit_Here
End Sub
```

Using the AdditionalData object, you can export any set of Access tables to an XML data file. To use this object, perform the following:

■ Declare an object variable as AdditionalData:

```
Dim objOtherTbls As AdditionalData
```

■ Create the AdditionalData object using the CreateAdditionalData method of the Application object and set the object variable to the newly created object:

```
Set objOtherTbls = Application.CreateAdditionalData
```

■ Use the AdditionalData object's Add method to add table names to the object:

```
objOtherTbls.Add "Orders"
objOtherTbls.Add "Order Details"
```

■ Pass the AdditionalData object to the ExportXML method:

```
Application.ExportXML ObjectType:=acExportTable, _
         DataSource:="Customers", _
         DataTarget:="C:\Learn_XML\CustomerOrdersDetails.xml", _
         AdditionalData:=objOtherTbls
```

5. Place the insertion point anywhere within the Export_CustomerOrder-Details procedure code and choose **Run | Run Sub/UserForm**. Access executes the procedure code and displays a message.

6. Click **OK** to clear the informational message.

7. Switch to Windows Explorer, locate the Learn_XML folder, and open the **CustomerOrdersDetails.xml** file. Notice that all the requested data was placed into one file.

8. Close the browser.

Now that you know how to export Access tables to XML, let's see how Access handles other objects. Custom Project 29-2 demonstrates how to export the Invoice report from the Northwind database to an XML file together with the presentation information and images.

◎ Custom Project 29-2: Exporting an Access Report to an XML Data File with ASP

This custom project uses the copy of the Northwind sample database you created in Hands-On 29-8.

Part 1: Creating a VBA Procedure to Export Invoice Data

1. In the Database window, choose **Tools | Macro | Visual Basic Editor**.

2. In the Visual Basic Editor window, choose **Insert | Module** to add a standard module to the current VBA project.

3. In the module's Code window, enter the Export_InvoiceReport procedure as shown below.

```
Sub Export_InvoiceReport()
    Application.ExportXML ObjectType:=acExportReport, _
            DataSource:="Invoice", _
            DataTarget:="C:\Learn_XML\Invoice.xml", _
            PresentationTarget:="C:\Learn_XML\Invoice.xsl", _
            ImageTarget:="C:\Learn_XML", _
            WhereCondition:="OrderID=11075"

    MsgBox "Export operation completed successfully."
End Sub
```

Take a look at the last two arguments of the ExportXML method used in the procedure above. ImageTarget specifies that images displayed on the Invoice report are to be placed in the Learn_XML folder. The WhereCondition argument specifies that we want only the data for Order 11075.

Part 2: Executing the VBA Code to Export Data

1. Place the insertion point anywhere within the Export_InvoiceReport procedure code and choose **Run | Run Sub/UserForm**. Access executes the procedure code and displays a message.

2. Click **OK** to clear the informational message.

3. Switch to Windows Explorer and locate the Learn_XML folder.

4. Notice that Access has created a number of files: Invoice.xsl (stylesheet), Invoice.xml (XML document), Invoice.htm (HTML document), and two image files (PictureLogo.bmp and NameLogo.bmp).

Part 3: Viewing the Invoice Page in the Browser

1. Double-click the **Invoice.htm** file in the Learn_XML folder.

    If you are using Internet Explorer, the file opens up as shown in Figure 29-17. When you compare this output with the original Access invoice report, you will notice that the invoice displayed in the browser is an exact image of the report displayed in the Access user interface.

2. Close the browser.

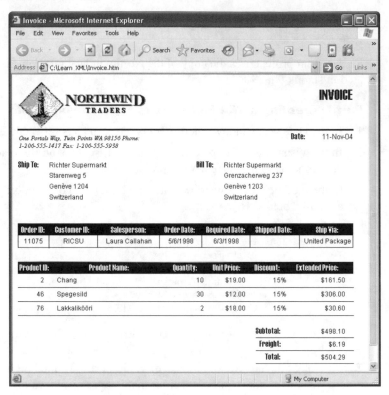

Figure 29-17: Viewing the exported invoice report in Internet Explorer.

Part 4: Examining the Content of the Invoice.htm File

1. In Windows Explorer, right-click the **Invoice** file and choose **Open With |
   Notepad**. The content of the Invoice file is shown below:

```
<HTML xmlns:signature="urn:schemas-microsoft-com:office:access">
<HEAD>
<META HTTP-EQUIV="Content-Type" CONTENT="text/html;charset=UTF-8"/>
</HEAD>
<BODY ONLOAD="ApplyTransform()">
</BODY>
<SCRIPT LANGUAGE="VBScript">
    Option Explicit

    Function ApplyTransform()
        Dim objData, objStyle

        Set objData = CreateDOM
        LoadDOM objData, "Invoice.xml"

        Set objStyle = CreateDOM
        LoadDOM objStyle, "Invoice.xsl"

        Document.Open "text/html","replace"
```

Taking Your VBA Programming Skills to the Web

```
            Document.Write objData.TransformNode(objStyle)
        End Function

        Function CreateDOM()
            On Error Resume Next
            Dim tmpDOM

            Set tmpDOM = Nothing
            Set tmpDOM = CreateObject("MSXML2.DOMDocument.5.0")
            If tmpDOM Is Nothing Then
                Set tmpDOM = CreateObject("MSXML2.DOMDocument.4.0")
            End If
            If tmpDOM Is Nothing Then
                Set tmpDOM = CreateObject("MSXML.DOMDocument")
            End If

            Set CreateDOM = tmpDOM
        End Function

        Function LoadDOM(objDOM, strXMLFile)
            objDOM.Async = False
            objDOM.Load strXMLFile
            If (objDOM.ParseError.ErrorCode <> 0) Then
                MsgBox objDOM.ParseError.Reason
            End If
        End Function

    </SCRIPT>
    </HTML>
```

Notice that when the htm page loads it executes the VBScript ApplyTransform function:

```
<BODY ONLOAD="ApplyTransform()">
```

The VBScript code uses a software component called the XML Document Object Model (DOM). The DOM offers methods and properties for working with XML programmatically, allowing you to output and transform the XML data. The XML DOM is automatically installed by Internet Explorer, as well as by Windows 2000/XP and Internet Information Services (IIS) 5.0.

The DOMDocument object is the top level of the XML DOM hierarchy and represents a tree structure composed of nodes. You can navigate through this tree structure and manipulate the data contained in the nodes by using various methods and properties. Because every XML object is created and accessed from the DOMDocument, you must first create the DOMDocument object in order to work with an XML document.

The ApplyTransform function above begins by setting an object variable (objData) to an instance of the DOMDocument that's returned by a custom CreateDOM function:

```
Set objData = CreateDOM
```

If you take a look at the CreateDOM function that appears at the bottom of the VBScript code, you will notice that a reference to the DOMDocument is set via the CreateObject method of the Server object. Because different versions of the MSXML parser may be installed on a client machine (DOMDocument5, DOMDocument4, DOMDocument, etc.), the function attempts to instantiate the DOMDocument object using the most recent version. If such a version is not found, it looks for older versions of the MSXML parser that may exist. It is extremely important that only one version of the DOMDocument is used, since mixing DOMDocument objects from different versions of the MSXML parser can cause ugly errors.

Once the DOMDocument object has been instantiated, the LoadDOM function listed at the bottom of the page is called. This function expects two parameters: objectDOM, which is the objData variable referencing the DOMDocument, and strXMLFile, which is the name of the file to load into the DOMDocument object. To ensure that Internet Explorer waits until all the data is loaded before rendering the rest of the page, the Async property of the DOMDocument is set to False:

```
objDOM.Async = false
objDOM.Load strXMLFile
```

The Load method is used to load the supplied file into the objData object variable. This method returns True if it successfully loaded the data and False otherwise. If there is a problem with loading, a description of the error is returned in a message box.

The Document object of XML DOM exposes a parseError object that allows you to check whether there was an error when loading the XML file or stylesheet. The parseError object has the following properties:

Table 29-2: parseError object properties

Property	Description
errorCode	Error number of the error that occurred.
filepos	Character position within the file where the error occurred.
line	Line number where the error occurred.
linepos	Character position within the line where the error occurred.
reason	Text description of the error.
srcText	The source (text) of the line where the error occurred.
url	URL or path of the file that was loaded.

After loading the Invoice.xml data file into the DOM software component, the ApplyTransform function repeats the same process for the Invoice.xsl file. After both files are successfully loaded, the transform is applied to the data using the TransformNode method:

```
Document.Write objData.TransformNode(objStyle)
```

The TransformNode method performs the transformation by applying the XSLT stylesheet to the XML data file. The result is the HTML document displayed in the browser as shown in Figure 29-17 earlier in this chapter.

2. Close the Invoice.htm file and exit Notepad.

Transforming XML Data with the TransformXML Method

So far you've learned how to use stylesheets to transform XML data files to HTML format to create a web page. While rendering XML files into HTML for display in a web browser is the most popular use of stylesheets, XML data files can also be transformed into other XML files using the XSLT transforms.

In this section we will learn how to use the TransformXML method to apply an Extensible Stylesheet (XSL) to an XML data file and write the resulting XML to another XML data file.

The TransformXML method takes a number of arguments that are presented in Table 29-3. In its simplest form, the TransformXML method looks like this:

```
Application.TransformXML DataSource:="C:\Learn_XML\InternalContacts.xml",
          TransformSource:="C:\Learn_XML\Extensions.xsl", _
          OutputTarget:="C:\Learn_XML\EmpExtensions.xml"
```

The above statement can be used inside a VBA procedure stub to programmatically apply the specified stylesheet.

Table 29-3: Arguments of the TransformXML method (in order of appearance)

Argument Type	Data Type	Description
DataSource (required)	String	Specifies the full path of the XML data file that will be transformed.
TransformSource (required)	String	Specifies the full path of the XSL stylesheet to apply to the XML data file specified in the DataSource argument.
OutputTarget (required)	String	Specifies the full path of the resulting XML data file after applying the XSL stylesheet.
WellFormedXMLOutput (optional)	Boolean	Set this argument to True to create a well-formed XML document. Set this argument to False to encode the resulting XML file in UTF-16 format. The default is False.
ScriptOption (optional)	AcTransformXMLScriptOption Use one of the following constants: **Constant** **Value** acDisableScript 2 acEnableScript 0 acPromptScript 1 acPromptScript is the default.	Use this argument to specify the action that should be taken if the XSL file contains scripting code.

Custom Project 29-3 demonstrates how to transform an XML data file into another XML file. We will start by creating a custom stylesheet named Extensions.xsl that will transform the InternalContacts.xml file (generated from the

Northwind database Employees table) into an XML file named
EmpExtensions.xml. Next, we will write a VBA procedure that exports the
XML source file and performs the transformation. Finally, we will import the
resulting XML data file into Access.

◎ Custom Project 29-3: Applying a Stylesheet to an XML Data File with the TransformXML Method

This custom project uses the copy of the Northwind sample database you created in Hands-On 29-8.

Part 1: Creating a Custom Stylesheet for Transforming an XML Source File into Another XML Data File

1. Open **Notepad** and enter the statements as shown below.

```
<?xml version="1.0"?>
<xsl:stylesheet version="1.0" xmlns:xsl="http://www.w3.org/1999/XSL/Transform">
<xsl:output method="xml" indent="yes"/>
<xsl:template match="/">
<dataroot>
<xsl:for-each select="//Employees">
<Extensions>
    <LastName>
        <xsl:value-of select="LastName" />
    </LastName>
    <FirstName>
        <xsl:value-of select="FirstName" />
    </FirstName>
    <Extension>
        <xsl:value-of select="Extension" />
    </Extension>
</Extensions>
</xsl:for-each>
</dataroot>
</xsl:template>
</xsl:stylesheet>
```

2. Save the file as **Extensions.xsl** in the Learn_XML folder. You must type
   the .xsl file extension to ensure that the file is not saved as text.

3. Close Notepad.

Take a look at the stylesheet shown above and notice that we have asked the
XSL processor to produce the output in XML format:

```
<xsl:output method="xml" indent="yes"/>
```

Next, we used the following instruction:

```
<xsl:template match="/">
```

This instruction defines a template for the entire document. The special pattern
"/" in the match attribute tells the XSL processor that this is a template for the
document root.

Because each XML document must have a root node, we proceeded to define <dataroot> as the document root. You can use any name you want for this purpose.

Next, we told the XSL processor to get all the Employees nodes from the source XML data file:

```
<xsl:for-each select="//Employees">
```

The first forward slash in the above instruction represents the XML document root. This is the same as:

```
<xsl:for-each select="dataroot/Employees">
```

Next, we proceed to extract data from the required nodes. We are only interested in three columns from the source XML data file: FirstName, LastName, and Extension. We create the necessary elements using the <xsl:value-of> tag with the select attribute specifying the element name:

```
<LastName>
    <xsl:value-of select="LastName" />
</LastName>
<FirstName>
    <xsl:value-of select="FirstName" />
</FirstName>
<Extension>
    <xsl:value-of select="Extension" />
</Extension>
```

We tell the XSL processor to place the defined elements under the <Extensions> node. When importing the resulting XML file to Access, Access will create an Extensions table with three columns: LastName, FirstName, and Extension. You can use any name you want when specifying the container node for your elements.

To finish off the stylesheet, we must write the necessary closing tags:

```
    </xsl:for-each>
    </dataroot>
  </xsl:template>
</xsl:stylesheet>
```

Now that you've got the stylesheet for our transformation, you can write a VBA procedure to export the source data and perform the transformation.

Part 2: Writing a VBA Procedure to Export and Transform Data

1. Ensure that the copy of the Northwind sample database you created in Hands-On 29-8 is open.

2. In the Database window, choose **Tools | Macro | Visual Basic Editor**.

3. In the Visual Basic Editor window, choose **Insert | Module** to add a standard module to the current VBA project.

4. In the module's Code window, enter the Transform_Employees procedure as shown below.

```
Sub Transform_Employees()
    ' use the ExportXML method to create a source XML data file

    Application.ExportXML ObjectType:=acExportTable, _
             DataSource:="Employees", _
             DataTarget:="C:\Learn_XML\InternalContacts.xml"

MsgBox "The export operation completed successfully."

    ' use the TransformXML method to apply the stylesheet that transforms
    ' the source XML data file into another XML data file
    Application.TransformXML DataSource:="C:\Learn_XML\InternalContacts.xml", _
             TransformSource:="C:\Learn_XML\Extensions.xsl", _
             OutputTarget:="C:\Learn_XML\EmpExtensions.xml", _
             WellFormedXMLOutput:=False

    MsgBox "The transform operation completed successfully."
End Sub
```

5. Run the **Transform_Employees** procedure.

The first part of the above procedure exports the Employees table from the Northwind database to an XML file named InternalContacts.xml. The second part of this procedure applies the Extensions.xsl stylesheet prepared in Part 1 of this custom project to the InternalContacts.xml data file. The resulting XML document after the transformation is named EmpExtensions.xml. A portion of this file is shown in Figure 29-18.

Figure 29-18: Partial contents of the EmpExtensions.xml file.

After transforming our source XML data file into another XML document, you can bring it into Access with the File | Get External Data | Import command.

Part 3: Importing the Transformed XML Data File to Access

1. In the Database window, choose **File | Get External Data | Import**.

2. In the Import dialog box select the **EmpExtensions.xml** file in the Learn_XML folder and click the **Import** button. Access displays the Import XML dialog box shown in Figure 29-19.

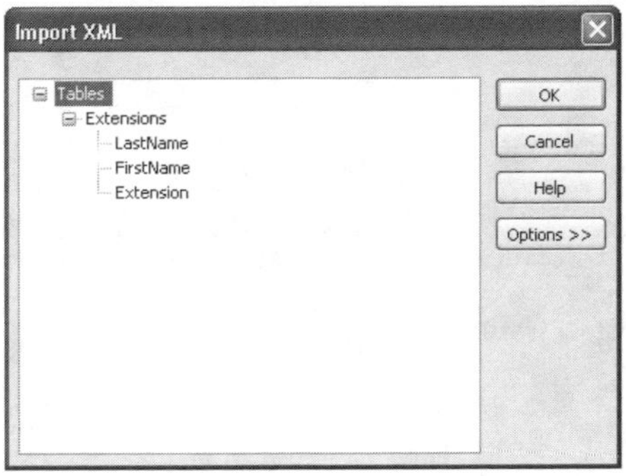

Figure 29-19: When you import the EmpExtensions.xml file, Access creates a new table named Extensions.

3. In the Import XML dialog box, click **OK** to perform the import.

4. Click **OK** to clear the confirmation message.

5. In the Database window, notice the appearance of the Extensions table. Open the **Extensions** table to view the following contents:

Extensions		
LastName	**FirstName**	**Extension**
Davolio	Nancy	5467
Fuller	Andrew	3457
Leverling	Janet	3355
Peacock	Margaret	5176
Buchanan	Steven	3453
Suyama	Michael	428
King	Robert	465
Callahan	Laura	2344
Dodsworth	Anne	452

6. Close the Extensions table.

A nice thing about XSLT transformations is that you can apply different stylesheets to the same XML data file to create and view the resulting document in different formats.

For example, let's assume that in the Extensions table you'd like to combine the LastName and FirstName columns into one column and sort the data by last name. You could create and apply the following Extensions_SortByEmp.xsl stylesheet to the InternalContacts.xml file to get the desired XML ouput:

```
<?xml version="1.0"?>
<xsl:stylesheet version="1.0" xmlns:xsl="http://www.w3.org/1999/XSL/Transform">
<xsl:output method="xml" indent="yes"/>
 <xsl:template match="/">
  <dataroot>
    <xsl:apply-templates select="dataroot/Employees">
       <xsl:sort select="LastName" order="ascending" />
    </xsl:apply-templates>
  </dataroot>
 </xsl:template>

 <xsl:template match="//Employees">
  <Extensions>
   <FullName>
      <xsl:value-of select="LastName" />
      <xsl:text> </xsl:text>
      <xsl:value-of select="FirstName" />
   </FullName>
   <Extension>
      <xsl:value-of select="Extension" />
   </Extension>
  </Extensions>
 </xsl:template>

</xsl:stylesheet>
```

The above stylesheet uses the <xsl:apply-templates> tag to tell the XSL processor to select the child elements of the dataroot/Employees node, and for
each child element, find in the stylesheet the matching template rule and process it:

```
<xsl:apply-templates select="dataroot/Employees">
     <xsl:sort select="LastName" order="ascending" />
</xsl:apply-templates>
```

The <xsl:sort> tag specifies how the resulting XML document should be
sorted. The select attribute of this tag is set to "LastName", indicating that the
file should be sorted by the LastName element. The order attribute defines the
sort order as ascending.

Next, in this stylesheet you can see the template rule that begins with the
<xsl:template> tag. Its match attribute specifies which nodes in the document
tree the template rule should process:

```
<xsl:template match="//Employees">
```

The "//Employees" expression in the match attribute is equivalent to
"dataroot/Employees".

Next, you need to define the document node in the output file as Extensions,
and proceed to define its child elements as FullName and Extension:

```
<Extensions>
  <FullName>
     <xsl:value-of select="LastName" />
     <xsl:text>, </xsl:text>
     <xsl:value-of select="FirstName" />
```

```
</FullName>
<Extension>
  <xsl:value-of select="Extension" />
</Extension>
</Extensions>
```

Because the FullName element should include the last name of the employee followed by a space and the first name, you can obtain the values of these fields with the <xsl:value-of> tag and use the <xsl:text> </xsl:text> tag pair to output a comma followed by a space between the last name and first name. Since there is nothing special about the Extension element, you can simply use the <xsl:value-of> tag to obtain this element's value.

Finally, complete the template and the stylesheet with the required closing tags:

```
  </Extensions>
 </xsl:template>

</xsl:stylesheet>
```

To apply the above stylesheet to the source XML file, you could write the following VBA procedure:

```
Sub Transform_ContactsSort()
    ' use the ExportXML method to create a source XML data file
    Application.ExportXML ObjectType:=acExportTable, _
            DataSource:="Employees", _
            DataTarget:="C:\Learn_XML\InternalContacts.xml"

    MsgBox "The export operation completed successfully."

    ' use the TransformXML method to apply the stylesheet that transforms
    ' the source XML data file into another XML data file

    Application.TransformXML DataSource:="C:\Learn_XML\InternalContacts.xml", _
            TransformSource:="C:\Learn_XML\Extensions_SortByEmp.xsl", _
            OutputTarget:="C:\Learn_XML\EmpExtensions.xml", _
            WellFormedXMLOutput:=False

    MsgBox "The transform operation completed successfully."
End Sub
```

After importing the EmpExtensions.xml file to Access, you should see the Extensions1 table in the Database window. When opened, this table displays a sorted list of employees with their extensions:

Extensions1	
FullName	Extension
Buchanan, Steven	3453
Callahan, Laura	2344
Davolio, Nancy	5467
Dodsworth, Anne	452
Fuller, Andrew	3457
King, Robert	465

Extensions1	
FullName	Extension
Leverling, Janet	3355
Peacock, Margaret	5176
Suyama, Michael	428

Importing to XML Using the ImportXML Method

Use the ImportXML method to programmatically import an XML data file and/or schema file. The ImportXML method takes two arguments, as shown in Table 29-4.

Table 29-4: Arguments of the ImportXML method (in order of appearance)

Argument Type	Data Type	Description
DataSource (required)	String	Specifies the full path of the XML file to import.
ImportOptions (optional)	aclmportXMLOption Use one of the following constants: Constant Value acAppendData 2 acStructureAndData 1 acStructureOnly 0	Specifies whether to import structure only (0), import structure and data (1) (default), or append data (2).

The following procedure will import the structure of the Extensions table from the EmpExtensions.xml file:

```
Sub Import_XMLFile()
    Application.ImportXML DataSource:="c:\Learn_XML\EmpExtensions.xml", _
            ImportOptions:=acStructureOnly

    MsgBox "The import operation completed successfully."

End Sub
```

Manipulating XML Documents Programmatically

You can create, access, and manipulate XML documents programmatically using the XML Document Object Model (DOM). The DOM has objects, properties, and methods for interacting with XML documents.

To use the XML DOM from your VBA procedures, take a few minutes now to set up a reference to the MSXML Object Library using the following steps:

1. Switch to the Visual Basic Editor window and choose **Tools | References**.

2. In the References window, select **Microsoft XML, v5.0** (see Figure 29-20) and click **OK**.

If you don't have version 5.0 installed, select the lower version of this object type library or upgrade your browser to the higher version so that the most recent library is available.

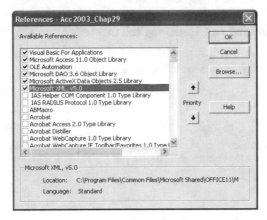

Figure 29-20: To work with XML documents programmatically, you need to establish a reference to the Microsoft XML object type library.

3. Now that you have the reference set, open the Object Browser and examine XML DOM's objects, methods, and properties (see Figure 29-21).

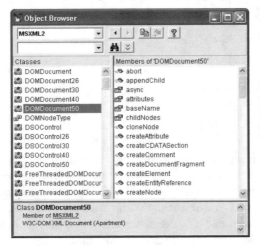

Figure 29-21: To view objects, properties, and methods exposed by the XML DOM (Document Object Model), open the Object Browser after setting up a reference to the Microsoft XML object type library (see Figure 29-20).

As mentioned earlier in this chapter (see Part 4 of Custom Project 29-2), the DOMDocument object is the top level of the XML DOM object hierarchy. This object represents a tree structure composed of nodes. You can navigate through this tree structure and manipulate the data contained in the nodes by using various methods and properties. The hands-on exercises in the following sections demonstrate how to read and manipulate XML documents by using VBA procedures.

Loading and Retrieving the Contents of an XML File

Hands-On 29-9 shows how to open an XML data file and retrieve both the raw data as well as the actual text stored in nodes.

⊙ Hands-On 29-9: Loading and Retrieving the Contents of an XML File

1. In the Visual Basic Editor screen, choose **Insert | Module** to add a new standard module to the current VBA project.

2. In the module's Code window, enter the ReadXMLDoc procedure shown below.

 Note: For this procedure to work correctly, you must set up the reference to the Microsoft XML object type library as instructed at the beginning of this section.

```
Sub ReadXMLDoc()
    Dim xmldoc As MSXML2.DOMDocument50
    Set xmldoc = New MSXML2.DOMDocument50

    xmldoc.async = False
    If xmldoc.Load("C:\Learn_XML\Shippers.xml") Then
        Debug.Print xmldoc.XML
        ' Debug.Print xmldoc.Text
    End If
End Sub
```

To work with an XML document, we begin by creating an instance of the DOMDocument object as follows:

```
Dim xmldoc As MSXML2.DOMDocument50
Set xmldoc = New MSXML2.DOMDocument50
```

The MSXML uses an asynchronous loading mechanism by default for working with documents. Asynchronous loading allows you to perform other tasks during long database operations, such as providing feedback to the user as MSXML parses the XML file or giving the user the chance to cancel the operation. Before calling the Load method, however, it's a good idea to set the Asynch property of the DOMDocument object to False to ensure that the XML file is fully loaded before other statements are executed. The Load method returns True if it successfully loaded the data and False otherwise. Having loaded the XML data into a DOMDocument object, you can use the XML property to retrieve the raw data or use the Text property to obtain the text stored in document nodes.

3. Position the insertion point anywhere within the code of the ReadXMLDoc procedure and choose **Run | Run Sub/UserForm**. The procedure executes and writes the contents of the XML file into the Immediate window as shown in Figure 29-22.

Taking Your VBA Programming Skills to the Web

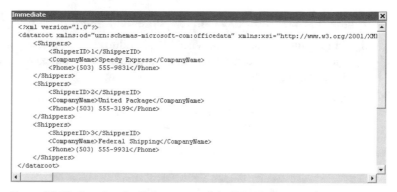

Figure 29-22: By using the XML property of the DOMDocument object you can retrieve the raw data from an XML file.

4. In the code of the ReadXMLDoc procedure, comment the first Debug.Print statement and uncomment the second statement that reads **Debug.Print xmldoc.Text**.

5. Run the ReadXMLDoc procedure again. This time the Immediate window shows the entry as one long line of text:

```
1 Speedy Express (503) 555-9831 2 United Package (503) 555-3199 3 Federal
        Shipping (503) 555-9931
```

Working with XML Document Nodes

As you already know, the XML DOM represents a tree-based hierarchy of nodes. An XML document can contain nodes of different types. For example, an XML document can include a document node that provides access to the entire XML document or one or more element nodes representing individual elements. Some nodes represent comments and processing instructions in the XML document, and others hold the text content of a tag. To determine the type of node, use the NodeType property of the IXMLDOMNode object. Node types are identified either by a text string or a constant.

For example, the node representing an element can be referred to as NODE_ELEMENT or 1, while the node representing the comment is named NODE_COMMENT or 8. See the MSXML2 Library in the Object Browser for the names of other node types.

In addition to node types, nodes can have parent, child, and sibling nodes. The hasChildNodes method lets you determine if a DOMDocument object has child nodes. There's also a childNodes property, which simplifies retrieving a collection of child nodes. Before you start looping through the collection of child nodes, it's a good idea to use the length property of the IXMLDOMNode object to determine how many elements the collection contains.

The following hands-on exercise uses the Shippers.xml file to demonstrate how to work with XML document nodes.

◎ Hands-On 29-10: Working with XML Document Nodes

1. In the same module of the Visual Basic Editor screen where you entered the ReadXMLDoc procedure in the previous hands-on exercise, enter the LearnAboutNodes procedure as shown below.

```
Sub LearnAboutNodes()
    Dim xmldoc As MSXML2.DOMDocument50
    Dim xmlNode As MSXML2.IXMLDOMNode

    Set xmldoc = New MSXML2.DOMDocument50
    xmldoc.async = False

    xmldoc.Load ("C:\Learn_XML\Shippers.xml")
    If xmldoc.hasChildNodes Then
        Debug.Print "Number of child Nodes: " & xmldoc.childNodes.length
        For Each xmlNode In xmldoc.childNodes
            Debug.Print "Node name:" & xmlNode.nodeName
            Debug.Print vbTab & "Type:" & xmlNode.nodeTypeString _
                                    & "(" & xmlNode.nodeType & ")"
            Debug.Print vbTab & "Text: " & xmlNode.Text
        Next xmlNode
    End If
    Set xmlDoc = Nothing
End Sub
```

Notice that the above procedure uses the hasChildNodes property of the DOMDocument object to check whether there are any child nodes in the loaded XML file. If child nodes are found, the length property of the childNodes collection returns the total number of child nodes found. Next, the procedure loops through the childNodes collection and retrieves the node name using the nodeName property of the IXMLDOMNode object. The nodeTypeString property returns the string version of the node type (for example, processing instruction, element, text, etc.) and the nodeType property is used to return the enumeration value. Finally, the Text property of the IXMLDOMNode object retrieves the node text.

2. Position the insertion point anywhere within the code of the LearnAboutNodes procedure and choose **Run | Run Sub/UserForm**. The result of running the LearnAboutNodes procedure is shown below:

```
Number of child Nodes: 2
Node name:xml
    Type:processinginstruction(7)
    Text: version="1.0" encoding="UTF-8"
Node name:dataroot
    Type:element(1)
    Text: 1 Speedy Express (503) 555-9831 2 United Package (503) 555-3199 3
        Federal Shipping (503) 555-9931
```

Retrieving Information from Element Nodes

Let's assume that you want to read the information from only the text element nodes. Use the getElementsByTagName method of the DOMDocument object to retrieve an IXMLDOMNodeList object containing all the element nodes. This method takes one argument specifying the tag name for which to search. To search for all the element nodes, use "*" as the tag to search for.

The following hands-on exercise demonstrates how to obtain data from XML document element nodes.

⊚ Hands-On 29-11: Retrieving Information from Element Nodes

1. In the Visual Basic Editor Code window, enter the following IterateThru-Elements procedure below the last procedure code (see Hands-On 29-10).

```
Sub IterateThruElements()
    Dim xmldoc As MSXML2.DOMDocument50
    Dim xmlNode As MSXML2.IXMLDOMNode
    Dim xmlNodeList As MSXML2.IXMLDOMNodeList
    Dim myNode As MSXML2.IXMLDOMNode

    Set xmldoc = New MSXML2.DOMDocument50
    xmldoc.async = False
    xmldoc.Load ("C:\Learn_XML\Shippers.xml")
    Set xmlNodeList = xmldoc.getElementsByTagName("*")
    For Each xmlNode In xmlNodeList
        For Each myNode In xmlNode.childNodes
          If myNode.nodeType = NODE_TEXT Then
            Debug.Print xmlNode.nodeName & "=" & xmlNode.Text
          End If
        Next myNode
    Next xmlNode
    Set xmlDoc = Nothing
End Sub
```

The IterateThruElements procedure retrieves the XML document name and the corresponding text for all the text elements in the Shippers.xml file. Notice that this procedure uses two For Each...Next loops. The first one (the outer For Each...Next loop) iterates through the entire collection of element nodes. The second one (the inner For Each...Next loop) uses the nodeType property to find only those element nodes that contain a single text node.

2. Position the insertion point anywhere within the code of the IterateThru-Elements procedure and choose **Run | Run Sub/UserForm**. The result of running the IterateThruElements procedure is shown below:

```
ShipperID=1
CompanyName=Speedy Express
Phone=(503) 555-9831
ShipperID=2
CompanyName=United Package
Phone=(503) 555-3199
ShipperID=3
```

```
CompanyName=Federal Shipping
Phone=(503) 555-9931
```

Retrieving Specific Information from Element Nodes

You can list all the nodes that match a specified criterion by using the selectNodes method. The following hands-on exercise prints to the Immediate window the text for all CompanyName nodes that exist in the Shippers.xml file. The "//CompanyName" criterion of the selectNodes method looks for the element named "CompanyName" at any level within the tree structure of the nodes.

⊚ **Hands-On 29-12: Retrieving Specific Information from Element Nodes**

1. In the Visual Basic Editor Code window, in the same module where you entered the previous procedures, enter the SelectNodesByCriteria procedure as shown below.

```
Sub SelectNodesByCriteria()
    Dim xmldoc As MSXML2.DOMDocument50
    Dim xmlNodeList As MSXML2.IXMLDOMNodeList
    Dim myNode As MSXML2.IXMLDOMNode

    Set xmldoc = New MSXML2.DOMDocument50
    xmldoc.async = False
    xmldoc.Load ("C:\Learn_XML\Shippers.xml")
    Set xmlNodeList = xmldoc.selectNodes("//CompanyName")
    If Not (xmlNodeList Is Nothing) Then
        For Each myNode In xmlNodeList
            Debug.Print myNode.Text
            If myNode.Text = "Federal Shipping" Then
                myNode.Text = "Airborne Express"
                xmldoc.Save "C:\Learn_XML\Shippers.xml"
            End If
        Next myNode
    End If
    Set xmlDoc = Nothing
End Sub
```

The SelectNodesByCriteria procedure creates the IXMLDOMNodeList object that represents a collection of child nodes. The selectNodes method applies the specified pattern to this node's context and returns the list of matching nodes as IXMLDOMNodeList. The expression used by the selectNodes method specifies that all the CompanyName element nodes should be included in the node list.

You can use the Is Nothing conditional expression to find out whether a matching element was found in the loaded XML file. If the matching elements were found in the IXMLDOMNodeList, the procedure iterates through the node list and prints each element node text to the Immediate window. In addition, if the node element's text value is Federal Shipping, the procedure replaces this value with Airborne Express. The Save method of the DOMDocument is used to save the changes in the Shippers.xml file.

2. Position the insertion point anywhere within the code of the SelectNodes-ByCriteria procedure and choose **Run | Run Sub/UserForm**. The result of running the SelectNodesByCriteria procedure is shown below:

```
Speedy Express
United Package
Federal Shipping
```

Note: When you run this procedure again you should see the following output:

```
Speedy Express
United Package
Airborne Express
```

Retrieving the First Matching Node

If all you want to do is retrieve the first node that meets the specified criterion, use the SelectSingleNode method of the DOMDocument object. As the argument of this method, specify the string representing the node you'd like to find. For example, the following procedure finds the first node that matches the criterion "//CompanyName" in the Shippers.xml file:

```
Sub SelectSingleNode()
    Dim xmldoc As MSXML2.DOMDocument50
    Dim xmlSingleNode As MSXML2.IXMLDOMNode

    Set xmldoc = New MSXML2.DOMDocument50
    xmldoc.async = False
    xmldoc.Load ("C:\Learn_XML\Shippers.xml")
    Set xmlSingleNode = xmldoc.SelectSingleNode("//CompanyName")
    If xmlSingleNode Is Nothing Then
        Debug.Print "No nodes selected."
    Else
     Debug.Print xmlSingleNode.Text
    End If
    Set xmlDoc = Nothing
End Sub
```

XML DOM provides a number of other methods that make it possible to programmatically add or delete elements in the XML document tree structure. Covering all of the details of the XML DOM Object Model is beyond the scope of this chapter. When you are ready for more information on this subject, visit the following web link: http://www.w3.org/DOM/.

Using ActiveX Data Objects with XML

In Chapter 16 you learned how to save ADO recordsets to disk using the Advanced Data TableGram (adPersistADTG) format. This section expands on what you already know about the ADO recordsets by showing you how to use ADO with XML. Since the release of ADO version 2.5 (in 2000), you can save all types of recordsets to disk as XML using the Extensible Markup Language (adPersistXML) format.

Saving an ADO Recordset as XML to Disk

To save an ADO recordset to a disk file as XML, use the Save method of the Recordset object with the adPersistXML constant. Hands-On 29-13 demonstrates how to create an XML file from ADO.

⊚ Hands-On 29-13: Creating an XML Document from ADO

1. In the Visual Basic Editor screen, choose **Insert | Module** to add a new standard module to the current VBA project.

2. In the module's Code window, enter the SaveRst_ToXMLwithADO procedure as shown below.

```
Sub SaveRst_ToXMLwithADO()
    Dim rst As ADODB.Recordset
    Dim conn As New ADODB.Connection

    ' change the path to point to the Northwind database on your computer
    Const strConn = "Provider=Microsoft.Jet.OLEDB.4.0;" _
        & "Data Source=C:\Program Files\Microsoft Office\" _
        & "Office11\Samples\Northwind.mdb"

    ' open a connection to the database
    conn.Open strConn

    ' execute a select SQL statement against the database
    Set rst = conn.Execute("SELECT * FROM Products")

    ' delete the file if it exists
    On Error Resume Next
    Kill "C:\Learn_XML\Products_AttribCentric.xml"

    ' save the recordset as an XML file
    rst.Save "C:\Learn_XML\Products_AttribCentric.xml", adPersistXML

    ' cleanup
    Set rst = Nothing
    Set conn = Nothing
End Sub
```

The above procedure begins by establishing a connection to the sample Northwind database using the ADO Connection object. Next, it executes a SQL SELECT statement against the database to retrieve all of the records from the Products table. Once the records are placed in a recordset, the Save method is called to store the recordset to a disk file using the adPersistXML format. If the disk file already exists, the procedure deletes the existing file using the VBA Kill statement. The On Error Resume Next statement allows bypassing the Kill statement if the file you are going to create does not yet exist.

3. Position the insertion point anywhere within the code of the procedure and choose **Run | Run Sub/UserForm**.

4. Open the **C:\Learn_XML\Products_AttribCentric.xml** file created by the SaveRst_ToXMLwithADO procedure and examine its content.

The web browser displays the raw XML as shown in Figure 29-23. Notice that the content of this file looks different from other XML files you generated in this chapter. The reason for this is that XML that is persisted from ADO recordsets is created in attribute-centric XML. Microsoft Office Access supports only element-centric XML. Therefore, in order to import to Access an XML file created from ADO, you must first create and apply an XSLT transformation to the source document. The stylesheet you create should convert the attribute-centric XML to element-centric XML that Access can handle (see Hands-On 29-14).

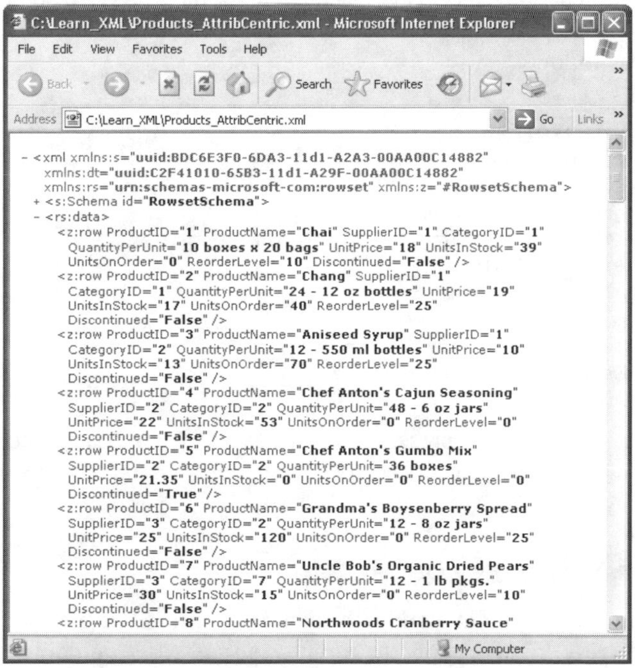

Figure 29-23: Saving a recordset to an XML file with ADO produces an attribute-centric XML file.

Attribute-Centric and Element-Centric XML

If you take a look at the XML file generated in Hands-On 29-13 (see Figure 29-23 above), you will notice that below the XML document's root tag there are two child nodes: <s:Schema> and <rs:data>.

The schema node describes the structure of the recordset, while the data node holds the actual data. Inside the <s:Schema id="RowsetSchema"> and </s:Schema> tags, ADO places information about each column: field name, position, data type and length, nullability, and whether the column is writable. Each field is represented by the <s:AttributeType> element. Notice that the value of the name attribute is the field name. The <s:AttributeType> element also has a child element <s:datatype>, which holds information about its data type (integer, number, string, etc.) and the maximum field length.

Below the schema definition, you can find the actual data. The ADO schema represents each record using the <z:row> tag. The fields in a record are expressed as attributes of the <z:row> element. Every XML attribute is assigned a value that is enclosed in a pair of single or double quotation marks; however, if the value of a field in a record is Null, the attribute on the z:row is not created. Notice that each record is written out in the following format:

```
<z:row ProductID='1' ProductName='Chai' SupplierID='1' CategoryID='1'
    QuantityPerUnit='10 boxes x 20 bags' UnitPrice='18' UnitsInStock='39'
    UnitsOnOrder='0' ReorderLevel='10' Discontinued='False'/>
```

The code fragment above is attribute-centric XML that Access cannot import. To make the XML file compatible with Access, you should have each record written out as follows:

```
<Product>
    <ProductID>1</ProductID>
    <ProductName>Chai</ProductName>
    <SupplierID>1</SupplierID>
    <CategoryID>1</CategoryID>
    <QuantityPerUnit>10 boxes x 20 bags</QuantityPerUnit>
    <UnitPrice>18</UnitPrice>
    <UnitsInStock>39</UnitsInStock>
    <UnitsOnOrder>0</UnitsOnOrder>
    <ReorderLevel>10</ReorderLevel>
    <Discontinued>False</Discontinued>
</Product>
```

The code fragment above represents element-centric XML. Each record is wrapped in a <Product> tag, and each field is an element under the <Product> tag.

Changing the Type of an XML File

Because it is much easier to work with element-centric XML files (and Microsoft Access does not support attribute-centric XML), you must write an XSL stylesheet to transform the attribute-centric XML file to an element-centric XML file before you can import an XML file created from an ADO recordset to Access.

The following hands-on exercise demonstrates how to write a stylesheet to convert an XML document from attribute-centric to element-centric.

Hands-On 29-14: Creating a Stylesheet to Convert Attribute-Centric XML to Element-Centric XML

1. Open **Notepad** and type the stylesheet code as shown below.

```
<xsl:stylesheet version="1.0"
 xmlns:xsl="http://www.w3.org/1999/XSL/Transform"
 xmlns:rs="urn:schemas-microsoft-com:rowset">
<xsl:output method="xml" encoding="UTF-8" />

    <xsl:template match="/">

    <!-- root element for the XML output -->
    <Products xmlns:z="#RowsetSchema">

      <xsl:for-each select="/xml/rs:data/z:row">
        <Product>
            <xsl:for-each select="@*">
              <xsl:element name="{name()}">
                 <xsl:value-of select="."/>
              </xsl:element>
            </xsl:for-each>
        </Product>
      </xsl:for-each>
    </Products>

    </xsl:template>
</xsl:stylesheet>
```

2. Save the above stylesheet as **AttribToElem.xsl** in the Learn_XML folder. Make sure to type the .xsl extension so the file is not saved as text. We will use this stylesheet for the transformation in the next hands-on exercise.

Notice that in the above stylesheet, the @* wild card matches all attribute nodes. Each time the <z:row> tag is encountered, an element named <Product> will be created. And for each attribute, the attribute name will be converted to the element name using the built-in XPath Name( ) function. Expressions in curly braces are evaluated and converted to strings. The select="." returns the current value of the attribute being read.

Applying an XSL Stylesheet

Now that you've created the stylesheet that can be used to transform an attribute-centric XML file into an element-centric file, you can use the transformNodeToObject method of the DOMDocument object to apply the stylesheet to the Products_AttribCentric.xml file created in Hands-On 29-13. The hands-on exercise that follows demonstrates how to do this. In addition, the procedure in this exercise will import the converted ADO XML file to Access.

⦿ Hands-On 29-15: Applying a Stylesheet to an ADO XML Document and Importing It to Access

1. Enter the following procedure below the procedure code you created in Hands-On 29-13.

```
Sub ApplyStyleSheetAndImport()
    Dim myXMLDoc As New MSXML2.DOMDocument50
    Dim myXSLDoc As New MSXML2.DOMDocument50
    Dim newXMLDoc As New MSXML2.DOMDocument50

    myXMLDoc.async = False
    If myXMLDoc.Load("C:\Learn_XML\Products_AttribCentric.xml") Then
        myXSLDoc.Load "C:\Learn_XML\AttribToElem.xsl"

     ' apply the transformation
       If Not myXSLDoc Is Nothing Then
           myXMLDoc.transformNodeToObject myXSLDoc, newXMLDoc

           ' save the output in a new file
           newXMLDoc.Save "C:\Learn_XML\Products_Converted.xml"

           ' import to Access
           Application.ImportXML "C:\Learn_XML\Products_Converted.xml"
       End If
     End If

     ' cleanup
     Set myXMLDoc = Nothing
     Set myXSLDoc = Nothing
     Set newXMLDoc = Nothing
End Sub
```

The above procedure begins by loading both the Products_AttribCentric.xml file (created in Hands-On 29-13) and the AttribToElem.xsl stylesheet (created in Hands-On 29-14) into the DOMDocument object. Next, the stylesheet is applied to the source file by using the transformNodeToObject method. This method is applied to a node in the source XML document's tree and takes two arguments. The first argument is a stylesheet in the form of a DOMDocument node. The second argument is another DOMDocument node that will hold the result of the transformation. Next, the result of the transformation is saved to a file (Products_Converted.xml) and the file is imported to Access using the ImportXML method, which was introduced earlier in this chapter.

2. Run the **ApplyStyleSheetAndImport** procedure.

3. Open the **Products_Converted.xml** file located in the Learn_XML folder. Notice that the Products_Converted.xml file content is now element-centric XML (see Figure 29-24).

4. In the Database window, locate and open the table named **Product**.

   The Product table was created by the ImportXML method in the ApplyStyleSheetAndImport procedure.

Taking Your VBA Programming Skills to the Web

Figure 29-24: This element-centric XML file is a result of applying a stylesheet to the attribute-centric ADO recordset that was saved to an XML file.

The original XML file is shown in Figure 29-23, and the stylesheet used in the transformation can be found in Hands-On 29-14.

Transforming Attribute-Centric XML Data into an HTML Table

As you've seen in earlier examples, after creating an XML file from an ADO recordset, the generated output contains attribute-centric XML. To import this type of output to Access you had to create a special stylesheet and apply the transformation to convert the attribute-centric XML to the element-centric XML that Access supports. But what if you simply want to display the XML file created from an ADO recordset in a web browser? You can create a generic XSL stylesheet that draws a simple HTML table for the users when they open the XML attribute-centric file in their browser.

Hands-On 29-16 demonstrates how to create a stylesheet to transform the attribute-centric XML file created in Hands-On 29-13 into HTML. The hands-on exercise that immediately follows performs the transformation by inserting a reference to the XSL stylesheet into the XML document.

◎ Hands-On 29-16: Creating a Generic Stylesheet to Transform an Attribute-Centric XML File into HTML

1. Open **Notepad** and type the stylesheet code as shown below.

```
<?xml version="1.0"?>
<xsl:stylesheet xmlns:xsl="http://www.w3.org/1999/XSL/Transform">

<xsl:template match="/">
<html>
<head>
<title>Using Stylesheet to convert attribute based XML to HTML</title>
<style type="text/css">
  .myHSet { font-Family:verdana; font-Size: 9px; color:blue; }
  .myBSet { font-Family:Garamond; font-Size; 8px; }
</style>
</head>

<body>
  <table width="100%" border="1">

    <xsl:for-each select="xml/s:Schema/s:ElementType/s:AttributeType">
      <th class="myHSet">
          <xsl:value-of select="@name" />
      </th>
    </xsl:for-each>

    <xsl:for-each select="xml/rs:data/z:row">
    <tr>
      <xsl:for-each select="@*">
         <td class="myBSet" valign="top"><xsl:value-of match="@*"/></td>
      </xsl:for-each>
    </tr>
    </xsl:for-each>
  </table>
</body>
</html>
</xsl:template>
</xsl:stylesheet>
```

The above stylesheet uses the feature known as Cascading Stylesheets (CSS) to format the HTML table. A style comprises different properties — bold, italic, font size and font weight, color, etc. — that you want to apply to a particular text (titles, headers, body, etc.) and assigns a common name to these properties. Thus, in the above stylesheet, two styles are defined. A style named myHSet is applied to the table headings, and a style named myBSet is used for formatting the text in the body of the table. Using styles is very convenient. If you don't like the formatting, you can simply change the style definition and get a new look in no time. Notice that to define a style, you must type a period and a class name. Using letters and numbers, you can define any name for your style class. After the class name, you need to type the definition for the class between curly brackets { }.

```
<style type="text/css">
    .myHSet { font-Family:Verdana; font-Size:9px; color:blue; }
    .myBSet { font-Family:Garamond; font-Size:8px; }
</style>
```

Notice that the definition of the class includes the name of the property followed by a colon and the property value. Properties are separated by a semicolon. A semicolon is also placed before the ending curly bracket (}). A style class can be applied to any HTML tag.

The example stylesheet shown above uses template-based processing. The following instruction defines a template for the entire document:

```
<xsl:template match="/">
```

The code between the initial and closing tags will be processed for all tags whose names match the value of the attribute "match." In other words, you want the pattern matching that follows to be applied to the entire document (/).

Next, a loop is used to write out the column headings. To do this, you must move through all the AttributeType elements of the root element, outputting the name attribute's value like this:

```
<xsl:for-each select="xml/s:Schema/s:ElementType/s:AttributeType">
<th class="myHSet">
<xsl:value-of select="@name" />
</th>
</xsl:for-each>
```

An attribute's name is always preceded by @.

Next, another loop runs through all the <z:row> elements representing actual records:

```
<xsl:for-each select="xml/rs:data/z:row">
```

All the attributes of any <z:row> element are enumerated:

```
<xsl:for-each select="@*">
<td class="myBSet" valign="top"><xsl:value-of match="@*" /></td>
</xsl:for-each>
```

The string @* denotes any attribute. For each attribute found under the <z:row> element, you need to match the attribute name with its corresponding value.

2. Save the above stylesheet as **AttribToHTML.xsl**. Be sure to type the .xsl extension so the file is not saved as text.

3. Close Notepad.

4. Open the **AttribToHTML.xsl** file in the browser to test whether it is well formed. If you made any errors while typing the stylesheet code, you must correct the problems before going on to the next section.

5. Close the browser.

Now that you are finished with the stylesheet, you need to link the XML and XSL files. You can do this by adding a reference to a stylesheet in your XML document as shown in Hands-On 29-17.

Hands-On 29-17: Linking the Attribute-Centric XML File with the Generic Stylesheet and Displaying the Transformed File in a Web Browser

1. Save the Products_AttribCentric.xml file as **Products_AttribCentric_2.xml**.
2. Open the **Products_AttribCentric_2.xml** file with Notepad.
3. Type the following definition in the first line of this file:

   ```
   <?xml-stylesheet type="text/xsl" href="AttribToHTML.xsl"?>
   ```

   The above instruction establishes a reference to the XSL file.
4. Save the changes made to the Products_AttribCentric_2.xml file and close Notepad.
5. Open the **Products_AttribCentric_2.xml** file in your browser. You should see the data formatted in a table (see Figure 29-25).

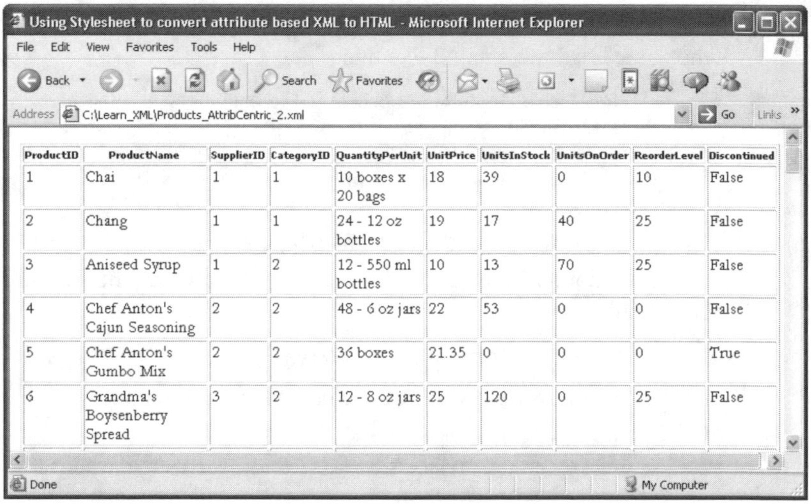

ProductID	ProductName	SupplierID	CategoryID	QuantityPerUnit	UnitPrice	UnitsInStock	UnitsOnOrder	ReorderLevel	Discontinued
1	Chai	1	1	10 boxes x 20 bags	18	39	0	10	False
2	Chang	1	1	24 - 12 oz bottles	19	17	40	25	False
3	Aniseed Syrup	1	2	12 - 550 ml bottles	10	13	70	25	False
4	Chef Anton's Cajun Seasoning	2	2	48 - 6 oz jars	22	53	0	0	False
5	Chef Anton's Gumbo Mix	2	2	36 boxes	21.35	0	0	0	True
6	Grandma's Boysenberry Spread	3	2	12 - 8 oz jars	25	120	0	25	False

Figure 29-25: You can apply a generic stylesheet to an XML document generated by the ADO to display the data in a simple HTML table.

Loading an XML Document in Excel

After saving an ADO recordset to an XML file on disk (see Hands-On 29-13 earlier in this chapter), you can load it into a desired application and read it as if it were a database. To gain access to the records saved in the XML file, use the Open method of the Recordset object and specify the filename, including its path and the persisted recordset service provider as "Provider=MSPersist." The following hands-on exercise demonstrates how to open a persisted recordset and write its data to an Excel workbook.

◎ Hands-On 29-18: From Access to Excel: Loading an XML File into an Excel Workbook

1. In the Visual Basic Editor window, choose **Insert | Module** to add a new standard module to the current VBA project.

2. In the module's Code window, enter the OpenAdoFile procedure as shown below.

```
Sub OpenAdoFile()
    Dim rst As ADODB.Recordset
    Dim objExcel As Excel.Application
    Dim wkb As Excel.Workbook
    Dim wks As Excel.Worksheet
    Dim StartRange As Excel.Range
    Dim h as Integer

    Set rst = New ADODB.Recordset

    ' open your XML file and load it
    rst.Open "C:\Learn_XML\Products_AttribCentric.xml", "Provider=MSPersist"

    ' display the number of records
    MsgBox "There are " & rst.RecordCount & " records " & _
            "in this file."

    Set objExcel = New Excel.Application

    ' create a new Excel workbook
    Set wkb = objExcel.Workbooks.Add

    ' set a reference to the ActiveSheet
    Set wks = wkb.ActiveSheet

    ' make Excel application window visible
    objExcel.Visible = True

    ' copy field names as headings to the first row of the worksheet
        For h = 1 To rst.Fields.Count
            wks.Cells(1, h).Value = rst.Fields(h - 1).Name
        Next

    ' specify the cell range to receive the data (A2)
    Set StartRange = wks.Cells(2, 1)

    ' copy the records from the recordset beginning in cell A2
    StartRange.CopyFromRecordset rst

    ' autofit the columns to make the data fit
    wks.Range("A1").CurrentRegion.Select
    wks.Columns.AutoFit

    ' save the workbook
    wkb.SaveAs "C:\Learn_XML\ExcelReport.xls"

    Set objExcel = Nothing
```

```
    Set rst = Nothing
End Sub
```

The above procedure is well commented, so we will skip its analysis and proceed to the next step.

3. Run the **OpenAdoFile** procedure.

   When the procedure is complete the Excel application window should be visible with the ExcelReport.xls workbook file displaying products retrieved from the XML file (see Figure 29-26).

4. Close the Excel workbook and exit Excel.

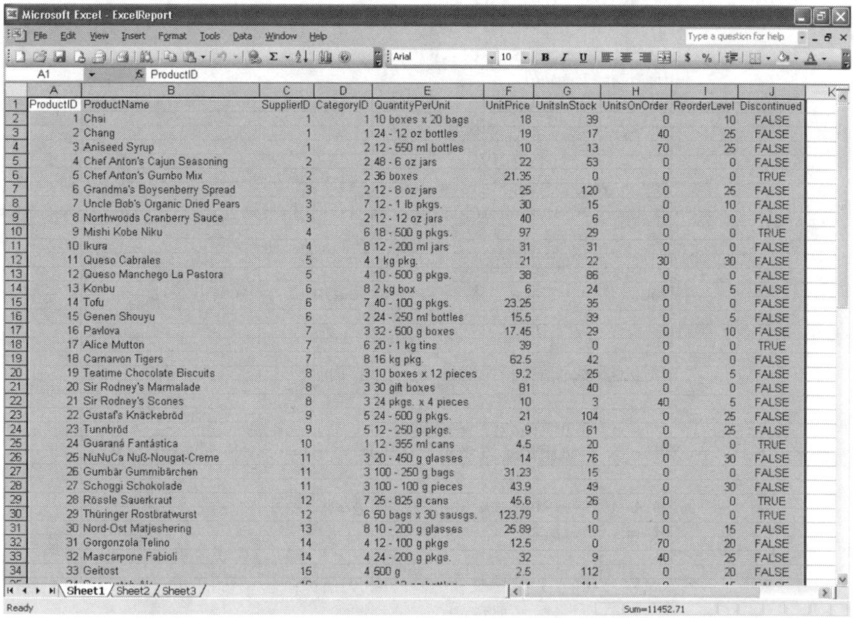

ProductID	ProductName	SupplierID	CategoryID	QuantityPerUnit	UnitPrice	UnitsInStock	UnitsOnOrder	ReorderLevel	Discontinued
1	Chai	1	1	10 boxes x 20 bags	18	39	0	10	FALSE
2	Chang	1	1	24 - 12 oz bottles	19	17	40	25	FALSE
3	Aniseed Syrup	1	2	12 - 550 ml bottles	10	13	70	25	FALSE
4	Chef Anton's Cajun Seasoning	2	2	48 - 6 oz jars	22	53	0	0	FALSE
5	Chef Anton's Gumbo Mix	2	2	36 boxes	21.35	0	0	0	TRUE
6	Grandma's Boysenberry Spread	3	2	12 - 8 oz jars	25	120	0	25	FALSE
7	Uncle Bob's Organic Dried Pears	3	7	12 - 1 lb pkgs.	30	15	0	10	FALSE
8	Northwoods Cranberry Sauce	3	2	12 - 12 oz jars	40	6	0	0	FALSE
9	Mishi Kobe Niku	4	6	18 - 500 g pkgs.	97	29	0	0	TRUE
10	Ikura	4	8	12 - 200 ml jars	31	31	0	0	FALSE
11	Queso Cabrales	5	4	1 kg pkg.	21	22	30	30	FALSE
12	Queso Manchego La Pastora	5	4	10 - 500 g pkgs.	38	86	0	0	FALSE
13	Konbu	6	8	2 kg box	6	24	0	5	FALSE
14	Tofu	6	7	40 - 100 g pkgs.	23.25	35	0	0	FALSE
15	Genen Shouyu	6	2	24 - 250 ml bottles	15.5	39	0	5	FALSE
16	Pavlova	7	3	32 - 500 g boxes	17.45	29	0	10	FALSE
17	Alice Mutton	7	6	20 - 1 kg tins	39	0	0	0	TRUE
18	Carnarvon Tigers	7	8	16 kg pkg.	62.5	42	0	0	FALSE
19	Teatime Chocolate Biscuits	8	3	10 boxes x 12 pieces	9.2	25	0	5	FALSE
20	Sir Rodney's Marmalade	8	3	30 gift boxes	81	40	0	0	FALSE
21	Sir Rodney's Scones	8	3	24 pkgs. x 4 pieces	10	3	40	5	FALSE
22	Gustaf's Knäckebröd	9	5	24 - 500 g pkgs.	21	104	0	25	FALSE
23	Tunnbröd	9	5	12 - 250 g pkgs.	9	61	0	25	FALSE
24	Guaraná Fantástica	10	1	12 - 355 ml cans	4.5	20	0	0	TRUE
25	NuNuCa Nuß-Nougat-Creme	11	3	20 - 450 g glasses	14	76	0	30	FALSE
26	Gumbär Gummibärchen	11	3	100 - 250 g bags	31.23	15	0	0	FALSE
27	Schoggi Schokolade	11	3	100 - 100 g pieces	43.9	49	0	30	FALSE
28	Rössle Sauerkraut	12	7	25 - 825 g cans	45.6	26	0	0	TRUE
29	Thüringer Rostbratwurst	12	6	50 bags x 30 sausgs.	123.79	0	0	0	TRUE
30	Nord-Ost Matjeshering	13	8	10 - 200 g glasses	25.89	10	0	15	FALSE
31	Gorgonzola Telino	14	4	12 - 100 g pkgs	12.5	0	70	20	FALSE
32	Mascarpone Fabioli	14	4	24 - 200 g pkgs.	32	9	40	25	FALSE
33	Geitost	15	4	500 g	2.5	112	0	20	FALSE

Figure 29-26: An ADO recordset persisted to an XML file is now opened in Excel.

Chapter Summary

This chapter has shown you that Microsoft Access 2003 makes it easy to work with XML files. Using Access built-in commands or programming code, you can both export Access data to an XML file and import an XML file and display the file as an Access table. You learned here what XML is and how it is structured. After working through the examples in this chapter, it's easy to see that XML supplies you with numerous ways to accomplish a specific task. Because XML is stored in plain text files, it can be read by many types of applications, independent of the operating system or hardware. You learned how to transform data from XML to HTML and from one XML format to another. You explored the ADO recordset methods suitable for working with XML programmatically. You were introduced to XSL stylesheets and XSLT transformations. All of these new methods and techniques you've studied here will need time to sink in. XML is not like VBA. It is not very independent. It needs many supporting technologies to assist it in its work. So don't despair if you don't understand something right away. Learning XML requires learning many other new concepts (like XSLT, XPath, schemas, etc.) at the same time. Take XML step by step by experimenting with it. The time that you invest studying this new technology will not be wasted. XML is here to stay, and future versions of Access are bound to offer even better integration with XML than the current 2003 version. Here are three main reasons why you should really consider XML:

- *XML separates content from presentation.*

  This means that if you are planning to design web pages, you no longer need to make changes to your HTML files when the data changes. Because the data is kept in separate files, it's easy to make modifications.

- *XML is perfect for sharing and exchanging data.*

  This means that you no longer have to worry if your data needs to be processed by a system that's not compatible with yours. Because all systems can work with text files (and XML documents are simply text files), you can share and exchange your data without a headache.

- *XML can be used as a database.*

  This means that you no longer need a database system to have a database. What a great value!

Index

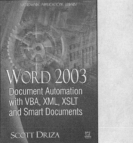

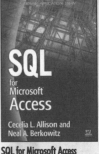